INTERNATIONAL DICTIONARY OF FOOD AND COOKING

INTERNATIONAL
DICTIONARY OF
FOOD AND COOKING

Ruth Martin

HASTINGS HOUSE *Publishers* NEW YORK 10016

First published in Great Britain 1973
by Constable and Company Ltd
10 Orange Street, London, WC2H 7EG
Copyright © 1973 by Ruth Martin

PUBLISHED 1974 BY HASTINGS HOUSE, PUBLISHERS, INC.

Library of Congress Cataloging in Publication Data

Martin, Ruth Marion (Somers) date
    International dictionary of food and cooking.

    1. Food — Dictionaries — Polyglot. 2. Cookery — Diction-
aries—Polyglot. 3. Dictionaries, Polyglot.
    I. Title.
    TX349.M33 1974   641.5'03   73-21522
    ISBN 0-8038-3388-1

Printed in the United States of America

To John
who helped so much

INTRODUCTION

The international nature of this dictionary indicates that it includes foods consumed in many countries. It does not claim to be wholly comprehensive; indeed, a dictionary which achieved this would run not to one volume but to many!

Purists and specialists in any one field will doubtless disagree with me on many points, such as whether "pilaff" rates one "f" or two, or whether cheddar cheese, being now a world-wide type, relinquishes the capital letter it once merited. But they will find, as I have found in the very many sources I have consulted, that experts disagree with one another to an astonishing extent and that consistency varies widely in any one book.

This dictionary, however, is not intended for the confident purist. It sets out to help the young housewife—or any student new to cooking—to understand basic terms and methods, and generally to clarify existing recipe books, whether English or American, both as regards simple, everyday meals or more adventurous dishes.

It seeks also to give a broad selection of overseas—particularly continental—cooking terms, styles and eating habits of other lands which have become of interest as a direct result of foreign travel.

Further, it aims to amuse and entertain the vast number of compulsive cookbook readers, as well as those interested in words themselves and what happens to them through usage and translation.

Historical sidelights are also included. For example, the "Lamb's wool" to which Shakespeare refers was a concoction of ale, wine, nutmeg, sugar and roasted crab apples; "Good Friday fritter" is a supper of fried rock limpets eaten traditionally on the Isle of Man each Good Friday.

Not least, I am sure, the army of crossword and competition addicts will find much in these pages to aid their search for that *bon mot* which leads to success.

RUTH MARTIN

à la (French) In the style of. (see separate entries)

à point (French) Done to a turn. Food cooked to the exact point of readiness.

a su salud (Spanish) Good Luck! A toast.

à votre santé, bonheur, et prospérité (French) To your health, happiness, and wealth. A toast.

aal (Afrikaans and Dutch) Eel.

Aal (German) Eel.

Aal grün mit Gurkensalat (German) Traditional Berlin summer dish of eel cooked in rich sauce and served with cucumber salad and boiled potatoes.

aal i gélé (Danish) Jellied eel.

aalsoep (Dutch) Eel soup, national soup of the Netherlands.

Aalsuppe (German) Eel soup.

Aalsuppe grün (German) Eel soup with added assorted herbs.

aardappel (Dutch) Potato.

aardappel puree (Dutch) Mashed potatoes.

aardappelsoep (Dutch) Potato soup.

abacate (Portuguese) Avocado.

abacaxi (Portuguese) Pineapple.

abaceria (Spanish) Grocery store.

abadejo (Spanish) Cod.

abaisse (French) Pie crust.

abaisser (French) To roll out, as for pastry.

abalone (American) Shellfish found in Californian waters.

abalone chowder (American) Abalone stewed with American corn, milk, onions and potatoes.

abat-faim (French) Literally, "hunger killer". Appetizer or soup served ahead of a meal.

abatis (French) Giblets. Edible entrails. Sometimes also head and feet.

abatis en ragoût (French) Giblet stew.

abats (French) Offal.

abatte (American) Thick double-edged knife used to flatten meat.

abattoir (French) Slaughter house.

abavo Indian pumpkin, used for making soup.

abbacchio (Italian) Milk-fed spring lamb.

abbacchio al forno (Italian) Roast spring lamb, a speciality of Rome.

abboccato (Italian) Generic term for sweet wine.

abelavis Egyptian melon.

abelmosk, abel-musk Indonesian herb whose seeds are used for flavouring coffee.

abendbrot (German) Evening meal.

abendessen (German) Evening meal; supper.

Abendmahl (German) supper.

abertam (Czechoslovakian) Sheep's-milk cheese.

Aberdeen Rich, creamy cheese, originating in Aberdeen.

Aberdeen Angus Breed of black polled cattle.

abernethy biscuit Plain, sweet biscuit, flavoured with caraway seeds.

abgerahmte Milch (German) Skimmed milk.

abgeschmackt (German) Insipid.

able (French) Fish of the bleak family.

ablette (French) Ablet, bleak. A very small white river fish.

ablette de mer (French) Whitefish.

abnehmen (German) To lose weight.

abondance (French) Diluted water-and-wine mixture.

abrelatus (Spanish) Tin-opener.

abricot (French) Apricot.

abricoté (French) (i) Candied apricot. (ii) Masked with apricot preserve.

abricoter (French) To cover a cake or sweet with apricot jam flavoured with apricot liqueur.

abricotine (French) Apricot brandy, a liqueur made from brandy, sugar and fresh apricots or apricot kernels.

absinthe Green alcoholic liqueur distilled from wormwood and flavoured with anise and other herbs. Habit-forming and dangerous to health, it has been banned in many countries. In France, its place has been taken by *Pernod* and other *pastis*.

abstainer One who abstains from drinking alcoholic beverages.

Abzugsabfüllung (German) Wine bottled where grapes were grown.

acacia Blossoms used for making (i) fritters (ii) a liqueur (ratafia)

acacia gum Basis of gum arabic, derived from tropical acacia and babul trees. Gum arabic is water-soluble and is used in making chewy gum drops, cough drops, etc.

acajou (French) Cashew, the tree yielding the cashew nut.

acaju (Brazilian/Portuguese) Cashew nut.

acanthus Plant from Southern France whose leaves, when young, are used in salads.

acarajé (Portuguese) Brazilian dish of beans covered with prawn sauce.

acarne Sea-bream.

acavus Variety of snail commonly found in French gardens and vineyards.

acciuga (Italian) Anchovy.

acciughe, all' (Italian) Food served in anchovy sauce.

accola (Italian) Marinaded fish similar to tuna fish.

accolade (French) Two chickens, fish or ducks arranged back-to-back on a serving dish.

accote-pot (French) Three-legged trivet.

acebuchina (Spanish) Wild olive.

acecinar (Spanish) To salt and dry meat.

acedira (Spanish) Sorrel.

aceite (Spanish) Oil.

aceite para ensaladas (Spanish) Salad oil.

aceituna (Spanish) Olive.

aceline (French) European fish rather like perch and prepared similarly for the table.

acepipes (Portuguese) *Hors d'oeuvres.*

acetarious Denoting plants used in salads.

acetary Acid pulp found in certain fruits.

acetic acid Chief constituent of vinegar obtained from fermenting ciders and wines. A dilute solution can substitute for white vinegar for pickling. Also used in very small quantities for making some sweets.

aceto (Italian) Vinegar.

aceto bianco (Italian) White vinegar.

aceto-dolce (Italian) Sweet-and-sour *hors d'oeuvre* of fruits and vegetables pickled in vinegar and preserved in honey and mustard.

aceto rosso (Italian) Red vinegar.

acetomel Sour-sweet syrup made from honey and vinegar used in preserving fruit, which then becomes *aceto-dolce* (Italian).

acetosa (Italian) (i) Food served in or with vinaigrette sauce (ii) Sorrel.

acetosella (Italian) Sorrel.

Achaia, Achaja (Greek) Sweet wine from Achaia in the Peloponnesus.

achar Pickled fruit and vegetables, strongly spiced, valued as a condiment throughout the Indian Archipelago and the West Indies.

achara (Filipino) Pickle (See achar)

ache de marais (French) Smallage; wild celery.

achinee (Greek) *Hors d'oeuvre* of sea-urchin roe.

achiote Crushed annatto seeds used in West Indian cooking to impart a golden-yellow colour to foods.

acid drop Hard, sharp, white sweet flavoured with tartaric acid.

acid food Foods such as cereals, cheese, eggs, fish, meats which contain varying amounts of chlorine, phosphorus or sulphur and leave an acid residue.

acid ice (American) Meringue-type mixture made of beaten egg whites, lemon juice and sugar.

acide (French) Acid, sharp, sour.

acido (Italian) Acid, sour, sharp.

acidulate To add lemon or vinegar to a dish and thus render it slightly acid.

acidulated Mineral waters charged with carbonic acid.

acon (French) Ancient tool still used by the mussel-farmers of *La Rochelle* to harvest their mussel beds.

acorn Fruit of the oak tree. Edible types are eaten raw or roasted in some countries, and acorn flour is used as a substitute for coffee.

acorn barnacle Small shellfish with delicate flesh, prepared like crab.

acorn squash (American) Acorn-shaped winter gourd vegetable with orange-yellow flesh.

acqua (Italian) Water.

acqua bianca (Italian) Liqueur containing flakes of silver, flavoured with cinnamon, cloves and nutmeg.

acqua d'oro (Italian) Liqueur containing flakes of gold and flavoured with angelica, cinnamon, cloves, lemon peel, etc., said to have been invented by the Italians in the 13th century and first introduced into France in 1533 by Catherine de Medici who became the wife of Henry II.

acqua minerale (Italian) Mineral water.

acquacotta (Italian) Thick Tuscan vegetable soup poured over thick slices of bread soaked in beaten egg.

acquadelle (Italian) Small edible fish found in the Adriatic.

acquavit (Scandinavian) Liqueur distilled from substances including potatoes, sawdust, grain; it is colourless, unsweetened, but usually flavoured with caraway seeds.

acquette (French) Spiritous and aromatic liqueur resembling *Danziger Goldwasser* made as silver-acquette or gold-acquette (See *acqua bianca* and *acqua d'oro*)

âcre (French) Sharp, piquante, pungent, tart.

acucar (Portuguese) Sugar.

Adam's ale Slang for water.

additive Any substance added to food for preserving, colouring, flavouring, emulsifying, stabilising, improving and processing. Although legally allowable, the use of additives is strictly controlled to prevent the inclusion of harmful substances.

addled egg Rotten egg.

ade Any beverage consisting of fruit juice and sweetened water such as lemonade, limeade, orangeade, etc; sometimes artificially flavoured and coloured.

adietar (Spanish) To diet.

adipose Fatty.

admiral Hot punch of claret sweetened with sugar, flavoured with vanilla and cinnamon, and thickened with egg-yolks.

adobado (Spanish) (i) Pickled pork. (ii) Pickled, curried, preserved.

adobo (Filipino) Stew of beef, chicken or pork simmered in water, then fried.

adobo a la monja (Filipino-Spanish) Chicken *adobo* with pineapple and tomatoes.

3

adobong labong (Filipino) *Adobo* of bamboo shoots, pork and prawns.

adobong pusit (Filipino) *Adobo* of squid.

adragante (French) Tragacanth.

adschempilave (Turkish) Dish of pickled meat stewed with rice.

adulterant Inferior substance added to another to increase bulk and reduce cost, with intent to defraud. The adulteration of food preparation and labelling is controlled by law, the manufacturer being compelled in many cases to state on the container the ingredients and respective quantities.

advocaat (Dutch) (i) Medicinal drink of eggs, rum and lemon-juice (ii) Liqueur made with brandy, egg yolks, sugar and vanilla.

æble (Danish) Apple.

æblegrød (Danish) Apple-sauce.

æblekage (Danish) Apple cake.

æg (Danish) Egg.

æg og sild (Danish) Egg and herring.

aeglé (French) Ugli (fruit).

aerate To put air into a commodity; to charge with air or carbon dioxide.

aerated bread Dough raised by mixing with carbonated water.

aerated flour Self-raising flour.

aerated water (i) Distilled water with purified air added. (ii) Carbonated water, used to add sparkle to soft drinks and wine cups. Natural aerated waters include Apollinaris, Perrier, Seltzer, Vichy, etc.

aéromètre (French) Hydrometer.

Afd Accelerated freezing and drying, the process of preserving cooked or raw foods at very low temperatures and vacuum-drying with radiant heat.

affetati misti (Italian) Mixed sliced cold meats and sausage.

affetato (Italian) Sausage or ham cut in slices.

affriander (French) To make a dish tempting by its appearance.

affriolé (French) (i) Fresh from the garden; fresh fruits or vegetables (ii) Appetising.

affrité (French) Ready to fry.

Africaine, à l' (French) Dishes using North African products such as aubergines, tomatoes, flap-mushrooms, usually cooked in oil and highly seasoned.

africain (French) Small dessert biscuit.

African ginger White ginger grown in Africa, India and other tropical places; pickled and preserved for export.

African peanut Peanut grown in West Africa.

African saffron Orange-coloured dye extracted from saffron flowers, used in colouring and flavouring rice and other foods.

after-dinner coffee See *demitasse*.

after-dinner drink Liqueur such as *Benedictine, Chartreuse, Cointreau, Curacao, Kummel*, or cordial, taken at the end of a meal.

after-taste Flavour which remains in the mouth after swallowing some beverages and foods.

agape Love feast. Meals eaten by the early Christians in memory of the Last Supper.

agar-agar Gelatinous extract from boiled red seaweed with powerful setting properties; used in canning and to thicken ice creams, jellies, soups and stews, particularly in vegetarian cookery; also called Chinese gelatine, Chinese isinglass or Japanese gelatine; it used to be produced mainly in those countries, Russia and the U.S.A., but is now manufactured in Britain.

agaric Family of fungi, containing many different types of mushrooms, both edible and poisonous.

agateware (American) Porcelain-enamelled iron or steel kitchenware, easy-to-clean and relatively unbreakable; used for cups, dishes, kettles, pans, etc., available in many colours.

agave South American plant whose pulp is fermented to make pulque and mescal. (See tequila)

agemono (Japanese) Fried food.

ägg (Swedish) Egg.

aglianico (Italian) Dry red wine from Camparia.

aglio (Italian) Garlic.

agneau (French) Lamb.

agneau de lait (French) Milk-fed baby lamb.

agnelet (French) Baby- or milk-fed lamb.

agnello (Italian) Lamb.

agnolotti (Italian) Tiny pasta turnovers filled with forcemeat, poached, and served with meat sauce and Parmesan cheese.

agonè (Italian) Freshwater shad.

agone d'Istria (Italian) Species of fish found in Italy's Lake Como and Lake Garda. Known as *sardina* in Italy, it is cooked (or salted) as for sardines.

agora (Greek) Market-place.

agoursi (French) Ridge cucumber.

agras (French) Continental drink originating in Algeria, made of pounded almonds and the juice of unripe grapes, slightly sweetened, served in a half-frozen condition.

agriote (French) Wild cherry.

agro dolce (Italian) Sweet-sour sauce made with vinegar, sugar, nuts, etc. See *aigre-douce*.

agua (Spanish) Water.

água (Portuguese) Water.

agua dulce (Spanish) Fresh water.

agua fresca (Spanish) Cold water.

agua minerale (Spanish) Mineral water.

agua potable (Spanish) Drinking water.

aguacate (Spanish) Avocado.

aguacate batido (Spanish) Avocado blended with lime juice and sugar.

aguamiel (Spanish) (i) Honey water. (ii) Mead. (iii) (South American) Sweet juice of the agave, aloe, century plant, sotol or maguey, the desert plants of South West America and Mexico. When fermented, *aguamiel* is known as pulque; distilled pulque becomes mescal, and re-distilled mescal becomes tequila.

aguardiente (Spanish) (i) Literally "fire-water", a generic term for molasses, cane sugar or wine distillations in Latin America, Spain and Portugal, including tequila, etc., (ii) Wine made from pomegranates.

aguaxima Brazilian pepper.

aguglia (Italian) Garfish.

agurkesalat (Danish) Cucumber salad.

agurksalat (Norwegian) Cucumber salad.

ahorn (German) Maple.

ai ferri (Italian) Grilled.

aigre (French) Sour or acid.

aigre au cédrat (French) Orangeade flavoured with the juice of mulberries acidulated with lemon juice, and sweetened with honey. Said to be a favourite beverage of Cardinal Richelieu.

aigre-douce (French) Sweet-sharp sauce, made with vinegar, sugar, pine kernels, almonds, chocolate, and small currants; served hot.

aigre-doux (French) Sour-sweet.

aigrefin, aiglefin, églefin (French) Haddock.

aigrelet (French) Sharp, sour.

aigrette (French) (i) Sour, piquant. (ii) Small *choux* paste cheese fritter.

aiguière (French) Ewer.

aiguillat (French) Dog-fish.

aiguille-à-brider (French) Larding-needle used for inserting strips of fat bacon into lean meat or breasts of birds.

aiguille-à-piquer (French) Larding needle.

aiguillette (French) Small strip of cooked poultry or meat.

aiguiser (French) To sharpen food either by making it acid with lemon juice or citric acid, or to spice it strongly.

ail (French) Garlic.

aile (French) Wing.

aillade (French) (i) Garlic sauce. (ii) Term also applies to other preparations made from garlic such as bread. *à l'aillade* — toasted bread rubbed well with garlic and sprinkled with olive oil.

aine (French) Top of sirloin.

aïoli (French) Thick garlic sauce.

air (Malay) Water.

airan (Russian) Uzbek summer sour-milk drink.

airelle myrtille (French) Whortleberry. Huckleberry. (i) (American) Savoury berry eaten freshly picked with savoury milk or a cream sauce. (ii) Small dark blue fruit, used as seasoning for certain dishes. Wine merchants use it to colour white wine, hence its French name, *teint-vin*.

airelle rouge (French) Red bilberry or cranberry. Dark red berry used for compôte, jellies, sauces, etc.

aiselle (French) Species of beetroot used as vegetable or in salads.

aitchbone Cut from the upper part of the leg of beef with a high proportion of bone. Usually roasted, but may also be braised or boiled, used in a stew, or salted and boiled.

ait-jannock (Scottish) Oatmeal short-bread.

ajedrea (Spanish) Winter savory.

ají (Spanish/American) Hot green capsicum pepper common to Andean countries of South America.

ajo (Spanish) Garlic.

ajouté (Frecnh) (i) Addition or mixture. (ii) Small garnish or side dish served with vegetable course.

akala Hawaiian plant yielding a berry tasting similar to the raspberry.

Akazie (German) Acacia.

akvavit Scandinavian liquor distilled from cereal grains, potatoes or sawdust, and flavoured with caraway seeds, often served before meals as an appetizer, quickly followed by a glass of beer.

ål (Danish, Norwegian and Swedish) Eel.

al fresco (Italian) Eating out of doors, as in a garden, in a porch, or beside a pavement.

al horno (Spanish) Oven-baked.

al modo de (Spanish) In the style of.

alaska, baked Sweet made from a scooped-out sponge base, filled with ice-cream and covered with meringue.

albacore Deep-sea tuna, the source of most canned tuna fish.

albana (Italian) Dry white wine from Emilia.

albana dolce (Italian) Dessert wine from Emilia.

albaricoque (Spanish) Apricot.

albemarle apple (American) Newtown pippin.

albicocca (Italian) Apricot.

albigeoise (French) Garnish of stuffed tomatoes and potato croquettes served with meat dishes.

albóndiga (Spanish) Forcemeat ball, with eggs and spices.

albondiguilla (Spanish) Small forcemeat ball.

alboronia (Spanish) Dish of tomatoes, aubergines, pimento and pumpkin.

albran (French) Young wild duck, cooked as for duck.

albrán (Spanish) Young duck.

albuféra, d' (French) (i) Poultry cooked in a Madeira-based sauce. (ii) Tartlets

filled with tiny balls of truffles and chicken stuffing, garnished with cock's kidneys, mushrooms and pickled tongue.

albumin, albumen Soluble protein which forms part of blood, milk and egg-white.

albumin powder Powder used instead of egg-whites to make meringues or royal icing.

albundigas (Spanish) (i) Mexican dish of cakes made from beef and bacon or veal and pork, served with Créole rice. (ii) Mexican soup with forcemeat *quenelles.*

alcachofa (Spanish) Artichoke.

alcaparra (Spanish) Caper.

alcarazas (French/Spanish) Water cooler

alcazar (Spanish) Pastry with almonds and apricot jam.

alcazuz (Spanish) Liquorice.

alcohol Intoxicating element of beers, whisky, wines, etc., produced by fermentation of fruits and grains; the ferments are then distilled into purer and more volatile forms.

alcohol (Spanish) Alcohol; liquor.

alcool (French) Alcohol.

alcorza (Spanish) Sugar-icing.

alderman's walk (i) Name formerly given to the centre cut of a haunch of mutton or venison. (ii) Best part of the under-cut (fillet) of a sirloin of beef. The name is supposed to be derived from a City Company's dinner, at which a City Alderman showed a special liking for this cut.

ale Alcoholic drink, light in colour, brewed from malt and hops. (See beer).

alecost See costmary.

alegar Vinegar derived from ale.

alénois (cresson) (French) Small garden cress.

alewife Variety of herring, named for its big belly. Also known as Allice and Round pompano.

alfredo, all' (Italian) Food served in a popular Roman sauce invented by a restauranteur of that city.

algae Plants which live in water, eaten in some countries, particularly Japan.

Algérienne, à l' (French) Dishes garnished with small tomatoes braised in oil, and sweet potatoes cooked in butter.

alginate Carbohydrates derived from seaweed used in jellies, soups, creams, fish and meat pastes to improve their texture or consistency.

alho (Portuguese) Garlic.

alicante Wine grape originally cultivated in the province of Alicante, Spain.

alice (Italian) Anchovy.

alici sott'olio (Italian) Anchovies in oil.

aliment (French) Food or food product.

alimentación (Spanish) Food; meals.

alimentar (Spanish) To feed.

alisander Plant of the parsley and celery order. Now almost forgotten, it used to be found wild near the sea coast of Great Britain. Before celery was known, it was used as a salad ingredient.

alivenca (Rumanian) Cottage-cheese dessert.

alkanet Bugloss.

Alkohol (German) Alcohol.

alkoholisch (German) Alcoholic.

alla (Italian) In the style of. (See separate alphabetical entries).

Allemande à l' (French) Dishes served with *Allemande* (German) sauce or garnished with German specialities such as pickled pork, smoked sausage, *sauerkraut* or potato dumplings.

Allemande sauce Rich version of *velouté* sauce, which is reduced to half quantity and thickened with egg-yolks and cream.

Allerlei (German) Dish of stewed early spring vegetables. A kind of *macédoine* of vegetables.

alligator pear Alternative name for avocado pear.

allodola (Italian) Lark.

all-purpose flour (American) Plain flour.

allspice (pimento, Jamaica pepper) Berry of the allspice tree, which combines the flavours of cinnamon, cloves and nutmeg; used for pickling or for seasoning fish and meat, used ground for curry powder, cakes, fruit, preserves, puddings, etc.

allumettes (French) (i) Sweet or savoury matchsticks of puff pastry cooked in the oven, served as an *hors d'œuvre.* (ii) Potatoes cut finely like matchsticks and baked or fried.

alma torte Apple cake named after the victory at the Alma River battle of the Crimean war.

almavica (Italian) Pudding, similar to semolina pudding.

almeja (Spanish) Clam.

almejón (Spanish) Mussel.

almendra (Spanish) Almond.

almendraro (Spanish) Macaroon.

Almeira Sweet, greenish-white grape.

almôço (Portuguese) Luncheon.

almond Fruit kernel of two similar trees. (i) The bitter almond, whose oil, after treatment to remove traces of poisonous prussic acid, is processed as a flavouring agent. (ii) The sweet almond, of which the two best types are Valencia and Jordan almonds. Whole almonds are salted and eaten as snacks, or sugar-coated as sweets. Also used to decorate cakes. Sliced or chopped almonds are used extensively in baked goods, sweets and savoury dishes. Ground almonds are added to cakes, biscuits, etc., especially macaroons and ratafias. They are also used in the making of almond cake-icing or marzipan. Almonds contain protein, fat and minerals, but little carbohydrate, and are the source of almond oil and pure almond essence.

almond, blanched Almond plunged into boiling water, drained and skinned by rubbing or pressing with the fingers. Used in cakes and baked goods, also in savoury dishes and as a decoration to sweets, ice-cream dishes, etc.

almond butter Butter flavoured with almonds.

almond cream Sweet made from eggs, butter, almonds and sugar.

almond, devilled Jordan almond blanched, fried in butter and strewn with cayenne pepper and salt.

almond essence Flavouring obtained from bitter almonds (after the extraction of almond oil) by fermentation and distillation, and used in cakes, biscuits and puddings.

almond mill Device for grinding dried blanched almonds.

almond oil Oil obtained by pressing almonds.

almond paste, almond icing Variations of almond paste made from ground almonds and fine sugar, bound together with egg. Placed on cakes before sugar-icing. Also known as Marzipan.

almond, salted Jordan almond blanched, dried, mixed with salad oil and salt, and baked in a slow oven till crisp.

almond sauce Blanched almonds in white sauce.

almond, sugared Almond coated with hard sugar, manufactured commercially rather than made domestically.

almond syrup Mixture of ground kernels of sweet and bitter almonds and barley or sugar syrup.

almôndega (Portuguese) Meatball.

almorzar (Spanish) To lunch.

almuerzo (Spanish) Lunch, mid-day meal.

aloe (i) Member of the lilaceous genus of trees and shrubs, including the American aloe, the agave. (ii) Purgative drug derived from some of the species.

Aloe (German) Aloe.

alosa (Italian, Spanish) Shad.

alose (French) Shad.

alouette (French) Lark.

aloyau (French) Sirloin of beef. Short loin of beef.

alphabet soup *Consommé* or soup containing small letters of macaroni.

alphabétique (French) Pasta letters used in soups, etc.

alpiste (French) Canary grass.

Alsace wine Dry white wines from Alsace, usually drunk while still young.

Alsacienne, à l' (French) Large cuts of meat and poultry garnished with Strasbourg sausage, braised *sauerkraut*, ham and boiled potatoes, typical of the food of Alsace.

Alse (German) Shad.

alter Kuhkäse (German) Sour-milk cheese, or "old cow" cheese.

alum Double sulphate of aluminium and potassium: astringent salt. Alum was used in confectionery and other preparations but is now prohibited by law.

aluminite Fireproof earthenware used for cooking utensils.

aluminium foil Thin, pliable sheets of aluminium available in different gauges, used to wrap foodstuffs and sold in a roll for covering oven dishes, etc.

alubia (Spanish) Bean.

alvéole (French) Wax cell of honeycomb.

alzavola (Italian) Teal.

amalgamer (French) Amalgamate. To mix several substances.

amande (French) Almond.

amande amère (French) Bitter almond.

amande cassée (French) Shelled almond.

amande douce (French) Sweet almond.

amande grillée (French) Roasted almond.

amande pralinée (French) Burnt almond.

amande salée (French) Salted almond.

amandes (pâté d') (French) Almond paste.

amandine (French) Food served with almonds; blanched, sliced, roasted, or in chips.

amarante (French) Amaranth (a kind of spinach). Cultivated in France for its flowers but the leaves of one variety are eaten in Italy.

amaretto (Italian) (i) Macaroon, almond cake (ii) Liqueur made from bitter almonds.

amargo (Spanish) Bitter.

amaro (Italian) Bitter.

amassette (French) Palette-knife.

amazake (Japanese) Sweet wine.

ambassadrice (French) (i) Fish — particularly sole fillets — rolled round stuffed crayfish, poached and served in a rich cream sauce (*Normande*) (ii) Small cuts of meat or poultry sautéed in butter and garnished with mushrooms, chicken livers, cock's combs, cock's kidneys and truffles, and served with Madeira sauce.

amberjack (American) Large fish of the genus *Seriola* found in the western Atlantic.

ambigu (French) Buffet ("ambiguous") meal. A meal where the meat and sweets are served at the same time.

ambroisie (French) Cold drink of milk, with vanilla or *Kirschwasser* flavouring.

ambrosia (i) Mythical food of the gods of Olympus. (ii) Nickname applied to any delicious food. (iii) (American) Fruit compôte topped with shredded coconut and whipped cream.

ameaux (French) Pastry made of puff paste and eggs.

amêijoa (Portuguese) Clam.

amer (French) Bitter.

amer piçon (French) Bitter liqueur made in France and mostly drunk as an apéritif.

Américaine, à l' (French) Dishes prepared with tomatoes fried in oil or butter and then puréed, spiced onions, shallots, garlic, parsley, chervil and tarragon, to which is added white wine or brandy.

American bread Bread enriched with soya flour.

American cheese United States version of Cheddar cheese.

American frosting Soft, quick-setting icing used on sponge mixtures and cakes.

American fried potatoes Hashed brown potatoes.

American lobster See Maine lobster.

American watercress Thin-leaved herb of the mustard family, found in mountain streams of the eastern United States, and suitable for salads and soups.

American wine Any wine made in the United States including the products of California, New York, Ohio, and Virginia.

americano Cocktail of angostura bitters, soda water, and vermouth.

amidon (French) Starch.

amiral, à l' (French) Fish dishes garnished with fried mussels, oysters, crayfish tails, truffles and peeled mushrooms.

amontillado Pale dry or medium-dry sherry, originating in Spain.

amoroso (Spanish) Dessert sherry wine.

amourettes (French) Spinal marrow cut in strips and crumbed or frittered.

Ampfer (German) Sorrel.

amphitryon (French) A host.

Amsel (German) Blackbird.

Amstel (Dutch) Beer brewed in Amsterdam.

amygdaline Substances which contain almonds.

anada (Spanish) Vintage wine.

anakajam (Malay) Indonesian dish made from young chicken.

analeptic Health-promoting restorative diet. Analeptics include beef tea, meat jellies, chocolate, wines, tapioca.

ananá (Spanish) Pineapple.

ananas (French) Pineapple.

Ananas (German) Pineapple.

ananasso, ananas (Italian) Pineapple.

anchoa (Spanish) Anchovy.

anchois (French) Anchovy.

ancholivette (American) Anchovy-stuffed olive.

anchovy Small fish of the herring family usually canned in white oil or preserved in brine. It should be used in small quantities only (because of the high salt content) for savouries, sauces, *hors d'œuvre*, garnishing and flavouring meat and fish dishes.

anchovy butter Boned anchovies pounded to a paste with butter, with added spice.

anchovy essence Flavouring for fish sauces and dishes, which should be used sparingly because of its strength.

anchovy paste Commercially-prepared mixture of pounded anchovies, vinegar, spices and water.

anchovy spear Small fork used for spearing anchovies and similar appetizers.

anchoyade (French) *Hors d'œuvre* based on anchovy paste.

anchusa See Bugloss.

ancienne, à l' (French) (i) Dishes — usually stews — served with mixed garnishes. (ii) Chicken or sweetbreads served in or with puff pastry.

Andalouse, à l' (French) Dishes prepared with tomatoes, sweet pimentos, aubergines, rice pilaff and chipolata sausages.

andouille (French) Large cooked sausage served cold and made of highly-seasoned pigs' intestines and chitterlings.

andouillette (French) (i) Forcemeat ball. (ii) A kind of small sausage. (iii) A *salpicon* of poultry or game wrapped in pigs' caul, and fried. (iv) Chitterlings.

anelletto gratino (Italian) Breadcrumbed cuttle-fish ring cooked in oil — a speciality of Sicily.

anello (Italian) Small pasta ring.

aneth (French) Dill.

aneto (Italian) Dill.

aneurin Vitamin B, now known as Thiamine.

ange (French) Angel fish. A fish of the shark or dog-fish family.

angel cake (American) Light, feathery sponge - type cake containing thoroughly-beaten egg whites into which cake flour is carefully folded.

angel food (American) Angel cake.

angel-fish Variety of dog-fish with delicate edible flesh.

angel pie (American) Baked meringue shell filled with berries and whipped cream over a layer of white cheese filling.

angel's kiss Cocktail made of layers of different coloured liqueurs such as green *crème de menthe*, brown *crème de cacao*, red cherry liqueur, etc.

angelica Tall plant of the parsley family. Chiefly cultivated on the Continent of Europe, especially in France. Its leaves can be used in salads. The hollow green stalks are candied and used for decorating iced cakes, cold sweets and ices. The seeds have medicinal uses.

angelica domestica (Italian) Angelica.

angel on horseback Oyster simmered in its own liquor, wrapped in bacon, grilled on a skewer and served on toast.

angelot (German) Variety of cheese.

angeln (German) To fish.

anglaise, à l' (French) (i) Food cooked simply in water or white stock — such as chicken and mutton; fish poached in stock; or fish coated with melted butter and grilled (ii) The term also applies to food dipped in a mixture of eggs, oil and seasoning, then coated with breadcrumbs and fried.

angler (American) Anglerfish. An ugly, rather poorly flavoured fish used in *bouillabaisse*.

angobert (French) Large cooking pear.

angostura Bitter flavouring extract used in medicines and in making cocktails. It has a high alcoholic content but is only used in small amounts, such as in "flavouring" a glass into which gin is then poured. ("Pink Gin")

Angoulême (French) Town in the Charente district of France famous for brandies and partridge *pâté*.

Angoumois (French) District of Central France famed for fish, meat and poultry

anguila (Spanish) Eel.

anguilla (Italian) Eel.

anguille (French) Eel.

anhydrated potato Cooked, peeled, and dehydrated white potato reduced to dry flakes; reconstituted to instant mashed potato by adding to boiling water.

anhydrated vegetables Cooked, peeled, and dehydrated vegetables, reduced to dry flakes; reconstituted by mixing with boiling water.

anice (Italian) Anise.

anijs (Dutch) Anise.

animal crackers (American) Animal-shaped arrowroot biscuits.

animella (Italian) Sweetbread.

animelle di abbacchio (Italian) Lamb's sweetbreads.

animelle di vitello (Italian) Veal sweetbreads.

animelles (French) Testicles, particularly of lambs and rams. Lamb's fry.

anis (Spanish) Anise.

anis (French) Generic term for *pastis*.

Anis (German) Anise.

anis vert (French) Aniseed.

aniseed, anise Sweet cumin. The seeds of the anise plant containing a volatile oil with a warm, sweet aromatic taste and smell. The oil is used as a flavouring for sweets, pastries, cordials and liqueurs. It also has certain medicinal properties.

aniseed cake Baked biscuit or cake flavoured with anise seeds.

anisette (French) Aniseed-flavoured sweet liqueur.

anisina (Italian) Anise-flavoured liqueur.

anitra (Italian) Duck.

anitra all'olive (Italian) Casseroled duck with olives.

anitra arrosto (Italian) Roast duck.

anitra con salsa arancio (Italian) Roast duck with orange sauce.

anitra in agrodolce (Italian) Duck in sweet-sour sauce.

anitra in creta (Italian) Duck baked in clay — speciality of Emilia-Romagna.

anitra selvatica (Italian) Wild duck.

anitrotto (Italian) Duckling.

Anjou (French) Large wine-flavoured yellow pear used for dessert, canning, or cooking.

anna potatoes (American) See *pommes anna*.

annatto Yellowish-red food colouring derived from a tropical tree of that name.

annette potatoes (American) See *pommes annette*.

anolini (Italian) Small stuffed ravioli from Parma, served in broth or with butter and cheese.

ânon (French) Fish of the haddock variety, cooked as for whiting.

ansjos (Norwegian) Anchovy.

Anrichte (German) (i) Sideboard. (ii) Dresser.

ansonica (Italian) Dry white Tuscan table wine.

antipasto (Italian) Dish served before the main dish in Italy — *hors d'œuvre* or appetiser.

antipasto alla genovese (Italian) *Hors d'œuvre* of raw young broad beans, salami and cheese.

antipasto di pesce (Italian) *Hors d'œuvre* of fish.

Anversoise, à l' (French) Dishes of meat, sweetbreads or eggs garnished with hop stalks in cream and fried potatoes.

aparador (Spanish) Sideboard.

apéritif (French) Aperitive; drink served before meals as an appetiser.

aperitivo (Spanish and Portuguese) Aperitive, appetizer.

apetito (Spanish) Appetite.

Apfel (German) Apple.

Apfel im Schlafrock (German) Apple fritter.

Apfelmost (German) Cider.

Apfelmus (German) Applesauce.

Apfelsaft (German) Apple-juice.

Apfelsine (German) Orange.

Apfelstrudel (German) Apple strudel. Flaky dough filled with apples, sultanas, sugar, margarine and lemon-juice, rolled and baked.

Apfelsuppe (German) Apple soup.

Apfelwein (German) Cider.

aphie (French) Onos, a Mediterranean fish prepared like whiting.

api (French) See *pomme d'api*.

apio (Spanish) Celery.

aplatir (French) To flatten (meat)

apogon (French) Cardinal fish, a Mediterranean species of mullet.

apollinaris Effervescent mineral water originally imported from a German spring of the same name.

appareil (French) Culinary term for prepared mixtures.

appel (Dutch) Apple.

appelbol (Dutch) Apple dumpling.

äppelkaka (Swedish) Apple .ake.

appellation contrôleé (French) French laws enacted to protect the good name and reputation of French wines.

appelmoes (Dutch) Applesauce.

äppelsoppa (Swedish) Apple soup.

appeltaart (Dutch) Apple pie.

äppelvin (Swedish) Cider.

appelwijn (Dutch) Apple cider.

Appenzeller (German) Cow's-milk cheese from the Appenzell Valley, Switzerland, marinated in cider or white wine before being aged.

appétissant (French) Appetising; something to whet the appetite; tempting.

appétit (French) (i) Appetite. (ii) Also the common French name for chives.

appetite Desire to eat, indicated in the stomach by a little weakness, sometimes accompanied by a little pain, and a slight sensation of lassitude. Meanwhile memory recalls such foods as please the taste, the stomach becomes sensitive, the mouth moist and the digestive powers ready for action.

appetitlich (German) Appetising, dainty, delectable.

appetitost (Danish) Buttermilk cheese first made in Denmark, now produced by many Danish-American communities

appetizer Foods or drinks served before meals to stimulate the appetite, usually salty or spicy; *apéritifs*, *canapés*, nuts, etc.

appetizer wine Dry sherries and vermouths served before meals, either by themselves or mixed in cocktails.

apple Fruit of a tree of the family *Roseacea*. The original apple of Britain is the crab. Several hundred varieties are now cultivated for dessert or for cooking in a large variety of ways — baking, stewing, preserving, etc. Most varieties have a low vitamin content but cooking apples are rich in pectin and are useful in helping jam made from low-pectin fruits to set.

apple *bonne femme* Apple, cored, filled with butter and caster sugar and baked in a little water.

apple brandy (Calvados) Spirit distilled from cider, widely drunk in Normandy and neighbouring apple-growing regions of Northern France. As "applejack" it is popular in parts of North America.

apple butter Sauce or jam made by stewing apples in water or cider, with added sugar and flavouring.

apple cake Soufflé-type dish made from apple pulp, eggs, sugar and cornflour or arrowroot and cooked in a pan of hot water, or *bain-marie*.

apple charlotte Pudding made of alternating layers of sliced apple and breadcrumbs (or sliced bread and butter) baked in the oven.

apple cider Beverage made from apple juice; hard or rough cider is alcoholic, sweet cider is less intoxicating; fermented cider is cider vinegar.

apple corer Utensil for removing apple cores; sometimes combined with an apple peeler or a device for sectioning apples.

apple crumble Pudding of sliced apple topped with flour, margarine and sugar blended until like breadcrumbs, baked to give a crusty top.

apple dumpling Apple wrapped in suet dough or short-crust pastry and cooked by baking, steaming or boiling.

apple florentine Traditional Bedfordshire Christmas dish of baked apples, sugar and lemon covered with rich pastry. The crust was cut after baking and hot, well spiced ale poured in.

apple fool *Purée* of apples (apple pulp), flavoured with cinnamon, clove, and sugar, mixed with new milk or cream.

apple fraise (or froise) Apple slices fried then cooked in batter in the frying pan.

apple fritter Cut-up or sliced apples coated in batter and fried.

apple hedgehog Dish of stewed apples (whole), the centres of which are filled with jam, arranged in the form of a hedgehog, decorated with shreds of almonds, covered with icing sugar, and browned in the oven.

apple juice Beverage obtained by pressing ripe apples.

apple meringue Similar to apple snow, but baked in a slow oven after being dressed on the dish.

apple mint Apple-flavoured mint used for flavouring or brewed as a digestive tea.

apple pandowdy (American) Apple pie made with molasses.

apple pie Apples covered with a pastry crust made from flour and shortening cooking fat, margarine, lard, butter or a mixture of lard and butter or margarine.

apple pudding Apples cooked in suet pastry.

apple pupton Pudding made with apple pulp, breadcrumbs, butter, eggs, and sugar, baked in a plain mould, and served with a hot fruit syrup.

apple snow Apple pulp or *purée*, sweetened, blended with stiffly beaten egg-white, piled into glasses and decorated to taste.

apple rum punch Beverage of rum, brandy, sugar, apple juice and spices poured over oranges stuck with cloves and baked; served warm.

apple tansy Kind of apple fritter. The batter, made of cream and eggs, is poured over partially-stewed apples. The fritters are fried in butter, and served very hot.

apple toddy Warm alcoholic drink containing cooked apple pulp.

applejack (American) Apple brandy, Calvados.

applesauce Sauce made from peeled, stewed apples, flavoured with sugar, lemon-juice, and cinnamon (optional); sometimes with added sherry and a little soft-cooked chopped onion.

apprêt (French) Prepared, cooked, dressed.

après-dîner (French) After dinner, afternoon, evening.

après-souper (French) After supper, evening.

apricoat (American) To cover a cake or sweet with a layer of apricot jam flavoured with apricot liqueur.

apricot Small delicious golden-yellow fruit, native of China, introduced into Europe by Alexander the Great. Popular as a dessert fruit but widely used for making flans, pies, ice-cream, etc.; also used for preserving and making brandy, it is high in vitamin A content.

apricot brandy (Sometimes called apricot gin) Liqueur made from apricots.

apricot nectar (American) Apricot juice.

Aprikose (German) Apricot.

apron (i) Small European fish with succulent flesh, resembling perch. (ii) Protective overgarment worn in the kitchen, usually tied round the waist.

apry (French) Apricot-flavoured liqueur.

aqua vitae (Latin) Literally "water of life". Distilled liquor such as aquavit or the French brandy *eau-de-vie*.

aquavit Colourless distilled alcohol known in various countries by sundry names such as *akavit, schnapps, eau-de-vie*, etc.

Arabian coffee Coffee brewed with cardamom seeds, honey or brown sugar and rose water.

arac (French) Spirit distilled from fermented rice, palmjuice or sugar and coconut milk.

arachide (French) Earthnut; peanut.

arachido (Italian) Peanut.

arachis oil Peanut oil.

aragosta (Italian) (i) Lobster. (ii) Crawfish.

araignée de mer (French) Spider crab.

arancia (Italian) Orange.

arancia affetata (Italian) Orange slices poached in liqueur.

aranciata (Italian) Orangeade.

arbenne (French) Snow partridge.

arbia (Italian) Dry white Tuscan table wine.

Arbois (French) Small town in the Jura giving its name to dry and sparkling white wines made in the area.

arbouse (French) Arbutus.

arbre à liqueur (French) Toddy palm.

arbutus Berry fruit of the cane apple, found in southern North America, Mexico and Southern Europe, used to make wine, spirits and the liqueur, *crème d'arbouse*.

Arcachon (French) Town on the Bay of Biscay famed for its oyster beds.

arcanette (French) Teal found in the Lorraine, highly regarded by gastronomes, with a flavour similar to wild duck and cooked in the same ways.

Archiduc, à l' (French) Dishes seasoned with paprika and blended with cream.

archil Paste made from lichen used for colouring pickled tongue.

Ardennaise, à l' (French) Dishes of small birds cooked in a casserole with juniper berries.

arenque (Spanish) Herring.

arête (French) Fishbone.

Arfensuppe mit Snuten und Poten (German) Hamburg speciality, thick pea soup made from pig's feet.

Argenteuil (French) District in France, Dept. *Seine-et-Oise*, celebrated for asparagus, *aspèrges d'Argenteuil*.

Ariègeoise, à l' (French) Dishes such as mutton or chicken garnished with pickled pork, green cabbage and red (kidney) beans.

arille, aril (French) Mace.

aringa (Italian) Herring.

aringa sott' olio (Italian) Herring fillets in oil.

arista (Italian) Roast loin (chine) of pork.

arista alla Fiorentina (Italian) Chine of pork roasted in water, not fat, with garlic, rosemary and cloves.

arista alla Perugina (Italian) Chine of pork roasted in water, with fennel.

Arles (French) Town in France (*Bouche du Rhône*), celebrated for its sausages, *saucissons d'Arles*.

Arlésienne, à l' (French) Dishes with a garnish based on tomatoes: (i) whole stewed tomatoes (peeled) with fried chicory hearts (ii) small tomatoes stuffed with rice pilaff, large olives stuffed with chicken forcemeat, new potatoes and anchovy butter, or (iii) sautéed tomatoes, fried aubergines and fried onion rings.

arm pot roast (American) Beef cut from chuck or neck.

arm steak (American) Thick braising slice from pork, beef or veal.

armadillo Small mammal native to South America, eaten as meat.

Armagnac (French) Brandy produced in the Armagnac area in southern France.

armoricaine Choice variety of oysters.

Armoricaine, à l' (Corruption) See *Americaine, à l'*

arnaki tis souvlas (Greek) Greek dish of whole roast baby lamb.

aroma Spicy fragrance.

aromates (French) Aromatics.

aromatics Plants, herbs etc. with bland or pungent aroma used in cookery or confectionery such as thyme, tarragon, bay leaves, chervil, dill, basil, cumin, fennel, etc.

arracacha American plant yielding a starch similar to arrowroot from its roots, which can also be cooked like yams and sweet potatoes.

arrack Spirit distilled from fermented dates, rice, palm juice or sugar and coconut milk.

arrière-goût (French) After-taste.

arroche (French) Orach or orache. Common name for certain plants such as mountain spinach, eaten as spinach.

arroser (French) To baste with gravy, sauce, oil, butter or dripping.

arrosto (Italian) Roast.

arrosto d'abbacchio (Italian) Roast spring lamb.

arrosto di vitello al forno (Italian) Oven-roasted veal.

arrosto di vitello ubbriacato (Italian) Pot-roasted veal.

arrowroot Easily digestible flour produced from the root of a tropical plant, used for thickening sauces and making puddings, porridge, sweets, etc., and flavouring biscuits.

arroz (Spanish) Rice.

arroz con bacalao (Spanish) Rice with codfish.

arroz con frijoles (Spanish) Rice with beans.

arroz con pollo (Spanish) Rice with chicken. Dish seasoned with garlic and coloured with annatto or saffron.

arsella (Italian) Mussel.

arsenic Element present in minute quantity in certain foods such as turnips, fish, egg-yolk, milk, etc., poisonous in overdose.

Artagnan, à l' (French) Meat and poultry dishes garnished with *cèpes*, stuffed tomatoes and potato croquettes.

artichaut (French) Artichoke.

artichaut (fond d') (French) Artichoke hearts which can be prepared and cooked in a variety of ways with sauces, in butter, etc.

artichoke (i) Chinese (or Japanese) artichoke: white spiral roots, eaten raw, or cooked and served with melted butter. (ii) Globe artichoke: resembling a large thistle when fully grown. The bud of the flower is the edible part, and the *fond* or bottom is particularly prized. Eaten boiled and served with melted butter or *vinaigrette* sauce. Leaves are pulled off singly, dipped in chosen dressing and sucked at the-soft end. The bottom, with the choke removed, is eaten with a knife and fork. They can also be sun-dried or pickled in brine. (iii) Jerusalem artichokes: knobby tubers, scrubbed, peeled and boiled in salted water with added lemon juice to preserve colour. Served with white sauce, or they can be baked in dripping to serve with roast meats.

Artois (French) Old province of France (*Pas de Calais*). Several dishes are called after this place.

aruba roast (American) Highly-spiced kid or lamb roasted and served with freshly shredded cucumbers; first introduced in the Dutch West Indian island of Aruba.

arza Arabian brandy made from mares' milk.

asado (Spanish) (i) Roast, roasted. (ii) A joint of meat.

asafoetida Oleo-gum resin extracted from *ferula foetida*, a plant found in Afghanistan and Persia which has some similarity to the onion family, though stronger and more crude. It is still used for curries in India.

Asbach (German) German brandy.

asciutto (Italian) Term applied to dry wines.

asco (Corsican) Seasonal cheese available October to May.

ascorbic acid Chemical name for Vitamin C.

ash Tree whose young shoots can be eaten in salads, its seeds preserved and its leaves used as the basis for a kind of lemonade with small alcoholic content

ash bread (American) Cornbread wrapped in cabbage leaves and baked in hot ashes or embers.

ashcake (American) Cornbread baked in hot ashes.

asiago (Italian) Cheese made from partly-skimmed cow's milk in the province of Vicenza.

asopao (Spanish) Puerto-Rican-style chicken and rice.

asparagi all'aglio (Italian) Asparagus cooked and served in garlic-flavoured hot oil.

asparagi, punte di (Italian) Asparagus tips.

asparago (Italian) Asparagus.

asparagus Edible shoots of the asparagus plant, (a member of the lily family), which are tied in bunches and boiled or steamed. Served cold in salads or hot with *hollandaise* sauce, melted butter, or grated cheddar cheese. It may be bottled and is obtainable canned and made into canned or packet soups.

asparges (Danish) Asparagus.

aspargessuppe (Danish) Asparagus soup.

aspèrge (French) Asparagus.

asperge (Dutch) Asparagus.

aspic Savoury jelly. Clarified stock fortified with meat or fish and vegetable flavouring, rendered gelatinous with calf's feet or gelatine. Used for cold *entrées*, for cold savouries, and for masking and garnishing.

aspic (Italian) Aspic jelly.

Aspik (German) Aspic jellly.

assaisonnement (French) (i) Seasoning. (ii) Dressing for mixed salad.

assaisonner (French) To mix; to season.

Assam Indian tea famous for its pungency.

assiette (French) (i) Plate. (ii) Term for *hors d'œuvre* which a plate is large enough to hold.

assiette Anglaise (French) Platter with a variety of cold meats and *charcuterie*, garnished with watercress, gherkins, etc.

assorti (French) Assorted.

astaco (Italian) Crayfish.

astakos (Gteek) Lobster, crayfish.

asti (Italian) Sparkling Italian wine in many varieties and qualities.

asti spumanti (Italian) Sparkling wine made from sweet muscat grapes originally grown in the Asti region of northwestern Italy.

asticciola alla calabrese (Italian) Skewer containing alternating beef, cheese, sausage and bread, oiled and grilled.

Astrakhan Russian province famed for its caviare.

astringent Commodity which causes puckering, tightening or contracting. Vegetable astringents such as bramble, lemon juice, quinces, etc. owe their property to tannin.

astroderme (French) Yellowish-pink fish with black and silver spots used in *bouillabaisse*.

atelet (French) See *Hatelet*. Small silver or wooden skewer used for decorative purposes.

Athénienne, à l' (French) Dishes usually flavoured with lightly-fried onion and garnished with aubergines, tomatoes and sweet pimentos.

athérine (French) Sand-smelt or silverside known also in France as *prêtre* and *faux éperlan*. A species of fish similar to smelts, distinguishable from the real smelt by the absence of the cucumber smell so peculiar to the latter. Though not so fine in flavour and taste, sand-smelts are both delicate and wholesome. All recipes suitable for bass can be used.

Atholl brose (Scottish) Beverage made of honey, water, whisky and oatmeal.

Atlantic coast hard-shell clam (American) Thick-shelled American clam found in the Atlantic Ocean; the largest ones are called Cape cods; the medium-sized, Cherrystones; and the smallest, Littlenecks.

atriplex Herbaceous plant of the spinach family, prepared like spinach, also known as Garden Orach or French spinach.

attereaux (French) Food, usually *hors d'œuvre* placed on skewers, coated with a sauce, breadcrumbed and deep-fried.

attendu (French) Term for dishes or beverages left to improve in flavour.

atum (Portuguese) Tuna.

atún (Spanish) Tuna.

au (singular) *aux* (plural) (French) To; in; with. See separate alphabetical entries.

au gratin (French) Sprinkled with breadcrumbs and/or cheese and browned in oven or under grill. (In English, the term implies a cheese topping, but this is not necessarily so in French usage, where *au gratin* means a brown top-crust.)

auberge (French) Inn.

aubergine (French) Eggplant. Egg-shaped fruit of a plant of the nightshade family, ranging in colour from yellow-white to purple. Skins are left on for baking and for some other dishes. Aubergines can be sliced, fried, grilled, sautéed, stuffed, used in fritters, soups and casseroles.

aubergiste (French) Inn-keeper; hotel-keeper.

aud man's milk (Scottish) Eggnog.

audit ale Strong ale, brewed originally at the Universities of Oxford and Cambridge and drunk at the "Audit Day" feasts.

Auflauf (German) *Soufflé* or puff; omelette or baked *soufflé* pudding.

Aufschnitt (German) Sliced cold meat or sausage.

aufwaschen (German) To wash the dishes.

aufzehren (German) To eat, to consume.

Aurillac (French) Town in the Auvergne region of France, centre of the production of *Cantal* cheese.

aurora (Italian) Basic white sauce, coloured and flavoured with tomato *purée*.

Aurore, à l' (French) (i) Sweetbreads, poultry or eggs served with a *velouté* sauce to which is added butter and tomato *purée*. (ii) A cheese made in Normandy.

aurum (Italian) Orange-flavoured liqueur.

Auslese (German) German wine produced from selected grapes.

ausnehmen (German) (i) To draw poultry (ii) To clean fish.

Ausschank (German) Pub, bar.

ausschmücken (German) To decorate, to garnish.

Auster (German) Oyster.

Australian baobab Cream-of-tartar tree.

Australian nut Macadamia nut.

autoclave Pressure-cooker.

automat Coin-operated machine dispensing beverages and foods.

Autrichienne, à l' (French) Dishes seasoned with paprika; sometimes fennel, sour cream or lightly-fried onion is also added, in Austrian-style cookery.

autruche (French) Ostrich.

Auvergne (French) Region of France noted for its high-quality meat, vegetables, dessert fruits, chestnuts and walnuts, as well as for its cabbage *potée* (soup).

Auvernat (French) Wine cultivated around *Orléans*.

avant-goût (French) Fore-taste.

ave (Portuguese and Spanish) Bird or fowl.

aveline (French) Hazelnut, filbert.

avellana (Spanish) Hazelnut, filbert.

avercake English oatcake.

avgolemono (Greek) Chicken soup thickened with eggs and flavoured with lemon juice.

Avignon (French) City of gastronomic fame in France.

avocado pear Pear-shaped fruit of a tropical and sub-tropical tree, When ripe, the pears are dark purplish green and the flesh is soft. A good source of Vitamin C, oil and calcium, they are usually eaten as *hors d'œuvre*, filled with a savoury mixture or with a *vinaigrette* sauce.

avocet Wading bird, cooked as for teal in France.

avoine (French) Oats.

Avola (Italian) Sicilian town renowned for its sweet almonds.

avondeten (Dutch) Supper.

ayapana South American plant whose leaves are used to make a tea-like infusion.

aythya (French) Pochard duck.

ayunar (Spanish) To fast.

azerole (French) Mediterranean medlar used for confectionery and jam: also for making a liqueur.

azeitão (Portuguese) Sheep's milk cheese.

azeitona (Portuguese) Olive.

azhabsanda (Russian) Steamed lamb and vegetables.

azote (French) Nitrogen.

azúcar (Spanish) Sugar.

azucarero (Spanish) Sugar-basin.

azy (French) Rennet made of skimmed milk and vinegar.

azyme (French) Unleavened bread.

azymous (French) Unleavened.

baalie (Scottish) Lightly baked thin oatmeal cake.

baba Very light yeast cake of flour, butter, milk and eggs flavoured with lemon, rum or kirsch, and usually containing currants. The name derives from the Polish, *babka*, although the cake is of a different kind.

baba au rhum (French) Rum-baba, a yeast-leavened cake soaked in rum, served hot or cold.

babawte (South African) Baked curry of minced beef.

babeurre (French) Buttermilk.

babines (French) (i) Pendulous lips of animals (ii) "Chops" (slang).

babka (Polish) Polish-Russian cake containing fruit, almonds, etc.

baboy (Filipino) Pork.

baby food Fruits, vegetables, and meats puréed, and sold in small jars or cans.

baby gouda Smooth, round, low-fat yellow cheese originating in the Netherlands, covered with red wax.

baby lamb See Lamb.

Babycham Brand name of a sparkling perry (pear cider)

bacalao (Spanish) Codfish.

bacalhau (Portuguese) (i) Codfish. (ii) Portuguese speciality dishes based on salt cod.

bacalhau do céu (Portuguese) Cod with olive oil, *béchamel* sauce and potatoes, garnished with hard-boiled eggs and onions.

bacardi Cuban-type "white" rum originally distilled in Cuba by the Bacardi family in 1862. Their product is said to have saved the life of the heir to the Spanish throne (Alfonso XIII) in 1892.

bacardi cocktail Mixed drink of bacardi rum, sugar, lime juice and grenadine syrup.

baccalà (Italian) Dried salt cod.

baccalà alla livornese (Italian) Tuscan dish of dried cod cooked with potatoes and tomatoes.

baccalà mantecato (Italian) *Puréed* salt cod.

19

Bacchus Roman god of wine.

Bachforelle (German) Brook trout.

bacile (French) Samphire.

bacillus bulgaricus (Latin) Essential element in yogurt and other fermented milks; the culture was named *bulgaricus* in honour of Bulgarian centenarians who attribute their longevity to eating yogurt.

backbone Spinal column or spine.

backen (German) To bake.

Backen (German) Baking.

Bäckerei (German) Bakery.

Backhendl (Austrian/German) Fried chicken.

Backhühn (German) Fried chicken.

backings Kind of fritter, best known in America, as a dish for breakfast.

Back'nbier (German) Baker's beer of Bayreuth, brewed in the bakeries as a side-line.

Backobst (German) Dried fruit.

Backpflaume (German) Dried plum; prune.

backspan (Scottish) Oatcake baking plate.

back spittle Long-handled wooden baking spatula.

Backsteiner (German) Literally "Brick-shaped" cheese similar to Limburger.

Backwert (German) Pastry.

bacon Sides and back of the pig, cured and smoked (The thigh, removed and cured separately, becomes ham). Bacon cured but not smoked is called green, fresh white or plain bacon. Its rind is white, its flavour milder than smoked bacon. Rashers and joints are now marketed in cellophane packs but this does not lengthen their keeping capacity. Rashers are grilled or fried, used in pies or puddings, or as accompaniment to poultry. Joints are boiled or baked, having been pre-soaked for several hours to remove excess saltiness.

bacon and cheese (American) Open sandwich combination often served with sliced cucumbers, sliced tomatoes, and potato crisps.

bacon dish Covered platter to keep bacon rashers warm until served.

bactericide Any substance capable of destroying bacteria.

badian Anise-flavoured fruit from China, used in liqueurs, confectionery, etc.

badimdzhan mussambe (Russian) Lamb and aubergine casserole.

Badisches Ochsenfleisch (German) Speciality dish of boiled beef with horseradish sauce, from the Black Forest region.

badminton cup Claret cup containing soda water, herbs, and sugar.

bael or Bengal quince Fruit of the orange tribe. Highly esteemed in India as a preserve, either as jam or as a syrup.

bagasse (French) Sugar cane.

bagna caôda (Italian) Piedmontese dish of a hot sauce made of oil, butter, truffles, anchovies and garlic, in which fresh vegetables (celery, artichokes, etc.) are dunked.

bagoong (Filipino) Shrimp or prawn paste.

bagration (French) French-style soup or salad named after 19th-century Russian general, Prince Pëtr Bagration, to whom Carême was chef.

bagration egg Egg cooked or served with macaroni.

bagration salad See *salade bagration*.

baht (Turkish) A toast — Good Luck!

baie (French) Berry.

baie de ronce (French) Blackberry.

bain de pied (French) Colloquial French term (literally "footbath") an excess of liquid, especially coffee overflowing from cup to saucer.

bain-marie (French) Double or multiple saucepan, used for cooking or keeping hot delicate dishes, such as sauces, which might disintegrate over direct heat. Used in the oven or on top of stove.

baiser (French) Small meringue joined to another by thick cream or other filling. Literally, "Kiss".

baissière (French) Wine sediment.

baisure (French) Delicate crust, "kissing" crust, where two loaves are attached.

bajet Species of oyster with edible but not very delicate flesh found on the west coast of Africa.

bajoue (French) Chap.

baka (Filipino) Beef.

bake Too cook over dry heat, usually in an oven, between 250 and 450 degrees Fahrenheit. Suitable method for meat, fish, poultry, cakes, pastry, bread, and certain fruits and vegetables.

baked alaska Meringue-covered sponge cake filled with ice cream and browned in a high oven.

baked apple Cored apple filled with white or brown sugar before baking; sometimes with added sultanas or raisins. Served with sour cream, whipped cream, ice cream or custard.

baked beans (i) American speciality. See Boston baked beans. (ii) Commercially marketed haricot beans in sauce based on the American original, and sold in cans.

baked beef bones Low-calorie slimming dish consisting of the baked lean meat left adhering to the bones, and the marrow within them.

baked egg Egg cooked in buttered ramekin dish in a hot oven until set.

bakehouse (American) Bakery.

bakemeat (American) Meat pie.

baker (i) Specialist in preparing and baking all kinds of breads, cakes, and pastries. (ii) (American) Vegetable serving dish without a cover.

baker's dozen Twelve plus one — extra one given to bring customers back again.

baker's yeast Maximum-growth yeast used for leavening dough.

bakery Establishment where bread and cakes are baked and sold.

bakeware (American) **baking ware** Heat-resistant utensils suitable for use in baking, such as pyrex-type glass or porcelain-coated steel.

Bakewell tart Open plate tart with a pastry base and a cake-type filling, originating in Bakewell, Derbyshire.

bakhlava (Russian) Layered pastry.

baking blind Method of baking pastry cases for flans, pies, etc. The container is lined with pastry, covered with greased greaseproof paper, half-filled with dried beans or crusts. The pastry is cooked in a hot oven until barely done, then the paper and filling are removed and the pastry returned to the oven to dry off and finish cooking. A hot filling can now be added, or the case may be cooled and filled later.

baking powder Raising agent used in cakes, etc.; a mixture of baking soda (sodium bicarbonate), an acid substance such as calcium phosphate or cream of tartar, and a starchy base, such as flour or cornflour. When a mixture containing baking powder is wetted and heated, carbon dioxide is given off and the mixture is 'aerated and increased in bulk.

baking-powder biscuit (American) Scone made with flour, shortening, baking powder, milk, salt and other ingredients such as cheese, ginger, etc.

baking soda Bicarbonate of soda (sodium bicarbonate).

baklava (Greek) Greek or Turkish dessert sweetmeat made from leaves of a kind of *strudel* paste, spread with butter and filled with crushed nuts. A sugar or honey syrup (often flavoured with lemon) is poured over the cooled, cooked pastry.

bakverk (Swedish) Pastry.

balachan Seasoning of small shrimps pounded with salt and dried in the sun. Widely used in Siam.

balantier (French) Wild pomegranate.

balaou (French) Small fish similar to the sardine, with delicate, easily digestible flesh, abounding in Martinique.

baldwin (American) American winter apple used for cooking, salads, or eaten raw.

Bâle, Basle Swiss city famous for its honey cakes, "leckerlies".

baleine (French) Whale.

baliste (French) Trigger-fish.

ball cheese (American) Pennsylvania-German sour-milk cheese.

balle (French) Ball.

ballotin (French) Variety of orange tree with a fruit similar to lemons.

ballotine (French) Small ball or roll of meat, fish or fowl.

balm Fragrant herb, having leaves with a flavour and scent of lemon. Used in punches, fruit drinks, etc., and added to stuffings, soups and sauces. The leaves may be dried.

baloney Corruption of Bologna, the famous Italian sausage.

Balsam (German) (i) Balm. (ii) Balsam.

balsam herb Costmary, or alecost.

balsamo (Italian) Balm, balsam.

balthazar Large wine bottle containing the equivalent of 16 ordinary standard bottles.

balyx (Russian) Salted or smoked sturgeon.

bambelle (French) Small fish of the carp family found in some Swiss lakes.

bamboo cocktail (American) Mixture of bitters, sherry, and vermouth.

bamboo juice Rice wine sold in a section of bamboo.

bamboo shoot Oriental vegetable delicacy, the leaf bud of the bamboo, a tropical arborescent grass. Bamboo shoots, which are available canned, are cooked alone or with other vegetables and extensively used in Chinese cookery.

bamies (Greek) Okra.

banana Fruit of a tropical tree. Of the 30 or so varieties, the two chief ones are the Jamaica or Plantain banana (long, largish, creamy-fleshed) and the Canary or Dwarf banana (smaller, shorter, with pinkish flesh and a richer, more aromatic flavour). The banana is rich in Vitamin C, contains other vitamins and has a high starch content. It is exported green and ripened in special warehouses. It is obtainable also in dried form. Bananas are eaten raw, or may be baked or fried or used in fritters, trifles, salads, jellies, etc.

banana (Italian) Banana.

banana bread Cakelike bread baked from dough containing mashed ripe bananas.

banana chips Thinly sliced fried and baked banana strips.

banana chutney Chutney made with sieved bananas, powdered curry, dates, crystallized ginger, etc.

banana cream pie Baked pie case filled with bananas in a custard mixture and topped with whipped cream.

banana flour Flour made from dried

ripe bananas, nutritious and easily digested.

banana fritter Banana dipped in batter and fried in deep fat.

banana ice cream Vanilla ice cream blended with banana pulp.

banana split Bananas cut lengthwise and topped with ice cream, chopped nuts, whipped cream and maraschino cherries.

banana squash (American) Taper-ended variety of winter squash.

banane (French) Banana.

Banane (German) Banana.

banane flambée (French) Sliced banana heated in syrup, sprinkled with rum, and set alight before serving.

banania (French) Banana - flavoured French liqueur.

Banbury cheese Very rich cheese sold in small soft rounds.

Banbury cake Traditional cake made of pastry with a filling of mixed dried fruits, etc.

babdeja (Spanish) Tray.

bandes des cervelas (French) Sausage strings.

bang (American) Ale and cider mixture spiced with ginger and nutmeg, often sweetened with sugar, which can be fortified with large measures of gin or whisky.

bangi Small tree growing in the Philippines, with green-coloured fruit the size of an orange.

banille (French) Small, long, tapering pod yielding a fragrant sweet juice often used in the manufacture of chocolate in place of vanilla, to which it is rather similar.

Bankett (German) Banquet.

banneton (French) See Cauf.

bannock (Scottish) Unleavened scone made of barley meal or oatmeal and cooked on a griddle or girdle, then often toasted till crisp.

banquet Elaborate meal consisting of many courses.

banquete (Spanish) Banquet; elaborate meal.

banquière, à la (French) Chicken, sweetbreads or *vol-au-vent* garnished with mushrooms, truffles, *quenelles* and Madeira sauce.

bantam fowl Very small fowl, so called because it was originally brought from Bantam, Java. Bantam eggs, though small, are of superior quality.

Bantu beer South African liquor brewed from corn, millet and other grains. Also known as "Kaffir beer".

Banyuls (French) Red dessert wine first grown near Banyuls in southern France.

baobab Tropical African tree yielding a sweet, slightly acid pulpy fruit known as "monkey-bread" because monkeys eat it. The Africans dry the leaves, powder them and mix with their food.

bap (Scottish) Breakfast roll made from a yeast dough, containing a little fat. Usually oval in shape, baps are brushed over with milk and water, then dusted with flour to give them their characteristic floury finish.

bar (i) Counter where drinks are mixed. (ii) Part of a licensed premises, i.e., public bar, private bar, saloon bar.

bar (French) Bass.

bar (Spanish) Bar.

bar-b-q (American) Slang abbreviation for barbecue.

bar de mer (French) Sea bass.

Bar-le-Duc (French) Town in Lorraine noted for red-currant preserves; also producing local red and white table wines.

bar noir (French) Black bass.

bar rayé (French) Striped bass.

bar spoon Long-handled stirring spoon used when mixing drinks.

bara lawr (Welsh) Bread made with seaweed.

barack (Hungarian) Hungarian apricot brandy.

baraquille (French) Patty filled with game, sweetbreads, etc. bound with sauce. Also prepared as rissoles.

barbabiètola (Italian) Beet, beetroot.

barbacoa (Spanish) Barbecue.

Barbados cream (American) Rum liqueur containing cinnamon, citrus fruit peel, cloves, mace, and brown sugar.

Barbados water (American) Cordial flavoured with rum, orange and lemon peel.

Barbantane (French) Dessert wine made in the Barbantane region of France. (*Bouches du Rhône*)

barbarano (Italian) Dry Venetian table wines, red or white.

barbarea Herb similar to cress and used in the same ways. Known as Herb of St. Barbara, winter cress and treacle wormseed. In the United States a variety is cultivated as winter cress and used as a salad green.

barbaresco (Italian) Dry red wine from Piedmont.

barbarin (French) Fish of the mullet family.

barbarine Variety of marrow, yellow and elongated, cooked as for marrow and cucumber. A squash in America.

barbarine (French) Passion-fruit, granadilla.

barbe (French) Literally, "beard" (i) Wattle (of a turkey, etc.) (ii) Fin (of a flat fish). (iii) "Mould" on preserves.

barbe de bouc (French) Plant resembling the salsify. It is boiled in seasoned water or stock, or baked.

barbe de capucin (French) Chicory.

barbe de jupiter (French) House-leek, a plant with succulent leaves that grows on walls and cottage roofs.

barbeau (French) Barbel.

barbecue (i) To roast meat, etc. on racks or spits over an open fire or in an oven. (ii) Open-air party with food cooked as in (i).

barbecue pit Trench for holding live coals and food to be barbecued.

barbecue rack Metal rack supporting a spit for turning fish, fowl, or meat above a bed of fuel.

barbecue sauce Highly seasoned basting sauce used in barbecuing.

barbel River fish of carp variety recognisable by the barbels around the mouth area. Eaten more on the Continent than in Britain. The flesh is insipid and bony but can be poached, fried, braised or baked. The hard roe is reputed to be poisonous.

barbera (Italian) Italian red wine made from Barbera grapes of northern Italy. (Piedmont) *barbera d'asti* (Italian) Sparkling red wine from Piedmont. See *Barbera*.

barberey (French) Small soft cheese resembling *Camembert*, sometimes known as *Fromage de Troyes*.

barberon (French) Salsify.

barberry Shrub with sharp red berries used in jellies and preserves. They can also be dried and candied. The unripe berries, when still green, can be pickled in vinegar, like capers.

barbillon (French) Young barbel.

barbio (Italian) Barbel.

barboteur (French) Duck, domestic.

barbotte, barbote (French) Common name for river burbot or eel-pout.

barbotte en casserole (French) Stewed eel-pout.

barbounia (Greek) Fried or grilled red mullet.

barbue (French) Brill.

barchette (Italian) Small pastry case, filled with savoury mixture for *hors d'œuvre*.

Barcelona nut Spanish-type filbert, usually kiln-dried.

barcolé (French) Speckled.

bard To cover poultry breasts with fat or fat bacon to prevent drying out during roasting.

bardé (French) Larded with bacon fat.

barding fat Slices of fat bacon or pork used to cover poultry before roasting.

bardolino (Italian) Dry red Venetian table wine.

Barford pudding 18th century boiled pudding made from beef suet, raisins, flour, sugar, eggs and nutmeg.

barge (French) Godwit.

Barigoule, à la (French) Artichokes stuffed with mushrooms. The name is said to derive from the barigoule mushroom found in the south of France.

baril (French) Small barrel.

barley Cereal grass cultivated for its seeds and used in cattle food, breakfast cereals, soups, and beverages. Barley is also malted and used to brew beer and distil whisky. See also pot barley and pearl barley.

barley flakes Pressed and flattened barley grains used for making milk puddings and gruel.

barley flour Ground hulled barley used for blending with other flours in baking bread, cakes, biscuits, pancakes, etc., also in infant and invalid foods and restricted diets.

barley grits Hulled barley broken into small particles and used in casseroles, cereals, meat loaves, hamburgers, and soups.

barley meal Wholemeal flour made by grinding barley coarsely; still used in some districts for porridge and gruel, also as an additive to a certain kind of bread.

barley sugar Transparent toffee made by melting and cooling cane sugar. Barley water was formerly used in its preparation, hence its name.

barley water Mixture of boiled pearl barley and cold water sweetened with brown sugar, with added lemon juice.

barley wine Strong ale brewed from barley.

barm Brewer's yeast. The scum of malt liquor.

barnacle Limpet mollusc found on sea rocks, eaten raw with *vinaigrette* sauce, or cooked like mussels.

barnacle goose Bird of passage with edible but indigestible flesh. Can be cooked as ordinary goose.

barnevelder (American) Fowl producing large eggs and tender meat, originating from *Barneveld*, Holland.

barolo (Italian) Fine red table wine from the Piedmont area of northern Italy.

baron d'agneau (French) Baron of lamb.

baron of beef The two sirloins of beef, left uncut at the bone and roasted.

baron of lamb or mutton Saddle and two legs, usually roasted or spit-roasted. (In America) Hindquarters (both legs and loins).

Barossa Valley Principal wine-growing district of Australia.

barquette (French) Oval-shaped tartlet shell.

barquillo (Spanish) Thin rolled wafer.

barracuda Fierce fighting fish of the Caribbean. The smaller, less voracious Pacific species has tasty flesh often grilled, fried, smoked or steamed.

barrique (French) Large cask or barrel, usually for wine.

barrel (i) Small cask used as container for brandy, oil, herrings, etc. (ii) Standard size beer container holding 36 gallons (British measure).

barrot (French) Small barrel containing anchovies.

Barsac (French) White wine from Bordeaux region in south-western France.

Barsch (German) (i) Bass. (ii) Perch.

barsez barszcz (Polish) Soup made of beetroot.

bartavelle (French) Red partridge.

bartend (American) To prepare and serve alcoholic drinks.

bartender (American) Person serving drinks in a bar, cocktail lounge, restaurant, tavern, etc. who is more knowledgeable about drinks than an ordinary barman.

bartender's shaker (American) Twin-compartment shaker used to keep ice and liquid separate until ready for pouring.

bartlett Large, yellow, bell-shaped eating pear.

basella Indian spinach. Edible tropical plant cultivated in Europe, prepared as for spinach.

baselle (French) Bassella.

basil Aromatic herb, used (sparingly) to flavour salads, fish, egg and tomato dishes. Basil vinegar is made by steeping the leaves in vinegar, and is used for flavouring when the fresh plant cannot be procured.

basilic (French) Basil.

basilico (Italian) Basil.

basket-fired tea Green tea grown chiefly in Japan; and prepared by a special method; the name implies the method of preparing the leaves for market.

Basler Leckerli (German) Popular dessert cake richly flavoured with honey and spice, called after the town of Basle, of which it is a speciality.

Basquaise, à la (French) Large cuts of meat garnished with fried flap mushrooms, potatoes and Bayonne ham.

bass Fresh- and saltwater fish of the perch order, sometimes called white salmon or salmon-dace. It is prepared and served as for brill, turbot or salmon.

Bass English ale.

basse-pâte (French) Under-crust.

Bassereau (French) Brand of sparkling Burgundy.

basset (French) Turnspit.

bassin (French) Shallow dish or large plate.

bassine (French) Deep pan or basin.

bastaple (Irish) Soda bread.

baste (i) To drip or pour liquefied fat on meat or poultry during the process of roasting, to prevent the outside of joints, birds, etc., from becoming excessively dry. (ii) To pour boiling water over poaching eggs.

basted egg Whole egg fried on one side and basted with fat until top is set.

baster Syringe-like device for basting roast meat or poultry by sucking up and expelling gravy or juice.

basterma (Russian) Caucasian dish of dried beef, hot peppers and fenugreek.

basting brush Long bristle brush for basting joints or poultry with gravy or other cooking juices.

basting spoon Long-handled spoon for pouring fats or juice over roasting meat or poultry.

bat Small mammal whose meat is highly regarded in the East, particularly China.

bat (French) French culinary term for tail of fish.

bataclan (French) Pastry dessert made of blanched almonds, sugar, vanilla, flour, eggs and rum; baked and then iced.

bâtarde, sauce (French) Butter sauce.

batata Sweet or Indian potato.

bateau (French) Boat-shaped *hors d' œuvre* dish.

batería de cocina (Spanish) Kitchen range.

bâton (French) (i) Bread-stick (ii) Various preparations shaped in the form of little sticks.

Bath bun Yeast bun containing candied peel and sultanas, originally made in the City of Bath, Somerset.

Bath chap Cheek and jaw-bone of the

pig, salted and smoked, so called because those coming from Bath were first to obtain a reputation as being the very finest.

Battelmatt (German) Emmenthaler type of cheese originating in northern Italy and Switzerland.

battenberg cake Two-coloured oblong cake, covered with almond paste.

batter Flour-and-liquid mixture used in making drop scones, cakes, and pancakes, and in coating for batter-fried foods such as fritters, etc.

batter pudding Baked unsweetened pudding made of eggs, flour, and milk, served as a first course or with roast meat, as Yorkshire Pudding.

batterbread See spoonbread.

battercake Pancake or flapjack.

batterie de cuisine (French) Complete kitchen equipment for preparing and cooking foods.

Bauch (German) Belly, stomach.

Bauden (German) Austrian sour-milk cheese.

baudruche (French) Sausage casing.

Bauernbrot (German) Farmer's bread. Usually a dark bread.

Baumkuchen (German) Pyramid cake.

bauple Macadamia nut.

Bavarian cream See *Bavarois à la crème*.

Bavaroise Hot drink, said to have been invented in Bavaria, which used to be served at evening parties. Made with eggs, sugar, hot tea and hot milk and flavoured with a liqueur or coffee, chocolate, orange, vanilla, etc.

Bavarois, à la (French) In Bavarian style.

Bavarois à la crème (French) Cold custard, Bavarian cream made from sugar, eggs and cream, flavoured with vanilla, almond, maraschino or other flavouring.

bavette d'aloyau (French) Thin flank or skirt of beef or veal.

bay salt Sea salt. Common salt obtained from sea water by evaporation, less pure than that obtained from salt wells.

baya (i) Philippine rice wine. (ii) (Spanish) Berry.

bayleaf Leaf of a species of the laurel-tree, known as the cherry laurel. Largely used as flavouring, it is includ-

ed in the *bouquet garni*. Bayleaf flavour should always be used in moderation in flavouring soups, stews, etc. It is extensively employed in Sweden and Russia in the preserving of anchovies and other fish.

Bayonnaise, à la (French) Garnished with anchovy fillets, gherkins, and braised button onions, as in *Bayonne* cookery.

Bayonne (French) Town in the Bas-Pyrenees noted for its salt hams, also for black puddings, citron preserve and chocolates.

Bayrisches G'frornes (German) Bavarian frozen beer.

beaked parsley Chervil.

beaker Wide-mouthed goblet.

bean Leguminous plant which comes in many varieties. The seeds (and in some cases the young pods) are eaten as a vegetable. The mature seeds, when dried, are known as pulses. They are a valuable food, the best vegetable source of protein and a good source of the vitamin B group. Sprouted peas and beans are a good source of vitamin C. Fresh green beans contain vitamins C and A.

bean curd Vegetable cheese popular in many Oriental countries.

bean flour Flour made from dried beans.

bean oil Soya bean oil.

bean pot Covered earthenware pot used for baking beans.

bean sprout Sprout of a legume seed, such as soya or mung. The beans are left for a few days in damp, warm conditions, when sprouting takes place. Rich in vitamin C.

bear Edible animal; its meat needs marinating to tenderise. Bear ham, cured as for pork ham, is common in the U.S.S.R. Bear's paw is the earliest Chinese delicacy.

bearberry Arbutus.

Béarnaise, sauce Rich white sauce with a basis of eggs, served with grilled meat or fish and made in several variations. Named after *Béarn*, France, birthplace of King Henry IV, a great *gourmand*.

beastings pudding Baked custard made

from the colostrum given by a cow shortly after calving.

beat To lift and turn an ingredient or mixture rapidly in an upward movement in order to introduce air, using a hand tool (spoon, fork, whisk) or an electric mixer. *Meat* Raw meat is beaten with a weighty tool to break down fibres and increase tenderness.

beater Utensil operated manually or by electricity for beating, mixing, stirring, or whipping.

béatille (French) Name for small titbit such as kidneys, mushrooms, sweetbreads, etc. used as garnishes.

Beauharnaise, à la (French) Small cuts of meat such as tournados garnished with small artichoke hearts, *Béarnaise* sauce, *purée* of tarragon and small potato balls, a dish said to be named for the family of the Empress Josephine.

Beaujolais (French) Ruby red wine originating from *Beaujolais* in the Burgundy region of France.

Beaune (French) Small French town (*Côte d'Or*) famous for its red and white wines such as *Pommard, Volnay, Beaune, Mersault* and *Puligny*.

Beauvilliers (French) (i) (*Antoine*) Name of a great *cuisinier* (1754-1871) author of *L'art du Cuisinier*, long a standard work. (ii) Spinach and stuffed tomato garnish for large cuts of meat. (iii) Light sponge cake, iced and filled with cream.

bébé (French) Very small optic measure used in France.

beber a la salud de (Spanish) To drink somebody's health.

beber como una cuba (Spanish) To drink like a fish.

bebida (Spanish) Beverage, drink.

bec-pointu (French) White skate.

bécar (French) Roe salmon.

bécasse (French) Woodcock.

bécasseau (French) Young woodcock.

bécassine (French) Snipe.

bécasse rôtie (French) Roast woodcock.

beccaccia (Italian) Woodcock.

beccaccia farcita (Italian) Stuffed, roasted woodcock.

beccaccino (Italian) Snipe.

becerro (Spanish) Bullock.

becfigue (French) Garden-warbler.

béchamel **sauce** Rich white sauce of coating consistency, used in many recipes for savoury dishes, recognised as one of the four foundation sauces.

bêche de mer (French) Trepang, sea slug.

Becher (German) Beaker, cup, goblet, mug.

Beck's German beer brewed in Bremen.

bécune (French) Sea pike.

bedstraw Plant with yellow flowering tops containing a substance used in the curdling of milk and applied to the preparation of Cheshire cheese.

beech nut Fruit of the beech tree used to flavour confections; can be eaten plain or salted like almonds.

beech oil High-quality oil extracted from beech nuts.

beef Meat of any adult bovine, the best deriving from an ox about two years old. The flesh should be deep red, the fat soft and creamy. Prime beef is firm, fine-textured, slightly moist, and without gristle. A source of protein, calories (particularly if there is plenty of fat) the B vitamins and iron, it is cut in various ways, according to region or country. Prime cuts (sirloin, ribs, top rump, aitchbone) are roasted; less tender joints can be pot-roasted (rib or topside) or braised or stewed (brisket, flank). Joints can also be pickled, then boiled (topside, silverside, aitchbone, brisket). Small prime cuts are grilled or fried, others braised, stewed or boiled according to cut and quality.

beef *bouillon* Beef stock, the basis of clear soups.

beef bread Pancreas of a cow or steer.

beef cattle Meat-producing breeds such as Aberdeen-Angus, Hereford and Shorthorn; usually shorter and stockier than dairy breeds.

beef essence Beef juice seasoned with salt, used in making beef stock or beef tea.

beef extract Beef-tea made of beef juice and other soluble parts of beef meat; used in sauces and stews.

beef fillet Undercut of sirloin.

beef glaze Concentrated beef stock boiled down to a syrupy consistency.

beef jerky (American) Beef cut into long strips and dried in the sun; sometimes prepared by seasoning and smoking. Said to be a corruption of the Indian word *charqui*, "smoked meat".

beef juice Liquid produced by quickly boiling raw beef and expressing the juice with a beef-juice press.

beef-juice press Utensil for extracting beef juice from boiled beef.

beef marrow Fatty filling of beef bones extracted by long cooking and spread on bread or used in baking and cooking.

beef (or ox) muzzle Offal cooked as for ox tongue.

beef olive Slice of steak, beaten, stuffed with forcemeat, skewered, browned then simmered slowly.

beef (or ox) palate Old-time dish cooked like calf's head, after blanching and skinning, or cut into pieces and deep-fried.

beef *ragoût* Rump, shoulder or rib of beef, browned then simmered slowly with vegetables.

beef *roulade* See *roulade*.

beef shank (American) Top part of rib of beef.

beef stroganoff Dish made with beef, onions, mushrooms, and sour cream, said to be named for Count Stroganoff, a 19th century Russian diplomat.

beefaroni (American) Beef and macaroni served in tomato sauce.

beefburger Hamburger made of minced beefsteak.

beefsteak Choice cut of beef from fillet or sirloin which is grilled or fried.

beefsteak *à l'américaine* Finely chopped raw beef fillet formed into flat cakes which are slightly hollowed to accommodate a raw egg.

beefsteak pie Cubed or sliced lean beef covered with a pastry crust. Kidney and/or mushrooms are often added.

beefsteak pudding Cut-up lean beef cooked in a basin or other receptacle which is lined and topped with suet pastry.

beefsteak society Founded in London by a John Rich in 1735, and lasted till 1867.

beef-tea Essence of beef, extracted by a slow process of cooking, as required. Served to children and invalids.

beer Alcoholic beverage made by fermenting malted barley with hops. Colour, strength and flavour are determined by methods of brewing and bottling. Light-coloured beers are called ales. Said to have originated in ancient Egypt, from whence it passed to the Greeks, Romans and Gauls, it is used in cooking for stews and similar dishes (replacing part of the stock or water in the recipe) and for helping to mature rich fruit puddings and cakes, such as Christmas fare.

beer comb Bone or plastic spatula for removing foam from tops of beer glasses and mugs.

beer yeast Brewer's yeast.

Beere (German) Berry.

beeregar (American) Beer vinegar.

beer-pull Dispensing-tap handle of a beer barrel.

Beerenauslese (German) Wine produced from individually picked grapes.

beestings First milk drawn from a cow after calving.

beet sugar Sugar produced from the white roots of sugar beets.

beetroot Root vegetable widely used in the manufacture of sugar. It can be served hot as a vegetable, served as a salad ingredient or garnish either pickled or freshly-boiled, or used to make an excellent soup.

béhague (French) Mutton raised on the salt marshes of France. Also termed *pré-salé*, the name is derived from the Marquis de Béhague, one of the great French sheep farmers.

beignet (French) Fritter. Anything dipped in batter or thin paste and fried in deep fat.

beignet de cerises (French) Cherry fritter.

beignet de crème frite (French) Cream fritter.

beignet de fromage (French) Cheese fritter.

beignet d'huîtres (French) Oyster fritter.

beignet de panais (French) Parsnip fritter.

beignet de pêches (French) Peach fritter.

beignet de pomme (French) Apple fritter.

beignet de ris de veau (French) Sweet-bread fritter.

bekmes (Russian) Grape syrup.

bel paese (Italian) Creamy mild dessert cheese.

Belag (German) Sandwich spread.

Belgian hare Small breed of rabbit often served in rabbit *ragoûts* and stews.

Belgian loaf Boat-shaped loaf with several slashes on the top and a crusty bottom.

Belgian pastry Layered pastry.

bell pepper Bell-shaped green pepper.

belle-alliance (French) Variety of winter dessert pear.

belle-angevine (French) Large variety of winter pear, not of top dessert quality.

belle-chevreuse (French) Variety of peach.

belle-et-bonne (French) Variety of cooking pear.

belle-garde (French) Early autumn variety of peach.

Bellelay (German) Soft rennet cheese from the Abbey of Bellelay, Berne, Switzerland; also known as Monk's-Head cheese.

Bellevue, à la (French) Dishes served in aspic, or masked with *chaudfroid* sauce and garnished with chopped aspic, truffles and tongue.

bellone (French) Large fig grown in Provence.

beluga White sturgeon fished from the Black and Caspian seas for its roe, which yields the best caviar.

Belvoir Castle bun Bun made for the Duke of Rutland from plain flour, butter, currants, milk, sugar and yeast.

ben cotto (Italian) Well done.

bénédictin (French) *Bénédictine*-flavoured iced sponge-type cake.

Bénédictine (French) Popular liqueur, sweet and aromatic, originated by the *Bénédictine* monks at *Fécamp* in Normandy in 1510 and still made by them.

bénédictine, à la (French) Eggs or poached fish garnished with a paste made from salt cod cooked in oil, with crushed garlic, sometimes with truffles added.

Benediktiner (German) *Bénédictine* liqueur.

benne cake (American) Sesame-seed cake.

benzoate of soda Food preservative.

beoreg (Russian) Strudel-dough pastry stuffed with a savoury filling.

berce (French) Cow-parsnip.

berenjena (Spanish) Aubergine.

bergamder (French) Species of duck.

bergamot (i) Aromatic herb of the mint family, used sparingly in salads, and for making medicinal tea. (ii) Fine variety of pear. (iii) Species of pear-shaped orange whose skin is used in making perfumes.

bergamot mint True mint of the genus *Mentha* noted for its faintly orange scent.

berinjela (Portuguese) Aubergine.

Berkshire White pig with black markings, originally developed in Berkshire.

berle, ache d'eau (French) Old name for wild celery; water-parsnip.

Berliner Kuhkäse (German) Berlin "cow cheese". Soft cheese flavoured with caraway seeds.

Berliner Pfannkuchen (German)   (i) Doughnut. (ii) Pan-cake.

berlingot (French) Kind of caramel sweetmeat.

berlinois (French) Ball-shaped light yeast cake similar to a doughnut.

Bermuda onion (American) Large sweet variety of onion.

Bernard, Emile Famous *chef de cuisine*, (1828-1897) Was chef for over 20 years to the Emperor William I. Co-author of *La Cuisine Classique*, a famous standard work on cookery.

Berry (French) Area of France famed for its sheep production and for fine wines.

berry Pulpy edible fruit such as the blackberry, blueberry, raspberry, strawberry, etc.

berry sugar (American) Caster sugar.

besaigre (French) Sour, tart. Usually referring to wine.

beschuit (Dutch) Biscuit.

beshow (American) Black cod.

besi (French) Variety of pear.

Besteck (German) Cutlery; set of knife, fork and spoon.

bétail (French) Livestock.

bête rousse (French) Wild boar between six and twelve months old. See wild boar.

bette (French) Mangel-wurzel.

bette commune (French) White beet.

betterave (French) Beet, beetroot.

between the sheets (American) Cocktail consisting of equal parts of brandy, curaçao, and rum, sometimes with lime juice added.

beurre (French) Butter.

beurré (French) Juicy dessert pears in several varieties.

beurre, au (French) With butter or done in butter, tossed or *sautéed*.

beurre de Montpellier (French) Montpellier butter. Edible green-coloured butter used mainly for decorative purposes.

beurre d'anchois (French) Anchovy butter.

beurre fondu (French) Melted butter.

beurre frais (French) Fresh butter.

beurre frit (French) Fried butter.

beurre, lait de (French) Buttermilk.

beurre mâitre d'hôtel (French) Butter blended with parsley, lemon juice and seasonings to accompany grilled meats and fish, also boiled vegetables.

beurre manié (French) Kneaded blend of butter and flour used in thickening sauces because it will not go lumpy.

beurre noir (French) Browned butter sauce seasoned with finely chopped parsley and wine vinegar, served with brains, fish, and some vegetables. Also served with eggs, but with the capers and butter omitted.

beurre noir, au (French) Anything done in butter which is cooked to a brown colour.

beurre noisette (French) Nut-brown butter. Butter melted over the fire until it begins to brown.

beurre salé (French) Salt butter.

beurre vert (French) Green butter. Butter softened and mixed with spinach; used for sauces and garnishes.

beurrée (French) Buttered or greased.

beverage Any liquid, other than water, which is consumed as a drink.

bezahlen (German) To settle (a bill).

bezieu soep (Belgian cuisine). Vermicelli and redcurrant soup.

Béziers (French) Town in the *Hérault* department of France regarded as the area's wine capital; also renowned for culinary specialities found in the *Languedoc*.

bhang (Indian) Intoxicant brewed principally from hemp.

bianco (Italian) White (wine).

bianco piceno (Italian) Dry white Umbrian table wine.

biancomangiare (Italian) Rice cooked in almond water.

biborate of soda (American) Borax.

bicarb Slang for bicarbonate of soda.

bicarbonate of soda Baking soda. Used as a raising agent in recipes where one of the ingredients is an acid and also where a darkening effect is desired, as with gingerbread or chocolate cake. Bicarbonate of soda was once used to conserve the colour of boiled green vegetables, but it was found to have a destructive effect on the vitamin C content. Added to the water used for cooking very acid fruit, it helps to save sugar, as it neutralises some of the fruit acid.

bicchiere (Italian) Glass (drinking).

biche (French) Hind doe.

bichique (French) Tiny fish found near Reunion Island, used for curry in Créole cookery.

Bickbeere (German) Bilberry.

biddies on a raft (American) Slang for poached eggs on toast.

biefstuk (Dutch) Beefsteak.

bien cuit (French) Well-cooked; well-done.

bier (Dutch) Beer.

Bier (German) Beer.

Bier, dunkles (German) Dark beer.

Bier, helles (German) Light beer.

bière (French) Beer.

Bierkanne (German) Tankard.

Bierstube (German) Tap room.

Biersuppe (German) Eggnog with beer.

bietjes (Dutch) Dish of hot beetroots.

bietola (Italian) (i) Beet. (ii) Spinach beet.

bife con batatas (Portuguese) Steak and chips.

biffstek (Swedish) Beefsteak.

Bifsteck (German) Beefsteak.

biftec (Spanish) Beefsteak.

biftec a la pobre (Spanish) Beefsteak served with two fried eggs, onion rings, and fried potatoes, speciality of Chile.

bifteck (French) Beefsteak.

bifteck frites (French) Steak and chips.

big-eyed herring Alewife.

big-eyed mackerel Chub mackerel.

big-necked clam (American) Gaper clam of the Pacific coast.

bigarade (French) (i) Rich sauce made with bitter oranges and served with duck or duckling. (ii) Seville orange, bitter orange.

bigaradier (French) Orange blossom tree (*citrus aurantium*).

bigarré (French) Vari-coloured.

bigarreau (French) Hard-fleshed cherry in red and white varieties.

bigarrure (French) (i) Rich stew made from pheasants, capons, etc. Literally, a variety of designs or colours. (ii) Insertions made in meat and filled with sliced meat of various kinds.

Bignon (French) Famous Parisian restaurateur.

bigoli (Italian) Venetian name for spaghetti.

bigorneau (French) Winkle, periwinkle.

bigos (Polish) Main course meal of *sauerkraut*, pork sausage, cabbage, mushrooms, etc., a Polish national dish.

bijane (French) Cold wine soup popular in *Anjou*.

bilberry Blueberry, whortleberry, whinberry and (in Scotland) blaeberry. A small, dark-blue berry which grows wild, and ripens in August or September. The berries have a delicious sharp flavour, are excellent for fritters, tarts, jams and jellies, and are a good source of vitamin C.

bill of fare Menu.

billete (Spanish) Bill.

billot (French) Chopping block.

biltong (South African - Afrikaans) Dried strips of meat which keep for years, and can be grated or sliced and eaten raw.

billy (Australian) Lidded metal can used chiefly for boiling water for tea.

bind To make a mixture hold together by adding cheese, cream, liquid, melted fat, eggs, gelatine, etc.

biotin One of the B vitamins.

birch beer Fermented sap of the silverbirch tree.

bird-grape wine (American) Wine made from fermented juice of bird grapes grown in the Bahamas and along the east coast of Florida and Georgia.

bird pepper Most pungent of all capsicum peppers.

bird's nest (edible) Nest constructed by a small species of swallow, the Salangane, found on the coast of China. There are two kinds, the black and white nests, the latter being much more rare. The Chinese regard these nests as a great delicacy, and make them into soup.

Bireweck (German) Alsatian pastry.

Birne (German) Pear.

birra (Italian) Beer.

birthday cake Cake baked in honour of someone's birday, often decorated with tiny candles and inscribed.

bis (French) Light brown.

biscotin (French) Small, hard, sweet biscuit.

biscotte (French) (i) Thin slice of brioche paste, baked, buttered and sugared, generally served with tea. (ii) Rusk of bread, rebaked in the oven.

biscottino (Italian) Small biscuit.

biscotto (Italian) (i) Rusk. (ii) Biscuit.

biscuit Originally, as the name implies, biscuit dough was baked twice to give the characteristic crispness and keeping capacity. There are innumerable varieties, both sweet and savoury, the commercial types being made in special ovens, but home-made biscuits can be produced with ordinary utensils and baked in a domestic oven.

biscuit (American) Scone.

biscuit (French) Biscuit.

biscuit cutter Sharp-edged utensil for cutting biscuits or scones from dough.

biscuit de reims (French) Savoy or finger biscuit.

biscuit glacé (French) Glazed biscuit, ice cream biscuit.

biscuitware Unglazed porcelain or pottery cups, mugs, plates and platters.

biset (French) Rock pigeon.

bishop (i) Hot drink usually made of mulled wine, spices, oranges and sugar, but varying from recipe to recipe. (ii) (American) Drink of sugar, fruit juice, soda water, Burgundy and rum, served with ice and seasonable fruit.

bisk Ancient dish made of wild and tame birds, sweetbreads, cocks' combs, etc.

bismarck herring Boned salt herring preserved in spices and wine vinegar, named after the 19th century statesman, Prince Otto von Bismarck.

bisque (French) Thick, rich soup based on a white stock made from fish or shell-fish.

Bisquit (French) Brand of champagne cognac.

bisquotin (French) See biscotin.

Bissen (German) Bite, morsel.

bistecca (Italian) Beefsteak.

bistecca alla cacciatora (Italian) Beefsteak in herbed wine and tomato sauce.

bistecca alla Fiorentina (Italian) Charcoal-grilled beef rib.

bistecca alla pizzaiola (Italian) Oven-cooked steak served with a hot tomato sauce, flavoured with herbs and peppers.

bistecchino (Italian) Hamburger.

bistik (Malay) Beefsteak.

bistro (French) Small tavern.

bitky (Russian) Meat balls served on toothpicks.

bitochky (Russian) Meatballs; meatcakes.

bitok Russian-style hamburger made of minced meat, tiny bits of bread, and onions, fried, then simmered in sour cream.

bitter (German) Bitter.

bitter chocolate (American) Unsweetened cooking chocolate.

bitter-sweet chocolate (American) Plain chocolate with added sugar, in place of some of the original fat content.

bitter cress Winter cress.

bitter melon East Indian cucumber-like vegetable, used in Chinese cookery.

bitter orange Species of orange with a very bitter and acid pulp, used in making marmalade. The essential oil of bitter orange is also used in cooking.

bitterballe (Dutch) Meat ball.

bitters Essence or liqueur made from bitter-flavoured aromatic herbs, spices, roots, barks etc. used in *apéritifs* and cocktails and as a flavouring. They are high in alcoholic content.

bivalve Edible two-shelled mollusc such as the clam, mussel, oyster, or scallop.

bizcochuelo (Spanish) Spongecake.

blåbærsuppe (Danish) Bilberry soup.

black abalone Species of dark-shelled abalone found in Pacific Coast waters.

black-and-white (American) Chocolate soda with vanilla ice cream.

black bass Freshwater game fish found in many parts of eastern North America

black bean (American) Mexican bean used for soup.

black bean soup (American) Soup made of black beans, celery, hard-boiled eggs, salt pork or bacon, and seasonings.

black beauty (American) Cheddar cheese made in Wisconsin, preserved in black wax coating.

black bread Dark coarse bread usually made from barley, cornmeal, and rye flours.

black bun See Scotch Bun.

black butter See *beurre noir*.

black caraway European herb used similarly to true caraway in baking, cooking, and salad making; also called black cumin.

black cock Male of the black grouse, or black game, a species of grouse common in the north of England.

black cod (American) Edible fish found in the North Pacific; also known as beshow or sablefish.

black coffee Coffee without cream or milk.

black crab (American) Edible land crab found in Florida and the West Indies.

black cumin Plant whose pungent seeds are used as a spice.

black-currant Small black juicy fruit of the black-currant bush widely used for puddings, desserts, preserves, ice-creams, cordials, etc. Made in France into popular liqueur called *cassis*, it is rich in vitamin C.

black-eyed pea Tiny white dried pea with a black spot in the centre, from a tropical leguminous vine, used in soups, etc. especially in America.

black game Black grouse.

black grouse, black game Species of grouse common in the North of England.

black jack (i) Name given to caramel, burnt sugar; sometimes used for colouring brown soups, sauces and gravies. (ii) Liquorice-flavoured toffee or chewing gum.

black mustard Species of mustard plant similar to the white mustard; the leaves are used for pickling and cooking; the seeds are made into condiments.

black olive Olive picked ripe.

black pepper Pepper with the outer husk of the seed left intact.

black pudding Sausage, popular in the Midlands and North of England, made of pig's blood, suet, breadcrumbs and oatmeal, usually sold ready boiled. It is then fried in slices and served with mashed potatoes or bacon.

black Russian Drink made of one part vodka, one part *kahlua* served on ice cubes.

black sapote Mexican variety of persimmon containing dark-fleshed, almost seedless fruit.

black sea bass Common sea bass.

black sloe Wild plum used in flavouring sloe gin.

black sugar (American) Liquorice juice.

black tea Fully fermented teas such as Congou and Orange pekoe.

black velvet Cocktail made of chilled champagne and Guinness in equal proportions.

black walnut Edible nut of a native American tree used in flavouring ice creams and sweets.

blackberry; (bramble) Black or dark purple edible berries from brambles of the genus *Rubus*. Blackberries are used in desserts, puddings, preserves, wines, etc. and their flavour blends particularly well with apple.

blackberry cordial Beverage made from blackberries.

blackberry dumpling Dumpling filled with blackberries.

blackberry *mousse* Mixture of blackberries, whipped cream, sugar, and egg whites.

blackberry shortcake (American) Sponge-type cake covered with blackberries and blackberry juice.

blackberry wine Alcoholic beverage made from fermented blackberry juice.

blackfin (American) Chub.

blackstrap (i) Final residue of sugar-cane processing, used in cattle food and industrial alcohol. (ii) (American) Drink of molasses-and-rum.

blackstripe (American) Drink of molasses and rum, crushed ice and nutmeg.

blade chop (American) Lamb chop, for grilling.

blade rib roast (American) Roasting joint of beef or veal cut from upper ribs. Also called Blade roast.

blade steak (American) Veal cut from the upper portion of the shoulder.

blaeberry Bilberry.

blanc (French) *Court bouillon* broth made of white meat, vegetables, flour and water.

blanc, au (French) Cooked white or with a white sauce, or cooked very gently so food does not brown.

blanc de blancs (French) Wine, especially champagne made from white grapes.

blanc de chine (French) "Chinese" white porcelain tableware.

blanc de noirs (French) White wine made from black grapes.

blanc d'oeuf (French) Egg white.

blanch (i) To bring food to the boil in water, to reduce a particular flavour, to whiten or preserve natural colour, (sweetbreads, kippers, etc.) (ii) To plunge into boiling water, (nuts, tomatoes, etc.) to remove skins.

blanchaille (French) Whitebait, a delicate little fish usually fried in deep fat.

blanchet (French) Cloth filter for straining syrups and other thick liquids.

blanchi (French) Blanched; parboiled.

blanchir (French) To blanch.

blanc-mange (French) White sweet cream set in a mould, made by boiling farinaceous substances in milk to the consistency of jelly. Originally a *maigre* soup, made of milk of almonds. It is wrong to add colouring matter to a *blanc-mange;* thus chocolate *blanc-mange* is incorrect.

bland (i) Buttermilk-and-water beverage. (ii) Smooth, mild-flavoured food.

blanquette (French) (i) Stew made of lamb, sweetbreads, veal or fowl, with a white sauce enriched with cream or egg-yolks. (ii) A white grape. (iii) A kind of pear.

blanquillo Edible sea fish rather like perch.

Blatterteig (German) Puff pastry.

Blaubeere (German) Blueberry, bilberry.

blaze To flame. To pour warmed brandy, rum, or whisky over food and set it on fire before serving.

blé (French) Wheat, corn.

blé noir (French) Buckwheat.

blé turquois (*blé de turquie*) (French) Maize. Indian corn.

bleach (American) (i) To whiten by parboiling or scalding. (ii) Celery whitened by banking earth round the stalks so the sun will not turn them green.

bleak Ablette. A small river fish with silvery scales, which can be fried.

blend To mix ingredients together until they are smooth. Usually applies to farinaceous or cereal-type foods which are mixed to a smooth paste with cold milk, water or stock before hot or boiling liquid is added, in order to prevent the formation of lumps.

blender Electrical device for blending foods and drinks, with rapidly-revolving blades set in the base of a mixing container. Used in preparing batters, dressings, *purées* and any dishes that call for intensive mixing.

blenny Small European and American scale-less fish which may be fried.

blet (French) Over-ripening of fruit.

blette (French) Strawberry spinach.

bleu, au (French) Fish blued by being cooked in vinegar or white wine.

bleu d'Auvergne (French) Blue mould cheese made from a mixture of goats', ewes' and cows' milk.

bleus Français (French) General name for French blue-mould cheese resembling *Roquefort* but less delicately flavoured.

blewit Variety of edible fungus.

blind, bake See baking blind.

blinchaty pirog (Russian) Pie of pancakes fried on one side only then placed in a casserole filled with minced beef, and hard-boiled eggs, or chicken in cream, topped with further pancakes and baked till brown.

blinchiky (Russian) Pancakes made of thin unleavened batter.

blini (Russian) Small pancake made with buckwheat flour and served with caviare and sour cream.

blintz (Jewish) Fried pancake stuffed with vegetable, meat, cheese or fruit filling.

bliny (Russian) Yeast-dough pancake often stuffed, or made into a layer cake with stuffings between the layers.

bloater (i) Salted and half-smoked herring made famous in Yarmouth, Norfolk. Bloaters may be baked in greased paper, poached or soaked briefly then dried and grilled, after filleting. (ii) (American) Chubb.

blødkogtæg (Danish) Soft-boiled egg.

blomkål (Swedish) Cauliflower.

blomkål gratin (Danish) Cauliflower *au gratin*.

blond (French) Light coloured, fawn.

blond de volaille (French) Clear or thickened chicken stock.

blonde de veau (French) Very rich veal broth, used for flavouring and enriching white soups and sauces.

blondir (French) To brown food very lightly, or to make a light *roux*.

blood and sand Cocktail of sweet vermouth, orange juice, cherry brandy and Scotch whisky.

blood orange Red-fleshed sweet orange.

blood pudding Sausage made of pig's blood and suet.

blood sausage Sausage containing dried blood as a principal ingredient.

bloody mary Cocktail of vodka, tomato juice, and seasoning, such as Worcester sauce.

bloomer loaf Long loaf with slashed top, enriched with milk, fat and sugar.

blue blazer (American) Drink of Scotch whisky and boiling water, ignited and poured from one mug to another, sweetened with sugar, invented by an American professor.

blue cheese Blue-veined cheese similar to that produced in *Roquefort*, France, Denmark or Norway.

blue crab (American) Common American crab found in coastal waters.

blue Dorset White crumbly cheese made in Dorset, which has a blue vein through it. Not widely known outside the county because it does not travel well.

blue fish (American) Edible Atlantic and Gulf of Mexico fish, also known as Skipjack or Skip mackerel because it sometimes leaps above the surface of the sea.

blue gage Blue plum.

blue gazelle Edible goat whose meat is cooked like roebuck.

blue gill (American) Bluegill bream or bluegill sunfish, a fresh water fish which is fried.

blue mould French cheese See *bleus Français*.

blue point (American) Small oyster dredged from the south shore of Long Island.

blue trout See *truite au bleu*.

blue vinny Local name for Blue Dorset cheese.

blueberry (American) Bilberry or whortleberry.

blueweed (American) Viper's bugloss, sometimes used in place of borage in U.S.A.

Blume (German) (i) Wine bouquet. (ii) Beer froth.

Blumenkohl (German) Cauliflower.

Blutwurst (German) Blood sausage.

boar Male swine.

boar's head Historical English Christmas dish. The custom of serving the boar's head still survives in some institutions.

boat Vessel for holding gravy, melted butter, sauce, etc.

boca chica (Spanish) Small sandwich or other light snack.

bocado (Spanish) Morsel; bite; mouthful

bocadillo (Spanish) Sandwich.

bocal (French) Wide-mouthed jar used for pickling or preserving.

Bockwurst (German) Solid type of Frankfurter sausage.

boda (Spanish) Wedding.

bodega (Spanish) (i) Grocery store. (ii) Warehouse. (iii) Wine cellar.

Bodensatz (German) Sediment, dregs, deposit.

body Qualities of strength and flavour possessed by good wines.

boels (Danish) Mild Danish cheese.

bœuf (French) Beef.

bœuf à la flamande (French) Beef in Flemish style.

bœuf à la mode en gelée (French) Cold braised beef in aspic.

bœuf bouillé (French) Boiled beef.

bœuf bourguignon (French) Beef cooked in the Burgundian manner, i.e., in red wine.

bœuf braisé (French) Braised beef.

bœuf braisé jardinière (French) Braised beef with mixed vegetables.

bœuf en daube (French) Spiced round of beef.

bœuf en persillade (French) Cold beef with parsley.

bœuf épicé (French) Spiced beef.

bœuf fumé (French) Smoked beef.

bœuf rôti (French) Roast beef.

bœuf salé (French) Corned beef.

bøf (Danish) Beefsteak.

bøf tatar (Danish) Tartar steak. Raw scraped beef mixed with capers and raw egg yolk.

bogavante (Spanish) Large-clawed lobster.

boga (Italian) Sea bream.

Bohne (German) Bean.

Bohnensalat (German) White bean salad.

Bohnensuppe (German) Bean soup.

boil To cook in liquid (stock, water,

milk, etc.) at 100°C or 212°F. Vegetables and pastas and certain puddings can be boiled fast but meat — once boiling point has been reached — should be allowed only to simmer at below 180°—190°, otherwise it shrinks and loses its flavour.

boiled egg Egg simmered in boiling water for 3 to 4½ minutes according to the degree of firmness required and the age of the egg. Fresh eggs take a little longer to set. Hard-boiled egg: Egg simmered in boiling water for 10-12 minutes.

boiled dinner (American) Meal consisting of beef or other meat, or fowl, boiled with vegetables.

boiled peanuts Favourite South American hot dish of green peanuts boiled in their shells in salt water, seasoned with tabasco sauce and black pepper.

boiled sweet Hard-textured sweet made from boiled sugar, glucose, an acid and a fruit or other flavouring.

boiler (i) Kitchen utensil for boiling food or water. (ii) Chicken over one year old whose flesh must be tenderised by boiling.

boiling point Temperature at which water boils, 212 degrees F., 100 degrees C.

boiling rings Polish sausages made of chopped pork and beef, and flavoured with garlic.

boisson (French) Beverage.

bok choy (Chinese) Chinese cabbage.

bokser (Hebrew) St. John's bread. Carob seed pod, or locust bean.

bol (French) Finger-bowl.

bolacha (Portuguese) Sea biscuit.

boldrô (Italian) Angler-fish.

bolée (French) Receptacle for drinking cider.

bolet (French) Boletus.

boletus Genus of fungi in both poisonous and edible varieties, the best-known being the *cêpe de Bordeaux*. highly esteemed in France.

bolillo (Spanish) Crusty roll.

bolita (Spanish) Fritter, "small ball".

boll (i) Measure of capacity used in Scotland and Northern England — in Scotland, 6 imperial bushels; in England varying between 2 and 6 bushels. (ii) Measure of weight containing 140 lb. flour.

Bollinger (French) Champagne first vinted by the Bollinger family in 1821, owners of vineyards in the *Ay* region of Champagne.

bolliti misti (Italian) Mixed boiled meats served with beans, vegetables and either green herb sauce or fresh tomato sauce.

bollito (Italian) (i) Boiled. (ii) Boiled meats and vegetables.

bologna (Italian) Large smoked sausage, made of bacon, veal, and pork suet; an Italian speciality principally manufactured at *Bologna*.

bolognese, alla (Italian) Rich meat sauce flavoured with wine, vegetables, chicken livers, served with butter and grated cheese.

Bols (Dutch) Dutch gin distillers founded in 1575.

bomba di riso (Italian) Dish of rice and pigeons.

Bombay duck Also called Bummelo, Bumbalo or Bumaloe fish; zoologists call it Harpodon. A fish found in the Indian waters, very nutritious, and possessing a peculiar yet delicate flavour. For export it is salted and cured, and is usually served with curry. In America and some parts of Europe it is considered a delicacy.

Bombay gelatine Agar-agar.

bombe (French) Iced pudding moulded into a bomb-like shape.

bombe glacée (French) Frozen dessert containing two or more mixtures served from a *bombe* mould.

bombe **mould** Utensil for shaping a *bombe*.

bombone (Spanish) Chocolate (sweet).

bon appetit (French) (i) Good appetite. (ii) Salutation meaning "Enjoy your meal".

bon goût (French) Good taste. An indication that something is properly seasoned and flavoured.

bon vivant (French) One who enjoys eating and drinking.

bonbon (French) Sweetmeat, confectionery.

Bonbon (German) Sweetmeat, *bonbon*.

bonbonnière (French) Sweet box or dish.

Bonbonniere (German) Box of sweets.

bonbon spoon Spoon for serving *bonbons*, candies, and nuts.

bon-chrétien (French) Cooking pear grown in two varieties, one summer, one winter.

bonded Liquor and other dutiable commodities kept in bonded warehouses under government supervision. Some wines, such as port, are aged in bond.

bondiola di Parma (Italian) Type of pork sausage.

bondon (French) Small whole-milk loaf-shaped cheese made in Normandy.

bone (i) Part of the skeleton of an animal, bird or fish. (ii) To remove the bones from fish, meat, or fowl.

bone china Translucent white chinaware made from a formula including bone ash.

bone glass Milk-white glassware made from a formula including bone ash.

bone porcelain Bone china.

bone marrow See bones.

boned chicken breast, French style (American) *Suprême* of chicken; chicken breast.

boneless Food served without bones.

bonensoep (Dutch) Bean soup.

bones Bones, the skeletal parts of fish and animals used to make stock to form the basis of soups, stews and sauces. The soft, fatty marrow of large bones can be extracted by long cooking and used as a spread on bread, toast, etc.

boning knife Short, sharp knife used for removing bones from fish, poultry and meat.

bonito (Spanish) Small species of tunny fish or tuna found in the Mediterranean, and off the Atlantic and North Pacific coasts.

bonne-bouche (French) Small savoury titbit.

bonne femme (French) (i) Dishes cooked in homely, simple style with garnishes of fresh vegetables, usually with mushrooms. (ii) Cream soup garnished with herbs.

bonnes-mares (French) Red wine of the *Côte d'Or*, France.

bonnekamp (Belgian) Bitters.

bonnet (French) Reticulum.

bonnet fleuk (Scottish) Brill.

bonnet-turc (French) Variety of pumpkin

bonnet de Turquie (French) Ancient pastry dish moulded into Turkish bonnet shape.

bonnet pepper Tropical American capsicum pepper plant yielding paprika and pimiento.

bonvalet (French) Cake almost identical to *Beauvilliers*.

bonvalet egg Egg served in hollowed-out bread *croûton* and masked with *velouté* sauce.

boops Mediterranean fish used in *bouillabaisse;* also fried or poached.

booze Slang for alcoholic drinks.

boque (French) Boops, a Mediterranean fish.

boquettier (French) Crab-apple tree.

bor (Hungarian) Wine.

borage Aromatic plant, used to flavour lettuce salads and iced drinks, claret cups, etc.; sometimes called cucumber herb, on account of its flavour. The plant has spiny leaves and blue flowers.

borax Hydrated sodium tetraborate, a mineral used as a cleaning agent and water softener.

Bordeaux Red or white wines first produced around Bordeaux in south-western France; a group of wines, including clarets, Sauternes, Graves, Barsacs, etc.

Bordeaux red Claret wine.

bordelaise, à la (French) (i) Dishes served with Bordelaise sauce with wine and marrowfat, or with additions of *cèpes*, *mirepoix* or artichokes and potatoes. (ii) The term also applies to various sweets and desserts, and to Bordeaux type cooking generally.

border Food arranged on a platter or turned out from a ring mould inside which other food is arranged for serving.

bordure (French) Edging of rice or mashed potatoes.

borecole Kale, Scotch kale.

börek (Turkish) Thin pastry dough filled with white cheese, egg, and parsley.

boric acid See borax.

borshchok (Russian) Stew of beets, onions, lemon juice, water and cubed beef.

bortsch (Russian) Russian or Polish soup in which beetroot forms the chief ingredient.

bosse de chameau rôti (French) Roast camel's hump, prepared only from very young camels.

Boston baked beans (American) See Boston beans.

Boston beans (American) Speciality dish of Boston, Mass. The beans, usually brown beans, are seasoned with molasses and salt pork and baked slowly in a special pot.

Boston brown bread (American) Steam-baked bread made with butter-milk, cornmeal, rye and wheat flour, molasses, and some raisins, usually served with baked beans.

Boston butt (American) Upper portion of lean shoulder of pork, usually roasted.

Boston cracker (American) Thick, hard, round, unsalted biscuit served with chowders and seafood dishes.

Boston cream pie (American) Double-layer cake filled with thick cream or custard and topped with chocolate icing.

botargo, bottarga, botterigo (Italian) (i) Relish prepared from tuna or mullet roe, served in thin slices with oil and vinegar or lemon. (ii) Grey mullet roe.

botella (Spanish) Bottle.

boter (Dutch) Butter.

boter melk (Dutch) Buttermilk.

boterkoek (Dutch) Rich shortbread.

bothan Illegal drinking club.

botijo (Spanish) Earthenware jar with handle and spout.

botte (French) Bunch, bundle.

bottiglia (Italian) Bottle. *Mezza bottiglia:* Half bottle.

bottled cream Double cream which has been commercially treated and packed to keep indefinitely.

bottled gas Butane or natural gas compressed into steel tanks for use in cooking where gas mains are not available.

bottled-gas stove Any range adapted to use butane or other bottled gas.

bottled in bond Liquor aged in a bonded warehouse.

bottle opener Utensil for prying metal tops from bottles.

bottle party Gathering where guests bring a contribution towards the alcoholic refreshments.

bottle rack Metal or wooden rack for storing bottles of wine at the correct angle.

bottling (i) Method of preserving food in bottles or jars by sterilisation and subsequent sealing. Vegetables should be sterilised in a pressure cooker before being placed in bottles. If correct procedure is followed bottled food will keep indefinitely. (ii) The science of dealing with wine.

bottling ring Rubber ring used to seal the jars of bottled food.

bottoms Dregs resulting from sedimentation of bottled wines.

botulism Food poisoning due to botulin spores present in food, fresh or canned.

boucané (French) Smoked.

bouché (French) Corked, stopped up.

bouchée (French) Small puff pastry case baked blind and filled with various foods, sweet or savoury.

boucher (French) Butcher.

bouchon (French) Cork.

boucon (French) Kind of veal *ragoût*.

boudanne (French) Cow's-milk cheese.

boudin (French) French sausage similar to black pudding, only much smaller.

boudin blanc (French) White sausage.

boudins de gibier (French) Game pudding

boudinade (French) Quarter of lamb stuffed with forcemeat.

bougras (French) Soup of the *Périgord* region using vegetables cooked in the water in which black puddings have previously been boiled.

bouillabaisse (French) Thick fish soup or stew made from Mediterranean fish cooked in white wine, olive oil with tomatoes, garlic, saffron, onions and herbs. The dish originated in Marseilles.

bouillant (French) Boiling.

bouilli (French) Fresh boiled beef. A national French dish.

bouillie (French) (i) Drink of farina and milk. (ii) Porridge of maize (Hasty pudding).

bouillir (French) To boil.

bouilloire, bouillotte (French) Boiler, kettle.

Bouillon (German) Broth, meat soup.

bouillon (French) Plain clear soup. Unclarified beef or veal broth.

bouillon cube Small cube containing compressed essence of beef or chicken, which is dissolved in hot water to make *bouillon*, or stock.

boujaron (French) Tot; small drink.

boukha (Arabic) Tunisian *eau-de-vie*.

boulanger (French) Baker.

boulangerie (French) Bakery.

boulangère, à la (French) Dishes served with fried onions and potatoes.

boule (French) Ball.

boule de neige (French) (i) Agaric. (ii) Ball-shaped, cream-covered cakes. (iii) Round-moulded ice cream *bombe*. (Also see Snowball (i))

boaleau blanc (French) Silverbirch. (See birch beer).

boulette (French) Small meatball rolled in egg-and-breadcrumbs and deep-fried.

bouquet (French) Aroma of a wine.

bouquet garni (French) Bunch of herbs, (sprig of parsley, thyme, a bayleaf, plus other herbs or piece of celery) bound into a faggot or tied in a muslin bag, and cooked with the liquid of casseroles, stews, sauces, etc., then removed and discarded before serving.

bouquetière, à la (French) Meat garnished with vegetables arranged in little "bouquets" round the serving-dish.

bourbon (American) Type of whisky originating in Bourbon County, Kentucky; modern bourbon is distilled from a fermented mash, mainly of Indian corn.

bourbon fog (American) Beverage of bourbon whisky, chilled black coffee and vanilla ice-cream.

Bourbonnais (French) Province of France noted for mineral waters, (Vichy) good quality meat, fish and vegetables.

bourdetto (Greek) Boiled fish with hot red pepper sauce.

boureka (Spanish) Paper-thin pastry *blintz* or *knish* filled with cheese, meat or spinach, and baked.

bourgeoise, à la (French) Large pieces of meat braised and garnished with carrots, small onions and diced lean bacon. The term indicates a modest kind of home cookery, simple but tasty and wholesome.

Bourgogne (French) (i) Burgundy wine. (ii) A rich brown sauce.

Bourgogne, à la (French) See *Bourguignonne, à la*.

bourgueil (French) Famous wine made from the grapes of the *Indre-et-Loire* area of France.

Bourguignonne, à la (French) Burgundian style dish of braised meat, eggs, fish or poultry cooked in red wine sauce and garnished with small onions and mushrooms.

bourguignote (French) *Ragoût* of truffles, usually served with game.

bourlghour (American) Cracked wheat, Bulgar wheat.

bourlghourlama (Armenian) Stew made of lamb, bulgar wheat and vegetables.

bourrache (French) Aromatic kitchen herb; also called cucumber herb, because of its peculiar flavour of cucumbers.

boutargue (French) See *Poutarge*.

bouteille (French) Bottle.

bouzy (French) White wine of the Champagne district.

Bovril Brand name for a commercially-prepared beef essence used in making beef tea, gravy and soup.

Bowle (German) (i) Bowl. (ii) Spice wine.

boyau (French) Casing sausage.

boysenberry Hybrid berry resembling a giant raspberry, developed by 20th century botanist, Rudolph Boysen.

bozbash (Russian) Substantial mutton-and-vegetable soup.

bra (Italian) Creamy soft mild-flavoured cheese originating in the Italian town of Bra.

braaivleis (Afrikaans) (i) Meat roasted on a spit. (ii) South African barbecue.

Brabançonne, à la (French) Dishes garnished with endives and potato croquettes; sometimes hop shoots cooked in butter or cream are also added.

brace Pair of game animals or birds such as partridge or ducks.

brachetto (Italian) Red table wine originating in the Piedmont area of Italy.

braciola, braciuola (Italian) Chop or cutlet.

braciola di maiale (Italian) Pork chop.

bracioletta (Italian) Small stuffed roll of meat (beef, veal, etc.)

braciuola alla Milanese (Italian) Veal chop.

Bradenham ham Sweet-cured ham, dark in appearance.

bragget Spiced and honeyed ale.

Brahma Large domestic fowl of Chinese origin, with pea combs and feathered legs.

brains Delicacies prepared from the substances within the skull of beef animals, calves, sheep and pigs. Brains must be very fresh. They are washed in cold salted water, cleared of bloodclots and left to soak in fresh cold water for at least an hour before being simmered with herbs, then fried or sautéed.

braise To cook by a combination of stewing, steaming and roasting, a method suitable for meat and vegetables, particularly the less expensive joints such as brisket or silverside of beef. Meat is first seared or browned quickly in a little fat to seal the juices, then simmered in a small amount of prepared liquid (stock, sauce, etc.) in a tightly-covered casserole or stewpan. An oven-cooked joint can be uncovered for the last 20 minutes of cooking to improve the flavour. Vegetables should also be browned lightly before braising.

braising pan Metal, earthenware or other fireproof vessel with a tight-fitting lid, suitable for slow-cooking. Before the days of oven cooking the original braising pans were rectangular, with deep covers into which live charcoals were placed.

bramble See Blackberry.

bramble jelly Preserve made from blackberries.

bran Outer husk of grains such as rye or wheat, which is removed by milling.

bran brack Old English cake made of caraway seeds, flour, sugar, eggs, butter, milk and yeast.

bran muffin (American) Scone made with bran, flour, eggs, molasses, and raisins.

brandade (French) (i) Dish of stewed haddocks. (ii) Dish of cod *à la provençale*, with garlic, parsley, lemon juice and pepper, beaten up with olive oil.

brander (Scottish) Gridiron.

brandered steak (Scottish) Grilled steak.

brandewin (French) Spirits distilled from wine.

brandied Fruit preserves, or other food flavoured with brandy.

brandied fruit Apricots, peaches, dates, figs, pears, etc., preserved in brandy-flavoured syrup.

brandy Spirit distilled from wine; the finest brandies are said to be those produced in the *Armagnac* and *Cognac* regions of France. The name derives from the German, *Branntwein* (literally, "burnt wine"). Colourless at first, brandy darkens in the cask as it matures.

brandy butter Thick butter sauce flavoured with brandy, used on rich puddings.

brandy sauce Sauce made from milk, arrowroot, egg yolks and brandy, or (richer) from cream, egg yolks and brandy.

brandy snap Crisp rolled biscuit which can be filled with cream.

Brankäse (German) Sour-milk curd cheese flavoured with beer.

Branntwein (German) Brandy.

branzino (Italian) (i) Bass. (ii) Pike. (iii) Perch.

brasato con lenticchie (Italian) Braised beef with lentils.

brasenose ale Punch made of heated ale and caster sugar with floating roasted apples, which used to be drunk in Brasenose College, Oxford, on Shrove Tuesdays.

brasière (French) Braising pan (also called *daubière*)

brasileira a (Portuguese) In Brazilian style.

brasserie Popular type of restaurant or

establishment where beef and cider are sold.

brassica Genus of Cruciferae which includes broccoli, brussels sprouts, cabbages, cauliflowers, radishes, and turnips.

Bratapfel (German) Baked apple.

Braten (German) Roast joint of meat.

braten (German) To roast, grill, bake or fry.

Bratenfett (German) Dripping.

Brathering (German) Grilled herring.

Brathühn (German) Roast chicken.

Bratkartoffel (German) Fried potato.

Bratpfanne (German) Frying-pan.

Bratwurst (German) Mild-flavoured frying sausage.

Bräu (German) Brew (Beer).

brauen (German) To brew.

Brauhaus (German) Brewery.

braune Ecke (German) Rye bread-roll.

Braunkohl (German) Broccoli.

Braunschweiger (German) Smoked liver sausage first made in Brunswick.

Brause (German) Fizzy drink.

Brauselimonade (German) Fizzy lemonade.

brawn Preparation of boned meat made from pig's head moulded and eaten cold. Sheep's head, veal and other meats may be used to make an economical brawn.

brazier Container for holding burning coals, over which open-flame cooking or barbecuing is done. Some have spits for turning meat above the coals, others have a barbecue oven over the turning spit.

Brazil nut Edible seed of a large tree native to Brazil. They have a distinctive, tough, angular shell and white kernels which are eaten plain or used in confectionery and cakes. Contain fat and protein.

Brazilian tea Maté from southern Brazil.

bread Staple food of the Western world made from flour, milk or water and a leavening agent (usually yeast) baked in many shapes, flavours and styles. It contains carbohydrate, protein, calcium and Vitamin B. Certain food values lost in milling are added to white bread in the baking process in Britain. White

bread is made from flour from which almost all the husk and germ has been extracted. Brown bread contains a higher proportion, and wholemeal bread retains all the germ and most of the husk. Bread is said to have been invented by the Egyptians or the Hebrews and that the Romans learned the skill of bread-making from the Greeks. See separate entries for Bloomer, Farmhouse, etc.

bread (American) To coat or cover with bread crumbs.

bread-and-butter pickles (American) Spiced relish made of thinly-sliced cucumbers and onions.

bread-and-butter plate Small plate used for serving bread and butter.

bread-and-butter pudding Pudding made from thin slices of buttered bread, milk, eggs, sugar, dried fruit and nutmeg, etc.

bread-basket (i) Woven basket for carrying and serving bread. (ii) Slang term for stomach.

bread bin Ventilated box made of metal, plastic, or wood used for storing bread, rolls, etc.

bread-board Wooden board for cutting bread, making sandwiches, slicing rolls, etc.

bread box (American) Bread bin.

bread fruit Large, greenish-yellow fruit of the bread-fruit tree.

bread knife Long-bladed knife with sharp scalloped or serrated edge for slicing bread or rolls, or cutting cake.

bread pudding Pudding made of flour, dried fruit, stale bread, eggs, milk, sugar and flavourings.

bread sauce Butter-and-milk sauce thickened with bread crumbs, and flavoured with onion and herbs.

bread stick Long crisp stick-shaped roll. *Grissini.*

breadcrumbs Crumbs of bread, either fresh or browned in the oven (raspings) used in puddings and savoury dishes; or as a topping; or as a coating for moistened food before it is grilled or fried. Fried crumbs can be served with roast game.

break flour (to) To stir cold liquid

gradually into flour until it becomes a smooth paste.

breakfast First meal of the day which breaks the night-time fast. Traditionally in Britain it consists of a cereal, hot or cold, and/or fruit juice, followed by a fried dish such as bacon and eggs, and concluded with toast and marmalade, accompanied by tea or coffee. Continental breakfast comprises coffee and rolls or *croissants* and butter. A good breakfast is considered important for alertness and efficiency but present day breakfast habits vary widely.

breakfast cereal Cooked or commercially prepared cereal such as porridge, oatmeal, cornflakes, puffed rice and shredded wheat.

breakfast food Breakfast cereal.

breakfast knife (American) Medium-size spreading knife.

breakfast plate (American) medium-size plate used for serving breakfast.

bream Species of fish. The fresh-water bream, seasonable from September to November is of rather coarse texture and flavour, but the sea bream has white, delicate-flavoured flesh and is at its best from June to December. Both varieties are best served baked with a savoury stuffing, but they may also be boiled, fried or grilled as for carp, or used in stew.

breast Tender white chest meat of chicken, duck, or other fowl; or the breast meat of beef, lamb, pork, etc. immediately below the neck.

breast of lamb Economical cut of lamb which can be roasted, braised or stewed.

brebis (French) Ewe.

Brechbohne (German) Kidney bean.

brèdes (French) Creole cookery of plants such as cabbage, spinach and lettuce simmered in a sauce.

breganze (Italian) Dry Venetian table wines, red and white.

Brei (German) Porridge.

Brennsuppe (German/Austrian) Brown soup.

Brésilienne, à la (French) In Brazilian style.

brésolle (French) (i) *Entrée* consisting of several kinds of meat. (ii) *Ragoût* of veal.

Bresse (French) Area of France famed for its poultry.

bresse bleu (French) Soft, blue-veined cheese resembling Gorgonzola, made near Lyons.

Breteuil, Baron de (French) A noted epicure of the reign of Louis XVI.

Bretonne, à la (French) Meat such as mutton garnished with haricot beans, whole or puréed.

Bretzel (German) Pretzel; crisp glazed biscuit baked in varying shapes.

brew (i) To prepare a beverage from hops and malt or other fermentable commodities. (ii) Beverage such as ale of beer.

brewer's yeast Yeast suitable for brewing ale and beer; also eaten as a food for its high protein and vitamin B content.

bret West-country name for brill.

brick cheese (American) Cheese of fairly firm texture shaped like a brick, with small holes and a rather sweet taste. Eaten raw and used in cooking, it may be either mild or strong. Some are weighted with bricks while maturing.

brick ice cream (American) Commercially packed ice cream sold in brick form.

brick sugar (American) Lump sugar.

bride cake Wedding cake.

brider (French) To truss poultry and game with a needle and thread.

bridge roll Small slim roll made with egg-enriched dough.

brie (French) Creamy, soft-textured, autumn-winter cheese made in Northern France from whole milk.

brié (French) Kneaded paste for biscuits, etc.

brier (French) To beat or flatten paste with a rolling-pin.

brife (French) Large portion of bread.

brifeur (French) *Gourmand*.

brignole (French) Species of dark-red cooking plum from Brignoles, a district in France.

brill European flat fish similar to turbot, with light and delicate flesh. It may be boiled whole; filleted and fried like sole; filleted and poached in a white wine sauce; or cut into steaks and baked with a little fat, seasoning and milk. In season all year, but best from April to August. Known in Scotland as "Bonnet Fleuk" and in the West Country as "Kike" and "Bret".

Brillat-Savarin (i) Famous French gastronome, Jean Anthelme Brillat-Savarin (1755-1826) auther of *La Physiologie du Gout*, "The Physiology of Taste"; his name is given to a method of preparing small pieces of lamb and mutton, garnished with stuffed *duchesse* potato and asparagus tips. (ii) Name of a Normandy cheese.

brin (French) Sprig.

brindis (Spanish) A toast; to drink someone's health.

brindza (Hungarian) Cheese made from goat's and sheep's milk popular in Hungary and throughout the Balkans.

brine (i) To remove water from vegetables such as cucumbers, tomatoes, etc. by sprinkling with salt, so that the vinegar in which they are pickled is not unduly diluted. (ii) To immerse in a salt-and-water solution meat which is to be pickled and vegetables which are to be preserved. (iii) Solution of salt and water for preserving food.

brinjaul Anglo-Indian name for eggplant or aubergine.

brinzen (Hungarian) Cheese made from ewes' milk mixed with rennet.

brioche (French) (i) Light roll of yeast dough made with butter and eggs, often in the shape of a large ball with a smaller one on top. Sometimes it contains currants and candied fruit. In France, the *brioche* is popular eaten hot for breakfast. (ii) Larger yeast dough cakes flavoured with cheese or filled with fruit.

brioli (Corsican) Polenta made from chestnuts and milk or cream.

brisket Meat carcase cut containing half the breast-bone with the commencement of the rib-bones attached on one side. The flesh consists of alternate layers of lean and fat. Generally applied to beef, it makes an economical

joint but requires slow cooking. When pressed and glazed it becomes Pressed Beef.

brisling Small Norwegian fish canned like sardines.

brisotine (French) Light *entrée* of forcemeat, etc.

brisquet (French) Brisket.

britannia Metal alloy of antimony, a little copper, tin and sometimes zinc used in making kitchen utensils. Similar to pewter in appearance.

britannia-ware Utensils made from Britannia metal.

Brittany Region of Northern France notable for fish, ground and winged game, dairy products and cider.

brittle Crisp sweetmeat such as almond brittle, peanut brittle, etc. made with sugar-syrup and nuts.

broad bean Green pod with large, creamy seeds. This is considered to be the original bean. When very young, the whole pod may be cooked, but in general the seeds only are eaten, cooked in boiling salted water and tossed in melted butter or served with parsley sauce.

broadbill (American) Edible swordfish.

broc (French) Wine pitcher.

brocard (French) Young roebuck.

broccio (Italian) Corsican cheese made from sour sheep's or goat's milk.

broccoletto di rape (Italian) Turnip top.

broccoli Type of cauliflower, in several varieties — white, purple sprouting and green-spouting. A good source of vitamin C. White broccoli (winter cauliflower) is cooked like cauliflower; the purple and green-sprouting (calabrese) kinds are cooked as for asparagus.

broccolo (Italian) Broccoli.

brochan (Scottish) Scots porridge.

broche, à la (French) Food cooked on a skewer or spit.

broché (French) Trussed and skewered ready for roasting.

brochet (French) Pike. Seasonable October to January. A fish to be found in almost all waters; much liked on account of its delicate flavour.

brochette (French) Skewer used for

grilling pieces of steak, lamb or veal, etc.

brocoli (French) Broccoli.

brød (Danish and Norwegian) Bread.

bröd (Swedish) Bread.

Brödchen (German) Small loaf.

brodettato alla romana (Italian) Lamb stewed with herbs and vegetables, served with a lemon-flavoured sauce thickened with eggs.

brodetto (Italian) Stew of mixed fish.

brodo (Italian) Broth; *consommé*.

brodo ristretto (Italian) Rich broth.

broeto di pesce (Italian) Venetian term for fish stew (*Brodetto*).

broil (American) To grill. To cook over or in front of a fire by direct heat. This old English word is now used exclusively for grilling in America.

broiler (i) Young chicken tender enough to be grilled. (ii) (American) The grill on or inside a cooker.

broiling dish, flat (American) Grill pan.

broiling rack (American) Grid of grill.

broken nut meats (American) Pieces of nuts, chopped nuts.

brolio (Italian) Bottled *chianti* of high quality.

Brombeere (German) Blackberry.

bronx (American) Cocktail made of gin, dry and sweet vermouth, and orange juice.

brood (Dutch) Bread.

broodkaas (Dutch) Hard flat "bread" cheese.

brook trout See Trout.

brose (Scottish) Scottish dish made by pouring boiling pot-liquor (or water) on oatmeal or barley meal, with small pieces of fat meat, fish or vegetables.

Brösel (German) Breadcrumb.

Bröselknödel (German) Breadcrumb dumpling.

Brot (German) Bread.

Brötchen (German) Small dinner roll.

broth Beef stock or broth. An unclarified gravy soup, with or without garnish.

brouet (French) Broth, soup.

brouet d'andouille (French) Tripe liquor.

brouillé (French) Scrambled, mixed, beaten up; usually applied to eggs.

brouilly (French) Famous red *Beaujolais* wine.

broussin (French) Mixture of soft cheese, pepper and vinegar.

broutes (French) Béarnaise dish made from cabbage.

brown (i) To seal in the juices of fish or meat by searing the surface. (ii) To finish off a dish by letting its outer surface cook uncovered to an even brown colour.

brown betty Baked sweet made from layers of buttered crumbs, apples spices, and sugar.

brown bread See bread.

brown butter Butter cooked to a brown colour.

brown gravy Gravy in which flour and drippings are blended and browned before liquid is added.

brown mustard Dark-coloured mustard.

brown rice Unpolished rice retaining some of the bran.

brown sauce Basic sauce made from fried onion in which flour is cooked to golden brown before stock and other vegetables are added. Used as a basis for *Piquante*, *Espagnole* and other sauces.

brown stew Steak, oxtail, liver or kidneys, floured, fried, then cooked slowly in a closely-covered vessel, with suitable flavourings.

brown stock Beef stock.

brown sugar (i) Demerara crystals, light or dark; powdered dark brown sugar is known as Pieces. (ii) (American) Very fine textured sugar, more like brown icing sugar.

brown trout (American) Variety of edible freshwater trout which can be grilled or fried or prepared as for cold salmon trout.

brownie (i) (American) Moist chocolate cake containing chopped nuts and cut into small squares. (ii) (Australian) Bread made of currants and brown sugar or molasses.

browning (i) Caramel. Liquid colouring matter made in the form of thick syrup by browning sugar nearly to burning point. (ii) See also Brown (to). (iii) See also Browning, gravy.

browning, gravy Colouring matter used to darken soups, gravies, etc. available in proprietary brands but homemade by spreading flour on a baking sheet and heating in the oven until it is brown, stirring frequently. It should be kept in a covered jar.

broye (French) *Béarnaise* dish prepared from white or roasted corn meal (maize flour).

broyé (French) Crushed or coarsely ground.

brugnon (French) Velvet skin peach or nectarine.

Brühe (German) Broth, meat soup.

brühen (German) To scald.

Brühkartoffel (German) Potato cooked in broth.

bruingebrande suiker (Dutch) Burned sugar; caramel.

brûlant (French) Burning, alight, burning hot.

brûlée (French) Burnt.

brun (French) Brown.

brun, au (French) Cooked in brown sauce

brunâtre (French) Brownish.

brunch Breakfast and lunch combined — a late morning meal.

bruncheon Brunch.

brunello di montalcino (Italian) Dry red Tuscan table wine.

brunkaalssuppe (Dutch) Green cabbage soup.

brunoise (French) (i) Method of shredding vegetables very finely. (ii) Vegetables cooked slowly in butter and used for making soups, stuffings, etc. (iii) Vegetables diced for addition to other dishes. (iv) Cookery typical of *Brunoy*, a French district (*Seine-et-Oise*) celebrated for its spring vegetables.

brunswick stew (American) Meat and vegetable stew; also called hunter's stew.

brush To coat thinly with butter, oil, or egg, before frying or grilling.

brussels biscuit Belgian-type rusk.

brussels cheese Skimmed-milk soft fermented cheese originating in Brussels.

brussels sprout Variety of the common cabbage. Small cabbage heads growing on the stem of the brussels sprout plant. In season from October to March.

Brust (German) Breast.

Bruststück (German) Brisket.

Brut (German) Fish-fry.

brut (French) Sharp or very dry champagne or wine.

Bruxelles (French) Brussels cheese.

Bruxelloise, à la (French) Meat garnished with Brussels sprouts and creamed potatoes.

bruyère, coq de (French) Heath cock.

bubble-and-squeak Old English dish, originally made from thinly sliced, diced or minced cold meat mixed with cold cooked potatoes and finely chopped cabbage or other greens and then fried; sometimes sprinkled with vinegar. Nowadays the meat is usually omitted.

bubble gum Chewing gum that can be blown into big bubbles.

bucarde, boucarde, bucardier (French) Cockle.

buccan (i) Caribbean word for a rack for roasting, smoking, and drying meat. (ii) Also the meat itself. Sea pirates ate buccan as their ration, thus becoming known as buccaneers.

bûche (French) Swiss roll.

bûche de Noël (French) Christmas yule log cake.

Büchsenfleisch (German) Tinned meat.

Buchweizen (German) Buckwheat.

buck Male deer, hare, goat, or rabbit.

buck rarebit Welsh rarebit with the addition of a poached egg placed on the top of the cheese.

buckhorn Whiting.

buckling Austrian smoked herring.

Bückling (German) Smoked herring, bloater, kipper.

buckwheat; Saracen corn A cereal-species of *Polygonum* grown in Europe for poultry and cattle feed. Can be milled or boiled whole. In America buckwheat is grown for human consumption and is available commercially as flour or as groats.

buckwheat cake (American) Pancake made of buckwheat flour.

buckwheat flour See buckwheat.

buckwheat groats (American) Roasted buckwheat, either whole or ground, used in casseroles, cereals, pancakes, soups, stuffings and kosher-style dishes.

buckwheat honey (American) Dark honey made from buckwheat.

buddego (Italian) Ligurian name for fish stew.

budding (Danish) Pudding.

budín (Spanish) Pudding.

budino (Italian) Pudding.

budino di mandorle (Italian) Almond pudding.

budino di pollo in brodo (Italian) Cream of puréed hard-boiled chicken eggs and cream served with chicken broth.

budino di ricotta (Italian) Cottage cheese with candied fruit and chopped nuts.

bue (Italian) Beef (ox).

bue de brasare (Italian) Braising beef.

Büfett (German) Sideboard, buffet.

buffet (i) Refreshment or sandwich bar. (ii) Sideboard. (iii) Informal meal at which guests serve themselves from dishes set out on counters or tables.

Bugey (French) Part of France famous for *Belley*, birthplace of Brillat-Savarin. Noted for crayfish, cheese, local wines, poultry and meat.

bugloss Common name for Anchusa, a plant whose flowers are used in salad and said to have tonic property.

bugnes (French) Rolled dough fritter fried in oil.

buisson (French) (i) Pyramid of food, said to be served *en buisson* (ii) Method of twisting pastry into a point.

buko (Danish) Cheese flavoured with ham, lobster, mushroom and prawns.

Bulgarian milk Fermented milk such as yogurt.

buljong (Swedish) Broth; *consommé*.

bull Male cattle. Flesh of young bulls is of good quality though a little tougher than beef.

bullace Fruit of a tree native to warm countries, but now also cultivated in more northern regions; the fruit is a kind of plum, much like the damson, but without its pleasant roughness of taste, and round in form whereas the damson is oval. Cooked as for damsons.

bullace gin Gin flavoured with bullace instead of juniper berries.

bullhead (American) Large-headed fresh-water edible catfish.

bullock Castrated bull, steer, or young bull.

bullrush Aquatic plant with edible roots and with leaves and shoots useable in salads.

bull's-eye (i) Very old sweetmeat made of boiled sugar, flavoured with peppermint and moulded into irregular striped pieces. (ii) (American) Drink made from rough cider and brandy.

bullshot Beverage of *consommé*, vodka, Worcester sauce, lemon juice and seasoning, mixed with ice.

bully beef Corned beef.

bumbo Kind of punch, made of spirits, etc.

bumbu (Malay) Spice.

bummalo Bombay duck.

bun (i) Type of sweet cake similar in texture to bread, made from a mixture containing yeast, sweetening and usually fat, currants and spice. Examples are cinnamon, currant, Chelsea, Bath and hotcross buns. (ii) Little cake, containing no yeast. (iii) Cream bun made of *choux* pastry.

bun loaf Bread enriched with milk, fat, sugar and fruit.

Bündenfleisch (German) Air-dried meat sliced paper-thin.

bung Cork or wooden stopper fitted into the bunghole of a barrel or cask.

bunion Earth nut.

Bunte oder Gepflückte Finten (German) Speciality of Lower Saxony, a dish of green and white beans, apples and carrots.

buntop (American) Frankfurter or hot-dog on a roll.

buñuelo (Spanish) (i) Fritter. (ii) Bun.

buñuelo de espinaca (Spanish) Spinach fritter, a Uruguayan speciality.

buon'appetito (Italian) (i) good appetite. (ii) A salutation meaning "Enjoy your food or meal".

Buranella, alla (Italian) Venetian dishes served with sauce made of fish or shell-fish caught around Burano.

burbot Freshwater fish with long fins, tail and barbels. Its liver is highly regarded by connoisseurs, and is prepared as for soft roes, also used in *pâtés*.

burdock Hardy perennial whose leaves have medicinal properties. Shoots and roots are cooked in Scotland.

burdwan Savoury dish of Indian origin made of re-heated poultry, venison, or meat.

burgall (American) Blue perch.

burette (French) Oil-and-vinegar cruet.

burger (American) Slang for hamburger.

bürgerliche Küche (German) Plain cooking.

burgoo (i) Sailor's dish of oatmeal, salt, butter and sugar. (ii) American stew of meat and vegetables.

Burgunderwein (German) Burgundy.

Burgundy Region of France yielding the best food and wine. Its capital, Dijon, is a city of *haute gourmandise*. In its various districts the highest quality poultry, fish, meat, *escargots*, and cheese are found. Its wines include *Nuits - St.- Georges, Beaune, Volnay, Pommard, Meursault* and *Puligny-Montrachet*.

Burgundy cheese Soft white cheese originating in Burgundy, France.

Burgundy sauce Sauce in several varieties but all having burgundy wine among their ingredients.

burnet Small shrub of the rose family whose cucumber-flavoured leaves are used in salads, sauces and soups. Also known as salad burnet.

burnt almond Roasted almond.

burnt-sugar colouring Caramel.

burrida (Italian) (i) Fish soup, speciality of Genoa. (ii) Cold fish soup of Sardinia.

burro (Italian) Butter.

burro, al (Italian) Buttered.

burst rice Rice put to boil in cold water; when boiling, the grains of rice will burst.

busecca (Italian) Stewed tripe and vegetables.

busecchina (Italian) Milanese soup of chestnuts, milk and wine.

bustard Large game-bird, usually roasted

butcher's broom Shrub whose bitter roots are used for *apéritifs*.

butcher's knife Medium-length, wide-bladed knife, for chopping and cutting.

butler's pantry Serving pantry between dining room and kitchen.

butt (i) British beer barrel holding 108 gallons. (ii) British cask containing 108 gallons of whisky or sherry.

butt (American) Ham shoulder or the thick end of a ham.

buttara (Italian) Cheese with a butter filling.

butter Fatty food extracted from the milk of mammals, made by churning the cream. Butter is versatile in that it can be used in many styles of cooking and flavoured in innumerable ways by blending with other foods such as chives, shellfish, garlic, mustard, nuts, etc.

Butter (German) Butter.

butter-and-honey cream Mixture of equal parts of butter and honey.

butter bean Large flat white dried seed of a plant similar to Lima beans, soaked and cooked as for Haricot beans, but for shorter periods.

butter boat Small gravy boat used for serving melted butter.

butter clam (American) Pacific Coast clam.

butter cream Cake filling or topping made by creaming butter and icing sugar, and flavouring to taste with coffee, chocolate, lemon, etc.

butter dish Small covered dish for serving butter.

butter icing Butter and icing sugar pounded to a soft consistency, flavoured, and used as a spread or topping for cakes, suitably decorated.

butter knife Blunt, broad-bladed knife for cutting, serving, and spreading butter.

butter lamb (Russian) Symbolic lamb moulded in butter, featured in the traditional Russian ritual Easter meal.

butter pat Ball or small rectangle or circle of butter.

butter sauce Flour-and-water sauce with added seasoning and butter.

butter spreader Butter knife.

butter sponge Rich spongecake made with butter. See Genoese sponge.

Butterbrot (German) Bread and butter.

buttercake (American) Layer cake made from recipe rich in butter.

buttercup squash (American) Turban winter squash with a sweet-potato flavour.

buttered eggs Scrambled eggs.

butterfat Fat content in dairy product such as cheese, milk, and ice cream.

butterfish (American) Small edible fish found along the Atlantic Coast.

butterfly chop (American) Specially trimmed pork chop.

butterhead (American) Small, close-leafed variety of lettuce.

butteriga (Italian) Tuna or mullet roe.

buttermilk That portion of the cream which is left after the butter has been made from it. Used in scones, cakes, etc. in conjunction with bicarbonate of soda as a raising agent. Also marketed as a cold drink.

buttermilk biscuit (American) Scone made with buttermilk instead of sweet milk.

buttermilk soup Flour blended with a little cold buttermilk and then added to heated buttermilk. Highly nutritive.

butternut American tree of the walnut family.

butternut squash (American) Acorn squash; a vegetable of the pumpkin family.

Butterreis (German) Buttered rice.

butterscotch (i) Variety of toffee, made from butter, sugar and water. (ii) Flavouring for puddings, cakes, etc.

Butterteig (German) Puff pastry.

buttery (i) Store-room for beverages and food. (ii) Name applied to some restaurants.

button onion Small pickled onion.

butyric acid Acid which turns butter rancid.

buvette (French) Refreshment-room or bar.

Buxton pudding Baked pudding of flour, milk, butter, sugar, eggyolks and lemon peel.

Byrrh French *apéritif* flavoured with bitter herbs and fortified with brandy.

C Celsius or centigrade (See centigrade).

caballa (Spanish) Mackerel.

cabaret Liqueur set of glasses and decanters on a tray or in a special cabinet.

cabaret (French) Inn or tavern.

cabaretier (French) Innkeeper.

cabbage Leafy vegetable in many varieties including white and red cabbage, savoy, turnip tops and kale. Cabbage, which contains vitamin A, iron, calcium and variable amounts of vitamin C, and is valuable as roughage, can be shredded and boiled to serve with main dishes, used in soups and salads, or stuffed. Red cabbage is pickled in salt. Cabbage was first introduced into Britain from Holland in the reign of Henry VIII.

cabbage head Compact top portion of a cabbage.

cabbage lettuce Round, cabbage-shaped lettuce.

cabbage palm Palm with edible buds used in salads or cooked as vegetables.

cabernet (French) Red wine grape grown chiefly in the Bordeaux region. Also produced in California.

cabillaud (French) Codfish.

cabinet cherry (American) Black cherry.

cabinet pudding Simple moulded pudding made from bread and butter, eggs, dried fruit, or, in richer version, with sponge cakes and *glacé* cherries.

cabinet wine Top-quality Rhine wine good enough for the vintner's own private cellar. From *Kabinett* (German)

cabob Shish-kebab.

cabrales (Spanish) Goat's-milk cheese.

cabri (French) Kid.

cabrito (Portuguese and Spanish) Kid.

cacao Tropical American palm tree yielding a bean from which chocolate is derived.

cacao (French, Italian and Spanish) Cocoa.

cacao butter Cocoa butter.

cacau (Portuguese) Cocoa.

cacciagione (Italian) Game, venison.

cacciatora, alla (Italian) Meat and

vegetable sauce flavoured with juniper and served with *pasta*.

cacciatore (Italian) Hunter.

cacciù (Italian) Catechu, cachou.

cacciucco (Italian) Tuscan soup of fish and red wine.

cacerola (Spanish) Saucepan.

cachaça (Spanish) Brazilian rum.

cachalot Sperm whale, a sea mammal whose flesh is sometimes eaten.

Cachar tea Indian teas from the Cachar district of Assam.

cachat (French) Provençal cheese made from ewe's milk and ripened with vinegar.

cachou (French) (i) See Catechu. (ii) Perfumed or aromatic tablet used to sweeten the breath, made from icing sugar catechu and gum tragacanth.

caciato (Italian) Sprinkled with grated cheese.

cacimperio (Italian) Cheese and meat omelette.

cacio (Italian) Cheese.

cacio fresco (Italian) New cheese.

cacio grattato (Italian) Grated cheese.

caciocavallo (Italian) Cheese made from skimmed cow's milk, sometimes smoke-cured. The cheeses are dried in pairs on either side of a pole like a rider astride a horse, hence the name which means "horse-cheese".

caciotto (Italian) Umbrian cow's milk cheese.

cactus candy (American) Confection containing prickly-pear leaves with the skin and spines removed.

cactus salad (American) Prickly-pear leaves divested of their needles and green skin and served as a salad.

caddy Small container for holding biscuits, crackers or more especially, tea.

cadelinha (Portuguese) Clam.

cadgery de saumon (French) Salmon kedgeree.

Caen (French) Town in France famous for its tripe and other delicacies (*à la mode de Caen*)

Caen, *à la mode de* (French) Tripe, seasoned with garlic and spices, cooked in cider and *Calvados* (apple brandy).

Caerphilly cheese Originally Welsh, this cheese is made from whole milk, pressed only lightly and eaten young. It is soft, white, bland and milky.

caesar salad (American) Salad of cos lettuce, olive oil, raw egg, grated cheese, bread *croûtons*, anchovies, and seasonings.

café (French and Spanish) (i) Coffee — a beverage prepared from roasted and ground coffee beans. (ii) small restaurant where coffee, tea and light refreshments are served.

café au kirsch (French) Coffee drink made with egg whites, *Kirschwasser*, sugar and ice.

café au lait (French) Hot coffee and hot milk poured simultaneously. In France, chicory is added for flavour.

café brulôt (French) Black coffee served with flaming brandy or cognac sometimes seasoned with cinnamon, cloves, lemon and orange peel, sweetened with sugar.

café chantant (French) Nightclub.

café com leite (Portuguese) Hot coffee and hot milk poured simultaneously.

café complet (French) Continental breakfast — coffee with hot milk, rolls, butter and preserves.

café con leche (Spanish) Coffee with milk; white coffee.

café crème (French) Coffee with cream.

café decaféiné (French) Coffee with caffeine extracted.

café double (French) Double-strength coffee.

café frappé (French) Iced coffee.

café glacé (French) Iced coffee.

café listo (Spanish) Latin-American instant coffee.

café nature (French) Black coffee.

café noir (French) Black coffee served without milk or cream.

café puro (Spanish) Black coffee.

café royale (French) Black coffee and cognac with sugar.

café turc (French) Turkish coffee.

café vierge (French) "Virgin" coffee made with whole-roasted coffee beans, unground.

cafetal (Spanish) Coffee plantation.

cafetera (Spanish) Coffee-pot.

cafeteria Self-service restaurant.

cafetière (French) Coffee pot.
cafèzinho (Spanish) Brazilian-style extra-strong coffee.
caffè (Italian) Coffee.
caffè freddo (Italian) Chilled or iced coffee.
caffè in grano (Italian) Coffee beans.
caffè macinato (Italian) Ground coffee.
caffeine White crystalline alkaloid substance contained in coffee, of which it is the active principle. Its main use is as a non-intoxicating stimulant, but too large a dose can induce nervous excitement and insomnia.
caffelatte (Italian) Hot coffee and hot milk poured simultaneously.
caguama (Spanish) Sea turtle.
caienna, pepe di (Italian) Cayenne pepper
caille (French) Quail.
caille farcie (French) Stuffed quail.
caille-lait (French) Cheese-rennet.
caille rôtie (French) Roast quail.
caillebotte (French) Curds. Curdled milk drained in a muslin bag and eaten fresh.
cailleteau (French) Young quail.
cailletot (French) Young turbot.
caillot-rosat (French) Variety of pear with a rose flavour.
caisse (French) Case; *ramekin* case, etc.
cajú (Portuguese) Cashew.
cake (i) Baked dough based on mixtures of flour, fat, sugar, eggs and flavourings, with additions of fruits and spices in certain recipes. The variation in size and type is infinite. (ii) (American) Desserts made either from an egg-butter-sugar combination or combinations of other wet or dry ingredients. Many countries have symbolic cakes baked or cooked to mark special dates or historic events. In Britain, Christmas cake, simnel cake, birthday cake and wedding cake are examples.
cake cover Cover of metal or plastic, used to protect a cake.
cake cooler (American) Cake rack.
cake decorator (American) Icing set or bag for use when decorating a cake.
cake filling Sweet mixtures of various flavours (chocolate, vanilla, coffee, orange, etc.) spread on split cakes or sponges.

cake flour (American) Special soft-wheat flour used in making cakes, waffles, and other baked goods requiring a light, fine texture.
cake icing Sugar or fondant mixture flavoured and spread over cakes, sponges, etc.
cake mix Packeted cake mixture, usually requiring only the addition of eggs and liquids.
cake pan (American) Cake tin.
cake rack Wire rack for cooling freshly baked cakes, tarts, etc.
cake spice Prepared blend of spices for mincemeat, pies, fruit cakes, spice cakes, etc.
cake tin Tin for baking cakes, usually of aluminium or coated sheet metal; available in many shapes and sizes, some with removable bottoms.
cakebox (American) Breadbin.
cakebread (American) Bread of sweetened, cakelike bread baked in the shape of cakes.
cala (American) Meat cut from below the shoulder or loin of pork.
calabash Tropical American tree with a melon-like fruit.
calabash nutmeg Fruit of a tropical tree *monodora myristica* used as for the true nutmeg.
calabrese, alla (Italian) Food served in a ginger-flavoured tomato sauce.
calamar (Spanish) Cuttlefish or squid.
calamar en su tinta (Spanish) Squid served in its own dark-purple ink.
calamaretto (Italian) Baby octopus or squid.
calamaro (Italian) Cuttlefish or squid.
calamary Squid.
calamus Sweet flag and its aromatic root.
calas Fritter-like West Indian sweetmeat made of eggs, flour, rice, sugar, and yeast, served very hot with a sprinkling of finely powdered sugar.
calcium Mineral present in milk, cheese, vegetables, pulses and cereals also in flour, eggs and fish, to a lesser extent; necessary for growth of bones and teeth.
caldo (Italian) Hot; warm.
caldo (Spanish and Portuguese) Clear soup, broth.

51

caldo asturiano (Spanish) Asturian soup.

caldo de carne (Spanish) Beef tea.

caldo de congrio (Spanish) Conger-eel soup.

caldo de gallina (Spanish) Chicken soup.

caldo verde (Portuguese) Green soup made of thinly-sliced cabbage and mashed potatoes.

calf Young bovine animal; female calves are heifers, males are bull calves.

calf meat Veal.

calf's crow Membrane covering the calf's intestines which can be cooked in various ways.

calf's brains Delicacy which must be well soaked and cleaned of blood before cooking in any of the numerous recipes available.

calf's ear Offal which should be well cleaned and blanched before cooking— braised, grilled, etc.

calf's foot Offal which must be soaked boned and blanched before serving in a number of ways — in sauces, fried, vinaigrette, etc. See also Calf's Foot Jelly.

calf's foot jelly Jelly made by boiling calves' feet slowly, then "clearing" the jellied stock by re-boiling with sugar, lemons, seasonings and brandy.

calf's head Offal which must be boned, soaked, blanched before cooking. It can then be cooked in a wide variety of ways — stuffed, cubed and fried, served with sauces, etc.

calf's heart Offal, which can be prepared as for calf's kidneys or cooked whole (braised, roasted, pot-roasted).

calf's kidney Offal which can be grilled, fried, escalopped, sautéed, etc.

calf's liver Offal suitable for cooking in sundry ways – fried, grilled, braised, etc.

calf's sweetbreads Calf glands, throat or pancreas, considered the most delicate of all white offal. Can be served in many ways – braised, escalopped, grilled, poached, in pastry cases, etc. The throat gland is the more delicate.

calf's tongue Offal which can be braised, poached, served with sauces etc.

calf's udder Offal widely used in Jewish cooking. Must be cooked and blanched before cooking.

calico bass (American) (i) Freshwater edible fish of the Great Lakes and Mississippi River. (ii) Pacific Coast sea bass.

calico bean (American) Kidney bean.

calico corn (American) Indian corn with mottled and variegated kernels.

calico crab (American) Red spotted crab found in shallow water along the Atlantic coast.

California dip Dry onion-soup mix blended with sour cream and eaten as a dip.

California sardine (American) Tiny edible fish also known as pilchard, found along the Pacific coast.

California wine (American) Wine grown in California from wines originally imported from Europe.

calipash Portion of glutinous meat to be found in the upper shell of the turtle.

calipee Glutinous meat found in the under part of a turtle's shell.

calisaya (Peruvian) Bitters made from chinchona bark, used in cocktails.

calmar (French) Squid.

caloric *punsch* Scandinavian liqueur made of rum and syrup.

calorie Unit of energy or heat-producing value of food. Large Calorie ('C') is the amount of heat needed to raise one kilogram of water by one degree centigrade. Small calorie ('c') is the heat necessary to raise one gram of water by one degree centigrade. Approximate calorie requirements obtained from food are established for individual needs and are used to regulate weight.

calostro (Spanish) Beestings.

caluso (Italian) Sweet wine from *Piedmont*.

calvados (French) Apple brandy, distilled from cider in Normandy.

camarão (Portuguese) Prawn.

camarão frito (Portuguese) Fried prawn.

camarón (Spanish) Prawn.

Cambacérès (Jean-Jacques, Régis de) (1753-1824) French High Chancellor under Bonaparte, famous for his table though an eccentric rather than a knowledgeable gastronome.

camel Mammal with one or two humps (dromedaries) eaten by Arabs while young and tender. The hump, feet and stomach are the most highly regarded, but the sirloin is sliced into escalopes, and the fillet is roasted after marination.

camel couscous Arabian dish in which camel meat is substituted for the more usual mutton.

camel pilaf Pilaf made from lean camel meat, taken from the fillet or sirloin of the young camel.

camembert (French) Soft cheese made from whole milk and attributed to a farmer's wife in the village of *Camembert*, France, where a statue stands to her memory. *Camembert* should yield to gentle finger-pressure but should not be runny. It should be kept at room temperature and never refrigerated.

camerain (French) Costly soup invented by an 18th century actor of that name.

cameriere (Italian) Waiter.

camarera (Spanish) Waitress.

camarero (Spanish) Waiter.

camomile Daisy-like herb with an aromatic scent and bitter flavour. The dried flower-heads are used to make a tisane, a camomile tea.

camote (Spanish) Sweet potato discovered by early Spanish explorers in the New World.

campagna, alla (Italian) Sauce made of minced beef and cottage cheese.

campanula Common field plant with edible root and leaves which must be picked before the stalk develops. Used in salads.

Campari (Italian) Brand of Italian vermouth, red in colour, and with a distinctive flavour produced by macerating herbs in the basic fortified wine. Its formula is a carefully guarded secret.

campeachy wood Mexican tree whose wood, when boiled, yields colouring matter (red/violet) used in making liqueurs and improving the colour of wines.

campine (French) Fat pullet from *Campine*, Flanders.

can Cylindrical metal container in which beverages and foods are preserved and sold.

Canada goose Wild goose of North America.

Canada potato (American) Jerusalem artichoke.

Canadian fruit pie Crumble topping over fruit.

Canadian style bacon (American) Bacon cut from loins and backs of pigs, boned and rolled.

Canadian whisky Light-bodied delicate blend of barley, corn, and rye whisky, distilled in Canada.

canapé (French) Bread or biscuit topped with tasty decorative spread, served at cocktail parties or as an *hors d'œuvre* before dinner.

canapé butter Spread made by mixing creamed butter with prawns, anchovies, chives, egg, horseradish etc. and used on *canapés*.

canard (French) Duck.

canard montmorency (French) Roast duck with cherries.

canard pressé (French) Pressed duck.

canard rôti (French) Roast duck.

canard sauvage (French) Wild duck.

Canary banana Small aromatic banana from the Canary Islands.

canary grass Genus of plant originating in the Canary Islands and cultivated for its seed which is rich in edible starch. Also known as canary grain, bird grain or spike grain.

canary pudding Basic steamed sponge pudding made from flour, fat, sugar and eggs, flavoured to taste (coffee, lemon, chocolate, etc.) or varied by the addition of fresh or canned fruit.

Canary wine Wine produced in the Canary Islands; some types resembling Madeira, sherry or port.

Cancalaise, à la (French) Dishes garnished with shrimps and oysters in *Normande* sauce, specialities of the little fishing port of *Cancale*.

Cancale (French) Small French fishing port famous for its oysters.

cancoillotte (French) Strong French cheese which is melted before serving.

candied Fruits, etc., crystallized or cooked in sugar or syrup until translucent.

candied angelica Stalks of angelica herb

candied with syrup, used as cake or dessert decoration.

candied apple (American) Toffee apple.

candied peel Grapefruit, lemon, lime, orange, tangerine or other citrus-fruit peel prepared by cooking in sugar and syrup. Used in cakes, puddings, mincemeat, etc.

candy (i) Sweetmeat made of crystallised sugar. (ii) (American) Toffees or sweets generally.

candy floss Coloured sugar spun into a light fluffy mass, usually twisted onto sticks and sold at fairs, carnivals, markets, etc.

cane (French) Hen duck.

cane juice Liquid yielded by crushed sugar cane, also called cane wine.

cane spirit Alcohol distilled from molasses often used as the basis for vodka, gin, etc.

cane sugar Sugar extracted from the sugar cane.

canela (Spanish) Cinnamon.

canello (Italian) Tube of *pasta*.

caneton (French) Duckling.

caneton à l'Alsacienne (French) *Nantes* duckling braised and served with *sauerkraut*.

caneton à la bigarade (French) See *Caneton à l'orange*.

caneton a l'orange or **à la bigarade** (French) Grilled or braised duckling served with a sauce made from Seville oranges.

canton rôti (French) Roast duckling.

cangrejo (Spanish) Crab.

canister Small container, for holding coffee, flour, salt, sugar, or tea.

canneberge (French) Cranberry.

canned food Food hermetically sealed in tins to preserve freshness. Storing time varies according to contents, but tins should be examined occasionally for signs of deterioration.

cannelé (French) Pastry crust or vegetables formed into decorative designs and shapes.

cannella (Italian) Cinnamon.

cannelle (French) Cinnamon.

cannelon or **canelon** (French) Small roll of puff pastry filled with savoury mince meat, fish, poultry or game.

cannelloni (Italian) Squares or tubes of pasta, stuffed with meat, cheese or fish or vegetable, baked with butter and cheese, or with a cream sauce and cheese.

canelloni ripieni (Italian) Stuffed *cannelloni*.

canning Process of preserving food in tins usually carried out commercially but apparatus is available for it to be done domestically.

cannolo (Italian) Rich cream-filled pastry horn.

cantal (French) Hard, strong cheese made in the *Auvergne*.

cantaloup (French) Cantaloupe melon.

cantaloupe Melon with hard rind and sweet orange-coloured flesh, originally grown in Cantalupo in central Italy.

cantarella (Italian) Sea-bream.

canteen (i) Bar, cafeteria or informal restaurant. (ii) Specially fitted box to accommodate cutlery. (iii) Container for liquid for outdoor use.

cantharelle (French) See *Chanterelle*.

cantina (Portuguese) Canteen.

cantina (Spanish) Wine cellar; saloon.

canton ginger Fine grade of ginger crystallized while still green.

Cantonware Blue and white porcelain china of a type exported from Canton, China.

canvasback (American) Highly esteemed wild duck, usually split and grilled.

cape cod (American) Largest hard-shell clam found along the Atlantic coast.

cape gooseberry Berry of a plant known in Britain as "Chinese Lanterns" and grown for house decoration. In hot countries the berries ripen and are made into preserves or eaten raw. With calyxes bent back, the fruit can be dipped into melted fondant and dried, then eaten as *petit fours*.

Cape grape Grape of South Africa used in wine making.

Cape wine South African wine made from native grapes.

capelan or **caplan** (French) Delicately flavoured fish of the cod family, resembling smelt.

capellini d'angelo (Italian) Long thin pasta, literally "angel's hair".

capendu (French) Red apple with a short stalk.

caper Unopened flower-buds of a plant which grows wild among the rocks of Greece and Northern Africa, and now cultivated in the south of Europe. They are imported from Italy, Sicily, and the south of France, after being pickled in salt and vinegar. The best are exported from *Toulon*. Used as seasoning, sauce flavouring and condiment.

capercailzie or woodgrouse Member of the grouse family, possessing a delicate flavour, usually cooked and served like grouse. The capercailzie is the largest of the gallinaceous birds of Europe about the size of small turkey, found in the north of Europe.

caperon (French) *Hautboy*, a large white strawberry.

capillaire (French) (i) Variety of fern. (ii) Syrup flavoured with orange-flowers etc. – *sirop de capillaire*.

capillotade (French) *Ragoût* of re-heated poultry.

capirotada (Mexican/Spanish) Bread pudding flavoured with cinnamon, pine nuts, bread and cottage cheese.

capitaine (French) Sea fish resembling carp and cooked in the same way.

capiteux (French) Heady, referring to wines rich in alcohol.

capitone (Italian) Large species of eel.

caplan (French) See *capelan*.

capocollo (Italian) Parma speciality of cured neck of pork.

capoletti (Italian) Triangular ravioli.

capon Castrated male chicken or rabbit.

caponata (Italian) Sicilian sweet-sour dish of aubergines, capers, olives, onions, celery, tomato sauce and fish.

capone (Italian) Sea hen; gurnard.

cappe (Italian) Variety of edible bi-valve molluscs including *tartufe di mare* (cockle).

cappelletti (Italian) (i) Type of soup. (ii) Stuffed *pasta* "hats" served in broth or with butter and grated cheese.

cappero (Italian) Caper.

cappone (Italian) Capon.

cappone ripieno (Italian) Stuffed, roasted capon.

cappuccino (Italian) Coffee - and - milk mixture served from an espresso machine.

câpre (French) Caper.

capretto (Italian) Kid; young goat.

capretto al forno (Italian) Roast kid.

capretto allo spiedo (Italian) Spit-roasted kid.

capretto ripieno (Italian) Stuffed, roast kid.

Capri (Italian) Delicate red wine originally produced on the Isle of Capri.

caprino (i) Argentinian goat's-milk cheese. (ii) Old Jamaican coffee-flavoured liqueur.

capriolo (Italian) Roe-buck.

capron (French) *Caperon*.

capucin, barbe de (French) Chicory.

capucine (French) Indian cress. Nasturtium.

capsicum Genus of a number of varieties of pepper. There are two main types; (a) hot, such as the chilli; (b) sweet, like those eaten as a vegetable. Capsicums can be green or red, and they vary considerably in size and shape.

caracol (Spanish) Snail.

carafe (French) (i) Wine decanter. (ii) Water bottle.

caraffa (Italian) Wine *carafe*.

carafon (French) Small *carafe*.

caramel See *caramel*.

caramel (French) (i) Toffee sweetmeat, soft or hard in texture, depending upon the temperature to which the mixture is boiled. (ii) Liquid colouring matter, made by browning until thick and dark brown. Commonly known as "Black Jack". Used as a flavouring and colouring agent in soups, gravies, puddings, etc., and used commercially in sauces, vinegars, wines, beers, etc. Also used for coating moulds for a kind of custard pudding, in which case the sugar is cooked to amber colour.

caramel fruit Sugar-glazed fruit.

caramelise (i) To cook sugar slowly until it turns brown and sticky (ii) To coat a cooking utensil or mould with browned sugar.

caramelvla (Dutch) Caramel custard.

carapace Shell of crabs, lobsters, and turtles, etc.

caraway Umbelliferous plant whose aromatic seeds are used as a pharmaceutical tonic and as a food flavouring in cakes, biscuits, etc. The seeds are used widely in European cookery, especially in Germany. In Scotland, they are sugared and known as "carvies" or "caraway comfits".

caraway comfit See caraway.

caraway loaf (American) Caraway cheese.

caraway oil Essential oil extracted from caraway seeds, and used in flavouring liqueurs, salad dressings, condiments and medicines.

caraway-seed biscuit (American) Scone sprinkled with caraway seeds.

caraway-seed bread Rye bread flavoured with caraway seeds.

caraway-seed roll Crisp baked roll topped with caraway seeds.

carbohydrates Compounds of carbon, hydrogen and oxygen (these last two in the same proportion as in water). They include sugars, starchy foods and cellulose and are converted by the body into energy. When carbohydrates are taken disproportionately to protein, the excess forms fat and leads to obesity.

carbon dioxide Gaseous compound formed by carbon and oxygen used in mineral and soda waters, also in drawing beer. Solid carbon dioxide is used in refrigeration in place of ice, thus saving space and avoiding humidity.

carbonada (Spanish) Stew of meat, fruit, and rice, speciality of Uruguay.

carbonada criolla (Spanish) Argentinian dish of beef stew baked in a pumpkin shell.

carbonado Ancient dish prepared from a fowl or joint of veal or mutton, roasted, carved, and cut across and across. The pieces were then basted with butter, sprinkled with breadcrumbs, and grilled. The term now applies to meat slashed crossways or before grilling.

carbonata (Italian) Stew of beef, herbs, onions etc. cooked in a casserole.

carbonated drink Drink infused with sparkle by means of carbon dioxide.

carbonated water Water charged with carbon dioxide; also known as Soda water and Sparkling water.

carbonated wine Wine charged with soda water.

carbonique (French) Carbon dioxide.

carbonnade (French) Casseroled beef stewed or braised in liquid, often incorporating beer.

carborundum stone Abrasive for sharpening knives, and other sharp-edged kitchen utensils.

carcase (i) Bone structure of a bird or animal. (ii) The body of the slaughtered animal.

carcasse (French) Carcase.

carcavelos (Portuguese) Sweet white Portuguese wine.

carciofino (Italian) Very young artichoke.

carciofo (Italian) Artichoke.

carciofo alla contadina (Italian) Stuffed seasoned artichoke, stewed in oil.

carciofo arrosto (Italian) Roasted artichoke with garlic.

carciofo bollito (Italian) Boiled artichoke.

carciofo fritto (Italian) Fried artichoke heart.

carciofo ripieno (Italian) Stuffed artichoke.

cardamine (French) Wild or bitter cress, tasting like watercress and used in salads.

cardamom Known as the "Seed of Paradise", a stimulant aromatic spice. The seeds of a plant of the ginger family, which grows abundantly in the mountain forests of the coast of Malabar; used in curries, cordials, cakes and confectionery.

cardamom oil Essential oil distilled from caramom seeds and used for flavouring.

cardamome (French) Cardamom.

carde (French) Edible portion of the cardoon. Mostly served braised or as a *purée*.

carde à la moëlle (French) Pieces of marrow braised with bacon.

cardinale, à la (French) (i) Fish garnished with mushrooms and sliced truffles. (ii) Fruits served with raspberry syrup and shredded almonds.

cardinal fish Variety of red mullet found in the Mediterranean.

cardinal sauce Red sauce served with

fish dishes, made from lobster butter, *béchamel* sauce, lemon juice and cream.

cardinaliser (French) To turn crustaceans red by plunging them in boiling water or stock.

cardio (Italian) Cockle.

cardo (Italian) Cardoon.

cardo di bietola (Italian) Swiss chard.

cardoon Plant of the thistle genus with edible leaf-stalks and roots. The blanched stalks are cooked like celery, the fleshy main root is boiled and served cold or in salads.

carême (French) Lent. A period of fasting imposed by the early Church to offset the gastronomic excesses of the winter.

Carême, Antonin Celebrated chef, born in Paris in 1784, died 1833; author of several culinary works, chef to the Prince Regent, George IV of England, and the Emperor Alexander I of Russia. Founder of classic French cookery – *la grande cuisine*.

caret (French) Green turtle.

cari (French) Curry.

cari (Italian) Curry powder.

cari de poulet (French) Chicken curry.

caribbean cabbage Root of the *arum esculeutum*, prepared as for swedes.

carline thistle Mountain plant with edible flowers used in salads. The root is used as a drug.

Carling Canadian ale and beef brewed in Toronto, Ontario.

Carlsberg Danish lager beer brewed in Copenhagen.

carmin (French) Crimson.

carmine Vivid red non-toxic food colouring derived from cochineal, and used in confectionery, icings, etc. (See cochineal).

carnation Flower whose petals are used to make a syrup and a ratafia.

carne (Italian) (i) Meat. (ii) Fruit pulp.

carne (Spanish) Meat.

carne asado (Spanish) Roast meat.

carne congelata (Italian) Frozen meat.

carne de carnero (Spanish) Mutton.

carne de cerdo (Spanish) Pork.

carne de cordero (Spanish) Lamb.

carne de membrillo (Spanish) Quince preserve.

carne de pluma (Spanish) Fowl flesh.

carne de vaca (Spanish) Beef.

carne fiambre (Spanish) Cold meat.

carne fredda assortita (Italian) Assorted cold cuts of meat.

carne in scatola (Italian) Canned meat.

carne salata (Italian) Corned Beef.

carne stufata (Italian) Stewed meat.

carne, sugo di (Italian) Meat, vegetable and wine sauce, served with *pasta* and grated cheese.

carne tritata (Italian) Minced meat.

carnero (Spanish) Sheep, mutton.

carniceria (Spanish) Butcher's shop.

carnier (French) Game-bag.

carob (American) Locust tree. Evergreen growing in Mediterranean areas, yielding seeds milled into flour used as a thickening agent. The seed pods are dried and ground into a fine powder used in cakes, biscuits, sweets, etc. Also known as St. John's bread.

carob flour (American) Flour milled from dried carob seeds.

carob powder (American) Fine-ground carob pods or locust beans.

carolina rice Long-grained angular rice, bright in appearance.

carolina tea (American) Indian tea.

caroni White rum distilled in Trinidad.

carota (Italian) Carrot.

carotene Reddish-yellow pigment present in yellow and green vegetables and fruit. Converted into vitamin A in the body.

carotte (French) Carrot.

caroube (French) Locust or carob tree yielding long beans with seeds. (See carob).

carp Fresh-water fish, not valued much as food in England, but popular in Chinese cooking and on the Continent. After washing well in running or salted water to remove the muddy flavour, it can be grilled or fried, stuffed and baked, or cooked in red wine.

carpa, carpione (Italian) Carp.

carpa (Spanish) Carp.

carpe (French) Carp.

Carpentras, à la Dishes garnished with truffles. The French district of *Carpentras* is famous for its well-flavoured truffles.

carpeau (French) See *carpillon*.

carpillon (French) Also called *carpeau*. (i) Small carp. (ii) Small non-spawning mullet, cooked as for carp.

carpion Variety of trout, and cooked in the same way.

carpione (Italian) Carp.

carrageen Purplish seaweed found off coasts of Europe and North America. Known as Irish moss when dried and bleached, it is used in making jellies and blancmanges, substituting for gelatine.

carré (French and Italian) Loin. The front part of the animal's hindquarter, with shank removed.

carré di vitello (Italian) Rib of veal.

carrelet (French) Flounder.

carrot Root vegetable rich in vitamin A, the B vitamins, sugar and calcium. Can be boiled, braised, served separately as a vegetable or incorporated in stews, soups, etc. or eaten raw in salads. Carrots were first introduced into England by Flemish gardeners in the reign of Elizabeth I and in the time of James I they were still so uncommon that they were worn in place of feathers on ladies' hats and sleeves.

carrot cake Cake made of carrots, eggs, nuts, and raisins.

carta (Spanish) Bill of fare.

carte, à la (French) Ordering individual dishes from a menu, rather than from a set combination (*table d'hôte*).

carte de vins (French) Wine list.

carte du jour, la (French) The bill of fare for the day; a list of daily dishes with the prices attached to each dish.

cartoccio, in (Italian) Food such as fish cooked in a paper case.

carvi (French and Italian) Caraway seed.

carvie (Scottish) Caraway seed, usually sugared.

carvie cake (Scottish) Oatmeal cake made with caraway seeds.

carving Cutting up meat and poultry to serve at table. Meat should be cut across the grain to achieve greater tenderness. Joints previously boned and stuffed are easier to carve than those still on the bone. Joints such as loin or neck should be chined rather than chopped, to facilitate carving, and meat and poultry should be skewered and tied into good compact shapes before cooking.

carving set Utensils for carving a joint or bird consisting of a carving fork, usually two-tined, with a finger guard; a carving knife, and a sharpening steel for honing the knife.

carviol Vegetable similar to cauliflower, best known and cultivated in Austria.

casaba Sweet melon with pale-yellow flesh and golden-yellow skin, named for the Turkish town of Kasaba where they were first grown.

casalinga (Italian) Adjective applied to any home-made dish or preparation.

casalinga, alla (Italian) Home-made tomato sauce to serve with *pasta*.

casanova (American) Celery-and-truffles salad.

case One dozen bottles (or its equivalent volume) of wines or spirits.

casein (i) Coagulated body-building substance of milk and certain leguminous plants. (ii) The curd of milk from which cheese is produced. Cheese is therefore an important flesh-forming food in a concentrated form.

caseralla (Greek) Soft creamy cheese.

casere (Greek) Sheep's-milk cheese.

casha (Indian) Dish consisting of a kind of cream flavoured with mace.

cashew Tropical American tree yielding crescent-shaped nuts.

cask Wooden container for wines and spirits.

cassareep Prepared juice of the cassava. The basis of many sauces and of the West Indian pepper-pot.

cassata (Italian) (i) (*Gelato*) Candied fruit-and-ice-cream confection (Neapolitan ice cream) (ii) (*Dolce*) A mould of *ricotta* cheese, candied fruit, and chocolate, with sponge fingers.

cassava Tropical shrub, also known as Ycca or Manioc. The food produced by its tubers, a staple in many African countries, also carries both names. When further refined, cassava yields both tapioca and farina.

casse (French) (i) Case, pan. (ii) Cassia.

casse à rôti (French) Dripping pan.

casserole (i) Covered dish made of glass, metal or earthenware, used for cooking composite meals. (ii) One-dish meal of meat or fish plus vegetables, sauce, *pasta*, etc.

casserole (French) (i) Saucepan. (ii) Dish with rice or potatoes shaped on a platter in casserole or timbale form.

casserole, à la (French) In casserole style.

cassia (i) Genus of shrubs yielding drugs and medicinal juices including senna and cascarilla. (ii) Bark used as a kind of coarse cinnamon.

cassis (French) (i) That part which is attached to the tail end of a loin of veal. (ii) Black-currant syrup or black-currant liqueur, popular in France.

Cassis (French) District in the *Bouches-du- Rhône* area giving its name to wine and liqueur.

cassola (Italian) Sardinian fish stew.

cassolette Small fireproof casserole for individual portions.

casson (French) (i) Broken loaf sugar. (ii) Broken cocoa-nibs.

cassonade (French) Moist brown sugar. Sugar which has not been highly refined.

cassoulet (French) Casserole dish made with haricot beans and meat, originating in the Carcassonne-Toulouse area of France.

castagna (Italian) Chestnut.

castagnaco (Italian) Thick fritter made with chestnut flour.

castagnola (Italian) Macaroon flavoured with chocolate and cinnamon.

castaña (Spanish) Chestnut.

castanha do Brasil (Portuguese) Brazil nut.

castelane (French) Variety of green plum similar to the greengage.

Castiglione, à la (French) Small pieces of meat garnished with slices of poached beef marrow, butter-sautéed aubergines and large, rice-stuffed, oven-baked mushrooms.

castle pudding Rich sponge mixture, baked or steamed in small dariole moulds or cups and served with jam sauce.

castradina (Italian) Venetian name for roast mutton.

castrato (Italian) Mutton.

Catalane, à la (French) Large pieces of meat served with rice pilaff and aubergines sautéed in oil.

catawba (American) Light red grape used in making sparkling white wine.

catchup Catsup or ketchup.

catechu Sap from a variety of acacia used in the making of *cachous*.

catfish (American) Freshwater and salt-water fish with whisker-like barbels and delicate flesh.

catfishburger (American) Hamburger made of catfish.

catsup Ketchup.

caudle Kind of gruel, with the addition of eggs, and sometimes beer, wine or spirits.

cauf (i) Baker's bread basket. (ii) Perforated receptacle used for keeping fish alive in water.

caul Membrane in the shape of a net covering the lower portion of an animal's intestines, used for encasing minced meat, sausages, salpicon, etc. Pork caul is the choicest.

cauli Slang for cauliflower.

cauliflower Plant of the cabbage family whose compact white flower head is usually boiled in salted water and served as a vegetable with a sauce, or broken into flowerets and eaten in salad.

caustic soda Sodium hydroxide; powerful cleansing agent used in dissolving fats and greases, and in cleaning stoves and ovens.

Cavaillon (French) Type of melon named for the French town in the *Vaucluse*.

cavedano (Italian) Chub.

cavendish Dwarf banana also known as the Chinese banana; cultivated extensively in Jamaica, and many parts of tropical America.

caviale (Italian) Caviare.

caviare Salted or marinated roe of fish of the sturgeon family, obtainable in various qualities. Caviare should be kept cold, and served with toast or on *canapés*, etc. as an *hors d'œuvre*.

cave (French) Cellar.

cave à liqueurs (French) Specially made chest fitted with a lock to store liqueurs.

cavoletto (Italian) Brussels sprout.

cavolfiore (Italian) Cauliflower.

cavolo (Italian) Cabbage.

cavolo di Brusselle (Italian) Brussels sprout.

cavolo marino (Italian) Sea kale.

cavolo romano (Italian) Broccoli.

cavolo rosso (Italian) Red cabbage.

cavour, à la (French) Small pieces of meat, such sweetbreads, escalopes, etc. dressed on circles of polenta and garnished with truffle slices and grilled mushrooms stuffed with chicken-liver *purée*.

cayenne pepper Pungent red powder derived from dried, ground capsicum fruits and used in cheese, egg, fish, and meat dishes, sauces, etc.

caza (Spanish) Game.

cazuela (Spanish) (i) Earthenware stewing pot. (ii) Vegetable dish prepared in a *cazuela*.

cc. Abbreviation for cubic centimetre.

cebada (Spanish) Barley.

cebolla (Spanish) Onion.

cece (Italian) Chickpea.

cece all'olio (Italian) Chick pea with olive oil.

cecil Old-fashioned variety of meat ball, flavoured with anchovies and lemon peel.

cecina (Spanish) Dry beef.

cédrat (French) Variety of citron-tree; its fruit is used for cakes, puddings, and ice-creams, and a special kind of oil is also prepared from this fruit.

cédratine (French) Corsican liqueur made from *cédrat* fruit.

cèfalo (Italian) Mullet.

céléri (French) Celery.

céléri rave (French) Celeriac.

celeriac or celery root Turnip-rooted celery, of which the root only is used; served as a vegetable, stewed in broth or served with melted butter.

celery Salad plant with crisp stalks eaten raw or dressed as salad. Cooked, it is served in various ways as a vegetable or in soups.

celery cabbage White-stalked vegetable with light green leaves; also called Chinese cabbage.

celery oil Oil extracted from celery seeds, and used in flavouring.

celery root (American) Celeriac.

celery salt Salt flavoured with dried and powdered celery, used in stews, salads, etc.

celery seed Ground aromatic seeds of a plant related to vegetable celery, and used to flavour stews, salads, fish and meat dishes, etc.

celestina (Italian) Clear soup served with *pasta* stars.

cellar Underground room cool, airy and dampish, used for storing wine.

cellaret Compartment or case for storing bottles of wine.

cellophane Transparent cellulose wrapping used to protect displayed foods but now largely superseded by plastic coverings which give greater protection.

Celsius See centigrade.

cena (Italian) Supper.

cena (Spanish) Supper, evening meal.

cendre, la (French) Ashes or embers. *Cuit sous la cendre* – cooked under the ashes.

cène (French) The Last Supper.

centigrade Temperature scale invented by Anders Celsius (1701-1744) now called Celsius by international agreement. On this scale water boils at 100 degrees and freezes at 0 degrees.

centopelle (Italian) Honeycomb tripe – the third stomach of a ruminant.

centre ham slices (American) Gammon rashers.

cépage (French) Variety of vine.

cèpe or *ceps* (French) Esculent boletus, an edible mushroom of yellowish colour, with an agreeable and nutty flavour, largely cultivated in the Bordeaux district.

cerdo (Spanish) Pork; pig.

cerdo asado (Spanish) Roast Pork.

cereal Seeds of such cultivated grasses as maize, oats, rye, rice, and wheat. Prepared in breakfast-food form, but used also in many cases for making flour, bread, etc.

cereza (Spanish) Cherry.

cerf (French) Deer, stag, hart. The meat of venison.

cerfeuil (French) Chervil.

cerise (French) Cherry.

cerises au vinaigre (French) Cherries in vinegar, ripe cherries bottled in caster sugar, cinnamon and wine vinegar.

cerneau (French) Kernel of a green walnut, usually prepared in salt-water. A red wine is also made from these kernels, called *vin de cerneaux*, which is drunk in the walnut season.

cerneau confit (French) Preserved green walnut.

cernia (Italian) Perch.

certosino (Italian) Honey cake filled with almonds and citron peel.

cerveceria (Spanish) (i) Brewery. (ii) Tavern or drinking house. (iii) Café.

cerveja (Portuguese) Beer.

cervelas (French) Saveloy – thick short smoked sausage made of pork, and seasoned with salt, pepper, and spices.

cervella (Italian) Brains – the contents of an animal's skull.

cervella di abbacchio (Italian) Lamb's brains.

cervella di maiale (Italian) Pork brains.

cervella di vitello (Italian) Calf brains.

cervellata (Italian) Saveloy, sausage.

cervelle (French) Brains – the substance within the skull of an animal.

cerveza (Spanish) Beer.

cerveza blanca (Spanish) Light beer.

cerveza floja (Spanish) Table beer, small beer.

cervo (Italian) Venison.

cestino (Italian) Small, savoury-filled puff or flaky pastry-case.

cetriolo (Italian) Cucumber, gherkin.

cevabçiçi (Yugoslav) Beef and veal sausages.

Ceylon cinnamon Bark of the cinnamon tree and high grade source of the spice used in cooking.

Ceylon tea Tea of a type originally produced on the island of Ceylon (See pekoe).

Chablis Small French town in the Yonne district famous for its white wines, and giving its name to a dry white Burgundy

chaboisseau (French) Large-headed Mediterranean fish used in making *bouillabaisse*.

chabot (French) Freshwater fish, sometimes wrongly called chub.

chafing dish Vessel for cooking or keeping food warm at table. The classic chafing dish comprises two pans, the lower of which contains hot water. Both are placed over heat. Modern chafing dishes are single dishes placed on a tripod over a source of heat to cook eggs, cheese fondue, etc.

chaine (French) Chine (of meat).

chair (French) Flesh.

chair à saucisse (French) Sausage meat.

chair blanche (French) White meat.

chair noire (French) Dark meat.

challah Plaited egg bread sometimes topped with sesame seeds, baked for the Jewish Sabbath and holidays.

chalop (Russian) Sour milk and herb soup served chilled in hot weather.

chalota (Portuguese) Shallot; scallion.

chalumeau (French) Drinking straw.

chambertin (French) Vineyard on the French *Côte d'Or*, producing a famous burgundy.

chambéry (French) Vermouth produced in the Savoy department of France.

chambrer (French) To remove wines from the cellar in order to bring them up to room temperature.

chameau (French) Camel.

chamois (French) Wild, goat-like animal whose flesh is eaten as venison and prepared as for roebuck.

chamomile Camomile.

champ Northern Irish dish of mashed potatoes, peas and onions.

Champagne French province which includes *Rheims*, *Épernay* and *Chalons-sur-Marne* with a world-wide reputation for its sparkling white wines which are blended to achieve perfection.

champagne World - renowned white wines from Champagne, France which are bottled before fermentation is complete and the carbonic acid gas left in solution creates the sparkling effect when the bottle is opened.

champagne cider Double - fermented cider; the first stage turning the apple juice into cider and the second turning the still cider into a sparkling beverage.

champagne cocktail Cocktail made of champagne, angostura, sugar, and lemon peel.

champagne cup Drink made from champagne, soda water, sugar, sliced oranges and balm.

champagne glass Stemmed glass (sometimes hollow-stemmed) holding 4 to 6 ounces of liquid.

Champagner (German) Champagne.

champagniser (French) To subject wines to the same treatment as in making champagne.

champagnisation Process of turning still wines into sparkling wines.

champãna (Spanish) Champagne.

champignon (French) Mushroom.

Champignon (German) Mushroom.

champignon au gratin (French) Baked mushroom.

champignon de prairie (French) Field mushroom.

champigny (French) Apricot-jam-filled puff pastry.

champoreau (French) Black coffee to which has been added a little rum, kirsch or brandy.

chanfaina (Spanish) Dish of lamb's liver, onions, breadcrumbs and seasoning.

channel bass (American) Edible bass found in the Gulf of Mexico and in South American coastal rivers, also called Red Drum.

channel cat (American) Catfish caught and eaten in southern United States.

chanquerettes (French/Spanish) Andalusian fish-fry.

chanterelle (French) Small yellow cup-like mushroom with a frilled edge.

Chantilly (French) (i) Whipped, sweetened and flavoured cream. (ii) Hollandaise sauce with added cream. (iii) Mayonnaise and whipped cream. (iv) Name given to various dishes and pastry confections.

chaomein (Chinese) Also called "Chow-mein". A Chinese dish of fried noodles topped with a mixture of meat, fish and vegetables fried together.

chap Cheek, especially of pig. (See Bath chap).

chapattie Pancake or *tortilla* from India and Ceylon, made of wheat flour and baked on a griddle over an open fire. A type of unleavened bread.

chapon (French) (i) Capon. (ii) A piece of bread boiled in soup. (iii) A crust of bread rubbed with garlic.

chaponneau (French) Young capon.

char Fresh-water fish, found in the English Lake district and in the lakes and rivers of Switzerland and the Savoy. It belongs to the same family as the salmon and trout, and has the same pink and oily flesh. It is cooked like trout.

charbonnée (French) Burnt.

charbonnier (French) Coal-fish.

charcuterie (French) (i) Pork butcher's shop. (ii) Pig's meat. (iii) Assortment of sausages, truffled pig's ears and feet, pig's liver, saveloy, etc.

charcutier (French) Pork butcher.

chard Edible leafstalks of the artichoke, cardoon or Swiss chard.

chardon (French) Wild thistle from which cardoons and globe artichokes derive.

chardoon Cardoon.

charentais melon Small melon with yellow-green skin, deep yellow flesh and a sweet, aromatic flavour.

Charente (French) Department of France famed for cognac brandy.

charged water Water charged with carbon dioxide; soda water or sparkling water.

charlotte (French) Two varieties of dessert, one made from sponge fingers, jelly and cream, the other from bread and fruit, usually apples. Savoury charlottes, using cheese can also be made.

charlotte de pomme (French) Apple charlotte, consists of thin slices of bread, steeped in clarified butter ranged in symmetrical order in plain moulds and filled with apple *purée*, and baked.

charlotte martinique (French) Strawberry ice cream and sponge fingers topped with whipped cream.

charlotte russe (French) Sponge fingers set in jelly in a mould, the middle filled with cream mixture.

charquican-chileno National dish of Chile made of lean beef and vegetables including pumpkin and pimentos.

charring Process of slightly burning on the inside a new or remade cask in which whisky is stored, and which is necessary for the correct maturing of the spirit.

chartreuse (French) (i) Originally, various kinds of vegetables or fruit, served in the shape of goblets set in aspic or jelly. (ii) Cooked game, small poultry, etc., cooked and dressed in Chartreuse style, either hot or cold. (iii) Fruit *macédoine* in a jelly shape with cream in the centre. (iv) Delicious and rather costly liqueur of a green or yellow colour. First distilled from many herbs by the monks of *Grande Chartreuse*, near Grenoble, France, in the 17th century.

chassagne-montrachet (French) An outstanding white Burgundy wine.

chasselas (French) Famous species of vine stock which gives its name to the grapes it produces.

chasseur (French) Small pieces of meat, fowl or eggs garnished with sliced, sautéed mushrooms flavoured with shallots and moistened with white wine.

chasseur sauce Rich, highly-seasoned brown sauce, usually containing white wine, mushrooms and shallots, served with meat, game or venison, etc.

châtaigne (French) Chestnut.

château (French) (i) Castle. (ii) Porterhouse steak. (iii) Stripped, buttercooked potatoes. (iv) Abbreviation for *Châteaubriand* sauce.

château potatoes Potatoes cut in strips, parboiled and braised in butter.

châteaubriand (French) (i) Method of preparing fillet of beef, named after Vicomte François de Châteaubriand, 19th century French statesman whose chef invented it. The grilled steak is served with sauce and butter-cooked potatoes. (*château* potatoes). (ii) Butter, meat-glaze and stock, water or wine sauce served with meat, especially steak.

châteauneuf-du-pape (French) Famous red wines from the *Vancluse* area of France.

châtelaine, à la (French) Large cuts of meat garnished with potato balls and artichoke hearts stuffed with chestnut *purée* and rice.

chatouillard (French) Method of cooking potatoes which are cut into long ribbons and fried.

chaud (French) Hot.

chaudeau (French) Sweet sauce served with puddings, etc.

chaudière (French) Soup kettle; cauldron.

chaudfroid (French) (i) Sauce made of béchamel sauce, cream and aspic, used to coat cooked meat, fish, poultry, galantine, etc., served as cold *entrées*. (ii) Sweet *chaudfroid* (equal quantities of melted lemon jelly and half-whipped cream) used to coat fruit as a cold sweet.

chaudron (French) Calf chitterlings.

chaufferette (French) Chafing dish.

chausse (French) Straining bag.

chausson (French) Round, flat, light pasty sometimes filled with jam; turnover.

chausson à la périgourdine (French) Flaky pastry turnover filled with *fois gras*, truffles and cognac.

chausson aux pommes (French) Apple turnover.

chayote (American) Vine of the gourd family with edible tubers and a large green pear-shaped fruit, eaten like marrow. Also called Custard marrow or Chow-chow.

cheddar cheese Whole milk hard cheese used for eating and cooking and made originally in Somerset; now also produced in various other parts of the country, also in Scotland, Canada, Australia, New Zealand and the U.S.A.; in fact, the name is now given to any cheese which undergoes the special "cheddaring" process. It varies from strong to bland and from whitish to orange-yellow.

chee keufta (Russian) Armenian raw lamb patties.

cheese Dairy product. Originally a way of preserving excess milk, cheese soon became a popular nourishing and valuable protein food in its own right. The milk curds are separated from the whey and some are fermented. Hard cheeses are pressed, soft cheeses allowed to ripen in moulds. The varieties, world-wide, are countless (See individual entries). Most usual types available among English cheeses are Cheddar,

Cheshire, Gloucester and Stilton, and from other countries: *French* Camembert, Brie, Pont l'Eveque, etc. *Dutch* Gouda, Edam, etc. *Italian* Parmesan, Gorgonzola, Bel Paese, etc. *Swiss* Gruyère, Emmenthal, etc.

cheese (preserve) Fruit *purée* boiled with sugar to make a stiff mixture; placed in small pots and left several months to mature before being served as jam or as relish with meat and other savouries.

cheese biscuit (i) (American) Baking-powder scone made with grated cheese. (ii) (English) Cracker-type biscuit eaten with cheese.

cheese board Small board, for cutting and arranging cheese.

cheese bread Cheese-flavoured bread.

cheese butter Butter-and-creamy-cheese mixture.

cheese-cloth (i) (American) Butter muslin. (ii) Fine, loose-textured material used in pressing cheeses.

cheese-cutter Cheese slicer.

cheese dream (i) Cheese, milk, and egg mixture spread on bread and toasted. (ii) Cheese-filled french toast. (iii) Toasted-cheese sandwich. (iv) Fried cheese sandwich.

cheese *fondue* Soft mixture of cheese, butter, eggs and seasoning which is usually served hot in a chafing dish and eaten by dipping into the mixture with bread, toast, crackers, etc.

cheese hoop Broad metal or wooden hoop into which curd is pressed during cheese-making.

cheese-knife Broad-bladed knife for cutting or spreading cheese.

cheese press Utensil for pressing cheese curd in a hoop or mould.

cheese-rennet Plants, such as yellow bedstraw, with the ability to curdle milk.

cheese-slicer Bladed utensil for slicing cheese and other foods.

cheese soufflé Baked dish consisting of *roux* sauce and grated cheese, lightened with beaten eggs.

cheese spread Processed cheese soft enough to be spread on bread, biscuits, etc., often flavoured with chives, onion, celery, etc.

cheese starter Lactic-acid bacterial culture such as rennet used in fermenting milk for cheese-making.

cheese straw Pastry finger flavoured with grated cheese.

cheese wafer Cheese-flavoured cracker-type biscuit.

cheeseburger Hamburger fried with a coating of melted cheese.

cheesecake Tartlet made of a very light and flaky crust, filled with a mixture of cheese-curd, or almond, etc.

cheesewich (American) Cheese sandwich.

chef (French) Skilled male cook who manages a large kitchen in a hotel, restaurant, etc.

chef-de-cuisine (French) Chief of the kitchen; head cook.

chef de rang (French) Waiter who has served his apprenticeship.

chela Large claw of a lobster or crab.

Chelsea bun Type of yeast currant bun, which pulls apart in a long continuous strip.

chemise (French) Robe, jacket (of potato).

chemisier (French) To coat a mould or a substance with aspic jelly.

chemisé (French) Lined (a mould coated with jelly, forcemeat, or paste).

chêne (French) Hickory nut.

chenelle di semolino (Italian) Semolina balls cooked in broth.

cherimoya (American) Sweet tropical fruit cultivated in tropical and subtropical America; custard apple.

cherries in vinegar Ripe cherries bottled in castor sugar, cinnamon, cloves and wine vinegar.

cherries jubilee Simmered, stoned cherries covered with their syrup thickened with arrowroot or cornflour, then topped with warm Kirsch, and set aflame at table.

cherry Fruit of the cherry tree in many varieties, the most popular grown in Britain being the large sweet White Heart and Black Heart (dessert cherries) and the Morello and Mayduke, two cooking varieties used in puddings, preserves, etc. For *Glacé* cherries see *Glacé* Fruit.

cherry bay Shrub whose rubbed leaves smell of bitter almonds.

cherry bean (American) Cow pea.

cherry bounce (American) Cherry-flavoured liqueur made of cider, rum, or whisky or diluted cherry brandy. (ii) Cherry brandy.

cherry brandy (i) Liqueur distilled from fermented cherries and their crushed stones. (ii) Liqueur made from spirit flavoured with cherries and their stones.

cherry cake Cake made of flour, fat, sugar, egg(s) and *glacé* cherries.

cherry *compôte* Stoned cherries, sugar and lemon juice stewed slowly without water until tender but unbroken.

cherry gin Cherry-flavoured gin.

cherry heering (Danish) Cherry liqueur.

cherry jam Cooking cherries and sugar made into a preserve.

cherry laurel (American) Cherry bay.

cherry liqueur Alcohol or brandy flavoured with black cherries.

cherry olive Pickled cherry served as an appetizer.

cherry phosphate Aerated soft drink flavoured with cherry.

cherry plum Small, round golden-yellow or red plum grown in various parts of Europe, including Britain. Known in France as the *Mirabelle* where a liqueur of the same name is made from the fruit. They are best stewed or made into tarts or preserved. The skins are tough, but can be slipped off easily when cooked.

cherry rum (American) Cherries steeped in rum.

cherry tomato Small-sized variety of tomato.

cherry whisky (American) Cherry-flavoured whisky liqueur.

cherry wine Fermented wine made from cherry juice.

cherrystone (American) Medium-sized hard-shell clam found along the Atlantic coast.

chervil Garden herb with an aniseed aroma and feathery leaves which turn almost purple in autumn. Used for salads and omelettes, soups and stews.

chervis (French) Skirret parsnip.

Cheshire cheese Hard cheese made from cow's milk first produced in Cheshire, and said to be the oldest English cheese. In two varieties, white and red (which is artificially coloured and generally milder). Blue veins sometimes develop in red Cheshire.

chesky (American) Cherry-and-whisky drink.

chesterfield soup Soup made with calf's tail and mushrooms with added ketchup and sherry.

chestnut Edible nut, fruit of the sweet (Spanish) chestnut tree, which can be boiled, mashed, roasted, made into flour, served as a vegetable, used to make a wide range of cakes, sweet and savouries. See also *marron glacé*.

chestnut bean (American) Chick pea.

chestnut *compôte* Chestnuts cooked in a light, vanilla-flavoured syrup with added liqueur, and served hot or cold.

chestnut stuffing Stuffing for poultry made of mashed boiled chestnuts, bread crumbs, flavourings and seasoning.

chevaine (French) Chub.

cheval blanc (French) *Château*-produced claret.

chevaler (French) (i) To place the components of a dish in symmetrical arrangement. (ii) Trimmed bread-slice topped with butter or fat pork and overlaid with chicken breasts.

chevesne (French) Chub.

cheveuse d'Ange (French) Sweetmeat prepared from young carrots.

chevrette, chevreau (French) Kid.

chevreuil (French) Roebuck, roe deer.

chevreuse (French) Small goose-liver tartlets.

chevrotin (French) Musk deer.

chewing gum Sweetmeat originally made of chicle (the latex of the sapodilla tree), to which syrup, sugar and flavouring are added.

chianti (Italian) Famous Italian red wine, light and fairly dry, from Tuscany.

chicago (American) (i) Cocktail made of brandy, sugar, angostura, champagne, curacao, and lemon peel. (ii) Pineapple soda or sundae.

chicha South American liqueur fermented from maize.

chiche (French) Chick-pea.

chick Newly hatched chicken.

chicken Domestic poultry high in egg production and tender of flesh. It is classified according to age and size: *Poussins*, very small, up to 2 lb. Broiler: Small, up to about 3½ lbs. Roasters: Cockerels up to 5 lbs., capons up to 8 lbs. Boilers: Older birds – 18 months or longer. Chicken is now obtainable in joints: wing, leg, breast, drumsticks. It is high in protein and the B vitamins and the ways of preparing it are innumerable. Frozen birds (or joints) are rather lacking in flavour because they are very young. They therefore need to be well seasoned or stuffed or served in a tasty sauce. Chicken joints can be grilled, fried, curried or baked; whole chickens roasted, stewed, steamed boiled, barbecued, according to age and size; chicken flesh, minced, served cold, in pies or in aspic, etc. etc. Chicken livers are obtainable in separate packs and form the basis of many delectable dishes. There are many classic chicken dishes such as Chicken Marengo, Chicken à la King, etc.

chicken à la King Diced chicken served in a sherried cream sauce.

chicken broth Soup made by simmering an old hen until all the goodness is extracted. A little vegetable and pearl-barley is sometimes added.

chicken gumbo (American) Creole soup of chicken or beef broth with vegetables and spices.

chicken halibut (American) Small halibut under 10 pounds.

chicken lobster (American) Tender young lobster.

chicken Marengo Jointed chicken browned in butter or oil and cooked in a sauce including tomato sauce, mushrooms, wine or sherry, garnished with pastry crescents or bread *croûtons*.

chicken Maryland Classic dish of chicken joints fried and served with sweet corn fritters, bacon rashers and fried bananas.

chicken *mornay* Chicken joints bread-crumbed and fried after dipping in a rich cheese sauce.

chicken Normandy Chicken stuffed or dressed with apples and cooked in cider.

chicken steak (American) Boneless chuck beef-steak.

chicken *suprême* Breast and wing of chicken cut when raw, then cooked in many ways – fried, stuffed, poached, sautéed, served with sauces and other garnishes.

chicken tetrazzini Chopped chicken flesh and mushrooms with cheese and spaghetti; named for the operatic soprano, Luisa Tetrazzini.

chickenburger (American) Fried patty made with chicken.

chick-pea Asiatic plant of the pea family with pods containing hard, parchment-yellow nutlike legumes, also called chestnut bean, dwarf pea, and garavance; chick-peas are now cultivated in many parts of the world and are popular in Mediterranean countries.

chicle Rubbery gum from a tropical American tree, the sapodilla, and used as the base of chewing gum.

chicorée (French) Endive.

chicory Plant also known as Succory and Endive. The young root is used as a vegetable, and the leaves as a salad. The roots are transplanted to a dark place for bleaching, and the fresh growth of leaves produces the well-known *Barbe de Capucin*, a salad much used in France. The mature root, roasted and ground, produces the chicory used to adulterate coffee. Chicory is found growing wild on the borders of British cornfields, but the plant is cultivated in all parts of Europe.

chicory gourilos Chicory or endive stumps used as an *hors d'œuvre* or cooked as a vegetable in butter, with cream or sauces, or grilled or fried, etc.

chien (French) Dog.

chiffon cake Very light cake made with vegetable oil instead of solid shortening.

chiffon pie Fluffy custard of gelatine, eggs, whipped cream, and flavouring, baked in a flan case and chilled.

chiffonnade (French) (i) Shredded herbs. (ii) Soup of herb leaves, finely shredded.

chiffonnade d'oseille (French) *Chiffonade* of sorrel leaves.

chiffonnade mélangée (French) Mixture of equal parts of lettuce and sorrel leaves shredded and used to garnish soups.

Chihuahua cheese White goat's milk cheese made in the border state of that name in northern Mexico.

chikhirtma (Russian) (i) Soup thickened with egg yolks. (ii) Dish of boned chicken or lamb topped with eggs and oven-baked.

chili (American) Chilli.

chill To cool without freezing.

chilli Small red capsicum pod, the source of cayenne or red pepper. Chillies are hot and pungent. Used in stews, sauces, pickles, etc. Ground chillies with no additives are called Powdered Chillies. Chilli Powder is composed of ground chillies blended with other spices, and therefore milder. Used in dishes like *Chilli con carne*.

chilli con carne (Spanish) Popular dish of chilli pepper sauce with minced beef.

chilli powder See Chilli.

chilli sauce Tomato sauce flavoured with red chilli peppers, onions, sugar, vinegar and spices.

chilli vinegar Sauce made with chilli peppers and vinegar.

chimney hook Pot-hook with teeth used to suspend pots and cauldrons over the fire.

china bean (American) Cowpea or black-eyed pea.

chinaware Fine tableware first imported from China in the 17th century.

chinchard Saurel, or horse-mackerel.

chine To saw through the ribs close to the spine and sever rib bones from backbone. Chining is preferable to chopping meat joints such as neck or loin. This makes them easier to carve, or they can then be boned and rolled.

chine of pork The chine, when cut from a small pig, consists of two undivided loins, and corresponds to a saddle of mutton. In a large pig whose sides are intended for bacon, the name applies to the spine or backbone, and the meat attached, the amount of which varies considerably according to locality.

Chinese anise See badian anise.

Chinese or Japanese Artichoke See artichoke.

Chinese banana Dwarf banana.

Chinese bean oil Soya bean oil.

Chinese cabbage Oval-hearted, close-leaved cabbage like a long cos lettuce. May be eaten raw in salad, cooked as for green cabbage or marinated like red cabbage.

Chinese cinnamon Cassia bark used in flavouring, pickling, and preserving.

Chinese gelatine Agar-agar.

Chinese gooseberry Delicious fruit with a brownish skin and green flesh.

Chinese lemon Citron.

Chinese mustard Herbaceous plant cooked like spinach; Indian mustard.

Chinese nut Litchi, lychee.

Chinese watermelon Wax fruit gourd about the size of a pumpkin; its white pulp is used in soups and stews.

Chineseburger (American) Hamburger patty containing rice.

chinois (French) (i) Pointed strainer with very fine holes, used for straining soups, sauces, and gravies. (ii) Chinese fruit like a small tangerine orange, generally sold in crystallised form.

chinook salmon (American) Largest and most important Pacific Ocean salmon, also called King salmon or Guinnat.

chiodo di garofano (Italian) Clove.

chiozzo (Italian) Gudgeon.

chip dip (American) Cocktail dip flavoured with bacon, cheddar cheese, garlic, horseradish, onion, etc.

chip potato (American) French-fried potato.

chipolata (i) Very small sausage, which may be baked, fried or grilled. Used to garnish meat dishes and to serve with roast poultry; also served on sticks as cocktail savouries. (ii) Small Italian sausage. Originally an Italian *ragoût*. (iii) Dishes which contain an addition of Italian sausages or a kind of mixed minced meat with which they are served as a garnish.

chipped beef (American) Dried salted beef sliced very thin.

chips Potatoes peeled, cut into strips and deep-fried. Other vegetables such as carrot, parsnip, etc. can also be cooked in this way.

chiqueter (French) To make small indentations with a knife round the rims of tarts, pastry cases, *gâteaux*, etc.

chitterlings Intestines of ox, calf and pig, used in manufactured meat products. Chitterlings are cleaned and usually boiled before being sold. If not, they should be washed thoroughly and simmered gently for about 2 – 3 hours until tender. They may be fried, baked or stewed in milk or stock with onions and other vegetables or stuffed with sage and onion stuffing before baking; or used as filling for pies, patties and turnovers.

chive Very small variety of onion with tender delicately - flavoured leaves. Minced or chopped, chives are used for flavouring salads and as a garnish for cold savoury dishes and soups.

chizza (Italian) Pastry square filled with cheese or anchovy.

chlodnik (Polish) Cold soup made from vegetables and yogurt.

chlorination Small quantity of chlorine added to water to disinfect and purify it for drinking.

choclo (Spanish) Ear of corn.

chocolade taart (Dutch) Chocolate cake.

chocolat (French) Chocolate.

chocolate Beans of the Theobroma cacao tree, manufactured and made into paste, cake, or powder for use in cakes, desserts, as a sweetmeat, a beverage, etc. The tree is a native of the West Indies and South America. The cocoa (or cacao) bean was held as a symbol of hospitality by the Siamese. In olden times it served as a current coin in Yucatan. Chocolate has been known as a favourite beverage for more than 400 years. Introduced into England in 1520 from Mexico, and sold in London coffee-houses in 1650.

chocolate (Spanish) Chocolate.

chocolate cake Light-textured mixture of flour, fat, sugar, eggs and chocolate, baked in a cake tin and iced or decorated.

chocolate chip Small piece of semi-sweet

chocolate cooked in cakes, biscuits, and desserts.

chocolate cream (i) Soft-centred sweet coated with milk or plain chocolate. (ii) Chocolate-flavoured dessert made with milk and eggs or gelatine, etc.

chocolate sauce Sauce made from plain chocolate, butter, sugar, water and flour or cornflour, sometimes with added egg.

chocolate *soufflé* Fluffy dessert made of chocolate, eggs, and cream.

chocolate syrup (American) Sweet syrup made with chocolate or cocoa, corn syrup, sugar, salt, and vanilla, used for flavouring and as a sauce.

chocolate truffle Sweetmeat of melted chocolate beaten into egg-yolk, butter cream and rum, formed into balls and rolled in chocolate vermicelli.

choesels (Belgian/French) *Ragoût* of tripe and pancreas – usually beef pancreas. A favourite dish in Brussels is *Choesels à la Bruxelloise* which incorporates Belgian beer. Other organs and meats, such as tail, kidneys, sweetbreads, breast and feet are also often added.

choisi (French) Choice.

choke apple (American) Crab-apple.

chokeberry (American) Astringent cherry native to North America, used in jams and jellies or eaten raw.

choke pear (American) Astringent pear used in cooking or preserving.

chop (i) To reduce food to small pieces by cutting with a sharp knife on a chopping board with a quick up-and-down action. (ii) To separate sections of meat by dividing the bones, as in neck, loin, etc. (iii) Small piece of meat either containing a rib bone (neck chop or cutlet) or cut from the chump or end of the loin, which can be grilled, baked, fried or braised according to age and quality.

chop suey (Cantonese/Chinese) Mixed stew of chicken, fish, meat, beansprouts, mushrooms, onions, water chestnuts, and soya bean seasoning. Literally, "bits and pieces", fried before stewing.

chope Beer goblet.

chopine (French) Half-bottle.

chophouse (American) Restaurant serving chops, steaks, and other meat dishes.

chopped meat (American) Minced meat, as used for hamburger, meat loaf, etc.

chopping block Butcher's solid hardwood block for chopping fish, meat or poultry.

chopping board Kitchen board for chopping meats and vegetables.

chops (i) Small pieces of meat (See Chop iii) (ii) Slang for lips, as in "licking chops" to indicate appreciation.

chopsticks Oriental eating sticks held between thumb and fingers.

chorizo (Spanish) Spiced pork or pork and beef sausage.

chota hazri (Indian) The first (or little) breakfast.

chou (French) Cabbage.

chou au café (French) *Chou* pastry puff filled with coffee-flavoured French pastry cream.

chou au chocolat (French) *Chou* pastry puff filled with chocolate flavoured French pastry cream.

chou au lard (French) Cabbage with bacon.

chou blanc (French) White cabbage.

chou caraibe (French) Caribbean cabbage.

chou de Bruxelles (French) Brussels sprouts.

chou de mer (French) Sea cabbage; sea kale.

chou de Siam (French) Another name for *chou-rave* or kohl-rabi.

chou farci (French) Stuffed cabbage.

chou frisé (French) Kale.

chou glacé (French) *Chou* pastry puff glazed with sugar.

chou navet (French) Swede.

chou rouge (French) Red cabbage.

chou vert (French) Green cabbage.

choufleur (French) Cauliflower.

chou-palmiste (French) Heart of palm.

chou-rave (French) Kohl-rabi.

choucroute (French) *Sauerkraut.*

choux chou, pastry Very light pastry of butter, water, flour and eggs used chiefly for *éclairs* and *profiteróles* and cream buns, rich fancy cakes and

fritters. The paste is piped through a forcing-bag onto greased tins.

chow-chow (i) Chinese preserve of ginger and orange peel and other fruits in syrup. (ii) Mixed vegetable pickle, containing mustard, sugar and spices. (iii) Chayote.

chow mein See chaomein.

chowder Thick soup or stew originating in France but now associated with America; made of fish and shellfish (particularly clams) with pork or bacon, corn and/or other vegetables.

chowder beer (American) Boiled black spruce bark, molasses, and water.

Christmas Family festival, December 25, at which traditional fare is eaten, roast turkey (or other poultry) plum (Christmas) pudding, mince pies, Christmas cake, etc., etc.

Christmas cake Rich cake made with many of the usual cake ingredients but including a high proportion of dried fruit, with crystallised cherries and peel, and almonds. Usually made well ahead of the festive season; "fed" with brandy occasionally, and finally covered first with almond paste, then royal icing, and decorated to taste.

Christmas pudding Rich traditional English pudding mix (called "Plum" pudding but not containing plums). Dried fruit, chopped almonds, grated apple and grated carrot are among the many ingredients (which vary slightly from recipe to recipe). Sometimes the mixture is moistened with ale instead of milk. The pudding is steamed or boiled for several hours well in advance of the holiday, then steamed or boiled again for a considerable period when required, served on a hot dish with a sprig of holly on top. It is served with brandy sauce, but can also be "flamed" by pouring a little warmed brandy or whisky over the pudding and setting it alight.

chromeware Chromium-plated kitchen utensils and containers.

chrysanthemum Plant whose edible flowers taste somewhat similar to those of the cauliflower but much more delicate. If shredded finely and mixed with a salad cream, they make a delicious salad. In Japan these flowers are a common article of diet. Almost every variety may be used, but those of a deep yellow are esteemed best for salad purposes.

chub Bony, carp-like fresh-water fish with a rather insipid flavour. It should be well-seasoned and is improved by stuffing with forcemeat.

chub mackerel (American) Small mackerel found in the North Atlantic.

chuck (American) Meat cut from around the neck and shoulder blade, including the first three upper ribs.

chuck wagon (American) (i) Horse- or mule-drawn kitchen used on Western cattle drives. (ii) Modern Western-style eating places.

chufa Sedge with small edible nutlike tubers.

chuleta (Spanish) Chop.

chuleta de cordero (Spanish) Lamb cutlet.

chum Dog salmon.

chunk honey (American) Honey in the comb.

chup oshi (Russian) Uzbek egg noodles.

churn (i) Machine used to make butter from whole milk or cream (ii) To agitate cream or whole milk in the butter-making process.

churn milk (American) Buttermilk.

churrasco (Spanish) Beef, pork, and sausages barbecued over an open fire.

churro (Spanish) Fritter.

chutney Indian condiment made of a variety of fruits, sugar, spices, and vinegar, served with curries, cold meat, etc.

chutney butter Chutney, butter and lemon juice well blended and used as a spread.

ciboule (French) Spring onion.

ciboulette (French) Chive.

cicorea (Italian) Chicory.

cider Refreshing beverage made from fermented apple juice. A drink of great antiquity, being traceable in Normandy back to Charlemagne. Cider is produced widely in the West Country, also in France and Germany. The fermentation process is the same as in making wine, and the cider is obtainable from the wood (either "rough" or "sweet") or bottled.

cider apple Any apple yielding apple juice suitable for cider making.

cider cup Beverage made of cider blended with tea or lemonade and flavoured with lemon or cinnamon, with added sugar, fruit and soda water to taste.

cider oil Mixture of cider and honey, also called Cider royal.

cider press Device for pressing apples to extract their juice for cider-making.

cider royal Mixture of cider and honey.

cider sauce Brown sauce blended with cider, seasoned, and served with baked ham.

cider vinegar Vinegar made from fermented apple juice.

cider wine (American) Sugared and spiced cider.

cidre (French) Cider.

ciervo (Spanish) Deer.

ciliegia (Italian) Cherry.

ciliegia amarena (Italian) Morello cherry.

cima alla genovese (Italian) Cold roast stuffed breast of veal.

cima di rape (Italian) Turnip tops.

cima di vitello (Italian) Breast of veal.

cimier (French) Saddle, haunch (generally used of venison).

cinder toffee (American) Crunchy toffee.

cinghiale (Italian) Wild boar.

cinghiale agrodolce alla Romana (Italian) Wild boar marinated in herbs and wine and cooked in sweet-sour sauce.

cinnamon Inner bark of a species of laurel growing wild in Java and Ceylon, but cultivated in the East and West Indies. Cinnamon has been in use from remotest antiquity, is mentioned in the Old Testament by a name which is derived from the Hebrew *Qinnàmon* – a reed or cane. Available in scroll or powder form, it is used for flavouring cakes, biscuits, sweet dishes, etc.

cinnamon-bark oil Light-coloured essential oil extracted from cinnamon bark for use in flavouring foods such as biscuits, cakes, etc.

cinnamon biscuit Biscuit flavoured with powdered cinnamon.

cinnamon bun (American) Cinnamon-and-sugar cake made from raised dough

cinnamon snail (American) Cinnamon bun baked in a coil.

cinnamon toast Toast sprinkled with sugar and cinnamon.

cinque terre (Italian) Dry white wine from Liguria.

cinzano (Italian) Brand of fine Italian vermouth originating in Turin in the 18th century.

cioccalata (Italian) Chocolate.

cioccalata amara (Italian) Bitter chocolate.

cioccalata in polvere (Italian) Powdered chocolate.

cioppino (Italian) Fish or shellfish stew resembling *bouillabaisse*.

cipolla (Italian) Onion.

cipollino (Italian) Shallot.

circassian walnut (American) English walnut.

ciruela (Spanish) Plum.

ciruela passa (Spanish) Dried plum; prune.

ciseler (French) (i) To make superficial incisions into the skin of fish to hasten cooking. (ii) To cut leafy herbs into *julienne* strips or into a *chiffonade*.

citric acid Acid used in small quantities for boiled sugar goods, obtained from the lemon and lime, also from other acid fruits, such as sour cherries, Seville oranges, raspberries, currants, etc. Commercially manufactured in clear crystals or white powder and is used to flavour drinks and fruit dishes, and to help set jams, etc.

citroen (Dutch) Lemon.

citron Fragrant fruit resembling the lemon, but longer and larger. In crystallised form its peel is added to cakes, puddings and biscuits; a slice of citron peel is the traditional decoration on Madeira cake.

citron (French) Lemon. The fruit of the lemon-tree or *citrus limonum;* a native of the North-West Indian Provinces. Introduced by the Arabs into Spain, from whence it spread over Europe, and is now cultivated in almost all the tropical and sub-tropical countries. An important culinary flavouring used in cakes, desserts, etc.

citronnade (French) Lemonade.

citronnat (French) Candied lemon peel.

citronné (French) Lemon-flavoured.

citronella Plant of the mint family with strong, lemon-like scent. Its flowers are used in making digestive liqueurs.

citronelle (French) Citronella.

citronnier (French) Lemon tree.

citrouille (French) Variety of vegetable-marrow, pumpkin or gourd.

citrus aurantium Tree whose leaves ("orange leaves") are used in making tisanes or teas. The flowers ("orange blossoms") are used for making distilled orange blossom water or essence of neroli, and in confectionery, medicine and perfumery.

citrus balotinum Variety of orange tree with fruit resembling lemons.

citrus bigardia (French) Seville orange.

citrus fruit Fruit from trees such as citron, lemon, orange, kumquat, tangerine, etc. used as a source of fruit juices and for flavouring cakes, puddings, etc.

city chicken (American) Small pieces of veal placed on skewers and braised.

ciupin (Italian) Ligurian fish stew.

civet (French) Stew made from furred game (hare, rabbit, etc.) also from feathered game or fowl, using the blood as an essential ingredient, and adding red wine.

civet de langouste (French) *Civet* of spiny lobster. (See *civet*).

civet de lièvre (French) *Civet* of hare. (see *civet*).

civette (French) Chive.

clabber Milk soured and thickened by fermentation.

clabber cheese Cottage cheese.

clabbered milk Curdled sour milk.

clafouti (French) Thick fruit pancake or pastry using black cherries.

claggum (American) Chewy molasses toffee.

clair (French) Bright; clear.

clairet or *clairette* (French) Light table wine.

clam Bivalvular shell-fish in many varieties, shapes and sizes. Hard and soft clams are common along the

North Atlantic American coasts and are baked, fried or steamed or eaten fresh as for oysters, used in chowders, dips, etc. Clams are rarely found in Britain but are imported in cans. Clams are cultivated along the French beaches of *Auray*, *Croisic* and the Bay of *Bourguef* and can be prepared as for oysters, mussels and other shellfish.

clam bar (American) Counter or restaurant where clams and other seafoods are served.

clam chowder (American) Thick stew of clams cooked in milk or tomatoes.

clam dip Clam spread.

clam juice Liquor left after clams have been steamed.

clam spread Minced clams, cream cheese, chopped onion, and Worcester sauce used as a sandwich spread or a cocktail dip.

clam steamer Double saucepan for cooking clams etc.

clambake (American) Outdoor party at which clams are baked on hot rocks.

clams en beignets (French) Clam fritters.

clams en soupe (French) Clam chowder.

claret English name for red Bordeaux wines, derived from the French *clairet*. The term originated in Scotland, where Bordeaux wines were largely consumed until the union with England, when a preferential tariff led to the exclusion of French wines in favour of port.

claret cup Decoction of sugar, water, claret and soda water flavoured with lemon, cucumber and oranges.

claret jelly Flavoured gelatine preparation made with half claret and half water and served as a party sweet.

clarete (Spanish) Claret.

clarifier Substance used to clarify a liquid.

clarify To clear fat or liquids by disposing of all suspended matter. Dripping is clarified by melting, straining, then adding twice its bulk of boiling water. The clean fat rises to the top and solidifies. Butter is clarified by heating and straining. Egg whites are used to clarify jelly, etc., etc.

clary Strong-scented sage formerly used in England as a pastry flavouring. One of the herbs used to make Italian vermouth.

clary sage Clary.

clayère (French) Oyster-fattening bed.

clayon (French) (i) Small rush or straw mat for serving food. (ii) Pastrycook's wire tray.

clear soup (i) Clarified stock, strong broth obtained by boiling meat, bones and vegetables. (ii) *Consommé*.

Clermont (French) Large cuts of meat garnished with stuffed potatoes and pickled pork or fried onions.

cleaver Broad-bladed chopper used by butchers.

clementine Hybrid produced by crossing the orange with the tangerine. The skin is more like orange peel but the fruit is almost seedless. It grows in North Africa.

clingstone Peach or plum whose flesh is not easily separated from the stone.

clipping-time pudding Old Cumberland rich rice pudding made at sheep-shearing time.

clisse (French) Small rush tray used in cheese-draining.

cloche (i) Cover used to keep dishes warm. (ii) Glass cover to keep cheese fresh.

cloche (French) Glass cover used in cooking.

clos de vougeot (French) Wines from the French village of *Vougeot* classed as delicate and among the outstanding Burgundies.

Close, Jean-Joseph (French) Famous 18th-century French pastry cook from Normandy.

clotted cream Thick substance obtained by alternately scalding and cooling cream skimmed from new, rich milk. Clotted cream is served chilled as a dessert with fruits or as a spread for bread, scones or cake. See Devonshire cream and Cornish cream.

clou de girofle (French) Clove.

clouter (French) To stud. To insert small pieces of truffle, bacon or tongue, into fowl, *poulards*, cushions of veal and sweetbreads. See also *contiser*.

clove (i) Aromatic spice, the unopened flower buds of a small evergreen shrub resembling the bay or laurel, cultivated in tropical America. The buds are gathered green, smoked by wood-fire and dried in the sun. Cloves are used for flavouring soups, stocks, meats, *ragoûts* and sweet dishes, and for flavouring stewed fruit such as apples or pears. In Holland, a delicious marmalade is made from green cloves. (ii) Segment of root bulb, i.e. clove of garlic.

clove July flowers syrup Old Midlothian recipe for syrup made from adding loaf sugar to the juice derived from boiling strong-scented carnation flowers in water for several hours.

clovisse (French) Variety of *palourde* or clam eaten fresh, or cooked as for mussels.

club cheese (American) Cheese made from cheddar or a mixture of cheese with added wine and spices.

club sandwich (American) Sandwich of three pieces of toast and two layers of filling, usually held together with toothpicks.

club soda (American) Soda water.

club steak (American) Small steak cut from the sirloin.

clupe (French) Genus of fish of the herring type, which includes the sardine, anchovy, brisling, pilchard, shad, etc.

clupeidae Genus of sea-and-fresh-water fish including shad, herring, sardine and anchovy.

clupes (French) See clupeidae.

coachman's cooler (American) Mixed fruit juices served in a tall glass.

coagulate To curdle or clot by chemical or natural reaction.

coal fish Variety of cod, prepared the same way. Also called Coley or Coalie.

coalie See coal fish.

Coalport English porcelain produced at Coalport in Shropshire.

coaster (i) Ring of silver or silver-plate fitting the inner diameter of round dishes, and used to hold the garnishes for the main dish. (ii) (American) Small pad or plate used to protect a table from wet glasses.

coat (i) To place a protective or decor-

ative covering over food, such as sauce in *chaud-froid* dishes. (ii) To cover with batter before frying. (iii) To cover a cooking utensil such as a spoon, in order to test the stage of cooking which has been reached.

cob Ear of sweet-corn.

cobbler (i) Fruit pie made with a thick top crust. (ii) Iced drink made of fruit, sugar and wine.

cobnut Type of hazel nut, of which Kentish cobs are considered the best, being very large and well-flavoured.

coburg cake Small cake containing syrup and usually flavoured with spices.

coburg loaf Round loaf, baked at the bottom of the oven.

coca Peruvian shrub (*Erythroxylon coca*) whose leaves yield an important narcotic and stimulant. Used as an infusion, a wine, an elixir, and in certain cakes.

coca-cola (coke) Popular drink which contains sugar, water, and carbon dioxide, but whose basic syrup ingredient is a well-kept secret. See cola.

coche-comedor (Spanish) Dining-car.

cochenille (Spanish) Cochineal.

cochevis (French) Copped or crested lark.

cochineal Deep red liquid colouring substance used for colouring creams, jellies, cakes, icing, etc., obtained from insects (coccus), indigenous to Mexico and Guatemala which are dried in an oven heated to 150 degrees Fahrenheit. It requires 70,000 insects to produce a pound (0.45 kilo) of the dye carmine.

cochlearia Type of cruciferous plant including the wild horse-radish whose young leaves (mustard-flavoured) are eaten in salad. Known as "scurvy grass" in American.

cochon de lait (French) Sucking-pig.

cochonnaille (French) Hog's or pig's pudding.

cocido (Spanish) (i) Cooked. (ii) Stew of beef, ham, chicken, sausage, a national dish of Spain.

cocina (Spanish) Kitchen.

cocinar (Spanish) To cook.

cock Mature male bird.

cock-a-leekie soup (Scottish) Popular

soup made from a fowl boiled with leeks.

cock ale Ancient dish, made of ale, minced meat of a boiled cock, and other ingredients.

cockerel Young cock.

cock's comb Rooster's comb, used as a garnish for *ragoûts*, etc.

cockle Nutritious shellfish, generally found on the seashore. The largest British cockles come from the Scilly Islands, the North Devon coast and the Hebrides. They should be washed and soaked before cooking.

cocktail (i) "Short" alcoholic drink, served very cold before lunch or dinner, consisting of a variety of ingredients shaken together (usually with ice) so that no one flavour predominates, and often decorated with lemon peel, cherry or olive. (ii) Non-alcoholic appetiser made from fish, fruit, fruit or vegetable juices, i.e., tomato juice, melon cubes, etc.

cocktail frank (American) Tiny frank-furter served for cocktail snacks.

cocktail napkin Small cloth or paper napkin, used when serving cocktails.

cocktail olive Small olive served on a plastic or wooden toothpick.

cocktail onion Tiny pickled onion used in certain cocktails, or speared onto a pick, with or without other titbits and served as an appetiser.

cocktail shaker Vessel for shaking liquids with ice in making cocktails.

cocktail strainer Strainer which fits the top of a cocktail shaker and separates ice, pulp, pips, etc. from drink being poured.

coco bean Variety of French bean.

coco de mer (French) Double coconut from huge palm trees in the Seychelles Islands. Thought to be the legendary "Bread of Life".

coco-plum Fruit of the tropical coco-plum tree which can be eaten fresh or preserved like prunes.

coco yam See taro.

cocoa Product of the cocoa tree native to tropical America, but also grown in other parts of the world. The fruit pod contains the seeds or beans which are allowed to ferment until the pulp drops off, then dried, and the hard outer skin removed. The beans are roasted and shelled, leaving the kernels or "nibs", which are ground and crushed between giant rollers, to a brown paste. Some of the fat (cocoa butter) is pressed out and the remaining dry cake reduced to a fine powder, sieved and blended into commercial cocoa powder.

cocoa butter See cocoa.

cocoa powder Soluble cocoa with reduced fat content.

cocoa shell Membraneous shell of husked cocoa bean used to prepare a chocolate-like beverage.

cocomero (Italian) Water-melon.

coconut Fruit of the coconut palm. From the fibre of the outer husk matting is made. The nut is shredded or grated and added to curries, pastry, and confectionery. It also yields coconut oil or coconut butter from its dried flesh (copra).

coconut ice Sweetmeat made from loaf sugar, desiccated coconut and milk, coloured to taste.

coconut milk (i) Strained infusion of grated coconut (known sometimes as "coconut cream") used to moisten curries, and to serve with fruit desserts, etc. (ii) The liquid found within the kernel when cracked open. This can be fermented to make palm wine.

coconut oil Extract from dried coconut flesh used in the manufacture of margarine and soap.

coconut pyramid Small cake made from sugar, desiccated coconut and egg-white.

coconut water The "milk" found within the coconut.

cocose (French) Butter made from coconut.

cocotte (French) (i) Small fireproof pan or dish in single portion size or larger. (ii) Cooking vessel in earthenware, glass, etc.

cocui (Venezuelan / Spanish) Cactus brandy.

cod Soft-finned white fish of the Northern seas, rich in vitamins A and D, eaten baked, boiled, grilled, flaked, smoked, etc. Salt cod needs soaking before cooking and special care in preparation.

cod-burbot Freshwater fish of cod type cooked as for river burbot. Also known as Burbot, Eel-pout and Coney-fish.

cod liver oil Pale yellow oil extracted from the fresh liver of the codfish.

cod roe The roe of the codfish. If raw, it should be tied in muslin, boiled, cooled and sliced, then coated and fried. Ready-bought smoked cod's roe is served as an *hors d'œuvre.*

cod sounds Cod air bladders, stewed in milk or served in a flavoured sauce.

cod's roe paste. Cooked, drained cod's roe stirred in butter over a gentle heat, seasoned, then pounded and sieved. Used for savoury biscuits, *canapés,* etc.

coda di bue (Italian) Oxtail.

coddled egg Egg cooked slowly in water just below boiling point.

codlin Good variety of cooking apple.

codling Young cod.

coenatio (Italian) Dining-room.

cœur (French) Heart.

cœur à la crème (French) Heart-shaped cream cheese served with cream and jam, or cream and sugar or salt.

cœur de palmier (French) Palm heart.

cœur de veau (French) Calf's heart.

coffee (i) Berry of a shrub, a species of the madder family. (ii) Beverage made from the berries when roasted and ground. Originally grown in Arabia; now cultivated in all tropical countries. Fine varieties come from Jamaica, Java and Mysore.

coffee bar Informal small eating house for drinks and snacks, etc.

coffee bread (American) Coffee cake.

coffee cake (American) Cake made of yeast dough, eggs, nuts, and sugar; often baked in a twist or braid with fruit fillings covered with a sweet glaze or icing.

coffee cocktail (American) Coffee-coloured cocktail made of brandy, port and sweetening, also sometimes a raw egg.

coffee cone Drip-filter coffee-maker with a central funnel shaped like a perfor-

ated cone for holding a filter paper and ground coffee.

coffee cream Single cream.

coffee cup Drinking cup designed to hold coffee.

coffee grinder Device for grinding or pulverizing coffee beans, also called a Coffee mill.

coffee ice Ice cream flavoured with coffee essence.

coffee mill Coffee grinder.

coffee ring (American) Ring-shaped coffee cake.

coffee royale (American) Coffee flavoured with rum, cinnamon, and whipped cream.

coffee service Ceramic or metal set consisting of coffee-pot, cream jug, sugar-bowl, and tray.

coffee set Coffee service as above, with cups and saucers.

coffee shop Small lunchroom or restaurant.

coffee spoon Small spoon for stirring an after-dinner coffee or *demitasse.*

cognac Brandy distilled from local wine in the Cognac district in west-central France.

Cognakpudding (German) Brandy Pudding.

coho Small salmon found in the North Pacific.

coil pottery Pottery built up with successive rolls of clay instead of by the action of the potter's wheel.

coing (French) Quince. A fruit used for *compôte* and marmalade.

coinguarde (French) (i) Liqueur distilled from quinces. (ii) Marmalade made from quinces and grapefruit.

cointreau (French) Orange-flavoured liqueur made in France, served after dinner and used for flavouring punches and cocktails.

coke Cola drink (See cola).

col (Spanish) Cabbage.

col fermentada (Spanish) Fermented cabbage.

cola (i) African tree yielding flat oblong seeds with tonic and stimulant properties. Used as a colouring (red) matter, and flavouring extract in wines, creams, etc. (ii) Soft drink made from cola seed (nut) extract, cola leaves, colouring and sweetening.

colander Perforated metal or plastic basket for straining green vegetables, macaroni, noodles, rice, spaghetti, etc.

colbert (French) Dishes named after Jean Baptiste Colbert, a statesman in the reign of Louis XIV of France, 1619-1683.

colazione (Italian) Meal.

colazione di mezzogiorno (Italian) Midday meal; lunch.

colazione, prima (Italian) Breakfast.

colby (American) Cheese similar to cheddar.

colcannon (Irish) Dish of cabbage and potatoes served hot with butter, similar to Bubble-and-squeak.

cold cellar Cold-storage area of a basement used for perishable foods.

cold cuts Assorted cheese and meats thinly sliced, often served at informal meals.

cold-meat fork Flat-tined serving fork.

cold slaw Cole slaw.

cole (American) Cabbage or sea kale.

cole slaw Raw shredded white cabbage tossed in a thin mayonnaise dressing.

colewort Variety of cabbage, originally the name of the wild plant from which all the cultivated varieties of cabbage are derived.

coley See coal fish.

colifidret (French) (i) Dry cake, made for birds. (ii) (Ancient usage) Decorative set-pieces for grand tables.

coliflor (Spanish) Cauliflower.

colin (French) Hake.

collar Boneless cut of bacon less expensive than gammon.

collard Smooth-leaf variety of cabbage.

collard greens Leaves of the collard boiled and served like spinach.

collared Pickled or salted meat which is rolled, boiled with suitable seasonings and served cold.

collation Light meal or refreshment, word deriving from the custom of reading the *Collationes* of Johannes Cassianus in monasteries while the monks were eating a small meal.

colle (French) Gelatine (synonym).

colle de poisson clarifiée (French) Isinglass.

college pudding Baked or steamed suet sponge pudding, containing flour, dried fruit, spice, breadcrumbs and eggs.

coller (French) To add dissolved gelatine to a preparation in order to give it body.

collet (French) Scrag-end of the neck of mutton or veal.

colli berci (Italian) Dry red or white table wine from Venetia.

collier's pie Staffordshire dish of flaky pastry filled with grated cheese, spanish onion and diced bacon.

collins (American) Summer cocktail, or highball, named for John Collins, London head waiter of the 19th century.

collins glass (American) Tumbler holding 10 to 14 ounces.

collop (i) Small piece or slice of boneless meat. (ii) Savoury dish of minced meat. (iii) Old-fashioned name for egg fried with bacon.

collop Monday Day preceding Shrove Tuesday when a traditional dish of eggs and meat collops used to be eaten.

colocasia Genus of plants of the arum family, native of the Moluccas (Spice Islands). In the West Indies its leaves are also eaten prepared as for cabbage.

colocynth A bitter cucumber.

colombe (French) Pigeon, dove.

Colombian coffee High-grade coffee grown in Colombia.

colombine (French) Croquette coated in semolina and Parmesan cheese.

colombo (Italian) Wild pigeon.

colonna (Italian) Dry white wine from Luzio.

colonne (French) Utensil for coring apples and cutting vegetables into column-shapes.

coloquinte (French) Colocynth, a bitter cucumber.

colouring (i) Thick syrup made of loaf sugar, fresh butter and a little water, simmered in a sugar boiler over a gentle fire till bright brown (ii) Matter used in cookery to give colour to cakes, icings, etc. of either vegetable or insect origin.

colza Variety of cabbage seed from which oil is extracted.

Columbia river salmon (American) Chinook or king salmon.

comb honey Honey in the comb.

combine To blend ingredients together.

comedor (Spanish) Dining-room.

comestible Article of food.

comfit (i) Fruits or vegetables preserved in sugar, brandy, or vinegar. (ii) Small sugared sweet usually with a centre of anise or caraway seeds.

comfrey Rough boraginaceous plant used in salads or cooked.

comice Large round yellow pear.

comida (Spanish) (i) Meal; food. (ii) Dinner.

comida almuerzo (Spanish) Lunch.

comida caliente (Spanish) Hot meal.

comida del mediodía (Spanish) Lunch.

comida fría (Spanish) Cold meal.

commis de rang (French) Assistant waiter. One who has served his apprenticeship but is not yet a *chef de rang* responsible for serving without supervision.

compiègne (French) Light yeast cake with crystallised fruit.

compote (French) Dish of fruit, fresh or dried, cooked whole or quartered, served in syrup, with added flavouring and liqueur.

compote bowl Decorative vessel of glass, metal or porcelain for serving *compote*.

compote composée (French) *Macédoine* of various fruits.

compote de marrons (French) Chestnuts cooked in light, vanilla-flavoured syrup with added liqueur and served hot or cold.

compote de pigeon (French) Pigeon stew.

compote glass Tall-stemmed glass used for serving *compote* or ice cream.

compote simple (French) One type of fruit cooked in syrup.

compotier (French) Deep dish set on a raised base and used as a centre-piece for serving fruits, *compotes*, or other cold desserts.

comprar (Spanish) To shop.

compressed yeast Cake of yeast combined under pressure with flour and starch.

con (Spanish and Italian) With.

con anitra (Italian) Food served in duck sauce.

con capperi (Italian) Food served in caper sauce.

coñac (Spanish) Brandy; cognac.

concasser (French) (i) To chop roughly with a knife (ii) To pound in a mortar.

conch Large marine gastropod mollusc with a spiral shell; served in appetizers, chowders, soups, and stews.

conchiglia (Italian) (i) Shellfish. (ii) Scallop.

concombre (French) Cucumber.

condé (French) (i) Sweet consisting of creamed rice combined with fruit and a red jam sauce. (ii) Flaky pastry strips topped with royal icing blended with chopped almonds.

condensed milk Canned milk evaporated and sweetened.

condiment Pungent seasoning for enhancing the flavour of food, i.e., ketchup, mustard, pepper, salt, spice, seasonings, etc.

condiment or condiments Common salt.

condiment set Matching containers and cruets for mustard, pepper, salt, olive oil, and vinegar, sometimes on a rack or tray.

condimento Italiano (Italian) Italian condiment. Combination of marjoram, oregano, rosemary, sage, savory, sweet basil, and thyme.

coneglio (Italian) Rabbit.

conejo (Spanish) Rabbit.

confection Sweetmeat.

confectioner's custard Thick sweet white sauce with added egg yolks used as a filling for cakes and sweet pastries such as vanilla slices.

confectioner's sugar (American) Icing sugar. Sugar pulverized and highly-refined for use in making sweets and icings.

confectionery Sweetmeats in great variety made from sugar.

confiserie (French) Confectionery.

confit (French) (i) Comfit. (ii) Pork, goose, duck, turkey, etc. cooked in its own fat and immersed in it to preserve it and keep from contact with air. A form of preservation.

confit de dinde (French) Preserved turkey.

confit d'oie (French) Preserved goose.

confit de porc (French) Preserved pork.

confiteria (Spanish) Confectioner's shop.

confitura (Spanish) Jam.

confiture (French) Preserved fruit, jam.

confiture de cerises (French) Cherry jam.

confiture de citron (French) Lemon jam.

confiture de courge (French) Pumpkin jam.

confiture de marrons (French) Chestnut jam.

conger eel Scaleless sea fish which grows to 8 feet long. Cooked like fresh-water eels when small (when large they are rather coarse). Fried, boiled, baked or made into soup.

congou Black tea from China.

congre (French) Conger eel, also called *Anguille de mer* (sea eel).

congress tarts Small pastry cases, spread with jam and filled with a mixture of ground almonds, sugar and egg; often decorated with a cross made of pastry strips or topped with *glacé* icing.

congroi (Spanish) Conger eel.

coniglio (Italian) Rabbit.

coniglio selvaggio (Italian) Wild rabbit.

conserve (i) Berries, fruits, or vegetables preserved in sugar. (ii) Preserve prepared from whole fruits or unbroken pieces of fruit retaining their original shape and suspended in syrup or jelly.

conserrar (Spanish) (i) To pickle or preserve. (ii) To can or tin.

consolante (French) Liquid refreshment (usually alcoholic) served to restaurant cooks while they are working.

consommé (French) Clear soup. The clarified liquor in which meat or poultry has been boiled, or the liquor from the stock-pot clarified, with or without meat and soup vegetables. Obtainable commercially in cans or as *bouillon* cubes. Garnishes and variations are innumerable.

consommé (Spanish) Clear soup.

consommé à l'alsacienne (French) *Consommé* with *sauerkraut* and strasbourg sausages.

consommé à l'écossaise (French) *Consommé* cooked with pearl barley and garnished with carrot, celery and leeks, cut into *julienne* strips and cooked in butter.

consommé à l'italienne (French) *Con-sommé* with fancy *pasta* (shells, letters, etc.) cooked and added.

consommé à la jardinière (French) *Consommé* garnished with cooked cauliflower sprigs and diced carrots and turnips.

consommé à la madrilène (French) Chicken *consommé* with tomato pulp sometimes with added diced cooked sweet pimentos.

consommé à la royale (French) *Con-sommé* garnished with steamed savoury custard cut into small shapes.

consommé all'uova (Italian) Clear soup thickened with egg yolk.

consommé au riz (French) *Consommé* poured over boiled rice.

consommé caldo (Italian) Hot clear soup.

consommé célestine (French) Chicken *consommé* garnished with small round slices of rolled pancake stuffed with finely chopped chicken and chervil leaves.

consommé fredo (Italian) Cold clear soup.

consommé julienne (French) *Consommé* with finely-shredded cooked vegetables.

consoude (French) Comfrey.

conta (Portuguese) Account; bill.

continental breakfast Coffee and hot rolls or *brioches*, with or without butter and preserves.

contiser (French) To insert small strips or pieces of truffle, ham, bacon, etc. into holes skewered in fillets of fish, poultry or game. See also *Cloûté*.

conto (Italian) Bill; account.

contre-filet (French) Slices of fillet of beef.

conversation (French) *Pâtisserie* made from puff pastry, almonds and cream, topped with royal icing.

coo-coo Barbados-style cornmeal pudding.

cook (i) One who prepares food. (ii) To prepare food for consumption by baking, boiling, grilling, frying, roasting, steaming, etc.

cookbook Reference work containing directions and recipes for food preparation.

cooker (i) Oven or stove for cooking food. (ii) (American) Pressure cooker.

cookery Art of preparing food for consumption.

cookie (American) Biscuit.

cookie cutter (American) Biscuit cutter.

cookie jar (American) Large covered jar of crockery or glass for holding biscuits.

cookie pan (American) Shallow tin for baking biscuits.

cookie press (American) Utensil for expressing biscuit dough in a special shape onto a baking tin.

cookie sheet (American) Flat rectangular metal plate for baking biscuits.

cooking Art of preparing food for enjoyment and nourishment, going back into antiquity.

cooking salt Salt that is less refined, therefore cheaper than table salt.

cookstove (American) Kitchen stove.

cooler (American) Room or refrigerator compartment for cooling food.

cooper Maker of casks for wines and spirits.

coot Water-bird with dark dry flesh, cooked as for wild duck. Regarded by the Church as Lenten fare.

copa (Spanish) Wine glass.

copeaux (French) (i) Small confections made from *langues-de-chat* type preparation, cooked, and twisted on sticks while still warm. (ii) Shavings as in *pommes en copeaux* (potato shavings).

copertina (Italian) Skirt (of beef).

coperto (Italian) Cover-charge in a restaurant.

coppa (Italian) Salami made from pig's head and rind.

coppa romana (Italian) Brawn.

copper-ware Kitchen utensils made of copper which being a good heat conductor, makes excellent cooking pans as the heat spreads evenly and cooks food right through. Many modern cooking utensils have copper-bottoms for this reason.

copra Dried kernel of the coconut, which yields coconut oil.

copracake Coconut cake.

copra kana (Hindi) Spiced coconut rice.

coprin (French) Shaggy ink-cap mushroom.

coq (French) Cock.

coq au vin (French) Chicken sautéed in butter and then simmered in red wine.

coq noir (French) Black game.

coq de bruyère (French) (i) Woodcock. A bird allied to the snipe. (ii) Heath cock – a name once applied to red game in the north of England.

coque de cacao (French) Cocoa shell.

coq en pâte (French) Dish which, despite its name, is usually made not from a cock bird but from tender chicken. The bird is stuffed and wrapped in pastry before cooking.

coque du Lot (French) Easter cake made in the *Lot* region of France.

coqueret (French) Strawberry-tomato.

coques à petits fours (French) Pairs of *petits fours* sandwiched together and glazed with fondant.

coquelicot (French) Red poppy whose leaves are sometimes used as a vegetable, like spinach, despite slightly narcotic properties.

coquetier (French) (i) Egg-cup. (ii) Dealer in eggs and poultry.

coquille (French) (i) Pastry shell moulded and baked to resemble a scallop shell and filled with creamed chicken, crab, or flaked fish. (ii) Charcoal-filled kitchen utensil over which joints are roasted on a spit.

coquillage (French) Shellfish; mollusc.

coquille St. Jacques (French) Scallop known as the pilgrim shell, which is fried, poached, served with various sauces, etc. Usually (but not necessarily) served in the shell.

coral Lobster ovary.

corata, coratella (Italian) Lights, intestines, pluck (of animals such as kid, veal, etc.)

corbeille (French) Basket.

cordero (Spanish) Lamb.

cordial (i) Originally a spirit sweetened and infused with flavouring and scenting agents, now more commonly known as a "liqueur". (ii) Sweet or concentrated fruit drink with no alcoholic content.

cordon bleu (French) (i) Ancient culinary distinction of a medal suspended on a dark blue ribbon, awarded to very skilful female cooks who passed an examination under the French Government, 1578–1830. (ii) Nowadays, a famous school of French cookery.

cordon rouge (French) Gastronomic distinction, granted by an English society of the same title to skilful cooks of both sexes, and to others who invented valuable articles of food or drink, also to writers of culinary and gastronomic works. The badge was a modelled white-heart cherry, suspended by a cherry-red ribbon.

core (i) Central membrane of fruit, vegetables, kidneys. (ii) (verb) To remove the central membrane and pips from fruit, or the central membrane from vegetables or kidneys. A special utensil for the purpose is a corer.

corer Curved sharp tool for removing fruit and vegetable cores, etc.

corette (French) Jew's Mallow, an Egyptian herb.

coriander Sweet, aromatic seed of an umbelliferous plant. The powdered seeds form one of the ingredients of curry-powder; also used in flavouring pickles, gin, liqueurs, medicines, etc. The whole seeds are used to make comfits.

coriandre (French) Coriander.

coriandro (Italian) Coriander.

coring knife Corer.

cork extractor Device for removing corks from bottle necks.

corkage Charge for opening and serving wine.

corked wine Wine whose cork has become infected.

corkscrew Pointed spiral metal device for removing corks from bottles.

corlieu (French) Curlew.

corme (French) Shad apple, from which a kind of cider is made in France.

corn (i) English term for grain – wheat, rye, oats, barley, maize, etc. (ii) Scottish term for oats. (iii) American term for maize, used widely in American cooking both as corn on the cob, and as flour for cakes, breads, batters, etc. also used in corn whisky-making. (iv) (verb) To cure in brine, "corn" is an old term for grain or small particle, and meat corning was originally done with salt granules.

corn dodger (American) Crusty corncake.

corn fritter Fritter made with cooked corn kernels.

corn grit (American) See hominy grits.

corn holder (American) Two-tined short-handled fork used for eating hot-corn-on-the-cob.

corn husk Leaves covering ear of sweet-corn.

corn liquor (American) Corn whisky.

corn mule (American) Slang for corn whisky, reputed to have the kick of a mule.

corn oil Oil expressed and refined from the germ of maize or corn. Used in salad oils and in the manufacture of some cakes and biscuits, also for deep-frying.

corn-on-the-cob Sweet-corn cooked and eaten on the cob.

corn oyster (American) Corn fritter made with green corn.

corn pone (American) Oval stick of corn-bread often made without milk or eggs.

corn popper (American) Deep, closed, sieve-like utensil for popping corn.

corn pudding Pudding made from kernel corn, eggs, and milk.

corn salad Variety of valerian (also called "Lamb's Lettuce") eaten in salad or cooked like spinach.

corn starch (American) Cornflour.

corn syrup Product, varying in colour from clear white to amber, manufactured from cornflour by treatment with an acid, and used as a table syrup or sweetening agent, but is less sweet than cane sugar. Used in baking, sweet-making etc. and served hot on waffles.

cornball (American) Sugar-coated pop-corn ball.

cornbread (American) Bread made from cornmeal and baking powder, sometimes eaten hot for breakfast.

corncake (American) Cornmeal bread baked in a frying pan or on a griddle; sometimes called Johnnycake or Hoe-cake.

corndab (American) Cornbread.

corne d'abondance (French) Cornucopia. Horn of plenty.

corned beef Cooked beef pickled in brine, and canned. Used as a cold meat, sliced, with salad; or in *ragoûts*, stews, curries, fritters, etc.

cornel Cornelian cherry.

cornelian cherry Small red fruit of sharp flavour used for pickling and making a jelly. Also called Cornel.

corner le diner (French) To blow the horn or sound the bell for dinner.

cornet (i) Hollow conical biscuit, made of thin, crisp wafer pastry, used to hold ice cream. (ii) Thin slice of ham or other meat, rolled into a horn shape. (iii) French butchery term for carcase larynx.

cornflour Inner part of the kernel of Indian corn or maize, very finely ground, used for making milk puddings and moulds and for thickening soups, sauces, and stews; also in some cakes, biscuits, etc.

cornichon (French) Gherkin.

Cornish cream Rich deep-yellow clotted cream made from new milk in Cornwall. The milk is left to stand for up to 24 hours then heated slowly until it raises a crust, then cooled and skimmed off. The commercial product should contain 48 per cent butter fat.

Cornish hen (American) Small hen usually cooked by grilling.

Cornish pasty Torpedo-shaped short pastry-case filled with raw meat and diced vegetables (onion and potato particularly).

Cornish split Yeast bun made in the West Country, which is halved and filled with jam and butter or cream.

cornmeal White or yellow sweet-corn, (maize) coarsely ground.

cornouille (French) Cornelian cherry.

cornstick (American) Cornbread baked in a mould to resemble a small ear of corn.

cornucopia (i) Conical metal shape for making pastry cones, (ii) Cone-shaped paper container for nuts and sweets.

coronado (Spanish) Baked meringue case filled with custard or light pudding and "crowned" with ice cream, whipped cream, and maraschino cherries.

coronata (Italian) White wine first made in Coronata, near Genoa.

cortese (Italian) Dry white wine from Piedmont.

coryphène (French) Bluefish.

cos Lettuce with long crisp leaves.

coscia (Italian) Leg.

cosciotto (Italian) Haunch, leg.

cosciotto d'agnello (Italian) Leg of lamb.

cosciotto di selvaggina (Italian) Haunch of venison.

costa di bue (Italian) Sirloin of beef.

costa di maiale (Italian) Pork chop.

costata (Italian) (i) Cutlet or chop. (ii) *Entrecôte*.

costermonger Old-fashioned London term for a seller of fruits and vegetables.

costmary Tansy-like herb whose leaves are used to flavour meats and salads, and to spice ale and beer.

costoletta (Italian) (i) Cutlet. (ii) Escalope.

costoletta alla Bolognese (Italian) Veal cutlet with melted cheese.

costoletta alla castellana (Italian) Ham and cheese with truffles sandwiched between two slices of veal, egg-and-bread-crumbed, and fried.

costoletta alla Milanese (Italian) Bread-crumbed veal cutlet.

costoletta alla Valdostana (Italian) Veal cutlet stuffed with *fontina* cheese and white truffles.

costoletta alla Viennese (Italian) *Wiener schnitzel*, veal cutlet.

costoletta d'agnello (Italian) Lamb cutlet.

costoletta di maiale (Italian) Pork cutlet or chop.

costoletta di vitello (Italian) Escalope or cutlet of veal.

costoletta di pollo (Italian) Chicken breast.

côte (French) Rib.

côté-à-côté (French) Dining side-by-side.

côte de bœuf (French) Beef rib.

cotechino (Italian) Boiled pork sausage, served hot, from Modena.

côtelette (French) (i) Chop or cutlet. (ii) Thin slice of lean meat.

côtelette au naturel (French) Plainly-cooked chop.

côtelette d'agneau (French) Lamb chop.

côtelette de mouton (French) Mutton chop.

côtelette de porc (French) Pork chop.

côtelette de veau (French) Veal cutlet.

cotherstone Stilton type rennet cheese originating in Yorkshire.

cotignac (French) Quince paste.

côtoyer (French) To turn meat so that all sides are exposed to the heat.

cotriade (French) Dish composed of water, potatoes and as wide a variety of fish as possible – a kind of *bouillabaisse* or thick fish soup/stew.

cottage cheese Cheese made from skimmed milk by the addition of a starter, rennet and salt; it is heated and then cooled. Very nutritious, with a high proportion of protein and calcium, it is used in baking, cooking and salads.

cottage loaf Loaf of bread consisting of two rounds joined together, a larger round topped with a smaller round.

cottage pie Similar to shepherd's pie, but using any minced meat.

cotton candy (American) Candy floss.

cottonseed oil Oil extracted from cottonseed and used in making margarine and vegetable cooking fats, salad oils, etc.

coucou (French) Cuckoo (edible). Prepared as for thrush on the Continent.

coucoumelle (French) Grisette, an edible mushroom.

cougloff (French) *Kugelhopf*, a German rich dough or yeast cake, with currants and raisins.

coulemelle (French) Edible cultivated fungus, *lepiota*, "parasol mushroom".

coulibiac (Russian) Dish of fishcake mixture wrapped up in *brioche* paste, and baked.

coulis (French) (i) (originally). The liquid juices which run from meat in cooking. (ii) Liquid seasoning used for brown and white stews and braises. (iii) Filtered soups, crustacean *purées* and certain creams.

coullis (French) Smooth sauce, highly but delicately flavoured, used for soups and *entrées*.

coupage (French) Commercial blend of wines.

coupe (French) (i) Cup, drinking vessel or goblet. (ii) Combination of fruit and ice cream served in a glass goblet.

coupé (French) Cut, broken, loose.

coupe à légumes (French) Vegetable cutter.

coupe glacée (French) Sundae; ice cream or water ice combined with fruit or other ingredients.

coupe pâte (French) Pastry cutter.

coupe St. Jacques (French) Liqueur-soaked fruit salad served in glass cups with ice cream on top.

couper en dés (French) To dice.

coupette (French) Small cup for serving fruit salad, prawn cocktail, etc.

courge, courgeon (French) Squash. Vegetable marrow.

courgette Variety of small vegetable marrow, cooked unpeeled, either whole or cut into pieces, then steamed, boiled or sautéed and served with melted butter and chopped parsley or tarragon.

courlis, corlis, corlieu (French) Curlew.

couronne (French) Crown. *En couronne*, to dish up in the form of a crown.

court-bouillon (French) Aromatic liquid in which fish or meat or vegetables are cooked or marinated. The ingredients vary, depending on the intended use, but often include olive oil, lemon or vinegar, onion, seasonings, carrots, celery, etc.

Courvoisier Brand name of Cognac said said to have been drunk by Napoleon.

couscous Arabian speciality made of steamed flour or other cereal, served with meat.

cousinette (French) Soup made from finely-cut mixed green herbs, such as spinach, sorrel, lettuce.

couteau (French) Knife.

couvert (French) (i) Collection of eating utensils set out on a laid table. (ii) Number of people present at a meal (i.e., 25 *couverts*) (iii) Fixed cover-charge in a restaurant.

couvert de table (French) Three utensils used by a diner – knife, fork, spoon.

Coventry godcake Triangular cake of puff or flaky pastry bestowed by old Warwickshire custom, by godparents as a blessing to their godchildren on New Year's Day.

cover See *couvert* (iii).

cowcress (American) Wild watercress.

cowfish (American) Horned trunkfish.

cow-heel Foot of beef animal used to

make nutritious invalid dishes, which are very gelatinous. Cow-heel is washed, boiled in milk and water flavoured with onion for up to three hours. The meat is taken off the bone, the liquid seasoned and thickened and poured over the meat. These feet can also be used to make savoury jelly or soup.

cow-parsnip Marsh plant whose young shoots are eaten like asparagus in Siberia. In Poland its leaves and seeds are made into beer.

cowpea (American) Black-eyed pea.

cowslip Sweet-scented flower used to decorate salads and to make syrup, vinegar or wine.

cozza (Italian) Mussel.

cozza in salsa piccante (Italian) Mussel in piquant sauce.

crab Edible crustacean of the *Decapoda* order, with broad carapace and pincered claw feet. It should be consumed as soon as possible after cooking and the meat can be served boiled, grilled, fried or curried in salads, fish cocktails, savouries, etc.

crab-apple Wild apple with small red fruit. It makes an excellent jelly which can be served as a preserve or with roast mutton as a substitute for redcurrant jelly.

crab foo yung Chinese omelette containing flaked crab, bean sprouts, eggs, onion and spices.

crabe (French) Crab.

crabe garni (French) Dressed crab.

crack stage Point in sweet-making when a little syrup dropped into cold water turns brittle which occurs when the temperature of the syrup reaches between 290 and 310 degrees Fahrenheit.

cracked cocoa Cacao nibs; roasted or dried cacao beans, shelled and separated from the sprouting germ.

cracked ice Ice broken into small pieces for use in drinks, particularly those which are shaken up before pouring and serving.

cracker Thin, crisp biscuit made of flour and water with an added flavour such as arrowroot or cheese.

Cracker Jack (American) Brand name for a molasses-coated popcorn.

crackermeal (American) Dry plain crackers crushed into a fine meal used in coating, stuffing, and topping foods.

crackling Outer skin or rind of meat (particularly pork) from which the under-fat has been rendered away and which itself has become crisp and crunchy.

crackling bread (American) Cornbread made with cracklings.

cracknel Hard, brittle type of plain biscuit made of paste which is boiled before being baked, causing it to puff up.

cradle Piece of equipment originally used to bring wine from a cellar without disturbing the sediment, but now often used to serve wine at table.

crakeberry Crowberry.

cramique (French) Belgian pastry, a kind of *brioche*, with raisins.

cranberry Fruit of a shrub growing in boggy regions, and resembling small cherries. Acid and astringent when raw, the berries develop a delicate flavour when cooked and are used in jellies, sauces, wines, etc.

cranberry butter Spread made from cranberries boiled and sieved or puréed and combined with sugar, grated orange rind, and lemon juice.

cranberry cocktail Chilled cranberry juice.

cranberry jam Cranberry sauce.

cranberry jelly Jelly made from cranberries, popular as an accompaniment to poultry.

cranberry sauce Relish made from de-pipped cranberries, served with turkey.

cranberry wine Wine made from fermented cranberries.

crapaudine, à la (French) Pigeons or poultry split, flattened and trussed to resemble a toad, then browned on each side under the grill, and served with gherkins.

craquelin (French) Crisp crunchy type of *pâtisserie*.

crawfish Crayfish.

crayfish (i) Correct name for fresh-water crustacean like a small lobster, with a delicate flavour. Served hot or cold, or used in soups, etc. (ii) Spiny lobster ("sea crayfish") a salt water crustacean, like a lobster but without claws and larger. Cooked as for lobster. Imported into Britain as "crawfish".

cream (i) Fatty part of milk used in making butter, cheese and clotted cream. *Single cream* has a minimum butter fat content of 18 per cent. *Double cream* has a minimum butter fat content of 48 per cent and can be whipped to fill cakes or decorate puddings, sweets, etc. *Canned cream* contains 23 per cent butter fat and does not whip. See also bottled cream. (ii) Cold sweet, made from whole cream or custard or puréed fruit mixed with cream. (iii) To beat ingredients together until they are soft and well-blended.

cream cheese Cheese made from cream which has been soured and drained in muslin.

cream crisp Palmier, a puff or flaky pastry cake sandwiched with cream or jam.

cream filling Custard or other creamy mixture used for filling cakes, cream puffs, *éclairs* or tarts.

cream horn Puff or flaky pastry wrapped round special cream horn tins, baked in a very hot oven and when cold, filled with a little jam or fruit and topped with whipped cream, or filled with any suitable sweet mixture.

cream nut (American) Brazil nut.

cream of tartar Acid salt used in baking powders and self-raising flour.

cream pie Thick cream or custard filling in pre-baked flan case.

cream puff Round of puff or flaky pastry filled with cream, custard or ice cream.

cream sauce Rich white sauce incorporating cream.

cream sherry Sweet brown sherry.

cream soda Aerated soft drink flavoured with sugar and vanilla.

cream soup Broth thickened with cereals, puréed vegetables, poultry, fish, etc. to which cream is added.

creamed butter Whipped-up butter.

crécy (French) Dishes (particularly soups and broths) prepared from carrots or garnished with carrots.

Named for the small French town of *Crécy*, Seine-et-Marne, renowned for the excellent quality of its carrots.

credenza (Italian) Sideboard, buffet. It derives its name which means "faith" or "credibility" from the fact that in earlier times it was used by food-tasters whose job it was to ensure that the food about to be served was not poisoned.

crema (Italian) (i) Custard. (ii) Cream. (iii) Cream soup.

crema (Spanish) Cream.

crema, alla (Italian) Food served with cream, butter and cheese.

crema caramella (Italian) Caramel cream.

crema d'asparagi (Italian) Cream of asparagus soup.

crema di fagioli (Italian) Cream of haricot bean soup.

crema di gallina, crema de pollo (Italian) Cream of chicken soup.

crema di piselli (Italian) Cream of green pea soup.

crema di pomodoro (Italian) Cream of tomato soup.

crema di porri (Italian) Cream of leek soup.

crema di sedani (Italian) Cream of celery soup.

crema di spinaci (Italian) Cream of spinach soup.

crémaillère (French) Chimney-hook.

crème (French) Cream.

crème, à la (French) In cream style. Dishes of meat or vegetables whose pan juices are mixed with fresh cream.

crème au beurre (French) Butter cream.

crème au citron (French) Lemon custard.

crème Bavaroise (French) Bavarian cream.

crème Chantilly (French) Sweetened whipped cream, flavoured with vanilla.

crème d'amandes (French) Almond cream made from almonds, sugar, butter and eggs.

crème d'avoine (French) Cream of oats, used for soups and puddings.

crème de banane (French) Banana-flavoured liqueur.

crème de cacao (French) Sweet, chocolate-coloured liqueur, with the flavour of cocoa.

crème de café (French) Coffee-flavoured liqueur.

crème de cassis (French) Black-currant liqueur.

crème de mandarine (French) Brandy and tangerine-peel liqueur.

crème de menthe (French) Sweet green liqueur, made of wine or grain spirit, and flavoured with peppermint.

crème de moka (French) Chocolate-and-coffee flavoured liqueur.

crème de noix (French) Walnut-flavoured liqueur.

crème de noyau (French) Liqueur containing crushed cherrystone flavouring.

crème de riz (French) (i) Finely-ground rice. (ii) White soup made of powdered rice.

crème de violette (French) Violet-flavoured and perfumed liqueur.

crème d'orange (French) Cherry and orange liqueur containing brandy.

crème d'orge (French) (i) Finely-ground barley. (ii) White soup made of fine barley.

crème double (French) Double cream.

crème du lait (French) Cream from milk.

crème faussée (French) Artificial cream made of vegetable oil.

crème fouettée (French) Whipped cream.

crème moulée à la vanille (French) Vanilla egg custard.

crème moulée au caramel (French) Egg-custard pudding in caramel sauce.

crème pâtisserie (i) French pastry cream. (ii) Confectioner's custard.

crème renversée (French) Caramel custard cooked in a *bain marie* and turned out when cold.

crème St. Honoré (French) Confectioner's custard with added beaten egg-whites.

crème vichyssoise (French) Cold cream soup of leeks and potatoes.

crémet (French) Cream cheese to which egg whites are added during preparation.

crémeux (French) Creamy.

Créole, à la (French) Creole-type cookery. (i) Dishes served with rice pilaf and garnished with sweet peppers and tomatoes. (ii) Sweet dishes usually prepared with rice and often flavoured

with orange; sometimes masked with chocolate.

Creole sauce Hot spicy sauce served with fish, meat, etc.

crêpe (French) French pancake.

crêpe aux champignons (French) Pancake with mushrooms.

crêpe suzette Thin pancake made with orange-flavoured batter and filled with an orange-flavoured cream containing curaçao. They are sometimes soaked with further curaçao and flamed before serving.

crépine (French) Caul.

crépinette (French) Savoury minced meat or poultry cake resembling a little sausage, wrapped in strips of fat bacon or pig's caul, and baked or fried.

crescent Crescent-shaped bun, roll or biscuit.

crescenza (Italian) Lombardy creamy cheese made from cow's milk.

crescione (Italian) Cress.

crescione d'acqua (Italian) Water-cress.

cress (i) Salad plant native to Great Britain which grows quickly and easily on any damp patch of ground. Rich in vitamins A and C. (ii) Alternative name for watercress.

cresson (French) Cress, a salad plant.

cresson de fontaine (French) Watercress.

crête de coq (French) Cock's comb.

crêtes (French) Giblets of poultry or game.

crever (French) To burst or crack, generally referring to rice.

crevette (French) Shrimp, prawn.

criado (Portuguese) Waiter.

crible (French) Kitchen utensil like a sieve but with bigger holes.

crimp (i) To decorate a piecrust edge by pinching it between the thumb and forefinger or pressing it with the tines of a fork. (ii) To slash a freshly caught fish so its muscles will contract and increase the firmness of the flesh.

Criollo (Spanish) Creole.

crispbread Type of bread made from crushed whole grains, such as rye and wheat, and formed into large, thin, brittle biscuits. Can be used as a base for cocktail savouries or *smørrebrød*.

croaker fish (American) Marine fish, in

several varieties, which makes a croaking noise when caught.

crochetta (Italian) Croquette.

crochetta di pollo (Italian) Chicken croquette.

crochetta di riso (Italian) Rice croquette.

crock Thick earthenware jar or pot.

crockery Articles made of thick earthenware.

croissant (French) Crescent-shaped pastry-like roll of very light consistency, made from a special yeast dough. Served hot for breakfast in France.

cromesqui Kromeski. Croquette shape of chicken, game, lobster-meat etc., rolled in a thin slice of bacon, dipped in batter and fried.

crop Part of the gullet of birds which is removed before cooking.

crookneck squash (American) Yellow summer squash with a curved top.

croquant (French) (i) Crunchy type of *petit-four*. (ii) Crisp, as in biscuits. (iii) Crackling.

croquantes (French) Transparent mixture of various kinds of fruit and boiled sugar.

croquembouche (French) Elaborate preparation made from a number of items– meringues, or fruits segments, or almond paste, or *profiterôles* all glazed with sugar which has been heated to the crack stage.

croque-monsieur (French) Fried sandwich of buttered bread filled with Gruyère cheese and lean ham.

croquet (French) Type of *petit-four* famous in the Bordeaux area of France.

croquette (French) Minced fowl, game, meat or fish, bound with sauce or egg, shaped into a small roll; generally egged, crumbed, and fried until crisp.

croquette de volaille (French) Chicken *croquette*.

croquignolle Parisienne (French) *Pâtisserie* made from flour, icing sugar and eggwhites, and flavoured to taste.

crosne de Japon (French) Chinese artichoke.

crostaceo (Italian) Shellfish.

crostino (Italian) Piece of buttered toast, or fried bread spread with *pâté*, cheese, shellfish or other savoury.

croustade (French) Shape made of fried bread or baked pastry crust filled with fish, game, *ragoût*, mince, or meat *entrées*.

croûte (French) (i) Crust. (ii) Thick piece of fried or toasted bread upon which *entrées*, etc., are served. (iii) Rind of cheese.

croûte au pot (French) Clear soup or beef broth with toasted or baked bread crusts floating on top.

croûton (French) Bread diced or cut into shapes and fried, and used for garnishing soups.

crow garlic (American) Wild onion.

crowberry Wild plant with black berries, which may be used like cranberries.

crowdy (Scottish) (i) Variety of oatmeal gruel. (ii) Type of cream cheese.

crown roast Loin of lamb or pork skewered into a circle with the bones forming a crown. The centre is filled with stuffing and each bone-end is decorated with a little paper frill.

cru (French) (i) Raw or uncooked. (ii) Word denoting wine from an important vineyard.

cruchade (French) Porridge made with cornmeal and milk or water.

crudités (French) Raw vegetables such as carrots, celery stalks, cucumbers, radishes, served as appetizers or meal-starters.

crudo (Spanish) Raw, uncooked.

cruet Vessels for serving olive oil, vinegar, and other condiments at the table.

cruller (American) Fancy-shaped bun or cake similar to a doughnut, made from baking-powder dough and fried in fat, then sugar-sprinkled.

crumble topping Rubbed-in plain cake mixture, used instead of pastry as a pie topping over fruit.

crumbs See breadcrumbs.

crumpet Soft yeast-mixture tea-cake with holes on top, baked on a girdle in special metal rings. Known as "pikelets" in the North of England.

crunch candy (American) Crisp and crunchy sweets.

crunchie Crisp biscuit, usually containing rolled oats.

crush To flatten and break into small particles crisp or hard items such as aromatic seeds or baked crusts.

crushed ice Tiny pieces of ice used in drinks.

crusher Utensil for crushing food or ice.

crust (i) Brown external part of food baked or roasted. (ii) Encrustation inside a wine bottle which forms as the wine ages.

crustace (French) Crustacean.

crustacean Aquatic creatures with shells such as prawns, crab, crayfish, lobster, etc.

crystal Top quality clear lead glass used in the production of fine glassware.

Crystal Palace pudding Recipe of 1851 for a cold sweet made from lemon jelly, fruit, eggs, milk, isinglass and flavouring, set in a mould.

crystallise To soak fruits or petals in syrup and leave to dry until a sparkling sugary finish is imparted.

cuba libre (Cuban/Spanish) Long drink of coca-cola and rum with ice and lemon.

Cubat, Pierre Celebrated chef to the Emperor Alexander II of Russia.

cube (i) To cut into cubes. (ii) Even, small square of meat, vegetables, etc. (iii) Concentrated small cake of broth or stock for making soup or *bouillon*.

cube soup (American) Broth made from beef, chicken, or vegetables, *bouillon* cubes dissolved in hot water.

cube steak (American) Tough beef sliced thinly and pounded with a steak hammer to make it tender.

cube sugar (American) Loaf sugar.

cubeb pepper Dried and pulverised berries of a climbing shrub, known to the Arabs in the Middle Ages. Used for medicinal purposes, but little in the kitchen, except in the East.

cubiertos (Spanish) Cutlery.

cuchara (Spanish) Table-spoon.

cucharilla (Spanish) Tea-spoon.

cuchillo (Spanish) Knife.

cuckoo Edible bird, prepared as for thrush on the Continent.

cucumber Gourd-type vegetable used in Britain for salads, garnishing and pickles, but in the East largely con-sumed as a staple article of food. (See gherkin).

cucumber sauce (i) Boiled and sieved cucumber added to hot *béchamel* sauce. (ii) Chilled, grated cucumber mixed with whipped cream and flavoured with vinegar and seasonings. Suitable for serving with boiled fish or mutton.

cucumber *vinaigrette* Thinly sliced cucumbers and onions soaked in sour cream and vinegar and served as an appetiser.

cuenta (Spanish) Account; bill; check.

cuillère (French) Spoon.

cuillère de cuisine (French) Wooden spoon especially recommended for stirring sauces.

cuire (French) To cook.

cuire à petit feu (French) To cook slowly; to simmer.

cuisine (French) (i) Kitchen. (ii) Cookery. (iii) National style of cooking, such as Italian *cuisine*, German *cuisine*, etc.

cuisinier (French) Cook who prepares, cooks, and dresses food.

cuisinière (French) (i) Woman responsible for the preparation and cooking of food. (ii) Small cooking-stove.

cuisse (French) Thigh.

cuisse de volaille (French) Leg of chicken or fowl.

cuisson (French) (i) Cooking of food. (ii) Cooking time. (iii) Liquid in which food is cooked.

cuissot (French) Haunch of pig, veal, beef, game, etc.

cuit (French) Cooked.

cuit à point (French) Done to a turn. Food cooked to perfection.

cuit sous la cendre (French) Food cooked under fire ashes or cinders.

cuivre (French) Copper.

culatta (Italian) Rump steak.

culinaire (French) Term applied to anything connected with the kitchen or the art of cooking. A good cook is called *une artiste culinaire*.

cullis (French) Coulis.

culotte (French) Rump, aitchbone of beef.

cultured milk Skimmed milk soured with lactic-acid bacteria.

Cumberland sauce Accompaniment made

from dry mustard, red-currant jelly, egg yolk and seasonings to serve with ham, braised tongue or cold beef or game.

cumin Plant of the parsley family related to the caraway whose aromatic seeds are used to flavour liqueurs, cordials, cheese and breads.

cumino (Italian) Cumin.

cumquat See kumquat.

cuore d'agnello (Italian) Sheep's heart.

cuore di bue (Italian) Ox-heart.

cuore di maiale (Italian) Pig's heart.

cuore di vitello (Italian) Veal (calf's) heart.

cup (i) Drink made from claret, cider or light white wine diluted with ice or soda water, and garnished with herbs and fruit as in champagne, cider and claret cups. (ii) Drinking vessel to hold coffee, tea, etc.

cup cake Small sweet sponge-type cake topped with sugar icing.

cup custard Egg custard served in individual custard cups and decorated with ratafia biscuits.

cup measure Standard measure. The British cup contains ½ pint (10 fl. ozs. – 28.4 centilitres) roughly comparable to a breakfast cup. The American cup contains 8 fl. ozs. (19.7 centilitres).

cuppa' Slang for a cup of tea.

curaçao (French) Liqueur made of the zest of the rind of the bitter orange, cultivated in the island of Curacao in the Dutch West Indies, and originally made there. Drunk as a liqueur and also used for flavouring creams, jellies, ices, etc.

curcuma (French and Italian) Turmeric.

curd cheese Cottage cheese.

curd knife Cheese slicer.

curds Solid part of milk coagulated with rennet, for the purpose of making cheese or junket. The liquid part is called whey.

cure To dry or smoke previously salted meat or fish.

cured Preserved with salt or by drying.

curly kale Variety of kale, cooked similarly.

currant (i) Dried, small stoneless grape, deriving originally from Corinth. Also imported from Australia, currants are used in fruit cakes, buns, biscuits, mincemeat, puddings and breads. (ii) A group of fresh fruits known as black, red and white currants. (See separate entries).

currant wine Wine produced from fermented currants.

curried (i) Food prepared with strong spices such as cardamom, pepper, tumeric, and ginger, and coloured with saffron. (ii) Food served in curry sauce.

curry (i) Indian condiment. (ii) Stew of meat, fish or fowl. (ii) Sharp spiced sauce. Curry, as a dish, is of immemorial use in India. Its constituents vary widely according to the part of India concerned. Curries are not always made with hot spices; some are quite mild.

curry paste Paste containing a mixture of finely ground spices, sometimes including spices not incorporated into curry powder. Often used in conjunction with curry powder for better effect. Obtainable in prepared form.

curry powder Mixture of finely-ground spices used in making curry.

curry sauce Sauce made from onions, seasonings, curry powder, curry paste, fruit, coconut milk, etc., used for re-heating cooked foods and making curried dishes.

cuscinetto (Italian) Baked cheese sandwich.

cush (American) Bread or crackers cooked in broth.

cushion Cut of meat nearest the udder in mutton or beef.

cushion lamb shoulder (American) Square-cut shoulder, often boned to form a "cushion roast".

cushion picnic shoulder (American) Square-cut shoulder of pork.

cusk Edible saltwater fish of the cod type, also known as Burbot or Torsk.

Cussy, à la (French) Dishes garnished with stuffed artichokes, truffles and cock's kidneys, served with port or Madeira sauce, named for the Baron de Cussy, who occupied an important post under Napolean I.

custard (i) Dish of milk and eggs sweetened and flavoured, parboiled, steamed or baked. (ii) Sweet sauce served with fruit or pudding, made from cornflour or proprietary brands of custard powder.

custard apple West Indian fruit with a pulpy yellow flesh reminiscent of custard.

custard cup Cooking cup of heat-resistant porcelain or glass for baking individual custards.

custard marrow See chayote.

custard pie (American) Cream pie.

custard tart Short-crust pastry flan cooked till set then filled with egg custard mixture.

cut-and-fold To fold in and mix sundry ingredients.

cut in To combine fat into other ingredients by cutting downwards with a knife.

cutlery (i) Sharp-edged cutting utensils such as knives, parers, etc. used in preparing and eating food. (ii) General term for eating utensils.

cutlet (i) Neck chop (best end) of mutton, lamb, pork or veal which is grilled, fried or braised. (ii) Small piece of chicken, lobster, salmon, or pheasant.

cutlings (American) Barley or oatmeal grits.

cuttlefish Cephalopod mollusc secreting an inky liquid in an internal shell. Its tough flesh is edible after vigorous beating.

cutturiddi (Italian) Rosemary-flavoured lamb stew.

cutting block (American) Chopping board or block.

cutting board Board of beechwood for meat cutting, with a groove to catch the juices.

cuvée (French) (i) Wine of a particular press made from a mixture of grapes. (ii) Special vintage of champagne.

cygne (French) Swan.

cygnet Young swan.

cymling (American) Variety of summer squash or marrow.

dab Small flat fish of the plaice and flounder species, with small dark spots, white underside and close-set scales. Cooked as for plaice.

dabchick Small moorhen or waterfowl.

dace (dare, dart) Small fresh-water fish of the carp family with coarse, rather tasteless flesh. It can be fried, grilled or baked whole.

dagang babi (Malay) Pork.

dagang goreng (Malay) Fried meat. Marinated beef strips.

dagang sapi (Malay) Beef.

dagh kebab (Turkish) Dish of skewered veal, onions and tomatoes flavoured with thyme.

dahlia Ornamental plant whose tubers are edible, cooked as for the Jerusalem artichoke which it approximates in flavour.

dainty Item of food which is particularly pleasing to the palate.

daikon (Japanese) Large radish eaten raw or cooked like turnips.

daiquiri Cocktail made of white rum, fresh lime juice and sugar syrup or grenadine named after the town in Cuba where American troops landed during the Spanish-American War.

dairy (i) Farm building where cream and milk are stored. (ii) Shop specialising in dairy products.

dairy butter Freshly prepared unsalted butter.

dairy cattle Milk-producing breeds such as Guernsey, Jersey, etc.

dairy cream Unadulterated cream.

dairy farm Farm devoted to the production of milk.

dairy product Milk product.

daisy (i) Common field flower whose young leaves and buds can be used in salad. (ii) (American) Cocktail of brandy, gin, whisky or rum with grenadine, lemon juice and sugar.

Dalmatian cherry Marasca cherry.

damascene Type of damson.

damasco (Portuguese) Apricot.

dame-jeanne (French) Demi-John, a large glass or earthenware bottle for storing wines, oils, etc. usually wicker-clad.

Dampfnudeln (German) Dish of dumplings of bread dough, enriched with butter, sugar and eggs which, after being partly cooked in milk, are steamed in the oven, and served with custard sauce, stewed fruit, etc.

damson Very small dark blue plum, which ripens in late summer. Damsons can be eaten raw if very ripe but are better cooked in such dishes as damson pie and pudding, or made into jam, jelly and cheese as their high acid and pectin content give a very good set.

damson cheese Preserve made by boiling damsons to a pulp, and then boiling again with an equal quantity of sugar. When cold it is of the consistency of cheese.

damson gin Damson-flavoured gin.

dandelion Wild plant with yellow flowers used for making wine. Its leaves may be eaten raw in salads or boiled and served as a vegetable.

dandelion spinach Chopped and boiled dandelion leaves.

dandelion wine Wine made from fermented dandelion flowers, flavoured with root ginger, orange, lemon and raisins.

Danish blue cheese Soft white cheese, veined with blue mould, sharp and salty in flavour.

Danish pastry Layered pastry with flaky texture and rich filling.

dansk kage (Danish) Danish cake; Danish pastry.

Danzig brandy *Danziger Goldwasser,* Danzig gold water.

Danziger Goldwasser (German) Citrus-peel-and-herb-flavoured liqueur containing tiny flecks of gold leaf.

dapur (Malay) Kitchen.

daragaluska (Hungarian) Dumpling.

dard (French) Dace.

dariole Originally the name of a small puff pastry cake, the word now means a small, cylindrical mould with sloping sides, used for making madeleines, individual sweets, savouries, etc.

darjeeling Orange pekoe black tea grown in mountains of northern India.

darne (French) Slice; middle cut of large fish, such as salmon or cod.

dartois (French) (i) Small snack served as an *hors d'œuvre* or light meal. (ii) Glazed puff pastry "sandwich" filled with almond cream.

dash Casual measurement of a few drops, or a pinch.

date Fruit of the date-palm, high in sugar content. Eaten as raw dessert or used in puddings, pies, etc. preserved in vinegar, or stuffed as a sweetmeat. The best quality dates come from Tunisia.

date fig Variety of fig, usually dried.

date plum Persimmon.

date sugar Sugar made from date-palm sap.

datte (French) Date, fruit of the date-palm.

Dattel (German) Date, fruit of the date-palm.

dattero (Italian) Date, fruit of the date-palm.

dattero di mare (Italian) "Sea-date" – small date-shaped shellfish eaten raw or served as for *moules marinière.*

dattero marinato (Italian) "Sea-date" (dattero) steeped in vinegar, oil, garlic.

daube, en (French) Meats or poultry braised or stewed.

daubière (French) Oval-shaped stewpan in which meats or birds are to be stewed or braised.

daucus Plant whose aromatic seeds are used in the preparation of some liqueurs.

daumont, à la (French) Method of serving large fish garnished with soft roe, mushrooms, crayfish tails with nantua sauce.

dauphine, à la (French) (i) Usually, a potato dish of deep-fried balls made of a mixture of *duchesse* potatoes and *choux* paste. (ii) Type of *beignet* or dough-nut.

daurade (French) Seafish about 18 inches long, resembling the bream, sometimes called sea bream (*brême de mer*). Its flesh is white and of good flavour. Baked, or cooked in white caper or tomato sauce, also fried. Not to be confused with *dorade.*

déboucher (French) To uncork a wine bottle.

débrider (French) To untruss a fowl after cooking.

decant To pour liquid gently from one vessel to another so as not to disturb the sediment.

décanteur (French) Glass - stoppered bottle into which wine is decanted.

decker: sandwich (American) Multiple sandwich of bread and fillings in layers. Double-decker: 3 layers of bread, 2 of filling. Triple-decker: 4 layers of bread, 3 of filling.

decoction Process of extraction by boiling a solid in water: i.e., meat boiled in water to yield stock.

découper (French) To carve; to cut in pieces.

Deddington pudden pie Old English dish made for the Deddington November Fair, of puff pastry filled with a cooked mixture of ground rice, milk, eggs, sugar, lemon rind and currants.

deep-dish pie (American) Fruit pie with top crust only, baked in a deep baking dish.

deep fat Hot fat used in deep-fat frying.

deep-fat fryer Deep utensil with a wire-mesh basket for holding food to be fried by immersion in deep fat.

deep freezer Cabinet or container for storing food at below-freezing temperatures

deep fry To fry in fat deep enough to cover the food.

deep fryer (American) Deep-fat frying pan.

deer Wild mammal, tender to eat only up to about one year old.

deg. Abbreviation for degree.

déglacer (French) To de-glaze; to dilute concentrated pan juices with soup, stock, cream or wine.

deglet nur Date of excellent quality and sweetness.

dégraisser (French) To remove the grease from soups, etc.

dehydrated food Dried food – fruit, meat, vegetables, etc.

déjeuner (French) (i) Breakfast (*petit* or *premier*) (ii) Lunch – the first main meal of the day.

déjeuner à la fourchette (French) Meat breakfast or luncheon.

déjeuner de noce (French) Wedding breakfast.

Delaware (American) Wine made from red Delaware grapes.

Delaware punch (American) Punch made of brandy, orange juice, and chilled Sauterne.

Delftware Blue and white porcelain pottery originally made in Delft, Holland.

delicacy Food or drink which is rare, luxurious or pleasing to the taste.

delicioso (Spanish) Delicious.

delicious Variety of red or golden apple, with a distinctive shape.

Delikatessaufschnitt (German) Cold cuts of meat.

Delikatesse (German) Delicacy; dainty.

Delikatessen (German) Ready-prepared foods, such as meat, fish and vegetables, salamis, pickled cucumbers, *sauerkraut*, herrings preserved by smoking or pickling.

delizioso (Italian) Delicious.

delmonico steak (American) Small steak cut from lower sirloin.

Demerara rum Rum distilled in the Demerara district of Guyana.

demerara sugar Originally indicating the cane sugar produced in Guyana, the term now refers to all crystallised, slightly-coloured cane sugars from the West Indies area.

demi-deuil, en (French) White meat such as veal, sweetbreads or fowl masked with *suprême* sauce and larded with truffles. Literally food "in half-mourning".

demi-deuil **egg** Soft-boiled or poached egg served in a pastry case filled with mushrooms.

Demidoff (French) Russian nobleman after whom several dishes were named, especially an elaborate method of preparing large poultry.

demi-Espagnole (French) See *demi-glace*.

demi-glace (French) (i) Brown coating sauce made by boiling and skimming *Espagnole* sauce and diluting with stock or soup. (ii) Variety of cream ice popular in Paris.

demijohn Large glass or earthenware bottle used for storing cooking oil, wines, etc.

demi-sec (French) Literally, "semi-dry" but usually indicative in the case of sparkling wines, of a sweet beverage.

demi-sel (French) Soft, whole-milk cheese.

demi-tasse (French) Small cup of black coffee or *bouillon*.

demoiselle d'honneur (French) Maid-of-honour cake.

den Tisch abräumen (German) Clear the table.

dénerver (French) To remove tendons, membranes, gristle, etc. from meat or poultry.

dent-de-lion (French) Dandelion. (Lion's tooth).

dente, al (Italian) Pasta cooked just enough to be somewhat firm to the bite.

dentice (Italian) Variety of seabream, an expensive fish.

dépecer (French) *Découper*. To carve; to cut in pieces.

Derby cheese Fine white and tangy cheese, with a pronounced flavour which ripens early and keeps well. Sage Derby is a variety flavoured and coloured with sage leaves.

dérober (French) To remove outer casing, skin or shell from food.

dés (French) Dice.

desayuno (Spanish) Breakfast.

D'Eslignac (French) French nobleman after whom a clear soup is named.

désosser (French) To remove the bones from meat, poultry or game.

despensa (Spanish) Pantry.

dessécher (French) To desiccate or dry up; to dehydrate.

dessert (i) In Britain, the final course of a formal meal, usually consisting of fresh, dried or crystallised fruits, sometimes preceded by ices, *petits fours* or fancy biscuits. (ii) In America, and sometimes in Britain, dessert denotes the pudding course.

dessert fork Round-tined fork slightly smaller than a dinner fork.

dessert knife Small knife used with dessert fork.

dessert plate Small plate for serving dessert.

dessert spoon Eating spoon smaller than a tablespoon and larger than a teaspoon.

dessert wine Sweet wine, fortified or unfortified, served at the end of a meal, or with fruit, ices, etc.

desservir (French) To clear the table.

desiccate To dry or dehydrate food in order to preserve it.

détendre (French) To lighten a mixture by the addition of liquid or eggs.

detergent Cleaning agent for emulsifying fats and greases for easy removal.

devil (i) To apply a highly seasoned and flavoured paste or a mixture of dry condiments to joints of poultry, cuts of fish, etc. and cook by grilling or frying. (ii) To cook as above and serve with *diable* sauce.

devil-fish Atlantic angler fish.

devilled ham Slices of ham spread with devilling butter made with Worcester sauce, and grilled.

devilled nut Nut such as almond, pecan, etc. blanched, fried in butter then, with Worcester sauce, chutney, salt and cayenne pepper added, stirred and cooked slowly for a few minutes.

devilling butter Mixture of butter, pepper, cayenne and lemon juice or Worcester sauce, for spreading on meat or fish to be "devilled".

devil's dozen Baker's dozen, 13 of anything.

devil's food (American) Dark rich chocolate cake.

Devizes pie Old Wiltshire dish made from calf's head, bacon, hard-boiled eggs, rich gravy, and covered with flour-and-water paste which is removed when the pie is cold.

Devonshire cream Clotted cream made as for Cornish cream.

Devonshire cream cheese Cheese made from rich whole cow's milk.

Devonshire split Yeast buns split and served hot with butter or cold with butter or cream and jam.

Devonshire stew Nineteenth - century West Country dish of potatoes, cabbage and onions cooked and shredded, mixed together and fried in beef dripping till brown.

dewberry Creeping blackberry. Species of the French *mûre des haies*.

dewberry flummery Type of custard made from dewberries, cornflour, lemon juice, sugar and water.

dextrose Form of glucose.

dholl, dhall Pulse somewhat similar to split peas or lentils, much used in India to make kedgeree, or a kind of porridge.

diabetic food Specially prepared food including beverages, jams and marmalades, chocolates and sweets containing reduced amounts of carbohydrate.

diable (French) Earthenware "devil" cooking utensil of two inter-fitting pans in which certain fruits and vegetables can be cooked without liquid.

diablé (French) Devilled.

diable (French) Devilled food (See devil).

diable de mer (French) Devil-fish.

diavolino (Italian) Small devilled rice or farina cake, fried.

dibs (Arabic) Wine juice reduced to a very thick and luscious syrup.

dice To cut food into small cubes.

dicke Bohne (German) Broad bean.

diet (i) Pattern of eating. (ii) Special eating regime followed for medical or cosmetic reasons.

diète (French) Diet.

diet cake (Scottish) Cake seasoned with cinnamon and lemon.

digby chick Kind of pilchard or small herring, called by fishermen "Nova Scotia sprats," named after Digby, a seaport in Nova Scotia.

digester Strong iron cooking-pot, the lid of which fits so tightly that the steam can only escape through a valve on the top.

digesteur (French) Digester.

Dijon Capital of Burgundy, France, famed for its gastronomy, including beef, and snails cooked *à la Bourguignonne*, mustard, ham, ginger-bread, etc.

dill Aromatic plant of the parsley family, used as a common pot herb in medieval times and as a witch's herb for spells, as well as an aphrodisiac. Its leaves and seeds have many uses as flavouring in sauces, soups, salads, egg and fish

dishes, pickles, etc. Dill seeds can also be used to make tea.

dill pickle Cucumber pickled in brine flavoured with dill seeds.

dill seed Seed of the dill plant.

dilute To thin by adding liquid.

dimple (American) New Orleans confection made of blanched almonds, egg whites, and sugar.

dinde (French) Turkey hen.

dinde farcie (French) Stuffed turkey.

dinde piquée (French) Larded turkey.

dinde rôtie (French) Roast turkey.

dindo (Northern Italian) Turkey.

dindon (French) Turkey cock.

dindonneau (French) Young turkey.

dîner (French) Dinner.

dîner de noce (French) Wedding feast.

dîner d'Andouille (French) Dinner of chitterlings, where the *Andouille* or chitterling sausage forms the *pièce-de-résistance*.

dîner mi-carème (French) Lenten dinner.

dinette Small-size dining area.

dining car Railway restaurant car.

dining room Room where meals are eaten.

dining saloon Room where food is served as aboard a ship.

dinner Principal meal of the day. The word is said to be a corruption of *dix-heures*, indicating the time at which the old Normans partook of their principal meal, which was 10 a.m. Since then the hour has got gradually later. *L'heure du dîner* dinner hour, in Henry VIII's time was at 11 a.m.

dinner fork Large fork used with the dinner knife.

dinner knife Largest-size eating knife used with dinner fork.

dinner music Music played during a meal.

dinner plate Large-size plate for serving the main course.

dip Soft savoury mixture of cream cheese or sour cream with added morsels of fish, onion, bacon, etc., eaten by dipping or "dunking" small savoury biscuits, potato crisps, short sticks of celery, etc. into the mixture.

diplomat (i) Sauce (see *diplomate*) (ii) Pudding made from sponge fingers, liqueur, jam, sugar and fruits.

diplomate (French) (i) Sauce flavoured with lobster butter, truffles, and brandy. (ii) Various dishes, so styled.

dish (i) Ceramic or glass dinnerware. (ii) Food prepared in a particular fashion.

dishcloth Cloth for washing dishes.

dish mop Short-handled small mop for washing-up.

dish rack (American) Plate-rack.

dish-rag Dishcloth.

dish towel (American) Tea-towel.

dishwasher Electrical appliance for washing and drying dishes.

disposal unit Electrically operated appliance connected to the waste pipe of the kitchen sink to grind up waste matter which is then flushed away.

dispensaire (French) Old-fashioned term for a cookery book.

dissect To cut or joint, as with a chicken.

dissolve Liquefy or melt.

distil To separate by vaporisation the more volatile components of a liquid.

distilled vinegar Colourless vinegar made by distilling ordinary vinegar.

dittany Aromatic herb secreting volatile oil.

diuretic Plant which promotes and increases the volume of urine (couch grass, asparagus, fennel, etc.)

diver Web-footed bird with tough and oily flesh.

Döbel (German) Chub.

dobule (French) Chub.

doce (Portuguese) Sweet; dessert.

dock Sorrel.

doe Adult female rabbit, antelope, deer, etc. The flesh (except rabbit) is marinated and prepared as for venison.

dog Domestic mammal with edible flesh. Eaten in certain countries. Chow dogs are specially fattened for the table in China.

dog salmon Large species of Pacific salmon.

dogfish (i) American catfish. (ii) Various fish of the shark family.

dog-rose See eglantine.

dog's nose Mixture of beer or stout and gin.

dolce (Italian) Sweet; dessert.

dolce latte (Italian) Mild veined cheese.

dolce-piccante (Italian) Bitter-sweet.

dolce verde (Italian) Italian blue-veined cheese served with dessert courses.

dolic Group of pulses which includes the soya bean.

dolma (Russian) Stuffed food, usually a vegetable such as cabbage, stuffed with meat and rice.

dolmadakia (Greek) *Dolmades*, stuffed leaves.

dolmades (Greek) Greek form of *dolma* with vine leaves substituted for cabbage leaves.

dolmas (Turkish) Dish of chopped meat, etc., wrapped in fig leaves and stewed.

domaci beli sir (Yugoslavian) Sheep's milk cheese cured in a sheepskin.

donkey (i) Mammal with tasty, edible flesh but not widely eaten in modern times. (ii) (Scottish) Savoury steamed oatmeal pudding.

done to a turn Food cooked to the exact point of readiness and perfection.

donzelle (French) Ophidium.

dooar Black tea grown in Dooar district of Bengal, India.

doppio formaggio, al (Italian) Food served with an extra quantity of cheese.

dorade (French) Fish found in tropical seas, and seen in aquariums, gold and red (*carassus doré*). Not to be confused with *daurade*.

dorata (Italian) *Daurade*, a species of sea-bream.

doratino di ricotta (Italian) Cheese fritter, sweet or savoury.

dorato (Italian) Food dipped in egg and flour and fried to a golden colour. (*Dorare:* to gild).

doré (French) Food brushed over with beaten egg yolks before baking. (*Dorure*).

dorée (French) John Dory fish.

dormant or *surtout de table* (French) Decorative objects which are left on the table to the end of a meal.

dormouse Small European rodent once regarded as a delicacy.

Dörrobst (German) Dried fruit.

Dorsch (German) Cod.

dorure (French) Yolks of eggs beaten and used for brushing over pastry, etc., to gild.

dot To cover the surface of a dish with small pieces of butter or margarine before cooking.

Dotter (German) (i) Egg Yolk. (ii) Cheese made of skimmed milk and egg yolks.

dotterel Wader bird cooked as for plover.

double boiler (American) Double saucepan.

double *consommé* (*Consommé* concentrated by prolonged cooking.

double cream Cream that has been standing 24 hours on the milk instead of 12.

double crème (French) Soft cream cheese, made with milk and added cream.

double decker Sandwich of 3 bread slices separated by 2 layers of filling.

double-fond (French) Double saucepan.

double Gloucester Close, crumbly well-flavoured cheese, round and flat in shape, so named to distinguish it from a milder Gloucester cheese (single Gloucester) now no longer made.

double saucepan Cooking utensil comprised of two pans. The food is put in the top pan and is cooked by heat from the boiling water in the lower pan, thus being safe from burning.

doubleburger (American) Two hamburgers on one roll.

doubler (French) (i) To fold over in two a piece of fish, meat or pastry. (ii) To cover pastries with another baking sheet as a protection from oven heat.

douce-amère (French) Bitter-sweet.

doucette (French) Corn salad.

dough Mixture of flour, liquid and other ingredients prepared stiff, firm or soft, according to the intended use. Dough is made for bread, cakes, biscuits, scones, pastry, etc.

dough cake Loaf or cake made from a yeast dough with added eggs, fat and fruit.

doughnut Yeast or baking powder round or ring-shaped cake made from slightly sweetened dough, cooked in hot fat and dredged with sugar.

doughnut joint (American) Cheap café.

douille mobile (French) Movable tube, adjusted on a forcing, or savoy bag, used in filling and decorating.

douillon (French) See rabotte.

Douro (Portugal) River around whose valley are grown the grapes from which port is made.

dovga (Russian) Dessert made from yogurt, spinach, rice and dill.

doux, douce (French) Sweet.

doyenne (French) Sweet, melting variety of pear.

doz. Abbreviation for dozen.

dozen Twelve of anything.

draff Refuse of malt after brewing from barley.

dragée (French) (i) Sweet made of fruit, nuts, etc., coated with hard sugar icing. (ii) Sugar almond.

dragon's eyes Far-Eastern fruit resembling lychees.

dragoncello (Italian) Tarragon.

drain To remove surplus liquid or fat from food by (i) a colander or sieve, (ii) placing on crumpled kitchen paper.

dram (i) Unit of avoirdupois weight. (ii) Colloquial Scottish term for a tot.

Drambuie Brand name for an aromatic liqueur made from Scotch whisky, heather honey and herbs.

draw (i) To eviscerate; to remove entrails. (ii) To pull out sinews.

drawn butter Melted butter.

dredge To coat or sprinkle with sugar, flour, seasoning, etc.

Dresdener Bierkäse (German) Sour-milk cheese flavoured with beer, originating in Dresden.

dress, to (i) To pare, clean, trim, etc. (ii) To dish up into good shape. Dressed vegetables indicate vegetables cooked in rich style and dished neatly.

dressage de plats (French) Presentation of food.

dressé (French) Dressed.

dried beef Beef dried, salted, and smoked.

dried fruit Fruit such as apples, apricots, figs, peaches, pears, prunes, raisins, etc., dehydrated by evaporation.

dried milk Milk dehydrated and powdered by evaporation.

dried peas Three varieties – split peas, yellow peas and chick peas, used for *purées*, as a vegetable, in soups, etc.

dried vegetables Vegetables concentrated and evaporated.

drikkevand (Danish) Drinking water.

drinking straw Hollow stem of straw, glass, etc. for imbibing cool drinks.

drip coffee (American) Coffee brewed in a filter coffee-maker.

dripping Fats and juices drawn from food, especially meat, during cooking.

dripping pan Tin or pan placed beneath roasting or grilling food to catch fat and juices.

drive-in (American) Restaurant serving food to motorists who drive in and eat in their cars at a counter or from portable trays.

drogheria (Italian) Grocery shop.

dromadaire (French) Dromedary.

dromedary Single-humped camel cooked as for camel.

drop scone Light batter cake cooked on a girdle (also known as Scotch pancakes).

dropping consistency Texture of a mixture for making cakes, puddings, etc. The test is made by filling a spoon with the mixture and tilting it sideways over the basin. It should drop from the spoon, unaided by shaking, in about five seconds.

drum Container for transporting liquids.

drumstick Lower part of the leg of poultry.

drupe (French) Any single-stoned fruit.

drupe See *drupe*.

dry (i) Characteristic of certain champagnes and wines denoting lack of sweetness. (ii) To dehydrate fruits and vegetables by exposure to heat.

dry curd Uncreamed unsalted cottage cheese used for baking or in salads, etc.

dry ice (American) Frozen carbon-dioxide gas used for refrigeration of perishable foodstuffs because it freezes at −109 degrees Fahrenheit.

dry Manhattan, Bronx (American) Cocktail made of blended whisky, dry French vermouth, angostura bitters, and maraschino cherry or lemon twist.

dry martini Cocktail made of gin and dry vermouth and served with a lemon twist or a small green olive.

dry-pack soup (American) Dehydrated soup, sold in packet form and reconstituted with water.

dry sack Good quality medium sherry.

du Barry (i) Rich puréed cauliflower soup. (ii) Oysters served in potato cases. (iii) Other dishes also named after Madame du Barry.

du jour (French) Food of the day, a restaurant term, as in *Plat du jour*, the chef's recommended dish of the day.

dubbelsmörgas (Swedish) Sandwich.

Dublin Bay prawn Largest prawn available in Britain, prepared as for scampi or used in salads, etc.

Dubois, Urbain Famous *chef de cuisine*, inventor of numerous dishes, author of "*La Cuisine Classique*," etc., for many years chef to the German Emperor William I (1818–1901).

Dubonnet Well-known French *apéritif*, made with sweetened fortified wine and sharpened with quinine, drunk neat, with ice and lemon, or made into a cocktail with vodka or gin.

Dubonnet cocktail Dubonnet and gin shaken with cracked ice.

duchesse (French) Winter variety of pear.

duchesse (French) (i) Potatoes puréed and blended with egg yolks. (ii) Dishes served with *duchesse* potatoes.

duchesse, petite (French) *Petit four* made of almonds, hazelnuts, egg whites, sugar and chocolate.

duck Web-footed bird in various wild and domestic varieties descended from the mallard. The Aylesbury duck is considered the best; the Rouen duck is larger but judged by some to be inferior in flavour although it is not bled, as are all other fowl, in order to impart a distinctive flavour and colour. Duck is roasted, braised, pressed, used for *pâtés*, salmis, etc.

duck egg Egg similar to hen egg but larger and richer, and more limited in use because of a tendency to contamination. Duck eggs should not be preserved or soft-boiled or used for meringues, and should be boiled for 14 minutes.

duck press (American) Device for pressing boned duck and other poultry.

duckling Young duck.

duckling à l'alsacienne Braised Nantes duck served with *sauerkraut*.

duel cheese Austrian rennet cheese made from cow's milk.

Duglère (French) Famous French chef who invented the method of serving soles dressed with *Béchamel* sauce and flavoured with tomato and fish essence, finished with fresh butter, and chopped parsley. He also created *pommes anna*.

dulce (Spanish) Sweet.

dulce de leche (Spanish) Milk dessert popular in South America.

dulces (Spanish) Sweets, confections, candy, chocolates.

dull Term indicating that a liquor or tea is cloudy.

dulse Edible red seaweed.

Dumas, Alexandre Famous French author, editor of the *Dictionnaire de Cuisine* (1803–1870).

dumb cake Traditional Isle of Man unleavened cake of flour and water baked in hot turf ashes. If eaten when walking backwards to bed, the girl will, according to legend, dream of her future husband.

dumpling (i) Ball or outer casing of dough, boiled or baked, made from suetcrust, shortcrust, yeast mixture or breadcrumbs. Boiled suet dumplings, plain or flavoured with herbs or cheese are served with stews. Sussex (hard) dumplings are made of flour, salt and water only. Fruit (i.e., apple) dumplings are shortcrust pastry wrapped round the fruit and baked. (ii) Forcemeat ball, *quenelle*.

Dunand Name of two famous chefs, father and son. Dunand the younger is accredited with the invention of *Chicken sauté Marengo*.

duncan Large pale-yellow variety of grapefruit thin-skinned and well-flavoured.

Dundee cake Rich fruit cake, decorated with almonds.

Dundee shortbread Flat rich crisp cake made of butter, eggs, flour and sugar.

dunelm Dish of braised mutton or veal, originating in Durham.

dungeness crab (American) Large well-flavoured crab found along the North Pacific coast.

dunking tray Large platter or tray holding an assortment of dips and dunks.

dunlop cheese (Scottish) Flat cheese similar to Cheddar, but moister and of a closer texture.

dünsten (German) To stew.

Dunstobst (German) Stewed fruit.

durazno (Spanish) Peach.

durazno en crema (Spanish) Peach in cream.

Durchschlag (German) Strainer, sieve.

durchsieben (German) To sift, to filter.

Durham Breed of shorthorn beef cattle developed in the county of Durham.

Duroc-Jersey (American) Large pig developed in America to produce red lard.

durra (Indian) Indian millet, a variety of sorghum grass grown for food.

dushab (Arabic) Favourite drink of the Arab epicure; a mixture of date wine and grape juice reduced to syrup.

dust To sprinkle lightly with cinnamon, flour, sugar, etc.

Dutch cheese Several varieties of cheese developed in Holland, the best-known being Edam and Gouda, but also including Dutch cheese and cottage cheese.

"Dutch courage" Saying which originated from the giving of gin to soldiers engaged in battle in the Low Countries.

Dutch cupboard (American) Dutch dresser.

Dutch gin Hollands; schnapps.

Dutch dresser Article of furniture with cupboards at the bottom and open shelving at the top, on which plates and other items of pottery are usually displayed.

Dutch macaroon Meringue-type cake made with egg-white, icing sugar and ground almonds.

Dutch oven (i) Roasting or toasting utensil with hooks which are attached to the bars of the grate. (ii) Heavy pot with well-fitting lid, for braising or cooking over open fires.

Dutch sauce *Hollandaise* sauce.

Dutch settle Seat with a hinged back which can be lowered onto the arms to make a table.

Dutch treat Meal or outing where each person pays his or her own expenses.

Dutchware blue (American) Delft pottery.

duxelles (French) Mushroom hash. Finely chopped mushrooms, sautéed with onion, shallots and seasoning and used for garnishing.

dwarf banana Small banana cultivated in Central America and the West Indies.

dwarf pea Chick pea.

earth almond Chufa.

earth apple Ancient name for Jerusalem artichoke.

earth ball Truffle.

earth chestnut Earth-nut.

earth-nut (i) Black-coated tuberous root tasting like chestnut, and used similarly. Its seeds can be substituted for caraway. (ii) Chufa or peanut. (iii) Another name for truffle.

earthenware Coarser varieties of dishes made from porous clay fired at low heat.

Easter biscuit Biscuit made from flour, sugar, butter, egg, ground cinnamon and currants for the Easter festival.

Easter egg (i) Hard-boiled egg with dyed or painted shell. (ii) Chocolate or confectionery moulded into egg shape and exchanged at the Easter festival.

eats Slang for food.

eau (French) Water.

eau de fleur d'orange (French) Orange-flower water.

eau de mélisse (French) Spirit distilled from Melissa or lemon balm.

eau de riz (French) Rice-water, a beverage for children and invalids.

eau de selz (French) Seltzer water, soda water.

eau de vie (French) Spirits of wine, old brandy, etc.

eau de vie de Dantzig (French) Danzig whisky; *Danziger Goldwasser.*

eau de vie de grain (French) Whisky.

eau de vie de prunelle (French) Sloe gin.

eau minérale (French) Mineral water.

ébarber (French) To remove the exterior parts of a piece of meat or fish.

ébouillanter (French) To scald.

ébullition (French) Liquid which has reached boiling point, as in *Chauffer à l'ébullition:* To heat until boiling.

écailler (French) To scale (a fish).

écale (French) Nut-shell.

écaler (French) To remove shells and outer casings from eggs, fruit, peas, beans, etc.

écalure (French) Peel of certain vegetables and fruits.

eccles cake Flaky, pastry cake with a

filling of dried fruit spices and peel moistened with melted butter and sugar.

échalote (French) Shallot. A mild onion used for seasoning soups, sauces, and salads, etc.

échaudé (French) Pastry made with dough which has been poached in water, then oven-dried.

échauder (French) To steep in boiling water. To scald, as with fowls or game, to facilitate the removing of the feathers or hair.

éclair (French) (i) Finger-shaped *choux* pastry filled with cream or confectioner's custard topped with coffee or chocolate icing. (ii) Savoury *éclair; choux* pastry with savoury filling.

éclanche (French) Shoulder of mutton.

écorce (French) Rind.

écorce de citron confite (French) Preserved lemon peel.

écorce d'orange confite (French) Candied orange peel.

écossaise, à l' (French) In Scottish style.

écosser (French) To shell (peas or beans).

écraser (French) To crush, as for seeds, breadcrumbs, etc.

écrémeuse (French) Milk and cream separater.

écrevisse (French) Crayfish, freshwater crustacean.

écuelle (French) Deep bowl or dish; porringer.

écume (French) Scum.

écumé (French) Skimmed.

écumoire (French) Skimming ladle or perforated spoon.

écureuil (French) Squirrel.

écuyer (French) Equerry. A title given to cooks in olden times.

edam cheese Round yellow, low fat Dutch cheese, weighing up to 5 lb. shaped by being pressed into a mould. Fairly dry and salty, it has a red wax outer casing.

edammer kaas (Dutch) Edam cheese.

eddike (Danish) Vinegar.

edelweiss camembert Pungent creamy Swiss-German cheese used as a spread on cocktail *canapés*, etc.

edible birds' nests See birds' nests.

edible frog Frog eaten in France and the south of Germany. The hind legs are considered a great delicacy, and in flavour resemble the flesh of a young rabbit.

edible snail See *escargot* (French).

eel Nutritious snake-like fish whose flesh has a particularly rich flavour. There are several kinds of eel, both fresh and salt water, but the silver eel is considered the best. Eels are baked, fried, pickled, smoked, stewed or jellied.

eel-pout Lotte or burbot.

ees eeghian (Greek) To your health! A toast.

eetzaal (Dutch) Dining room.

effervescence Gas released in a liquid.

effeuiller (French) To strip a plant of its leaves and flowers.

egg Important food items supplying protein, fat, calcium, iron and vitamins. Those from the domestic fowl are most popular and can be poached, fried, scrambled, baked and boiled, used in cakes, sweets, desserts, puddings and made into an enormous variety of dishes. Other eggs used for cooking are duck's eggs, goose eggs, turkeys' eggs, plovers' eggs and penguin eggs, the latter two being regarded as great delicacies. An easy way to test the freshness of eggs is to place them one by one in a tumbler of water. The fresher the egg, the nearer the bottom of the glass it will stay An egg that floats is almost certainly bad. Eggs (not duck or goose eggs) can be preserved or pickled. See seperate entries for boiled, poached eggs, etc.

egg albumen Egg white; protein.

egg-and-crumb To coat food such as fish, rissoles, cutlets, etc. with beaten egg and roll in breadcrumbs before frying.

egg apple Eggplant, aubergine.

egg-beater Rotating blades operated electrically or by hand, used in beating eggs, whipping cream, etc.

egg-bread (American) (i) Golden-yellow batter-bread or spoonbread. (ii) Egg *challah*.

egg cheese Semi-hard Finnish cheese made by adding eggs to the curds.

egg cooler (American) Egg holder.

egg-cup Small cup just big enough to hold a boiled egg.

egg *en cocotte* Egg oven-baked in a dish standing in warm water.

egg-fruit Eggplant, aubergine.

egg-holder Wire basked used for boiling eggs so that they may be easily removed for cooling.

egg nog Nutritious beverage made of eggs, cream or milk, sugar, and flavouring, sometimes fortified with brandy, rum, whisky, or wine, and usually served with a dash of cinnamon or nutmeg.

egg-plant Aubergine.

egg-plum Firm, well-flavoured fruit, "Magnum bonum", in two kinds: red, and yellow-and-white, both egg-shaped and both found in several varieties under different names.

egg poacher Shallow pan with hollowed upper tray to hold eggs cooked by means of water boiling in the lower part of the pan.

egg pop (American) Egg nog.

egg powder Dried eggs.

egg roll (spring roll) Traditional Chinese New Year food of a dough square filled with chicken, mushroom and bean sprouts, and fried to golden brown.

egg sauce White or cream sauce containing chopped hard-boiled eggs.

egg slicer Utensil with fine steel wires for slicing a hard-boiled egg with a single movement.

egg timer (i) Hour-glass-shaped device for timing the boiling of eggs, made so that the sand runs from the top to the bottom section in three minutes. (ii) Clock-work device which can be set to time eggs and other cooking.

egg white White or albumen part of the egg, used for making icings, meringues, and light cakes.

egg yolk Yellow centre of an egg, used in making custards, sauces, and garnishes, etc.

egghot (American) Hot beverage made from beer, cinnamon, raw eggs, and sugar.

eggwich (American) Slang for egg sandwich.

églantier (French) Wild rose whose fruit (hips) is used for preserves.

eglantine Dog-rose or wild rose. The fruit (hips) is used to make syrup and preserves.

égouter (French) To drain.

égoutture (French) Drippings.

égrapper (French) To remove grapes, and berries from their stalks.

égrener (French) To detach corn or other grain from its stalk.

égrugeoir (French) Salt-grinder.

égruger (French) To grind.

Ei (German) Egg.

Ei in Schale (German) Egg in the shell, boiled egg.

Eidotter (German) Egg-yolk.

Eierbecher (German) Egg-cup.

Eierkuchen (German) (i) Omelette. (ii) Pancake.

Eierpunsch (German) Egg-flip.

Eierspeise (German) Dish prepared with eggs.

Eiersalat (German) Egg salad.

Eiersosse (German) Eggsauce.

Eigelb (German) Egg-yolk.

Ein Dunkles (German) Brown ale. Literally, "One dark".

Ein Helles (German) Light ale. Literally, "One light".

Einbecker Bier (German) Beer brewed in Lower Saxony.

Einbrenne (German) Soup-thickening.

Eingemachtes Kalbfleish (German) Veal stew with white sauce and capers, a speciality of the Black Forest area.

einkochen (German) To preserve.

einpökeln (German) To salt or pickle.

einsalzen (German) To salt, cure or pickle.

einschmelzen (German) To melt down.

Eis (German) Ice; ice cream.

Eisbein (German) Pig's trotters.

Eisbein in Gelee (German) Jellied pig's trotters.

Eiswein (German) Rare "ice wine" made from grapes still frozen by frost.

Eiweis (German) (i) Egg-white. (ii) Albumen.

ekneck kataif (Turkish) Meal porridge.

élan (French) Elk, moose.

eland Large deer.

Elbing (German) Cow's milk cheese originating in northern Germany.

elbow macaroni Angled pieces of macaroni.

elder Mancunian dish of boiled cow's udder.

elderberry Small black berry of the elder-tree found all over Europe, Northern Africa, and Asia. Used for making a wine which, drunk hot at night, has a reputation as a preventative of and cure for colds.

elderberry wine See elderberry.

elderflower Flower of the elder tree used to make wine and tisanes and to flavour preserves.

elderflower wine See elderflower.

electric knife Electrically vibrated knife used for cutting bread, slicing cheese, carving meat, etc.

electric mixer Domestic utensil for beating, whisking, blending, and mixing, often with attachments for slicing, shredding, juice-extracting, mincing, and pulping.

electricidad (Spanish) Electricity.

électricité (French) Electricity.

Elektrizität (German) Electricity.

electronic cookery High-speed method of cooking by which food is subjected to high-frequency electric waves which penetrate to the middle of the mass and cook from the inside to the outside.

elephant Large mammal yielding edible but leathery flesh. Its trunk and feet are considered delicacies.

elettricità (Italian) Electricity.

Elijah's cup (Jewish) Cup of wine placed on the table at Passover for the prophet Elijah.

elixir (i) Liquid made by dissolving certain elements in alcohol. (ii) Wine containing a high level of alcohol.

elmassia (Turkish) Dish, made from calves' feet.

elver Young eel.

emballer (French) To wrap food in a caul or cloth before cooking.

émincé (French) (i) Finely sliced or shredded. (ii) Dish made from thinly sliced left-over meat and covered with sauce.

émincer (French) To slice or shred finely.

Emmenthal cheese Swiss hard cheese named after the Emme valley. Made from whole or semi-fat milk, with holes or "eyes" which are large and plentiful.

Made like Gruyère but creamier and less pungent.

émonder (French) To blanch. For example, to plunge almonds in boiling water to remove their skins.

empanada (Spanish) Meat pie.

empanadilla (Spanish) Small pie or patty.

Empire wine Wine produced in the British Commonwealth.

empotage (French) Collective expression for all the ingredients in a braising pot.

emulsin Enzyme obtained from bitter almonds.

emulsion Mixture of liquid ingredients such as milk and water, oil and wine.

en (French) In, served in, *en tasse* – in a cup, etc.

en chemise (French) With the skin or "shirt" on, as in potatoes boiled or baked unskinned.

en couronne (French) To dish food up in the form of a crown.

en croûte (French) Encrusted, wrapped or enclosed in paste prior to cooking.

en denier (French) Term applied to potato crisps because of their shape. (From *denarius* – coin).

en dés (French) Cut into dice shapes.

en fête (French) Table set in festive style.

en la mesa (Spanish) On the table.

en lata (Spanish) Tinned, canned.

en papillote (French) Fish, meat or birds wrapped in greased paper, in which they are cooked and sent to table.

en serviette (French) Food served in a napkin.

en tasse (French) Served in cups. Chiefly applied to clear soups.

enamelware Kitchenware covered with a vitreous enamel coating.

enchilada (Spanish) Mexican tortilla, filled with chicken, fish, meat, prawns or vegetables and served with a chili sauce and grated cheese.

enchilada de carne (Spanish) Meat *enchilada*.

enchilada de gallina (Spanish) Chicken *enchilada*.

enchilada de legumbres (Spanish) Vegetable *enchilada*.

enchilada de pescado (Spanish) Fish *enchilada*.

enchilada-fish South African cold fish

curry. Cod, cut into steaks, is first fried to a deep brown and then pickled in curry, vinegar and Spanish onions for several days.

endaubage (French) Supplementary ingredients which go into the braising pot.

endive (i) Chicory. (ii) Curly-leaved close-type lettuce.

endive (American) Chicory.

endive (French) Chicory.

endive à la flamande (French) Chicory with butter.

endive à la meunière (French) Chicory with brown butter.

endive au jus (French) Chicory in gravy.

Endivie (German) Endive, chicory.

eneldo (Spanish) Dill.

Engadine Whole-milk cheese originating in the Engadine valley in Switzerland.

Engelwurzel (German) Angelica.

Englisches Bier (German) Ale.

English bamboo Pickle made from the young shoots of the elder-tree, salted and dried, with a pickle vinegar poured over them.

"English Frontignac" Elderflower wine.

enrich To add nutrients to food often to replace those lost in manufacturing or refining processes.

enrober (French) To coat.

ensalada (Spanish) Salad.

ensalada de apio (Spanish) Celery salad.

ensalada de arroz (Spanish) Rice salad.

ensalada de frutta (Spanish) Fruit salad.

Entchen (German) Duckling.

Ente (German) Duck.

entrecuisse (French) Thigh of poultry or feathered game; the upper part of the leg as distinct from the drumstick.

Entre-deux-mers (French) Area of France between the Dordogne and the Garonne which gives its name to certain red and white wines.

entrecôte (French) Sirloin steak cut from the middle part of the loin or sometimes the rib of beef.

entrée (French) (i) In Britain, a main course served before the roast (if any). (ii) In America the main course. (iii) Originally a course of dishes or corner dish for the first course. (iv) Also the conventional term for hot or cold side dishes. (v) Also defined as dishes generally served with a sauce.

entrelarder (French) To cook slices of meat with alternate layers of pork fat.

entremés (Spanish) (i) Relish; side dish. (ii) *Hors d'œuvre.*

entremets (French) (i) In earlier times, dainty dishes of vegetables or hot and cold sweets and after-dinner savouries served as second course. (ii) Modern usage: sweets served after the cheese course.

Enzian (German) (i) Gentian. (ii) Herb brandy.

enzyme Protein substance produced by living cells which, with co-enzymes, acts as a catalyst (changing another substance without changing itself), e.g., B vitamins which oxydise carbohydrates into sugar.

epanada (Spanish and Portuguese) Panada.

épaule (French) Shoulder.

épaule d'agneau (French) Shoulder of lamb.

épaule de mouton (French) Shoulder of mutton.

épergne (French) Decorative table centre-piece with several glass or silver or porcelain bowls attached, and used for serving pickled delicacies or cooked fruit, ices, etc.

éperlan (French) Smelt, a fish akin to the salmon family.

éperlan frit (French) Fried smelt.

épiaise de marais (French) Red nettle.

épice (French) Spice, seasoning. Aromatic plants or their seeds.

epicure One addicted to the luxury of eating and drinking.

épigramme (French) (i) Culinary term for small fillet of poultry and game, and breast of lamb or mutton, prepared as an *entrée.* (ii) Dish of alternate cutlets of the neck and breast.

épinard (French) Spinach.

épine d'hiver (French) Winter variety of eating pear.

Epiphany Twelfth night, or Feast of the Kings, celebrated in France with a special dough or pastry cake.

éponger (French) To dry parboiled, drained vegetables on a cloth.

Epping sausage 19th century skinless sausage of pork, suet, sage and other herbs, lemon, nutmeg and egg.

équille (French) Sand-eel, cooked as for smelt.

érable (French) Maple-tree.

erbarrosto (Italian) Mixed dried herbs.

erbazzone (Italian) Vegetable and spinach soup served with cheese and butter.

Erbse (German) Pea.

Erbsenbrei (German) Split pea *purée*.

Erbsensuppe (German) Pea soup.

Erdapfel (German/Austrian) Potato.

Erdapfelcroquette (German/Austrian) Potato croquette.

Erdapfelknodel (German / Austrian) Potato dumpling.

Erdapfelpuree (German/Austrian) Potato *purée*.

Erdapfelsalat (German/Austrian) Potato salad.

Erdapfelschmarren (German / Austrian) Fried potatoes.

Erdapfelsuppe (German / Austrian) Potato soup.

Erdbeere (German) Strawberry.

Erdbeere in Ribiselsaft (German) Strawberry in red-currant juice.

Erdbeerschnitte (German) Strawberry slice pastry.

Erdnüss (German) Peanut.

Ersatz (German) Substitute beverage or food which imitates the original.

ervy (French) Soft cheese resembling *Camembert* made in the Champagne district of France.

erwtensoep (Dutch) Pea soup.

escabescia (Spanish) Dish of highly seasoned partridges.

escalfado (Spanish) Poached.

escallop Scallop.

escalope (French) Collop. Thin round steak of veal usually egged, crumbed, and fried.

escargot (French) Edible snail, considered a delicacy in China and France. The Continental edible snail differs both in colour and size from the usual garden snail of Britain. Not greatly esteemed as a food in Britain, the edible snail was brought here from southern Europe in the 18th century, and is still found in chalk-soil districts.

escarole (French) Dark green, broad-leaved salad plant eaten raw or cooked as for endive (chicory).

Escoffier, A. (1847–1935) Celebrated French *maître chef*, author of *A Guide to Modern Cookery* and other cook books.

Eskimo pie (American) Brand name of an ice cream coated with chocolate.

espadon (French) Swordfish.

Espagnole (French) Rich brown "Spanish" sauce; the foundation of many brown sauces; classified as the main brown grand sauce, or *sauce mère*.

espárrago (Spanish) Asparagus.

especialidad (Spanish) Speciality.

espinaca (Spanish) Spinach.

Essen (German) Meal.

essence (i) Extract from any food substance. (ii) Solution of essential oils or flavouring ingredients in alcohol. (iii) More commonly, the synthetic preparations marketed as essences, such as almond, lemon, etc. which are less delicate than the originals of (ii) but are considerably cheaper and are acceptable for use in cooking cakes, sweets, biscuits, etc.

essence d'ail (French) Garlic essence.

essence d'amandes amères (French) Bitter almond essence.

essence d'anchois (French) Anchovy essence.

essence de champignons (French) Mushroom essence.

essence de gibier (French) Essence of game.

essence de persil (French) Parsley essence.

essence of game Game stock reduced to thick meat jelly.

Essig (German) Vinegar.

Essig-gurke (German) Gherkin (pickled).

est! est! est!!! (Italian) Dry and dessert wines from Lazio.

estagnon (French) Drum.

estaminet (French) (i) Smoking room in a coffee house. (ii) Basement tavern.

estomac (French) Stomach.

estómago (Spanish) Stomach.

estouffade (French) (i) Method of cooking meats slowly with very little liquid, in a covered stewpan. Braised, stewed or steamed. (ii) Clear brown stock.

estragon (French) Tarragon.

esturgeon (French) Sturgeon. A very large fish, usually salted and smoked. The roe is caviare.

étouffé, étuvé (French) See *estouffade* (i) and *étuver.*

étourneau (French) Starling, cooked on the Continent as for thrush.

étuver (French) To cook food in a covered pan without moistening but with added butter, fat or oil.

evaporated milk Unsweetened canned milk reduced in bulk by evaporation and then sterilised, used in cooking and as a substitute for cream.

Everton toffee Hard, brittle sweetmeat similar to butterscotch but also containing evaporated milk or cream and cream of tartar.

eve's pudding Baked sponge pudding with a fruit foundation.

Evian water Bottled alkaline mineral water first found at Evian-les Bains in France.

eviscerate To degut, to remove the entrails of an animal.

ewe (i) Female sheep whose flesh is cooked when young as for mutton. (ii) Female goat.

ewe cheese Cheese made from ewe's milk.

ewe's milk Milk with a higher proportion of protein, fat and sugar than cow's milk, used in making continental cheeses such as *Roquefort, Brousses, Cachat*, etc.

ewer Vessel for holding water used at table.

exocet (French) Flying-fish.

exocoetus Flying-fish, prepared as for mackerel.

expresso coffee Coffee prepared under pressure in coffee bars, etc.

extra-fin (French) Of the best quality.

extra sec (French) Very dry, usually applied to champagne.

extract Essence obtained by heat, distillation, evaporation, etc. Commercially manufactured and sold in concentrated form as proprietary brands. Meat extracts (natural juices and mineral salts) are used to flavour soups and gravies, as also are yeast extracts, which are similar in flavour.

extractor (i) Utensil for squeezing juice from fruits, meats, and vegetables. (ii) Device for removing corks from bottles.

extrait (French) Extract.

extrait de malt (French) Malt extract.

extrait de soja (French) Soy sauce.

extrait de viande du commerce (French) Commercially prepared meat extract for domestic use.

F Abbreviation for Fahrenheit, the temperature scale on which water freezes at 32 degrees and boils at 212 degrees, devised by Gabriel Fahrenheit, 18th century German physicist.

faar i kaal (Scandinavian) Braised lamb and cabbage.

face of the rump (American) Rump steak.

fadge Barley pancake.

faggeto (Italian) Beech-nut.

faggot (i) Savoury preparation of pig's liver, fat pork, onions, breadcrumbs, herbs, etc., usually covered with caul, and slowly baked in a tin. The mixture is divided into squares, usually before cooking. (ii) Sprigs of parsley and thyme and a bayleaf tied together with twine, and removed from a dish such as a casserole before serving.

fagianella (Italian) Young pheasant.

fagiano (Italian) Pheasant.

fagiano alla crema (Italian) Pheasant cooked in butter and cream.

fagiano arrosto tartufato (Italian) Pheasant stuffed with truffles and roasted.

fagiolino (Italian) French bean, string bean.

fagiolino rampicanto (Italian) Runner bean.

fagiolo, fagiuolo (Italian) Haricot bean.

fagot (French) See *bouquet garni* or faggot (ii).

fagou (French) (i) Pancreas. (ii) Calf's sweetbreads.

faience Highly coloured glazed earthenware crockery which takes its name from the Italian town of Faenza.

faire la cuisine (French) To cook or to dress food.

faire revenir (French) To fry or brown lightly without actually cooking.

faire suer (French) To cook meat in a covered stewpan with no liquor except the juices which ooze from the meat.

faire une fontaine (French) To make a hollow in the flour in the mixing bowl or piled on the table.

fairy shrimp (American) Freshwater prawn, so called because of its delicate colouring.

faisan (French) Pheasant.

faisán (Spanish) Pheasant.

faisan piqué (French) Larded pheasant.

faisandage (French) Red meat which is "high".

faiselle, faisselle (French) (i) Basket used for draining cheese. (ii) Table used for draining apple residue after brewing cider.

falernian wine Wine produced in Campagna, Italy, (Falerno rosso, Falerno bianco) immortalised in verse by the poet Horace.

fallow-deer Wild ruminant whose meat, when young, is delicate. The flesh of older animals needs to be marinated. Cooked as for venison.

falstaff (American) Beer brewed in St. Louis, Missouri.

fan (Chinese) Rice.

fanche (Chinese) Dining car.

fanchonnette (French) Small egg custard tartlet covered with meringue.

fanfre (French) Pilot fish.

fannings Coarse siftings of tea.

fantail mullet (American) Edible fish popular in Florida and the West Indies.

fantail shrimp (American) Large prawn split lengthwise and fried.

fantasie (French) (i) Description on labels of synthetic products. (ii) Bread sold by the piece rather than by weight.

fanting (Chinese) Dining room.

far (French) (i) Porridge made from hard wheat flour. (ii) Flan made in Brittany.

faraona (Italian) Guinea-fowl.

faraona alla creta, al coccio (Italian) Guinea-fowl baked in clay.

faraona arrosta (Italian) Roasted guinea-fowl.

faraona incrostata (Italian) Guinea-fowl in a pie.

faraona ripiena (Italian) Stuffed guinea-fowl.

farce (French) Forcemeat or stuffing, from the Latin word *farcire* to fill, to stuff. From this is derived the word *farcimen*, the sausage. A *farce* need not necessarily contain meat.

farci (French) (i) Southern French dish of cabbage stuffed with sausage meat or other forcemeat. (ii) Filled; stuffed.

farfalla (Italian) *Pasta* "butterfly".

farfallino (Italian) Small bow of *pasta*.

farfel (Jewish) Kosher dumpling made of egg barley, served in *consommé* or soup.

farina Meal made from cereal grains or starchy roots and used for puddings, soups, and breakfast cereals.

farina (Italian) Flour.

farina di grano nero (Italian) Buckwheat flour.

farina di riso (Italian) Ground rice.

farinaceous food Food which consists largely of starch – such as bread, potatoes, oatmeal, flour, macaroni, semolina, etc.

farine (French) Flour.

fariné (French) Powdered or dredged with flour.

farine de riz (French) Ground rice.

farinière (French) Flour bin.

farineux (French) Farinaceous food.

farl (Scottish) Triangular oatmeal cake, similar to a bannock.

farmer cheese (American) Pressed cheese made of skimmed or whole milk, as made on farms.

farmhouse bread Loaf enriched with milk (and sometimes fat) with a floury top. Baked in a tin.

faro (Italian) Dry red Sicilian table wine.

farstufning (Swedish) Lamb stew.

Fasan (German) Pheasant.

Faschingskrapfen (German / Austrian) Viennese carnival doughnuts eaten from January to Lent.

fascine (French) Bundle, such as a bundle of asparagus.

faséole, féverole (French) Species of kidney-bean.

fat Substance with a low melting point, valuable as fuel food. Derived from meats, dairy products, oily fish, nuts, etc. Fats are used widely in cooking for frying, baking, etc. and making cakes and puddings. They include butter, margarine, suet, lard, dripping, olive oil, nut oil, etc.

fattoush (Arabian) Mixed salad.

fabonne (French) Bean *purée* soup seasoned with savoury herbs and added vegetables.

fausse tortue (French) Mock turtle soup.

faux, fausse (French) Mock, false, as *fausse tortue*, mock turtle.

fava (Italian) Broad bean.

faverolle (French) Regional name for haricot bean in France. (Also *favorette, farviole, fayot, fayol*).

Favre, Joseph Famous 19th century chef and writer on *cuisine*.

fawn Young of the roe deer, prepared as for roebuck.

fayol, fayot (French) French kidney-bean, fried, haricot bean.

feather fowlie (Scottish) Chicken-and-ham soup with cream and egg yolk.

fecula Starchy flour obtained from potatoes, rice, etc., used for thickening soups, sauces, etc.

fécule (French) Very fine flour used for binding soups and sauces.

fécule de mais (French) Cornflour.

fécule de marante (French) Arrowroot.

fécule de pommes de terre (French) Potato flour.

fécule de riz (French) Rice flour.

fedelino (Italian) Ribbon of *pasta*.

fegatino (Italian) Small piece of liver, usually cooked on a spit.

fegatino di pollo (Italian) Chicken's liver.

fegato (Italian) Liver.

fegato di bue (Italian) Ox-liver.

fegato di vitello (Italian) Calf's liver.

Feige (German) Fig.

Feigwurz (German) Fennel.

feijão (Portuguese) Bean.

feijoada (Portuguese) Brazilian dish containing beans, meat, and rice.

Feinschmecker (German) Gourmet.

Fenchel (German) Fennel.

fendre (French) To split, as *fendre un poulet pour griller*, to split a chicken for broiling.

fennel Aromatic plant in several species, used in fish sauces. Fennel seeds, which resemble anise are used to flavour pickles, pastries, liqueurs, etc.

fennel-water Liqueur made from fennel seeds.

fenouil (French) Fennel.

fenouillette (French) Fennel-water, a liqueur made from fennel seeds.

fenugreek Leguminous plant whose ground seeds are used in curry-powder. Fenugreek, cultivated in India as a fodder-plant, derives its name from

Fœnum Grœcum, Greek hay. It resembles celery in flavour.

fenugrec (French) Fenugreek.

fer (French) Iron.

féra (French) Type of salmon found in the lakes of Switzerland and Austria.

ferchuse (French) Burgundian speciality made from the lungs, heart, and liver of pig simmered in red wine and stock or water.

Ferkel (German) Piglet.

fermentation Chemical change brought about by the action of bacteria. Fermented foods include beers, vinegars, bread, sour milk. Accidental fermentation can result from bad storage or incomplete sterilisation, as in the case of jams, fruits, etc.

fermière, à la (French) Meat braised or pot-roasted slowly with vegetables.

fernet-branca (Italian) Brand of Italian bitters used in cocktails and said to have medicinal properties.

ferri, ai (Italian) Meat cooked on an iron griddle.

fersk suppe og kjøtt (Norwegian) Soup made with beef, carrots and cabbage.

Fest (German) (i) Feast. (ii) Festival.

feta, fetta (Greek) White goat's milk cheese, often served as a meal starter with olives, tomatoes and fresh bread.

fête (French) Festive celebration.

fête champêtre (French) Garden party.

Fett (German) Fat, grease, lard.

fetta (Italian) Slice.

fettucina (Italian) Ribbon of *pasta*.

feuillantine (French) Finger of baked puff-pastry.

feuillé (French) Dish decorated with leaf-shaped garnishing.

feuillage (French) Leaves.

feuilletage (French) Puff-paste.

feuilleton (French) Thin slice of veal or pork, stuffed and braised.

fève (French) Broad bean.

fève d'Espagne (French) Name sometimes used for scarlet runner or string bean.

fiambre (Spanish) Cold meat.

fiambrera (Spanish) Lunch-basket.

fiaschino (Italian) Small wine flask.

fiasco (Italian) Wide-based, straw-covered wine bottle or flask.

fiasque (French) Long-necked wine flask with a straw covering. (*Fiasco* – Italian).

fiatole (French) Mediterranean fish, flat and broad, cooked as for turbot.

ficelle, à la (French) Tied with string.

fico (Italian) Fig.

fideo (Spanish) Thin noodle.

fidget (or fitchett) pie Old English farmhouse pie of potatoes and mutton or bacon, apples, stock and seasoning, covered with short crust pastry.

fieldfare Migratory bird of the thrush tribe, found in England in winter, and once cooked in pies.

field-poppy oil Oil extracted from the seeds of the white poppy and used as for olive oil.

fiesta (Spanish) (i) Feast-day. (ii) Entertainment. (iii) Party.

fig Fruit of the fig-tree, which comes in many varieties. Its fleshy exterior encloses a large number of small seeds. Figs are eaten raw, or cooked as for apricots; dried artificially or in the sun and used in fruit salads, or stewed, or in cakes, puddings, etc. In the Middle East figs are used to make a fermented drink and spirit.

fig banana (American) Small tropical American banana with a fig-like flavour.

fig-bird Small delicate southern European bird, prepared like ortolan or plover.

fig (or fag) pie Lancashire Mothering Sunday delicacy which appears in other parts of Britain during Lent, probably associated with the withering of the fig-tree after Jesus's triumphal entry into Jerusalem.

figaro (French) Cold sauce which is a mixture of mayonnaise and tomato.

figer (French) To coagulate.

figue (French) Fig.

figue (or figuier) de barbarie (French) Prickly pear.

filatello (Italian) *Pasta.*

filbunke (Swedish) Soured milk.

filé (French) Spun, stringed, as in *sucre filé*, spun sugar.

filet (French) Fillet.

Filet (German) Fillet (of meat).

filet de bœuf (French) Fillet of beef.

filet de chevreuil (French) Fillet of venison or roebuck.

filet de sole (French) Fillet of sole.

filet de veau (French) Fillet of veal.

filet en chevreuil (French) Mutton cooked and served in imitation of venison.

filet-mignon (French) Small daintily-cut fillet of beef, etc.

filete (Spanish) Fillet of steak.

filete de ternera (Spanish) Veal fillet.

filetto (Italian) Fillet.

filetto alla tartara (Italian) Steak *tartare*.

filetto di maiale (Italian) Pork fillet.

filetto di pollo (Italian) Breast of chicken.

filetto di sogliola (Italian) Fillet of sole.

filetto di tacchino (Italian) Slice of turkey breast.

filled cheese Cheese with butter fats removed and other fats added.

filled milk Milk whose cream has been replaced by other fat such as vegetable oils.

fillet (i) Under-cut of a loin of beef, mutton, veal, pork, and game. (ii) Boned breasts of poultry. (iii) Boned sides of fish.

fillet of flounder Boned flounder.

fillet of plaice Boned plaice.

fillet of sole Boned sole.

fillet steak Under-cut of sirloin, usually grilled or fried, shaped into rounds, or *tournedos* and served with sauce and garnishes.

filmjölk (Swedish) Sour milk.

filo dough Paper-thin dough used in *strudels*, etc.

filter To strain liquid through a fine metal filter or through cloth or paper.

filter coffee Coffee made in a vessel with a fine filter and allowed to drip slowly through into cup or jug.

filter paper Porous paper for use in a filter device.

financière, à la (French) Poultry and meat dishes garnished with cock's combs, cock's kidneys, sweetbreads, *quenelles*, truffles and mushrooms.

fines herbes (French) (i) Originally a mixture of herbs – parsley, chervil, tarragon, chives. (ii) More generally, chopped parsley only.

finger-bowl Individual basin of warm water for rinsing fingers while at table.

finger roll Bread baked in long rolls.

fining Clarification of wine and other beverages.

finnan haddie (Scottish) Smoked haddock.

fino (Spanish) Word indicating the dryest types of sherry.

finocchio (Italian) Fennel, eaten raw like celery, or braised or served *au gratin*.

finocchiona (Italian) Sausage flavoured with fennel, a speciality of Tuscany.

finte Fish similar to the shad and cooked in the same ways.

fior di latte (Italian) Fresh, unsalted *mozzarella* cheese.

fired Oven baked.

firkin Barrel containing (i) 9 gallons of British beer, (ii) 56lbs. of butter.

firlot (Scottish) Old Scottish dry measure equal to the fourth part of a boll. (See boll).

firmity Frumenty.

Fisch (German) Fish.

fischietto (Italian) Thin macaroni, a variety of *pasta*.

Fischkelle (German) Fish-slice.

Fischmilch (German) Soft roe.

Fischrogen (German) Roe.

fish Harvest of the sea and a prime source of food – natural, nutritious, and in enormous variety. An important source of protein and vitamins A and D, fish is classified according (a) to shape or (b) type, which may be fat or non-fat. Fish quickly deteriorates and should therefore be used as soon as possible after being caught. Modern freezing methods make fish available at all times. Cooking is as varied as the food itself – straightforward boiling, poaching, baking, frying, and made up into particular dishes with the aid of other ingredients and with the addition of suitable sauces.

fish and chips Fried fish and French-fried potatoes, one of the national dishes of Britain, particularly England.

fish cake Patty or *croquette* made of cooked fish and boiled potatoes seasoned, bound, egg-and-crumbed, and fried or baked.

fish chowder Thick fish soup made with onions, potatoes, seasoning, etc.

fish custard (Scottish) Dish made from filleted fish, eggs, milk, and salt.

fish flour Dried fish meal.

fish fry (American) Picnic where fish are caught, fried, and eaten on the spot.

fish-house cooler (American) Nick-name for Delaware punch.

fish-house punch (American) Eighteenth-century Philadelphian drink based on rum, brandy, sugar water and bitters, now served in many variations.

fish kettle, fish boiler Oval metal utensil with a removable grid on which fish is placed to cook over or in water or *court-bouillon*.

fish knife Wide-bladed knife with pointed tip.

fish mousse Flaked, seasoned fish mixed with gelatine and cream and set in a mould.

fish pie Cooked white fish mixed with white sauce, seasoned with salt, pepper, parsley and a little onion, and topped with a layer of creamed potato, then browned in the oven or under the grill.

fish spread Sandwich spread made of processed fish mixtures.

fishball Mixture of mashed potatoes and fish, usually cod, halibut, flounder or similar white fish, shaped into balls, coated with egg and breadcrumbs, and deep fried.

fishburger Hamburger made of fish.

fishmonger Man who sells fish.

fishes' eggs Fish roe. The roe of sturgeon and sterlet is used for caviare; that of salmon for red caviare, that of mullet for *poutargue*. Other edible fishes' eggs include shad and herrings.

fisk (Danish, Norwegian and Swedish) Fish.

Fisole (German/Austrian) French bean.

Fisolensalat (German) French bean salad.

fissurelle (French) Gasteropod mollusc species found in temperate and tropical waters, and prepared as for octopus.

fizz Effervescent beverage.

flageolet Pale green seed of a choice variety of haricot or kidney bean. Fresh beans are cooked like peas, dried beans are first soaked then cooked in salted water, tossed in butter and sprinkled with parsley.

flagon Large bulbous vessel of ceramic, glass, or metal for holding liquors and wines.

flake To separate food like fish into small particles.

flaky pastry Rich pastry suitable for meat pies, jam puffs, etc., in which the fat is divided into four and added to the other ingredients in separate operations.

flamande, à la (French) Large cuts of meat with diced belly of pork, carrots, potatoes and braised cabbage.

flamber (French) (i) To drench food with spirit, such as brandy and then ignite it. (ii) To singe poultry or game before cooking.

flame tokay Bright red grape originating in Hungary.

flameware Ovenware which can be exposed to high heat or direct flame without breaking.

flamiche (French) Leek tart made in Burgundy and Picardy.

Flammeri (German) Blancmange.

flamri (French) Semolina pudding made with eggs and white wine.

flamusse (French) Burgundian cheese-flavoured pastry.

flan Open pastry case baked in a tin ring or circle, filled with a sweet or savoury mixture and served either hot or cold.

flan (French) Custard tart or cream preparation in pastry.

flan (Spanish) Caramel custard.

flan case Baked case of flan pastry filled before cooking, or baked "blind" and filled when cold.

flan de cerises (French) Cherry flan.

flan pastry Rich shortcrust pastry of flour, salt and fat blended with an egg yolk, used for making sweet and savoury flans.

flanc (French) Side dish served at large dinners.

flanc, flanchet (French) Flank of beef or codfish.

flank of veal or beef Flesh between the breast and the leg, used principally for stewing.

flannel scone Scotch pancake.

flannelcake (American) Griddlecake or qancake.

flapjack (i) Cookie-type biscuit made from a mixture of fat, sugar, rolled oats and golden syrup. (ii) (American) Pancake.

Flasche (German) (i) Bottle. (ii) Flask.

flatfish Marine fish, (halibut, flounder, sole, etc.) which swims on one side of its broad flat body.

flatten To beat meat such as steak, escalope, etc. with a beater or mallet to make it more tender and easier to cook.

flatware Tableware such as forks, knives, and spoons.

flavouring Addition of herbs, spices, essences, wines, liqueurs etc. to food to enhance taste.

flaxseed Seed of the flax plant which yields linseed oil and a coarse meal.

flead Residue left from rendering pork lard, used in cakes.

flead cake Old Kentish delicacy of a light crisp cake made from flead, flour, salt and cold water.

Fleisch (German) Meat.

Fleischbrühe (German) (i) Meat broth. (ii) Beef tea.

Fleischer (German) Butcher.

Fleischhacker (German) Butcher.

Fleischmesser (German) Butcher's knife.

Fleischpastete (German) Meat pie.

flensje (Dutch) Thin pancakes.

flétan, grand flétan (French) Halibut.

fleuron (French) Small fancy-shaped piece of puff, flaky or rough-puff pastry used for garnishing.

flip Drink of eggs beaten with sugar, beer or wine, and some spirit.

flitch Side of pork, salted and cured.

floating island (i) Custard topped with "islands" of meringue or whipped cream. (ii) Old French sweet of sponge cake sliced and soaked in Kirsch, spread with apricot jam, currants and chopped almonds, re-assembled into original shape and coated with Chantilly cream.

fløde (Danish) Cream.

flødeis (Danish) Ice cream.

flødeskum (Danish) Whipped cream.

florence fennel Sweet fennel.

Florentine, à la (French) Fish or eggs served on a bed of buttered, stewed spinach topped with mornay sauce and sprinkled with grated cheese.

Florentine egg Egg (soft-boiled or poached) served on spinach and covered with mornay sauce.

flounder (i) Small flat sea-fish, resembling plaice, (and cooked in the same way) but of poorer texture and flavour. (ii) (American) Plaice.

flour (i) Crushed or de-husked grain reduced to powder. Wheaten flour is made from wheat (and, because of its gluten content, is most suitable flour for bread-making), cornflour from maize or Indian corn, rice flour from rice. Rye, buckwheat and oatmeal are among other flour-producing cereals. White flour keeps better than wholemeal and the food properties lost in the refining process are replaced – calcium, iron, thiamin and nicotine acid. Wholemeal flour contains the whole wheat including the germ. This goes rancid after a while which is why wholemeal flour does not keep. Wheatmeal flour retains a small portion of the husk. Stone-ground flour is produced by grinding the grains between stones instead of rollers, thus keeping a 100% extraction. Flour is a staple food in most temperate countries and is used in an enormous range of dishes and culinary preparations. (ii) To flour: To dredge food with flour before frying, or to sprinkle flour on a board to prevent pastry from sticking when rolled.

flourcake (American) Doughnut.

fluid ounce Liquid measure, 1/20th pint (English), 1/16th pint (american), 2.84 decilitres (metric).

flúido (Spanish) Fluid.

fluke (American) Flounder or plaice.

flukie (Scottish) Flounder.

flummery Old English cold sweet dish, made mainly of cereals, originally of oatmeal set in a mould and turned out. Dutch flummery is made with gelatine or isinglass, egg yolks, and flavourings; Spanish flummery is made of cream, rice flour, cinnamon and sugar.

Flunder (German) Flounder.

flundra (Swedish) Flounder.

flute (i) To decorate by grooving, (i.e., pastry). (ii) To cut vegetables into decorative designs. (iii) Short-stemmed narrow glass correct for serving champagne.

flûte (French) Finger-shaped roll.

flynder (Danish) Flounder.

flyndre (Norwegian) Flounder.

focaccia (Italian) (i) Tart. (ii) Bun. (iii) Cake.

focaccia di vitello (Italian) Veal rissole.

focaccina (Italian) Tartlet.

fofo de bacalhau (Portuguese) Fish ball.

fogosch **or** *fogàs* (Austro-Hungarian) Fish of delicate flavour, found in Hungarian and Austrian lakes. Usually served with paprika or *Hollandaise* sauce.

foie (French) Liver.

foie de veau (French) Calf's liver.

foie-gras (French) Fat goose liver, chief ingredient of *pâté de fois gras*.

folgaga (Italian) (i) Coot. (ii) Moorhen.

fold in, to To add ingredients to a whisked mixture in such a way that it retains its lightness, as in making meringues, *soufflés*, etc. The extra ingredient is sifted onto the mixture and gently turned in by use of a metal spoon folding the mixture over but taking care not to disturb the air bubbles more than necessary. It cannot be done with an electric mixer but is essentially a hand process.

folle-blanche (French) White grapes from *Charentes* used in brandy distillation.

fond (French) (i) Strong gravy, meat stock. (ii) Bottom, as in *fond d'artichaut*, (artichoke bottom).

fond blanc (French) Chicken or veal stock.

fond brun (French) Beef, game, or lamb stock.

fond de cuisine (French) Stocks and broths, the basis of all fine sauces, stews, soups, etc.

fonda (Spanish) Inn, eatinghouse.

fondant (French) Soft, melting sweetmeat; dessert bon-bon.

fondu (French) Melted.

fondue (French) (i) Preparation of melted

cheese, originally made in Switzerland. (ii) Cheese savoury.

fondue fork Long-handled fork for dipping bread into cheese, *fondue.*

fonduta (Italian) Dish of melted cheese, egg yolks, milk and butter, with truffles. Speciality of *Piedmont.*

fontaine (French) Fountain. Spring. *Faire une fontaine* – to make a well or hollow in the flour in the bowl or on the table.

Fontainebleau (French) Northern French town renowned for its grapes and cream cheese.

fontina (Italian) Soft goat's-milk cream cheese.

food mill Colander with rotating pressure plate which pulps food into a smooth mass.

food poisoning Illness caused by eating food (i) contaminated by bacterial infection or (ii) with added toxic material or (iii) containing natural poisons, as in certain fungii.

food press Food mill.

fool Dessert made of puréed fruits and whipped cream.

forbidden fruit (i) Small shaddock so named from a legend that it may have been the fruit which Eve took in the Garden of Eden. (ii) American grape brandy and grapefruit juice liqueur.

force (i) To grow fruit and vegetables under glass to ripen early (ii) To press food such as cream or icing through a forcing bag to decorate dishes.

forced cabbage Eighteenth-century dish of stuffed cabbage simmered in broth.

forcemeat (i) Pounded or finely minced meat, etc., for stuffing meat or birds. (ii) Veal stuffing, usually consisting of suet, parsley, breadcrumbs, etc. (iii) Other stuffings, such as sage and onion, oyster, chestnut and truffle also rate as forcemeat.

forchetta (Italian) Fork.

forefoot of pork (American) Forequarter of a pig.

forehock Cut of bacon which includes bone and knuckle. The meat is well-flavoured but coarser in texture than gammon. Often sold boned and rolled,

but the bones are excellent for soup-making.

foreleg ham Meat from below the ham or shoulder of legs of pork.

Forelle (German) Trout.

forequarter of lamb Shoulder, breast and neck of lamb.

foreshank (American) Meat cut from the top part of the front leg.

forestière, à la (French) Small cuts of meat and poultry garnished with morels, bacon and diced fried potatoes.

foret (French) Gimlet.

fork Eating tool with tines, first manufactured in England in 1608: its use was ridiculed at the time.

fork luncheon Mid-day meal.

formaggio (Italian) Cheese.

forno (Italian) (i) Oven. (ii) Bakehouse.

forno, al (Italian) (i) Food baked or oven-roasted. (ii) Pasta boiled then oven-baked with cheese and butter, or with a sauce.

forshmak (Russian) Appetizer of mashed potatoes and hashed meat or herrings.

fortified wine Wine strengthened by the addition of grape brandy or other spirit. In this category are port, sherry, Madeira, etc.

forum (Latin) Market place.

forum boarium (Latin) Cattle market.

forum olitorium (Latin) Vegetable market.

fosset (French) Wine-cask peg.

fouace (French) Hearth-cake.

fouet (French) Food whisk.

fouetté (French) Whipped with a whisk, as for cream.

fouler (French) To press food through a strainer or sieve.

foulque (French) Coot.

four (French) Oven.

four, au (French) Baked or cooked in the oven.

fourchette (French) Fork.

fourneau de cuisine (French) Kitchen stove.

fournou (Greek) Octopus cooked in sauce.

fourré (French) (i) Food coated with sugar, cream, etc. (ii) Filled or stuffed birds, etc.

fowl Edible domesticated bird – chicken, capon, turkey, etc.

fragola (Italian) Strawberry.

fragola, fragolina di bosco (Italian) Wild strawberry.

fragolina di mare (Italian) Small squid, known as "little sea strawberry", used in *frutti di mare*.

fraisage (French) Dough-kneading.

fraise (French) (i) Strawberry. (ii) Strawberry-flavoured cordial. (iii) Mesentery of a calf or lamb. (iv) Fleshy excrescence (wattle) under the throat of a turkey.

fraise de veau (French) Mesentery of calf – the membrane enveloping the intestines, cooked like calf's head.

fraiser la pâte (French) To plait; to roughen or ruffle pastry.

fraisure (French) See *fressure*.

framboise (French) (i) Raspberry. (ii) Sweet spirit flavoured with raspberries.

frambuesa (Spanish) Raspberry.

Française, à la (French) In French style.

Francatelli Eminent chef (1805–1876), author of *The Cook's Guide* and *The Modern Cook*, pupil of A. Carême, chef at the Reform Club, and to Queen Victoria.

francolin Wild bird of the eastern Mediterranean countries – Sicily, Greece, etc. – cooked as for partridge, which it resembles.

frangipane Cream puff pastry made with butter, egg yolks, flour, and milk, used with forcemeats and poultry.

frangipane cream Cream made with eggs, sugar, and macaroons or ground almonds, used in desserts, as flan filling, etc.

frank (American) Frankfurter.

frankental Black dessert grape originating in Germany.

frankfurter (i) Beef or beef-and-pork sausage hot dog. (ii) Continental smoked pork sausage.

Frankfurter Wurst (German) Frankfurter sausage.

frappé (French) Drink served in a chilled glass with crushed iced edging, or with finely crushed ice.

Frascati (Italian) White wine from Lazio in both sweet and dry varieties.

frascati, à la (French) Meat dishes garnished with slices of *foie gras*, truffles, mushrooms and asparagus tips.

freccia rossa (Italian) Red and white dry and dessert wines from Lombardy.

free house British public house not owned or controlled by a brewery.

freeze To reduce food to a temperature at which water would solidify into ice.

freeze-dry To freeze by rapid evaporation at low pressure, subsequently drying by evaporation of moisture from the ice.

freezer (i) Cabinet for storing frozen foods at low temperature. (ii) Section of a refrigerator used as above.

freezing point Point where water freezes – 32 degrees Fahrenheit or 0 degrees Celsius on the centigrade scale.

French and scarlet runner beans Also known as String, Stick, Kidney, Wax, Waxpod or Snap beans. Members of the haricot family, French beans are the more delicate of the two. The pods of young fresh beans are eaten with the immature seeds. But pods can be left to mature on the plants and the seeds then removed and eaten fresh or dried. Fresh whole runner beans are sliced and cooked in boiling salted water until tender, then tossed in butter. French beans need merely to be topped and tailed.

French bread Crisp-crusted bread baked in an elongated loaf and made from water dough.

French chop (American) Trimmed rib chop.

French dressing Salad dressing of olive oil and vinegar, garlic, salt, etc.

French endive (American) Chicory.

French-fried potato Potato cut into strips and fried in deep fat; chips.

French-fry cutter Utensil for cutting potatoes into strips.

French fryer Deep pan with wire-basket for deep-fat frying.

French ice cream (American) Frozen custard made of cream and egg yolks.

French mustard Mustard paste made from powdered dark mustard seeds, flavoured with herbs and spices and mixed with vinegar or wine.

French pancake (American) Thin pancake rolled up and served with preserve or cinnamon and sugar.

French pastry Puff pastry filled with confectioner's custard, preserved fruit or whipped cream.

French pea Tiny pea, *petit pois*.

French roll French bread baked in finger rolls.

French spinach (American) Orach, also known as Sea Purslane.

French toast (i) Bread dipped in egg and milk, and fried. (ii) Bread toasted on one side only and buttered on the reverse side.

French vermouth Dry vermouth.

fresa (Spanish) Strawberry.

fresas con nata (Spanish) Strawberries and cream.

fresco (Spanish) (i) Fresh. (ii) New laid (as of eggs).

fresh butter Unsalted butter.

fressure (French) Haslet, or fry, as in pigs fry, or lamb's fry.

fressure d'agneau (French) Lamb's lights.

friand (French) (i) Epicure. (ii) Dainty morsel.

freux (French) Rook.

friandise (French) Small dessert dainty, sweet, *petit four*, etc.

friar's omelette Baked omelette prepared with apples stewed to a pulp, eggs, and sugar.

fricandeau (French) (i) Topside of veal. (ii) Loin of veal larded with bacon fat and braised or roasted. (iii) Braised fillets of fish – mainly sturgeon or tuna.

fricandelle (French) Cake of minced veal or beef, flavoured and fried.

fricasseau (Italian) Veal *fricassée* or stew.

fricasseau di pollo (Italian) Chicken *fricassée*.

fricassée (French) Stew of meat, poultry or vegetables served in a creamy white sauce. When used as a means of using up left-overs, the cooked food should be added to the hot sauce and re-heated before serving.

fridge Refrigerator (colloquial).

fried banana Sliced banana sautéed in butter and sprinkled with sugar.

fried cake Doughcake such as cruller, doughnut, etc. cooked by frying in fat.

fried egg Egg broken into a pan containing hot fat and basted to achieve even cooking on top and underside.

frigate mackerel Small sea fish related to the tuna fish and not a true mackerel.

frijol (Spanish) Bean.

frijole negro (Spanish) Black bean.

frijoles refritos (Spanish) Beans cooked, then mashed into a smooth paste.

frikadelle (Danish) Meat ball.

frill Paper decoration placed on the bone end of a chop or on the bone ends of a crown roast of meat.

frío (Spanish) Cold.

frire (French) To fry.

frisé (French) Curled. As *chou frisé* – curled Savoy cabbage.

frit or frite (French) Fried.

friteau (French) Food – usually small pieces – dipped in frying batter, and fried in deep fat.

frito (Spanish) Fried.

fritot (French) Fritter made with small pieces of meat or poultry sweetbreads or brains.

frittata (Italian) Omelette.

frittatina imbottita (Italian) Small stuffed pancake.

frittella (Italian) Fritter, pancake, rissole, etc. Fried food, stuffed or filled, sweet or savoury.

fritella di segala (Italian) Spiced rye-flour roll, fried in oil.

fritter Food dipped in batter and fried. Fritters can be savoury (made with meat, etc.) or sweet (made with fruit such as apple or banana).

fritto (Italian) Fried.

fritto di pesce (Italian) Mixed fish-fry.

fritto di scampi (Italian) Fried prawn.

fritto misto (Italian) Mixed fry, in several varieties of offal and vegetables, cheese, chicken, fish, cut into small pieces, dipped in batter and deep-fried.

fritto misto mare (Italian) Mixed seafood fry.

frittura (Italian) Fritter.

frittura di pesci (Italian) Fried fish.

friture (French) (i) Fat, which may be oil, lard or dripping, in which articles are fried. (ii) Process of deep frying.

friture à l'Italienne (French) Italian dish, *Fritto Misto* – assorted fried foods.

frizzante (Italian) *Petillant* wine.

frizzle To fry or bake until crisp and curled at the edges.

frog See edible frog.

froid (French) Cold.

frokost (Danish) Luncheon.

frokost (Norwegian) Breakfast.

frollare (Italian) To soften, tenderise or hang meat.

fromage (French) Cheese.

fromage à la crème (French) See *coeur à la crème*.

fromage à la pie (French) Cheese made from whole or skimmed milk unfermented and eaten fresh at once. Cream may be added.

fromage blanc (French) Whole-milk white rennet-treated cheese, eaten fresh in summer.

fromage bleu (French) Bleu cheese.

fromage de chèvre (French) Goat's-milk cheese.

fromage de cochon (French) Hogshead cheese. Brawn.

fromage de monsieur (French) Soft French cheese, made in Normandy.

fromage de soja (French) Soya bean curd.

fromage de tête de porc (French) Hog's head cheese, or pork brawn.

fromage fort (French) Savoury, strong-smelling preparation of milk, cheese, salt and herbs packed into glazed stone jars, topped up with white wine and brandy, sealed and left to ferment.

fromage glacé (French) Ancient expression for an ice cream, or frozen pudding in the form of a cheese.

fromageon (French) White sheep's milk cheese made in the South of France.

fromager (French) To add grated cheese to sauces, stuffings, etc.

froment (French) Wheat.

fromenteau (French) Dessert grape.

fromentée (French) Frumenty.

Frontignan Small town in the *Hérault* district of France from whence comes a heavy muscatel wine of that name.

frosted fruit Fruit such as grapes or currants dipped in egg-white or syrup then tossed in fine sugar and dried on a rack.

frosting (i) Culinary term for making certain dishes appear like frost. Whipp-

ed whites of egg are spread roughly over the dish, dredged with castor sugar, and baked in a cool oven. (ii) (American) Icing.

froth To dredge meat joints in flour and heat briskly after basting to give a brown finish.

frozen food Perishables subjected to quick freezing and stored in freezer cabinets.

frozen pudding Ice pudding.

Frucht (German) Fruit.

Früchte in Backteig (German) Fruit in batter.

fructose Sugar contained in honey and fruit juices.

frugt (Danish) Fruit.

Frühstück (German) Breakfast.

fruit (i) (Botanical) Ovary of a growing plant. (ii) (Culinary) The edible part of a plant. The three main types are (a) Stone fruits – plum, cherry, etc. (b) Berry fruits. (c) Citrus fruits – orange, lemon, etc. Rhubarb, also regarded as a fruit, is in a separate category. Fruit is high in food value, and can be eaten in a wide variety of dishes as well as a form of dessert.

fruit (French) Fruit.

fruit cake Rich cake containing flour, fat, sugar, eggs, dried fruit, nuts, spices, etc. and sometimes flavoured with brandy or rum for special occasions.

fruit cocktail Mixed diced fruits served in syrup as a first course or as dessert.

fruit cup Dessert consisting of diced assorted fruits and nuts, topped with ice cream or whipped cream.

fruit de mer (French) (i) Shellfish. (ii) Dish of cold shellfish pieces.

fruit drink Beverage made from fruit juices.

fruit fool Stewed fruit (rhubarb, berries, etc.) sieved into a *purée* then, when cool, added to cream, served in a bowl or individual sundae glasses and decorated with chopped nuts, ratafia biscuits, etc. An economical version can be made by substituting custard for cream.

fruit frais (French) Fresh fruit.

fruit juice Juice extracted from fruit.

fruit kernel Soft, usually edible centre of the hard nut or stone found in fruit.

fruit knife (i) Small knife for coring, paring, or slicing fruit. (ii) Small table knife usually silver, for peeling and cutting fruit.

fruit salad Assorted fruits, usually chosen in contrasting colours and shapes. It can consist of different canned fruits, or fresh fruits, or a mixture of both.

fruit sec (French) Dried fruit.

fruit soup Cold soup made from berries, apples, peaches, pears, etc.

fruit squeezer Device for expressing fruit juices.

fruit wine Wine fermented from fruit other than grapes.

fruktvin (Norwegian) Fruit wine.

fruiterie (French) Fruit-shop.

fruits rafraîchis (French) Fruit salad.

frullo (Italian) Whisk (for eggs, etc.)

frumenty Wheat placed in a stone jar, covered with thrice the quantity of water, put in a hot oven for a short while, left there for 24 hours, which process will burst the husks and set the wheat into a thick jelly. Milk and sugar can be added to it as a breakfast food; whipped with beaten eggs; or mixed with fruit and cream and used as a sweet. In its time, frumenty has been used as a staple food, and was once a traditional Lord Mayor's dish.

fruta (Spanish) Fruit.

fruta en compota (Spanish) Stewed fruit.

fruta en conserva (Spanish) Tinned fruit.

frutería (Spanish) Fruiterer's shop.

frutta (Italian) Fruit.

frutta acerba (Italian) Unripe fruit.

frutta cotta (Italian) Stewed fruit.

frutta di mare (Italian) Seafood.

frutta e dolci (Italian) Dessert.

frutta fresca (Italian) Fresh fruit.

frutta in scatola (Italian) Tinned fruit.

frutta sciroppata (Italian) Fruit in syrup.

fruttata (Italian) Tart of candied fruits.

frutteto (Italian) Fruit orchard.

frutti di mare (Italian) Dish of small assorted fish and shellfish.

fruttiera (Italian) Fruit dish.

fry Testicles of animals, particularly lambs and sheep, which are a culinary delicacy when fried, fricasséed, etc.

fry, to To cook in hot fat, butter or oil. (i) Shallow-fry, using a small quantity of fat, for chops, steak, pancakes, etc. (ii) Deep-fry, using sufficient to cover the food, as for croquettes, potato chips, etc.

frying pan Round shallow pan with long handle for frying, often specially coated to prevent sticking.

fudge Sweetmeat made from sugar, butter, milk, cream and flavouring, with additions such as chopped nuts, *glacé* or dried fruit, chocolate, vanilla, honey, etc.

fuego (Spanish) Fire.

fuente (Spanish) Dish.

Füllung (German) Stuffing.

fumage (French) Process of smoking meat, fish, cheese, etc.

fumé (French) Smoked. (Hams, bacon, fish, etc.)

fumet (French) (i) Liquid produced by boiling foods such as chicken, fish or game in stock or wine, and used for flavouring (ii) Pleasant smell, as of cooking. (iii) Bouquet (of wine).

fungho (Italian) Mushroom.

fungho ripieno (Italian) Stuffed mushroom.

fungus Mushroom, toadstool, boletus, etc. Many fungi are edible but some are poisonous, so careful identification is essential. Their food value is slight but their flavour is an excellent addition to grilled dishes, casseroles, etc.

funnel Hollow tube-ended cone for pouring liquids and powders into containers.

funnel cake Fried cake made by dropping egg batter through the spout of a funnel.

fusil (French) Sharpening steel.

fusillo (Italian) *Pasta* shaped into thin "corkscrews".

fût (French) Tun, or large cask.

fylld blømkal (Norwegian) Stuffed cauliflower.

G

Gabel (German) Fork.

gadelle (French) Western French name for red-currant. Normandy: *gade*.

gaelic coffee Irish coffee.

Gaillac (French) White wines from the Tarn district of France.

gal Abbreviation for gallon.

galantina (Italian) Galantine.

galantine Type of meat loaf.

galantine (French) (i) Dish of white meat, rolled, pressed, and glazed, served cold. (ii) Fowl or breast of veal, boned, and stuffed with forcemeat.

galantine de dinde (French) Boned turkey or turkey *galantine*.

galathée (French) Shell-fish species resembling crayfish, cooked as for lobster or crayfish.

galerie (bordure) de plat (French) See coaster. (i)

galette (French) (i) "Twelfth cake" – a round cake made from flaky pastry. (ii) Small roll made with egg-and-cream dough.

galettoire (French) Girdle (or griddle) pan.

galichon (French) Small iced almond cake, an *Aix* speciality.

galimafrée (French) Medieval *ragoût* made of cold meat or poultry.

Gallerte (German) Gelatine.

galleta (Spanish) Biscuit.

galley Ship's kitchen, or food compartment aboard an aircraft.

galley oven Oven in a ship's galley.

galley range Cooking stove in a ship's galley.

galliano (Italian) Pale yellow Italian liqueur.

gallimaufry See *gallimafrée*.

gallina (Italian) Hen.

gallina (Spanish) Chicken.

gallina bollita (Italian) Boiled fowl.

gallina en chicha (Spanish) Chicken in red wine sauce, dish of El Salvador.

gallina faraona (Spanish) Guinea-hen.

gallinaccio (Italian) Turkey-cock.

gallinaccio brodettato (Italian) Roman dish of turkey-cock stewed with wine

121

and vegetables, served in an egg-yolk-thickened sauce.

gallinella (Italian) (i) Pullet. (ii) Moorhen

gallo (Italian) Cock.

gallo di brughiera (Italian) Wood-grouse.

gallo di montagna (Italian) Grouse.

gallon Liquid measure containing four quarts or eight pints. (Metric: 4.545 litres).

galuiha rechiada (Portuguese) Stuffed capon.

galuska (Hungarian) Soft noodles.

Gamay (French) Famous vine with a high grape yield, named for a village in Burgundy.

gamba (Spanish) Prawn.

gambellara bianco (Italian) Dry white table wine from Venetia.

gamberetto (Italian) (i) Shrimp. (ii) Small prawn.

gambero (Italian) (i) Crayfish. (ii) Large prawn.

gambra (French) European partridge, cooked as for British partridge.

gambrel Butcher's hook for hanging meat, carcasses, etc.

game Wild birds and animals hunted and eaten as food. In Britain the only game animals are deer and hare. Birds include pheasant, partridge, grouse, ptarmigan, etc. which come under the Protection of Birds Act 1954 and can only be taken in specified seasons.

game-bag Bag or net to hold game.

gammelost (Norwegian) Milk cheese.

gammon Hind-quarter of a cured side of bacon cooked whole and served as a ham, or cut into large rashers and grilled, fried or baked.

ganga (French) Pyrenees hazel grouse.

ganier (French) Judas tree.

gans (Dutch) Goose.

Gans (German) Goose.

ganso (Portuguese and Spanish) Goose.

gantois (French) Flemish spiced pastries made from butter and egg dough.

gaper (American) Large clam with a shell that gapes at each end.

gar, garfish, garpike Slender, edible fish with green bones, found off most European coasts.

garance (French) Madder-wort.

garavance Chick-pea.

garbage disposal unit Electrical device attached to waste pipe of a kitchen sink which grinds down waste food matter, so that it is flushed away.

garbanzo (Spanish) Chick-pea.

garbure (French) Rich broth of the Béarnaise district of France containing bacon, bread, cabbage, smoked sausage and seasoning.

garçon (French) Waiter.

garçon de salle (French) Restaurant waiter.

garde manger (French) (i) Larder or meat safe. (ii) Person in charge of the cold meat room or larder; larder cook.

garden warbler Small bird greatly prized as a delicacy in France.

gardevin (French) Large bottle or decanter for containing and serving wine.

gardon (French) Roach.

garganega (Italian) Sweet and dry varieties of a white table wine from Venetia.

gargotage (French) Badly dressed victuals.

gargote (French) Common or cheap restaurant.

gargotier (French) (i) Keeper of a common cookshop. (ii) One who cooks badly.

garibaldi biscuit Square or oblong biscuit made by sandwiching dried fruit between two thin layers of sweet pastry.

garide (Greek) Shrimp.

garlic Bulblike root-plant with a pungent taste. Like onions, chives, and shallots, it possesses medicinal virtues and is used as flavouring in soups, stews, salads, forcemeats, etc. Each bulb is made up of smaller bulbs called "cloves". Garlic is said to have been cultivated from earliest times and formed part of the rations of the Egyptian pyramid builders. Roman soldiers were given garlic as an excitant.

garlic bread French or Italian bread or rolls spread with garlic butter and heated.

garlic butter Butter flavoured with crushed garlic cloves.

garlic dill pickles Cucumbers pickled in brine flavoured with dill and garlic.

garlic toast Wholemeal bread slices lightly toasted then spread with garlic *purée*, sprinkled with breadcrumbs and browned in the oven.

garlic mustard Tall hedge plant with a garlic-like smell.

garlic oil Olive or salad oil infused with garlic.

garlic powder Pure garlic concentrate.

garlic salt Salt flavoured with powdered garlic.

garlic wine vinegar Wine vinegar flavoured with garlic.

Garnele (German) Shrimp.

garni (French) Garnished.

garnieren (German) To garnish.

garnish To add decorative touches to prepared dishes, i.e., sprigs of watercress or parsley, chopped nuts, fried *croûtons*, pastry *fleurons*, radish "roses" etc.

garniture (French) Garnish.

garretto di vitello stufato (Italian) Stewed veal hock and vegetables.

Gartenkresse (German) Mustard and cress.

garum (Latin) Variety of condiment made from pickled fish, much prized by the Romans, who are said to have made it from fish gills, intestines, etc.

gås (Danish, Norwegian and Swedish) Goose.

Gasthaus (German) Inn, hotel, public house.

Gasthof (German) Inn, hotel.

Gastmahl (German) Banquet.

gastronome Person knowledgeable about fine beverages and good food; an epicure.

gastronomie (French) Gastronomy. Art of good eating.

gastronomy Art of good eating.

gâteau (French) Elaborate cake or sweet with a sponge, biscuit, or pastry base and added fruit, jelly, cream, etc. as decoration.

gâteau chocolat au rhum (French) Chocolate cake with rum.

gâteau de noce (French) Wedding cake.

gâteau de potiron (French) Pumpkin pudding.

gâteau des rois (French) Twelfth-night cake.

gâteau sablé (French) Sand cake.

gâteau St. Honoré (French) Short-crust or biscuit pastry with an edging of *choux* paste, topped, when cooled, with a custard and cream mixture, and decorated with *choux* pastry balls and *glacé* cherries or crystallised petals.

gâteaux assortis (French) Assorted cakes.

gaufre (French) Wafer; waffle; a light biscuit, baked or fried in specially-constructed *gaufre* moulds of two plates, operated by handles.

gaufrette (French) Wafer biscuit.

gaufreuse (French) Pastry wheel.

gaufrier (French) Waffle iron.

gauloise (French) Small cake made of almond sponge mixture then spread with apricot jam and grilled chopped almonds.

gauloise, à la (French) Garnish of cock's combs and kidneys served (a) with soup, (b) with *vol-au-vents*.

gayette (French) Provençal sausage made from pork liver and bacon.

gazpacho (Spanish) Famous Andalusian cold soup based on raw vegetables, tomatoes and garlic.

geai (French) Jay, a bird regarded on the Continent as a delicacy when young.

geans (French) Species of cherry in many varieties, used to make *guignolet*, a liqueur speciality of *Angers*.

Gebäck (German) (i) Pastry. (ii) Roll. (iii) Cake.

Gebackener Aal (German) Speciality eel dish of the Rhineland.

gebaken (German) Baked.

Gedeck (German) (i) Place laid at table. (ii) Menu.

gefilte fisch (Jewish) Stewed or baked fish stuffed with a mixture of fish meat, breadcrumbs, and eggs.

Geflügel (German) Poultry.

Gefrorene (German) Ice cream.

gefüllt (German) Stuffed.

gefüllte Kalbsbrust (German) Stuffed breast of veal.

gefüllte Schweinerippchen (German) Pork chops stuffed with raisins, apples and toast laced with rum.

gehaktnest (Dutch) Meat loaf of minced beef, pork, or veal stuffed with breadcrumbs, eggs, onions, and spices.

gekocht (German) Boiled.

gekochtes Ei (German) Boiled egg.

gelant (French) Jellied or partly frozen.

gelatine Protein substance made chiefly from calves' heads, cartileges, tendons, etc., and marketed in powdered, flaked or sheet form. Used in table jellies, and for making aspics, desserts, etc.

gelatin dessert (American) Sweet jellies, flavoured and set in moulds.

gelato (Italian) Ice cream.

gelato di tutte frutti (Italian) Ice cream filled with candied fruit, peel, etc.

gelbe Rübe (German) Carrot.

gelée (French) Jelly.

Gelee (German) Jelly.

gelée au salop (French) Salop (or salep) jelly.

Geleemasse (German) Gelatine.

gelinotte (French) Hazel-hen, hazel-grouse.

gemischter Salat (German) Mixed salad.

Gemüse (German) Vegetable.

Gemüsehandler (German) Greengrocer.

Gemüsepudding (German) Vegetable pudding.

Gemüsesalat (German) Vegetable salad.

Gemüsesuppe (German) Vegetable soup.

gemyse (Danish) Vegetables.

gendarme (French) (i) Pickled herring. (ii) Hard Swiss sausage.

génépi (French) Wormwood.

genevrette (French) Juniper wine.

genièvre (French) (i) Gin. (ii) Juniper-berry. A blue-black berry, with an aromatic flavour, used as a flavouring in marinades, etc., also in syrups and liqueurs. The essential oil flavours gin, *Hollands, Schiedam, Schnapps,* etc.

genipap (American) West Indian fruit with a green skin and purplish juice, used in many tropical American preserves.

Genoa cake Rich fruit cake decorated with almonds.

Genoese sponge Light, rich mixture of flour, butter, sugar, eggs, used as the basis for fancy iced cakes or *petits fours,* or served as an undecorated sponge cake.

Genoise fine (French) Butter sponge cake.

Genovese, salsa (Italian) White wine sauce containing tomatoes, chopped veal, mushrooms and other vegetables.

gentian Species of plant used in the preparation of *apéritifs,* also to make *gentiane.*

gentiane (French) *Apéritif* liqueur distilled from the gentian root.

Gentsche waterzooi (Flemish) Belgian fish soup.

geoduck (American) Large chowder clam found along the Pacific Coast.

geräucherter Hering (German) Smoked herring, bloater.

gerboise (French) See jerboa.

Gericht (German) (i) Food course. (ii) Dish.

German beefsteak (American) Chopped meat eaten raw with chopped fresh onion and lemon juice, or topped with a raw egg, which is the original Hamburg steak.

German pancake (American) Stiff-batter pancakes fried lightly, then baked to a fluffy consistency.

German pound cake Similar to Genoa cake, but with less fruit and no almonds.

German sausage Many different varieties of smoked cold sausage, made of pork, veal, beef, liver, bacon or blood (usually a mixture of two or more of these ingredients) salt, spice and garlic.

German toast (American) French toast.

German-fried potatoes (American) Par-boiled potatoes fried in a pan.

germano (Italian) Wild duck, mallard.

germon (French) White-fleshed Mediterranean tuna-fish.

géromé (French) Whole milk rennet cheese made in the Vosges.

geronnene Milch (German) Curdled milk.

geröstet (German) (i) Roast. (ii) Grilled.

Gerste (German) Barley.

Gerstenschleim (German) Barley water.

Gerstensuppe (German) Barley soup.

gervais (French) Best known of the French *petit-suisse* cheese – creamy, unsalted, made from whole milk.

gesalzener Hering (German) Pickled herring.

Geschirr (German) Crockery.

Geschmack (German) Taste, flavour.

Geselchtes (German) Smoked pork.

gésier (French) Gizzard.

gesse (French) Vetch.

Getränk (German) Drink, beverage.

Getreide (German) Wheat, corn.

Gevrey-chambertin (French) Famous burgundy.

gevulde kalfsbors (Dutch) Stuffed breast of veal.

Gewürz (German) Spice (herb).

Gewürznelke (German) Clove.

Gex (French) Blue-veined whole milk cheese made in *Gex* (Ain).

gezouten haring (Dutch) Salt herring.

gezuckert (German) Candied.

ghee Clarified butter much used in Eastern cookery.

gherkin Pickled fruit of a small variety of cucumber, used in mixed pickles, as an accompaniment to cold meats and in savouries, sauces, etc., and as a garnish for cocktail titbits and cold savoury dishes.

ghiaccio (Italian) Ice.

giant bass (American) Edible black sea bass.

giant rock (American) Large edible clam.

gibelotte (French) Rabbit-stew.

gibier (French) Game; animals taken in the chase.

giblets Edible entrails of poultry such as the heart, kidney, gizzard and liver, also the neck. In French cookery the term includes the head, combs, feet, tail, wattles, etc. Hearts and gizzards are used in making gravies, and chicken, duck, and goose livers have long been considered delicacies. Cocks' combs and kidneys are often used for garnishes.

gibson (American) Cocktail made of gin and dry vermouth and served with a cocktail onion.

gigot (French) Leg of mutton.

gigot à l'ail (French) Leg of mutton with garlic cloves inserted. Garlic is sometimes boiled in three separate waters before being inserted, to modify the strong taste and penetrating flavour and smell.

gigot à sept heures, gigot à la cuillère (French) Leg of mutton which has been cooked for seven hours, when it may be carved with a spoon.

gigot d'agneau (French) Leg of lamb.

gigue (French) Haunch (of game).

gild To glaze.

gill Liquid measure, usually interpreted as a quarter pint but in some parts of Britain, particularly in the North, it often means a half pint. (Metric: 1.42 decilitres).

gilthead Any of several brilliantly-coloured marine fish such as the Mediterranean sea bream or the conner.

gimblette (French) Kind of French pastry biscuit prepared in the shape of a ring, similar to *croque-en-bouche*.

gimlet (i) Pointed steel tool for piercing casks, etc. (ii) American highball of soda water, limejuice, sugar and gin or vodka. (iii) British colonial drink of gin and lime cordial in equal proportions, well shaken.

gin Colourless spirit distilled from rye and barley or maize and flavoured with juniper berries; used as the basis of many cocktails, such as Martini, Gin Sling, Pink Gin and Bronx, and for various other long and short drinks.

gin and It Gin and Italian vermouth.

gin and tonic Gin and quinine water served with lemon or lime peel.

gin buck (American) Gin-based highball containing ginger ale and lemon or lime juice.

gin fizz Cocktail of dry gin, lemon juice, sugar and soda-water.

gin rickey (American) Highball of gin, soda water, and lime juice.

gin sling Drink of gin, Angostura bitters, lemon juice, sugar, mixed with ice and topped with water.

gin sour Drink of gin, lemon juice, powdered sugar, and orange bitters, with or without soda-water.

ginebra (Spanish) Gin.

ginepro (Italian) Juniper.

gingembre (French) Ginger.

ginger Root-stock of a plant native to the East and West Indies, although the Jamaican variety is considered the best. In the East, the young green shoots are preserved and crystallised. The dried roots are ground into powder which is used widely in cooking – for cakes, puddings, biscuits. Whole root is used in pickling and jam-making.

ginger ale Carbonated soft drink,

sweetened and flavoured with ginger, often used in punches or to dilute whisky or brandy.

ginger beer Slightly alcoholic effervescent ginger-flavoured, fermented beverage. Used alone or in punches.

ginger brandy Ginger-flavoured liqueur.

ginger cake Gingerbread.

ginger nut Crisp biscuit flavoured with ginger and other spices, brown-coloured and with a cracked surface.

ginger oil Aromatic essential oil extracted from ginger root.

ginger pop (American) Ginger ale.

ginger shortbread Shortbread mixture of plain flour, butter and sugar, with added ground and chopped ginger. Cooked as for shortbread.

ginger wine Ginger-flavoured fermented beverage with a moderate alcoholic content.

gingerade Ginger-flavoured soft drink.

gingerbread Moist brown cake flavoured with ginger and containing treacle or golden syrup; usually served cut into squares, decorated with preserved ginger. The proverb "Taking the gilt off the gingerbread" arose when treacle was substituted for honey in the 15th century. In order to disguise the darker colour of the treacle produced, the gingerbread was covered with gold leaf or gilt paper.

gingersnap Ginger nut.

ginkgo Maidenhair tree yielding a kernel used for flavouring in Japanese cookery.

ginseng Chinese medicinal herb.

girofle, clou de (French) Clove.

giraumont (French) West Indian pumpkin cooked with other gourds or used in salads.

girdle, griddle Thick, solid sheet of cast metal, usually round and slightly convex, with a half-hoop handle. Largely used in Scotland and the North of England for making drop scones, potato cakes, teacakes, etc. over the fire or other source of heat.

girdlecake Drop scone.

girella Small coloured marine fish used in *bouillabaisse*.

girelle (French) Girella.

gitane, à la (French) Dishes cooked usually in Spanish "Gypsy" fashion, with tomatoes.

gizzard Second stomach of a bird.

gjoetøst (Norwegian) Sweet-flavoured brown cheese.

glace (French) (i) Ice. Ice-cream. (ii) Concentrated stock – i.e., meat glaze.

glacé (French) (i) Glazed. Anything iced or frozen, or having a smooth and glossy surface. (ii) Drink served very cold from the refrigerator or by the addition of ice cubes.

glace à la vanille (French) Vanilla ice cream.

glace à rafraîchir (French) Ice put in drinks, etc.

glace aux fruits (French) Fruit ice.

glace de sucre (French) Icing sugar; mixed with white of egg it is called royal icing, (*glace royale*).

glace de viande (French) Meat extract or glaze. Stock or gravy reduced to the thickness of jelly; used for glazing cooked meats, etc., also for strengthening soups and sauces. (See also *extraits de viande du commerce*).

glacé fruit Fruit preserved by impregnation with a concentrated sugar syrup, used in cakes and sweet dishes, as a decoration, and as a dessert to serve at the end of a formal meal.

glacé icing Simple glossy icing made from icing sugar and water, with added flavouring.

glace royale (French) Royal icing. See *glace de sucre*

glacière (French) (i) *Timbre à glace*. Ice box. Refrigerator. (ii) Sugar-dredger.

Glas (German) Glass, tumbler.

glasieren (German) To glaze, or ice cakes, etc.

glasiert (German) Iced, glazed, frosted.

glasierte Kastanie (German) Glazed chestnut.

glass Transparent or translucent material used for tableware, cooking utensils, bottles and drinking vessels.

glassware Kitchenware and tableware made of glass.

glasswort Samphire.

Glasur (German) Icing (cake).

glayra Aromatic liqueur based on Scotch whisky.

glaze To coat a dish with a substance which imparts a glossy surface, i.e., jam or syrup glaze for flans, etc., egg-and-milk glaze for pastry, aspic jelly for meat and fish moulds, etc.

globe artichoke See artichoke.

glögg (Swedish) Hot drink of spiced red wine, with added brandy and sweet sherry.

Gloucester cheese See double Gloucester.

Gloucester pudding Steamed flour, suet, apple and mixed-peel pudding.

glucometer Tool for measuring the sugar-density of wines, syrups, etc.

glucose Basic simple sugar found in its natural state in many fruits, especially grapes, and in cane sugar. Commercial glucose is used in making sweets and some jams, and to increase the sugar content of wines and beers. All starches and sugars are converted to glucose during digestion.

Gluhwein (German) Mulled wine.

gluten Protein substance found in flour, which enables it to be made into bread. It may be isolated by washing flour in a muslin bag under running water to extract the starch.

gluten bread Wheat-flour bread, high in gluten and low in starch content, used for diabetics.

glutton (i) One who habitually eats to excess. (ii) Common name for the wolverine.

glycerine Colourless sweetish oily syrup used in confectionery, diabetic foods, and as an additive to royal icing to keep it moist.

glycerol Glycerine.

gnoccho (Italian) (i) Dumpling made of potato, flour, semolina or polenta (maize flour). (ii) *Chou* paste forced through a forcing bag into short lengths, poached and served in a white sauce.

gnoccho di patate (Italian) Potato dumpling.

gnoccho leggiero (Italian) Cheese noodle.

gnummarielli (Italian) Baby lamb entrails, spit-roasted.

goat's beard Wild salsify

goats' milk Milk from the goat, widely used for making cheese, milk puddings, and for other ordinary household purposes. Also for feeding babies allergic to cows' milk. It has a high percentage of fat and protein and a somewhat strong flavour.

gobelet (French) Goblet.

goblet (i) Bowl-shaped stemmed glass. (ii) Round silver drinking vessel.

goby, black Tiny delicate ocean and river fish in several varieties fried as for gudgeon.

godard, à la (French) Garnish for poultry and large meat cuts, containing *quenelles*, sweetbreads, truffles, and cock's combs, named for 19th century French composer, Benjamin Godard.

godiveau (French) Rich veal forcemeat *quenelles* used as a garnish.

godwit Marsh-bird, cooked in France as for woodcock.

goéland (French) Colloquial name for seagull, once eaten as Lenten fare and cooked as for goose, though with rather unpalatable flesh.

goémon (French) Seaweed.

goque (French) Speciality of *Angevin*, vegetable-stuffed beef rolls simmered, cooled, sliced and fried.

golas (Italian) Goulash.

gold apple Tomato.

gold flakes Tiny flakes of gold used for garnishing liqueurs and elegant pastries.

golden berry Cape gooseberry.

golden buck Buck rarebit. Welsh rarebit topped with a poached egg.

golden delicious Sweet yellow eating apple.

golden egg roll Bread roll made with egg yolks, vegetable dye, or saffron.

golden guinea Sparkling muscatel wine.

golden oriole Small European bird cooked in France as for lark.

golden syrup Light-coloured syrup containing various sugars, with added flavouring and colouring matter. Syrup is not quite as sweet as sugar, since it contains more water and glucose. Used to sweeten and flavour cakes, ginger-breads and puddings, to make sauces, as a filling for tarts.

Goldwasser (German) Colourless, potent

liqueur, flavoured with aniseed and orange, decorated with minute particles of gold leaf or other yellow substance. See *Danziger Goldwasser*.

golubsty (Russian) Cabbage.

gombaut, gombo Gumbo.

gomme (French) (i) Gum. (ii) Heavy sugar syrup.

goober (American) Peanut.

goober pea (American) Peanut.

Good Friday fritter Limpet collected from the rocks on the Isle of Man and traditionally fried for Good Friday supper.

goose Domesticated acquatic bird traditionally eaten at Michaelmas, also at Christmas. Geese should be eaten at not more than a year old. Roasted and served with apple or gooseberry sauce, or prepared in a variety of ways in French *cuisine* and Continental cookery. Goose livers have an excellent flavour and are made into *pâté de foie gras*.

goose egg See egg.

gooseberry Fruit of a prickly shrub yielding green berries, smooth or hairy according to variety, some of which redden deeply on ripening. Used as a dessert, and for making pies, puddings, sweets, preserves, etc.

gooseberry fool See fruit fool.

gooseberry sauce Sieved stewed gooseberries, served with goose, duck, mackerel, etc.

gooseberry vinegar Old English brew of water, gooseberries and sugar, not worked with yeast, but left to stand in a barrel for a year and in bottles for a further year before use.

gora (Russian) Small undeveloped grapes remaining on the vine after harvest.

gorcock Grouse.

goret (French) Porker – a young pig of six months, no longer suckling.

Gorgonzola Semi - hard blue - veined cheese, with a strong flavour, originating from the small town of Gorgonzola near Milan.

gorgot (American) Wheat kernels.

gosling Young goose.

Gouda Mild full-fat Dutch cheese, large, round and yellow, from Gouda, Holland.

goudale (French) *Garbure* soup with added red or white wine, in *Béarnaise* cookery.

goudse kaas taart (Dutch) Flan filled with Gouda cheese, eggs, milk and ham.

Gouffe, Jules Famous chef (1807–1877) who learned his craft under Carême and afterwards established a renowned restaurant on the *rue St. Honoré* in Paris. He published several books of cookery.

gougère (French) Burgundian egg-and-cheese pastry cake.

gougnette (French) Fried yeast doughnut.

goujon (French) Gudgeon.

goula pois, pois goulu (French) Pea of which the pod is also eaten.

goulash (Hungarian) Beef stew made with onions and paprika, in many variations.

goullasch (Italian) *Goulash*.

gourd Vegetable of the same family as the marrow, pumpkin and squash, in hundreds of varieties, some edible.

gourilos (French) Stumps of endive and chicory.

gourmand (French) Ravenous eater; a glutton.

gourmet (French) Epicure. A good judge of food and a connoisseur of wines.

gourmet exotica Unusual foods, usually canned, pickled, or otherwise preserved, such as chocolate-covered ants, and bear steaks.

gournal (French) Gurnet or gurnard.

goût (French) Taste or savour. The sense of tasting.

goûter (French) (i) Afternoon meal; a meat tea. (ii) To taste or to relish.

goveda supa (Yugoslavian) Beef soup.

goyave (French) Guava.

gragnano (Italian) Dry red wine from Campagna.

graham bread (American) Bread baked from graham or whole-wheat flour and resembling a granary loaf.

graham cracker (American) Wholemeal biscuit made of whole-wheat or graham flour.

graham flour Whole-wheat blend of flours invented in the 19th century by an American food reformer, Sylvester Graham.

grain (i) Small hard seed of corn. (ii) Smallest British measure, 1/7,000th of one pound avoirdupois.

graine de sureau (French) Elderberry.

graisse (French) Fat, suet, grease.

graisse à friture (French) Frying fat, usually made from clarified suet.

graisse de vins (French) Defect in certain white wines known as "ropiness".

gram Metric unit equal to 0.035 ounce.

gramolates (French) Type of water ice cream.

grana (Italian) Characteristic fine-grained cheese of Emilia.

grana padana (Italian) Parmesan-type cheese.

grana reggiano (Italian) Hard, pungent grating cheese made from whole milk, similar to Parmesan.

granada (Spanish) Pomegranate.

granadilla Passion fruit. Edible fruit of the passion flower, in many varieties, with delicious and refreshing flavour. Served as a dessert fruit, or made into ices, creams, jelly, etc.

granary loaf Tin-baked bread made from malted grains mixed with wheatmeal flour.

Granatapfel (German) Pomegranate.

granatina (Italian) "Cutlet" of minced beef and egg, crumbed and fried.

grancevola (Italian) Large Adriatic crab.

granchio (Italian) Crab.

granchiolino (Italian) Small crab.

grand marnier (French) Orange-flavoured golden-brown French liqueur based on fine cognac.

grand veneur (French) Brown sauce served with game and venison.

grande champagne (French) Cognac distilled in the *Charente-Maritime* department of France.

grandine syrup See *grenadine*.

granita (Italian) Sweet of crushed ice over which flavouring such as coffee, chocolate, fruit, etc. is poured.

granita di caffé (Italian) Cold coffee poured onto crushed ice.

granité (French) Light water ice.

Granny Smith Green eating apple.

grano (Spanish) Grain, cereal.

Grantham gingerbread Puffy round white gingerbread biscuits which used to be made for Fairs in Lincolnshire and Norfolk.

granulate To form or crystallize into grains.

grape Fruit of the vine, grown in enormous variety, but low in food value. Wine grapes are, generally, smaller than dessert grapes. Certain varieties are dried to form raisins, sultanas and currants, used in cakes, confectionery, puddings, pastries, etc. Grapes can be made into grape jelly.

grape juice Juice expressed from grapes.

grapefruit Large yellow-skinned citrus fruit originating from China and the East. Its slightly bitter flavour makes it popular as an appetizer. It can be mixed with other fruits for fruit cocktails and salads and also made into preserves.

grapefruit juice Juice expressed from the grapefruit, available canned, sweetened and unsweetened.

grapefruit knife Small knife with a curved and serrated blade for coring and sectioning grapefruit.

grapefruit spoon Spoon with a serrated edge for removing sections of citrus fruit, especially grapefruit.

grappa (Italian) Brandy or gin, made from distilled wine.

gras (French) Fat, plump.

gras, au (French) (i) Dressed with rich meat gravy. (ii) Cooked in rich gravy or sauce.

grasa (Spanish) Fat, grease.

gras-double (French) Tripe.

grate To shave food into small particles or shreds for easier digestion or assimilation; or for making decorative or savoury toppings, such as chocolate on desserts or cheese on savoury dishes or salads, etc.

gratella (Italian) Grill, gridiron.

grater Utensil with a rough surface for grating food.

grateron (French) Rennet.

graticola, alla (Italian) (i) Grilled food. (ii) Food grilled over charcoal.

gratin (French) Food baked with an encrusted or browned surface; such as breadcrumbs strewn over meat, fish, macaroni cheese and similar dishes, and browned under the grill or in the oven. In Britain, *au gratin* usually refers to food with a cheese-flavoured crusty top.

gratinata, **pasta** (Italian) Macaroni cheese.

gratiner (French) To brown the surface of the contents of a dish.

gratton (French) Small square of pork fat and skin, cooked for a long time until the skin is crisp and the square has risen like a small fritter.

Graupe (German) Groats.

gravenche (French) Lake fish of the salmon family, cooked as for river-trout.

Graves (French) Red and white wines produced from the vineyards of the *Graves* district of Bordeaux.

gravlaks (Norwegian) Smoked salmon.

gravlax (Swedish) Marinated or pickled salmon.

gravy (i) Juice obtained from meat in cooking, especially from roasting joints. (ii) Brown sauce made from meat juices to serve with roasts and grills (See gravy sauce).

gravy boat Boat-shaped receptacle with a pouring lip and a handle, used for serving gravy.

gravy browning See browning.

gravy sauce Sauce made from drippings of meat, with added thickening agent, water and seasoning.

grayling Freshwater fish of the trout family and cooked similarly. It is found principally in the rivers in the north of England.

grease Rendered animal fat.

greben (Jewish) Cracklings rendered from chicken or goose fat.

greco (Italian) Dry white table wine from Umbria.

greco di tufo (Italian) Dry white table wine from Campania.

Greek olive Ripe black olive preserved in brine and olive oil.

Greek salad Salad of vegetables, feta cheese, anchovies, capers, etc. in an oil and vinegar dressing.

green butter Savoury spread for biscuits, sandwiches, etc. Made from pounded, sieved watercress, mixed with creamed

butter, flavoured with salt and cayenne pepper.

green *Chartreuse* Stronger of the two liqueurs invented in the 17th century by the Carthusian monks in the Grenoble area, who used well over 100 herbs in its making. The other, less potent, is yellow *Chartreuse*.

green corn (American) Tender ears of sweet corn.

green crab Edible crab found in tidal waters.

green duck Young duckling.

green ginger Young shoots of the reed-like ginger plant, used fresh in oriental cooking, also preserved in syrup or crystallised and served as a dessert.

green goose Young goose (gosling) not more than four months old.

green laver Edible seaweed.

green olive Unripe olive pickled in brine and vinegar, sometimes stoned and stuffed.

green onion (American) Scallion, spring onion.

green pea Pea, grown in pod.

green pepper Immature fruit of the red pepper, used as a garnish for savoury dishes or salads, or stuffed with a savoury mixture and grilled or baked.

green tea Chinese tea leaf processed to preserve the green colour. Rather astringent in taste.

greengage Yellow-green plum, with a fine flavour. The most famous is the variety *Reine Claude*. Greengages are mainly used as a dessert fruit, but may also be boiled, stewed, and made into tarts, puddings, and jam.

greengrocer Dealer in fruits and vegetables.

greengrocery Fresh fruits and vegetables.

grenade (French) Pomegranate. The fruit of the pomegranate tree (*grenadier*), largely used for preserves, jellies, and syrup.

grenadin (French) Small heart shaped slice of veal larded and braised.

grenadine (French) Syrup made from the expressed juice of the pomegranate, and sugar. Also known as Grandine syrup.

grenki (Russian) Bread slices topped with

grated cheese and melted butter, heated to melt and brown the cheese and served with *bortsch.*

grenouille (French) Edible frog.

gressin (French) Dietary bread.

grey mullet Coastal fish with delicate white flesh, cooked as for bass.

greyfish Dogfish, shark or pollock.

grianneau (French) Young grouse.

griddle (American) Girdle.

griddle cake (American) Girdle cake.

gridiron, grill Grating placed before or over the fire; used for broiling or grilling.

Griesknödel (German) Semolina dumpling.

Griess (German) (i) Semolina. (ii) Groats

Griessuppe (German) Semolina soup.

griglia, alla (Italian) Grilled.

grignon (French) Piece of dry, hard-baked bread.

gril (French) Gridiron or grill.

grill To cook over or under an open flame or other direct heat.

grill Gridiron.

grillade (French) Grilled meat.

grille (French) Cake rack or tray.

grillé (French) Grilled.

grillette (French) Collop of grilled pork.

grillroom Restaurant specialising in grilled meats.

grilse Young salmon which has been to sea once, cooked as for larger salmon.

Grimod de la Reynière Famous gastronome, (1758–1838), author of the *Almanac des Gourmands.*

grind (i) To reduce to powder or small particles by means of a food mill, etc. (ii) (American) To mince or crush into small pieces or flakes.

grinder (American) Mincer or electric food pulveriser.

grindstone Circular stone set in a stand and turned to sharpen cleavers, knives, etc.

griotte (French) Dark-red "Armenian" or Morello cherry used for *compôte* and jam.

grisette (French) Edible mushroom.

griskin (i) Chine of pork. (ii) Thin piece of pork loin.

griskin of pork Top of the spare-rib. In a small pig the griskin and spare-rib

are not separated, sometimes called chine of pork.

grissini (Italian) Breadsticks; pencil-shaped rolls baked until hard and crisp, and eaten with cocktails or at lunch or dinner.

gristle Part of the connective tissue of an animal body, forming the soft skeleton which supports the other tissues and organs. Its principal constituent, collagen, is converted into gelatine by prolonged cooking.

grits (American) See hominy.

griva (Italian) (i) Thrush. (ii) Blackbird.

grive (French) Thrush.

grivelette (French/Spanish) Small thrush from San Domingo.

groats Hulled and coarsely-crushed grain of oats used for making porridge, gruel and broth.

groentesoep (Dutch) Vegetable soup.

grog Beverage of spirits (usually rum), hot water, and sugar.

grondin (French) Generic name of many varieties of small fish including gurnard, roach, etc.

grongo (Italian) Conger-eel.

grønnsaker (Norwegian) Vegetables.

grønsager (Danish) Vegetables.

grönsaker (Swedish) Vegetables.

gros-sel (French) Coarse salt.

groseille (French) Currant, red, white or black.

groseille à macquereau (French) Gooseberry.

grosse-pièce (French) Large joint of meat or poultry.

ground chuck (American) Minced beef.

ground meat (American) Minced meat.

ground rice Pulverised rice (less fine than rice flour) used for milk puddings, moulds, etc., and for giving a drier texture to cakes and added crispness to biscuits.

ground round steak (American) Minced beef taken from the U.S. cut, round of beef.

ground nut Peanut.

groundnut (peanut) oil Clear oil extracted from peanuts and used both in cookery and as a table oil for salads, etc.

grouper (American) Edible fish of the bass type.

grouse Moor fowl in several varieties but usually referring to the Scotch or Red grouse of which the shooting season runs from August 12 to December 10. Cooked by roasting, or in pies, etc. after being well hung. Other varieties are: Black grouse (cooked as for (pheasant) Hazel grouse or hazel hen, (cooked as for partridge) and the best-known variety in France. American varieties include Ruffed grouse, Blue grouse, Black grouse, Prairie chicken.

groux (French) Gruel made from buckwheat flour.

grovbrød (Norwegian) Rye or brown bread.

groviera (Italian) *Gruyère* cheese.

gruau (French) (i) Husk of the wheat in which the grain is encased. (ii) Gruel made from oatmeal or fine potato pasta.

gruau d'avoine (French) Oatmeal.

gruel Thin porridge generally made of finely-ground oatmeal, but also of barley and other farinaceous foods.

grüne Bohne (German) (i) Green bean. French bean. (iii) String bean.

Grünersalat (German) Lettuce.

Grünkohl (German) Kale.

grunt (American) (i) Tropical edible fish. (ii) New England dessert of biscuit dough and fruit.

Grünwarenhandler (German) Greengrocer.

Grünzeug (German) (i) Greens. (ii) Herbs.

Gruyère (i) Swiss village celebrated for its cheese. (ii) Emmenthaler-type hard Swiss cheese, honey-combed with holes and well flavoured. Now gruyère-types of cheese are made all over Europe and in America. (iii) *Crème de Gruyère*. Processed mild-flavoured cheese, sold in foil-wrapped triangles.

grytstek (Swedish) Pot roast.

guacamole (American) Mashed avocados, tomatoes, onions and lime juice, often used as a dip.

guancia di maiale (Italian) Bath chap.

guava Tropical and sub-tropical seeded fruit of the guava tree, made into jams and jellies or eaten raw.

guava nectar Canned guava juice.

guayaba (Spanish) Guava.

gudgeon Small, delicately-fleshed lake and river fish, usually cooked as for smelts, fried or grilled after soaking in salted water.

guéridon (French) Small pedestal serving table.

Guernsey Brown dairy cattle originally bred in Guernsey, Channel Islands, yielding milk with a high cream content.

Gugelhupf (German) Yeast cake with raisins and almonds, baked in a fluted tin.

guignard (French) Variety of small plover.

guignette (French) (i) Sand-piper. (ii) Mollusc, the *littorine*.

guimauve (French) Marshmallow plant.

guineo (Cuban-Spanish) Banana.

guinguette (French) Restaurant or pleasure garden where music and dancing are provided.

guinea fowl Bird of the turkey species with delicate flesh and bluish-grey plumage with white dots. It has the advantage of being in season all the year; it should be well hung before roasting, and well basted to avoid dryness.

Guinness Rich dark stout originally brewed in Dublin, from barley, water, hops and yeast, the yeast having been passed down in direct line from the original yeast first used two hundred years ago.

guisado (Spanish) Stew.

guisante (Spanish) Pea.

guisar (Spanish) To cook.

guiso (Spanish) Dish.

Gulasch (German) *Goulash*.

gulasch di selvaggina (Italian) Game goulash.

gulf flounder Edible flatfish from the Gulf of Mexico.

Gullasch (German/Austrian) *Goulash*.

Gullaschsuppe (German/Austrian) *Goulash* soup.

gulyás (Hungarian) *Goulash*.

gum (i) Sticky substance obtained from various trees and plants which hardens on exposure to the air. (ii) Sweetmeat containing gum or an equivalent, usually flavoured with fruit (and for cough lozenges a medicinal ingredient as well).

gum arabic Acacia gum used in jujubes, pastilles and gum-drops, also in medicines.

gum tragacanth Gum obtained from the tragacanth plant and used to make lozenges firm and chewy, also used in ice-cream powders and for thickening creams, jellies, pastes, and stiff Royal icing.

gumbo (i) Okra, the annual pod of a tree of the hibiscus family used for soups and pickles, also eaten as a vegetable. (ii) (American) Soup thickened with gumbo or okra pods.

gungo pea (i) Tropical pea resembling the green pea, found in greenish-brown pods. (ii) Dried pea of above, brown in colour, cooked as for haricot beans. Used in African and West Indian cookery.

Gurke (German) (i) Cucumber. (ii) Pickled gherkin.

Gurkensalat (German) Cucumber salad.

Gurkensalat mit Rahm (German) Cucumber salad with sour cream.

Gurkensosse (German) Pickled cucumber sauce.

gurneau (French) Species of gurnet and cooked similarly.

gurnet, gurnard Fish in many varieties, the red, the piper, the streaked, the grey, and the little gurnard, which emit a grunting sound when caught. The red gurnet or gurnard is caught in trawls on the west coast of England at all seasons of the year. Cooked as for haddock.

gusta (Spanish) Menu.

gustar (Spanish) To taste, to try.

gusto (Spanish) (i) Taste. (ii) Pleasure.

gut (i) Alimentary canal of animals, etc.
(ii) To clean out the inside of a fish, removing entrails before cooking.

gut durchgebraten (German) Well-done meat.

guten Appetit (German) Good appetite.

Guyenne (French) Large province of France including the *Gironde, Dordogne Lot, Aveyron, Lot-et-Garonne, Tarn-et-Garonne*. Famous especially for truffles, garlic, *Roquefort* cheese, geese and duck livers and allied products, and for good red and white wines, as well as *Armagnac*.

gymnètre (French) Cod-like Mediterranean fish, cooked as for cod.

gypsy bread Fruit bread made with black molasses.

haba (American) Broad bean, lima bean.

Habanera (Spanish) Food prepared with many spices, often called *à la Habanera* (Havana-style).

habiller (French) To dress food.

hachage (French) Chopping of food.

haché (French) Minced meat, finely sliced meat. See also *hachis*.

hachee (Dutch) Beef hash.

hacher-menu (French) To mince meat finely.

hachis (French) Hash. (i) Hashed meat. A favourite form of redressing cooked meat. (ii) Chopped food.

hachoir (French) Mincer or chopper.

hackberry (American) Small sweet berry used for making preserves.

Hackbrett (German) Chopping-board.

Hackfleisch (German) Mincemeat.

Hackmesser (German) (i) Cleaver. (ii) Meat knife.

haddie (Scottish) Haddock.

haddock Fish resembling the cod but smaller and distinguished by a dark spot on either side of the body beyond the gills (said in legend to be the thumb and forefinger marks of St. Peter when taking tribute money out of the mouth of a fish of this species). Haddock is cooked as for cod but the flesh is dryer. Haddock is also commercially smoked and as such makes excellent savoury meals. Most famous are the Scottish Finnan Haddies.

Haferbrei (German) Porridge.

Haferflockensuppe (German/Austrian). Oat soup.

Hafergrütze (German) Oatmeal, ground oats.

haggis National dish of Scotland. A kind of globular liver sausage made from the liver, lights and heart of a sheep, finely chopped, mixed with oatmeal, suet and seasoning, then inserted in a sheep's paunch and boiled for several hours.

Hahn (German) Cockerel.

hake Long and slender white marine fish, with a pointed snout and large mouth; its flesh is close-textured and

135

delicately flavoured. Hake is available all the year round, and is cooked as for cod.

halaszle (Hungarian) Fish stew.

halbran, halebran (French) Young wild duck cooked as for duck.

half-and-half (American) Half cream, half milk.

half-moon (American) Perch-like edible marine fish of the Pacific.

half om half (Dutch) Sweet brownish-red liqueur.

half pint Liquid measure containing (British) 10 fluid ounces, (American) 8 fluid ounces.

half pound Dry measure containing 8 ounces.

halibut Very large North Atlantic flatfish. Best for flavour when young (about 3 lb.) in season from March to October. Larger ones are best from August to April. Halibut can be grilled, steamed, cooked as for brill or served with a piquant sauce.

halibut liver oil Oil extract from halibut, a particularly rich source of vitamins A and D.

halleves (Hungarian) Cod stewed with root vegetables.

halva (Turkish) Sweetmeat made of crushed almonds or crushed sesame seeds mixed with honey or syrup.

halva (Russian) Sweetmeat made of butter, flour, sugar and nuts (optional).

ham (i) Correctly, the hind leg of pork, when it is salted and dry-cured, or smoked. (ii) Term also applied to the meat from pork shoulder similarly treated. (See separate entries for York ham, etc.)

ham hock Cut of ham just above the foot.

ham shoulder Cut taken from front leg of pork.

hamantaschen (Jewish) Three-cornered pastry filled with prunes or poppy seeds, baked for the Jewish feast of Purim in memory of their deliverance from the plot of Haman.

hambre (Spanish) Hunger.

Hamburg (i) German breed of poultry. (ii) Variety of black grape.

hamburger Meat patty made of minced beef, pork and beef combined, or minced vegetables, baked or grilled and served on a round bread roll, plain or garnished.

hamburger press Device for shaping hamburgers.

hamburger roll Soft round white sliced bread roll on which hamburgers are served.

hamburger steak Beef hamburger.

Hamchen (German) Knuckle of pork.

hamkins North of England term for hand of pork.

Hammel (German) Mutton.

Hammelfleisch (German) Mutton.

Hammelkeule (German) Leg of mutton.

hamper (i) Large basket, used to contain food eaten on picnics. (ii) Food put together in presentation form.

Hampshire (i) (American) Breed of white-and-black belted pigs. (ii) Mutton-producing, hornless sheep originally bred in Hampshire.

hanche (French) Haunch, as applied to leg and loin part of venison, mutton or lamb.

hand cheese (American) German type sour-milk cheese.

hand of pork Fore-leg of a pig, an economical joint which can be salted and boiled, roasted or used for savoury dishes.

hang To expose meat or game to the air (suitably protected) in order to allow the meat to "ripen" before cooking and thus become tender when cooked.

hansa (Norwegian) Type of beer from Bergen.

hanya (Arabic) "Good health!"

har chow fun (Chinese) Fried rice with prawns.

hard cake Old Yorkshire tea-cake made of flour, butter, lard, baking powder, volatile salts and cold water.

hard sauce Sauce served with Christmas and other rich puddings, made with butter and castor or brown sugar and flavoured with brandy or rum, which becomes firm when cold.

hardbake Sweetmeat made of almonds, molasses and sugar.

hard-ball stage Stage in sweet-making when the syrup, as it is dropped into cold water, forms a hard ball, (245 deg. F to 250 deg. F.).

hard-boiled Cooked until hard, (usually applied to eggs).

hard-crack stage As hard-ball stage but at temperature 325 deg. F.

hardkogt aeg (Danish) Hard-boiled egg.

hardekookt eier (Dutch) Hard-boiled egg.

hard-shelled clam (American) Quahog.

hardtack Hard unsalted ship's biscuit or bread made of flour and water.

hardware Household and kitchen equipment.

hare Wild animal resembling the rabbit in appearance but larger and with darker, richer flesh. When paunched, skinned and jointed it is jugged, roasted, braised, or used for *fricassée* or soup.

hareng (French) Herring.

hareng frais (French) Fresh herring.

hareng fumé (French) Smoked herring, bloater.

hareng mariné (French) Pickled herring.

hareng salé (French) Salt herring.

hareng saur (French) Kippered herring.

harenguet (French) Sprat.

haricot (French) (i) Bean. (ii) Stew of meat and beans.

haricot bean Name given to a wide range of plants of which the best known is the French or kidney bean. In Britain the name applies particularly to the dried white seeds of dwarf or climbing haricot bean plants. They can be served as a vegetable or used in soups, stews, etc. They require pre-soaking and long, slow cooking. Other varieties of haricot beans are green, purple, brown or red, and vary widely in size.

haricot de lima (French) Lima bean.

haricot flageolet (French) Flageolet bean, a variety of kidney bean.

haricot mutton Thick meat stew or *ragoût*, using neck of mutton with the breast attached.

haricot rouge (French) Kidney bean.

haricot vert (French) French bean, green bean.

harina (Spanish) Flour.

haring (Dutch) Herring.

haringsla (Dutch) Herring salad.

harput keufta (Russian) Armenian stuffed meat balls.

harvard beets (American) Sweet-and-sour dish of small whole beets served hot in vinegar-flavoured sauce.

harvest fish (American) Edible fish found in warm Atlantic waters.

Hase (German) Hare.

Haselnuss (German) Filbert, hazelnut.

Hasenklein (German) Jugged hare.

Hasenkuchen (German) Hare *pâté*.

Hasenpfeffer (German) Stew of hare meat marinated in pickling spices and vinegar.

hash (i) Dish of left-over chopped meat and chopped vegetables, usually potatoes, browned in a frying pan. (ii) Diced, cooked left-over meat, re-heated in a well-flavoured sauce.

hash house (American) Low-class or cheap café.

hashed-brown potatoes (American) Parboiled potatoes, chopped and fried until brown.

haslet Pig's fry.

hasty pudding (i) Simple pudding of boiled milk and sugar, with tapioca, sago, semolina or flour to thicken, served hot with sugar, jam or treacle. (ii) American dessert of cornmeal, milk and molasses.

hâtelet (French) Small silver skewer garnished with cut vegetables, truffles, mushrooms, cock's combs, etc., used for ornamenting dishes.

hatelette, hatelle (French) Small pieces of meat roasted on a skewer.

hâtereau (French) Sliced pig's liver, wrapped in pig's caul and cooked on skewers.

hâteur (French) Formerly an officer in the Royal kitchens, whose duty it was to see that all meat was properly prepared and correctly dressed.

hâtiveau (French) (i) Early pear. (ii) Also other early fruits.

haunch Hindquarters of ox or venison.

Hauptmahl (German) Main meal; dinner.

Hausen (German) Sturgeon.

Haut-Brion (French) Highly esteemed Bordeaux wine from the Graves district of France.

haut goût (French) (i) Fine taste, high

flavour, strong seasoning. (ii) (Scottish) Bad or tainted.

Haut-sauternes (French) White Bordeaux wines.

hautboy Species of white strawberry, delicately flavoured.

havercake (Scottish) Oatcake.

haw Hawthorn berry.

hay box cookery Method of cooking food slowly without constant attention, by padding a large wooden box with clean hay, and making two or three holes to fit saucepans. The food is brought to boiling point before being placed in the box and re-heated before serving.

hazel hen, hazel grouse Game bird, the ruffed grouse, with white tender flesh of unique flavour, prepared as for partridge.

hazelnut Fruit of the hazel nut or cobnut tree found all over Europe. Cultivated varieties include the Filbert, Cob, and Barcelona. Hazelnuts are used as dessert and for flavouring and decorating cakes, biscuits, confectionery, etc.

head Animal head (calf, pig, etc.) containing a large amount of well-flavoured meat, especially the tongue and brains. The remaining meat can be made into pies, scalloped dishes, brawn, etc.

head cheese (American) Brawn. Jellied mould made of boiled beef, lamb or pig offal meats: feet, heads, hearts, and tongues.

head lettuce (American) Variety of lettuce with a compact head.

heady Descriptive term for wines rich in alcohol which "go to one's head".

health food Fruits, nuts, and other special products, sold chiefly in health-food stores.

health salad (American) Salad of apples, carrots, and cucumbers cut into strips, seasoned with lemon juice and salt, and served with sour cream.

heart Offal. The hearts of sheep, calves and bullocks require trimming, soaking in salted water and long, slow cooking. They can be roasted, baked or stewed.

hearth-cake Pastry of unleavened dough baked under the ashes in the hearth, made in all French provinces.

heather ale Mild Scottish brew of heather blossoms, honey, hops, spices, and yeast.

heavy cream (American) Double cream.

Heber (German) Siphon.

Hecht (German) Pike.

hedgehog Insect-eating mammal with prickly exterior. Edible, usually baked.

hedgehog tipsy cake Eighteenth-century cold sweet made from shaped sponge cake soaked in wine or fruit juice, with apricot jam powdered chocolate, blanched almonds, and served surrounded by syllabub.

Hefe (German) Yeast.

Hefeteig (German) Leavened dough.

Heidelbeere (German) Bilberry, blueberry.

Heidelbeerstrudel (German) Bilberry *strudel.*

heifer beef Meat from a young cow.

heilbot (Dutch) Halibut.

Heilbutt (German) Halibut.

Heineken (Dutch) Beer brewed in Rotterdam.

helado (Spanish) Ice cream

helfar (Spanish) To freeze.

helgeflundra (Swedish) Halibut.

helianthi (French) Sunflower.

helleflynder (Danish) Halibut.

helleflyndre (Norwegian) Halibut.

helva (Arabic) Halva.

hen Female domestic fowl.

hen tureen Tureen made of glazed pottery in the form of a hen sitting on a basket of eggs.

Henne (German) Hen.

herb Plant with no woody stem above ground; aromatic plant used in cooking to improve the flavour of soups, stews, etc. Herbs are best used fresh but can be dried for winter use. See separate entries for basil, marjoram, thyme, etc.

herb butter Fresh herbs (chopped parsley, thyme, tarragon, chives, etc.) added to creamed butter and used as a savoury sandwich spread, or, with added lemon juice, as a sauce for fish or meat.

herb bouquet See *bouquet garni.*

herb-ivy Species of chive used to flavour salads and sauces.

herb vinegar Young, fresh, dry herbs (mint, tarragon, thyme, etc.), placed in a jar, covered with vinegar, left for about 3 weeks, shaken at intervals, then strained and bottled.

herbes (French) Herbs.

Hering (German) Herring.

hérisson (French) Hedgehog.

hermit (American) Biscuit containing molasses, brown sugar and cinnamon.

hermitage (French) Rich, purple-red Rhône valley wine, with a special bouquet.

Herr Ober! (German) Waiter!

herring Small marine food fish, rich in protein, fat and vitamins A and D, caught in great quantities in northern waters, at their best from June to December. A good source of protein, they are fried, grilled, canned, etc. and are preserved as bloaters, kippers, rollmops, salt herrings. Herring roes make a delicious savoury.

hervido (Spanish) Steamed.

Heurigen (German) Light Austrian wine.

hibachi (Japanese) Portable brazier for grilling food over a charcoal fire.

hickory nut (American) Type of walnut grown in North America, the best known being the pecan nut, used in cakes, biscuits, and confectionery.

hickory-smoking (American) Hams, bacon and cheese smoked over hickory-wood shavings.

hielo (Spanish) Ice.

hígado (Spanish) Liver.

high tea Substantial knife-and-fork meal served with tea from about five p.m.

highball (American) Tall drink, usually iced, made from brandy, gin, rum, vodka, or whisky, with added Coco-Cola, ginger ale, soda water, or plain water.

higo (Spanish) Fig.

Himbeere (German) Raspberry.

Himbeergeist (German) Raspberry brandy.

Himbeersaft (German) Raspberry juice.

hind Female red deer.

hindbær med fløde (Danish) Raspberries with cream.

hindle wakes Lancashire recipe for an old boiling fowl steamed after being stuffed with prunes soaked in lemon juice.

hindquarter Hind leg and loin of a side of meat.

hipogloso (Spanish) Halibut.

hippocras Mediaeval wine drink, sweetened with honey and flavoured with herbs and spices.

hirino tis souvlas (Greek) Roast sucking pig.

Hirn (German) Brains.

Hirn Salat (German) Brain salad.

Hirnsuppe (German) Brain soup.

hirondelle (French) Swallow.

Hirschkeule (German) Haunch of venison.

Hirse (German) Millet.

hiyar salatasi (Turkish) Cucumber salad.

hocco Gallinaceous bird with white delicate flesh, found in equatorial Central America and bred in France. Cooked as for turkey, which it resembles.

hochepot (French) Mixed stew made of pigs' ears, tails of beef, mutton, and bacon, etc., with sliced vegetables.

hochequeue (French) Wagtail.

hock (i) Strictly, the wine made at Hochheim, in Germany but now the term for white wines from the Rhine districts, such as *Liebfraumilch*, (ii) Joint of meat from the leg, as in hock of bacon.

hoecake (American) Corncake, so named because early in American history corncake was baked on the heated blade of a hoe.

hog Domesticated swine.

hog banana (American) Red-skinned cooking banana.

hog chitterlings Pig's intestines.

hog pudding French sausage made of pork.

hog trotters Pig's feet.

hogen mogen (American) Strong liquor.

hog-fish Spiny-headed fish used in *bouillabaisse* or other fish soups also known as "Sea Devil".

hog-flesh Pork.

hog-meat Pork.

hog-plum West Indian tree of the

cashew family, the fruit being relished by hogs.

hog's fat Fat from pig's kidneys and fillet, used in making Black puddings.

hog's grease Hog fat or pork lard.

hogshead (i) (British) Beer barrel holding 54 gallons. (ii) Cask containing 56 U.K. gallons of rum or 54 gallons of sherry, or 46 gallons of claret.

hog's head cheese Pork brawn.

Hollandaise (French) Sauce made with butter, egg-yolks, and lemon juice or vinegar, served with eggs, fish and vegetables. *À la Hollandaise* – in Dutch style.

Holland gin Dutch gin.

Hollands Gin distilled in Holland from barley, malt, rye and juniper berries. The best known is Schnapps.

hollyhock Plant yielding a nourishing starch flour from its roots.

holothurie (French) Sea slug.

Holstein-friesian Black-and-white dairy cattle, originally developed in Friesland, Holland; the breed gives the highest milk yield, although the milk has a low butterfat content.

holubsti (Russian) Ukranian stuffed cabbage.

Holunderwein (German) Elderberry wine.

Holzapfel (German) Crabapple.

homard (French) Lobster.

home-brew Home-made alcoholic beverage.

home-freezing Preserving food, after correct preparation, in a freezer unit operating at –18 deg. C.

hominy (American) Maize grits used for porridge, etc.

hominy grits (American) Grains of hominy served at breakfast.

homogenised milk Milk pumped through a fine aperture at high pressure to break down the fat and distribute it evenly so that no "cream" forms on top.

hone To sharpen (knife blades, etc.)

hone (Danish) Chicken.

honey Natural liquid sugar prepared by bees from flower nectar, used mainly as a preserve but also in making sweetmeats and substituting for sugar in cakes, puddings, etc. It is obtainable (a) in the comb, (b) as a clear honey and

(c) solid. The latter is clear honey which has solidified.

honey bee (American) Cocktail of Jamaica rum, honey, and lime juice.

honey cake Cake made with honey used in part substitution for sugar.

honeycomb (i) Second stomach of a ruminant, the reticulum. (ii) Mass of waxy cells formed by bees and used by them to store honey.

honeycomb mould Light dessert egg jelly with added whipped egg white, which sets into a jelly layer topped with a fluffy "honeycomb" layer.

honeydew melon Smooth-skinned oval melon with sweet fragrant greenish flesh.

honey-pot Variety of grape.

Hongroise, à la (French) Dishes cooked in Hungarian style with cream sauce seasoned with paprika.

Honig (German) Honey.

Honigkuchen (German) Gingerbread.

Honigwabe (German) Honeycomb.

hooch Slang for rough liquor, usually illicit.

hood Metal canopy above an oven or range to absorb excess heat and cooking fumes.

hop Ripened bitter catkin-like flower of the hop vine used to flavour medicines and beer. The tender male shoots are eaten as a vegetable in France and Belgium.

hopping John (American) Southern States stew of beans or black-eye peas, bacon and red peppers.

hop-shoot See hop.

hora de comer (Spanish) Dinner-time.

horchata (Spanish) Almond-flavoured soft drink.

horehound Herb yielding an extract for flavouring cakes, etc., once used in cough mixtures.

horn chestnut Water chestnut.

hors d'œuvre (French) Small cold or hot snacks served as an appetizer at the beginning of a meal, consisting of either a single item or a mixture of foods and tit-bits.

hors d'œuvre **dish** Special dish divided into sections for serving mixed *hors d'œuvre*.

horseflesh Horsemeat, prepared for human consumption in many parts of Europe, but in Britain used only as food for domestic animals.

horsemeat Meat cut from the carcase of a horse.

horseradish Species of scurvy grass with a root of peculiarly hot flavour, which makes an excellent relish, stimulating the appetite and promoting digestion. Used grated as a garnish and in sauces.

horse's neck Long drink of ice cubes, ginger ale and a long spiral of lemon peel. A "Stiff Horse's Neck" is made by adding a dash of Angostura bitters and two measures of spirits.

hortatiza (Spanish) Vegetable.

hot buttered rum Drink composed of dark rum, hot water, sugar, cloves and a dab of butter.

hot cake (American) Thick batter pancake.

hot-cross bun Yeast bun (traditionally served for breakfast on Good Friday) flavoured with spice and with a cross on top, made by (a) cutting the buns with a knife before putting them to prove, (b) marking a cross with pastry trimmings which are removed after the the bun is cooked, or (c) by forming cross with candied peel.

hot dog (American) Hot cooked pork' or frankfurter sausage served in a soft bread roll.

hot plate (i) Flat top surface of a cooker. (ii) Similar plate, heated independently, for keeping food hot.

hot-pot Baked stew or casserole dish made with meat or fish topped with a layer of potatoes, which is browned by removing the lid 20 to 30 minutes before cooking is completed.

hot pot (Dutch) Pork chops and potatoes.

hot sandwich Hot roll, bap, or bread toasted on one side only and filled as required.

hot toddy Drink consisting of hot water, whisky, lemon, cloves, cinnamon and sugar.

hot water crust pastry Pastry for raised pies, such as pork pies, made by pouring lard melted in milk or water over the flour and mixing to a paste.

hotch-potch Stew of pigs' ears and tails, breast of beef, breast and shoulder of mutton, together with mixed, sliced vegetables.

hotchpotchsoppa (Swedish) Thin stew.

hothouse products Food such as grapes, tomatoes, etc., grown out of season under glass by special forcing methods.

houblon (French) Hop (vine).

howtowdie (Scottish) Boiled chicken with poached eggs and spinach.

hr. Abbreviation for hour.

huckleberry (American) Whortleberry; a black or dark red fruit resembling the blueberry and used for pies, preserves, ice cream, etc.

huerta (Spanish) (i) Kitchen garden. (ii) Orchard.

hueso (Spanish) (i) Bone. (ii) Fruit-stone.

huevo (Spanish) Egg.

huevo cocido (Spanish) Boiled egg.

huevo duro (Spanish) Hard-boiled egg.

huevo escalfado (Spanish) Poached egg.

hueve estrellado (Spanish) Fried egg.

huevo frito (Spanish) Fried egg.

huevo pasado por agua (Spanish) Soft-boiled egg.

huevo revuelto (Spanish) Scrambled egg.

huevo y tocino (Spanish) Bacon and egg.

huffkin Traditional English tea-bread from Kent, thick, flat and oval, with a hole in the middle.

huguenote (French) Pipkin.

Huhn (German) Chicken.

Hühnchen (German) Pullet, chicken.

Hühnerbrühe (German) Chicken broth.

Hühnersalat (German) Chicken salad.

Hühnersuppe (German) Chicken soup.

huile (French) Oil.

huile, à l' (French) Done in oil or served with oil, vinaigrette, etc.

huile blanche (French) Poppyseed oil.

huile de crustaces (French) Shellfish oil.

huile de mais (French) Corn-oil.

huile de noix (French) Walnut oil.

huile d'œillette (French) Field-poppy oil, also known as *olivetti*.

huile d'olive (French) Olive oil.

huile de palme (French) Palm oil.

huile de sésame (French) Sesame oil.

huilier (French) Condiment set.

huître (French) Oyster.

huître de Zélande (French) Zeeland oyster.

huître en coquille (French) Oyster served in its shell.

huître en cheval (French) Oyster rolled in a bacon slice, grilled, and served on toasted or fried bread *croûte*.

huître frite (French) Fried oyster.

huître marinée (French) Pickled oyster.

huîtrier (French) Oyster-catcher.

hull (American) To remove the husk of a fruit or seed, or the stem of strawberries, tomatoes, etc.

hulled millet (American) Millet.

huller (American) Metal tweezers for removing fruit stems.

hulluah (Indian) *Compôte* of sugar, butter, milk, almonds, pistachio nuts, raisins and fruit, sometimes flavoured with spirit such as whisky.

humbug Cushion-shaped hard, boiled sweet, usually flavoured with peppermint.

hummer (Danish, Norwegian and Swedish) Lobster.

Hummer (German) Lobster.

hummer salat (Danish) Lobster salad.

Hummermayonnaise (German) Lobster with mayonnaise.

Hummersalat (German) Lobster salad.

humpback salmon (American) Small pink species of salmon found in rivers from Alaska to California. In the breeding season, the male develops a large dorsal hump.

hung beef Beef hung till tender, then salted, rolled tightly in a cloth, and hung up for about three weeks, till it becomes dry. If smoke-dried it will keep for a long time.

Hungarian paprika Red paprika grown in Hungary.

Hungarian pepper Hungarian paprika.

hunger Need for food.

hunter's beef Lincolnshire dish of stuffed, pot-roasted beef.

hunter's pudding Nineteenth-century Suffolk baked pudding of flour, suet, sugar, milk, raisins and eggs.

hûre (French) (i) Boar or pig's head. (ii) Head and shoulders of some large fish.

hûre de sanglier (French) Wild boar's head.

hush puppy (American) Deep-fried cornmeal batter fritter.

husk (i) Most nourishing part of the wheat encasing the grain, rich in gluten. (ii) Outer casing of oats, not used in bread-making.

hutspot (Dutch) Beef hotpot.

huzarensla (Dutch) "Huzzar's" salad of cubed cooked beef, potatoes, beet, chopped hard-boiled eggs and gherkins, tossed in mayonnaise and served on lettuce.

hvitkålsoppa (Swedish) White cabbage soup.

hydromel Drink of honey and water flavoured with herbs and spices which, when fermented, becomes mead.

hydrometer Instrument for measuring density.

hyldebærsuppe (Danish) Elderberry soup.

hyson Variety of Chinese green tea.

hyssop (i) Plant of the mint family with pungent, aromatic leaves, used in salads, soups, etc. (ii) (American) Several varieties of wormwood.

hydrogenated fats Vegetable oils solidified by the action of hydrogen, used as shortening.

icaque (French) Coco-plum.

ice (i) Frozen water, used to chill drink or food or to keep it fresh. (ii) Ice-cream.

ice bucket Container for holding ice to chill champagne or other wine.

ice cellar (American) Underground room or basement where foods and refreshments are kept on or near ice.

ice chest Icebox, ice compartment, or portable icebox.

ice chipper Ice fork with short tines for chipping ice off a block.

ice-cream Frozen sweets made with a foundation of rich milk, cream or evaporated milk and flavoured with fruit juice, etc., used in conjunction with fruit, whipped cream, fruit syrup, nuts, etc., to make sundaes, ice puddings, *parfaits*, etc. Water ice – see separate entry.

ice-cream cone Crisp conical wafer biscuit used for holding ice cream.

ice-cream freezer Device for mixing and freezing custards, ice creams and water ices.

ice-cream scoop Utensil for serving individual portions of ice cream in neat round balls.

ice-cream soda Soda water or other carbonated beverage topped with ice cream.

ice-cream-soda spoon Long-handled spoon.

ice crusher Utensil for crushing chunks or cubes of ice.

ice cube Small square of ice made in the freezer compartment of a refrigerator, used mainly for chilling drinks.

ice fork Ice chipper.

ice pick Pointed steel utensil for chipping ice.

ice tongs Hooked tongs for handling large blocks of ice.

ice tray Shallow tray with a removable grating for making ice cubes.

ice tub Ice bucket.

ice water Water chilled with ice.

iceberg lettuce (American) Crisp, firm, round lettuce with large broad leaves.

icebox (American) Refrigerator.

iced *bombe* Ice-cream mixture frozen in a *bombe* mould, and when unmoulded, decorated with whipped cream, *glacé* cherries, nuts, etc.

iced coffee Coffee served ice cold with cream and sugar, and a little brandy as an optional extra.

iced pudding (i) Cold sweet made of ice-cream mixture frozen as for iced *bombe*, (ii) Sweet consisting of a block of ice-cream on a sponge base covered with a sweet omelette or meringue mixture and browned briefly in a very hot oven. Also known as Baked Alaska when meringue mixture is used.

iced tea Tea served ice cold, usually with lemon.

Iceland moss Lichen resembling Carrageen moss, but darker in colour, which grows on barren mountains in Iceland and other northern regions, sometimes used in cooking in the same way as Carrageen moss.

ichang (Chinese) Black tea from China.

ichiba (Japanese) Market.

ichthyophagy Practice of eating virtually nothing but flesh.

icing Sweet covering for cakes, biscuits, pastry, etc., made with icing sugar and white of egg, or icing sugar and water, flavoured and coloured according to taste. See also butter icing.

Idaho potato (American) Large potato baked in its jacket and served with sour cream.

idria (Italian) Water jar; pitcher.

iechyd da (Welsh) Good health! A toast.

igname (French) Yam.

iguana Type of lizard whose flesh is highly regarded by *gourmets* in South and Central America. The eggs are also eaten dried, pickled or fried.

il conto (Italian) The bill.

Ile de France (French) Region of France which incorporates Paris and which includes among its culinary specialities *andouillettes*, pig's liver *pâté*, glazed Paris ham, chicken *Bercy*, duckling *Nantais*, lark *pâtés* of *Étampes*, sugared almonds of *Melun*, and cheeses *Coulonniers* and *Brie*

ile flottant (French) See floating island.

Imbiss (German) Snack, light meal.

Imbiss-stube (German) Snack bar.

imbottiti (Italian) Stuffed pasta.

imbriquer (French) To overlap pieces of food to produce a decorative effect.

immersion heater Electrical apparatus with a heating element immersed in water.

impastare (Italian) To knead into a dough.

impératrice, à l' (French) Name given to a variety of dishes and cakes, e.g., a cold rice dessert, rice *à l'imperatrice*.

imperia salad See *salade impéria*.

imperial (i) Variety of plum. (ii) Large bottle for wine or spirits holding about $1\frac{1}{2}$ gallons.

imperial club (American) Canadian cheddar cheese.

impériale, à l' (French) Dishes garnished with kidneys, cock's combs, truffles, *foie-gras*, etc. in "Imperial" style.

impromptu (French) Improvised meal.

in vino veritas (Latin) In wine is truth.

incise To make light cuts into the skin of fish with a sharp knife before grilling or frying.

inciser (French) To incise.

Indian arrowroot Nutritious starch extracted from the rhyzomes of a tropical plant.

Indian bread Corn-bread or maize-bread.

Indian corn Maize.

Indian cress Nasturtium.

Indian fig Prickly pear.

Indian gram Chick-pea.

Indian kale Taro.

Indian maize Indian corn.

Indian meal Ground maize, cornmeal.

Indian mustard See Chinese mustard.

Indian nut (i) (East Indies) – Betel nut. (ii) (South America) – Pine nut.

Indian pudding (American) Baked pudding of milk, molasses, cornmeal, sugar, spices, butter, and eggs.

Indian rice (American) Wild rice.

Indian shuck bread (American) Batter made of ground maize wrapped in corn husks and boiled.

Indian tea Black tea imported from India.

Indienne, à l' (French) Indian-style dishes containing curry and chutney, served with rice.

indivia (Italian) Endive, chicory.

Indonesian isinglass Agar.

inferno (Italian) Red dry table wine from Piedmont.

infuse To extract flavour by steeping in liquid, e.g., in making tea, coffee, etc.

infuser (French) To infuse.

Ingwer (German) Ginger.

inkfish Cuttlefish or squid.

insalata (Italian) Salad.

insalata alla russa (Italian) Salad of chopped cold cooked vegetables in mayonnaise. (Russian salad).

insalata composta (Italian) Mixed salad.

insalata con tartufi (Italian) Salad of celery hearts, endive and sliced white truffles, in oil and vinegar.

insalata cotta (Italian) Salad of cold cooked vegetables.

insalata di bietole rosse (Italian) Beetroot salad.

insalata di carne (Italian) Salad of meat chopped and mixed with cold cooked vegetables, lettuce, hard-boiled egg, etc.

insalata di cetrioli (Italian) Cucumber salad.

insalata di lattuga (Italian) Lettuce salad.

insalata di legumi (Italian) Vegetable salad.

insalata di lingua di bue (Italian) Salad of chopped beef tongue and chopped vegetables.

insalata di patate (Italian) Potato salad.

insalata di pesce (Italian) Salad of white fish and shell fish.

insalata di pomodoro (Italian) Tomato salad.

insalata di riso e pollo (Italian) Rice and chicken salad.

insalata di stagione (Italian) The salad in season.

insalata di tonno (Italian) Tuna-fish salad.

insalata di uova (Italian) Egg salad.

insalata frutta di mare (Italian) Shellfish salad.

insalata mascherata (Italian) Mixed salad masked with mayonnaise.

insalata mista (Italian) Mixed salad.

insalata verde (Italian) Green salad.

insect Small invertebrate creature. Some insects are edible though disregarded by western countries. Among insects eaten in the near and middle East are grasshoppers, locusts, bumble

bees, silkworm chrysalises and white ants.

insecte comestible (French) Edible insect, such as grasshoppers, bumble bees, locusts, etc.

intercostata di manzo (Italian) Rib steak of beef.

interiora (Italian) Offal.

interlard To thread lardoons into certain meat cuts such as fillets of beef, veal chops, and poultry.

intingolo (Italian) (i) Gravy. (ii) Stew.

invert sugar Mixture of glucose and fructose resulting from hydrolysis (breakdown by water) of cane sugar. Also produced by ferment (as honey), or by boiling with acid (as jam).

involtino (Italian) Thin slice of veal and ham rolled, skewered and cooked in butter or oil.

iodine Element necessary in minute amount to prevent goitre, usually present in sufficient quantity in drinking water, fish and some vegetables such as watercress and onions.

iota triestina (Italian) Soup made of pig's trotters, smoked pork, beans, potatoes and pickled cabbage.

iridée (French) Iridescent seaweed.

iridescent seaweed Rainbow-coloured edible seaweed eaten raw in salad or cooked as for French beans.

Irish coffee Hot coffee and Irish whisky topped with whipped cream.

Irish mist Irish honey - and - whisky liqueur.

Irish moss Carrageen.

Irish soda bread See soda bread.

Irish stew Irish national dish of mutton stewed in white stock with potatoes and onions.

Irish turkey (American) Slang for corned beef and cabbage.

Irish whisky or whiskey Barley-malt-and-grain whisky distilled in Ireland, and matured for not less than seven years.

Irlandaise, à l' (French) Irish-style dishes containing potatoes either introduced during the process of cooking or served as a garnish.

iron Essential mineral component of the blood, derived from certain foods such as meat, liver, eggs, green vegetables, dried fruit and sometimes from drinking water.

ironware Cooking utensils made of iron.

ische bone Aitch-bone.

Ischia (Italian) *Rosso* (red) or *Bianco* (white) table wines from Campania.

ise-ebi tempura (Japanese) Deep-fried lobster.

Isigny (French) Small French town in Calvados renowned for its butter.

issues (French) Animal pluck.

isinglass Agar-agar. Pure, almost tasteless form of gelatine derived from the air-bladder tissue of fish, especially sturgeons; used to clarify beer and wine and to replace gelatine in jellies and table creams.

isvand (Danish) Ice water.

isvann (Norwegian) Ice water.

isvatten (Swedish) Ice water.

Italian chestnut Sweet chestnut.

Italian dressing Salad dressing of olive oil, wine vinegar, pepper, salt, and other seasonings.

Italian marrow Courgette, baby marrow.

Italian paste Dough used in making *pasta*.

Italian vermouth Sweet vermouth.

Italienne, à l' (French) Usually an Italian-style dish made entirely or partly of macaroni or similar *pasta* with added Parmesan cheese or tomato, or both.

iudabah (Arabic) Dish of rice stewed in rich chicken stock, and sweetened.

ive (French) Herb ivy.

izard Wild Pyrenean goat, cooked as for roebuck.

izmir keufta (Russian) Minced lamb patties in tomato sauce.

jabalí (Spanish) Wild boar.

jabiru Aquatic bird of Brazil.

jabot (French) Crop of a bird.

jacana Genus of tropical wading birds.

jack plum (American) Java plum, the Jambolana.

jack rabbit (American) Long-eared hare.

jack salmon (American) Wall-eyed perch.

jacket potato Potato scrubbed, dried, pricked and baked in a fairly hot oven till soft, then split and buttered.

jackfruit Edible tropical fruit of the breadfruit genus. Its seeds can be roasted and eaten as a snack.

jacobin (French) Nickname of *quenelle* of custard, fashionable during the French Revolution; after the Restoration the name was changed to *Royale*.

jagger, jagging-iron Wheel fastened to a handle, used for cutting pastry into fancy shapes.

jaggery (i) Coarse brown sugar made from palm juice. (ii) Brown cane sugar.

jaiba (Cuban-Spanish) Crab.

jalapeño (Mexican) Hot green and yellow capsicum pepper.

jalea (Spanish) Jelly.

jalea de carne (Spanish) Aspic jelly.

jalea de guayaba (Spanish) Guava jelly.

jalousie (French) Small puff-paste cake.

jam Confection or conserve of fruit, made by boiling fruit with sugar to its setting point (approximately 220 degrees F.)

jam biscuit (American) Scone filled with jam and rolled up before baking.

jam buttie Lancashire name for a jam sandwich.

jam sauce Boiled mixture of jam, sugar, water and lemon juice used with sponge or suet puddings, or other sweets.

Jamaica apple Cherimoya.

Jamaica banana Large yellow banana from the West Indies.

Jamaica cucumber Gherkin.

Jamaica ginger Superior grade of ginger, originally developed in Jamaica.

Jamaica plum Hog-plum.

Jamaica rum Dark rum produced in Jamaica, used as an alcoholic drink and for flavouring in cakes, etc.

Jamaican pepper Powdered berries of the pepper myrtle shrub; allspice.

Jamaican tangelo Ugli.

jambalaya Creole dish of spiced rice and vegetables cooked with meat, usually ham.

jambe de bois (French) Clear soup containing piece of leg on the bone. As the meat cooks and falls away the bone resembles a wooden leg, floating. This gives the name to the dish.

jambolana Java plum, fruit of the rose-apple tree.

jambon (French) Ham.

jambon de York (French) York ham.

jambon froid (French) Cold ham.

jambonneau (French) (i) Very small ham. (ii) Ham foreleg.

jamón (Spanish) Ham.

jamón gallego (Spanish) Thin-sliced Galician smoked ham.

janhagel (Dutch) Spiced biscuit.

jantar (Portuguese) Dinner.

Japan tea Light unfermented tea.

Japanese artichoke See artichoke.

Japanese date plum Japanese persimmon.

Japanese gelatine Agar-agar.

Japanese isinglass Agar-agar.

Japanese medlar Loquat.

Japanese oyster Large oyster transplanted from the Orient to the Pacific Coast off North America.

Japanese persimmon Large persimmon native to Japan. See persimmon.

Japanware Lacquer-coated boxes, canisters, trays, etc.

Japonaise, à la (French) (i) Dishes containing Chinese artichokes. (ii) Iced *bombe* of peach ice-cream and tea-flavoured mousse.

japonica apple Fruit of the ornamental japonica tree, sometimes added (peeled and sliced) to fruit pies, because of its scented flavour. It is also made into preserves either alone or used with other fruits such as apples, etc.

jar Wide-mouthed container.

jar opener Utensil with opposing grips for turning difficult screw caps.

jarabe (Spanish) Syrup.

jardinière (French) Mixture of spring vegetables; vegetables stewed down in their own juices.

jardinière, à la (French) Dishes garnished with fresh vegetables, carrots, turnips, peas, beans, etc.

jarlsberg (Norwegian) Semi-soft cheese made from pasteurised milk.

jarra del agua (Spanish) Water-jug, pitcher.

jarret (French) Knuckle of meat.

jarret de bœuf (French) Shin of beef.

jarret de veau (French) Knuckle of veal.

jarro para la leche (Spanish) Milk-jug.

jaseur (French) Waxwing.

jasmin(e) Powerfully scented plant used in oriental cookery.

jasmine tea Tea leaves mixed and fired with jasmine petals.

jaune d'œuf (French) Egg yolk.

jaune-mange (French) Yellow-coloured egg-jelly made from eggs, white wine, lemons, sugar, and gelatine.

Jause (German/Austrian) Austrian-style afternoon tea; coffee with whipped cream, tea, pastries, sandwiches, etc.

Java plum Fruit of the rose-apple tree, from the East Indies.

Java tea Medicinal brew made from an East Indian plant.

Jean de Carême (**John of Lent**) Famous cook under Pope Leo X, nicknamed "John of Lent" in consequence of a celebrated *soupe maigre* which he used to prepare for the Pope.

jellied Congealed, gelatinous.

jellied *bouillon* Clear soup set with gelatine and served cold.

jellied *consommé* Clear broth set with gelatine and chilled.

jellied eggs Eggs (poached or softboiled) set in meat jelly in a dish or in individual moulds.

jellied soup Broth, *consommé*, etc. set with gelatine.

jelly (i) Preserve of strained fruit-juice boiled with sugar and bottled as for jam. (ii) Gelatinous dish, sweet or savoury, such as *consommé*, aspic, flavoured jelly dessert, etc. (iii) Sugar-coated soft sweetmeat, fruit flavoured, or Turkish Delight, marshmallow, etc.

jelly bean Small oval jelly sweet covered with a glazed coating, coloured and flavoured.

jelly doughnut (American) Doughnut filled with jellied preserve.

jelly glass (American) Medium-size tumbler for holding homemade jelly.

jelly powder Powdered gelatine.

jelly roll (American) Swiss roll.

jelly roll pan (American) Swiss roll tin.

jerboa Small rodent found in Europe and southern America, cooked as for squirrel.

Jerez (French) Sherry wine.

Jerez (Spanish) Sherry wine.

jeroboam Very large wine bottle. In champagne terms, it is equivalent to a double magnum.

jerked beef Beef cut into thin slices and dried in the sun.

jerky (American) See beef jerky.

jernik-kalwasi (Russian) Dish of semolina, milk, and honey.

Jersey Tan-and-white milking cattle bred on Jersey in the Channel Islands.

Jerusalem artichoke See artichoke.

Jerusalem cucumber Gherkin.

Jerusalem melon Egyptian melon with succulent flesh used for ices, desserts, etc. or eaten plain. The seeds are used to make sedative and tranquillising drinks.

Jerusalem pickle Pickled gherkin.

Jerusalem potato Jerusalem artichoke.

jesse Very bony fish similar to and cooked as for carp.

jésuite Small flaky pastry triangle cooked with almond paste and sprinkled with *praline*.

jésus (French) Swiss pork liver sausage.

jet de houblon (French) Hop shoot, edible flower of the male hop plant, served as a vegetable or a garnish.

jetée (French) Throw, as in spinning sugar by throwing.

jicama (American) Mexican turnip plant used sliced in salads, or served boiled with melted butter sauce.

jigger (American) Liquid measure containing $1\frac{1}{2}$ fluid ounces.

Johannisbeere (German) Red-currant.

Johannisbeerkuchen (German) Speciality red-currant tart.

Johannisbeersosse (German) Red-currant sauce.

Johannisberg (German) Dry white wine made from the large Riesling and small Riesling vines grown in the Prussian village of this name.

John Collins (American) Highball of dry gin, powdered sugar and lemon juice poured over ice cubes and topped with soda-water. Said to be named for the head waiter of a London hotel in the 19th century.

john dory Oddly shaped oval flat-fish with delicate flesh, cooked either whole by braising, poaching or grilling, or filleted and cooked as for sole or turbot. Also used in *bouillabaisse*. The name is said to derive from *jaune dorée*, indicating the golden yellow colour of the body on which is found a distinctive round black mark ringed by a light grey circle.

johnny-cake (i) (American) Soda bread made of cornmeal, eggs, milk. (ii) (Australian) Country bread made of baked or fried wheat meal. (iii) (English) Piece of dough shaped like a man or a boy, with currants for eyes, mouth and coat-buttons.

joint (i) Cut of meat prepared for the table from animal carcase, such as lamb, pig, etc. (ii) To cut a carcase anatomically, e.g., to cut a chicken into four or eight.

joinville, à la (French) (i) Method of cooking sole fillets. (ii) *Gâteau* of flaky pastry and raspberry jam. Dishes named for the third son of Louis Philippe I of France, Prince de Joinville.

jolerie (French) Small sweet-water fish similar to perch.

jonathan Bright-red dessert and cooking apple.

Jordan almond Sweetmeat, a sugar-coated almond, white or pastel coloured.

jordbær (Norwegian) Strawberry.

joubarbe (French) Jupiter's beard.

joue de porc (French) Pig's cheek; Bath chap.

judas tree Tree of the Caesalpinia family bearing rose-coloured, scented flowers that are pickled in vinegar.

149

jug Large or small vessel of earthenware, china or glass, equipped with a handle and a narrow pouring lip.

jugged Brown stew of hare or other game, cooked in a jar with just sufficient stock or sauce to cover, and then stewed at even temperature in a *bain-marie* or in the oven.

jugo (Spanish) (i) Juice. (ii) Marrow.

jugo de naranja (Spanish) Orange juice.

jugo de piño (Spanish) Pineapple juice.

jugo de tomate (Spanish) Tomato juice.

juice Natural liquid squeezed from herbs, fruits, vegetables or meats.

juicer Utensil for expressing juices from fruits, vegetables, etc.

juicy Juice-filled.

jujube (i) Shrub of the buckthorn family whose fruit is dried and eaten as a sweetmeat. (ii) Chewy sweetmeat made of gelatine or gum arabic, water and sugar, with added colouring and flavouring.

julekake (Norwegian) Christmas cake.

julep (i) (Arabic) Ancient cooling drink containing mucilage and opium, etc. (ii) (American) Mixed drink of bourbon whisky, sugar and fresh mint served in a frosted glass.

julienne (French) (i) Clear vegetable soup first made in 1785 by Jean Julien, a noted French chef who left his fortune to the poor of Paris, made from *consommé* with added finely-shredded, butter-cooked vegetables. (ii) Food cut into strips or fine shreds.

jumble (i) (British) Small rich biscuit flavoured with lemon, almond, etc. and baked in "S" shape. (ii) (American) Sugar biscuit filled with jam or mincemeat.

jumbo peanuts Large-size peanuts.

jumbo shrimp (American) Very large prawns.

jumbo size Biggest size available.

junge Henne (German) Pullet.

"jungle juice" Poor quality or raw spirits.

juniper berry Small, dark, purple-blue fruit of the juniper tree used to flavour gin, sauces, etc. and also used in medicine.

juniper juice (American) Slang for gin.

juniper wine Medicinal drink made from juniper berries.

junket (i) Easily-digested dessert made of curds produced by treating lukewarm milk with rennet and flavoured to taste; suitable for children and invalids; often served with fruit in place of custard. Also used to make cheese cakes. (ii) (Old English: juncate) Cream cheese made in a rush basket.

junket tablet Rennet tablet used to curdle milk when making junkets or similar puddings.

jupiter's beard Several fleshy-leaved plants, such as the house-leek or wild artichoke, and the edible white stonecrop.

jurançon (French) Wine, red and – more popular – white, made in a small French town of that name in the Basses-Pyrénées.

jus (French) (i) Juice pressed from fruits, herbs, vegetables or meats. (ii) The liquid expressed from lightly grilled beef. (iii) Broth. (iv) Gravy from roast meat diluted with clear soup and reduced by boiling.

jus, au (French) Food served in its own juice.

jus d'ananas (French) Pineapple juice.

jus de citron (French) Lemon juice.

jus de fruit (French) Fruit juice.

jus de fruit rouge (French) Red fruit juice.

jus d'herbes vertes (French) Herb juices from raw plants such as watercress, parsley, etc.

jus de pommes (French) Apple juice.

jus de rôtis (French) Gravy of the roast joint.

jus de tomates (French) Tomato juice.

jus de viande (French) Meat juice.

jus d'orange (French) Orange juice.

juter (French) To baste.

juvia South American name for Brazil nut.

k Abbreviation for kilo or kilogram.

kaas (Dutch) Cheese.

kaastruffel (Dutch) Cheese truffle.

kabâb (Persian) Roast; roast meat.

Kabeljau (German) Cod, codfish.

Kabeljausteak (German) Cod steak.

kabiljo (Swedish) Cod.

Kabinett (German) Term indicating high-quality wine.

kabob, kebab, kebob Skewered pieces of meat marinated and roasted over an open fire.

kabuni (Albanian) Raisin and rice dessert.

Kadaver (German) Carcase.

kærnemælk (Danish) Buttermilk.

kærnemælkskoldskal (Danish) Cold buttermilk soup.

kaffe (Danish, Norwegian and Swedish) Coffee.

Kaffee (German) Coffee.

Kaffee mit Milch (German) Coffee with milk.

Kaffee mit Schlagobers (German) Coffee with whipped cream.

Kaffeecreme (German) Coffee butter cream.

Kaffeeglasur (German) Coffee icing.

Kaffeekanne (German) Coffee-pot.

Kaffeeklatsch (German) Coffee gossips. Social gathering for ladies with refreshments of coffee, chocolate flavoured with vanilla and beaten up with egg and cream, various wafers, cakes, etc.

Kaffeekuchen (German) Coffee cake.

Kaffeemühle (German) Coffee-grinder.

Kaffeesatz (German) Coffee grounds.

kaffir beer See Bantu beer.

kaffir bread (South African) Pith of the cycad plant.

kaffir corn (South African) (i) Sorghum, a tropical grass akin to sugar-cane. (ii) Millet.

kage (Danish) Cake.

kagne (French) Kind of vermicelli.

kahlúa (Spanish) Coffee - flavoured liqueur from Mexico.

kahvi (Finnish) Coffee.

kail (Scottish) Kale.

kail brose (Scottish) Broth of kale, oatmeal, vegetables, and meat.

kail gully (Scottish) Large knife for cutting kale.

kailcannon (Scottish) Pie of mashed potatoes and fried cabbage.

kailyard (Scottish) Kitchen garden or cabbage patch.

kaimak (Russian) Dessert similar to cream custard.

Kaiserfleisch (German/Austrian) Viennese dish of smoked sucking pig, eaten raw or cooked.

Kaiserschmarrn (German / Austrian) Viennese omelette sprinkled with sugar and raisins.

kajmar (Yugoslavian) Serbian cream cheese.

Kakao (German) Cocoa.

kaki (French) Persimmon.

kakku (Finnish) Cake.

kakoretsi (Greek) Sausage roasted on a spit.

kalakukko (Finnish) Baked fish.

kalamarakia (Greek) Fried squid.

Kalb (German) Calf.

kalbasá saséski (Russian) Salami sausage.

Kalbfleisch (German) Calf meat; veal.

Kalbsbraten (German) Roast veal.

Kalbsfrikassee (German) Veal *fricassée*.

Kalbsgulasch (German) Veal goulash.

Kalbsgullasch (German/Austrian) Veal goulash.

Kalbshaxe (German) Knuckle of veal.

Kalbskeule (German) Leg of veal.

Kalbskotelett (German) Veal chop.

Kalbsmilch (German) Calf's sweetbread.

Kaldaunen (German) Tripe.

kaldomar (Swedish) Stuffed cabbage roll.

kale Green, curly-leaved vegetable of the cabbage family which does not form a head. A rich source of vitamin C, it is prepared and cooked like cabbage, and used in soups.

kalfkott (Swedish) Veal.

kalop (Swedish) Collop.

kal rulader (Norwegian) Stuffed cabbage.

kålsoppa (Swedish) Cabbage soup.

kaltes Geflügel (German) Cold poultry.

kaltschall (Russian) Fruit salad well moistened with liqueur, wine or syrup.

kalvehjerte (Danish) Calf's heart.

kalvekjøtt (Norwegian) Veal.

kalvkød (Danish) Veal.

Kandiszucker (German) Sugar candy.

kangaroo Austrian mammal with edible flesh.

kangourou (French) Kangaroo.

Kaninchen (German) Rabbit.

Kanne (German) Can, mug, tankard, pot.

kans (Indian) Grass allied to sugar-cane.

kanten Agar-agar jelly.

Kapaun (German) Capon.

Kaper (German) Caper.

Kapernsosse (German) Caper sauce.

kapushiak (Polish) Cabbage soup.

karab (Russian) Ewe's milk cheese.

Karaffe (German) Decanter, carafe.

kari (French) Curry.

karidopita (Greek) Nut cake.

karnemelk (Dutch) Buttermilk.

Karotte (German) Carrot.

Karottensalat (German) Carrot salad.

karp (Swedish) Carp.

Karpfen (German) Carp.

kartoffel (Danish) Potato.

Kartoffel (German) Potato. ·

Kartoffelbrei (German) Mashed potatoes.

Kartoffelpuffer (German) Potato pancake.

Kartoffelpüree (German) Mashed potato.

Kartoffelsalat (German) Potato salad.

Kartoffelsuppe (German) Potato soup.

Käse (German) Cheese.

Käsebrot (German) Cheese bread.

Käseplatte (German) Assorted cheeses.

Käsestrudel (German) Cheese *strudel*.

kasha (Russian) Baked or braised cereal such as buckwheat, barley, millet, oatmeal, etc.

kasha varnishkas (Jewish) Buckwheat groats with noodles.

Kasseler Rippchen (German) Smoked pork chops.

Kasserolle (German) Casserole, stewpot.

Kastanie (German) Chestnut.

kasza (Polish) Buckwheat groats.

kaukauna (American) Hickory-smoked processed cheese containing caraway seeds.

kava (i) Species of pepper. (ii) Narcotic drink prepared from its root and stem.

Kaviar (German) Caviare.

kavirma palov (Russian) Uzbek lamb pilaff.

kazmag (Russian) Flat bread of un-leavened egg dough.

kebab (Turkish) Skewered meat grilled over hot embers.

Kebob See *Kebab.*

kebbock (Scottish) Cheese.

kedgeree (i) Indian dish of curried fish and rice. (ii) Onion-flavoured, spicy Indian dish of rice or lentils and fish. (iii) Anglo-Indian dish of rice, smoked fish and hard-boiled eggs, served for breakfast or as a light meal during the day.

keeling (Scottish) Codfish.

keftede (French) Hamburger steak.

keftede (Greek) Spiced meat ball.

keftes-kebabs (Turkish) Small pieces of raw meat skewered, grilled and served with rice pilaff and gravy.

keg Cask for holding beer, etc. usually containing 10 gallons, but varying in size.

keg beer Beer which has been pasteur-ised and placed in strong kegs con-taining the gas to force the beer out.

Keks (German) Biscuit.

kelkel Slice of sole, dried and salted.

Kelle (German) Ladle.

Kellner (German) Waiter.

kelner (Dutch) Waiter.

kelp Large brown edible seaweed, rich in iodine.

kelt Salmon that has just spawned.

kennebec (American) Large white po-tato grown along the Kennebec River in Maine, U.S.A.

Kentucky bass (American) Black bass.

Kentucky ham (American) Ham salted and hung in smoke from a fire of corn cobs, hickory bark, or sassafras wood.

kephir, kefir (Russian) Fermented cow's, goat's or ewe's milk of Caucasian origin.

Kern (German) (i) Nut kernel. (ii) Fruit stone.

kernmilk (Scottish) Buttermilk.

kerosene, kerosine (American) Paraffin oil obtained from shale or by distill-ation of petrol, used in lamps and cooking stoves.

kerosine stove Cooking stove fired by kerosine.

kerrie kool sla (Dutch) Curried coleslaw.

kesäkeitto (Finnish) Vegetable soup.

keshka (Russian) Porridge of cracked wheat and beef or chicken.

Kessel (German) Kettle.

ketchup (i) Spiced sauce named for the main ingredient, tomato. (ii) Mush-room. (iii) Unripe walnuts.

ketmie Okra.

kettle Vessel for heating or boiling liquids, often with spout and lid.

kettle of fish Riverside picnic at which freshly-caught salmon are cooked and eaten on the spot.

keufta (Russian) Meat ball or patty.

key-lime pie (American) Pie made with small limes from the mangrove thickets of the Florida Keys.

kg. Abbreviation for kilo or kilogram.

khadja puri (Russian) Georgian dish made of cheese and bread served as a first course or dessert.

khana (Hindi) Dinner; food.

khleb (Russian) Bread.

kholodnik (Russian) Cold soup of herbs, *kvass,* fish, cream, cucumber, etc.

kibble To grind or chop coarsely.

kichel (Jewish) Biscuit.

kickshaw Fancy food, delicacy, luxury.

kid Young goat, popular as food in some Mediterranean regions. It is usually roasted whole, after marinating in vinegar, oil and seasonings, to impart flavour and counteract the tendency to dryness.

kid-glove orange (American) Orange such as the tangerine or mandarin with easily removable skins.

kidney Offal meat from edible animals ranging from the rabbit to beef animals, rich in protein and iron. Used to flavour meat pies and puddings, also in stews, casseroles, curries, soups, omelettes, etc. Ox kidneys need slow cooking but those of smaller animals such as the lamb, pig, calf, can be grilled or fried.

kidney bean See French bean.

kidney chop Loin chop containing part or all of the kidney.

kielbasa (Polish) Sausage, similar to *Knackwurst* or saveloy.

kike West-country name for brill.

kilderkin British beer barrel holding 18 gallons.

kilic baligi sisde (Turkish) Swordfish on a spit.

kilki (Norwegian) Small fish similar to anchovies (and served in the same ways) found in northern waters.

kilo Kilogram, a unit of metric measure equalling 2.21 pounds.

kimali burek or *beurreck* (Russian and Turkish) Pancake, stuffed, rolled and fried, popular as an *hors d'œuvre*.

king salmon (American) Chinook or quinnat salmon, found along the North Pacific coast.

kingfish Several species of white, firm-fleshed fish found in all oceans, cooked as for tuna.

kip (Dutch) Chicken.

Kipferl (German) Crescent roll.

kipper Herring split, salted and dried in smoke, then grilled, baked, fried or poached. Filleted and boned kippers are used for savoury snacks, sandwiches, etc.

kippis (Finnish) Cheers! A toast.

kir Mixture of chilled *chablis* and *cassis*.

kirin (Japanese) Rice beer brewed in Tokyo.

Kirsch, Kirschwasser (German) Brandy made in Germany and Switzerland, from a cherry base which can be added to fruit salads, ices, trifles, etc.

Kirsche (German) Cherry.

Kirschenknödel (German) Cherry dumpling.

Kirschenstrudel (German) Cherry *strudel*.

Kirschsaft (German) Cherry juice.

kishka (Jewish) Beef intestinal skin stuffed with a savoury mixture of onion, paprika, seasonings, flour and matzo meal, roasted and served, sliced, with roast meat or poultry.

kishri, kitchri (Indian) Kedgeree.

kissel, kizel (Russian) Pudding made of fruit juice or fruit and sugar thickened with cornflour or potato starch.

kissing-crust Pale soft crust where one loaf touches another during baking.

kitchen brush Bristled tool for cleaning kitchen and tableware made of wire for scouring pots and pans, of nylon for cleaning glass and chinaware, and of nylon for other purposes such as scrubbing vegetables, etc.

kitchen equipment Entire range of utensils and tools needed in the preparation and cooking of food.

kitchen pepper Mixture of finely-powdered ginger, cinnamon, black pepper, nutmeg, Jamaica pepper, cloves and salt.

kitchen shears Strong scissors with serrated edges for poultry-bone cutting, meat trimming, and vegetable cutting; some can also remove screw tops.

kitchen tool set Rack holding cooking tools such as long-handled fork, spoon, spatula, slotted spoon, ladle, etc.

kitchen utensil Tool used in food preparation.

kitchener Ancient name for cook, but now only applied to a kitchen apparatus, usually the old-fashioned solid fuel cooking stove.

kitchenware Tools, utensils, and hardware used in the kitchen in the preparation of food.

kizil (Russian) Cornelian cherry made into a syrup.

kjøttpudding (Norwegian) Minced meat hash.

Kleie (German) Bran.

Klops (German) Meat dumpling.

Kloss (German) Dumpling.

Klosterkäse (German) Small pungent cheese.

klukva (Russian) Variety of cranberry.

knäckebröd (Swedish) Rusk.

Knäckebrot (German) Crispbread.

Knackwurst (German) Saveloy sausage.

knaidel (Jewish) Dumpling; matzo ball.

knead To work dough with floured hands, folding and pressing until the required consistency is obtained. Scone and pastry doughs need less firm handling than bread dough.

Kneipe (German) Pub; saloon.

knekkebrød (Norwegian) Thick rye cracker biscuit.

Kneten (German) To knead (dough).

knife Cutting implement with blade and handle, varying in shape and size according to its type – carving, paring, slicing, chopping, etc.

knife box Compartmented box or drawer

divider for separating knives, forks and spoons.

knife-rest Small silver or glass utensil to support the knife and prevent soiling the tablecloth.

knish (Jewish) Small dough dumpling filled with cheese, minced meat or poultry, or potatoes and onions, and baked in the oven.

Knoblauch (German) Garlic.

Knöchel (German) Knuckle, joint.

Knochen (German) Bone.

Knödel (German) Dumpling.

knuckle Ankle joint of meat, usually pork or veal, used for stews and stock, or stewed and eaten with vegetables.

kobu (Japanese) Seaweed used in soups and stews.

Koch (German) Cook, chef.

kochen (German) To cook, to boil.

Kochsalz (German) Common salt.

Kochtopf (German) Saucepan.

kød (Danish) Meat.

koekje (Dutch) Sweet biscuit.

Koffein (German) Caffeine.

koffie (Dutch) Coffee.

koffietafel (Dutch) Lunch.

kogt oksebryst (Danish) Boiled brisket of beef.

Kognac (German) Brandy.

Kohl (German) Cabbage.

kohl-rabi Vegetable, with a turnip-like globe stem topped with curly green foliage. Primarily a summer vegetable, it may be clamped for storage with leaves removed, like the potato.

Kohlsprossen (German) Brussels sprouts.

Kokosnuss (German) Coconut.

Kokosroulade (German) Coconut roll pastry.

kola (French) Cola.

koláčeki (Czech) Small buns filled with a cooked mixture of apples, apricots, prunes, dates, nuts, and poppyseeds.

koldt bord (Danish) Cold collation of dishes ranging from smoked fish to meats, salads, and cheeses.

kolokithakia yemista (Greek) Courgettes stuffed with minced meat.

Kölsch (German) Light local beer of the Cologne and Dusseldorf areas.

kombu (Japanese) Kelp.

komijnekaas (Dutch) Spicy cheese flavoured with cumin.

Kompott (German) Stewed fruit.

Konditor (German) Confectioner, pastry cook.

Konditorei (German) Pastry shop.

Konfekt (German) Chocolates.

Konfitüren (German) Candied fruit.

Königinsuppe (German) Cream of chicken soup.

Königsberger Klops (German) Spiced sweet-and-sour meatball stewed in caper sauce.

konjak (Swedish) Brandy; cognac.

Konserve (German) Canned food, preserve.

Konservierungsmittel (German) Preservative.

koofthas (Indian) Mince of meat or fowl, curried, shaped into balls, and fried.

kool (Dutch) Cabbage.

Kopfsalat (German) Lettuce.

korf (Swedish) Sausage.

Korinthe (German) Currant.

Korn (German) Grain, cereal.

Kornbranntwein (German) Corn brandy, whisky.

kosher food Jewish food prepared in accordance with their religious dietary rules, usually sold at special shops and stores.

kosher pickle Fresh cucumber cured in brine-filled wooden kegs with garlic, spices, and vinegar.

Kost (German) Food, fare.

Kostlich (German) Delicious.

Kotelett (German) Chop.

kotlety (Russian) Meat cutlets made from chopped or minced meat.

kotopoulo (Greek) Roast chicken.

köttbullar (Swedish) Meatball.

kouglof (French) *Kugelhøpf.*

koulibiak (Russian) Pastry loaf stuffed with fish or meat.

koulitch (Russian) Currant bread traditionally baked just before the Russian Easter festival.

koumiss, kumiss (Russian) Fermented mare's milk, made originally in Turkestan and Tartary by adding brewer's yeast, honey and flour to milk. Nutritious and easily digested, it is effervescent when fermented and has a small alcoholic content.

kourabi (Swedish) Favourite sweetmeat served with coffee.

Krabbe (German) Crab.

Kraftbrühe (German) Broth, *consommé*, meat soup, beef tea.

krakowska (Polish) Roasted pork sausage, flavoured with garlic.

Krapfen (German) Doughnut.

Krauskohl (German) Savoy cabbage.

Kraut (German) Plant; vegetable, especially cabbage.

Krauterkäse (German) Green cheese.

Krautertee (German) Herb tea or infusion.

Krautknödel mit Speck (German) Cabbage dumplings, with bacon.

Krautsalat (German) Cabbage salad.

Krautstrudel (German) White cabbage *strudel*.

Krebs (German) Crayfish.

kreeft (Dutch) Crayfish.

Kren (German/Austrian) Horseradish.

kreplach (Jewish) Small triangular noodle-dough dumplings stuffed with cheese, chicken, liver or chopped meat, and served in soup.

Kresse (German) Cress.

kriter (French) Fine sparkling wine whose secondary fermentation takes place in the bottle.

Krokette (German) Croquette.

kromeski (Polish) Croquette of minced meat, game or poultry, wrapped in calf's udder or bacon, and fried.

krona pepper Well-flavoured, non-pungent mild red pepper seasoning, used in cooking and as a condiment.

krug (French) Highly-rated brand of champagne.

Krug (German) Jug, pitcher.

krupenik (Russian) Barley and mushroom soup.

krupnik (Polish) Drink of honey and hot vodka flavoured with cinnamon, citrus rind, cloves, and vanilla.

Kruste (German) Crust.

Krustig (German) Crusty (pastry, bread, etc.)

Kuchen (German) Cake-bread of soft yeast dough, with varied toppings such as raisins with fried breadcrumbs,

sliced apple with cinnamon and sugar, etc.

Kuchenmeister (German) Chef, head cook.

Kuchenteig (German) Cake-dough.

Kuchenzettel (German) Bill of fare.

Kuchlein, Kücken (German) Young chicken; pullet.

kufta (Egyptian) Meat croquette.

kugel (Jewish) Baked dish of eggs and bread, barley, potatoes, rice or fish, or cabbage, served as a separate course, or as an accompaniment to meat or poultry; or (if sweet) as a dessert.

Kugelhopf (German) Rich dough or yeast cake, with currants and raisins.

kugelhupf, kuglhupf (French) Alsatian raised-dough cake baked in a mould lined with shredded almonds.

kugelis (Lithuanian) Potato pudding.

Kühlschrank (German) Refrigerator.

Kühltruhe (German) Deep-freeze.

Kühlung (German) Refrigeration.

Kukuruz (German/Austrian) Maize, sweetcorn.

kulebiaka (Russian) Large square of pastry stuffed with meat, hard-boiled eggs and flavourings.

kulich (Russian) Traditional Easter cake made from risen dough.

kulinarisch (German) Culinary.

kumle (Norwegian) Raw potato dumpling.

Kümmel (German) (i) Caraway seed. (ii) Colourless liqueur flavoured with caraway seeds and cumin.

Kümmelkase (German) Cheese, flavoured with caraway seeds.

kumminost (Swedish) Cumin cheese.

kumquat, cumquat Small yellow subtropical fruit similar to the mandarin orange, with juicy pulp and a bittersweet flavour, eaten raw as dessert, also cooked or preserved.

Kunstbutter (German) Margarine.

Kürbis (German) Gourd, pumpkin.

kurini (Russian) Ewe's milk cheese.

kurkkukeitto (Finnish) Cucumber soup.

kvass (Russian) Beverage made from fermented rye, also added to soups.

kyckling (Swedish) Chicken.

kylling (Danish and Norwegian) Chicken.

kypare (Swedish) Waiter.

l'addition (French) Restaurant bill, account.

la carte (French) Menu.

la cuenta (Spanish) Bill, account.

La Varenne (French) Famous 17th century French chef who wrote the first planned cookery books.

Lab (German) Rennet.

Labrador herring (American) Common herring of the North Atlantic.

labre (French) Labrus, a genus of fishes.

labrus European seafish of brilliant colouring but indifferent flavour and texture, used in *bouillabaisse*.

lache (French) Small, delicate marine fish, cooked as for smelt.

Lachs (German) Salmon.

lacquerware Japanned ware.

Lacrima Christi (Latin) Sweet delicate wine "Tear of Christ" made from grapes grown on the slopes of Mount Vesuvius, in red, white or *rosé* varieties.

lactaire (French) Lactary.

lactary Agaric-type fungus containing milky juice. Only some lactaries are edible, others are poisonous.

lactic acid Acid present in sour milk and other fermented substances.

lactic ferment Microbe which produces lactic acid in milk.

lactique (French) Lactic acid, lactic ferment.

lactometer Graduated densimeter showing the density of milk so that the cream content can be calculated.

lactose Sugar found in milk though less sweet than sugars from other sources such as cane, etc. It is obtained by evaporating whey.

ladies' fingers (i) Okra. (ii) Boudoir biscuits or sponge fingers.

ladle Deep-bowled dispensing spoon usually on a long handle used for serving liquid or semi-liquid food such as soup.

ladog (French) Variety of herring found in Lake Ladoga, in Russia.

Lady Baltimore cake (American) White

layer cake, iced and filled with chopped figs, nuts, and raisins.

Lady Westmorland's soup Old English name for water in which young cabbage has been boiled.

Lagacque (French) Famous restaurateur of the French Revolution, whose establishment was in the garden of the *Tuileries*.

lagar (Portuguese) Large stone vat in which the grape-juice for port and other wines is pressed.

lager (i) Light beer of low alcoholic content; brewed by slow bottom-fermentation method, and stored, or "lagered" before clarification. (ii) Original name for a cellar in which beer was matured.

lagopède (French) Lagopus.

lagopus Pyrenean or snow partridge, cooked as for grouse.

Laguipière (French) Eighteenth century master of French cookery who died in the 1812 Retreat from Moscow.

Laib (German) Bread.

lait (French) Milk.

lait, au (French) With milk, or cooked in milk.

lait d'amande (French) Almond milk.

lait de coco (French) Coconut milk.

lait de poule (French) Egg-nog.

lait de soja (French) Soya milk.

laitance (French) Soft roe of a fish.

laiterie (French) Dairy.

laiteron (French) Sow-thistle.

laitiat (French) Drink made by steeping wild fruit in whey.

laitue (French) Lettuce.

laitue printanière (French) Spring lettuce.

lake salmon (American) Large trout found in many Canadian and Alaskan lakes.

Ladritze (German) Liquorice.

laks (Danish and Norwegian) Salmon.

lamantin (French) Sea-cow, the walrus.

lamb Meat from a sheep under one year old. It should be light-coloured and firm-textured, with a fair proportion of white fat in the joints. Prime joints such as leg, loin and shoulder are usually roasted; loin chops are grilled. Cheaper cuts – best end of neck and middle neck – will also roast, as will breast but this requires slow cooking. These latter cuts are also suitable for braising and stewing. So, too, is scrag end, and this makes good broth or soup. Sheep over one year old is mutton (see entry). Milk-fed lamb is lamb killed before weaning.

lamb-and-kidney pie Pastry crust baked over lamb meat and kidneys.

lamb chop Chop cut from loin, rump or neck of a lamb carcase.

lamb loaf Baked loaf made from minced lamb.

lamb mint (American) Peppermint or spearmint herb; common garden mint.

lamb pie Stewed lamb and vegetables baked in pastry.

lamb shoulder Meat cut from the upper foreleg of a lamb carcase.

lamb's fry (i) Lamb's liver, sweetbread, heart and inner fat. (ii) Lamb's testicles.

lamb's lettuce Hardy annual winter salad plant of the valerian family, used in salads; also known as Corn salad.

lamb's stove Lamb's head, its jaws stuffed with lamb's lights, spinach, onion, and parsley, cooked slowly in good stock.

lamb's wool Old English drink referred to in Shakespeare's plays made from ale, wine, nutmeg, sugar and roasted crab-apples.

lamballe (French) Term usually applied to a broth made by adding to a *purée* of fresh pea soup a rather thick *consommé* containing tapioca.

lambanog (Filipino) Popular locally-brewed spirit of the Philippines, much drunk at celebrations of all kinds.

lambick Belgian beer, rather sour to the taste and very intoxicating.

Lambrusco (Italian) Dry red table wine with a fizzy quality but usually of low alcoholic content.

lambstones Parts removed in the castration of young rams, cooked and served like lamb's sweetbreads, and considered a delicacy.

Lamm (German) Lamb.

lammestel (Norwegian) Roast lamb.

Lammkeule (German) Leg of lamb.

Lammkotelett (German) Lamb chop.

lamper (French) (Colloquial) To swig or toss back drink or wine.

lampern Small lamprey; cooked like eels.

lampone (Italian) Raspberry.

lamponi con crema (Italian) Raspberries with cream.

lampreda (Italian) Lamprey.

lamprey Type of eel, once considered a great delicacy, which is prepared as for eels, but requires longer cooking.

lamproie (French) Lamprey.

lampsana Type of endive eaten raw in salads.

Lancashire cheese Hard, round yellow cheese with a crumbly texture resembling Cheshire cheese.

Lancashire hot-pot Casseroled dish of mutton and onions topped with sliced potatoes. See hotpot.

lançon (French) Sand-eel.

Landpartie (German) Picnic.

landrail Corncrake, an edible bird of good flavour, eaten on the Continent.

Landwirtschaft (German) Agriculture.

langosta (Spanish) Rock or spiny lobster.

langosta con mayonesa (Spanish) Lobster mayonnaise.

langostino (Spanish) Baby crayfish.

langouste (French) Spiny-lobster crayfish, a salt-water crustacean.

langoustine (French) Baby crayfish.

langue (French) Tongue.

langue de bœuf (French) Ox tongue.

langue de chat (French) (i) Flat, finger-shaped sweet biscuit. (ii) Piece of chocolate shaped as above.

langue de veau (French) Calf's tongue.

Languedoc (French) Region of south-western France renowned for its food, especially poultry, fish, soups, etc. It stretches from the *Haute Loire* and the *Haute Garonne* to the Mediterranean coast.

Languedocièenne, à la (French) Dishes usually served with a garnish of tomatoes, aubergines and *cèpes*.

Langueste (German) Spiny lobster.

languier (French) Smoked hog's or pig's tongue.

lapereau (French) Young wild rabbit.

lapereau rôti (French) Roast baby rabbit.

laphroaig (Scottish) Malt whisky from Islay, western Scottish isle.

lapin (French) Rabbit.

lapin de garenne (French) Wild rabbit.

lapin sauvage (French) Wild rabbit.

lapje (Dutch) Steak.

Lapland cheese Dumbell-shaped cheese made in Lapland from reindeer milk.

lapsang souchong Variety of black tea grown in China and possessing a smoky flavour.

lapsha (Russian) Noodles.

lapskaus (Norwegian) Hash.

lapwing Bird of the plover family: the Peewit, eaten on the Continent.

lard (i) Melted internal pig fat, strained and stored in air-tight containers. The best (or "leaf" lard) comes from the abdomen or round the kidneys. Commercial lard derives from fat from all parts of the pig. Lard is used for frying, or for cake and pastry-making. (ii) To insert strips of fat or bacon rind into meat or poultry before cooking to keep it moist.

larder Cupboard for storing food.

larder (French) To lard.

larding needle Tool used for larding meat, poultry and game (See lard (ii))

lardoire (French) Larding needle.

lardon (French) Lardoon.

lardoon Strip of larding fat threaded into meat or poultry.

lardy cake Cake made with risen bread dough, lard, sugar and dried fruit.

large jigger (American) Liquid measure containing two fluid ounces.

lark Small wild bird now rarely eaten in England but still trapped in nets on the Continent and regarded as a delicacy; roasted, grilled, made into pies, etc.

lasagne (Italian) Wide ribbons of pasta served with meat and tomato sauce, and cheese.

lasagne verdi (Italian) Noodles dyed green with spinach water.

lata (Spanish) (i) Tin plate. (ii) Tin can.

latex Milky sap of certain plants, sometimes used in cooking or drunk as a beverage.

latke (Jewish) Pancake.

Latour (French) *Château* wine from the

vineyards of *Pauillac* and the *Gironde*.
latte (Italian) Milk.
latte di gallina (Italian) Egg-flip.
latteria (Italian) Dairy.
lattice tart Flan or pastry shell filled with fruit or cream and criss-crossed with narrow pastry strips.
lattuga (Italian) Lettuce.
lau lau (Hawaiian) Mixture of meat and fish wrapped in banana leaves, roasted and steamed in a bed of coconut charcoal.
Lauch (German) Leek.
laurier (French) Bayleaf.
lavaret (French) Fish of the salmon family found in deep lakes, and cooked as for river and salmon trout.
laver Nutritious marine alga or seaweed, growing on rocks on the sea coasts, cooked like spinach, and served as an accompaniment to roast meat. Of the three varieties: (the purple, the green, and the sea lettuce) the purple laver is esteemed the best.
lax (Norwegian) Smoked salmon.
lax (Swedish) Salmon.
layer cake Sponge cake baked in two or more separate tins, then sandwiched with butter icing, jam, cream or other filling and decorated with sugar, or icing.
Layon (French) Slopes bearing the vineyards of *Anjou* (France).
lazy susan Revolving circular tray; sometimes divided into compartments to hold various items such as condiments, preserves, nuts, etc.
lb. Abbreviation for pound, derived from *libra* (Latin – pound).
leaf lettuce (American) Variety of loose headed lettuce with crisp, curly edges.
leaf mustard Herbaceous plant cooked like spinach.
lean Fat-free, or with little fat.
leaven (i) Piece of sour dough retained to ferment the next batch of bread; a method used before yeast was obtainable. (ii) Fermenting agent such as baking powder, yeast or sour dough.
lebanon (American) Spiced red sausage originally made by Pennsylvania Germans in Lebanon, Pennsylvania.
Leber (German) Liver.

Leberaufstrich (German) Liver spread.
Lebergullasch (German/Austrian) Liver *goulash.*
Leberkäs (German) Paste made from beef, pork and liver, a speciality of Munich.
Leberknödel (German) Liver dumpling.
Lebersuppe (German) Minced liver soup.
Leberwurst (German) Liver sausage.
Lebkuchen (German) Traditional Christmas cake containing citron, ginger, honey, nuts and spices.
leche (Spanish) Milk.
leche asada (Spanish) Custard made with cognac, eggs, and milk.
lèchefrite (French) Dripping-pan.
lechería (Spanish) Dairy.
lechero (Spanish) Milkman.
lechón (Spanish) Sucking pig.
lechuga (Spanish) Lettuce.
lecithin Fat containing phosphorus found in brains, egg yolks, etc.
leckach (Jewish) Honey cake.
Leckerbissen (German) Delicacy, titbit.
leckerlie Spiced biscuit of Swiss origin containing flour, fat, sugar, honey, almonds, peel and spices.
lecythos Narrow-necked Greek vase for holding oil.
leechee Lychee nut.
leek Mild-flavoured, non-bulb-forming vegetable of the onion and garlic family, used in soups and stews; also served as a vegetable, preferably coated with cheese or white sauce. The leek is the national emblem of Wales and, with boiled fowl, forms the famous Scottish dish "Cock-a-leekie".
lees Wine dregs or sediment.
leftovers Food remaining after a meal, which should be stored with care and used up as quickly as possible.
leg of lamb Cut of meat from the hind leg of a lamb carcase, usually roasted.
Leghorn Small breed of domestic fowl, originating in Leghorn (Livorno), Italy, with white feathers and yellow legs.
legumbre (Spanish) Vegetable.
légume (French) Vegetable.
legume (Italian) Vegetable.
legume Plant group including beans, peas, and lentils.

legumi all'aceto (Italian) Antipasto of vegetables served with oil and vinegar.

legumin Protein substance found in peas, beans and lentils.

Leicester cheese Mild cheese similar to Cheddar but of a looser texture, and coloured with annatto to a deep orange.

leipa (Finnish) Bread.

leitão assado (Portuguese) Roast suckling pig.

leite (Portuguese) Milk.

leite creme con farófias (Portuguese) Custard with meringue.

lemon Fruit of the lemon tree, *citrus limonum*, cultivated in warm countries, usually gathered when green and ripened in special storehouses. An excellent source of vitamin C, its acid and pectin content assist in marmalade and jam-making. The rind and juice are used to flavour many sweet and savoury dishes and the juice can replace vinegar in salad dressings.

lemon balm Herb of the mint family, used in sauces, stuffing, drinks, etc.

lemon curd Preserve made from lemons, eggs, butter and sugar; used in puddings, pies, and as a spread.

lemon custard Custard cream made with milk that has been boiled with lemon zest.

lemon gin Gin flavoured with lemon instead of juniper berries.

lemon grass Perennial oriental grass yielding a lemon-scented essential oil.

lemon jam Preserve made from lemons and sugar.

lemon meringue pie Short-crust pastry shell filled with a soft mixture of cornflour, eggs, lemon juice and rind, butter and sugar, and topped with whisked egg whites and sugar to form a meringue.

lemon phosphate Soda water flavoured with lemon syrup.

lemon sole Flatfish found from the North of Scotland to the Mediterranean, but abundant in the English Channel and in season all the year round. Smaller than ordinary soles and of poorer flavour and texture, lemon soles are cooked as for other fish, particularly frying and grilling.

lemon squash Drink made with sweetened lemon pulp with added colouring.

lemon thyme Strongly flavoured herb used for flavouring stuffings, etc., sometimes as substitute for lemon.

lemon twist Thin slice of lemon slit and twisted over the edge of a cocktail glass as a garnish.

lemon verbena (American) Small wild shrub whose leaves are used to flavour cold drinks.

lemonade (i) True lemonade is a refreshing drink made from the juice of lemons, the essence of the rind, sugar, and water; sometimes the white of egg and sherry is added, especially if intended as an invalid drink. (ii) Commercial preparation of glucose, aerated water and citric acid.

lengua (Spanish) Tongue.

lenguado (Spanish) Sole; flounder.

lenteja (Spanish) Lentil.

lenticchia, lente (Italian) Lentil.

lentil Pulse vegetable; a leguminous seed about half the size of a pea. In the East, especially in Egypt, they have long been a staple item of diet and are mentioned in the Scriptures as far back as the days of Jacob. Grown all over south Europe and in the U.S.A. they contain carbohydrate and are a good source of protein (legumin), vitamin B, iron and calcium, and come in three varieties, red, yellow and dark green. They are used in soups and stews, and are rendered more digestible by rubbing through a sieve, which removes their outer coating.

lentil soup Soup made from lentils, carrots, onions and other vegetables.

lentille (French) Lentil.

lentisk Bush grown in the Greek archipelago. Its fruit yields an edible oil, and its trunk a resin used to flavour the spirit, *raki*.

Léognan (French) Red wine from the commune of *Léognan* in the Graves region of France.

Léoville (French) Red Bordeaux from the *Medoc* region of France.

lepiota Edible cultivated fungus.

lepidosteus Lake and river fish of Central America, with bonelike scales, cooked as for pike.

lepre (Italian) Hare (game).

Lerche (German) Lark (bird).

lessare (Italian) To boil or stew.

lesso (Italian) Boiled.

letchi (French) Lychee.

lettuce Green plant, with succulent leaves, in several species and many varieties. Although used chiefly as a salad, it can be cooked and served as a vegetable.

lettuga (Italian) Lettuce.

levain (French) Leaven, ferment. Dough or batter prepared with yeast before mixing it with the rest of the flour.

levantar la mesa (Spanish) To clear the table.

leveret Young hare.

leverpostei (Norwegian) Liver pie.

leverpostej (Danish) Liver *pâté* made of cooked and seasoned liver.

levraut (French) Young hare.

levreteau (French) Young hare.

levûre (French) Yeast.

liaison (French) Thickening agent such as agar-agar, arrowroot, cornflour, eggs or flour.

liard (French) Food cut into thin rounds, such as potato crisps.

liche (French) Lichia, a Mediterranean fish similar to tuna fish.

lichee nut See Lychee.

lichia Mediterranean fish similar to tuna fish and cooked in like manner.

licor (Spanish) (i) Liquid. (ii) Strong drink or spirits.

licorice, liquorice Perennial herb of Europe and Asia, the roots of which are used for flavouring sweets, medicines and beverages.

lié (French) Thickened, bound; applied to creams, soups, and sauces.

Liebig, Baron Justus von (German) Famous chemist who invented and greatly increased the popularity of beef extract.

Liebfraumilch (German) General term for German wines.

liebre (Spanish) Hare.

liederkranz (American) Pungent Ger-man-American cheese resembling Limburger.

Liégeoise, à la (French) Food cooked with juniper flavouring, popular in the *Liège* region of Belgium.

lietiniai (Russian) Lithuanian meat-stuffed pancakes.

lievito (Italian) Yeast.

lièvre (French) Hare (game).

lièvre en civet (French) Jugged hare.

light bread (American) White bread.

lights, lites Lungs of sheep, bullocks or pigs, generally used for feeding pets but occasionally used in soups and stews.

Likör (German) Liqueur.

Lillet (French) Apéritif, red or, more usually, white, made in the *Garonne* area of France and first made by a family of that name in 1872.

lima (Spanish) Lime.

lima bean Bean of the haricot variety, originating in South America. The green or white seeds may be eaten fresh or dried.

Limabohne (German) Lima bean.

limande (French) Dab, flatfish.

limande sole (French) Lemon sole or dab.

limandelle (French) Well-flavoured flat fish cooked as for brill or sole.

limburger cheese Semi-hard fermented Belgian and German cheese with a strong flavour and smell.

lime Pale yellow, round fruit from the citrus lime tree, native to Asia but grown in many warm countries. It has a high acid content, and its rind and juice are used in the same way as that of lemons. Limes make excellent preserves and drinks, and were used in the British navy to prevent scurvy before the discovery of vitamins. This gave rise to the nickname of "Limeys" given to our sailors by other countries.

lime blossom Dried flowers of the lime (linden) tree. Used to make a delicate tea or tisane, said to have medicinal properties.

lime juice cordial Beverage made from crushed whole limes, the resulting juice being concentrated, with citric acid, sugar, colouring and preservatives added. Used to dilute gin or rum or with iced water.

lime juicer (American) Utensil for expressing juice from limes.

lime phosphate Soda water flavoured with lime syrup.

lime pickle Pickled lime condiment served with soups, meat, etc.

limeade Beverage of lime juice, sugar, and water.

limequat (American) Citrus hybrid of lime and kumquat.

limon Hybrid citrus fruit of lime and lemon.

limon (French) Lime.

limón (Spanish) Lemon.

limonada (Spanish) (i) Lemonade. (ii) Lemon squash.

Limonade (German) Lemonade.

limonata (Italian) Lemonade.

limone (Italian) Lemon.

limousine, à la (French) Dishes garnished with specially-cooked red cabbage.

Limoux, blanquette de (French) Rather heavy, sparkling wine made at *Limoux* in the *Aude* (France).

limpet Small, single-shelled fish found adhering to rocks, prepared and cooked like the cockle, periwinkle or mussel.

Lincoln cheese Soft cream cheese originally produced in Lincolnshire.

ling (i) Large fish of the cod family, usually salted. (ii) Name given to varieties of American hake or burbot.

lingua (Italian) Tongue.

lingua con salsa verde (Italian) Tongue in parsley ("green") sauce.

lingua di bue (Italian) Ox-tongue.

lingua in agrodolce (Italian) Tongue in sweet-sour sauce.

lingua piccante (Italian) Spiced tongue.

lingue (French) Ling.

linguine (Italian) Narrow "little tongue" macaroni ribbons.

linnet Small bird which feeds on hempseed and is eaten on the Continent, prepared as for lark.

linot, linotte (French) Linnet.

Linse (German) Lentil.

Linsenpuree (German) Lentil *purée*.

Linsensalat (German) Lentil salad.

Linsensuppe (German) Lentil soup.

Linzertorte (German) Austrian cake first made in Linz, containing almonds, apricots, and chopped nuts.

lion Lion-meat is rarely eaten although it is edible. Its basic tastelessness is overcome by marinading, and is then cooked as for beef.

liptauer (Hungarian) Tasty cheese made of goat's milk, flavoured with paprika, capers, peppers, etc.

lipto (Hungarian) Sheep's milk cheese.

liq Abbreviation for liquid.

liqueur Composite alcoholic drink made from a mixture of spirits and syrups. Liqueurs are very numerous and vary in their alcoholic strength. They include *Kummel, Chartreuse, Bénédictine* and *Curaçao*. Home-made liqueurs are derived from fruit steeped in alcohol or spirits, and are often called *ratafias*.

liqueur cellar Specially-made chest, fitted with a lock, for storing liqueurs.

liqueur d'or (French) Colourless French liqueur containing flecks of gold leaf.

liqueur jaune (French) French liqueur imitating yellow *Chartreuse*.

liqueur verte (French) French liqueur imitating green *Chartreuse*.

liqueur wine Any wine which is both sweet and alcoholic, such as Madeira, Muscatel, Malmsey, *Frontignan*, drunk mainly as an *apéritif* and used in cooking and confectionery.

liquid pepper seasoning (American) Tabasco sauce.

liquido (Italian and Spanish) Liquid, fluid.

liquor (i) Distilled beverage with a high alcoholic content such as gin, rum, vodka, or whisky. (ii) Broth or gravy.

liquorice, licorice Plant whose roots are used in medicine and to make various sweets. (See licorice).

liquorist Maker of liqueurs.

lista de platos (Spanish) List of dishes; menu.

lista de pratos (Portuguese) List of dishes; menu.

lista de vinos (Spanish) Wine-list.

lista delle vivande (Italian) List of food; menu.

lit (French) Bed. Thin slice of meat or vegetables spread in layers.

litorne (French) Field-fare.

litre (French) Liquid measure equalling 1.7C English pints.

littleneck (American) Small hardshell clam

livèche (French) Lovage.

liver Abdominal animal gland used as food, the choicest being that of lamb, veal and chicken. These are best fried and served with bacon or in a mixed grill. Ox liver requires slow cooking, as in a casserole; pig's liver is used in sausage-making but can be also fried. Liver is high in food value, containing protein, vitamins A and B, and iron.

liver *à la crême* Calf's liver sliced and stewed with vegetables, with added cream and vinegar.

liver paste *Pâté* made from cooked, sieved liver.

liver pudding Liver sausage.

liver *wurst* Liver sausage.

livestock Cattle, sheep, lambs and pigs raised for food.

Livornese, alla (Italian) Food served with a thick tomato sauce, often containing mushrooms and cheese, a speciality of the *Livorno* (Leghorn) area.

llama South American ruminant edible mammal, cooked as for beef.

lo mein (Chinese) Soft noodles.

loach Small river fish of the carp family, prepared like smelt.

loaf Moulded or shaped mass of food-stuff, such as bread, cooked meat, sugar, etc.

loaf cake Cake baked in a rectangular loaf tin.

loaf cheese Loaf-shaped processed cheese.

loaf sugar Sugar compressed into cubes; lump sugar.

lobio (Russian) Haricot beans.

lobscouse Stew or hash of meat and vegetables or biscuit, as served to sailors.

lobster Highly-esteemed edible crustac-ean of the crab family found along European shores and in other oceans and seas. Lobster meat can be served with a simple oil and vinegar dressing or mayonnaise-type sauce, but can also be served hot in many dishes – curried, *au gratin*, scalloped, in omel-ettes, etc.

lobster *à l'américaine* Sautéed lobster combined with onions, tomatoes, herbs, dry white wine and brandy and served in the shell with a sauce made from the coral, butter, lemon juice and parsley.

lobster *bisque* Fish soup made of lobster.

lobster biscuit (American) Scone dough rolled out, filled with chopped and seasoned lobster meat, rolled up, and baked.

lobster butter Lobster coral pounded with butter and used to make lobster *bisque*, cardinal sauce, etc.

lobster coral Spawn of the hen lobster.

lobster mayonnaise Lobster meat cut into small pieces and mixed with mayonnaise sauce, served on lettuce and topped with sliced hard-boiled egg.

lobster newburg Dish of lobster meat cooked with cream, egg yolks, sherry or Madeira.

lobster thermidor Lobster meat in creamy sauce, baked in its shell, with a crumb-and-cheese top, grilled to brown.

lobster tureen White earthenware tureen with a cover made in the shape and colour of a lobster.

locksoy Macaroni made with rice flour and flavoured with soy sauce.

locro Argentinian stew.

locust bean Fruit of a Mediterranean shrub, much used in the Near East; also called carob or St. John's Bread, used to make a kind of flour and also a syrup. (See carob).

lodge Place for storing wine.

Löffel (German) Spoon.

lofschotel (Dutch) Baked endive.

loganberry Purplish-red succulent fruit, larger and more acid than the rasp-berry, used to make tarts, pies and preserves. Ripe loganberries can be served for dessert.

loin Back portion nearest the leg of an animal.

loin chop Chop cut from the lower back or loin of a carcase of lamb, pork, etc.

loksh (Jewish) Noodle.

lollipop Hard sweet on a stick.

lombata (Italian) Loin (of meat).

lombata di bue (Italian) Sirloin of beef.

lombata di vitello (Italian) Loin of veal.

lombatello (Italian) Fillet.

lombo (Italian) (i) Loin. (ii) Sirloin.

lombo de bue (Italian) Fillet of beef.

lombo di maiale (Italian) Loin of pork.

lombo di vitello (Italian) Loin of veal.

lomo (Spanish) Loin or chine of meat.

lomo de cerdo (Spanish) Loin or chine of pork.

lomo de cordero (Spanish) Loin of lamb.

lomo de ternera (Spanish) Loin of veal.

lone star (American) Beer brewed in San Antonio, Texas.

long bean (American) Kidney bean.

long clam (American) Soft clam.

long drink Drink served in a tall glass, usually diluted with aerated liquid or water.

Long John Well-known brand of Scotch whisky.

long pepper Spice similar in taste and smell to ordinary pepper, used in making curry-powder and pickles.

longchamp (French) Broth made by cooking shredded sorrel and vermicelli in *consommé* and adding a *purée* of green peas.

longaniza (Spanish) Pork sausage, sliced.

longe (French) Loin.

longe de veau (French) Loin of veal.

lonza (Italian) Cured pork fillet.

loquat Japanese species of medlar, with small yellow fruit, used for jams and jellies.

Lorbeer (German) Bay (herb).

Lorbeerbaum (German) (i) Bay-tree. (ii) Laurel-tree.

Lord Barrington's plum pudding Nineteenth-century boiled pudding made from eggs, milk, breadcrumbs, suet, raisins, currants and nutmeg.

Lord John Russell's pudding Mid-19th century iced pudding of eggs, milk, isinglass, loaf sugar, cream, brandy, peel, cherries, preserved pineapple and dried fruit.

Lord Sandy's sauce Worcestershire sauce.

lords and ladies Wild arum whose tuberous root yields an edible starch.

lorgnette (French) (i) Fried onion ring. (ii) Small dessert biscuit. (iii) Candied fruit.

loriot (French) Golden oriole, small bird trapped and eaten on the Continent.

Lorraine (French) District of France of high gastronomic repute. Famed, among many other dishes, for its *Quiche*, (a tart filled with eggs, cream and lean bacon). Cheeses, pastries, waffles, pork products, (including the black pudding of Nancy) are among the many products of the area. Also wines in great variety.

lote Eel-pout, a freshwater fish prepared like eels or lampreys.

lotte or *burbot* (French) Eel-pout, burbot. (See lote).

lotte de rivière (French) Burbot.

Lotvarik (German) Apple butter.

louche (French) Soup-ladle.

Louis XIV French monarch in whose reign Epicureanism began to flourish.

Louis XVI Epicure in whose reign restaurateurs first became professional men; he introduced the potato, first as a flower, then as a food.

Louis XVIII French monarch who re-introduced gastronomy as a fine art after the Revolution. Himself a cook, he is said to have invented *Truffes à la purée d'ortolans*.

loukomade (Greek) Sweet fritter.

loukoumi (Greek) Oriental confection of chopped almonds and corn syrup.

loup de mer (French) Sea bass.

love apple Early name for tomato.

lovage (i) Herb of the cow parsley family. Its shoots are candied like angelica, as roots and seeds used for flavouring a liqueur. (ii) (Scottish lovage) Herb with a celery flavour used in stews, etc.

love in disguise Eighteenth-century dish of stuffed braised calf's heart brushed with egg yolk, coated with crumbs mixed with cooked vermicelli, and then browned in the oven.

low-calorie food Foods low in energy-producing fats and starches.

low wines First distillation of Scotch whisky.

Löwenbräu (German) Strong lager beer brewed in Munich.

Löwenzahn (German) Dandelion.

lox (Jewish) Kosher-style smoked red salmon.

loza (Spanish) Crockery.

lozenge Hard sweet or cough drop.

luccio (Italian) Pike.

lucine (French) Clam.

lucine papillon (French) Soft clam.

Lucullus Famous Roman epicure and field-marshal, Lucius Licinius Lucullus, 114–57 B.C. Said to have once given a banquet costing £20,000.

luganiga (Italian) Spiced pork sausage.

lumaca (Italian) Snail.

lumaca di mare (Italian) Winkle.

lump sugar Sugar compressed into cubes; loaf sugar.

lunch, luncheon Mid-day meal, which can be a sandwich or snack-type repast, or a more susbstantial meal of several courses.

lunch-box Container for carrying lunch to school or work.

lunch cake Rather plain, but substantial fruit cake.

luncheonette (American) Place where snacks and coffee, milk, tea, and soft drinks are served.

lunchmobile (American) Mobile lunch wagon designed for serving people at small factories, etc.

lunchroom (Dutch) Place where tea and cakes, ice cream, sandwiches and soft drinks are served.

Lunel (French) Sweet, dessert muscatel wine made in the *Hérault*, Southern France.

lustreware Highly glazed earthenware with an iridescent copper-coloured sheen.

lutfisk (Swedish) Cod soaked in mild solution of lye until the bones dissolve to become part of the flesh.

luting Pastry strip used to seal the lid onto a dish in which game or other preserve has been potted.

luzinzeth (Arabic) Sweet cake delicacy consisting of a thin shell of pastry containing a rich almond stuffing and delicately-flavoured cream, served in sauce of sweet melted butter.

lye hominy (American) Hominy grits hulled by soaking in lye solution.

lychee (litchi) Fruit of a tree of Chinese origin, with a scaly red-brown covering and white pulpy flesh which is acid yet sweet. Available in cans, also in fresh form.

Lyonnais (French) Important fruit-producing region of France, also noted for game, fish, poultry and *Lyons* sausage.

Lyonnais, à la (French) Food garnished with or containing shredded fried onion.

maatjes haring (Dutch) Fresh herring pickled in spices, sugar and vinegar.

macademia Nut of an Australian evergreen, similar to the sweet almond, used in confectionery, roasted and salted.

macaron (French) Macaroon.

macaroni Farinaceous food; a variety of *pasta* originating in Italy. Served simply with butter and grated cheese, as a savoury dish such as macaroni cheese, added to soups and stews, or made with milk and sugar into a pudding.

macaroni cheese Cooked, broken macaroni topped with cheese sauce and browned.

macaroni salad Cold cooked macaroni combined with salad dressing, and ingredients such as cucumber, onion, pepper, tomato, lettuce.

macaroni vongole (American) Macaroni, spaghetti, or other *pasta* served with a clam sauce.

macaroon Cake or biscuit made of almond paste, egg white, flour, and sugar, baked on rice paper.

maccherone (Italian) Macaroni.

maccherone alla chitarra (Italian) Macaroni cut on coiled steel wires to resemble guitar strings.

maccherone alla marinara (Italian) Macaroni cooked with garlic and olive oil.

macchinetta del caffé (Italian) Dripstyle coffee-making machine.

macco (Italian) Mash of beans.

mace Outer husk of the nutmeg, used in both "blade" and powder form in sauces, soups, stews and curry powder, and occasionally in a *bouquet garni*.

mace (Italian) Mace.

mace butter Nutmeg butter.

macédoine (French) (i) Mixture of various kinds of diced vegetables or fruits. (ii) Assortment of ripe fruit embedded in jelly and set in a mould. (iii) Fruit salad flavoured with liqueurs and syrup.

macédoine de fruits (French) Fruit salad.

macedonia di frutta (Italian) Fruit salad.

macellaria (Italian) Butcher's shop.

macerate To soften food by steeping in liquid.

macéré (French) Steeped, macerated, or soused.

mâche (French) Lamb's lettuce. Corn or field salad.

macintosh (American) Red cooking and eating apple grown in Canada and northern U.S.A.

macis (French) Mace.

mackerel Round, oily-fleshed fish in season from October to July (though best in April, May and June) with a silvery underside and distinctive blue-black markings on the back. Rich in protein, certain vitamins and minerals, it should be eaten when really fresh. It can be smoked, salted, soused, or steamed, grilled, fried or baked, with a suitable sauce such as parsley, gooseberry or mustard.

Mâcon (French) Town in Burgundy, France, renowned for its Burgundy wines.

Mâconnaise, à la (French) Various meat dishes flavoured with red wine typical of *Mâcon* cookery.

macque, pain de la (French) French pastry, made like cream puffs.

macreuse (French) Widgeon, a black water-fowl of the wild duck family.

mad apple Early name for the eggplant, or aubergine.

Madeira Sweet, dark and robust forti-fied wine originating in the Portuguese island of Madeira off the West African coast. Used as a beverage and also to flavour sauces and ices, etc.

madeira cake Rich cake containing no fruit and flavoured only with lemon. Candied citron peel is placed on the top during baking.

madeira nut (American) English wal-nut.

madeira sauce Rich brown sauce flav-oured with Madeira wine and served with roast dark meats or smoked meats.

Madère, vin de (French) Madeira wine.

madder-wort Plant used in dyeing, from which a kind of beer is also made.

madeleine Small fancy cake baked in a *dariole* mould and coated with jam and coconut.

madeleine (French) Sponge cake baked in a scallop-shaped mould.

maderisation Spoiling of wine by over-exposure to air. White wines are especially susceptible. Otherwise known as Oxidation.

Madras Term generally applied to a dish flavoured with curry or chutney.

Madras tea Black tea produced in Madras province, Southern India.

madrilène, à la (French) (i) Clear soup flavoured with tomato juice. (ii) Dishes flavoured with tomato juice.

maduro (Spanish) Ripe.

mælk (Danish) Milk.

Magdalen College butter Oxford recipe for a spread made from boiled parsley mixed with pounded anchovies and butter.

maggiorana (Italian) Marjoram.

maggiordomo (Italian) Majordomo; but-ler, chief steward.

magistères (French) Nourishing soups invented by Brillat-Savarin.

magnum Large wine bottle containing about 1/3 gallon.

magnum platter (American) Large wood-en serving platter designed also to be used as a carving board.

magpie Black and white bird not now eaten in Britain but very common in France and often used there for stock-making.

maguey Mexican plant of the agave species used as a vegetable and also to make pulque or tequila.

Mahl (German) Meal.

Mahlzeit (German) Mealtime.

maia Balkan name for fermented milk used in the making of yogurt.

maiale (Italian) Pork.

maiale al latto (Italian) Pork stewed in milk.

maiale marinato (Italian) Pork marinated in flavoured wine and cooked in the marinade.

maid of honour Small tartlet with a filling made from flavoured curds. Best known flavouring is that of almonds and brandy.

maigre, au (French) Dishes prepared without meat. Lenten dishes.

Maine lobster (American) Large-clawed lobster fished from Labrador to Cape Cod but chiefly off the coast of Maine; also called American lobster.

Maintenon (French) Name of the Marchioness Francoise d'Aubigne, a great patroness of cooks. Several dishes are called *à la Maintenon*. The dish *Côtelettes de veau à la Maintenon* is said to have been invented by this lady to tempt Louis XIV's failing appetite when he was advanced in age.

maionese (Italian) Mayonnaise sauce.

maionese all'aglio (Italian) Garlic-flavoured mayonnaise sauce.

maionese verde (Italian) Green mayonnaise sauce, coloured with spinach.

maïs (French) Maize; Indian corn.

Mais (German) Corn; maize, sweetcorn.

mais frais au naturel (French) Boiled corn-on-the-cob.

maison, à la (French) Strictly, dishes prepared on the premises of the restaurant or hotel concerned, but often used more generally.

maito (Finnish) Milk.

Maitrank (German) May drink. A delicious German beverage, of hock or other white wine, flavoured with woodruff, lemon, bay leaves, and sugar.

maître d'hôtel (French) Person in charge of the dining-room in a hotel or restaurant.

maître d'hôtel (French) (i) Dishes quickly and plainly prepared in which parsley is used as the principal flavouring. (ii) Flavouring butter, mixed with chopped parsley and seasoned with lemon juice, pepper, and salt. Served on grilled meats. (iii) White sauce flavoured with lemon and parsley.

maíz (Spanish) Corn.

maize Indian corn in several varieties, including sweetcorn, flour corn and popcorn. It is grown enormously in the U.S.A. for human and animal consumption, also in southern Europe and parts of Africa and Asia. Maize is used to make corn syrup, corn oil, flour, custard powder, porridge, hominy, hominy grits, polenta, etc.

maize oil Corn oil.

majolica Richly ornamented Majorcan pottery.

Majoran (German) Marjoram.

majordomo Butler or head steward.

Makrele (German) Mackerel.

Makrone (German) Macaroon.

Malabar almond Edible East Indian almond.

Malaga Spanish dessert wine from Andalucia, white (which is goldencoloured) and red, used also in cooking and confectionery-making.

malart, malard (French) Mallard, the common wild duck.

malaxer (French) To knead or soften.

malic acid Organic acid found in apples and other unripe fruit, also in some vegetables.

malique (French) Malic acid.

mallard Wild duck which can be roasted or braised. In season September to January.

mallow Plant with emollient properties in its leaves, which can be eaten in salad, or cooked as a vegetable like spinach.

malmsey Sweet dessert wine imported from Sardinia, Sicily, Madeira, and the Canary Islands, and drunk as an *apéritif;* it also replaces Madeira, etc., to flavour sauces, etc.

malt Barley which has been allowed to germinate so that its starch is converted into dextrin and sugar, then kiln-dried. High in carbohydrates and protein, it is used in brewing and distilling, making cakes, bread, puddings, malted milk powder and medicines. Malt syrup is made by evaporating malted barley at a low temperature.

malt and date loaf Loaf-shaped cake made from flour, syrup, milk, egg, dates, bicarbonate of sugar and malt extract.

malt bread Bread made of flour, yeast, syrup, fruits, sugar, milk and water and malt extract.

malt vinegar Vinegar made from malted grain.

malt whisky Whisky made from malted barley.

malted milk Milk drink containing malt powder and flavouring.

maltese orange (American) Blood orange.

maltose, malt sugar Simple sugar formed as the result of the action of maltose upon starch.

malvasia del vulture (Italian) White Italian wine in sweet and sparkling varieties.

Malvern water Pure bottled water from around Malvern, Worcestershire, often used with gin and whisky in preference to ordinary tap water which is now chemically treated.

malvoise, vin de (French) Malmsey.

Malz (German) Malt.

mamaliga (Rumanian) National porridge-type dish of corn, meal, and sheepmilk cheese.

mammee Aromatic fruit of the West Indian mammee-tree, also known as mammee apple.

mammee sapota Tropical marmalade tree, or its fruit.

mammelle (French) (i) Breast. (ii) Udder.

mämmi (Finnish) Traditional Easter pudding of rye malt and rye meal boiled, seasoned, baked and served cold with cream and sugar.

manatee See sea-cow.

manchet Seventeenth - century bread made from flour, ale and salt, or from flour, yeast, butter, egg, sugar and salt, shaped by hand and not baked in a tin.

manchette (French) Paper cutlet frill.

manchon (French) (i) Small flaky pastry cake baked in the shape of a muff. (ii) Almond paste *petit four* biscuit, rolled, filled with butter cream and dipped at each end into finely shredded green almonds.

mandarijntje (Dutch) Tangerine.

mandarin oil Oil extracted from mandarin oranges, used for flavouring.

mandarin orange Type of orange, larger and sweeter than the tangerine, grown in Mediterranean countries.

mandarina (Spanish) Tangerine orange.

mandarine (French) (i) Tangerine. (ii) Mandarine.

Mandarine (German) (i) Mandarin orange. (ii) Tangerine.

mandarino (Italian) Tangerine.

Mandel (German) Almond.

mandelbrot (Jewish) Almond-flavoured pastry roll baked, cut in slices and browned.

mandelbund (Norwegian) Almond cake.

Mandeltorte (German) Almond pastry.

mandlen (Jewish) Small pieces of baked dough served with soup.

mandoline (French) Shredder and slicer.

mandorla (Italian) Almond.

mandorlato (Italian) Almond paste.

mandorlo (Italian) Almond-tree.

mange-tout (French) Variety of sweet peas, wax, and butter beans, of which the pod is also eaten.

mangel worzel, mangold Coarse beet, mainly grown for cattle food but can also be cooked like swede or turnip.

mangle (French) Fruit of the mangrove.

mango Tropical fruit rather like a big pear, with orange-yellow flesh and spicy yet acid flavour. Ripe mango is eaten as a dessert fruit; green mango is used in fruit salads, and in pickles and chutney. Mango figures extensively in Indian cookery.

Mangold (German) (i) Beet. (ii) Mangel-wurzel.

mangosteen Dark brown, orange-shaped tropical fruit with spots and rose-coloured pulp.

mangue (French) Mango.

Manhatten (American) Cocktail made of sweet or dry vermouth, rye whisky, curaçao and a dash of angostura bitters, stirred over ice cubes.

Manhatten-style clam chowder (American) Chowder made with tomatoes in place of cream or milk.

manier (French) To knead; to mix with the hands.

manioc Tropical plant, from the root of which tapioca and cassava are derived.

manna croup, manna kroup, manna groats Russian semolina, much esteemed for making puddings, obtained from the hard wheats or grains of manna grass of Odessa and Taganrog.

manos de ternera (Spanish) Calf's feet.

manqué (French) Sponge-type cake

popular in Paris and baked in a special "*manqué*" mould. Said to have been invented by accident when a classic cake-mix being prepared by a pastry-cook, failed.

mansard (French) Wood-pigeon, ring-dove.

mansikkatorttu (Finnish) Strawberry tart.

mante de mer (French) Sea mantis, quill fish.

manteca (Spanish) (i) Lard, grease, fat, butter. (ii) Pulpy parts of fruit.

manteca de cerdo (Spanish) Lard.

manteca de cacao (Spanish) Cocoa butter.

mantecada (Spanish) (i) Buttered toast. (ii) Kind of cake.

mantecado (Spanish) (i) Butter-cake. (ii) French ice-cream.

mantecato (Italian) (i) Type of ice cream. (ii) Venetian dish of puréed salt cod.

mantelikokkare (Finnish) Almond custard, a dessert served with fruit sauce.

mantequilla (Spanish) Butter.

manzana (Spanish) Apple.

manzanilla (Spanish) Pale sherry.

manzo (Italian) Beef.

manzo arrosto (Italian) Roast beef.

manzo bollito (Italian) Boiled beef.

maple cream Sweetmeat made by boiling together syrup and cream.

maple honey Light-coloured maple syrup reduced to the consistency of honey.

maple sugar Sugar obtained by boiling down maple syrup.

maple syrup Sap from various maple-tree species boiled down to a syrup used on pancakes and waffles and to flavour ice creams, confectionery, cakes, puddings, etc.

maple syrup frosting (American) Icing made with maple syrup, boiling water and egg-whites.

maquereau (French) Mackerel.

maquereau grillé maitre d'hôtel (French) Grilled mackerel with parsley butter.

marabout (French) Very large coffee-pot.

marasca (Italian) Dalmatian cherry used in making *maraschino* liqueur.

maraschino Cherry brandy liqueur made from a small, sour, black cherry (Marasca) grown in Dalmatia.

maraschino (Italian) Maraschino liqueur.

maraschino cherry Stoned cherry preserved in maraschino liqueur, used to garnish desserts, custards, cakes, etc.

marasquin (French) Maraschino.

marasquin de zara (French) See Zara.

marble cake Cake made with light and dark mixtures half blended so as to give a marbled effect.

marbré (French) Marbled. Effect achieved with certain cakes and gelatine dishes.

marc (French) Distilled wine, not necessarily matured.

marc de raisin (French) Semi-hard French cheese with a crust of grape-skins and pips replacing the usual rind.

marcassin (French) Wild boar under six months old, marinated and cooked as for pork.

marché (French) Market.

maréchale, à la (French) Method of preparing small cuts of poultry and meat. Cuts are dipped in egg-and-breadcrumbs and fried in butter before garnishing with green asparagus tips and truffles.

marée (French) Collective name for all seafood and crustaceans sold in a fish market.

marena (Italian) (i) Morella cherry. (ii) Drink made from the same.

Marengo (French) Chicken served in a sauce made from olive oil, wine or water, tomatoes and mushrooms, originally created after the Battle of Marengo on June 14, 1800 by Napoleon's chef who hurriedly assembled what ingredients were available to make a meal. His version included fried eggs and crayfish, but not mushrooms.

Marennes (French) Small port on the south-eastern coast of France, famous for green and white Marennes oysters.

mare's-tail Hard-stemmed field-plant whose new shoots are tender and cooked like asparagus, or pickled in vinegar.

margarine Edible fat manufactured

originally from mixed animal fats but now primarily from vegetable oils such as palm, groundnut, cottonseed, soya bean, sunflower, etc. It is enriched by added vitamins and given a buttery taste by the addition of a milk culture. Margarine is widely used to replace butter and in cakes and baking with 50% lard in pastry-making.

margarita (American) Cocktail of tequila *cointreau*, lime or lemon juice, and sugar; served with a wedge of lime dipped in salt.

margaux (French) Wines from the Bordeaux region.

marguerite (American) Small cupcake made with flour, fat, pecan nuts and brown sugar or molasses.

maridaki (Greek) Whitebait.

marignan (French) Popular Parisian pastry cake soaked in liqueur-flavoured syrup and topped with meringue.

marigold Garden herb, a native of Spain, introduced into England in 1573 and once used in salads and in making cordials.

marinade Mixture of oil, wine, vinegar or lemon juice and herbs in which meat or fish is soaked before cooking, to impart flavour and to tenderise. Especially useful for cuts of meat which are not of top quality.

marinade (French) Marinade.

marinara, alla (Italian) Food marinated and cooked in wine, herbs, etc.

marinare (Italian) To pickle or marinade.

marinate To soak in brine or seasoned marinade.

mariné (French) (i) Marinated. (ii) Pickled, cured.

mariner (French) To marinade or pickle.

marinière (French) (i) Method of preparing mussels and other shell-fish. (ii) Fish dishes cooked in white wine and garnished with mussels.

marisco (Spanish) Shellfish.

marjolaine (French) Marjoram. Herb of strong aromatic flavour in several varieties, used fresh or dried for game seasoning, flavouring sauces, forcemeat, etc. The sweet or knotted marjoram is a native of Portugal.

marjoram Aromatic herb of the mint family used fresh or dried to season salads, soups, and other dishes. See *marjolaine*.

marknad (Swedish) Market.

markt (Dutch) Market.

Markt (German) Market.

marmalade (i) Preserve made from Seville oranges, traditionally served at breakfast in Britain, but also used in making puddings, sauces, etc. (ii) The term marmalade also applies to preserves made from other fruits such as lemons, quinces, pears, grapefruit, etc. It derived originally from Portugal (*Marmalada*) where the preserve was made from quinces.

marmelade (French) (i) Marmalade. (ii) Fruit stewed for a long time until reduced to a thick *purée*. The term originated in Portugal.

Marmelade (German) (i) Marmalade. (ii) Jam.

marmellata (Italian) (i) Marmalade. (ii) Jam.

marmellata di albicocca (Italian) Apricot jam.

marmellata di ciliegie (Italian) Cherry jam.

marmellata di fragole (Italian) Strawberry jam.

marmelo (Portuguese) Quince. The origin of the word "marmalade" which initially meant quince jam.

marmite (French) (i) Stockpot: copper, iron or earthenware lidded cooking vessel with or without feet, depending on whether used on a cooking stove or in a hearth. (ii) A brand of yeast food extract used to flavour soups, stews, and savoury dishes.

marmite à pression (French) Pressure-cooker.

marmite de vapeur (French) Steam kettle.

marmite norvégienne (French) Hay-box (for slow cooking).

marmite, petite (French) Clear, savoury broth.

Marone (German) Edible chestnut, fruit of the sweet- or true chestnut tree.

marquer (French) To prepare, and arrange in a stewpan or braising pan, a piece of meat ready for cooking.

marquise (French) Tender and sweet variety of pear in season in France during November and December.

marron (French) Chestnut.

marron glacé (French) Candied, glazed or sugar-dipped chestnut.

marron grillé (French) Roast chestnut.

marrone (Italian) Edible chestnut, fruit of the sweet or true chestnut tree.

marrone candite (Italian) Candied or glazed chestnut.

marrow (i) Delicate tissue contained within the hollow bones of animals, used in soups, stews, etc. or eaten in jellied form. (ii) Gourd in several varieties of colour and shape, cooked as a vegetable, or filled with a savoury stuffing and baked as a main dish; also used for preserve-making or with apple in fruit pies. Although low in nutritional value, marrows are popular baked, fried, steamed or boiled and, when sealed with wax at the end, keep well for winter use.

marrow-bone Animal bone containing marrow which can be utilised in various ways. (See marrow (i))

marrow jam Marrow-flesh cooked with lemon juice and rind, root ginger and sugar until set, then potted and covered.

marrow scoop Long thin spoon used for extracting marrow from bones.

Marseillan (French) Wine, known as onion-skin (*pelure d'oignon*) made in the *Hérault* town of that name.

marshmallow Elastic, spongy sweetmeat, white or tinted in pale colours, made from sugar, egg-white, glucose and gelatine or gum arabic. Marshmallows can be used in ice creams, jellies, etc. Marshmallows were originally made from the roots of the plant of that name.

marshmallow sauce Sugar, water and chopped marshmallows, folded into beaten egg-white.

marrow pudding Dish from the Scottish borders of a baked pudding made with white breadcrumbs, milk, eggs, beef marrow, currants, raisins, sugar and spices.

Marsala Fortified wine resembling sherry and Madeira, made from grapes grown near Marsala, in Sicily.

marsh hare (American) (i) Small hare found along the south-eastern American coast. (ii) Name for muskrat sold as game.

marsouin (French) Porpoise.

martin-sec (French) Winter pear used for cooking.

martin-sire (French) November pear with yellow flecked skin.

martini cocktail (i) Sweet martini: gin and Italian vermouth. (ii) Dry martini: gin and French vermouth. (iii) Mixed martini: gin and French and Italian vermouth.

Martinique Island in the Lesser Antilles renowned for its sugar-cane, rum, coffee, cocoa and spices.

marzipan, marchpane (i) Almond paste. (ii) Delicate dessert dainties made from almond paste. Name is said to be derived from *Marci Panis* – bread of St. Mark.

mascotte (French) Genoese cake iced with butter cream and pounded roast hazel-nuts.

mascotte, à la (French) Small cuts of meat or poultry garnished with quartered sautéed artichoke hearts, truffles, and small, butter-cooked potatoes.

mash Crushed malt and hot water from which, ultimately, spirit can be distilled or beer made.

masher Kitchen utensil for mashing potatoes and other foods.

mask (i) To cover or coat any kind of cooked meat with rich gravy or savoury jelly. (ii) To sauce a dish which is ready for serving. (iii) To coat the inside of a mould with sweet or savoury jelly or *chaudfroid* sauce.

maslin Bread made with mixed flours, especially rye and wheat.

mason jar Wide-mouth glass jar used for home preserving.

masquer (French) To cover or mask food with mayonnaise or other thick sauce.

masséna, à la (French) Steaks garnished with artichoke hearts stuffed with *Béarnaise* sauce and poached beef bone-marrow.

massenet (French) Garnish. See *masséna, à la.*

massepain (French) Marzipan; almond paste.

massette (French) Bullrush.

massillon (French) Tartlet-shaped almond paste *petit-four.*

mastiquer (French) To masticate; to chew.

maté South American tea, (Yerba de Maté) made from the leaves and green shoots of a species of holly.

matefaim (French) Coarse pancake intended to dull the edge of appetite.

matelote (French) Rich brown fish stew with wine and herb flavouring. Usually prepared from fresh-water fish – carp, tench, pike, eel, etc.

Mateus rosé (Portuguese) Light and very popular Portuguese *rosé* wine.

matignon (French) *Fondue* of vegetables used to garnish other dishes.

maton (French) Local name for curdled milk.

matsal (Swedish) Dining room.

matties (Scottish) Immature herring, a Scottish delicacy.

maturing The storing of wines and spirits in casks or bottles to improve their quality. The system varies according to the liquor concerned and requires skill and knowledge.

maturo (Italian) Ripe.

matzo, matzoth, matza (Jewish) Large thin brittle biscuit of unleavened bread traditionally eaten during the Passover. It commemorates the flight from Egypt when the Jews did not have time to let their bread rise.

matzoon (Armenian) Fermented milk.

maubêche (French) Sandpiper, a small bird eaten on the Continent.

Maulbeere (German) Mulberry.

mauve (French) (i) Mallow plant. (ii) Gull.

mauviette (French) Common name for a fatted lark (*alouette*).

mauvis (French) Redwing.

mavrodaphne (Greek) Greek liqueur.

May drink Spring-time white wine cup of German origin, flavoured with May flowers. Also called May Bowl or May wine.

mayonnaise (French) (i) Thick cold sauce made of yolks of eggs, oil, and vinegar; a salad sauce or dressing. Said to have been invented by the chef to the *Duc de Richelieu*, after the victory of *Mahon* (*Mahonnaise*). (ii) Fish or poultry dish covered with *mayonnaise* sauce and garnished with lettuce hearts, hard-boiled eggs, etc.

mazagran (French) (i) Glass of black coffee, sugar, and iced water. (ii) Baked tartlet lined with *duchesse* potatoes.

mazapán (Spanish) Marzipan.

mazarin Cake filled with candied fruit and glazed with kirsch-flavoured apricot coating.

mead Fermented liquor of honey and water with wild flowers or spices to flavour. The word "honeymoon" is derived from the old English custom of drinking mead as the special beverage for thirty days after the wedding feast.

meal Dish or dishes consumed at any one time.

meal-planning Arranging of meals in an order which takes into account all the factions concerned – season, weather, food availability, finance, numbers to be catered for and personal tastes, as well as colour, texture and flavour of the dishes contemplated.

mealie South African name for (i) Maize. (ii) Maize cake or corn-cake.

mealy pudding Oatmeal pudding served with grilled sausages, bacon, herrings, etc.

measuring cup Glass or metal vessel marked to indicate common cooking measurements. The American standard cup holds 8 fluid ounces, the British, 10 fluid ounces.

measuring jug Glass or metal vessel with a pouring lip marked to show fluid ounce and pint divisions.

measuring spoons Set of spoons made in graduated sizes. Both British and American sets are available.

meat Flesh (i.e. muscle tissue) of animals consumed as food. A source of protein, fat, vitamins A, B and D, iron, potassium and phosphorus. The term includes the flesh of all edible animals such as elephant or deer as well as the more commonplace pig (pork) ox (beef) calf (veal) lamb (lamb) sheep (mutton) and rabbit.

meat chopper (American) Mincer.

meat cleaver Implement used to split carcases in half, and to cut up meat.

meat extract Animal flesh minced, boiled, skimmed, filtered and evaporated. Used to make drinks or to add food value and flavour to soups, stews, gravies, etc.

meat grinder (American) Mincer.

meat loaf Minced meat, breadcrumbs, and other ingredients such as onion, seasonings, etc. shaped into a loaf and baked.

meat pie Meat baked in gravy under a pastry crust.

meat pudding Traditional English dish of suet pastry used to line and top a basin filled with meat and gravy, tied down with greaseproof paper and a cloth, and steamed or boiled.

meatball Minced meat shaped into a ball and grilled, fried, steamed, or boiled and served alone or in combination with other food.

méchoui (Arabic) Meat of a young animal roasted on charcoal embers or, in some parts of Morocco and Tunisia, braised in a glazed earthenware oven.

medaglione (Italian) Small round "medallion" of meat.

médaillon (French) Medallion. Small round or oval slice of meat such as *tournedo* of beer, collop of mutton, beef, poultry, etc.

medlar Fruit of the medlar tree, only eaten when thoroughly ripened and softened after keeping. Brown-coloured and similar to a large rose-hip, medlars are eaten raw or used to make preserves.

medlar cheese Preserve made from medlars, lemons, and sugar.

Médoc (French) Region in the *Gironde* producing full-bodied red wines of great reputation.

Meerettich (German) Horseradish.

Mehl (German) Flour.

Mehlfeister (German) Flour paste.

Mehlspeise (German) Pudding, sweet.

Mehlsuppe (German) Sweet-sour soup made with flour.

mejillón (Spanish) Sea mussel.

mekong Siamese rice whisky.

mela (Italian) Apple.

melacotogna (Italian) Quince.

melagrana, melagranata (Italian) Pomegranate.

melaine (French) Colouring matter.

mélange (French) (i) Mixture. (ii) (American) Coffee and cream served in a tall glass.

melanzana (Italian) Eggplant, aubergine.

melanzana alla marinara (Italian) Cold boiled aubergine or eggplant seasoned and dressed with oil, vinegar and garlic.

melanzana alla parmigiana (Italian) Eggplant or aubergine baked with cheese and tomatoes.

melanzana alla romagna (Italian) Aubergine or eggplant sliced and baked with a meat sauce, basil and cheese.

melanzana farcita (Italian) Stuffed eggplant or aubergine.

mélasse (French) Molasses.

melba (i) Peach melba. (ii) Melba toast. (iii) Melba sauce. Named for Dame Nellie Melba, world-famous singer.

melba sauce Raspberry sauce served with Peach melba and other desserts.

melba toast Very thin dry slice of toast.

melette (French) Sprat.

melissa Plant, known as lemon-balm with a mint-like leaf, used for flavouring and for making a spirit, *eau de mélisse*.

mélisse (French) Lemon balm, or melissa.

melitzane (Greek) Fried aubergine.

melk (Dutch and Norwegian) Milk.

melocotón (Spanish) Peach.

meloen (Dutch) Melon.

melon Plant and fruit of the cucumber genus, grown in several varieties such as cantaloupe, honeydew, charentis and water melon. Consisting mainly of water and low in calories, melons make a refreshing meal starter or dessert, and can also be pickled.

melón (Spanish) Melon.

melon baller Utensil with a small round

bowl for scooping out balls of melon flesh and other fruits and vegetables.

melon d'eau (French) Water-melon.

melon de malabar (French) Siamese pumpkin, cooked as for ordinary pumpkin.

melon fruit Papaya.

melon musqué (French) Musk-melon.

melon pickle Preserve made with melon, sugar and vinegar, and flavoured with cloves and cinnamon.

Melone (German) Melon.

melone (Italian) Melon.

melongena Aubergine.

melongène (French) Aubergine, eggplant.

melt To convert a solid into a liquid over gentle heat, e.g. ice or fat.

melting point Temperature at which a solid or semi-solid melts; ice turns to water at 32 degrees Fahrenheit (zero Centigrade).

melt, milt (i) Edible spleen of a meat animal. (ii) Soft roe of a fish.

meluggine (Italian) Crab apple.

membrillo (Spanish) Quince.

mendiants (French) Dessert of mixed almonds, hazel nuts, figs and raisins.

menta (Italian, Portuguese and Spanish) Mint.

menthe (French) Mint.

Mentonnaise, à la (French) Food, particularly rock-pool fish, cooked with tomatoes, black olives and garlic, in the style of Menton.

menu (French) Bill of fare. Literally, minute detail of courses. A list of the dishes which are to be served at a meal, first used in 1541.

menú (Spanish) Menu.

menu-gibier (French) Small game, such as partridges, grouse, pheasants, etc.

menu rôti (French) Small roast birds.

menue viande (French) Fowl and game.

menus droits (French) Pig's ears served as an *entrée*.

mercado (Portuguese and Spanish) Market.

mercato (Italian) Market.

mercatus (Latin) Market.

Mercurey (French) Wine made from grapes grown in the commune of *Mercurey* in the Saône-et-Loire district of France.

mère de sole (French) Plaice-like fish, cooked similarly.

mère de vinaigre (French) Mother of vinegar, the thick film which forms during the acidulation of wine.

mère goutte (French) Wine made from juice of grapes when first crushed and before they go into the press.

merenda (Italian) Snack.

merendero (Spanish) Lunchroom, café.

merga (Arabic) Sauce served with *couscous*.

merienda (Spanish) (i) High-tea. (ii) Light meal.

merienda campestre (Spanish) Picnic.

meringa (Italian) Meringue.

meringue (i) Small *pâtisserie* made of egg-whites and sugar, slow-baked and filled with cream or served with ice-cream or other desserts, or served for afternoon tea. (ii) Egg-white and sugar topping to a pie or other dessert.

merise (French) Wild cherry.

merisier (French) Wild cherry tree from whose fruit *Kirschwasser* is made.

merlan (French) Whiting.

merlango, merlano (Italian) (i) Small cod. (ii) Whiting.

merle (French) Blackbird.

merluche (French) (i) Hake. (ii) Dried cod. (iii) Dried hake.

merluccio (Italian) Hake.

merluza (Spanish) (i) Cod. (ii) Hake.

merluzzo (Italian) (i) Hake. (ii) Cod. (iii) Whiting.

mermelada (Spanish) (i) Jam. (ii) Preserve. (iii) Marmalade.

mermelada de naranja (Spanish) Orange marmalade.

merrythought Wishbone of poultry.

merry widow (American) Cocktail made of dry vermouth, Dubonnet, and lemon twist.

merveille (French) Small pastry made from deep-fried dough cut in different shapes and sprinkled with vanilla-sugar when cooked.

mesa (Spanish) Table.

mésange moustache (French) Reed bird, or rice bird, the Java sparrow, highly regarded as a delectable morsel, and called rice bird because of its depredations in the rice fields.

mescal Alcoholic drink made in Mexico and South America from the maguey or American sloe or agave. It tastes of bitter almonds.

mesentery of calf Membrane enveloping the intestines, cooked as for calf's head.

mesero (Spanish) Waiter.

mess (i) Dish of food. (ii) Number of persons who cater or eat together, especially in the Services.

Kesser (German) Knife.

messire-jean (French) Fragrant russet-coloured autumn variety of pear.

metabolism Sum total of chemical changes of living matter; the process by which food is passed into the blood stream and converted and absorbed.

metaxas (Greek) Sweet brandy liqueur.

metélt (Hungarian) Dry noodles.

metheglin (i) Ancient name for mead. (ii) Medieval herbal drink.

methuselah Large wine bottle containing the equivalent of 8 standard bottles.

mets (French) Any food prepared for the table; the meal, or dish.

Mettwurst (German) Bologna sausage.

meunière, à la (French) Fish floured and fried in butter, sprinkled with lemon juice and parsley, with the cooking butter poured over it when served.

meursault (French) White Burgundy from the *Beaune* slopes in France.

Mexican rabbit (American) Baked dish of cheese, eggs, green peppers, and tomatoes.

Mexican snapper (American) Red snapper, a type of bass.

Mexican tea (American) Kind of tea made with the ambroissier shrub, said to have restorative and medicinal properties.

Mexicanburger (American) Hamburger containing chilli.

mezcal (Spanish) Mescal.

meze (Greek) Appetizers.

mezza bottiglia (Italian) Half-bottle.

mezzo fiasco (Italian) Round-bottomed, straw-covered bottle, containing one litre of wine.

miche (French) Loaf, usually round.

miche de pain (French) Loaf of bread.

mickey finn Adulterated liquor with a disastrous after-effect. "Knock-out drops".

middagmåltid (Danish) Midday meal.

middagsmål (Swedish) Midday meal.

middlings Outer coating of grain, finely or coarsely ground, and used for animal feed.

midia dolma (Turkish) Mussels stuffed with seasoned rice and cooked in olive oil.

mie de pain (French) Soft bread; crumbs.

miel (French and Spanish) Honey.

miele (Italian) Honey.

miette (French) (i) Crumb of bread. (ii) Morsel.

mignardise (French) (i) Decorative pastry puff. (ii) Small dainty dish.

mignon (French) (i) Very small portions of fillets, *filet mignon*, etc. (ii) Delicate, dainty.

mignonette (French) Coarsely-ground white pepper-corns which resemble mignonette seed.

mignonne (French) (i) Kind of peach. (ii) Variety of pear.

migraine (French) Wine made from grapes grown near *Auxerre*, France.

mijoter (French) To cook slowly; to simmer gently over a small fire.

milanais (French) Small cake spread, when cooked, with apricot jam and coated with aniseed-flavoured icing.

Milanaise, à la (French) (i) Food dipped in egg and breadcrumbs mixed with Parmesan cheese, and fried. (ii) Dishes garnished with macaroni, cheese, pickled tongue, mushrooms and truffles blended in tomato sauce. (iii) Method of preparing macaroni.

Milch (German) (i) Milk. (ii) Soft fish-roe.

milch cow Dairy cow.

milchik (Jewish) Dairy dishes.

Milchkaffee (German) Coffee with milk.

Milchkäse (German) Curd.

mild-and-bitter Mixture of mild and bitter ales or beers.

milk Mammary fluid of female mammals such as the cow, ewe, and goat. Cow's milk is the one most widely used for domestic purposes and forms an important food because it contains almost all the constituents required by the human body. It is subject to many processes: pasteurising, homogenising, sterilising, etc., as well as drying into powdered form, condensing, evaporating, or souring to make cream cheese, scones, etc. Milk is the basis of many puddings and desserts, drinks and beverages, etc. and, because of its importance, is closely monitored by authority.

milk bar Snack bar specialising in milk drinks, ice cream sodas, etc.

milk chocolate Confectionery made from cocoa beans, milk, and sugar.

milk fat Butterfat.

milk-fed lamb See lamb.

milk jelly (i) Dessert made with milk, sugar, lemon rind and gelatine. (ii) Commercially-prepared jelly made up into a dessert with milk or milk and water.

milk powder Dried milk.

milk pudding Hot sweet made from whole milk and a grain (whole, crushed or ground), sugar and flavouring, such as spice or fruit, baked or boiled.

milk punch Beverage of milk and rum or whisky, with added sugar and nutmeg.

milk shake Cold drink of milk, ice cream and coffee, chocolate or fruit flavouring.

milk toast Hot buttered squares of toasted bread served in warm milk and seasoned or sweetened.

milkfish (American) Edible fish of the Pacific, similar to the herring, also available smoked and canned.

milkglass Opaque or translucent glassware with a milky appearance.

milkweed (American) Sow-thistle.

mill Small machine for pulverizing foods such as breadcrumbs, herbs, coffee, etc.

millas, miliasse (French) Porridge, similar to Polenta, made in the *Languedoc* region of France from cornmeal (maize) flour or from a mixture of wheat and maize flours. Also used to make sundry sweets.

millecanton (French) Small fish like whitebait, found in Lake Geneva;

cooked as for whitebait. In season during July and August.

mille-feuille (French) "Thousand-leaves" puff-pastry slice or cake split and filled with jam and cream, topped with *glacé* icing.

millefoglie (French) *Millefeuille*, "thousand leaves", flaky pastry.

millet Cereal high in carbohydrate and protein, which forms the staple food in parts of Africa and Asia. It is husked and made into porridge or ground into meal; also fermented to make an alcoholic drink. Millet flour is used for cakes, pastry, etc.

millet meal Meal ground from hulled millet.

milliasson (French) Small cake made with millet flour, sugar, eggs, and lemon flavouring.

milt (i) Soft roe of fish. (ii) Edible spleen of a meat animal.

mimosa salad Salad made from a wide variety of ingredients but topped with sieved hard-boiled egg-yolks.

mince (i) To divide food finely by chopping or passing through a mincing machine. (ii) Meat, either cooked or raw, which has been treated as above and is thus made easy to assimilate. It can be mixed with cereals, vegetables or pulses to make it go further, served with potato rings and garnished with tomatoes, mushrooms, etc., or made into meat patties, rissoles, and so on.

mince-pie Traditional English Christmas fare, a small pastry patty filled with mincemeat.

mincemeat Preserve used as a filling for mince pies and tarts, and in steamed suet or sponge puddings. Originally it included cooked lean beef, though now this is omitted except in America, and it usually consists of dried fruits, peel, suet, sugar, spices, orange and lemon, apple, brandy, etc. varied to taste.

mincer (i) Machine, hand-turned or electric, for mincing meat, etc. (ii) (American) Hand-mill grinder for mincing parsley, hard-boiled eggs, cheese, peel, vegetables, etc.

mineral water (i) Natural spring water

containing local salts and minerals and thought to have medicinal properties. Some waters, such as Vichy and Seltzer, water, are bottled and sold. (ii) Commercially, the name given to various aerated liquids, such as soda water, lemonade, etc.

minerals Chemical substances necessary for the efficient working of the body, including iron, calcium, copper, iodine, cobalt, fluorine, sulphur, potassium, sodium, phosphorus and magnesium.

minestra (Italian) Thick soup.

minestrina (Italian) Broth with small pieces of *pasta* served in it.

minestrone (Italian) Soup containing diced vegetables, beans, chick-peas, macaroni and vermicelli. Served with Parmesan cheese.

minguiche (Spanish/American) Mexican soup containing cheese, sour cream, green peppers and onions.

minnow Small edible freshwater fish, prepared like whitebait.

Minorca Black variety of domestic fowl originating on the island of Minorca.

mint Small aromatic plant in several varieties, including garden mint, spearmint, peppermint and pennyroyal. Used in flavouring dishes, making sauces, and included in commercial preparations of chewing gum, toothpaste, etc. Mint can be used fresh or dried, and is the traditional accompaniment to roast lamb. (See mint sauce).

mint jelly Preserve made from cooking apples, mint, sugar, lemon juice and colouring.

mint julep Drink made of bourbon whisky, sugar, sprigs of mint, water and ice.

mint sauce Sauce made from chopped mint, sugar, water and vinegar, served principally with lamb or mutton.

minuta (Italian) Bill of fare.

minute, à la (French) (i) Dishes which are hurriedly prepared. (ii) Anything cooked in the quickest possible style, such as omelettes and grills.

minute steak Steak about a quarter-inch thick which can be cooked in a very short time.

Minze (German) Mint.

mique de mais (French) Small cornmeal (maize flour) dumpling made with pork fat, poached in salt water and eaten in the *Périgord* area of France as an accompaniment to many dishes; also fried in butter as a sweet.

Mirabeau, à la (French) Grilled meat garnished with anchovy fillets, anchovy butters, stoned olives and tarragon leaves, named for the revolutionary, Mirabeau.

mirabelle (French) (i) Small yellow-red plum, sweet and juicy, a cross between a greengage and a very luscious plum, but much smaller. Used fresh or dried to make *compôtes*. (ii) Liqueur made from this fruit.

mirepoix (French) Foundation preparation of diced vegetables, herbs, and bacon, for brown soups and sauces, braised meats, etc. Name is said to be derived from the Duc de Mirepoix.

mirin (Japanese) Rice wine resembling sherry.

mirliton (French) Tartlet with a basis of puff-paste and filled with a custard mixture, speciality of Rouen.

miroir, au (French) (i) Dishes with a bright finish. (ii) Eggs baked in the oven so that the white forms a polished film on top.

miroton (French) Stew made from previously cooked meats.

Mischung (German) Blend, mixture.

mise en bouteille (French) Bottled, as applied to wines.

mise en place (French) (i) Putting things in place. (ii) Preparing the kitchen for cooking a meal.

misof (Armenian) Meat and vegetable stew.

Mispel (German) Medlar tree and fruit.

mission olive (American) Californian olive used for oil and for pickling.

misto (Italian) Mixed.

misto carne fredda (Italian) Mixed cold meats.

misto di arrosti (Italian) Assortment of roast meats.

mistra (Italian) Anise-flavoured liqueur.

mitilo (Italian) Mussel.

mitonner (French) To steep and simmer bread in soup for a long time.

Mittagessen (German) Lunch.

mix To stir ingredients until well blended.

mixed grill Meal of assorted grilled meats, such as steak, kidney, sausage, cutlet, with garnish of mushrooms, tomatoes, and watercress.

mixed-herb vinegar Vinegar flavoured with a combination of herbs such as basil, bay leaf, rosemary, tarragon and thyme. Used in sauces and salad dressings, etc.

mixed spice Blend of ground or powdered spices such as cinnamon, nutmeg, mace, cloves, coriander, caraway or ginger; used in flavouring puddings, biscuits and cakes.

mixed whole spices Blended, unground spices used for pickling and preserving meats, vegetables, etc.

mixing bowl Round bowl for blending, mixing and preparing foods.

mixing glass Heavy-sided glass for mixing drinks.

mixto (Spanish) Mixed.

mjölk (Swedish) Milk.

mizú (Japanese) Water.

Mocha (i) Strong fine coffee originating in Mocha on the Red Sea, used mainly in blended coffee. (ii) Mixture of coffee and chocolate flavours, used in cakes, icing, ice creams, etc.

mocha cake Cake of Genoese mixture filled and topped with mocha icing.

mochatine cake Portion of cake or *petit four* of Genoese mixture filled with butter icing and covered with fondant icing, both mocha-flavoured.

mochi (Japanese) Rice cake.

mock caviare Early 19th-century recipe of anchovies, parsley, and chives, pounded with olive oil, salt and lemon juice, spread on toast.

mock chicken Veal or other meat prepared to taste like chicken.

mock (imitation, synthetic) cream Substitute for whipped cream, either commercial or home-made.

mock cutlet Savoury mixture of meat, fish, eggs or vegetables shaped into cutlets, coated and fried.

mock duck (i) Meat, such as pork or shoulder of lamb, carved to resemble a duck. (ii) Economy dish of sage and onion stuffing, shaped and baked.

mock fritter See *pain perdu.*

mock turtle soup Brown soup made from calf's head, alleged to resemble real turtle soup.

mode, à la (French) (i) (French) Large cuts of braised beef. (ii) (American) With ice cream.

moëlle (French) Marrow of bone.

moëlle de bœuf (French) Beef bone-marrow.

Mohn (German) Poppyseed.

Mohnkuchen (German) Poppyseed cake.

Möhre (German) Carrot.

Mohrenkopf (German) Chocolate *éclair.*

Mohrrübe (German) Carrot.

moisten To add liquid such as broth, wine, stock, etc. to dishes like stews, *ragouts*, braised food, etc.

mojarra (American) Edible, round Caribbean fish.

moka (French) (i) Mocha (as in icing, flavouring, etc.) (ii) Strongly flavoured coffee (See Mocha).

Mokka (German) Mocha coffee.

molasses (i) Thick, brown, treacly drainings from raw sugar. (ii) Syrup obtained from the sugar during refinement. Molasses drained from beet sugar is very bitter and is mainly used in cattle feed. Molasses from cane sugar is pleasant-tasting and is used in making rum.

molé (Spanish) Mexican *fricassé* of meat or turkey with chilli sauce.

Molkerei (German) Dairy.

Molke (German) Whey.

mollet (French) Soft, i.e., *œuf mollet,* soft-boiled egg.

Molluske (German) Mollusc.

monaco (French) (i) *Consommé* of clear chicken broth thickened with arrowroot, garnished with a cheesy cake cut in small rounds. (ii) Cream of chicken soup, garnished as above.

monastine (French) Yellow liqueur resembling yellow Chartreuse in flavour.

Monbazillac (French) Rich white wine from a commune of that name in the Dordogne, France.

monkey nut Peanut.

monosodium glutamate Crystalline salt used to accentuate the flavour of meat foods, stock, soups, etc.

monselat (French) Dishes whose ingredients include artichoke hearts and truffles, sometimes with butter-fried potatoes.

mont-blanc (French) Sweet made from chestnut *purée* and *Chantilly* Cream.

mont-bry (French) Garnish of small spinach cakes cooked in Parmesan cheese, with *cèpes* in cream.

mont-cenis (French) Large semi-hard French cheese with blue veins, made from whole milk and ripened in cellars.

mont d'or (French) (i) White Swiss wine. (ii) French cheese, now made from cow's milk but originally made from goat's milk.

mont-frigoul (French) Soup in which semolina forms the chief ingredient.

monte bianco (Italian) Dessert of sweetened, puréed chestnuts covered in whipped cream.

monte cristo (French) Another name for *Montpensier gâteau.*

montglas (French) *Salpicon* made from *foie gras* and pickled tongue with mushrooms and truffles, used to fill tartlets, *vol-au-vents*, etc.

montgolfier, filet (French) Fillet distended by blowing out into a balloon-shape, said to have been invented by the Montgolfier brothers who sent up the first fire balloon in 1783.

montilla (Spanish) Light, dry, fortified wine taken as it is, or made into sherry.

monteith Punchbowl of the 17th or 18th century, fluted and scalloped and usually made of silver, for cooling punch glasses.

montilla (Spanish) Dry sherry from Córdoba, southern Spain.

montmorency (French) Bitter variety of cherry, cultivated near Paris.

montmorency (French) Dishes, cakes or sweets flavoured with cherries.

montone (Italian) Mutton.

Montpellier French city, capital of the *Hérault*, renowned for its culinary specialities such as lobster cardinale, stuffed mussels, and squid in hot, spicy red sauce.

Montpellier butter Edible green-coloured butter used principally for decoration of cold dishes.

montpensier (French) (i) Garnish of asparagus tips and truffles. (ii) Butterdough flan filled with an almond meringue mixture.

Montrachet (French) Famous white wine from the *Côte d'Or*, France.

moonshine Liquor distilled illegally. See poteen.

moorfowl, moorgame, moorcock (i) (Scottish) Grouse. (ii) Black game.

moorhen, waterhen Small waterfowl.

moose, elk Large deer, with edible flesh, prepared as for deer.

moque (French) Belgian confectionery of butter, sugar, molasses, flour and cloves.

mora selvatica (Italian) Blackberry.

morango (Portuguese) Strawberry.

moray Carnivorous fish, similar to the eel and cooked in the same manner.

Morchel (German) Morel, edible fungus.

morel Fungus found in woods and orchards, said to possess great stimulating properties; used as garnish for *fricassées*, and for soups and sauces. Can be simmered or fried in butter.

Morelle (German) Morello cherry.

morello cherry Dark red rather bitter cherry, used in cooking but not as dessert. Suitable for flans, pies, preserves, etc. also used to make cherry brandy.

morena (Spanish) Brown bread.

morgenmad (Danish) Breakfast.

morille (French) Morel, edible fungus.

morillon (French) (i) Black grape. (ii) Blue-winged duck.

moringa Horse-radish tree, an Egyptian shrub bearing edible pods yielding an oil used in perfumery.

mornay (French) Dishes coated with mornay sauce.

mornay sauce Rich creamy cheese sauce, served with eggs, vegetables, fish, and chicken.

mortadella (Italian) Large pink sausage made of beef and pork seasoned with pepper-corns and containing squares of white fat; made in Bologna, Italy.

mortadella di campotosta (Italian) Sausage more highly spiced than the Bologna *mortadella* and strongly garlic-flavoured.

mortadelle (French) *Mortadella* sausage, largely manufactured in Bologna, Italy, but also made in France.

mortar Bowl of metal, wood, stone or marble used for crushing and pounding food with the aid of a pestle.

mortier (French) Mortar.

mortifie (French) Term applied to well hung meat and game.

mortifier (French) To hang (game or meat).

morue (French) Salt cod.

morue sèche, morue verte (French) Salted fish, usually cod.

moscatello (Italian) (i) Muscatel grape. (ii) Wine made from Muscatel grapes.

moscovite (French) (i) Term applied to various sweets such as jellies, creams, etc. usually made in a moscovite mould (a hexagonal mould with a hinged lid) (ii) Ice cream or *bombe* made in a mould, as above, and filled with fruit and *Chantilly* cream.

Moscow mule (American) Mixed drink of vodka, ginger beer and lime or lemon juice.

Moselhect (German) Pike cooked with grated cheese and cream, a speciality of the Moselle region.

Moselle Clear dry wines similar to hock made in the Moselle valley.

mossberry Cranberry.

Most (German) (i) Cider. (ii) New wine.

mostarda (Italian and Portuguese) Mustard.

mostaza (Spanish) Mustard.

mostelle (French) Delicate Mediterranean fish, cooked as for whiting.

mote, moti Indian fish curry.

mother of vinegar Thick film which forms during the acidulation of wine.

motza Matzo.

mou (French) Animal lights.

mouflon (French) Mountain sheep.

mouille bouche (French) Bergamot pear.

mouiller (French) To add broth, water, or any other suitable liquid, during the cooking of meats.

mouillette (French) Toast dipped in liquid.

moulage (French) Moulding food into a shape.

mould (i) Sweet or savoury close-textured dish shaped in a mould, usually served cold. Sweet moulds can be set with cornflour or gelatine and savoury ones with gelatine or aspic. (ii) Hollow receptacle for shaping food. (iii) Minute organism which grows as "whiskers" or spots on the surface of meat, cheese, jams and cooked food. Mould indicates that food is stale or has been badly stored. It can be scraped off cheese and lifted from jams, etc.

moule (French) (i) Mould (the receptacle) (ii) Mussel.

moulin (French) Mill, food mill.

moulin-a-vent (French) Red Burgundy wine from *Maçon*.

moule marinière (French) Cooked, shelled mussel served in a sauce made from the cooking liquid, thickened with egg yolks and cream (or fat and flour).

mountain ash Tree bearing the bright red rowan berry, sometimes used in apple sauce, or for a jelly to serve with game.

mountain mint (American) Aromatic herb of the mint family, also called basil mint.

mountain oyster (American) Edible animal testicle.

moussache (French) Manioc flour used in making tapioca.

moussaka (Greek) Dish made of alternate layers of aubergine minced meat, and *courgettes*.

mousse (French) Light creamy dish, hot or cold, sweet or savoury thickened with cream, eggs or gelatine, and flavoured with coffee, chocolate, fruit, etc., or, when savoury, with fish, cheese, etc.

mousse au chocolat (French) Chocolate mousse containing egg, sugar, double cream, chocolate and vanilla.

mousseau (French) Type of bread made from wheat flour.

Moussec British effervescent wine made from French grape juice.

mousseline (French) (i) Dish containing whipped cream. (ii) Small mould of poultry, game or fish, enriched with cream. (iii) Sponge-cake made with flour, cornflour, fine sugar, egg yolks and beaten egg whites, usually filled with flavoured cream.

mousseline sauce (i) *Hollandaise* sauce to which beaten egg or whipped cream has been added, to accompany fish or certain vegetables. (ii) Sweet sauce made from egg, sugar and sherry beaten over hot water, and served with sponge puddings and fruit, etc.

mousseron (French) Type of white mushroom, principally used for *ragoûts*. Also known as St. George's Agaric.

mousseux (French) General term for French sparkling wine, except Champagne.

moussoir (French) Swizzle-stick for drinks.

moustille (French) Semi-sparkling wine.

moutarde (French) Mustard.

moutardelle (French) Type of horse-radish, used similarly.

moût (French) Unfermented wine.

mouton (French) Sheep; mutton.

Mouton cadet (French) (i) Popular claret from Bordeaux. (ii) Also in a white version.

Mouton-Rothschild château (French) Famous and costly claret from the Bordeaux region.

moyeau (French) Egg-yolk.

mozo (Spanish) Waiter.

mozzarella (Italian) Round white cheese made from buffalo milk. When fresh, it is soft and moist. When matured and dried, it is rather rubbery and is used for cooking, particularly in *pizza*.

mozzarella in carrozza (Italian) *Mozzarella* cheese sandwich dipped in egg batter and fried.

msg Abbreviation for monosodium glutamate.

muffin (i) (English) Thick, flat, round yeast cake made from soft dough and baked on a girdle. Toasted and eaten usually at tea-time. (ii) (American) Quick bread made from egg batter and cooked in special muffin tins.

muffin pan (American) Baking tin with cavities for small cakes, individual batter puddings, etc.

mufle de bœuf (French) Ox cheek.

muge, mulet (French) Grey mullet.

muggine (Italian) Mullet.

muguet angumeux (French) Solomon's seal.

mugwort Wormwood; aromatic bitter plant used as a flavouring.

muisje (Dutch) Coloured sugar-coated confection served at teatime.

mulberry Fruit similar to the blackberry but larger, and with red berries ripening to a deep purple. Eaten raw with sugar, stewed in syrup, bottled, made into pies, flans, wine. Combined with apple, they can also be used for jams or other preserves.

mulberry wine Wine made from mulberries, sugar and yeast.

mulgikapsad (Russian) Estonian pork with sauerkraut.

mull To heat ale, cider, sherry, claret, etc. with spices or sugar. The traditional method is to insert a red hot poker into the brew.

mulled wine Red wine, port, brandy, a clove-stuck lemon, lemon-peel, cinnamon and nutmeg heated to near boiling point and served in mugs with added brown sugar.

mullet Salt-water fish, of several species, particularly: (i) Red mullet. Bright pink, and at their best from April to October. The firm and white delicate flesh should be grilled or baked. (ii) Grey mullet, with a greenish back, a silvery underside. When large they are cooked as cod; small ones may be cooked as for red mullet.

mulligatawny (i) Indian curry soup. (ii) Paste made of curry; derives from Tamil, *molegoo* (pepper) and *tunnee* (water).

mum Beer brewed from malted wheat or from oat or bean meal. (See *Mumme*).

mumbled hare Minced, cooked hare's meat, flavoured, spiced, and acidulated, put into a stew-pan with beaten eggs and butter, and cooked to a thick consistency by constant stirring.

Mumme (German) Beer made without hops, dark and bittersweet, made in Lower Saxony. (See mum.)

Münster Firm yellow whole-milk cheese flavoured with anise or caraway seed, often coated in red wax and originating in Münster, Germany.

mûr (French) Ripe.

mûre (French) Mulberry.

mûre de ronce, mûre sauvage (French) Blackberry.

murena, morena (Italian) (i) Sea-eel, moray. (ii) Lamprey.

murène (French) Moray, sea-eel.

muscade (French) Nutmeg.

muscadelle (French) Musk pear.

Muscadet Sweet white wine made from muscat grapes, grown in the Loire and elsewhere.

muscadine Muscat grape used for wine-making.

muscat (French) Muscadine. A white or black grape (muscadine grape) with a musty flavour, used for making Muscadet wine.

Muscat de Rivesaltes (French) Strong liqueur wine made at *Rivesaltes*, in the *Pyrenees-Orientales*.

muscatel (i) Large, juicy, sun-dried raisin from Spain, used in cookery or served as a dessert, especially at Christmas when it is usually accompanied by blanched almonds. (ii) Sweet white wine made in France, Spain and Italy from muscat grapes also called Muscadet.

Muschel (German) Mussel.

muscolo (Italian) Mussel.

muscovado Unrefined sugar, left after evaporating the cane juice and draining the molasses away.

museau de bœuf (French) Beef or ox muzzle, cooked as for ox tongue.

mush (American) Boiled cornmeal seasoned with salt, resembling Polenta.

mushimono (Japanese) Steamed food.

mushroom Edible fungus in many varieties the best-known being the field mushroom, horse mushroom and fairy ring mushroom. Low in food value, mushrooms are nevertheless highly regarded for their flavour which enriches casseroles, omelettes, grills, stews, soups, etc. They can be sautéed, baked or grilled and served on toast, etc. Cultivated mushrooms are used in the same ways.

mushroomburger (American) Vegetarian hamburger made of minced and seasoned mushrooms.

musigny (French) Name associated with some of the great wines of Burgundy.

musk deer Small Indian deer, edible when young, and cooked as for kid.

Muskatnuss (German) Nutmeg.

muskellunge (American) Large North American freshwater pike, a game fish.

muskmelon Common melon, in several varieties including cantaloupe.

muslin bag Bag used to hold ingredients to be infused but not released into a dish, as, for example orange and lemon pips when making marmalade.

mussel Greenish-black bivalve mollusc found along sea coasts and in rivers and streams. They must be fresh (alive) when purchased, thoroughly washed, scrubbed, scraped before cooking in water until the shells open. The "beard" and any foreign bodies are then removed. They can be served plain with vinegar or lemon juice, served in a sauce, added to soups, stews and fish dishes, fried, curried, etc., etc. See *moule mariniere*, etc.

mussel brose (Scottish) Mussels cooked in milk, water and oatmeal.

mussel plum Dark purple plum resembling a mussel shell in shape.

must Unfermented grape juice. which is treated with yeast and turned into wine.

mustard (i) Seeds of a plant, *Sinapis nigra* (black) and *Sinapis alba* (white or yellow) pulverised and used as a relish or condiment. English mustard was first manufactured at Durham in 1729. (ii) Condiment, see mustard sauce.

mustard and cress Hardy white mustard seedlings grown in conjunction with garden cress, for use in salads, as a garnish, or as a sandwich filling in conjunction with other items such as cheese or chopped, hard-boiled egg.

mustard greens Green leaves of various mustard plants, used in salads.

mustard pot Small jar used for serving mustard sauce. often with matching spatula or spoon.

mustard sauce (i) Condiment made from ground mustard seed, made in a variety of ways. English mustard, first manufactured in 1729, is sold as a fine powder and is mixed with milk or water. French mustards are sold in paste form, having been flavoured and then mixed with verjuice (Dijon mustard) or vinegar or unfermented wine (Bordeaux mustard). Other specialist mustards include Cremona mustard from Italy, containing crystallised fruit. (ii) Sauce made with butter, flour, water and vinegar, and flavoured with mustard powders, to serve with fish and other dishes.

mustard seed Small seed of the mustard plant, ground into powder for use in gravies, pickling, sauces, etc., and as a condiment.

mustard spinach Indian mustard.

mustèle (French) Mediterranean fish similar to burbot and cooked in the same way. Its liver is regarded as a great delicacy.

Mutterschaf (German) Ewe.

mutton Flesh from the carcase of a sheep more than one year old. Prime joints (leg, shoulder, loin) are suitable for roasting as well as for other cooking methods. Cutlets can be fried, grilled or braised. Breast can be stewed, or stuffed and baked. Sheep's head and trotters are stewed. Mutton flesh should be red and close-grained, with firm white fat.

mutton chop Chop cut from the ribs of a sheep's carcase. Can be grilled, braised, baked, etc.

muttonburger (American) Hamburger made of mutton.

myost (Norwegian) Light-brown whey cheese, the national cheese of Norway.

myrte (French) Myrtle.

myrtille (French) Bilberry.

myrtle Fragrant evergreen shrub whose berries were once used widely in stews and wines. The pepper myrtle yields berries which, when powdered, are known as Jamaican pepper.

na zdorovie (Russian) To your health! A toast.

naartje (Africaans) Cape orange, small-ish fruit about the size of the mandarin.

nabo (Spanish) Turnip.

Nachtessen (German) Supper, evening meal.

Nachtisch (German) Dessert.

Nachtmahl (German/Austrian) Night meal; supper.

nage, à la (French) Method of preparing shell fish such as crayfish and lobster in *court bouillon.*

nagelkaas (Dutch) Skimmed milk cheese flavoured with cloves and cumin seeds.

nagerecht (Dutch) Dessert.

Nahe (German) District of Germany famed for good wines.

nahit (Jewish) Chick-peas.

Nahrung (German) Nourishment.

Nahrungsmittel (German) Victuals, provisions, food.

nalésnik (Polish) Rolled pancake.

nalysnyky (Russian) Ukranian dish of cheese-filled pancakes.

namaycush (American) Lake salmon.

Nantais (French) (i) Small almond biscuit. (ii) Nantes duckling.

napery Table linen; napkins, tablecloths, etc.

Napfkuchen (German) Pound-cake, large cake.

napkin Square of paper or fabric used at table for wiping mouth and fingers.

napkin ring Hollow ring for holding an individual napkin.

Naples biscuit Ladyfinger or boudoir biscuit.

Napoleon *Mille-feuille* pastry filled with custard or whipped cream and iced.

Napoleon brandy (i) Liqueur brandy casked during era of Napoleon I. (ii) Term applied to any very old brandy.

Napoletana, alla (Italian) Dish with tomato sauce, a speciality of Naples region.

Napolitaine (French) Naples or Neapolitan style, a term applied to various dishes, notably a tricoloured ice cream. (See neapolitan).

napolitain (French) (i) Neapolitan. (ii) Rich iced almond cake.

nappe (French) Tablecloth.

nappé (French) (i) Covered lightly; food masked or coated thinly with sauce or jelly. (ii) Food dipped in coating.

narang (Arabic) Orange.

naranja (Spanish) Orange.

naranjada (Spanish) (i) Orangeade. (ii) Orange squash.

naranjillada (Spanish) Orange-juice drink.

Narbonne (French) Town in the Aude district, one of the centres of French viticulture.

narcisse (French) Narcissus.

narcissus Plant grown from bulbs which are edible, and cooked as for Jerusalem artichokes.

narsharab (Russian) Sharp syrup of cooked pomegranate juice.

narval (French) Narwhal.

narwhal Acquatic whale-like mammal with a canine tooth; eaten as food by Greenlanders, but chiefly known for the oil extracted from its fat.

Näscherei (German) Sweetmeats, dainties.

naseberry plum Sapodilla.

nasello (Italian) (i) Hake. (ii) Whiting.

nasi (Malay) Boiled rice.

nasi goreng (Malay) Spicy Indonesian dish of fried rice with added pork fillet, chicken, fish, prawns or other seafood.

Nassau royale Fine, unique liqueur invented in the Bahamas.

nasturtium Indian cress. A native plant of Peru, now widely grown. The round, hot-flavoured leaves are eaten in salads. The yellow, orange or red flowers may be used to garnish salads. The green, berry-like seeds are pungent and, when pickled, can substitute for capers.

nata (Spanish) Cream.

natillas (Spanish) Custard.

native Oyster taken from the oyster beds off the coast of Essex and Kent.

natural brown rice Rice hulled by a special process, to preserve the germ and retain the high-protein content.

nature, au (French) Food served in its natural state – raw, uncooked, or unseasoned, or very simply and plainly cooked.

Naturschnitz (German) Fried veal cutlet.

nau de morue (French) Cod sounds or swimming bladders.

navarin (French) Lamb or mutton stew or *ragoût*, with potatoes and onions.

navel orange Seedless orange with a navel-like depression on the outside, and a fleshy plug within.

navet (French) Turnip.

navette (French) Wild turnip.

navy bean (American) Haricot bean (white, dried).

navy-bean soup (American) Thick vegetable soup of haricot beans, carrots, celery, milk, onions, parsley, tomatoes and seasoning.

nazdar (Czechoslovakian) Good luck! A toast.

neapolitan Sweets, cakes, ices, etc., made with layers of two or more colours, each appropriately flavoured, and served so that the different colours show to the best advantage.

neapolitan ice cream Ice cream brick made of three or four varieties, such as chocolate, vanilla and strawberry ice.

neapolitan sandwich Lengthwise alternating slices of white and brown bread spread with different fillings, cut across to display the striped effect.

neat Cattle – ox, cow or bull.

neat's foot Foot of a calf or ox.

neat's foot oil Oil obtained from the feet of oxen.

neat's tongue Tongue of a calf or ox.

nebuchadnezzar Huge wine bottle containing the equivalent of 20 standard bottles.

nectar (i) Mythical beverage of the Greek gods. (ii) Sweet liquid of flowers, collected by bees in making honey.

nectarine Smooth-skinned type of peach in both free and cling-stone varieties, eaten fresh as dessert fruit or cooked as for peaches.

needle (i) Larding needle, a tool for passing thin strips of bacon fat into meat, poultry, etc. (ii) Trussing needle, a pointed tool for trussing poultry and game.

nèfle (French) Medlar.

nèfle d'Amérique (French) Sapodilla.

negroni Drink of gin, sweet vermouth and campari served over ice and topped with soda water.

negus Hot mixture of port, claret or sherry, sugar, nutmeg, and lemon juice, called after Colonel Negus who invented it in the reign of Queen Anne.

neige (French) Snow. Whites of egg beaten to a stiff froth.

neige de Florence (French) Delicate *pasta* used in clear soup.

Nelke (German) Clove.

Nelson's blood Royal navy term for rum.

neludko Ice cherry *petit four*.

nemour (French) Tartlet of flaky pastry filled with jam and *chou* paste.

Nepal pepper Yellowish pepper, largely grown in Hindustan, similar to Cayenne and Guinea pepper but less hot, and with a sweet, pungent flavour.

néroli (French) (i) Volatile oil extracted from orange-blossom and used in confectionery and liqueurs. (ii) Small light cake made of almonds, eggs, sugar, candied orange peel and orange flower water.

nespola (Italian) Medlar.

nespola di Giappone (Italian) Loquat (Japanese medlar).

nesselrode Iced pudding, flavoured with candied fruits and chestnuts, invented by Mony, chef to the famous Count Nesselrode. The name Nesselrode usually indicates the presence of chestnuts.

nest (i) Edible, basket-shaped arrangement of food, such as match-stick potatoes, or meringue cases filled with titbits. (ii) Swallow's nest found in grottoes in Jave and Malaya, and prized by Chinese gourmets as a delicacy; usually served in soup. (iii) Set of kitchen bowls, casseroles or measuring spoons in graduated sizes, fitting one into another.

nettle Hedgerow and field weed with a stinging action. Young nettles, which have a pleasant, slightly bitter taste, may be cooked as a vegetable and served with butter or cream, or made into soup.

nettle soup Young stinging nettles washed, cooked, sieved and added to thin white sauce.

neufchâtel (French) Soft French cheese made from whole or skimmed milk according to type. Dark yellow in colour, it is also called Boudon.

neutral spirit Unflavoured spirit added to gin, vodka, etc: also called "Silent spirit".

nevera (Spanish) Refrigerator; ice-box.

New England clam chowder (American) Chowder made with milk.

New England dinner (American) Salted, smoked beef boiled with vegetables.

New Hampshire red (American) Breed of domestic poultry developed from Rhode Island Red chickens.

New Jersey tea (American) Deciduous shrub, redroot, a member of the buckthorn family formerly used as a tea substitute.

New York cut (American) Cut of beef including the hipbone.

New York dressed (American) Poultry prepared for market with feet, head, and viscera included.

New York State wine (American) Wine produced in New York State, often from native American varieties of grapes.

newburg, *à la* (American) Food served in a sauce made from butter, cream, egg yolks and sherry or Madeira.

newburg sauce (American) Brandy, butter, cream, egg yolk, and wine sauce.

newtown pippin Green apple of excellent flavour, originating in Devonshire, and taken across the Atlantic two centuries ago and named after Newtown, Long Island, U.S.A.

niçoise (French) Method of preparing dishes with tomatoes and garlic among the ingredients.

niçoise **salad** See *salade niçoise*.

nicotinic acid One of the vitamin B group, niacin.

nid (French) Nest.

nid d'hirondelles de Chine (French) Chinese birds' nest.

Nieheimer Hopfenkäse (German) Sour milk "hop" cheese originating in the north German town of Nieheim.

Niederungskäse (German) Rennet cheese

Niere (German) Kidney.

Nierenbraten (German) Roast loin.

Nierenfett (German) Suet.

niersoep (Dutch) Kidney soup.

nigella Black cumin. Plant of the *renunculus* family yielding aromatic or pungent seeds which are used as a spice.

nigelle (French) Nigella; black cumin.

nightcap Grog, mulled wine or beer, or other hot drink, taken before going to bed.

nightshade Plant in several varieties, some of whose leaves can be eaten like spinach, although others are poisonous or narcotic.

nimono (Japanese) Boiled food.

niokes, niokies (Russian) Farinaceous dish of semolina or Indian corn flavoured with grated cheese, cream, etc.

nip Sip or small serving of drink.

nitrogen Essential element in all protein foods.

Nivernais (French) French province renowned for meat, poultry, root vegetables and table wines.

Nivernaise, à la (French) Garnish of cut carrots and glazed onions, served with meat dishes.

niverolle (French) Snow bird.

nivette (French) Variety of peach.

njure (Swedish) Kidney.

noble rot Fungus which forms on over-ripe grapes left on the vines after the main harvest. These are then used to make very sweet wines.

noce (French) Wedding.

noce (Italian) Nut, walnut.

noce americano (Italian) Brazil nut.

noce del Brasile (Italian) Brazil nut.

noce di cocco (Italian) Coconut.

nociolino (Italian) Filbert, cob or hazelnut.

Nockerln (German) Little Dumpling.

nog Drink such as Egg Nog, Rum Nog, etc.

noggin (i) Liquid measure, usually $\frac{1}{4}$ pint. (ii) Portion or ration of liquid.

Noilly Prat Dry French vermouth.

noisette (French) (i) Hazel-nut. (ii) Small nut or kernel. (iii) Small round piece of lean meat, such as lamb or mutton cutlet, with bone and fat removed. (iv) Part taken from the middle, such as a *noisette* of beef tenderloin, i.e. a slice cut from the centre.

noisette **butter** Butter heated in a pan until light hazelnut colour.

noisette **potatoes** Potatoes shaped with a ball-scoop and cooked in butter until pale brown.

noisette **sauce** *Hollandaise* sauce with *noisette* butter added.

noisettine (French) Small cake consisting of two oval layers of short pastry filled with hazelnut-flavoured cream.

noix (French) Nut; walnut.

noix de Brésil (French) Brazil nut.

noix de coco (French) Coconut.

noix de muscade (French) Nutmeg.

noix de palme (French) Palm nut, from which palm oil is extracted. Fruit of the Eléis of New Guinea.

noix de veau (French) Veal knuckle; veal or cushion.

nokedli (Hungarian) Dumpling.

nøkkelost (Norwegian) Dark goat's milk cheese flavoured with caraway seeds.

non maturo (Italian) Unripe.

nonnat, nonat (French) Small fish, similar to whitebait, and cooked in the same way.

nonnette (French) Small round iced gingerbread.

nonpareille (French) (i) Small capers pickled in vinegar. (ii) Coloured sugar granules used for cake decoration. (iii) Sugar-coated chocolate drop. (iv) Large variety of pear.

noodles (i) Type of *pasta* made of flour, eggs and water originating in Italy, and cut into long, flat, narrow strips. They can be served, broken, in soups; or as an accompaniment to a main course in place of potatoes; or, topped with meat or tomato sauce, as a main course in themselves. (ii) Chinese Noodles: Pasta "strings" made from wheat and rice flour, and served in a meat sauce, or in soup, or fried.

nopal (Spanish) Edible prickly-pear cactus.

nopalitos (Spanish) Mexican dish of prickly-pear cactus leaves.

noque (French) Small dumpling made of eggs, butter and flour, poached in boiling, salted water; served in soup, or sprinkled with Parmesan cheese and butter.

nordost (Swedish) Tangy, mellow whole-milk cheese.

norelle (French) Nightshade.

Norfolk dumpling, drop dumpling, spoon dumpling Batter-ball made of flour, eggs, milk, etc. dropped into boiling water from a spoon.

Normande, à la (French) (i) Method of serving food, especially fish, braised in white wine, garnished with shrimps, oysters, crayfish, etc. (ii) Small cuts of meat or poultry with cider poured over them.

Normandy French province renowned for butter, cream, apples, cider, fish, etc. Cheese of the region include *Neufchâtel, Pont l'Evêque* and *Camembert.* Culinary specialities include *Soupe Normande* and the Madame Poularde *omelette aux coques,* tripe, duckling *à la Rouennaise.* etc.

Normandy sauce White sauce made with fish liquor, butter, egg yolk, and lemon juice, served with fish dishes.

northern spy (American) Red winter cooking and eating apple.

norvégien (French) Kirsch-flavoured cake made from butter, cornflour, sugar, eggs, sweet almonds and apricot kernels.

Norvégienne, à la (French) (i) Surprise pudding of ice cream inside a hot casing. (ii) Method of serving cold fish or shell fish.

nouet (French) Muslin bag.

nougat (French) Sweetmeat made with sugar, honey, almonds, pistachios, and other nuts, often coloured pink-and-white.

nougatine Chocolate-covered nougat.

nougatine cake Layered square of Genoese cake and praline cream, iced with chocolate fondant icing.

nouilles (French) Noodles.

nourrir (French) To enrich by adding butter, cream, oil, etc to other ingredients.

noyau (French) (i) Fruit stone. (ii) Liqueur originally made in France, flavoured with cherry-stone kernels which impart a bitter almond flavour.

nubbin Small or imperfect ear of corn.

nubian Dark-purple plum.

Nudeln (German) Macaroni, vermicelli, noodles.

Nudelsuppe (German) Noodle soup.

nuez (Spanish) Nut.

Nuits St. Georges (French) Burgundian commune producing excellent wines.

nun's sigh See *soupir de nonne* or *pet de nonne.*

nun's toast Fried bread.

Nuss (German) Nut.

Nussbügel (German) Pastry filled with almonds, hazelnuts or walnuts.

Nusskipfer (German) Nut biscuit.

Nusskuchen (German) Nutcake.

Nussstrudel (German) Nut *strudel.*

Nusstorte (German) Nut cake, pastry or tart.

nut Hard-shelled dry fruit or fruit seed, such as Brazil, cashew, hazel, pecan, peanut, etc.

nut butter Paste made from crushed nuts.

nut forcemeat Stuffing made of breadcrumbs, egg, herbs and ground or finely chopped nuts, used for poultry, etc.

nut-gall Fruit of a species of sage bush, also of a ground ivy.

nut margarine Margarine made from coconut and peanut oils.

nut oil Oil derived from nuts such as coconut oil, peanut oil, walnut oil, etc.

nut pine Edible pine seed.

nutcracker Hinged, double-handled device for cracking nuts.

nutcracker set Set of implements consisting of a nutcracker and picks to remove the nutmeats from the shells.

nutmeat Kernel of a nut, extracted when the shell is broken.

nutmeg Seed of a tropical tree native to the Molucca islands but cultivated in Indonesia. The husk around the seed is dried as mace; its kernel is the nutmeg, used for oil extraction, or exported whole for use in baking, and other cooking.

nutmeg cream Cream flavoured with sugar, vanilla and grated nutmeg.

nutmeg grater Small metal utensil for grating whole nutmegs, some made also with a container to hold nutmegs.

nutpick Sharp-pointed implement for picking nut meats out of their shells.

nutrient Chemical component of food which produces energy, makes or repairs tissue and/or regulates the body processes.

nutrition (i) Food. (ii) Process of nourishing. (iii) Science of food and the study of essential food factors in human life.

nutritionist Specialist in nutrition.

ny ka py (Chinese) Chinese whisky-type spirit made from millet and flavoured with herbs.

oat groats Hulled oats used as a cereal.

oats Cereal, *avena*, containing all the nutrient properties of wheat. The seeds are husked and the grain ground or rolled in various ways to produce different grades of rolled oats or oatmeal, including the specially treated quick-cooking type. Oatmeal has a low gluten content.

oatcake Thin, flat oatmeal pancake, baked on a griddle or girdle.

oatmeal Ground or rolled oats, used in breads, cakes, biscuits, and porridge.

oatmeal bannock See bannock.

oatmeal porridge Breakfast cereal made from oatmeal.

oatmeal soup Oatmeal simmered in stock, milk or water, with butter, egg yolk and cream added.

oba Species of African mango yielding a white oily almond with a cocoa-like flavour.

obed (Russian) Dinner.

Ober, Oberkellner (German) Head waiter

obiad (Polish) Dinner.

oblade Mediterranean fish similar to bream.

oblong roaster (American) Roasting tin of oblong shape.

o'brien potatoes (American) French-fried potatoes cooked with chopped onions, peppers and pimientoes.

Obst (German) Fruit.

Obst in Weinegelee (German) Fruit in wine jelly.

Obstkuchen (German) (i) Fruit tart. (ii) Fruit cake.

Obstsalat (German) Fruit salad.

Obstsoufflee (German) Fruit *soufflé*

oca (Italian) Goose.

oca arrosta (Italian) Roast goose.

occa, oka, oxalis South American plant with edible tubers now grown in Britain and Europe, which can be fried in butter, served in gravies, etc.

ocean perch (American) Rosefish, large salt water edible fish, red or orange in colour when mature.

Ochsenmaulsalat (German) Cold meat

salad with onions, oil, vinegar and spices, a speciality of Nurenburg.

Ochsenschwanz (German) Oxtail.

Ochsenschwanzsuppe (German) Oxtail soup.

Ochsenzunge (German) Ox tongue.

odorat (French) Smell.

oebithera Herbaceous plant with edible roots cooked like salsify.

œillet (French) Carnation.

oenology Science of wine production.

œuf (French) Egg.

œuf à la coque (French) Boiled egg.

œuf à la neige (French) Snow egg.

œuf brouillé (French) Scrambled egg.

œuf de Pâques (French) Easter egg.

œuf de pluvier (French) Plover's egg, popular in France but prohibited in Britain.

œuf de vanneau (French) Lapwings' egg, popular in France but prohibited in Britain.

œuf dur (French) Hard-boiled egg.

œuf farci (French) Stuffed or devilled egg.

œuf frit (French) Fried egg.

œuf mollet (French) Soft-boiled egg.

œuf poché (French) Poached egg.

œuf sur le plat (French) Fried egg.

œffrier (French) Wire egg-holder.

œufs de poisson (French) Fishes' eggs; roe.

Ofen (German) Oven, stove.

off-licence Premises licensed in Britain to sell wines and spirits to take away for consumption elsewhere.

offal Edible internal parts of an animal – ox, cow, calf, pig, sheep, including the following: lamb's and pig's fry, brains, chitterlings, feet or trotters, heads, hearts, kidneys, liver, ox-palate, ox-tail, sweetbreads, tongue, tripe. Prepared and cooked in an enormous number of ways to provide tasty, nutritive dishes. (See separate entries).

ognonnade (French) (i) Stew containing a large proportion of onions. (ii) Finely chopped onion, cooked in butter or white wine.

ogurtsy (Russian) Ridge cucumber.

Ohio wine (American) Wine produced in Ohio, U.S.A., often from native American grapes grown on islands in Lake Erie.

oie (French) Goose.

oignon (French) Onion.

oil Fat of animal, vegetable or mineral origin which is liquid at normal temperature. It does not mix with water but can be emulsified. Vegetable oil such as ground nut, sun-flower and corn are used in most cooking processes. The best known and most expensive is olive oil. Fish oils such as cod and halibut are valued for their A and D vitamin content. Mineral oils are not usually taken except for medicinal purposes.

oil of almonds Oil extracted under pressure from sweet and bitter almonds, used in confectionery.

oille (French) (i) Ancient French soup. (ii) French version of the Spanish *olla-podrida*. (iii) Pigeon and chicken stew cooked with beef and vegetables.

oilstone Whetstone moistened with oil, for sharpening cutlery.

oiseau (French) Bird.

oison (French) Gosling, young goose.

ojen (Spanish) Spanish *pastis*.

oka See occa.

Oka cheese Cheese made by Trappist monks at Oka, Quebec, Canada.

okolehao (Hawaian) Spirit brewed from sugar-cane mash, rice lees and taro root.

okra Pod-yielding plant of the mallow family, grown in the East and West Indies, America, India, and the Mediterranean countries. The young pods, which resemble immature cucumbers, are used as a vegetable, also in soups and stews. Also known as Gumbo and Ladies' fingers.

okroshka (Russian) Type of cold salad-soup made with cucumbers and spring onions, with left-over meat, (or with mixed vegetables) and buttermilk or sour milk.

oksesteg (Danish) Roast beef.

øl (Danish and Norwegian) Beer.

Öl (German) Oil.

öl (Swedish) Beer.

oladky (Russian) (i) Cottage cheese fritters. (ii) Thick pancakes.

olandese (Italian) *Hollandaise* sauce.

old crow (American) Popular brand of bourbon whisky.

old-fashioned (American) Cocktail made of whisky (usually bourbon) and soda, with bitters, sugar, lemon peel, and a little fresh fruit.

old-fashioned glass (American) Short broad tumbler for serving old-fashioned cocktails.

Old grand-dad (American) Well-known brand of bourbon whisky.

old tom gin (American) Gin sweetened with sugar syrup.

oleo margarine (American) Margarine.

olio (Italian) (i) Oil. (ii) Olive oil.

olio di arachide (Italian) Peanut or groundnut oil.

oliva (Italian, Portuguese, and Spanish) Olive.

olive (i) Fruit of the olive-tree, used (often stuffed with pimentoes) as an *hors d'œuvre* and as a garnish for sauces, stews, salads, etc. There are several varieties. Those imported from Spain are the largest and most highly esteemed. Olives may be picked green or when fully ripe and black. (ii) Small piece of meat, stuffed, rolled and braised.

olive (French) Olive.

olive, meat Small piece of meat rolled round stuffing or forcemeat and usually braised.

olive cream cheese Soft cream cheese mixed with chopped green olive.

olive oil Oil obtained from ripe olives, used in salad dressings, mayonnaise, marinades and batters and for greasing casseroles or for frying food. It is chiefly imported from Spain, Italy and the South of France.

olla (Spanish) Earthenware jar, jug or stewing-pot with a wide mouth and looped handles, used for making *olla podrida*.

olla podrida (Spanish) Highly seasoned Spanish stew cooked in an *olla* and containing pork, chicken or other meat, chopped vegetables, chick-peas, etc.

oloroso (Spanish) Full-bodied golden sherry of good bouquet and flavour.

Olympia (American) Beer brewed in Olympia, Washington, U.S.A.

omble, omble, chevalier (French) Fresh-water fish of the salmon family, found in Swiss lakes and rivers, in season during January and February.

ombre (French) Grayling. Fresh-water fish, resembling a trout.

ombre de mer, ombrine (French) See *umbrine*.

ombrina (Italian) Grayling.

Omelett (German) Omelette.

omelet (American) Omelette.

Omelett (German) Omelette.

omelette Dish of beaten eggs cooked in butter, folded over and served, savoury or sweet. Savoury omelettes are filled with one or more of any variety of additions – cheese, chopped ham, cooked fish, diced vegetables, mixed herbs, diced frankfurters or meat, mushrooms, etc. A sweet omelette has sugar and flavouring added in place of seasonings, and served with fruit, preserves, etc. A *soufflé* omelette is made by whisking the whites separately and then folding into the beaten yolks before pouring into the omelette pan.

omelette (French and Italian) Omelette.

omelette à la ciboulette (French) Chopped spring onions added to beaten egg mixture and cooked as for omelette.

omelette à la Norvégienne (French) Baked Alaska.

omelette alla parmigiana (Italian) Cheese omelette.

omelette au confiture (French) Omelette with jam.

omelette au fromage (French) Cheese omelette.

omelette au lard (French) Omelette with bacon.

omelette au sucre (French) Omelette made with sugar added to beaten egg-mixture then sprinkled with sugar or glazed under the grill after normal cooking.

omelette aux champignons (French) Omelette with mushrooms.

omelette aux courgettes (French) (i) Thin slices of marrow or *courgettes* sautéed in butter, covered with beaten eggs and cooked flat. (ii) Diced, sautéed marrow or *courgettes* added to egg mixture and cooked as for plain omelette.

omelette aux crevettes (French) Shrimp or prawn omelette.

omelette aux épinards (French) Leaf spinach sweated in butter, mixed with eggs, beaten and cooked like a pancake.

omelette aux fines herbes (French) (i) Omelette with herbs. (ii) Omelette flavoured with parsley.

omelette aux fraises (French) Kirsch- or rum- and sugar-steeped strawberries folded into cooked omelette egg mixture and glazed under the grill.

omelette aux pointes d'asperges (French) Omelette with asparagus tips.

omelette di funghi (Italian) Mushroom omelette.

omelette dubarry (French) Omelette containing fried cauliflower flowerets, cooked as a pancake.

omelette pan (i) (British) Frying pan with curved and rounded side. (ii) (American) Half-round hinged pan, the mixture being poured into the lower half, and covered by the top half which shapes the omelette.

omelette panachée (French) Large omelette folded over a smaller one which has been made from eggs mixed with thick tomato pulp or puréed spinach.

omelette parmentier (French) Omelette with diced potatoes, cooked flat or fluffy.

on the rocks Beverage served with ice cubes but without water or soda, usually applied to alcoholic drinks such as whisky.

onager Central Asian wild ass, prized as game.

onion Pungent edible bulb of the lily family, varying in size and flavour, grown throughout the world, eaten as a vegetable and used to flavour soups, stews, *rechauffés*, and sauces. Onions can be boiled, fried, baked, stuffed and pickled, and used in salads.

onion powder Concentrate derived from dehydrated fresh onions.

onion tureen Pottery tureen fashioned like a huge onion and used for serving sauces and soups.

onopordon Wild artichoke.

onos Mediterranean fish prepared like whiting.

ontbijt (Dutch) Breakfast.

oolong Partially-fermented tea which combines the characteristics of green and black teas.

open-faced pie Flan or tart.

open sandwich Single slice of bread used as a base for cold meat, cheese, salad items in whatever variety is required.

ophidium Small Mediterranean eel-like fish used in *bouillabaisse*.

Oporto Portuguese town which is the headquarters of the port wine trade and from whence it is shipped.

oporto (Spanish) Port wine.

opossum (American) Edible marsupial whose flesh resembles that of rabbit.

oppvarter (Norwegian) Waiter.

optic Measuring device used in British public houses for serving spirits.

orach, orache Garden plant such as mountain spinach cooked as for true spinach.

orange Citrus fruit of an evergreen tree growing in hot climates in many countries, and having a high vitamin C content. Sweet oranges are eaten as dessert, and used as a flavouring agent in baking, fruit salads, jellies, sorbets, confectionery, etc. Their juice is expressed for use as a beverage, consumed by itself or with spirits such as gin or rum; orange juice is also bottled, frozen and canned commercially. Bitter oranges come mainly from the Seville area of Spain and are used to make marmalade and other preserves. Orange peel is crystallised or candied; it also yields orange oil.

orange ambrosia Sliced oranges dotted with flaked coconut and sprinkled with rum.

orange bitters Extract of bitter-orange.

orange blossom (i) Flower of the orange tree which, together with its leaves, can be used as an unfusion. (ii) Cocktail of gin, orange juice, honey or sugar, and ice.

orange blossom water (American) Orange flower water.

orange-flower water Flavouring distilled from orange blossoms, used in making sweets and pastries.

orange gin Orange-flavoured gin.

orange juice Juice expressed from an orange, used as a meal-starter, in drinks, sweets, etc.

orange mint Bergamot mint.

orange oil Extract derived from the peel of bitter and sweet oranges.

orange peel, candied Skin of the orange, free from pith, blanched, put into syrup and cooked.

orange pekoe Small-leaved black tea from Ceylon, India and East Africa.

orange snow Orange jelly whipped before setting, with stiff egg whites folded in.

orange whisky Orange-flavoured liqueur made with a whisky base.

orange wine Wine made by fermenting orange juice or orange peel.

orangeade Drink made from fresh oranges and served cold, available in proprietary brands or made at home.

orangeado (American) Candied orange peel.

orangeat (French) Finely-chopped, candied orange peel.

Orange (German) Orange.

Orangensaft (German) Orange juice.

orangine (French) Genoese *gâteau* flavoured with orange peel and iced with orange-flavoured fondant icing.

orata (Italian) Daurade, gilt-head, seabream.

oregano Wild marjoram, *origanum*, herb of the mint family, which is much used in Italian and South American cookery.

oreille (French) Ear.

oreille de porc (French) Pig's ear.

oreille de veau (French) Calf's ear.

orge (French) Barley.

orgeat (French) Beverage originally made from barley, now made from almonds and sugar.

oriental salad See *salade orientale*.

orientale, à l' (French) Dishes such as fish, eggs and vegetables, cooked with tomatoes and garlic and spiced with saffron.

origan (French) Wild marjoram, oregano.

origano (Italian) Wild marjoram, oregano.

Originalabfüllung (German) Wine bottled where the grapes were grown.

Orly, à l' (French) Batter-fried fish fillets served with tomato sauce.

orohova potica (Yugoslavian) Raisin-and-nut pie.

Orpington Breed of domestic poultry, white, black or buff, originating from the Orpington district of Kent.

ørred (Danish) Trout.

ørret (Norwegian) Trout.

ortaggo (Italian) (i) Pot herb. (ii) Green vegetable.

ortanique Citrus fruit, a cross between an orange and a tangerine which comes from Jamaica.

ortolan Delicately flavoured wild bird, caught in nets on the Continent and fattened in captivity before being killed for the table. It is usually roasted, its breast covered with vine leaves.

ortolano (Italian) Ortolan.

orval Clary.

orvale (French) Clary.

Orvieto (Italian) Sweet and dry white wines made around the central Italian town of that name.

orzo (Italian) Barley.

os (French) Bone.

os de moëlle (French) Marrow-bone.

oseille (French) Sorrel.

osseter Species of sturgeon.

osso-bucco (Italian) (i) Marrow-bone. (ii) Dish made from knuckle of veal cut into pieces, sautéed and stewed with garlic, onion and tomato. The meat is served on the bone, with spaghetti or rice.

osso di prosciutto (Italian) Hambone.

ost (Danish, Norwegian and Swedish) Cheese.

Osterei (German) Easter egg.

Ostertorte (German) Easter cake.

ostión (Spanish) Large oyster.

ostra (Spanish) Oyster.

ostrica (Italian) Oyster.

ostrich Large bird whose flesh was prized by the Romans but forbidden to Jews and Moslems.

oswego cheddar (American) Cheddar

cheese made in western New York State.

oswego tea (American) Mint-like herb whose leaves were brewed into a medicinal tea by the Oswego Indians.

otard (French) Celebrated cognac stored in the cellars of the castle of the town of Cognac.

ottopode (Italian) Octopus.

ouglie (French) (i) Thin pastry. (ii) Dessert biscuit.

ouha (Russian) Clear fish soup.

ours (French) Bear.

outarde (French) Bustard.

ouzo (Greek) Liqueur flavoured with aniseed. Greek *pastis*.

ovale (French) Oval; egg-shaped.

ovár (Hungarian) Firm, orange-coloured cow's-milk cheese.

oven (i) Arched cavity or enclosed chamber for cooking in dry heat. (ii) Part of a domestic cooker, using either gas, electricity or solid fuel. Some modern electric cookers have the oven situated separately from the hotplate instead of being combined in one piece of apparatus.

oven-dressed Poultry prepared for market and ready for cooking as all bleeding, cleaning and removal of inedible offal has been done.

ovenware Tempered glass and pottery cooking utensils made to withstand heat.

ovo (Portuguese) Egg.

ox (i) Castrated male bovine. (ii) General name for male or female domestic cattle, (bull or cow).

ox-belly Tripe.

ox cheek Fleshy side of ox head.

ox liver Beef liver, similar to calves' liver, less delicate.

ox palate Old-time favourite dish of beef or ox palate soaked, blanched, skinned, and cooked as for calf's head, or cut into pieces, marinaded and deep fried, or used to make a *fricassée*.

ox tongue Tongue from beef animal cooked in various ways and served hot or cold. A good source of protein, as are other ox products.

oxalis See occa.

oxe (Swedish) Beef.

Oxford sauce Sauce made from redcurrant jelly, port, orange, lemon, mustard and ginger, served with venison.

Oxford sausage Nineteenth-century skinless sausage of pork, veal, suet, bread, herbs, nutmeg and lemon and egg.

oxheart (i) Certain varieties of cherries. (ii) (American) Variety of cabbage with a large oval head.

Oxo Commercial product of flavoured fluid beef juice used in making bouillon, gravy, etc.

oxtail Skinned beef tail meat used for soups and stews, said to have been first used by a starving member of the French nobility during the 1793 Reign of Terror.

oxtunga (Swedish) Ox tongue.

oxydation See maderisation.

oxymel Syrup made from four parts honey to one of vinegar.

oyster Marine bivalve mollusc with a flat, rough grey shell. Although usually eaten raw (for which purpose the Essex and Kent natives are best) oysters are also baked, fried and used in soups, stews, etc. Portuguese and American oysters are now cultivated in Britain for cooking purposes.

oyster bar Restaurant specialising in serving oysters.

oyster-catcher Wading bird with delicate flesh when young. Prepared as for plover.

oyster cracker Small round dry biscuit served with chowders and seafood cocktails, etc.

oyster fork Small three-tined fork for eating seafoods.

oyster knife Thick-bladed short narrow knife in a wooden handle used in opening clams, oysters, etc.

oyster plant Salsify.

oyster rockefeller (American) New Orleans method of grilling oysters on rock salt and serving with a highly-seasoned sauce.

oz. Abbreviation for ounce.

Paarl Town and surrounding area on Cape Province, which is the centre of the South African wine trade.

pabrica Paprika.

pabst (American) Beer brewed in Milwaukee, Wisconsin.

pabulum (Latin) Food.

pacaret (Spanish) Wine of the Jerez district of Spain.

Pacific herring (American) Herring species found in the North Pacific.

Pacific mackerel (American) Edible fish caught along the Pacific Coast.

Pacific sardine (American) Californian sardine.

paella (Spanish) (i) Internationally-famed Spanish dish of rice, with other ingredients such as chicken, shellfish, peas, garlic, tomatoes, pimientos, etc. varying in content according to region and ingredients available. (ii) Two-handled iron frying pan in which this dish is traditionally cooked.

paella Valenciana (Spanish) Valencian *paella* considered the best of all the

paellas and made of clams, chicken, mussels, peppers, prawns, chick-peas and tomatoes, etc. served on a bed of saffron rice.

Pago Sheep's milk cheese originating on the island of Pago, Yugoslavia.

pah jook (Korean) Rice and beans.

paillasse (French) Food grilled over the hot cinders of a charcoal fire.

paille (French) Straw.

paillé (French) Straw-coloured.

paille au parmesan (French) Cheese straw.

pain (French) (i) Bread. (ii) Small piece of forcemeat.

pain bis (French) Brown bread.

pain d'épice (French) Gingerbread.

pain de Gênes (French) Genoa cake.

pain de seigle (French) Rye bread.

pain de volaille (French) Small moulds of finely-pounded chicken *purée* or forcemeat.

pain doré (French) French toast.

pain grillé (French) Toast.

pain perdu (French) Mock fritters made

of milk or cream-soaked pieces of bread, fried in butter and sprinkled with sugar and cinnamon, or spread with jam.

pain rôti (French) Toast.

pain sans levain (French) Unleavened bread.

"painted ladies" Fillets of cod, smoked and dyed.

pak-choy (Chinese) Variety of cabbage.

palacsinta (Hungarian) Pancake.

palais de bœuf (French) Ox or beef palate.

palate of ox See ox-palate.

Palatinate Wine-growing district of Germany especially famous for its sweet wines.

Palestinian citrus Citron.

palet de dames (French) Small dry water-iced *petit four* flavoured with lemon or orange rind, or vanilla or other flavouring.

palette-knife Knife with large, flat, flexible blade used to pick up paste in pastry-making; also to spread icing, etc.

palillo (Spanish) Toothpick.

pallottolina in brodo (Italian) Cheese dumplings served in broth.

palm butter Palm kernel oil, in a solid state.

palm heart Tender shoot of palm, cooked as for asparagus.

palm kernel oil Extract from palm nut kernel. Solid at normal temperatures, palm oil is used for cooking in Africa, but elsewhere mainly in the manufacture of soap and margarine.

palm oil Soft oil extracted from palm fruit pulp, especially the oil palm, used in making margarine.

palm sugar Sugar made from the sap of certain palm trees.

palm wine Beverage made of fermented palm sap, particularly date and coconut.

palma Term applied to sherry, meaning "fine and dry".

palmae Family of trees of which the fruit, nuts, terminal shoots (cabbage palm) and stem interior (sago) are used in cooking.

palmier (i) Cake of puff or flaky pastry, sandwiched together in pairs with cream or jam, and sprinkled with icing sugar. (ii) Palmae.

paloma (Spanish) Pigeon.

palombella (Italian) Wood pigeon.

palombe (French) Wood pigeon.

palombo (Italian) (i) Dog-fish. (ii) Ring dove.

palomet Species of mushroom.

palourde (French) (i) Clam. (ii) Variety of vegetable marrow.

palpuszta (Hungarian) Aromatic soft cheese.

pámpano (Spanish) Pompano.

pamplemousse (French) (i) Grapefruit. (ii) Shaddock.

Pampelmuse (German) Grapefruit.

pan Baking or cooking utensil made of metal or heat-resistant glass.

pan (Japanese) Bread.

pan (Spanish) Bread.

pan bazo (Spanish) Brown bread.

pan blanco (Spanish) White bread.

pan de centeno (Spanish) Rye bread.

pan de maíz (Spanish) Corn bread.

pan duro (Spanish) Stale bread.

pan pepato (Italian) Gingerbread.

pan tierno (Spanish) Fresh bread.

panaché (French) Two or more kinds of fruits, meats, vegetables, or ice creams, mixed together.

panada (i) Paste of beaten, soaked breadcrumbs used in making forcemeat, stuffing balls, etc. (ii) Thick *roux* sauce for binding rissoles, fishcakes, etc. and as a basis for *soufflés*, etc.

panade (French) Panada.

panadería (Spanish) Baker's shop.

Panadlsuppe (German/Austrian) White bread soup.

panais (French) Parsnip.

panata (Italian) Bread soup, panada.

panato (Italian) Food fried in breadcrumbs.

panbroil (American) To grill food in a pan under an open flame so that the juices are retained.

pancake Thin, flat cakes of batter fried in a small quantity of lard, served with lemon and sugar, or filled with a sweet or savoury mixture. French pancakes are lighter because the eggs for the batter are separated and the whites whipped stiffly before being added to the mixture. American pancakes are usually served with butter and sugar. Scotch pancakes are usually served cold.

pancake skillet (American) Griddle or pan for frying pancakes and other foods.

pancalier (French) Spring cabbage from the town of Pancagliere in Italy, from whence it was brought to the royal gardens at Versailles by La Quintine, first gardener to Louis XIV.

pandekage (Danish) Pancake.

pandorato (Italian) Bread soaked in beaten egg and milk, then fried until golden-brown.

pane (Italian) Bread.

pané (French) Food breaded, crumbed, dipped or rolled in breadcrumbs.

pane al olio (Italian) Oil bread, made as rolls.

pane al latte (Italian) Milk bread.

pane di segale (Italian) Rye bread.

pane grattato (Italian) Breadcrumbs.

pane integrale (Italian) Brown bread.

pane raffermo (Italian) Stale bread.

panecillo (Spanish) Roll.

panela Inferior brown sugar produced in Latin American countries, used in baked goods, confectionery, soft drinks, etc.

paner à la panure (French) To coat with breadcrumbs.

panetière (French) Lattice-carved sideboard dresser.

panetteria (Italian) Baker's shop.

panetto (Italian) (i) Small loaf. (ii) Bread roll.

panetto de pollo (Italian) Chicken rissole.

panettone (Italian) Milanese sweet cake made of yeast-raised mixture including dried fruit, candied peel, etc.

panfish (American) Any fish suitable for frying, usually hand-caught.

panforte (Italian) Sienese ginger cake containing nuts, candied peel, etc.

panfry To fry food in a pan with very little fat.

panicum Millet milled into flour and used to make a kind of meal with milk or stock.

panier (French) Wicker basket with handle which certain foods are fashioned to resemble, i.e., pulled sugar *paniers* for serving *petit fours*, *bombes*, etc., and potato *paniers*, ribboned and fried potatoes in which other fried foods are arranged.

panier en pommes-de-terre (French) See *panier*.

panier en sucre tiré (French) See *panier*.

panieren (German) To roll in breadcrumbs.

paniert (German) Breaded, crumbed.

panino (Italian) Roll.

panna (Italian) Cream.

panna, alla (Italian) Food served with cream.

panna montata (Italian) Whipped cream.

panne (French) Fat from pigs, used in black (blood) pudding.

pannekake (Norwegian) Pancake.

pannekoek (Dutch) Pancake.

pannequet (French) French pancake, spread with cream, preserve, sauce or other mixture, rolled or folded, sprinkled with icing sugar and glazed under a grill or in the oven.

pannkaka (Swedish) Oven-baked pancake.

panocha (Spanish) Raw sugar.

panoufle (French) Butchery term for under-part of the top of the sirloin.

panthay khowse (Burmese) Chicken and noodles.

pantin, petit (French) Small patty filled with pork forcemeat.

pantothenic acid One of the B group of vitamins.

pantry (i) Larder for storing food. (ii) Small room between kitchen and dining-room used for storing tableware.

panure (French) Breadcrumbs, grated crumbs, or bread raspings used to coat food.

panurette (French) Preparation of grated rusks, used for crumbing, for coating the inside of moulds, and for decoration in place of lobster coral.

pão (Portuguese) Bread.

pâon (French) Peacock.

pap Soft, mushy food such as bread soaked in milk, etc.

papa (Spanish/American) Potato.

papa rellena (Spanish/American) Stuffed potato.

papain Enzyme derived from papaya with meat-tenderising properties.

papaw American shrub in several varieties yielding a type of custard fruit. Not to be confused with Paw-paw or Papaya.

papaya, pawpaw Tropical fruit originating in South America but now grown elsewhere, varying in type, colour and size. Eaten raw like melon when ripe. When not ripe, cooked as a vegetable. It yields an enzyme, papain, which possesses the unique property of tenderising meat, and is thus used as the basis of meat-tenderising powders.

paper-towel Rolled, absobent, perforated paper, for kitchen use.

paper-towel holder Device for holding paper towels.

papero (Italian) Gosling.

papershell (American) Soft-shelled pecan nut.

papier dentillé (French) Lace paper.

papillote (French) (i) Paper frill placed on end bones of cutlets, chicken *suprêmes*, etc. (ii) Small joints of meat covered in heart-shaped pieces of oiled white paper, and oven-cooked. (iii) Sweetmeats wrapped in gold or silver paper.

pappardelle (Italian) Ribbon macaroni in rich sauce, served especially with jugged hare.

pappilan hätävara (Finnish) Dessert of berries, crumbs, and whipped cream.

paprica (Italian) Paprika.

paprika Hungarian red pepper, a sweet capsicum, (pimento), less pungent than the Spanish pepper, powdered and used as a condiment, also as a seasoning in Hungarian goulash.

paprika butter Butter-sauce coloured and flavoured with paprika.

Paprika Hühner (German) Chicken cooked with paprika.

paprikás (Hungarian) Dish containing paprika and sour cream.

pâquerette (French) Daisy. (Edible).

paraffin Hydrocarbon derived from petroleum, in both solid and liquid form. In solid form (paraffin wax) it is used to seal jars of home-made preserves or in making bases or supports for dishes. Liquid paraffin does not go rancid and assists other fats to resist doing so, when it is mixed with them. It is used in making chocolates. Not to be confused with the fuel oil (English) used for heating and lighting.

paraffine (French) Paraffin.

Paraquay tea Maté.

paramach (Russian) Fried meat pastries, a Tartar dish.

parasol mushroom Edible fungus growing as large as a dinner plate. Must be grilled or fried rapidly to prevent toughness.

parata See paratha.

paratha, parata, paratta Indian unleavened, slightly flaky bread or pancake, shallow-fried in ghee or oil until puffy, and served hot.

paratta See paratha.

parboil To cook partially by boiling, before finishing the cooking process by some other method such as shallow-frying.

parch To brown in dry heat.

parched corn Roasted or dried ears of maize.

pare To remove the outer skin of fruits and vegetables.

parer Sharp-bladed kitchen tool for paring fruits and vegetables.

parer (French) To trim, to pare food, to improve appearance, etc.

pareve (Jewish) Foods, such as eggs, fruit, matzos, and vegetables, neither dairy nor meat products, which do not contravene the Jewish dietary laws.

parfait (i) Frozen sweet made with beaten eggs, similar to mousse. (ii) Ice-cream layered with fruit, syrup and whipped cream.

parfait-amour (French) Violet-coloured liqueur flavoured with grated peel, citron, coriander, and cinnamon.

parfait glass Tall, narrow glass used for serving parfaits.

paring knife Small-bladed knife used for paring fruits and vegetables.

Paris-Brest Parisian speciality of a

crown-shaped pastry made with *choux* paste, filled with praline butter cream and sprinkled with almonds.

parisien (French) Sponge *gateau* baked in a tin with a central hole. It is cut into layers, spread with *frangipane* cream, and the hole filled with crystallised fruits. Finally, the cake is covered with meringue.

Parisienne, à la (French) Garnish which includes small potato balls cooked and tossed in meat jelly and sprinkled with parsley.

parkerhouse roll (American) Rolled yeast dough folded off-centre and named after the Parker House Hotel, Boston.

parkin Oatmeal gingerbread, eaten traditionally in Yorkshire and Lancashire on November 5th, Guy Fawkes Day.

parliament cake Thin ginger biscuit.

Parma ham Sweet-flavoured cured Italian ham, which is cut wafer thin and eaten uncooked as an *hors d'œuvre*.

Parmentier Antoine Augustin Parmentier (1737–1817) who introduced the potato into France in 1785, during the reign of Louis XIV. He also invented many different ways of cooking potatoes.

parmentier (French) Method of preparing dishes, with potatoes as one ingredient.

parmentier egg (i) Egg baked in a halved baked potato (ii) Egg broken into a dish of fried diced potato, then baked.

parmentier soup Potato-and-leek soup made with these vegetables, fried, simmered in stock, then sieved.

parmesan (French) Food served with grated parmesan cheese.

parmesan cheese Hard Italian cheese made from partially-skimmed milk, originating in Parma, Northern Italy, used grated in cooking, and for garnishing soups, salads, etc. Obtainable in the piece, or ready-grated in packs.

parmigiano (Italian) (i) Parmesan cheese. (ii) Dishes served or seasoned with parmesan cheese.

parr Very young salmon.

parsley Hardy biennial plant with bright green leaves, used as a flavouring and as a garnish. It grows in four varieties, common, curly-leaved, celery-leaved, and turnip-rooted. Native to Sardinia it was introduced into England in 1548.

parsley flakes Dehydrated parsley leaves.

parsley jelly Parsley and sugar mixture boiled until it sets.

parsley sauce White *roux* sauce with added chopped parsley.

parsley wine Wine made from parsley heads, sugar, yeast, oranges and lemon.

parsnip Root vegetable available from autumn to spring. It can be boiled and served in pieces, or mashed with butter; roasted round the joint, made into parsnip chips, or cooked in strips and coated with batter flour for fritters. Parsnips are also used for wine-making.

parsnip chips Parsnip prepared and fried like potato chips.

parsnip wine Wine made by fermenting parsnips, sugar and yeast.

parson's nose Poultry rump, considered a delicacy.

partridge Game bird in several varieties found nearly all over the world. The English bird, taken from September to February, has a finer flavour than the French partridge, the latter being known by its red legs. Usually roasted (stuffed or otherwise), the breast covered to prevent drying out.

parures (French) Meat trimmings.

pasa (Spanish) (i) Raisin. (ii) Plum.

pascal (American) Green-stalked celery.

pashka (Russian) Traditional Easter dessert of cream cheese, sour cream, butter, sugar, nuts and dried fruit served cold garnished with berries, nuts or crystallised fruits.

paska (Russian) Elaborate Ukranian cake made at Easter.

passarelle Dried muscatel grapes.

passata (Italian) Mash; *purée*.

passata di mele (Italian) Apple sauce.

passata di patate (Italian) Mashed potato.

passata di verdura (Italian) Sieved vegetable soup.

passe-crassane (French) Fragrant variety of winter pear.

passe-pomme (French) Three varieties of August-ripening apple: White, Red and Jerusalem.

passe-purée (French) *purée*-presser.

passe-tout grain (French) Red Burgundy wine made from mixed, unselected grapes.

passer (French) (i) To pass a sauce, soup, vegetable or meat through a tammy cloth, sieve, or strainer. (ii) To fry in butter over a quick fire so as to form a crusty surface on meats or vegetables which are to be finished by some other cooking process, such as stewing or braising.

passera (Italian) Flounder.

passerillage, passarillage (French) The process of turning Passarelle (dried muscatel grapes) into raisins.

passerino (Italian) Plaice.

passion fruit Granadilla, edible fruit of the passion flower tree, eaten as a dessert. Its juice is used in cups, punches, etc.

passoire (French) Colander; strainer.

Passover bread Matzo.

Passover wine Traditional sweet red wine prepared for the Jewish Passover.

pasta Paste originated in Italy, made from hard-wheat flour and rolled and cut or otherwise formed into a great variety of shapes and sizes; for example, macaroni, vermicelli, spaghetti, ravioli, canneloni, alfabeto, tagliatelli, etc. It can be served as a main dish with a sauce, added to soups, or used for savoury dishes such as spaghetti cheese. Rich in carbohydrates and usually served with protein (meat, cheese).

pasta alimentaria (Italian) Alimentary paste.

pasta asciutta (Italian) Dry dough.

pasta frolla (Italian) Fine short pastry.

pasta in brodo (Italian) Spaghetti in broth.

pasta Italiana (Spanish) Italian paste, such as macaroni, spaghetti, etc.

pasta sfoglia (Italian) Puff paste.

paste (i) Dough, pastry. (ii) Pounded meat or fish, blended with other ingredients and used as a spread.

pastel (Spanish) Cake, pastry.

pastel con pasas (Spanish) Plum cake.

pastel de carne (Spanish) Meat pie.

pastel de pescado (Spanish) Fish pie.

pastelería (Spanish) Pastry-cook's shop.

pastelillo (Spanish) Small pastry.

pastelito (Spanish) Small pastry.

pastelito de coco (Spanish) Coconut tart.

pastelón (Spanish) (i) Large pie. (ii) Pigeon or meat pie.

pastèque (French) Watermelon.

pasterma (Russian) Alternative spelling for *basterma*.

Pastete (German) Patty, pie, pastry, tart.

pasteurisation Process of sterilisation by heat developed by the 19th century French chemist, Louis Pasteur.

pasteurised homogenised milk Milk pasteurised and pumped through a fine aperture so that the fat content is evenly distributed throughout instead of forming a layer of cream at the top.

pasteurised milk Milk treated to high heat then rapidly cooled to below 50 degrees F (10 degrees C) before bottling, in order to reduce milk-souring organisms and destroy disease-carrying organisms.

pasticceria (Italian) Cake and pastry shop.

pasticcio (Italian) (i) Pie, pastry. (ii) Cake.

pasticcio di maccheroni (Italian) (i) Macaroni cheese. (ii) Pie filled with macaroni, cheese and sauce.

pastillage (French) Gum paste, for ornamental confectionery.

pastille (i) Small round sweetmeat, made from dissolved sugar and flavouring. (ii) Medicated or gum lozenge.

pastina (Italian) Tiny pasta shape used in soups.

pastina in brodo (Italian) Tiny pasta shapes in broth.

pastis (French) (i) Alcoholic beverage, high proof, yellow in colour and turned cloudy by the addition of water to dilute. Drunk as an *apéritif*. (ii) Yeast-raised cake from the *Béarnais* region made of flour, melted butter, eggs, castor sugar and brandy.

pastitsada (Greek) Macaroni meat pie in tomato sauce.

pastorella (Italian) Soft, bland cheese.

pastry (i) Preparation for making baked goods such as pies, flans, etc. made from flour and shortening. See separate entries for rough-puff, flaky, puff pastry, etc. (ii) Name loosely applied to fancy cakes, such as meringues, *éclairs, mille-feuilles*, rum babas, cream horns, etc.

pastry bag (American) Forcing bag.

pastry blender Kitchen tool with thin wire blades curved into a semi-circle and fixed into either end of a wooden handle, used to blend or cut lard or other shortening into flour, ready for pastry-making.

pastry brush Soft-bristle brush for applying glazes to the top of bread, dough or pastry before baking.

pastry crimper Tool used for pinching the edges of tarts, pies, etc.

pastry cream, French Custard of eggs, sugar, flour, milk and flavouring used as filling for cakes, pastries, etc. Also called confectioner's custard.

pastry flour Flour made from finely-milled wheat with a low gluten content.

pastry fork Four-tined fork with one sharp-edged tine, used for eating soft, creamy cakes and pastries.

pastry jagger (American) Pastry wheel.

pastry mix Ready-prepared mixture for making pies, tarts, etc.

pastry tube Forcing tube; nozzle of forcing bag through which dough or icing is expressed into fancy shapes.

pastry wheel Device for trimming pastry.

pasty Small meat pie or savoury turn-over.

pata (Spanish) (i) Leg, foot. (ii) Duck.

pataca (Spanish) Jerusalem artichoke.

patasca (Spanish) Argentinian dish of pork and maize.

patata (Italian and Spanish) Potato.

patata al latte (Italian) Potato cooked in milk.

patata bollita (Italian) Boiled potato.

patata dolce (Italian) Sweet potato.

patata foglia (Italian) Potato chip.

patata frita (Spanish) Chipped potato.

patata frita a la inglesa (Spanish) Potato crisp.

patata fritta (Italian) Fried potato, chips.

patata passata (Italian) Mashed potato.

patata tenera (Italian) New potato.

patate (French) (i) Potato. (ii) Sweet potato.

patay (Spanish) Spanish-American dry paste made from carob beans.

pâte (French) General term for doughs, pastry, sweet pastes, batters, etc.

pâté (French) (i) Pie; pasty; a savoury meat pasty, or a raised or fruit pie. (ii) Liver paste, meat paste, fish paste, etc. used as a spread on rusks, etc. for *hors d'œuvre*, meal starters and snacks.

pâte à chou (French) *Choux* pastry.

pâte à frire (French) Frying batter.

pâte alimentaire (French) Italian paste used in *pasta*.

pâte croquante (French) Crisp almond and sugar paste.

pâte d'amandes (French) Almond paste.

pâte d'anchois (French) Anchovy paste.

pâte d'arachide (French) Peanut paste.

pâte de bifteck (French) Beef-steak pie.

pâte de cailles (French) Quail *pâté* or paste.

pâté de corbeau (French) Rook pie.

pâté de foie gras (French) Well-known delicacy prepared from the livers of fat geese, a speciality of the *Périgord* district of France.

pâté de guimauve (French) Marshmallow pastry.

pâté de guimauve (French) Marshmallow (sweetmeat).

pâté de marrons (French) Confection of blanched and pounded chestnuts, cooked and mixed with apricot jam, then cut into squares and dried.

pâté de piment (French) Red pepper paste.

pâté de Périgord (French) Pie made in the Périgeux region of France, containing the truffles for which the area is celebrated.

pâté di fegato (Italian) Liver *pâté* or paste.

pâté di fegato di pollo (Italian) Chicken liver *pâté* or paste.

pâte feuilletée (French) Puff paste.

pâte frisée (French) Short crust paste.

pâte pastillage (French) Gum paste.

patella Limpet, an edible univalve gastropod mollusc eaten raw.

patelle (French) Patella.

patience Vegetable similar to spinach, with a mild flavour and a slight acidity like sorrel leaves.

pâtisser (French) To make pastry.

pâtisserie (French) (i) Pastry. (ii) Fancy cakes and pastries. (iii) Pastry-making. (iv) Tea-room. (v) Pastry-cook's shop.

pâtissier (French) Pastrycook.

patissière noix (French) Culinary term for round of veal, or chump end of loin of veal.

Patna rice Long-grain variety of rice from the Ganges valley in India, used for savoury dishes, particularly curries.

pato (Portuguese and Spanish) Duck.

patronnet (French) Apprentice pastry-cook.

patte d'ours (French) Bear's paw.

patty (i) Small pie or *vol-au-vent* of puff paste, filled with game, fish, meat, etc. (ii) (American) Small pie or flat cake made of meat, fish, potato, etc.

patty pan Pan or tin for baking patty pies.

patty shell Round shell of puff pastry baked blind to hold a sweet or savoury filling.

paua New Zealand abalone.

pauchouse (French) Dish of mixed freshwater fish flambéed with brandy and garnished with pork breast and onions.

Pauillac (French) Commune in the *Gironde*, France, famous for its milk-fed lamb.

paunch (i) Belly. (ii) To remove entrails from rabbits, hares, etc.

paupiette (French) Thin rolled slice of meat stuffed with forcemeat.

pavé (French) (i) Savoury mixture set in a square mould and coated with jelly. (ii) Square cake, either iced sponge or spiced cake.

pavé d'entremets (French) Sweet *pavé*. (See *pavé*).

pavie Clingstone peach.

pavezno (Spanish) Young turkey.

pavlova Australian dessert created in honour of the famous ballerina, Pavlova. A light meringue flan, with built-up sides to suggest a ballet dancer's *tutu* filled with fresh cream and fruit.

pavo (Spanish) Turkey.

pavo real (Spanish) Peacock.

pavot (French) Poppy.

pawpaw See papaya.

paysanne, à la (French) Poultry or meat braised and garnished with bacon and buttered vegetables.

pazar (Turkish) Market.

pazuly leves (Hungarian) Bean soup.

pea Seed of a leguminous plant. A popular vegetable in many varieties: garden peas, field peas, black-eyed peas, chick-peas, etc.

pea bean (American) Small white variety of shell bean.

pea flour Flour made from dried ripe peas, used to thicken sauces and as a basis for soup.

pea soup Thick soup of dried green peas soaked and cooked with a ham bone or turkey carcase, or with vegetables and added milk.

peaberry Small round coffee seed.

peach Delicious fruit of a tree of the *Rosaceae* family, eaten raw, preserved, stewed, or dried, or used in pies, flans, jams, ice creams, etc. It was introduced into Europe by the Romans but is said to have originated in China.

peach leather (American) Confection made of dried and sugared peach pulp.

peach melba Composite sweet invented by Escoffier and named to honour the opera singer, Dame Nellie Melba. Sundae glasses are lined with ice cream on which is placed a halved peach, covered with Melba sauce or raspberry *purée*.

peach wine Wine made from peaches, sugar, yeast, oranges and lemon.

peacock Fowl of the pheasant family. In the Middle Ages it was a dish of much importance but is now rarely eaten. It is cooked as for pheasant.

peanut, ground nut, monkey nut Seed of a leguminous plant native to Brazil and cultivated in many tropical and sub-tropical countries. Peanuts are eaten like nuts, made into peanut butter, and used in sweetmeats, cakes, biscuits, etc. They yield an oil used as a substitute for olive oil, and are rich in protein and fat.

peanut brittle Crunchy sweetmeat of peanuts stirred into a hot syrup and cooled until hard.

peanut butter Spread made from ground peanuts, salt and vegetable oil, available commercially in two styles; one is smooth, the other incorporates small pieces of peanuts which give a crunchy consistency. Used on rusks, toast, bread, etc. also incorporated into certain cake and biscuit recipes.

peanut butter cookies Small cakes made of flour, spices and peanut butter.

peanut flour Flour made from ground peanuts.

peanut oil Oil extracted from peanuts and used in cooking, salad-dressings, etc.

peanut paste Paste made from blanched, pounded peanuts.

pear Fleshy fruit in a wide variety of sizes, colours and flavours. Some varieties make excellent dessert but when over-ripe they loose their juicy quality and become "sleepy", i.e., mushy and discoloured. Pears can also be stewed, baked, dried and otherwise preserved, and used to make a wide variety of sweets, combined with ice cream, cream, custards, rice, etc. From pears are made the fermented beverage, perry or pear cider.

pearl barley Grain which is steamed, rounded and polished in the mill, after the removal of the husks. Used for thickening soups and stews and for making barley water and puddings.

pearl hominy (American) Medium-size pellets of hominy.

pearl onion Silverskin onion. Tiny white onion pickled and served in cocktails or used to garnish salads, casseroles, etc.

pearl tapioca Round, finely-ground pellets of tapioca.

pearlware Pearly white china.

pease brose (Scottish) Type of porridge made with pea flour or meal.

pease porridge Very thick pea soup.

pease pudding Split peas soaked then boiled in a cloth until soft.

peau de porc (French) Crackling.

pebrada, pebre (Spanish) Sauce made of pepper, vinegar and garlic.

pecan (American) Tree of the walnut family, yielding a well-flavoured nut; pecan nuts are eaten plain or used in cakes and confections in the same way as walnuts which they largely resemble, except that their shells are longer, brownish red and brittle.

pecan pie (American) Open pie filled with mixture of pecans, butter, corn syrup, eggs, and sugar.

peccary Species of South African wild pig, prepared as for wild boar.

pêche (French) Peach.

pêche cardinal (French) Peaches, stewed and drained, served on strawberry ice and covered with iced redcurrant jelly.

pêche melba (French) Peach melba.

pechuga (Spanish) Breast of fowl.

peck Dry measure containing 8 quarts, solid measure.

pecorino (Italian) Variety of sheep's milk cheese.

pecten Genus of bi-valve mollusc, with rounded shells, such as scallops.

pectin Jelly-forming carbohydrate substance, found in the cell walls of many plants such as apples, citrus fruits, sugar beet. In combination with sugar it causes jam to set.

pectine (French) Pectin.

peel (i) Outer skin of fruit and vegetables. (ii) To remove the outer skin of vegetables and fruit such as potatoes and apples.

peensoep (Dutch) Carrot soup.

peigne (French) Pectin.

peixe (Portuguese) Fish.

pejapalo (Spanish) (i) Haddock. (ii) Stockfish.

Pekin Large white duck originating from Peking, China.

pekoe Black tea of uniform leaf-size grown chiefly in Ceylon and India.

pelican Large, web-footed water-fowl

with a "storage sack" for fish below its bill. Its flesh is coarse and oily but it is eaten in some countries.

Pellkartoffel (German) Potato cooked in its jacket.

pelmeny (Russian) Stuffed dumplings.

pelures (French) Edible trimmings, such as truffle or mushroom parings.

pemmican (i) Dried buffalo or deer meat, powdered and mixed with melted fat; a concentrated food used by North American Indians and later by trappers and other adventurers. (ii) Modern emergency ration of dried beef, flour, salt and sweetening.

pendre la crémaillère (French) Literally, "to hang up the chimney hook". Symbolic expression to indicate the first meal served in a new home or household.

penguin Genus of sea-fowl of the Antarctic regions.

penguin egg Very large egg similar in texture and flavour to plovers' eggs.

pénide (French) Sugar cooked with a decoction of barley, twisted and manipulated so that it becomes opaque, thus differing from the transparent barley sugar.

pennyroyal European wild mint, less aromatic and more pungent than peppermint or spearmint; sometimes used as condiment.

pensión (Spanish) (i) Cost of board and lodging. (ii) Boarding house.

penuche (American) Brown-sugar candy.

pepato (Italian) (i) Peppered, spiced. (ii) Spiced Sicilian cheese made from cow's and goat's milk.

pepe (Italian) Pepper.

pepe di Caienna (Italian) Cayenne pepper.

pepe in grano (Italian) Peppercorn.

pepe macinato (Italian) Ground pepper.

pepperone (Italian) Capsicum; chilli, pepper.

peperone gratinato (Italian) Pimento stuffed, crumbed and oven-baked.

peperone sott'aceto (Italian) Pickled chilli or capsicum.

peperoni (Italian) Highly seasoned sausage.

pepino (Spanish) Cucumber.

pepita (Spanish) (i) Pip, seed. (ii) Roasted and salted pumpkin seed.

pepper (i) Seed-bearing fruit of the pepper plant, a genus of vine-like shrubs. The berries are picked before ripening. Black pepper is obtained from the whole seeds which are greenish-black and wrinkly. White pepper is obtained from those seeds with the outer coating removed which makes it less pungent. Both are used in cooking and as a condiment. Unground pepper seeds are used in pickling. (ii) Vegetable. Fluted pear-shaped fruit of the capsicum plant, with a shiny skin and varying in colour from green to yellow or red, according to variety and ripeness. Used stuffed with savoury filling, or cut into strips or rings as a garnish.

pepper pot (i) Perforated container holding the condiment pepper. (ii) (American) Highly-spiced West Indian stew of fish or meat and vegetables.

pepper shaker (American) Pepper pot.

pepperbox (American) Pepper pot.

peppercorn Unground pepper seed which retains its flavour better than ground pepper. Used for flavouring soup, stews and pickles and to grind in a pepper mill as a condiment. See pepper (i).

peppergrass Cress of the genus *Lepidium*, similar to watercress and used for salads.

peppermill Hand-operated mill for grinding whole peppercorns, to use as a condiment or in cooking.

peppermint European plant, similar to garden spearmint but more aromatic, from which an oil and a flavouring essence are made. Peppermint is used as a flavouring for confectionery, drinks and some desserts, also medicinally.

peppermint glacial (American) Digestive cordial made from wine alcohol flavoured with mint essence.

peppermint humbug Sweetmeat made of demerara sugar, golden syrup, butter, cream of tartar, water and peppermint oil. By dividing the mixture and pulling one part till pale-coloured, the humbugs can be given a striped appearance.

peppermint oil Flavouring extract derived from peppermint.

peppernut (American) Christmas sweetmeat made of highly spiced and sugared dough.

peppersteak (American) Beefsteak baked in pepper sauce.

pepolino (Italian) Thyme.

pepsi-cola Popular soft drink of American origin.

pepsin Digestive enzyme obtained from the gastric juices of vertebrates, often used as a digestive aid.

pequeno almoço (Portuguese) Breakfast, little lunch.

pera (Italian, Portuguese and Spanish) Pear.

pera al forno (Italian) Baked pear.

pera caramellata (Italian) Sugar-dipped or caramalized pear.

perch Firm-fleshed fresh-water fish of delicate flavour, in season from June to February, but seldom seen in the fishmonger's shop. Perch should be cooked as soon as possible after catching and may be grilled or fried in butter or baked in stock and white wine.

perche (French) Perch.

percolate To filter liquid in order to extract its essence.

percolateur (French) Coffee percolator.

percolator Coffee-pot in which boiling water in the lower section ascends and filters over the coffee grounds in the perforated basket above, until the required strength of coffee is obtained.

perdiz (Spanish) Partridge.

perdiz blanca (Spanish) Grouse.

perdreau (French) Young partridge.

perdrix (French) Full-grown partridge.

perejil (Spanish) Parsley.

perelada (Spanish) High-quality Spanish sparkling wine.

perfect Cocktail comprised of equal quantities of gin and sweet and dry vermouth, shaken with ice.

Périgourdine, à la (French) Dishes garnished with truffles, typical of the *cuisine* of the *Périgord* area of France.

periwinkle (i) Winkle, an edible gastero-

pod gathered by the shore at low tide. (ii) Creeping evergreen woodland plant.

Perlgraupe (German) Pearl-Barley.

perle di orzo (Italian) Pearl-Barley.

perles de Nizam, perles du Japon (French) Special variety of large pearl barley.

Perlhuhn (German) Guinea-fowl.

pernice (Italian) Partridge.

pernice al forno (Italian) Oven-roasted partridge.

pernice alla crema (Italian) Partridge casseroled in cream.

pernice arrosto (Italian) Roast partridge.

pernod (French) Best-known of the French *pastis* – a yellow alcoholic liquor which goes cloudy when diluted with water.

perrier (French) Brand of mineral water.

perry Pear cider, a fermented beverage made in a similar way to apple cider.

persil (French) Parsley.

persillade (French) Garnish of chopped parsley.

persiller (French) To sprinkle a dish with parsley.

persimmon Date plum. The fruit of a tree of Japanese origin, also grown in Mediterranean countries and in America. Persimmons are similar in shape to a tomato, with yellow or orange-coloured pulp; the best varieties are seedless. The unripe fruit is astringent, the ripe fruit bitter-sweet. Persimmons are stewed when very ripe, used for flavouring ices and jellies and for making preserves.

pestle Wood, metal or porcelain tool used, with a mortar, to pound food.

pertsovka (Russian) Vodka infused with pepper.

peru (Portuguese) Turkey.

pesca (Italian) Peach.

pesca (Spanish) Fishing.

pesca alla Melba (Italian) Peach Melba.

pesca ripiena (Italian) Baked, stuffed peach.

pescaderia (Spanish) Fishmonger's shop.

pescadilla (Spanish) Whiting.

pescado (Spanish) Caught fish.

pescado frito (Spanish) Fried fish.

pescanoce (Italian) Nectarine.

pescar (Spanish) To fish.

pesce (Italian) Fish.

pesce affogato (Italian) Poached fish.

pesce all'agliata (Italian) Fish in garlic sauce.

pesce arrosto (Italian) Spit-roasted fish.

pesce cane (Italian) Dog-fish.

pesce in insalata (Italian) Fish salad.

pesce in umido (Italian) Fish stewed with herbs and vegetables.

pesce marinato (Italian) Marinated fish.

pesce persico (Italian) Perch.

pesce ripieno (Italian) Stuffed fish.

pesce San Pietro (Italian) John Dory.

pesce spada (Italian) Swordfish.

pescheria (Italian) Fishmonger's shop.

pescheria minuta (Italian) Whitebait.

pesciaiola (Italian) Fish-kettle.

pescolini (Italian) Whitebait.

pèse sirop (French) Saccharometer; instrument for measuring concentration of sugar solutions.

pestle Club-shaped implement used to crush or pound food in a mortar.

pet de nonne (French) *Soufflé* fritter.

Petersilie (German) Parsley.

petillant (French) Term which applies to wines which are not truly sparkling yet not actually still, such as Portuguese *rosé* wines, etc.

petit déjeuner (French) Breakfast.

petit four (French) Very small, rich, sweet cake or biscuit served at the end of a dinner, or with morning coffee or afternoon tea. Candied fruits, marzipan and other sweetmeats are sometimes served as *petits fours*.

petit-houx Butcher's broom shrub.

petit lait (French) Whey.

petit pain (French) Bread-roll.

petit pain fourré (French) Small roll scooped out and stuffed with various kinds of savoury *purées;* served as savoury or side dishes.

petit-pâté (French) Patty or small pie.

petit poussin (French) Young chicken, usually roasted, fried, sautéed or grilled.

petit quiche au fromage (French) Small quiche lorraine tart with Gruyère cheese among the ingredients.

petit quiche au jambon (French) Small quiche lorraine tart with added ham.

petit salé (French) Bacon. Lean salt pork.

petit suisse (French) Unsalted cream cheese made from whole milk.

petit saumon (French) Salmon grilse.

petit vol-au-vent d'huîtres (French) Oysters in a pastry case.

petite beurre (French) Sweet butter biscuit.

petite gruyère (French) Foil-wrapped processed cheese.

petite marmite (French) (i) Soup containing beef broth, lean beef, marrow bones, stockpot vegetables, and cabbage balls, served in the small pottery casserole in which it has been cooked, often finally sprinkled with cheese. (ii) The vessel itself.

petits-pieds (French) Collective term for all small birds such as larks, thrushes, ortolans, etc.

petits pois au beurre (French) Green peas cooked in butter.

petits pois verts (French) Small green peas.

pétoncle (French) Scallop.

pets-de-nonne (French) Ancient name for queen fritters or small *beignets soufflés*.

pettitoes Scottish term for pig's trotters.

petto (Italian) Breast.

petto d'agnello (Italian) Breast of lamb.

petto di bue (Italian) Brisket.

petto di pollo (Italian) Chicken breast.

petto di tacchino (Italian) Turkey breast.

petto di vitello (Italian) Breast of veal.

pewter-ware Kitchen utensils and tableware made of pewter.

pez (Spanish) Fish, still alive.

Pfanne (German) Frying-pan.

Pfannkuchen (German) (i) Fritter. (ii) Fried rounds of *brioche* dough sandwiched together with apricot *purée*.

Pfau (German) Peacock.

Pfeffer (German) Pepper.

Pfefferkuchen (German) Gingerbread.

Pfefferminz (German) Peppermint.

Pfefferpotthast (German) Westphalian spicy stew of beef, onions, bay leaves, breadcrumbs and peppercorns.

Pfeffernuss (German) Traditional spicy, iced Christmas biscuit with black pepper and other spices in the mixture.

Pfeilwurz (German) Arrowroot.

Pfirsich (German) Peach.

Pflaume (German) Plum.
Pflaumenkuchen (German) Plum tart.
Pflaumenstrudel (German) Plum *strudel*.
pheasant Choicest of the game birds, at its prime in October and in season until February 1st. It originated in Asia Minor. The hen is considered the best eating. The birds should be hung for about a week and are roasted, casseroled, etc.
Philadelphia pepper pot (American) Highly-seasoned stew of tripe, meat and dumplings.
philernum West Indian liqueur, also suitable for cups, punch and flavouring.
phoque (French) Seal.
phosphate Carbonated water flavoured with fruit syrup.
phosphore (French) Phosphorus.
phosphorus One of the essential body minerals, a constituent of bones and teeth.
phylloxera Aphid which attacks the roots of vines and which once threatened the entire wine-growing areas of Europe, especially France. American roots were found to be resistant to the parasites, so European vines were grafted onto American roots and the situation was saved.
phytic acid Compound of phosphorus found in bran and the outer part of cereal grains, haricot and butter beans, dried peas, almonds, Brazil nuts and cobnuts.
picadillo (Spanish) Meat and vegetable hash.
picarel (French) Small Mediterranean fish prepared like anchovy.
piccalilli Mixture of onions, cauliflower, cabbage, cucumbers, tomatoes and spices, pickled in a mustard sauce.
piccione (Italian) Pigeon.
pichet (French) Wood or ceramic container for wine, etc., with a handle.
pichola (American) Stew made of fresh pork, tomatoes, onions and chillies with added hominy, speciality of Arizona.
picholine (French) Large green table olive, eaten as *hors d'œuvre*.
pickerel Young pike.

Pickert (German) Westphalian speciality – a dough made of buckwheat flour and grated potatoes, fried in a pan.
pickle (i) Combination of vegetables or fruits, or both, preserved in spiced vinegar. (ii) To preserve fruit, vegetables, fish or meat in vinegar, brine or dissolved salt.
pickle fork Two-tined fork for spearing pickles.
pickled cabbage Red cabbage shredded, covered in salt for 24 hours then drained, packed in jars and covered with vinegar.
pickled cauliflower Florets of cauliflower boiled briefly and covered in spiced vinegar.
pickled cherry Unstoned cherry preserved in sugared, spiced vinegar.
pickled cucumber (i) Cubed cucumber, brined before covering with spiced vinegar. (ii) Small cucumber, pickled whole, as in (i).
pickled egg Hard-boiled egg preserved in spiced white wine or cider.
pickled onion Small onion preserved in spiced vinegar.
pickled walnut Green walnut soaked and re-soaked in brine, then dried until black, finally packed into jars and covered with hot spiced vinegar.
pickling cabbage Red cabbage.
pickling cucumber Cucumber suitable for pickling, usually small, smooth and fairly uniform in shape and size.
pickling spices Blend of whole spices (clove, cinnamon, allspice, coriander, mustard, pepper, etc. etc.) used when pickling fruit and vegetables.
pickling vinegar Vinegar to which pickling spices have been added.
picnic Outing into the country or at the sea, combined with an *al fresco* meal.
picnic ham (American) Ham cut from below the shoulder of pork or ham.
picnic hamper Basket for conveying picnic food, beverages, cutlery, dishes, glasses, napkins, etc.
pie Meat, fish or fruit baked in a dish covered with pastry. The earliest form of pie is the pasty which is made without a dish.

pie (French) Magpie, common in France, and often used to make stock.

pie (Spanish) Foot.

pie-crust Pastry dough.

pie-crust mix Ready-prepared pastry mix needing only water to form a dough.

pie pan Shallow receptacle, usually round, for baking a pie.

pie plate Pie tin or pan.

pie shell Pie crust baked "blind", and later filled with sweet or savoury food.

pièce de résistance (French) Principal joint or other important dish of a dinner.

pièce montée (French) Centre-piece, set piece; mounted piece.

pied (French) Foot.

pied d'agneau (French) Lamb's foot.

pied-au-cheval (French) Variety of large oyster.

pied de porc (French) Pig's trotter.

pied de mouton (French) Sheep's trotter.

pied de veau (French) Calf's foot.

piede di maiale (Italian) Pig's trotter.

piémontaise, à la (French) Meat and poultry dishes garnished with *timbales* of risotto and truffles.

pierna (Spanish) Leg.

pierna de cabrito asada (Spanish) Roast leg of kid.

pierna de cordero asada (Spanish) Roast leg of lamb.

pig fries Pig entrails or testicles.

pig in a blanket One food wrapped up and cooked in another, such as liver or oyster in bacon; pork sausage in pastry, etc.

pig's bladder Part of animal intestines which is cleaned, blown up, dried and used for big sausage skins or for wrapping lard.

pig's cheek Part of pig's head, pickled and cured to form Bath chap.

pig's ear Rarely eaten as a separate dish, pig's ear is cooked with trotters and used in sausages and other commercial preparations such as pork pies, etc.

pig's feet Trotters or feet of a pork carcase, usually boiled or pickled.

pig's fry Heart, liver, lights, and other interior parts of a pig, fried or stewed, casseroled or made into faggots.

pig's knuckles (American) Bacon hocks.

pigeon Grain-eating bird in many species, drawn and prepared for the table like other birds – roasted, casseroled, grilled, etc., and used to make *mousses* etc. Pigeon's liver contains no gall, and can therefore be left in the bird.

pigeon de Bordeaux (French) Bordeaux pigeon.

pigeonneau (French) Pigeon, squab.

pigeonneau au cresson (French) Squab with water-cress.

pigfish (American) See triggerfish.

piggvar (Swedish) Turbot.

pignoli, pignon (French) Kernel of the pine cone, used in place of almonds and pistachios.

piirakka (Finnish) Rye pastry crust filled with a rice cream.

pike Fresh-water fish with a long head and scaly body, dry flesh and many bones. Pike may be fried or grilled, cooked in wine, or stuffed and baked to improve the flavour.

pike-perch Delicate, white-fleshed fish of the *Percidae* family found in central and Eastern Europe and in some French rivers.

pikelet (i) North of England name for a crumpet. (ii) Girdle cake.

pilaff Dish originating in the Middle East, of rice with meat, fish or poultry, prepared in various ways in different countries.

pilau (French and Italian) Pilaff.

pilchard Small fish of the herring family and similarly prepared. Nutritionally valuable, pilchards are canned in oil or in tomato sauce. Young pilchards are known as sardines.

pilé s kesteni (Bulgarian) Chicken with chestnuts.

pilet (French) Pintail duck.

pilon (French) Pestle.

pilot biscuit Hardtack.

pilot bread Hardtack.

pilot burner Small flame which burns continuously in gas appliances, to light the larger burners when required.

pilot cracker Hardtack.

pilot-fish Fish similar to mackerel and cooked in the same ways.

Pilsner (Czechoslovakian) Famous Czech lager originating in the town of Pilsen.

Pilz (German) Mushroom.

piment (French) Green or red pepper.

Piment (German) Allspice, pimento, Jamaican pepper.

pimento Allspice, Jamaica pepper.

pimento (Italian) Sweet pepper.

pimienta (Spanish) Black pepper.

pimiento (Spanish) (i) Red pepper, sweet and pungent, used in salads as a vegetable, and a garnish. (ii) Cayenne pepper.

pimpernelle (French) Salad-burnet, a herbaceous plant.

Pimms Proprietary "long" drink called Pimms' Cup, made with various bases: No. 1: gin and bitters; No. 2: whisky; No. 3: brandy; No. 4: rum; No. 5: rye whisky; No. 6: vodka. The exact compounds are closely-guarded secrets.

pin British beer barrel containing 4½ gallons.

pina (Spanish) Pineapple.

pina colada (Spanish) Chilled pineapple.

pinbone steak (American) Steak cut from sirloin.

pince (French) (i) Pastry crimper. (ii) Tongs.

pincer (French) (i) To brown food, such as meat or vegetables, in fat before adding liquid. (ii) To pinch up the edges of pies, tarts, etc.

pincée (French) Pinch (of salt, etc.).

pinch Amount of salt or other seasoning that can be held between the fore-finger and thumb.

pine nut Edible seed of various pine cones, used as a substitute for almonds and other nuts.

pineapple Much esteemed dessert fruit, native of South America, first imported to Europe about the middle of the 18th century. Eaten raw, canned, used in sweet dishes, cakes, ices, etc.

pineapple cheese (American) (i) Cheese shaped and coloured like a pineapple. (ii) Cream cheese flavoured with pineapple.

pineapple stick Pineapple cut into sticks

for use in cocktails, long drinks, or salads.

pineapple surprise Whole pineapple hollowed, its flesh chopped, mixed with strawberries or other suitable fruits, and returned to the shell.

pineau, pinot (French) Small grapes, black or white, used to make the best Burgundy wines.

pinée (French) Top-quality dried cod.

pingouin (French) Penguin.

pinion Poultry wing.

pink gin Cocktail of gin and angostura bitters.

pink lady Cocktail of apple brandy, gin, grenadine syrup, lemon juice, and egg white.

pinole Variety of wheat-corn, roasted. Used as a substitute for coffee in the East, also sometimes added to coffee as a flavouring.

piñon (Spanish) Pine nut.

pinot (French) See *pineau*.

pinson de neige (French) Snow bird.

pintade (French) Guinea-fowl. A bird of the turkey species with bluish-grey, spotted plumage.

pintadeau (French) Guinea chick.

pintail Common migratory bird found in the north of England and Europe, and prepared as for wild duck.

pinto bean Spotted pink shell-bean grown in western United States as a vegetable and as animal food.

pinwheel Pastry, biscuit or *canapé* filled, rolled up like a Swiss roll, and cut into slices.

pinwheel sandwich Single slice of moist bread cut length wise from the loaf, filled with a spread, as for Rolled sandwich, then cut in sections, re-sembling Swiss roll.

pipa (Spanish) Hogshead (of wine).

pipe (i) To decorate food such as cakes, sweets, desserts, galantines, etc., with cream, butter, icing, etc., as suitable, pressing through the nozzle of an icing bag or similar tool. (ii) Cask containing 115 gallons of port wine.

piperade (French) Basque dish made of cooked onions, sweet peppers, and tomatoes with eggs added to make a fluffy *purée*.

pipit Small edible bird cooked as for larks on the continent.

pipkin Old-fashioned cooking pot, with or without feet.

pippin Dessert apple in many varieties including Cox's Orange, Golden, Newtown, etc.

piquage de viandes (French) Interlarding.

piquante (French) Sharp of flavour, stimulating, pungent or sour.

piquante sauce Well-flavoured sharp sauce, served with vegetables, fish, re-heated meat dishes, etc.

piqué (French) Larded.

piquepoult (French) Wine made in the *Gers* Department of France, from which Armagnacs are distilled.

piquer (French) To lard. To insert strips of fat bacon, truffles, tongue, etc., into lean meat, poultry, game or fish.

piquette (French) (i) Wine of second or third pressing obtained by flooding grape-husks with warm unsweetened water. (ii) Mediocre wine.

pir (Slav) Feast.

pirozhky (Russian) Sour-cream or egg dough turnovers stuffed with meat, chicken, cheese or other filling.

pirozhnoye (Russian) Pastry.

pis (French) Udder.

Pischinger Torte (German / Austrian) Viennese chocolate wafer named after its inventor.

pisco (Spanish) Chilean or Peruvian anisette of high alcoholic content.

pisco **sour** (American) Mixed drink of *pisco* and lime juice.

pisello (Italian) Pea.

pisello seccho (Italian) Dried pea.

pismo (American) Hard-shell clam found along the coast of central and southern California.

pissaladière (French) Flan filled with anchovies, onions, and black olives, a speciality of the Nice region.

pissalat (French) Provençal condiment made from pickled fish fry.

pissenlit (French) Dandelion.

pistache (French) Pistachio nut.

pistache, en (French) Method of preparing leg of mutton in south-west France by garnishing with cloves or garlic.

pistachio nut Fruit of a tree grown in Southern Europe, Asia Minor, and Mexico. Its small green kernel, sweet and delicate in flavour, is shelled and blanched, chopped or sliced and used to decorate sweets, cakes and ices.

pistole (French) Variety of plum, stoned and sun-dried like prunes.

pistou (Italian) Thick soup of vegetables and vermicelli, containing also tomatoes, oil, basil and garlic.

pit (American) (i) To take the stones out of fruit. (ii) Fruit stone.

pitcaithly bannock (Scottish) Shortbread in flat, round cakes made from a paste of flour, butter, sugar, almonds, peel, and caraway seeds.

Pithiviers (French) Town near Orléans, France, famous for its pastry, especially lark pies and almond-*gâteaux*, and for its honey.

piti (Russian) Lamb soup.

piviere (Italian) Plover.

pivni polevka (Czechoslovakian) Beer soup.

pizza (Italian) Savoury flan of yeast dough filled with spiced tomato sauce, cheese, and olive oil, garnished with anchovies, sliced sausage, mushrooms, olives etc. Naples is famous for its *pizza*.

place mat Oblong mat of cotton, linen, plastic, or straw used in place of a tablecloth.

plaice Marine flat-fish with red spots on its dark side, varying from a small dab to a fish of about 10 pounds. The medium-sized fish have the best flavour and can be cooked whole or filleted, baked, grilled, fried, etc.

planche à découper (French) Cutting-board.

plaisir (French) Small cone-shaped wafer, served with ice-cream dishes.

plaki (Greek) Cod baked in oil with garlic and raisins or currants.

plank (American) To cook meat or fish on a plank of wood, usually oak, to give a special flavour.

planked steak (American) Steak grilled and served on a well-seasoned plank and garnished with vegetables.

plantain (i) Tropical fruit closely

resembling a banana. The better, ripe fruit has sweet, soft flesh and can be eaten raw. The coarser varieties, and the unripe fruit, can be baked, boiled, or fried. (ii) British weed which was dried and made into a drink before tea was introduced. Its leaves are used in salads.

planter's punch (American) Mixed drink of dark rum, grenadine, curaçao, pineapple sticks, maraschino cherries and soda water. The actual recipe has no fixed formula and tends to be varied to suit individual preferences.

plaque à rôtir (French) Roasting-pan.

plat (French) Dish.

plat du jour (French) Dish of the day, a restaurant's ready-to-serve speciality.

plátano (Spanish) Banana.

plate Small round receptacle usually of porcelain or china, to hold food. Silver, pewter and glass plates are also used in certain circumstances, but these tend nowadays to be reserved for ornamental rather than practical purposes.

plate of beef (American) Cut of beef between the brisket and the flank.

plate-pie Double crust pie with sweet or savoury filling.

platillo (Spanish) Saucer.

platine (French) Small shallow baking pan.

plato (Spanish) (i) Plate. (ii) Course.

plato de carne (Spanish) Meat dish.

plato del dia (Spanish) Special dish of the day.

plato frio (Spanish) Cold dish.

plato vegetariano (Spanish) Vegetarian dish.

Platte (German) Plate.

platter Large flat plate for serving a main course.

plätter (Swedish) Pancakes made on a griddle, *pannkaka*.

Plattfisch (German) Plaice.

pleurote (French) Genus of fungi, of which the species *argonane* or *pleurote du panicaut* is edible.

plie (French) Plaice.

plombière (French) Rich ice cream made with almonds, eggs, and whipped cream.

plonk Slang for any cheap table wine.

plover Small wading bird in several species. Highly esteemed as a game bird, some gastronomes declare it should be cooked undrawn. Its eggs are considered a delicacy.

pluche (French) Garniture for soups. The leaves of parsley, chervil, tarragon, lettuce, and sorrel, cut into fine shreds.

pluck (i) To remove the feathers from a fowl. (ii) Entrails and offal removed from an animal or bird.

plum Stone fruit in many hundreds of varieties, ranging in colour from gold to purple, and varying considerably in size. Some are suitable for dessert, some for cooking, and some may be used in either way. The types known as gages are the best for dessert. Special varieties of plums are grown for drying as prunes. Plums are used for pies, baked and steamed puddings, flans, fruit salad, etc. They may also be pickled, dried, bottled or preserved.

plum brandy Distillate of plum wine, called *slivovitz* in Slav countries.

plum duff Steamed or baked pudding containing currants or raisins but not plums.

plum pudding Christmas pudding containing no plums; but usually including flour, currants, sultanas, raisins, lemon, eggs, suet, breadcrumbs, spices, and some ale, stout, brandy or wine.

plum tomato Small oval cherry tomato.

pluvier (French) Plover. A game bird whose eggs are esteemed a great delicacy.

pluvier doré (French) Golden plover.

Plymouth gin Famous gin made in Devon, less aromatic than Hollands, but more so than London dry gin.

Plymouth rock (American) Type of poultry developed in America and named for the rock where the Pilgrims landed.

poach To cook in liquid, simmering just below boiling point. A method of cooking usually applied to eggs and *quenelles* of fish, meat or game.

poached egg Egg cooked (i) in buttered individual pans in a poacher by standing over boiling water till lightly set, or (ii) in water.

poacher (i) Egg-poacher. (ii) Illegal catcher of birds and fish.

po'-boy sandwich (American) Sandwich made with a loaf of French bread cut length-wise and filled with lettuce, cheese, ham, etc.

pochard Migratory duck from Northern Europe, much prized for its flesh by connoisseurs and hunted during its flights across France. Cooked as for any wild duck.

poche (French) Forcing bag.

poché (French) Poached.

pocher (French) To poach.

pochouse (French) Freshwater fish stew cooked in white wine with butter, bacon, mushrooms and onions, and served on toasted, baked or fried bread.

podvarku (Yugoslav) Baked *sauerkraut*.

poêlage (French) Method of cooking in a covered pan with butter or other fat; pot-roasting.

poêle (French) Cooking pot or pan.

poêler (French) Mode of braising meat, etc., in a fire-proof earthenware pan.

poêlon (French) (i) Metal or earthenware long-handled pan for cooking sugar. (ii) Small skillet.

poffertje (Dutch) Fritter.

pogne de romans (French) Sweet brioche eaten hot or cold, served with red-currant jelly.

poi Polynesian taro-root paste.

point, à (French) Cooked to perfection.

pointe de culotte (French) Top of the rump.

pointe d'asperge (French) Asparagus tip.

poire (French) Pear.

poiré (French) Perry, pear cider.

poire belle Hélène Ice-cream topped with half a canned pear covered in chocolate sauce and decorated with chopped almonds.

poireau (French) Leek.

pois (French) Pea or peas.

pois cassés (French) Split peas.

pois chiche (French) Chick-pea.

pois et riz (French) Peas and rice.

pois mangetout (French) Sugar pea, or edible-podded pea.

pois sec (French) Dried pea.

poisson (French) (i) Fish. (ii) The fish course of a dinner.

poisson-chat (French) Catfish.

poisson d'eau douce (French) Freshwater fish.

poisson de mer (French) Marine fish; saltwater fish.

poissonier (French) (i) Fishmonger. (ii) Restaurant chef in charge of all fish dishes other than straight-forward grills or fries.

poissonière (French) Fish-kettle; fish pan.

poitin (Irish) Poteen. Whisky illicitly distilled from barley, potatoes, or molasses.

Poitou Region of France famed for *pâté de fois gras*, poultry, game pork, mutton, fish and shellfish, vegetables and walnuts, etc. etc.

poitrine (French) (i) Breast. (ii) Brisket of beef.

poivrade (French) (i) Method of preparing some meats, especially minced game. (ii) Small young artichokes, eaten with salt. (iii) Peppery sauce.

poivre (French) Pepper.

poivré (French) Peppered.

poivre de Cayenne, poivre rouge (French) Cayenne pepper prepared from the seeds of chilli or capsicum pods, grown in Cayenne (Guiana), and Guinea, Africa, the latter being more pungent.

poivre de Guinée (French) Guinea pepper.

Pol Roger Famous brand of champagne said to have been the favourite of Sir Winston Churchill.

Poland China (American) Black pigs with white markings, a cross-breed of Polish and Chinese swine.

polenta (Italian) Substantial cornmeal or maize porridge; a staple food in some parts of Italy. It is cooled, cut up into pieces, fried and served with bacon, etc.

polenta dulce (Spanish) South American cornmeal cream flavoured with anise, cinnamon, and vanilla.

polipo (Italian) Octopus.

Polish ham Ham produced in Poland,

usually strong-flavoured, smoked and aged.

Polish pickles Cucumbers pickled in alum, garlic, onions, vinegar, and spices.

Polish sausage Minced beef and pork sausage flavoured with garlic.

pollastrino (Italian) Very young chicken (*Poussin*).

pollastro (Italian) Spring chicken.

pollastro alla cacciatora (Italian) *Ragoût* made with young chicken, mushrooms, onions, herbs, etc.

polleria (Italian) Poulterer's shop.

polished rice See rice.

pollo (Italian and Spanish) Chicken.

pollo al forno (Italian) Oven-baked chicken.

pollo al latte (Italian) Chicken cooked in milk.

pollo al vino blanco (Italian) Chicken with white wine.

pollo all'olive (Italian) Chicken cooked with olives.

pollo alla cacciatore (Italian) Stewed chicken.

pollo alla diavola (Italian) Grilled chicken.

pollo arrosto (Italian) Roast chicken.

pollo asado (Spanish) Roast chicken.

pollo con arroz (Spanish) National dish of chicken with rice.

pollo con rosmarino (Italian) Chicken sautéed with rosemary.

pollo fritto (Italian) Fried chicken.

pollo imbottito (Italian) Stuffed roast chicken.

pollo in casseruola (Italian) Casseroled chicken.

pollo in gelatina (Italian) Cold chicken in aspic.

pollo in salsa picante (Italian) Chicken cooked in white wine and vinegar.

pollo lesso (Italian) Boiled chicken.

pollo ripieno (Italian) Stuffed chicken.

pollo tartufato (Italian) Chicken stuffed with truffles.

pollo tonnato (Italian) Chicken with tuna-fish sauce or mayonnaise.

pollock, pollack Large marine white fish of the cod family caught in various species off the Atlantic coasts of Europe and near Newfoundland.

Cooked as for cod. Also known as Coal-fish or Rock-salmon.

polmone (Italian) Lung (offal).

polmone di vitello (Italian) Calf's lung.

Polonaise, à la (French) Vegetables garnished with melted butter, parsley and hard egg-yolks.

polony (Italian) Sausage made of partly-cooked bacon, pork, veal or sometimes beef, with cereal, herbs and seasonings.

polpa (Italian) (i) Fruit pulp. (ii) Animal flesh.

polpetta (Italian) Croquette, rissole.

polpetti See *poupeton*.

polpettina (Italian) Meat ball, usually served in a tomato sauce.

polpettina di pesce (Italian) Small fishcake.

polpettone (Italian) (i) Hash. (ii) Meat roll or loaf.

polpo (Italian) (i) Octopus. (ii) Inkfish.

polpo affogato (Italian) Stewed octopus or inkfish.

polpo in purgatorio (Italian) Octopus or inkfish served in a hot, spicy tomato sauce.

pølse (Norwegian) Sausage.

polypodium Species of edible ferns.

polyporus Very large species of European mushrooms, edible but rather tough-fleshed.

polyunsaturate Fat, oil, or shortening containing many insoluble fat globules which do not remain in the body as other fats tend to do.

pomace (i) Residue of fruit such as grapes, apples, etc., after the juice has been extracted. From it is made pectin, used to set jellies, jams, etc. It is also used to make *eau de vie*. (ii) Apples crushed for cider-making.

pomaceous Resembling, relating to or consisting of apples.

pomme (i) Apple. (ii) Fruit constructed like an apple.

pomegranate Fruit of a tropical tree with great thirst-quenching properties, found in South America and the Mediterranean area. When freshly picked it is larger than an orange but when imported the outer rind has shrunk to a hard yellow-red skin encasing the pulpy red grains within. The squeezed-out fruit is strained for use in drinks or in flavouring ices, etc. It is made into wine in Iran, and into a liqueur, *Aguardiente*, in Mexico.

pomelo (i) Shaddock. (ii) Type of grapefruit, with pinkish flesh.

pomeroy, pomroy Old-fashioned variety of apple.

pomiculture Fruit-growing.

pomiferous Bearing apples, pomes or other fruit.

pomme (French) Apple.

pomme au four (French) (i) Baked apple. (ii) Baked potato.

pomme cannelle (French) Custard apple.

pomme d'amour (French) Tomato.

pomme d'api (French) Small red and white French dessert apple.

pomme de terre (French) Potato.

pomme de terre en robe de chambre (French) Potato baked in its skin or, literally, "dressing-gown".

pomme farcie (French) Stuffed potato.

pomme nouvelle (French) New potato.

pomme sauvage (French) Wild apple; crab apple.

Pommery (French) Famous champagne firm.

pommes allumettes (French) Matchstick potatoes.

pommes anna (French) Thin round slices of potato cooked in butter and shaped into a cake.

pommes annette (French) Finely-shredded potatoes cooked as for *pommes anna*.

pommes chips (French) Potato chips.

pommes de terre duchesse (French) Duchess potatoes; potatoes puréed with egg-yolk.

pommes de terre en pailles (French) Straw potatoes.

pommes frites (French) French-fried potatoes.

pommes parmentier (French) Diced potatoes fried in hot fat until crisp and golden outside, and soft within.

pommes purées (French) Mashed potatoes.

pommes sautées (French) Sautéed potatoes.

pomodoro (Italian) Tomato.

pomodoro, al (Italian) With tomato sauce.

pomodoro ripieno (Italian) Stuffed tomato.

pompano (i) Expensive, fine-flavoured species of tropical marine food fish found in the Atlantic and the Caribbean. (ii) Small bluish or greenish fish found along the Pacific coast.

pompano en papillote (French) Pompano cooked in metal foil or paper.

pompelmo (Italian) Grapefruit.

pomponnet (French) Small pouch-shaped rissole filled and fried in deep fat.

ponche (Spanish) Punch.

ponche de pina (Spanish) Pineapple punch.

pone (American) Oval-shaped cornmeal bread or cake.

poner la mesa (Spanish) To set the table.

Pont l'Évêque (French) Softish fermented pale yellow cheese made from whole or skimmed milk.

pont-neuf Puff pastry tartlets filled with *frangipane* cream and crushed macaroons.

Pontet-canet (French) Vineyard in the Bordeaux region producing fine red wine (*Médoc*).

pony Small whisky glass.

poor knights of Windsor *Pain perdu*.

poor knights pudding *Pain perdu*.

poor man's goose Casserole dish made from liver, onions and potatoes.

pop Slang for soft fizzy drink.

popcorn Variety of Indian corn or maize whose kernels pop open when heated, and form odd shapes. It can be eaten with melted butter and salt, or coated with sugar.

popcorn popper (American) Hinged-lid wire basket with a long handle for popping corn over an open flame. A lidded frying-pan used over a gas or electric burner can substitute.

pope Fish which resembles the perch in size, appearance, and flavour. Also known as ruffe.

pope's eye (i) Small circle of fat found in the centre of a leg of pork or mutton. (ii) In Scotland, the primest rumpsteak.

pope's nose Parson's nose.

popover (i) Batter or Yorkshire pudding

baked in individual patty tin, served with roast beef. (ii) Individually-baked batter, as in (i) but with added sweet or savoury flavouring such as (a) fruit, for a sweet course, or (b) onion, bacon, cheese, etc., for a savoury course.

poppy seed Flower seed used in stuffings, cakes, bread, etc. The capsule which contains the seed is the source of opium.

poppyseed oil Oil extracted from the seeds of the black, purple or white poppy, used for cooking and at table.

porc (French) Pork.

porc-épic (French) Porcupine.

porc frais (French) Fresh pork.

porc salé (French) Salted pork.

porcelain Delicate, translucent ceramic used in making decorative pottery and table-ware. Hard-paste porcelain is of Chinese origin dating back to 200 B.C., soft-paste porcelain is French in origin.

porchetta (Italian) Roast sucking-pig.

porco (Italian) (i) Pig. (ii) Pork meat.

porcupine Spiny mammal whose flesh makes good eating, especially when young.

porgy (American) (i) Marine food fish of the sea-bream family, found along the Atlantic and Mediterranean coasts. (ii) General name given to many other fishes such as pinfish, scups, spadefish, surf fish, etc.

pork Fresh pig meat, as distinct from cured pig meat, i.e., bacon and ham. Pork should be firm-fleshed with white fat, and should be well-cooked to prevent food poisoning. Prime joints such as loin, leg, shoulder (blade bone) are usually roasted. Chops are baked, grilled or fried. Cheaper cuts such as belly and hand are usually boiled or stewed, often pickled. They can also be baked. Pork pieces are used to make pork pies, galantines, etc. Pork meat is widely used for sausages.

pork loin Side cuts of pork.

pork pie Raised pie made with hot-water crust and filled with pork meat.

pork side Pork loin.

pork tenderloin (American) Pork fillet.

porkburger Hamburger made of pork meat.

porker Pig of six months of age, no longer suckling.

porpoise Short-snouted genus of the dolphin family whose meat is eaten in some parts despite its oily nature. The oil is the porpoise's main value, and is extracted.

Porree (German) Leek.

Porreesalat (German) Leek salad.

porridge (i) Breakfast dish of Scottish origin, made from fine, medium or coarse oatmeal, pin-point or quick cooking oats. Served in Scotland with salt but elsewhere usually taken with sugar, honey or syrup. (ii) Thick soup of maize, buckwheat or split peas.

porringer Bowl or dish for eating porridge.

porro (Italian) Leek.

port Fortified red wine, traditionally drunk after dinner. It is made from grapes grown in the Douro Valley of Portugal and shipped from Oporto. The main types are: Vintage: (one particular year's wine); Tawny: (lighter in body and colour, a blend of several different years); Ruby: (light red, a single-year product, or a blend); White: (a white fortified wine somewhat similar in taste to port).

porte-couteau (French) Knife-rest.

port-salut, *port du salut* (French) Delicious creamy yellow whole-milk French cheese, first made in a Trappist monastery near Laval and now made in Trappist monasteries elsewhere.

porter Dark-brown malt beer, to which molasses can be added to make stout.

porterhouse steak Thick steak cut from the middle of the ribs of beef.

porto (French and Portuguese) Port wine.

Portugaise (French) (i) Portuguese-style cooking, usually a dish of which tomato forms a part. (ii) Tomato fondue.

Portwein (German) Port wine.

Porzellan (German) China.

posel (Welsh) Curdled milk.

posset Hot drink made of sweetened or

spiced milk curdled with treacle, ale or wine, etc., once used as an aid in the cure of colds and for nursing mothers, etc.

postre (Spanish) Dessert.

pot Deep handled cooking vessel in ceramic, enamelware, or metal.

pot-ale Refuse from a grain distillery.

pot-au-feu (French) Economical and wholesome beef broth. The standard dish in France, and the origin of beef stock.

pot ball Dumpling.

pot barley Scotch or hulled barley; most nutritious because only the outer husk is removed. Used in soups and stews, it requires lengthy cooking to make it tender.

pot cheese Cottage cheese.

pot de crème (French) Vanilla- or chocolate-flavoured soft custard topped with whipped cream.

pot herb Stew vegetable such as carrot, onion, etc.

pot liquor (American) Broth of boiled meat or vegetables.

pot pie (American) Chicken or meat and vegetables, covered with a pie crust, and baked.

pot-roasting Slow-cooking by steam in a covered pan, suitable for less tender or dubious roasting joints. The surface is browned in fat, then cooked over a little water to which vegetables are added.

pot still Traditional, centuries-old vessel used in distilling such spirits as malt whisky, cognac, etc.

potable (French) Drinking.

potable (Spanish) Drinking.

potac (French-Canadian) Potato.

potage (French) Thick soup.

potage ambassadeur (French) Pea, sorrel and rice soup.

potage andalouse (French) Tomato and tapioca soup.

potage au lièvre (French) Hare soup.

potage au queue de bœuf (French) Oxtail soup.

potage au salop (French) Salep soup.

potage au vermicelle (French) Noodle soup.

potage aux huîtres (French) Oyster soup.

potage bavarois (French) Bavarian soup, sliced sausage in lentil soup.

potage bonne-femme (French) Leek and potato soup.

potage clair (French) Clear soup.

potage crème de céléri (French) Celery soup.

potage crème de haricots verts (French) French (string) bean soup.

potage crème d'orge (French) Cream of barley soup.

potage crème de poireaux (French) Leek soup.

potage d'artois (French) White bean and vegetable soup.

potage d'aspèrges (French) Asparagus soup.

potage de betterave (French) Beetroot soup.

potage de champignons (French) Mushroom soup.

potage de gibier (French) Game soup.

potage de homard (French) Lobster soup.

potage de tête de veau (French) Mock turtle soup. Also called *fausse tortue.*

potage de tomates (French) Tomato soup.

potage de volaille (French) Chicken soup.

potage freneuse (French) Turnip soup.

potage lié (French) Cream, *purée* or *velouté* soup.

potage parmentier (French) Potato cream soup, so called because Parmentier introduced potatoes into France.

potage portugais (French) Tomato soup.

potage purée à la reine (French) Cream of chicken soup.

potage purée de lentilles (French) Lentil soup.

potage purée de marrons (French) Chestnut soup.

potage purée de topinambours (French) Jerusalem artichoke soup.

potage Saint Germain (French) Fresh pea *purée* soup.

potage velours (French) Smooth carrot and tapioca soup.

potager (French) (i) Soup-pot. (ii) Cooking stove. (iii) Kitchen garden.

potaje (Spanish) Thick soup.

potaje de garbanzos (Spanish) Chicken-pea soup.

potato Much-used tuber, native of South

America and introduced into Europe in 1584. For some 200 years it was an expensive delicacy but as cultivation widened and improved it became the staple diet of poorer people, particularly the Irish. Potatoes vary widely in type, consistency and season, and yield more calories than other vegetables. They are prepared in countless variations on baking, boiling and frying, used in soups, stews and many other dishes such as salads, griddle cakes, etc., etc.

potato alcohol Potato spirit, distilled from fermented potatoes.

potato ball Small potato croquette.

potato bean (American) Yam bean.

potato cake Mashed potatoes, butter and flour formed into a patty and fried.

potato chips (i) Peeled potatoes cut into strips and deep-fried. (ii) (American) Potato crisps.

potato crisps Thinly-sliced potatoes crisped in deep fat and dried; some have special flavours added such as cheese, onion, bacon, etc.

potato croquette Puréed potatoes bound with egg, shaped into small corks, egged-and-crumbed, and fried in deep fat.

potato flakes Anhydrated potatoes, finely flaked.

potato flour Flour prepared from potatoes by cooking, drying, and milling.

potato masher Tool to mash up cooked potatoes. Usually a long-handled utensil with a perforated chromium plate which is pressed down into the potato, so that it is squeezed through the apertures. A pastry cutter with thin wire blades can also serve to mash potatoes.

potato pancake Pulped or grated raw potatoes added to pancake batter and cooked in the usual way.

potato quenelle Puréed potatoes mixed with egg and flour, shaped into balls or cork-like rolls and cooked in boiling salted water, then drained and buttered.

potato salad Cubed, boiled potatoes tossed in salad dressing, sometimes with added chives, chopped celery, onions, and seasoning.

potato spirit Alcohol distilled from fermented potatoes.

potato whisky Potato alcohol.

potée (French) (i) Food cooked in an earthenware pot. (ii) Soup made with pork and vegetables.

poteen, potteen, potheen Illegally distilled liquor, made under cover of night, often by moonlight. Commonly known as "moonshine".

potet (Norwegian) Potato.

potheen See poteen.

potiron (French) Pumpkin.

potpourri (French) Stew of various kinds of meats and spices.

potrock (Russian) Thick soup.

pottage Thick meat or vegetable soup usually containing a pulse or cereal.

potted Fish or meat pounded into a fine paste, seasoned, and canned, or packed in jars and covered with clarified butter. Used as spreads on cocktail *canapés*, in sandwiches, etc.

potted cheese Cheese made from ripened cheddar cheese, butter, condiments, wine, or other spirits and packed in pots.

pottery Coarse ceramic ware used in making kitchen utensils such as casseroles, etc.

pottinger Old-English name for an apothecary or spice merchant.

pottle (i) Half-gallon measure. (ii) Chip basket for strawberries.

pottle pot Half-gallon drinking vessel.

potware Crockery.

pouchong tea Oolong tea scented with gardenia, jasmine, or magnolia.

pouchouse Stew made of freshwater fish. See *pochouse*.

pouding (French) Pudding.

pouding à la mælle (French) Marrow pudding.

pouding à la semoule (French) Semolina pudding.

pouding au chocolat (French) Chocolate pudding.

pouding au pain (French) Bread pudding.

pouding au pain bis (French) Brown bread pudding.

pouding au sagou (French) Sago pudding.

pouding au tapioca (French) Tapioca pudding.

pouding au vermicelle (French) Vermicelli pudding.

pouding aux amandes (French) Almond pudding.

pouding de cabinet (French) Cabinet pudding.

pouding de fruits (French) Fruit pudding.

pouding de Noël (French) Christmas pudding, plum pudding.

pouding de riz au plat, dit à l'Anglaise (French) English rice pudding.

pouding de semoule (French) Semolina pudding.

pouding Ecossais (French) Scotch pudding, oatmeal pudding.

pouding glacé (French) Iced pudding.

pouding roulé à l'Anglaise (French) English suet-roll pudding.

pouding soufflé aux marrons (French) Chestnut souffle pudding.

poudre d'ail (French) Powdered garlic.

poudre de cacao soluble (French) Cocoa powder.

poudre de levure (French) Baking powder.

Pougues (French) Saline mineral water, from *Pougues*, in the department of *Nievre*, France.

pouilly fuissé (French) Famous dry white Burgundy wine.

pouilly fumé (French) Dry white wine from the Loire.

poularde (French) Fat pullet; a chicken about 7 or 8 months old that has not started to lay eggs.

poule (French) Hen.

poule au pot (French) Boiled chicken.

poule au riz (French) Chicken with rice.

poule d'eau (French) Water-hen, moorhen.

poule de neige (French) White grouse.

poulet (French) Young cock chicken.

poulet à la crapaudine (French) Spread-eagle chicken.

poulet à la reine (French) Fine specimen of young chicken.

poulet de grain (French) Spring chicken.

poulet dinde (French) Young turkey.

poulet froid (French) Cold chicken.

poulet en casserole (French) Chicken browned in butter in an earthenware casserole, then covered and allowed to cook very slowly, basted occasionally.

poulet rôti (French) Roast chicken.

poulette (French) Young hen.

poulette, à la (French) (i) Method of preparing dishes in a white sauce made of stock, cream, butter, flour, egg-yolks, and chopped herbs. (ii) White stew.

pouliot (French) Pennyroyal mint.

pouillard (French) Young partridge.

poulpe (French) Octopus.

poultry Domesticated species of birds (chicken, turkeys, ducks, etc.) bred for their eggs or for the table.

poultry needle Long thin needle for sewing up fish, meats, and poultry after stuffing.

poultry seasoning Blend of herbs such as parsley, marjoram, sage and thyme used to stuff meat, chicken, turkey, etc.

poultry shears Strong scissors for cutting up or jointing a poultry carcase.

pound Unit of weight equalling 16 ounces. (Metric: 0.45 kilos).

pound cake Fruit cake, so named because the main ingredients were originally measured in equal quantities of one pound.

poupart (French) Large crab, found along the coasts of France. Also called *Fourteau*.

poupelin (French) *Choux* paste *gâteau* filled with *Chantilly* cream, fruit mousse or ice cream.

poupeton, polpetti (French) Slices of meat such as veal stuffed with minced meat, and braised.

pouring batter Batter made thin enough to be poured.

pourpier (French) Purslane.

pourriture (French) Rot, decay.

pousse-cafe (French) Mixed drink made of layers of liqueurs and spirits which do not blend because of their different specific gravities.

poussin (French) Very young chicken, spring chicken.

poussoir (French) Sausage-making machine.

poutarge, poutargue, (properly boutargue) (French) Botargo.

pouter Large-breasted pigeon.

powdered coffee Instant coffee.

powdered milk Dehydrated milk, skimmed or whole.

powdered sugar (American) Icing sugar.

praire (French) Clam.

prairie chicken (American) Species of grouse, cooked as for other species.

prairie oyster Drink of whole raw egg, Worcester sauce, lemon juice or vinegar, and seasoning, given to invalids and also to "hangover" sufferers, intended to be swallowed at a gulp.

pragoon (French) Ruscus.

praline Confection of nuts and caramelised sugar.

praliné (French) (i) Layered cake filled and covered with praline butter cream and sprinkled with almonds. (ii) Flavoured with burnt almonds.

praline (French) Name of a French sweet, an almond encased in sugar.

pranzo (Italian) Meal.

pranzo di legumi (Italian) Vegetable platter.

pranzo di manzo (Italian) Beef pot-roast served with Italian sauce.

pratelle (French) Variety of cultivated large pinkish mushroom.

prawn Large shrimp obtainable all the year round, but at its best during the spring and summer and usually sold ready boiled; also obtainable in cans and jars and packeted frozen. Prawns are used in salads, sauces, scalloped and curried dishes, savouries and cocktails. The famous Dublin Bay prawn is used for Scampi.

prawn cocktail Prawns served with shredded lettuce and mayonnaise sauce, as an appetiser or first course of a meal.

pre-heat To heat an oven before use so that it will have reached the correct temperature when the food is put in for cooking.

pré-salé (French) Young sheep fattened in meadows bordering the sea-coast. The flesh tends to be darker than that of ordinary animals.

Preignac (French) White wine from the *Preignac* district in the *Gironde*, France.

Preiselbeere (German) (i) Cranberry. (ii) Bilberry.

prêle (French) Mare's tail, a common field plant whose young shoots are eaten like asparagus.

présent (French) Dutch cheese.

présentoir (French) Dish upon which a tureen, vegetable dish, etc. rests.

preservative Substance which retards or arrests fermentation or other decomposition of food. The principal permitted preservatives are: Sulphur dioxide (in jam, fruit preparations, sausage-meat, drinks, including beer and cider, etc.); Benzoic acid (pickles, sauces, soft drinks, etc.) Sodium and Potassium nitrate (bacon, ham); Propionic acid, Sorbic acid (for flour products). The term 'preservative' does not strictly apply to vinegars or other traditional means of preserving food.

preserve (i) Jam, jelly or other conserve made from fruit or vegetables. (ii) To subject food to a preservation method in order to keep it in good condition and to prevent decomposition.

preserve jar Jar or pot for storing home-made preserves.

preserving Methods of keeping food in good condition by heating, refrigeration, drying or placing in salt, vinegar, sugar or other chemicals. Bottling and freezing are other means of preservation.

press (i) Culinary tool which extracts juice from fruit or meat. (ii) To pass food through a strainer, pressing it through with a large wooden spoon.

presse (French) Food press, such as a lemon-squeezer, etc.

pressed beef Boned brisket beef, salted, cooked, pressed and glazed.

Presskopf (German) Jellied mould of offal meats.

pressoir (French) Appliance for pressing grapes, apples, etc.

pressure cooker Hermetically-sealed, lidded saucepan which cooks foods at a higher temperature than that achieved by ordinary methods. The escape of steam is controlled, and the temperature and the pressure inside the cooker rise above normal levels, resulting in shorter cooking time. A suitable cooking method for non-prime cuts of meat and poultry; also for soups, preserves, root and pulse vegetables. Egg custards can also be pressure-cooked successfully and in a fraction of the time they normally require.

présure (French) Rennet.

prêtre (French) Small French marine fish with delicate flesh and a silvery star-like mark on its sides.

pretzel Glazed brittle, hard, salted biscuit, originating from Germany, formed into a loose knot and often served with beer.

pretzel bender (i) Baker accomplished in bending pretzel dough into shapes. (ii) Machine which performs this task.

pretzel press Utensil for shaping pretzel dough.

prezzemolo (Italian) Parsley.

prickly pear Watery, refreshing fruit of various types of cactus plants, eaten raw, or stewed, or used for making alcoholic beverages.

prima colazione (Italian) Breakfast.

prima costoletta (Italian) Loin chop.

primeiro almoço (Portuguese) Breakfast.

primeur (French) Early forced vegetable or fruit.

primost (Norwegian) Creamy whey cheese.

primrose Plant whose yellow flowers can be used to decorate a salad which includes its leaves.

primrose vinegar Vinegar made from sugar, water, primrose flowers and yeast, matured in the cask.

primus Portable stove for outdoor cooking.

principio (Spanish) Entrée.

printanier (French) Collection of early spring vegetables, cut small or into little balls, used as a garnish, or in the form of a *macédoine* of vegetables.

printanière, à la (French) Meat cuts garnished with spring or mixed vegetables.

pris (French) Set, as in the case of jellies, custards, etc.

probar el vino (Spanish) To taste the wine.

processed cheese Medium-soft cheese made from cheeses such as Cheddar, Dutch or Gruyère. After the rind is removed the cheese is ground, melted and mixed with emulsifiers and colourings, before being moulded into shapes and finally wrapped in foil.

profiterole (French) (i) Type of light cake, originally baked in hot ashes and then filled with cream. (ii) Small ball of *choux* paste garnished with whipped cream and served with chocolate sauce.

promessi (Italian) Soft cream cheese.

proof Alcoholic strength of a liquid.

proost (Dutch) Cheers! A toast.

propina (Spanish) Tip, gratuity.

prosciutto (Italian) Thinly-sliced ham.

prosciutto affumicato (Italian) Smoked ham.

prosciutto con melone (Italian) Parma ham served with iced melon.

prosciutto cotto (Italian) Cooked ham.

prosciutto crudo (Italian) Raw ham.

prosciutto di Parma (Italian) Most famous of Italian hams.

prosit (German) Cheers! Here's to your health! A toast.

protective foods Foods, such as dairy produce, eggs, meat, fish, vegetables, fruit and cereals, rich in the minerals and vitamins which regulate the body and help to keep it healthy.

protein The most important nutrient for body-building and repair, carbon, hydrogen, oxygen, nitrogen and other elements in the form of amino acids. Animal protein is derived from meat, poultry, game, fish, cheese, eggs, milk, etc. Vegetable protein is found in nuts, cereals, pulses, soya beans, etc.

prove To allow bread to rise for the second time before cooking.

provençale, à la (French) Preparations characterised by use of garlic and/or tomato, typical of the cooking of Provence.

Provence French region, bordering the Mediterranean, rich in culinary specialities of fish, seafood, vegetables, cheeses, wines, fruits, etc. Garlic is the basis of most Provençal dishes but the garlic grown in the area is less strong than that grown farther north.

provisiones (Spanish) Provisions; groceries.

provola (Italian) Buffalo-milk cheese.

provolone (Italian) Buffalo or cow's milk cheese made in many shapes and sizes.

prugna (Italian) Plum.

prugna cotta (Italian) Stewed prune.

prugna seccha (Italian) Dried plum. Prune.

prune Dried plum in several varieties ranging from small to large in size. A source of vitamin A, prunes are slightly laxative and are used in a wide variety of sweets and puddings, also (stuffed) as a cocktail savoury.

prune (French) Plum.

prune butter Prunes sweetened, boiled, sieved, flavoured with cinnamon and cloves, and used as a spread.

prune de damas (French) Damson plum.

prune de Reine-Claude (French) Greengage.

prune whip Sweet made of strained prune pulp, sugar, and egg white.

pruneau (French) Prune.

prunelle (French) (i) Sloe; wild plum. (ii) Pale-green, sloe-flavoured liqueur.

pt. Abbreviation for pint. (American: 20 fl. oz; British: 16 fl. oz. Metric: 0.57 litres).

ptarmigan Small wild bird of the grouse family, found in Northern Europe, and in season from August 12th to December 10th. It turns white during the winter months and is also known as white grouse, willow or rock partridge and mountain grouse. Its flavour is not so fine as that of grouse, but it is served in the same way.

ptomaines Principles found in decayed or tainted food which cause food-poisoning.

puchero (Spanish) (i) Cooking pot. (ii) Stew.

puchero de carne (Spanish) Meat stew.

pudding (i) Savoury dish such as steak and kidney pudding, Black pudding, etc. (ii) Sweet-course dish hot or cold, usually fairly substantial, such as baked pies, tarts, sponge mixtures

steamed or baked, suet crust mixtures, milk and cereal dishes, custard and breadcrumb mixtures, egg dishes such as soufflés, batters, etc. (iii) Creams and jellies, fruit sweets, moulds, ice cream dishes, etc.

pudim (Portuguese) Pudding.

puerco (Spanish) Pork.

Puerto Rican molasses Dark-coloured molasses, slightly rum-flavoured.

puff pastry Rich pastry made with equal quantities of butter and flour, suitable for any dish requiring a very light crust. The fat is formed into a flat cake and rolled into the flour-and-water dough.

puffer Fritter made with flaked-oats batter, and cooked in a frying pan.

puits d'amour (French) French pastry made of puff paste and filled with confectioner's custard.

pulë me orrë (Albanian) Chicken with walnuts.

pulled bread Soft part of a loaf pulled into pieces while hot, and baked in a moderate oven until crisp.

pullet Young female chicken.

pulp Soft, fleshy parts of vegetables or fruit rubbed through a sieve to form a *purée*.

pulpe (French) Pulp.

pulpeta (Spanish) Oven-baked slice of veal covered with a savoury mixture of garlic, herbs, olives and hard-boiled eggs bound with sherry.

pulpo (Spanish) Octopus.

pulque Mexican fermented beverage made from agave sap or juice of the maguey plant.

pulse Dried legume seed such as beans and peas, lentils, etc., high in protein content.

pultöst (Norwegian) Mountain farm cheese made from sour milk.

Pumpernickel (German) (i) Black bread. (ii) Westphalian rye-bread.

pumpkin Large, golden gourd cooked as a vegetable, puréed as a pie-filling, or used for making soups, preserves or salads. Pumpkin seeds can be salted, roasted and eaten as a snack.

pumpkin pie Pumpkin flesh puréed and

blended with eggs, milk, sugar and seasoning, and baked in a pie shell.

pumpkin-pie spice (American) Ginger, clove and cinnamon finely ground and used to flavour pumpkin pies, sweet-potato pies, biscuits, etc.

pumpkin seed Seed of the pumpkin, roasted and salted.

punch Mixed beverage, served hot or cold, with a base of wine, milk, cider, ale, lager, champagne or tea, with added whisky, rum, brandy or sherry or a liqueur. Non-alcoholic fruit punches are made with a ginger-ale or soda base, and pieces of fruit can be added to either type. Punch derives its name from the Hindu word "panch" meaning five, because the Hindus made their punch from five ingredients – sugar, spice, lemon juice, arrack and water.

punch à la romaine (French) Soft white ice made from lemon-juice, water, white of egg, sugar, and rum. It is served in goblets between courses and assists the digestion.

punch au rhum (French) Rum punch.

punch cup Handled cup for serving punch from a bowl.

punch glacé (French) Iced punch.

punch marquise (French) Punch of sweet white wine and cognac, flamed, and served with lemon sliced.

punchbowl Large silver, porcelain or glass bowl for mixing and serving punch, usually with matching cups and ladle.

puncheon (i) British beer barrel holding 72 gallons. (ii) Cask containing 100 gallons of rum or 120 gallons of brandy.

punsch (Swedish) Liqueur made of flavoured and sweetened arrack.

punt e mes (Italian) Distinctive vermouth drunk as an *aperitif*.

punta di asparago (Italian) Asparagus tip.

punto, al (Italian) Food cooked neither under- or over-done. Literally, "done to the point".

purée (French) (i) Smooth pulp, sauce or soup. (ii) Mashed vegetables or fruits. (iii) Cooked, pounded and sieved meat or fish. (iv) To pound or sieve meat, fish, fruit or vegetables.

purée Bretonne (French) Haricot beans cooked in *Bretonne* sauce of puréed onions.

purée d'oursins (French) Sea-urchin *purée*.

purée d'ail (French) Garlic *purée*.

purée de betteraves (French) *Beetroot purée*.

purée de cervelle d'agneau, de veau (French) Puréed lamb or calf's brains.

purée de courgettes (French) Baby marrow (*courgettes*) *purée*.

purée d'épinards (French) *Purée* of spinach.

purée d'estragon (French) Tarragon *purée*.

purée de fèves fraiches (French) Broad bean *purée*.

purée de flageolets secs (French) Dried bean *purée*.

purée de fois de veau (French) Calf's liver *purée*.

purée d'huîtres (French) Oyster *purée*.

purée de laitues (French) Lettuce *purée*.

purée de legumes (French) Vegetable *purée*.

purée de marrons (French) Chestnut *purée*.

purée de piments doux (French) Sweet pepper *purée*.

purée de pois (French) Pea soup.

purée de pois cassés (French) Split pea *purée*.

purée de pois chiches (French) Chick-pea *purée*.

purée de pois frais (French) Fresh pea *purée*.

purée de pommes de terre (French) Potato *purée;* mashed or creamed potatoes.

purée de ris de veau (French) Sweet-breads *purée*.

purée de topinambours (French) Jerusalem artichoke *purée*.

purée de volaille (French) Chicken *purée*.

purée soubise (French) Onion *purée*.

purée - presser Utensil for pressing through *purées* of meat, vegetables, etc.

purgatorio, in (Italian) Food served in a peppery, highly flavoured tomato sauce.

puri (Hindi) Type of chapatti made in India for special occasions.

purl Old-fashioned winter drink of spiced ale, or ale, milk and spirits.

purpoo mulligatawny (Hindi) Curry soup made in Ceylon and India.

purslane Herb used in salads, soups, pickles and sauces, also as a pot herb.

First introduced into England from America in 1652.

"push out the boat" Expression meaning to take your turn at buying a round of drinks.

pusher Child's eating utensil with which food can be pushed onto a fork.

Puter (German) Turkey-cock.

Pyrex Proprietory brand name of a range of heat-resisting glass ovenware.

pyridoxine One of the vitamin B group.

qt. Abbreviation for quart (British: 32 fl. oz; American: 40 fl. oz.) Metric: approx. 1.14 litres).

quab (Russian) River fish.

quadrillé (French) Thin strips of paste laid across tarts, so as to form a chequered pattern.

quaglia (Italian) Quail.

quaglia al vino bianco (Italian) Quail cooked in white wine.

quaglia alla griglia (Italian) Quail bacon-wrapped and grilled.

quaglia arrosto (Italian) Roast quail.

quahog (American) Edible Venus mollusc, the common hardshell clam of the North American Atlantic Coast, also known as round clam.

quaich (Scottish) Two-handled drinking cup.

quail Small migratory bird in several species throughout the world. The European common quail is protected in Britain and is no longer classed as a game bird. The Japanese quail is now being raised for consumption.

Quails can be roasted, stuffed, braised, devilled, served cold, in aspic, etc., etc.

quaker bread (American) Twin loaves of bread baked in a double bread tin.

quantity cooking Preparing food in large amounts, with special equipment and recipes.

Quark (German) Curds, cream cheese.

Quarkkäse (German) Cottage cheese.

Quarkkloss (German) Cottage-cheese dumpling.

quart Liquid measure containing 2 pints, or 32 fl. oz. (American: 40 fl. oz.) Metric: approx. 1.14 litres.

quarter One-fourth part of a meat carcase including either the forequarter or the hindquarter.

quartern loaf Original British standard loaf of bread which used to weigh 4 lb.

quartier (French) Quarter.

quartier d'agneau (French) Quarter of lamb.

quartier de devant (French) Forequarter.

quartier de derrière (French) Hindquarter.

quartier de lard (French) Flitch of bacon.

quasi (French) Cut from the rump of veal.

quass, quas, quaas (Russian) Beer made of rye or bread, or of apples or pears.

quassia bitters Bitters made from the bark and wood of the *Quassia amara* tree.

quassia cup Infusion of quassia chips, flavoured with orange peel, borage and spices, sweetened, and fortified with alcohol.

quatre épices (French) Well-known mixture of four spices – nutmeg, ginger, cloves and white pepper.

quatre mendiants (French) Dessert of figs, raisins, nuts and almonds.

quatre quarts (French) Pound cake mixture made up of equal parts of its four ingredients: butter, eggs, flour, sugar.

que apreveche (Spanish) Good appetite! A toast.

queen cake Small, light, rich cake, containing flour, butter, sugar, eggs, peel and dried fruit and baked in patty tins or paper cases.

queen conch Tropical shellfish used in salads, chowders and stews, whose shell is used to make cameos.

Queen Henrietta Maria's marmalade of cherries Preserve made for King Charles the First's queen from cherries, red-currants, raspberry juice and sugar.

queen of puddings Pudding of breadcrumbs soaked in custard and topped first with jam or fruit, then with meringue.

queen olive Large oval Spanish olive with elongated stone.

Queensland nut Macadamia nut.

queijadinha de amêndoas (Portuguese) Small almond cheese cake.

queijo (Portuguese) Cheese.

queijo da ilha (Portuguese) Firm cheese made in the Azores.

quenelle (French) Forcemeat dumpling. Small ball or oval of minced fish or meat bound with eggs and added to sauces or used as a garnish. It can be cooked in boiling stock or water, or coated with egg and crumbs and fried. Served as an *entrée* or as a garnish.

quenelle de veau (French) Minced veal dumpling.

queso (Spanish) Cheese.

queso de bola (Spanish) Dutch cheese, such as Edam.

queso de crema (Spanish) Cream cheese.

queso gallego (Spanish) Soft creamy cheese made in the province of Galicia.

quetsch (Alsatian) White, potent brandy, distilled in Alsace from the *quetsch* plum and flavoured with its kernels.

queue (French) Tail.

queue d'écrevisse (French) Crayfish tail.

queue de bœuf (French) Oxtail.

queue de mouton (French) Sheep's tail.

queue de veau (French) Calf's tail.

quiche (i) Savoury custard tart, originating in Lorraine, and a speciality of Alsace and Lorraine, where many variations can be found. (ii) Erroneously, also applied to some sweet custard tarts served as a sweet.

quiche Lorraine (French) Savoury egg custard tart with cheese and bacon or ham among the ingredients.

quick bread (American) Scones leavened with baking powder and not kneaded.

quick-freezing Rapid commercial process of freezing food whereby ice crystals formed are too small to damage the food cells. The results are better than those obtained by home-freezing which, being slower, forms larger crystals. Colour, flavour and texture are preserved by quick-freezing.

quick oven Hot oven.

quignon (French) Wedge of bread from a large French loaf.

quillet (French) Famous Parisian pastry made with sugar, eggs, flour, powdered vanilla, and filled with an orgeat – (almonds and sugar) – flavoured butter cream.

quince Yellowish astringent fruit of a tree of the apple family, and resembling apples or pears according to variety. The fruit is not suitable as dessert but can be baked or cooked in tarts and makes excellent fruit butter, jam or jelly, either by itself or mixed with apples, pumpkin, marrow or cranberries. (See *marmelo*).

quince compote Preserve made from quinces cooked in vanilla syrup.

quince jelly Preserve made from quinces, water and sugar.

quince water Ratafia liqueur flavoured with quince.

quinine water Tonic water.

quinnat King salmon.

quinta (Portuguese) Wine estate.

quintal Variety of cabbage.

quire pancake Pancake made from an 18th century recipe for a rich batter with added nutmeg and sack or sherry.

Quitte (German) Quince.

quoorma (Hindi) Very mild Indian curry preparation.

qutaif (Arabic) Arabian dish similar to pancakes, which are made as thin as possible, fried in almond oil, served with a rich syrup, and sprinkled with rose water.

rabano (Spanish) Radish.

rabarbaro (Italian) Rhubarb.

rabarbe (Danish) Rhubarb.

rabarbersuppe (Danish) Rhubarb soup.

rabbit Small rodent of the hare family with delicate flesh which makes good eating in either tame or wild varieties. The rabbit's white meat contains a high amount of animal protein and a low fat content. Rabbit is roasted or fried only when young, otherwise cooked as for meat – stewed, braised, made into pies, moulds, terrines, fricassées, etc., etc.

rabiole Variety of kohl-rabi or turnip.

rable (French) Back or loin part of rabbit or hare.

rabotte (French) Baked fruit dumpling, usually made with apple or pear. Also called *douillon*.

racahout, racachou (i) Arabian beverage prepared like drinking chocolate, made from the flour of roasted edible acorns, cocoa, potato flour, rice flour, sugar, powdered orchid root and vanilla. (ii) Thin gruel given to invalids.

racimo de uvas (Spanish) Bunch of grapes.

racine (French) Root; root vegetable.

rack (American) (i) Rib portion of a meat carcase, or the neck and forequarter. (ii) Arrack.

rack of lamb (American) Best end of neck.

raclette (French) Swiss dish of cheese melted over an open fire and eaten with boiled potatoes, a speciality of the canton of *Valais*.

racoon, raccoon Small wild animal of the American forests, cooked as for wild rabbit.

radicchio (Italian) Chicory; endive.

radicchio rosso (Italian) Red chicory.

radice (Italian) Radish.

Radieschen (German) Radish.

radikia me ladi (Greek) Boiled dandelion greens.

radis (French) Radish.

radish Small red or white-and-red

vegetable with a characteristic, slightly hot flavour, which should be eaten while young and tender and is best served raw in salads. Larger radishes may be boiled (unpeeled) in salted water until tender and served with a white or parsley sauce. As a garnish, radishes are sliced thinly, or cut into "roses" or "lilies". Radish tops may be cooked in salted water as a green vegetable.

radish rose Radish cut and opened in water to form a "rose" for garnishing salads and other dishes.

rafano (Italian) Horseradish.

raffinade (French) Best quality refined sugar.

Raffinade (German) Refined sugar.

raffiné (French) Purified.

raffineria (Italian) Sugar-refinery.

raffinerie (French) Sugar refinery.

rafraîchir (French) To refresh; to cool.

ragbröd (Swedish) Ryebread.

ragoule (French) Agaric (edible) fungus, also called *barigoule*.

ragoût (French) Rich, seasoned stew of meat, fish or poultry and vegetables, browned in a little fat then gently simmered.

ragoût de mouton (French) Mutton stew.

rahat lakoum Turkish delight.

Rahm (German) Cream.

rahmig (German) Creamy.

Rahmkäse (German) Curd.

Rahmpudding (German) Cream pudding

Rahmschnitzel (German) Veal or pork fillet, with sour cream or cream and lemon juice.

raidir (French) To sear food in hot fat.

raie (French) (i) Skate. A flat sea-fish, in season October to April. (ii) Ray.

raifort (French) Horseradish.

rail Small wading bird, the rail or water-rail, which can be cooked as for widgeon or quail.

rainbow trout Food and game fish with coloured skin, imported into Europe from California.

raised crust See raised pie.

raised pie Pie made with hot-water crust pastry which becomes firm during baking and, when cold, is filled up with stock which sets into a jelly. Usually served cold.

raisin Dried white or black grape in several varieties and grown in many countries including Spain, Australia and South Africa. Muscatels are seeded and are best in flavour, the choice Malaga ones are eaten as dessert with almonds, especially at Christmas time. Some varieties are seedless but either type can be used in cakes, pastries, pies, pudding etc., as well as used for wine-making.

raisin (French) Grape.

raisin de corinthe (French) Currant.

raisin de Malaga (French) Dried muscat grapes eaten as dessert or used in cakes and puddings.

raisin scone Baked scone dough containing raisins.

raisin sec (French) Dried grape, raisin.

raisiné (French) Jam made by reducing grape juice to a jelly consistency, often with fruit added.

raising agent Means of introducing an air or gas into food such as bread, cake, pastry or pudding, so that they rise during cooking. This can be yeast, or a chemical reaction between an acid and an alkali, such as cream of tartar or tartaric acid and bi-carbonate of soda, baking powder, or can be a manual process such as whisking ingredients over hot water.

raiton (French) Small skate.

raki (i) Liqueur made in Greece and the Levant from grapes or plums. (ii) Arrack, Turkish alcoholic beverage distilled from wine and flavoured with aniseed.

rakia Central European liqueur made from full-flavoured grapes.

rale (French) Rail.

ram Male sheep.

rambour, rambourg (French) Variety of red or white baking apple originating in the *Rambour* (Somme) district of France.

ramekin (i) Small fireproof china or glass dish in which a savoury or *entrée* is served. (ii) Cheese fritter or finger.

ramequin (French) Ramekin.

ramereau (French) Young wild wood-pigeon.

ramier (French) Wild wood-pigeon.

rampion Plant with an edible tuberous root prepared like salsify, and leaves that are cooked like spinach or eaten in salads.

rana (Italian) Frog.

rana dorata (Italian) Egged-and-fried frog's leg.

rancid Rank-smelling or rank-tasting oil, butter, or other fat that is in process of going bad.

rancio (French) Red or *rosé* sweet wine of the Midi, tasting similar to Madeira.

range (i) (British) Kitchen stove using solid fuel. (ii) (American) Kitchen stove.

rangette (American) Small stove, usually portable.

rangpur Sour variety of mandarin orange.

Ranhofer, Ch Noted 19th-century chef of Delmonico's Restaurant, New York, author of *The Epicurean*, Franco-American cook book.

rapa (Italian) Turnip.

rape Turnip-like plant (*Brassica napus*) whose foliage is used for animal fodder. Its seeds yield an oil used in soap-making and also as a lubricant.

râpé (French) Abbreviation for *fromage râpé* – grated cheese.

râper (French) To shred or grate.

rarebit Welsh or buck rarebit or rabbit. Toast topped with melted cheese, (Welsh rarebit) sometimes with added poached egg (Buck rarebit).

rascasse (French) Hog-fish.

rasher Thin slice of bacon.

raspberry Fruit allied to the bramble; there are two kinds, red and white, both are eaten as dessert or used for compôtes, tarts, jams, cream, *mousses*, etc., also for making a delicious brandy.

raspberry fool Strictly, puréed, sweetened raspberries mixed with cream, but a more economical version contains custard or a mixture of cream and custard.

raspberry vinegar Acidulated syrup of raspberries.

raspberry wine Wine made from raspberries, sugar and yeast.

rassolni (Russian) Salted cucumber soup.

rastegaï (Russian) Yeast-dough patty crimped at each end, filled with a savoury mixture but with the middle unsealed or "unbuttoned", which is the meaning of the name in Russian.

ratafia (i) Flavouring essence made from the essential oil of almonds. (ii) Cordial or liqueur flavoured with fruit kernels such as cherries, peaches, almonds, etc. (iii) Sweet biscuit resembling macaroons.

ratatouille (French) Vegetable dish of aubergines, cucumbers, peppers, tomato and onion, cooked in olive oil.

ration Food allowance or portion.

raton (French) Variety of cheesecake.

raton-laveur (French) Racoon, or raccoon.

ratonnet (French) Small skewer of meat, generally mutton.

Raute (German) Rue.

ravanello (Italian) Radish.

rave (French) Root vegetable.

ravier (French) Small *hors d'œuvre* fish.

ravigote (French) (i) Highly seasoned white herb sauce, served hot or cold. (ii) Salad dressing of chopped green herbs, garlic, olive oil and wine vinegar.

ravigote butter Green coloured butter, made by adding fresh aromatic herbs such as tarragon, parsley, chives, etc., to creamed butter; served with grilled meat, etc.

ravioli (Italian) Small squares of *pasta*, filled with a well-seasoned, savoury minced mixture, cooked like macaroni and served with tomato sauce and grated cheese, or used as a garnish for soups.

ravioli alla fiorentina (Italian) Cheese ravioli.

ravioli alla vegetariana (Italian) Vegetable-filled *ravioli* in tomato sauce.

razorback (American) Wild pig, descendant of domestic pigs hunted in many parts of the Southern States.

razza (Italian) (i) Ray. (ii) Skate.

Rebe (German) Vine.

Rebensaft (German) (i) Grape-juice. (ii) Wine.

Rebfleisch (German) Venison.

Rebhuhn (German) Partridge.

reblochon (French) Creamy ewe's milk cheese made in the Savoy.

receta (Spanish) Cookery recipe.

réchaud (French) (i) Chafing dish or hot-plate used to keep food warm, or to prepare sauces or *crêpe suzettes* at the table. (ii) Small portable stove.

réchauffé (French) (i) To re-heat. (ii) Cold meat, fish, poultry, etc., re-warmed or re-dressed.

recheio de castanha (Portuguese) Chestnut forcemeat. Poultry stuffing.

recherché (French) Choice or rare.

Rechnung (German) Bill; account.

recipe Ingredients and instructions for preparing a dish.

recrépi (French) (i) Food re-shaped, usually applied to fish. (ii) Decorated pastry edge.

recuire (French) To re-cook, a term used for pastry preparations where the mixtures are cooked in two operations.

recuite (French) Cheese made with whey.

red Bordeaux Claret produced near Bordeaux in southwest France.

red cabbage Species of the common cabbage with dark red leaves, chiefly used for pickling, but also prepared as a vegetable, shredded finely and stewed with rich broth, sometimes with chestnuts.

red-cabbage casserole Red cabbage cooked with apple, onion, bacon, vinegar, sometimes with added caraway seeds and red wine.

red-currant Fruit of a bush yielding clusters of small red translucent berries, in season in high summer. High in vitamin C content they can be bottled, frozen, stewed, made into pies, puddings, summer sweets, jelly (for use with mutton and other meat) and in conjunction with fruits such as raspberries. They make excellent jam because of their high pectin content. When fully ripe they can, like whitecurrants, be eaten as dessert.

red-currant jelly Preserve made from cooked, strained red-currants and sugar, served with roast mutton and other meats.

red delicious Bright-red eating apple.

red fish (American) Species of mullet found off the Atlantic coast.

red grouper (American) Edible fish whose flesh reddens on maturity, found along the Atlantic coast of America.

red grouse See grouse.

red gurnard Mediterranean fish, a variety of red mullet, prepared in the same way.

red herring Smoked and salted whole herring, its flesh turned reddish in the curing process.

red Malaga Large grape first grown in the Malaga area of southern Spain.

red mullet Delicate, highly esteemed fish, at its best from April to October, sometimes called "the woodcock of the sea". According to some connoisseurs this fish should not be gutted and the trail eaten after grilling or baking.

red nettle Plant whose edible roots can replace the Chinese artichoke.

red pepper See Pepper (Condiment).

red pepper paste Red peppers pounded with onion and ginger, macerated in oil and used in Creole cookery.

red pontiac (American) Red-skinned white potato.

red snapper (American) Brightly-coloured edible fish caught in the Atlantic from Long Island to Brazil.

red table wine General term for red burgundies, clarets, chiantis, etc.

redstart Bird of passage, much prized as game on the Continent, and cooked as for Lark.

reduce To boil a mixture in an open pan so as to reduce the liquid and concentrate the flavour.

reduire (French) To boil down; to reduce; to boil liquid gradually to a desired consistency.

redwing Small thrush-like bird, eaten on the Continent.

reeve Female ruff, a kind of small sandpiper.

reflector oven Oven whose heat is intensified by reflection from the inside metal surfaces.

réforme, à la (French) (i) Garniture for lamb cutlets devised by the chef of the Reform Club, London, consisting of finely-cut strips of cooked carrots, truffle, ham, and hard-boiled white of egg. (ii) Brown sauce containing above items as garniture, with added port wine and red-currant jelly.

refresco (Spanish) Cold drink.

refresh To pour cold water over cooked vegetables to preserve their colour before they are re-heated.

refrigerator (i) Domestic appliance which chills food but does not freeze it except in the compartment specially designed to do so. (ii) Store chest or chamber containing ice. (iii) Refrigerating plant employed to maintain provisions at a low temperature.

refrigerator bag Plastic bag for storing salads and other foods in a refrigerator.

refrigerator dish Covered container for storing food in the refrigerator.

refroidi (French) Cooled; chilled.

régal (French) Banquet; feast.

régalade, à la (French) The skill of pouring liquid direct from a bottle into the mouth without letting it touch the lips.

Regenpfeiter (German) Plover.

régime alimentaire (French) Diet.

regimen Diet.

regimen alimentico (Spanish) Diet.

réglisse (French) Liquorice.

Reh (German) Roe; venison.

Rehkeule (German) Haunch of venison.

re-heated food See *réchauffé*.

rehoboan Large wine bottle containing the equivalent of six standard bottles.

Reims District of France famous for its champagnes.

reina (Italian) Bream.

reindeer Large, heavy deer native to the Arctic regions, esteemed for its flavour though inferior to deer or roebuck. Cooked as for roebuck. Reindeer tongues are considered a great delicacy.

reindeer cheese Rennet cheese made in Finland, Norway, and Sweden from reindeer-milk.

reine (French) (i) French variety of chicken. (ii) Sauces, *purées*, and soups made with cut-up chicken.

reine-claude (French) Greengage. A deliciously flavoured green variety of plum. Its French name derives from Queen Claude, wife of Francois I, its English name from the fact that Sir William Gage, of Hengrave Hall near Bury St. Edmunds, obtained and cultivated cuttings from the French queen.

Reineclaude (German) Greengage.

reinette (French) Russet apple.

reinsdyrstek (Norwegian) Roasted reindeer.

Reis (German) Rice.

Reisauflauf (German/Austrian) Austrian rice pudding.

Reissuppe (German) Rice soup.

rekening (Dutch) Bill; account.

relâcher (French) To thin a *purée* by adding a liquid.

relevé (French) Course of a formal dinner known as the "remove", consisting of large joints of meat, animal game or large fish.

reliefs (French) Remains, or leftovers, of a meal.

religieuse (French) (i) *Gâteau* of cream-filled *éclairs* built into a pyramid set on a sweet pastry base and decorated with piped cream. (ii) Puff pastry spread with jam and currants and covered with criss-crossed pastry strips.

relish Condiment, sauce or pickle taken with a meal to give added flavour and zest.

relleno (Spanish) Filled; stuffed.

remolacha (Spanish) Beetroot.

remondou (French) Belgian cheese also known as "*fromage piquant*".

remonter (French) To add a condiment to a sauce or stew, or alcohol to a wine.

rémoulade (French) Highly spiced mayonnaise sauce made with hard-boiled egg yolks and containing gherkins, capers, anchovy essence, chives, etc., and served with salads, asparagus, artichokes and cold fish or meat.

remove Course of a formal dinner comprising of roasted meat or animal game, or sometimes large cuts of fish.

renaissance, à la (French) Garnish of small heaps of new vegetables set round a roast.

rendan santan (Malay) Chicken or meat dish flavoured with coconut and ginger.

render (i) To extract fat from meat trimmings by melting. (ii) To clarify fat by melting.

Renke (German) Salmon trout.

renne (French) Reindeer.

rennet Preparation made from calf's stomach which curdles milk into a clot (junket) and is also used to form the curds in cheesemaking. Vegetable rennet with milk-coagulating properties is found in certain plants, including the thistle, yellow bedstraw and common fig.

renversé (French) (i) Turned out on a dish. (ii) Caramel custard known as *crème renversée*.

repas (French) Meal.

repassé (French) Strained repeatedly.

repère (French) Paste of flour and egg-white used to join decorations together or fix them onto a dish.

repollo (Spanish) Cabbage.

requin (French) Shark.

restaurant Public establishment serving food, a comparatively recent development since, up to the 18th century, food was only obtainable at inns. In 1765 a Parisian soup-maker called his soups "restaurants", i.e., restoratives, but it was not until 1783 that the next true restauranteur set up in business, a Frenchman called Beauvilliers who established a new trend in eating out.

restaurante (Spanish and Portuguese) Restaurant.

restaurateur Person responsible for the running of a restaurant, who may or may not be the actual owner.

restauratiewagen (Dutch) Dining car.

restauratvagn (Swedish) Dining car.

restes (French) Leftovers.

restoran (Russian and Turkish) Restaurant.

resutróan (Japanese) Restaurant.

retes teszta (Hungarian) *Strudel.*

reticulum Second stomach of a ruminant. Also known as honeycomb tripe.

retsina (Greek) Well-known resin-flavoured wine.

Rettich (German) Radish.

réveillon (French) (i) Feast held in France on Christmas Eve after Midnight Mass, consisting of a very elaborate supper often provided by the wealthy and most generous members of the town or village. The chief dish is usually *boudin noir* – black pudding. (ii) Also a feast held on New Year's Eve, St. Sylvester's Night.

revel bun Bun made in the 19th century for an anniversary feast, from flour, butter, cream, brown sugar, eggs, currants, saffron, and nutmeg.

revenir, faire (French) To fry or brown lightly without actually cooking.

reverdir (French) To put back the green colour of vegetables lost in cooking by immersing in a solution of copper sulphate – a practice which has from time to time been forbidden.

Rhabarber (German) Rhubarb.

Rhabarberknödel (German) Rhubarb dumpling.

Rhabarberkuchen (German) Rhubarb cake.

Rhabarberstrudel (German) Rhubarb strudel.

Rhenish Food and wine from the valley of the Rhine.

Rheinsalm (German) Rhine salmon.

Rhine wine Light dry dinner wine produced in the Rhine valley.

rhinoceros Huge herbiferous pachyderm of Africa and Southern Asia whose flesh is edible and preferred by the natives to elephant meat.

Rhode Island greening (American) Green or yellow cooking apple.

Rhode Island red American breed of general-purpose domestic poultry with brownish-red plumage.

rhubarb Garden plant, strictly speaking a vegetable cooked and eaten like fruit. The stalks vary from green to red and are best picked when young. Rhubarb, which has a pleasant flavour but little food value, can be bottled and is used to make pies, puddings, fools and similar sweets, also jam. The leaves should be discarded as they are poisonous.

rhubarb vinegar Vinegar made from water, sugar, rhubarb and yeast, matured in a barrel for one year and bottled for another year before use.

rhubarb wine Wine made from rhubarb, sugar and yeast.

rhubarbe (French) Rhubarb.

rhum (French) Rum.

rhum, au (French) Food flavoured with rum.

rhyton Greek drinking vessel in the shape of a horn.

rib chop, Frenched (American) Trimmed veal cutlet.

rib-eye steak (American) Choice steak cut from prime ribs of beef.

rib roast, rolled (American) (i) Roasting joint from rib of beef. (ii) Roasting joint of loin of veal.

rib steak (American) Grilling or frying cut from the rib of beef.

ribaude (French) Baked apple dumpling.

ribbon Well-beaten sugar and egg-yolks which form a fold like ribbon.

Ribeauville (French) White wine from *Ribeauville* in the *Haut-Rhin*.

ribes (Italian) (i) Red, black or white currant. (ii) Gooseberry.

ribier (French) Type of large black grape originally grown in France.

riblette (French) Rasher, slice.

riboflavin One of the vitamin B group, once known as B$_2$.

Ricard (French) Brand of *pastis*.

ricco de mare (Italian) Sea urchin.

rice (i) Edible grain from a cereal grass which originated in India and China, and spread to Europe and America. In milling, the outer husk is removed and later the inner skin. This "polished" rice is thus deprived of its vitamin B and nicotine acid content. Peoples who use rice as their staple diet only eat the rough or unpolished product, otherwise they contract beri-beri. Modern methods of marketing rice aim to preserve the food value of rice by steaming before milling so that the vitamin B and nicotine acid are absorbed by the grain before it is polished. Rice comes in several varieties with differing shapes, sizes and colour – Carolina rice, Java rice, Patna rice, Japanese rice, Indo-Chinese rice, etc., and is used to make ground rice and rice flour. Rice is used extensively in both sweet and savoury cooking, for pilaffs, risottos, puddings, cold sweets etc., etc. (ii) To force, through a perforated utensil such as a sieve.

rice-bird Java sparrow, known as rice bird because of its depredation in the rice fields.

rice boiler (American) Double saucepan.

rice flour Flour milled from rice.

rice milk Rice and milk gruel or porridge.

rice paper Thin, semi-transparent, edible paper made from the pith of a Chinese plant, on which macaroons and similar delicate cakes are baked.

rice pudding Rice baked with milk, sugar and butter, sprinkled with nutmeg.

rice water Beverage served to infants and invalids and made by boiling rice in water.

rice wine (i) Wine made from rice, raisins, yeast and sugar. (ii) Very potent wine resembling sherry made in China.

ricer (American) Special perforated utensil through which food is passed, to "rice" it, i.e., to form strings which are the size of rice in diameter and which break up into rice-like particles.

riche, à la (French) Fish, particularly sole, served with *sauce riche* (containing brandy and lobster butter) created at the Parisian *Café Riche*, no longer in existence.

Richebourg (French) Burgundy wine from the *Beaune* district of France.

richlieu (French) (i) Garnish of stuffed tomatoes and mushrooms, braised lettuce and roast potatoes. (ii) Method of preparing fish fillets by egg-and-crumbing, frying in butter and serving with *maître d'hotel* butter and truffles. (iii) Large pastry layered with jam and *frangipane* cream.

ricotta (Italian) Mild sheep's milk cottage cheese, often blended into *pasta* dough.

ricottina (Italian) Small *ricotta* cheese.

riddle Kitchen utensil similar to a sieve but with bigger holes.

riddle bread Yorkshire oatcake.

rieska (Finnish) (i) Flat rye bread made without yeast. (ii) Casserole dish.

Riesling (German) High-quality white grapes used for wine-making in Germany, Austria and Alsace and other European countries. The wine of this name originated in the Rhine valley but is now also produced outside Europe.

rigatoni (Italian) Ribbed or fluted pasta.

rigodon (French) Burgundian flan served either as an *entrée* with ham or bacon filling, or as a sweet, with a fruit *purée* filling.

rijsttafel (Dutch) Elaborate Indonesian meal consisting of a mound of rice garnished with curried chicken, prawns, vegetables, etc.

rillauds, rillettes (French) Potted meat preparation made from pork, also from goose and rabbit, and differing slightly in content and method of making from one area of France to another.

rind Outer skin of fruits such as oranges, lemons, etc., widely used as flavouring in cookery.

Rinde (German) (i) Rind, peel. (ii) Bread-crust.

Rinderbraten (German) Roast beef.

Rindfleisch (German) Beef.

Rindfleisch in Kohl (German) Beef and cabbage.

Rindfleisch mit Ananas und Kirschen (German) Beef with pineapple and cherries.

Rindfleischsalat (German) Beef salad.

Rindsuppe (German) Beef broth.

ring Border.

ring mould Ring-shaped utensil for moulding food.

Ringelblume (German) Marigold.

Rinnen (German) Pomeranian sour-milk cheese flavoured with caraway seeds.

riñone (Spanish) Kidney.

rioja (Spanish) Strong brand of Spanish wine.

ripieno (Italian) Stuffing, for meat, poultry, etc.

Rippchen mit Sauerkraut (German) Pork ribs in sauerkraut, a speciality of Frankfurt.

Rippenspeer (German) Spare-rib.

ris (Danish, Norwegian, Swedish) Rice.

ris (French) Sweetbread.

ris d'agneau (French) Lamb's sweetbread.

ris de veau (French) Calf's sweetbread.

ris de veau piqué (French) Larded sweetbread.

risi e bisi, risi pisi (Italian) Thick soup of rice and peas flavoured with ham, onion and celery.

riskrem (Norwegian) Pudding made from boiled rice, whipped cream, almonds, vanilla, and sugar.

risi pisi (Italian) See *risi e bisi*.

riso (Italian) Rice.

riso e zucca (Italian) Rice with pumpkin.

riso verde (Italian) Rice with spinach.

rissole Small croquette or round cake, made of cooked minced meat or pounded fish bound with mashed potatoes or panada sauce, coated with egg and breadcrumbs and fried in hot fat.

rissole (French) Pastry filled with a savoury mixture and deep-fried or baked.

rissolé (French) Well-browned, fried, or baked; covered with crumbs.

rissolette (French) Small rissole, usually made with thin pancake rather than the pastry used in *rissoles*.

risotto (Italian) Rice dish. Rice cooked in meat broth and then flavoured in many ways.

risotta alla marinara (Italian) Mussel and prawn *risotto*.

risotto alla milanese (Italian) Saffron *risotto*.

risotto con funghi (Italian) Onion and mushroom *risotto*.

risotto con tartufi (Italian) Truffle *risotto*.

risotto di frutti di mare (Italian) Shellfish *risotto*.

risotto di gamberi (Italian) Prawn or crayfish *risotto.*

risotto di vongole (Italian) Clam *risotto.*

ristorante (Italian) Restaurant.

riz (French) Rice.

riz à la crème (French) Creamed rice.

riz à l'indienne (French) Blanched, well-rinsed and dried rice, as served with curries and other strongly-seasoned dishes.

riz au blanc, au beurre (French) Boiled rice with butter.

riz au gras (French) Rice cooked in *pot-au-feu* broth or other rather fatty white stock.

riz au lait (French) Rice cooked in milk.

riz au safran (French) Saffron rice.

rizzared haddie (Scottish) Sun-dried haddock.

roach Fresh-water fish of the carp family with white flesh which turns red when cooked. It is usually fried or grilled, and is in season from September to March.

roast (i) To cook food in an oven or on a spit (spit-roasting) so that the inner juices are sealed by the outer coating being heated and forming a crust. Roast meats and poultry should be basted frequently unless covered with roasting foil or film. (ii) The food so cooked.

roast slicer (American) Carving knife.

roaster Chicken of 4 to 8 lbs, usually caponised, tender enough for roasting.

roasting jack Electric or hand-operated device for turning a roasting spit.

roasting pan Pan used for roasting food in an oven.

roasting rack Wire rack placed inside a roasting pan to hold the roasting meat above its drippings.

rob (Arabic) Fruit juice evaporated to the consistency of honey.

rob roy Cocktail of equal parts of sweet vermouth and Scotch whisky shaken with ice.

robalo (Spanish) Haddock.

robe de chambre, en (French) (i) Paper cases filled with light iced cream. (ii) Potatoes cooked and served in their jackets. Literally, "in dressing-gown".

Robert (French) Brown spicy sauce usually served with pork, invented by an 18th century Parisian restaurant keeper, Robert Vinot.

robin Small bird, prepared on the Continent as for larks and eaten on a skewer. The American robin is about twice the size of the European variety.

robine (French) Variety of pear, also known as *royale* and *muscat d'août.*

robiola (Italian) Soft cream cheese, sometimes blended with olive oil.

Rocamadour Pilgrimage centre in the *Lot* (France) which gives its name to a small cheese made of ewes' milk.

rocambole Plant which bears "fruits" at the top of its stem, resembling garlic, but not so pungent.

rock cake Plain bun or small cake made from a dryish cake mixture containing fruit and spice, baked in small heaps on a tin or baking sheet.

rock cornish game hen (American) American game bird.

rock lobster Spiny lobster.

rock pigeon (American) Wild pigeon, cooked as for domestic pigeon.

rock salmon Pollock.

rocket cress Strong-smelling wild plant with smooth leaves, white or pale yellow flowers and a piquant flavour, used as a salad seasoning.

rocket salad (American) Winter cress, a kind of watercress.

rockfish (American) Name used for many different species of fishes including the striped bass, and the Caribbean groupers.

rockfish muddle (American) Fish stew made of rockfish, salt pork, butter, eggs, cream crackers, onions, and tomatoes, a speciality of North Carolina.

rodaballo (Spanish) Turbot.

rode kool (Dutch) Red cabbage.

rødrød med fiøde (Danish) Summer sweet of red berry juices thickened with potato flour and served with cream and sugar.

rødkal (Danish) Red cabbage.

roe Spawn or milt of a fish, often cooked with the fish but in some cases used to make separate savouries or made-up dishes.

roebuck Venison.

Rogen (German) Fish-roe.

Roggen (German) Rye.

rognon (French) Kidney.

rognon de coq (French) (i) Cock's kidney. (ii) Cock's kernel.

rognon de mouton (French) Sheep's kidney.

rognon de veau (French) Calf's kidney.

rognone (Italian) Kidney.

rognone di bue (Italian) Ox-kidney.

rognone di maiale (Italian) Pig's kidney.

rognone di vitello (Italian) Calf's kidney.

rognonnade (French) Cut of veal with the kidney adhering to it, usually roasted or baked.

rognures (French) Remnants; parings; trimmings.

Rohkostplatte (German) (i) Vegetable plate. (ii) Vegetable salad.

Rohrzucker (German) Cane-sugar.

roi des cailles (French) Landrail, cooked as for quail.

rökt al (Swedish) Smoked eel.

roll Yeast dough made into small round, elongated or fancy-shapes.

roll out To spread pastry to an even thinness by means of a rolling-pin.

rolled oats Oatmeal. Husked oat kernels flattened with heated rollers.

rolled rump (American) Roasting or braising cut from the rump of beef (top of the round).

rolled rump roast (American) Roasting or braising cut of veal.

rolled sandwich Single slice of moist bread spread with a filling and rolled, or rolled round an asparagus tip.

rolling pin Roller used for flattening and spreading pastry dough; usually made of wood, or glass, but sometimes of ceramics with a hollow centre into which water or ice can be placed to keep the dough cool whilst being processed.

rollmop Filleted rolled herring marinated in seasoned white wine or packed in brine, often stuffed with onion and/ or gherkin. Eaten as *hors d'œuvre*.

Rollmops (German) Soused herring.

rolpens (Dutch) Minced beef and tripe cooked in a roll and served with fried apples.

roly-poly Suet-crust pastry rolled out into a strip, spread with mincemeat, jam, syrup or a savoury mixture, rolled up like a Swiss roll, and steamed in a cloth, or cooked in a straight-sided jar, or baked in a long tin.

romaine (American) Long-leaved cos lettuce.

romaine (French) Cos lettuce.

Romanée (French) Wine from the commune of *Vosnos-Romanée*, France.

romarin (French) Rosemary.

rombo liscio (Italian) Brill.

rombo maggiore (Italian) Turbot.

Rome beauty (American) Reddish-yellow cooking apple grown near Rome, New York.

rompre (French) To work paste or dough two or three times. Literally, to break.

ron (Spanish) Rum.

rook Type of crow, edible when still a fledgling and used to make rook pie.

room (Dutch) Cream.

roomijs (Dutch) Ice cream.

root beer Drink made from dandelion, sassafras, etc.

root vegetable Vegetable such as the carrot, turnip, swede, parsnip, salsify and beetroot whose root is the chief part which is eaten. Root vegetables are mostly eaten cooked, but some, such as carrot and radish, can be served raw in salad. Radishes are in the root vegetable category but are usually eaten raw.

rootie (Hindi and Malay) Bread.

rope Bacterial contamination of bread dough which makes it turn "ropy" in hot, moist conditions.

ropiness Defection in certain white wines, resulting from pressing the grapes as soon as they are gathered, and corrected by the addition of tannin during clarification.

Roquefort (French) Famous, superbly-flavoured ewe's milk cheese made in the town of Roquefort, Southern France. The blue mould comes from the special breadcrumbs mixed into the curds, and the cheeses, which should have a greyish crust, are stored in the natural caves of the area (Causses) for up to 40 days, then left to ripen further before sale. Other "Roquefort-type" cheeses are produced elsewhere, some of cow's milk, but the name is reserved for the original.

roquette (French) Rocket cress.

Roquevaire (French) Liqueur wine made at *Roquevaire*, Bouches-du-Rhône.

roquille (French) Orange peel, candied and used in confectionery.

rosbif (French, Italian and Spanish) Roast beef.

rosbif freddo (Italian) Cold roast beef.

rose hip Red fruit of the dog-rose used in making jellies, sauces, beverages, etc. High in vitamin C content.

rose hip syrup Syrup made from rose hips, sugar and water, with a high vitamin C content.

rose petal Flower petal crystallised as a cake or cold sweet decoration.

rose water Distillation from rose petals or a preparation from rose oil giving flavour and aroma to sweets such as Turkish Delight.

rosefish Large red saltwater edible fish found along the northern coasts of America and Europe.

rosmarino (Italian) Rosemary.

rosemary Aromatic perennial evergreen shrub of the mint family whose narrow, hard leaves are used, fresh and dried, as seasoning.

rosemary wine Wine made from rosemary flowers and leaves.

Rosenkohl (German) Brussels sprout.

rosette (American) (i) Piece of veal, boned, rolled and sold on skewers, for braising. (ii) Sugar-water rosette-shaped fried cake or waffle.

rosette (French) Sausage made around Lyons, France, and eaten uncooked.

rosette iron (American) Long-handled baking iron shaped like a rosette.

rosetto (Italian) Red sea bream.

Rosine (German) Raisin.

Rosmarin (German) Rosemary.

rosolio (French) Red liqueur made from raisins in Italy and France.

rospo (Italian) Angler-fish.

rossini (French) Garnish of truffle and *fois gras* for small cuts of meat.

rossini salad See *salade rossini.*

rossolis (French) Sundew, an aromatic plant whose leaves are used in salads or cooked as a vegetable.

rossolis (Italian) Rosolio liqueur.

rossolye (Russian) Mixed salad of boiled potato, raw onion, cooked carrot, herring, meat, cooked beef and hard-boiled egg, with a sour-cream dressing.

rostbiff (Swedish) Roast beef.

Rostbraten (German) Pot roast, roast meat.

rösten (German) Roasted, grilled or toasted food.

rosticceria (Italian) Cooked-meat shop, delicatessen.

Rostkartoffeln (German) Fried potatoes.

rôt (French) (i) Roast course, either meat, poultry or game. (ii) Dish following the *entrée.*

rota (Spanish) Wine made in the North of Spain.

rotary beater (i) Electrically-driven rotating blades or wires for beating eggs, etc. (ii) Hand-operated tool of revolving blades for mixing and beating.

Rotauge (German) Roach.

rote Rübe (German) Beetroot.

rotengle (French) Freshwater fish (*gardon rouge*) similar to roach and prepared in the same way.

rôti (French) Roasted meat, poultry or game.

rôtie (French) Toast.

rôtie à l'ail (French) Garlic toast.

rôtir (French) To roast.

rôtis au four (French) Oven-roasting.

rôtis à la brioche (French) Spit-roasting.

rôtissage (French) Roasting.

rôtisserie (French) (i) Part of the kitchen where roasts and grills are prepared. (ii) Cooking appliance with a rotating spit for cooking meat, poultry, etc.

Rotkohl (German) Red cabbage.

Rotkraut (German) Red cabbage.

Rotkrautsalad (German) Red cabbage salad.

Rotwein (German) Red wine, claret.

rouelle (French) Thick slice of veal cut from the leg.

Rouennaise (French) Dishes cooked in the style of Rouen.

rougail (French) Highly-spiced condiment used particularly in Creole cooking, made from tomatoes, green apples, egg plants, or fish, etc.

rouge, au (French) Food served with or finished in red sauce.

rouge de rivière (French) Shoveller duck, usually roasted.

rouge-gorge (French) Robin.

rouge-queue (French) Redstart.

rouget, rouget barbet (French) (i) Red mullet. (ii) Various fresh-water fishes with reddish scales.

rough-puff pastry Quick method of making flaky pastry for pies, sausage rolls, etc., in which the fat is cut small and mixed with the other ingredients before being rolled 3 to 4 times. This does not rise as much as puff or flaky pastry so is less suitable for *vol-au-vent* cases, *bouchées*, etc.

roughage Carbohydrate passing through the body without being assimilated (though necessary for bulk), such as the fibrous material from vegetables and cereal foods.

roulade (French) (i) Rolled piece of veal or pork. (ii) Slice of meat stuffed with forcemeat and rolled.

rouladine (French) Small roll.

roulé (French) Rolled-out cake mix spread with jam, rolled up and sprinkled with praline and toasted almonds.

roulette (French) Pastry wheel.

round (American) Silverside. Meat cut from the centre of the hind leg of a meat carcase.

round bone (American) Hip bone, used in stewing or stock-making.

round clam (American) Common hard-shelled clam, or quahog.

round fish All fish other than flatfish.

round potato (American) Irish potato.

round radish (American) Turnip radish.

round steak (American) Meat cut from the hindquarters of beef, the top side and silverside, usually minced for hamburgers or forcemeat.

rousselet (French) Russet pear.

roussette (French) Fritter made from a thick paste of flour, eggs, milk, orange blossom water and *eau de vie*, cut into rounds and fried.

roussi (French) Ancient term for *roux*.

roussir (French) To colour food by turning it in smoking hot butter or other fat.

rout cake biscuit Old English confection similar to *petits fours* served at "routs" or evening parties.

rowan jelly Jelly made from the bright red fruit of the mountain ash, served with game, or sieved and added to apple sauce.

roux Mixture of melted butter and plain flour, used for thickening soups and sauces. There are three kinds of *roux*. white, fawn, and brown, the colour being determined by the length of cooking time.

royal (French) Egg custard used for garnishing clear soups.

royal fizz Gin fizz made with eggs, gin, and soda water.

royal icing Icing made from egg whites and icing sugar, used for coating cakes that are to be decorated; it is usually applied over a coating of almond paste, and hardens in keeping.

royal jelly Food fed to certain bee larvae by worker bees, which causes them to become queen bees; it is said to be beneficial to human health.

royal macadamia (American) Hawaiian-grown macadamia nut.

royal worcester Fine English china or porcelain made in Worcestershire by royal warrant.

royale, à la (French) Name applied to many dishes, sweet or savoury, hot or cold, garnished, decorated or sauce-coated.

royan (French) Delicately - flavoured small fish similar to the sardine, caught off Royan, South of France.

røyktlaks (Norwegian) Smoked salmon.

rsvp Abbreviation for *répondez, s'il vous plait*. (French: Please reply) which appears on formal invitations.

rub in To blend or incorporate fat into flour by cutting the fat into small pieces and rubbing it into the flour with the fingertips until like bread-crumbs – a process for producing short-textured cakes, pastry, etc. This manual operation has largely been superseded by the use of either a hand tool with very fine wire blades, or the electric mixing machine.

ruban (French) Ribbon.

Rübe (German) Turnip.

Rubenzucker (German) Beet sugar.

ruby port Blend of young port wines with older vintages.

rudder fish See stromateus.

rue Strong-scented, bitter Mediterranean shrub whose leaves are finely chopped as a flavouring for salads, stews, etc.

ruff Type of small sandpiper, formerly considered a delicacy and cooked like woodcock.

ruffe Fish resembling the perch in size, appearance and flavour. Also known as pope.

rugbrød (Danish) Ryebread.

Rühre (German) Scrambled egg.

rum Spirit distilled from molasses or other sugar-cane residue, chiefly in the West Indies and the Caribbean. It is usually coloured with caramel and often flavoured with fruits such as prunes and raisins. Used for making hot and cold punches, flavourings, syrups and rum butter, as well as being drunk as a beverage, often diluted with orange squash or black-currant syrup.

Rum (German) Rum.

rum and coke Drink of rum and coca-cola.

rum baba Cake made of sweet yeast dough soaked in rum sauce.

rum collins (American) Tom Collins drink containing rum instead of gin.

rum crustas (American) Iced rum served in a glass lined with lemon peel.

rum daiquiri Cocktail of rum, lime juice, sugar syrup and crushed ice.

rum nog Dark rum mixed with an egg, sugar and milk, shaken with ice and sprinkled with nutmeg.

rum rickey (American) Drink of soda water, lime juice, and rum.

rum toddy Toddy made with rum.

rump Cut of meat from the back of the sirloin of beef.

rump roast (American) Silverside of beef.

runcible spoon Broad-pronged pickle fork. A nonsense word used by Edward Lear in "The Owl and the Pussycat".

Runkelrübe (German) Beetroot.

runner bean String bean, scarlet runner.

rusa Indian grass from which an aromatic oil is distilled.

ruscus Plant similar to asparagus whose young shoots are prepared as are hop shoots.

rusk (i) Slice of bread or cake baked crisp in the oven. (ii) Type of tea biscuit. (iii) Commercial product for young children and invalids.

russet Brownish-green eating apple.

Russian dressing (American) Piquant salad dressing of a sharp ingredient, such as pickle or horseradish, blended with mayonnaise, sometimes with added onion, pimento or caviar.

Russian salad (i) Mixed vegetables cut into dice or strips, with added pickled tongue, cooked mushrooms, sausage, truffles and lobster or crawfish meat, cut to match. (ii) Simple mixture of diced cooked vegetables, tossed in mayonnaise.

Russian tea Strong China tea with added hot water and lemon and rum or jam.

Russian turnip (American) Rutabaga, swede.

Russian walnut (American) English walnut.

russinkaka (Swedish) Raisin cake.

russula Edible fungus prepared like mushrooms.

rusty Word applied to bacon, meaning it has stood too long.

"rusty nail" Drink composed of Scotch whisky and Drambuie.

rutabaga Large yellow turnip; swede.

rye Hardy cereal, next in importance to wheat. As its gluten content is low it needs to be mixed with other flours in bread-making, otherwise the bread is heavy and damp. Rye flour is used for cakes and biscuits. In America, rye whisky is distilled from the grain, and in Russian it is made into *kvass*.

rye bread Close-textured loaves made from rye and wheat flours in varying proportions, which cause colour varia-tions. Sometimes flavoured with cara-way seed.

rye whiskey Whisky made from rye grain, or a blended whisky in which rye grain predominates. Also known as American whiskey.

sabayon (French) Light frothy sweet sauce composed of sherry or other white wine, sugar and eggs. French version of *Zabaglione* (Italian).

sablage (French) Sanding, a type of table decoration, with different coloured sands spread on the table cloth to form designs.

sablé (French) Delicate short-cake pastry originating in Normandy.

sable fish (American) Black cod.

sablier (French) Egg-timer.

sabot au sang (French) Old-time stew.

sabra Modern liqueur distilled from Jaffa oranges and flavoured with chocolate.

saccharin White crystalline powder, manufactured from coal tar, with sweetening properties but no food value. It is used by slimmers and diabetics in cooking, drinks, etc.

saccharometer Instrument for measuring concentration of sugar solutions.

Sachertorte (German) Rich pastry filled with preserves and topped with chocolate icing.

sack Various wines used during the Middle Ages, particularly those produced in the Canary Islands.

sack posset See posset.

sacristain (French) Small puff pastry shaped like a paper twist.

saddle of mutton or lamb Whole upper back portion of the animal, from the end of the loin to the best end of neck; a prime roasting joint, but large for present-day requirements and therefore usually cut into smaller joints.

safflower Herb of the thistle family yielding oil from its seeds which is classed with other vegetable oils as poly-unsaturated, and used for cooking. Its flowers are dried and powdered for use in drugs, dyes, foods and cosmetics.

safflower oil See safflower.

safran (French) Saffron.

safrané (French) Food which contains saffron or is saffron-coloured.

saffron Powder derived from the dried

247

stigmas of the common crocus, used as a colouring agent in some cakes, buns, etc., also in *bouillabaisse*, curries and rice dishes. Saffron is orange-yellow, aromatic and slightly bitter. It is expensive because an enormous number of blooms are needed to produce even a small quantity. Originating in Asia Minor, it is now cultivated in southern Europe. From the 16th to the 18th century it was grown in Essex and gave its name to the town of Saffron Walden.

Saft (German) (i) Juice. (ii) Gravy (meat).

sage Strongly-flavoured herb in several varieties with grey-green leaves and a slightly bitter taste. The leaves are used to flavour meat dishes, stuffings, soups, salads, milk puddings, etc. The flowers may be used in salads.

sage tea Infusion of fresh or dried sage and boiling water.

sagne (Italian) Pasta.

sago Starchy, grain-like substance obtained from the pith of the sago palm, used to thicken milk puddings, fruit moulds and soups.

sago pudding Milk pudding made of eggs, milk and sago.

sagou (French) Sago.

saguin (American) Philippine banana.

Sahne (German) Cream.

saignant (French) Bloody; underdone, as for steak.

saigneux (French) Neck of veal or mutton.

saindoux (French) Unsalted pork fat.

Saint-Émilion (French) Small commune of the *Gironde in Libourne*, France, celebrated for its wines of good colour, marked bouquet and aromatic character.

St. George's agaric Small spring and autumn mushroom, cooked as for cultivated mushrooms.

Saint-Germain (French) (i) Thick soup made with fresh peas. (ii) Garnish with peas as the principal ingredient. (iii) Variety of pear.

Saint-Honoré (French) Parisian speciality cake with a pastry lining and iced *choux* and cream filling.

Saint-Jacques (French) See *coquille Saint Jacques*.

St. John's bread Carob bean.

St. John's wort Hypericum genus of bitter-tasting plants with resinous and aromatic fragrance. Infusions are made from its flowers, and the plant was once used to produce a liqueur.

Saint-Michel (French) Layered Genoese cake, cream-filled and covered, with a coating of chopped roasted almonds.

St. Pierre (French) Fish found in British seas. See John Dory.

St. Raphael (French) Famous *apéritif* wine.

Sainte-Menehoud (French) District of the Marne, France, famed for pork products and its speciality of pig's feet.

saisir, faire (French) To seize; to cook meat over a brisk fire so that it retains its juices.

sake (Japanese) Traditional "rice wine" of Japan, drunk warm and served in small porcelain cups.

sal (Spanish) Salt.

sala da pranzo (Italian) Dining-room.

sala de jantar (Portuguese) Dining-room.

salad (i) Raw herbs, edible plants, raw and cooked vegetables, eggs, meat, or fish seasoned with oil and vinegar or other salad dressing. (ii) Mixture of fruits (fruit salad).

salad basket Wire or plastic basket in which to shake and drain lettuce, cress, etc.

salad bowl Large bowl of china, glass, plastic, porcelain, or wood for mixing salad ingredients.

salad burnet Perennial herb whose leaves are used in salads, like water-cress. Their flavour is rather like cucumber.

salad dressing Piquant blend of vinegars, seasonings, spices etc., with or without egg-yolks and other ingredients, for serving with salads, or for tossing salad greens: French-dressing, mayonnaise, *vinaigrette*, sour-cream dressing, yoghurt dressing, etc., etc.

salad fork (i) Small fork for eating salad. (ii) Large serving fork, usually part of a set of salad servers.

salad oil Corn oil, peanut oil, safflower oil, etc., used for salad dressing.

salad servers Pair of matching tools, usually in fork and spoon style, with long handles, for serving salad from a bowl.

salad soup *Gazpacho.*

salada, salado (Spanish) Salty.

salade (French) (i) Green salad, particularly lettuce. (ii) Salad.

salade bagration (French) Artichoke bottoms and celeriac cut in strips, mixed with macaroni and seasoned with tomato-flavoured mayonnaise.

salade cancalaise (French) Poached oysters in lettuce "shells".

salade composée (French) Mixed salad.

salade cressonière (French) Watercress and potato salad.

salade de betteraves (French) Beetroot salad.

salade de choucroute (French) German *Sauerkraut* salad.

salade de crustaces (French) Shell-fish salad.

salade de fruits (French) Fruit salad.

salade de homard (French) Lobster salad.

salade de laitue (French) Lettuce salad.

salade de langouste (French) Spiny lobster salad.

salade de légumes (French) Vegetable salad.

salade dubarry (French) Cooked cauliflower flowerets, radishes and shredded watercress, seasoned with a dressing oil, lemon juice, chives, salt and pepper.

salade flamande (French) Seasoned chicory, potatoes, and oven-cooked onions, garnished with salt herring.

salade impéria (French) Lettuce leaves filled with a mixture of truffles and asparagus tips.

salade niçoise (French) Mixture of potatoes, French beans, tomatoes, anchovies, capers, olives, chervil and tarragon; a speciality of Nice.

salade orientale (French) Seasoned mixture of cooked rice, onion, sweet peppers, tomatoes and black olives.

salade rossini (French) Oil and vinegar, lemon juice, seasoning, and truffles.

salade russe (French) Russian salad.

salade simple, à servir crue (French) Raw salad of one herb or vegetable, plus appropriate dressing.

salade simple, à servire cuite (French) Plain salad of one cooked herb or vegetable, plus appropriate dressing.

salade variée (French) Mixed salad.

saladier (French) Salad dish or bowl.

salaison (French) Salting, brining.

salamander (i) Oven in which food is glazed or browned very rapidly. (ii) Utensil made of rods heated and used for the above purpose.

salamandre (French) (i) Salmander. (ii) Breadcrumbs fried in butter.

salambo (French) Small cream-filled *chou* paste cake.

salame (Italian) Salami.

salami Dry spicy sausage made in Italy, Hungary and other European countries from finely-chopped beef and pork, moistened with red wine. The sausages are air-dried or smoked, and keep for a long time. Salami is eaten as an *hors d'œuvre* or with other cold meats and salads, etc.

salangange Far Eastern sea-swallow whose nests are used for soup, broths, etc. Exported to Europe as swallows' nests.

Salat (German) Salad.

salata (Greek) Salad.

salata (Italian) Salting: immersing in brine.

Salbei (German) Sage.

salçali köfte (Turkish) Beef balls in tomato sauce.

salchicha (Spanish) Small sausage.

salchichería (Spanish) Sausage-shop, delicatessen.

salchichón (Spanish) Large sausage.

salcochado (Spanish) Boiled.

salé (French) Salt, salted; corned.

sale (Italian) Salt.

sale di sedano (Italian) Celery salt.

salep Edible substance obtained from dried orchis tubers from the East and near East. Prepared as a jelly or soup.

salep jelly Jelly made with salep, water, cinnamon and fruit juice.

salep soup Soup of salep, vegetable stock, tarragon and soya sauce.

saler (French) (i) To salt; to season with salt. (ii) To cure in salt.

saleratus (American) Potassium or sodium bicarbonate used in baking powder.

salgemma (Italian) Rock-salt.

salicoque (French) Prawn.

salière (French) Salt cellar.

salignac (French) Cognac.

salisbury steak (American) Hamburger made from best beef.

salle-à-manger (French) Dining-room.

sallet Old English for salad.

Sally Lunn Variety of tea-cake, slightly sweetened and raised with brewers' yeast, served hot and buttered. Sally Lunn was a citizen of Bath who, in the 18th century, used to make and sell in the streets of Bath tea-biscuits known as Sally Lunns.

Salm (German) Salmon.

salmagundi Old English supper dish of meat, salad ingredients, hard-boiled eggs, pickles, etc.

salmi, salmis (French) Brown *ragoût* made of partly-roasted game.

salmigondis (French) *Ragoût* of reheated meat.

salmon Round fish of up to 30 lbs, living in the sea but spawning in rivers, prized for its tasty reddish flesh. It is taken from British rivers from February to August, imported throughout the year and obtainable also in canned and smoked form. Salmon can be cooked whole or cut into steaks, served hot or cold, boiled, grilled or baked, used in salad dishes, etc., etc. Canned salmon comes in three grades. The best, or red salmon, can be used in place of fresh fish, but the lower grades are more suitable for making fish moulds, cakes, etc. Smoked salmon is sold ready to eat, being an expensive delicacy, is used mainly as an *hors d'œuvre*, in salads, sandwiches, on *canapés*, etc.

salmón (Spanish) Salmon.

salmon paste (i) Potted fish-paste containing salmon, sold in jars and used as a tea-time or savoury spread.
(ii) (American) Smoked salmon made into a paste for *canapés*, etc.

salmon *soufflé* See *soufflé de saumon*.

salmon trout Sea fish with pink flesh, in season from March to August, and cooked like salmon or trout.

salmone (Italian) Salmon.

salmone affumicato (Italian) Smoked salmon.

salmone scozzese (Italian) Scotch salmon.

salo (Russian) Salt pork.

saloir (French) Salting tub.

salonu nerede (Turkish) Dining-room.

salop See Salep.

saltpetre (French) Saltpetre.

salpicon (French) One or more ingredients diced and bound with a sauce and used to fill pastry cases, *canapés*, etc., or made into croquettes or rissoles. Savoury *salpicons* can be made of poultry, game, fish, meat, vegetables, etc. Sweet *salpicons* are made of fresh or candied fruits soaked in liqueur.

salsa (Spanish and Italian) Sauce.

salsa de perejil (Spanish) Parsley sauce.

salsa mayonesa (Spanish) Mayonnaise sauce.

salsa picante (Spanish) Highly seasoned sauce.

salsiccia (Italian) Spiced sausage.

salsifis (French) Salsify.

salsify White root vegetable also known as vegetable oyster and oyster plant, similar to parsnip, with a sweetish flavour said to resemble that of oysters, hence its other names. Salsify is cooked as a vegetable, served in sauces, with cream, etc., also used to flavour meat pies, or made into fritters. Wild salsify ("goat's beard") is a field plant. Its young shoots are eaten in salads and its roots cooked as for salsify. See also scorzonera.

salt Sodium chloride, a chemical compound essential to life, mined or obtained by the evaporation of sea water. Salt is required in most cooking recipes. (See cooking salt, table salt, bay salt). Flavoured salts are also made commercially, such as celery salt and onion salt.

salt butter Butter with added salt, once a necessary method of preservation but now popular for its own flavour.

salt cellar Container for holding salt

at table, strictly an open container with a small spoon or scoop, but also the upright bottle-shaped kind in glass, china or metal with a hole in the top for pouring.

salt fish Cod, ling and other large fish salted when newly caught and either kept in pickle or dried by air.

salt grinder Small wooden mortar or mill used to grind rock salt to powder.

salt herring Herring put down in barrels with alternate layers of salt.

salt of soda (American) Sodium bicarbonate.

salt pork Portion of a pig carcase cured in brine.

salt-rising bread Bread made from dough leavened with a fermented mixture of flour, salted milk, soda, and sugar.

salt shaker (American) Salt cellar.

salt spoon Small spoon for serving salt from an open salt cellar.

salted nuts Nuts such as pecans, walnuts, almonds, etc., blanched, fried in butter until brown then drained and dredged with table salt.

saltimbocca (Italian) Slivers of veal and ham braised with anchovies.

salting Method of preserving meat, fish, butter, beans, etc., by wet salting (pickling) or dry salting.

salting tub Tub or vat of varying size used to immerse food in brine.

saltpetre Potassium nitrate, piquant and slightly bitter in taste, used sparingly in the salting industries to impart good colour to meat.

salud, pesetas, y amor (Spanish) Health, wealth, and love! A toast.

saludable (Spanish) Wholesome (food or drink).

salumeria (Italian) Delicatessen, cooked meat shop.

salute (Italian) Health! A toast.

salver Tray, usually made of silver, for serving beverages and food.

salvia (Italian) Sage.

Salz (German) Salt.

Salzfass (German) Salt-cellar.

Salzgurke (German) Pickled cucumber.

Salzkartoffel (German) Boiled potato.

Salzlake (German) Brine.

Salzstange (German) Poppyseed bread roll sprinkled with rock salt.

sambal Tasty side-dish accompaniment to Indian and Pakistan dishes, particularly curries, consisting of grated coconut, fried French beans, tomatoes, peppers, etc.

sambal goreng (Indonesian) Green pepper and prawn dish served with sautéed onions.

Samos (Greek) Sweet wine made on the Greek island of that name.

samovar (Russian) Brass, copper or silver utensil for preparing tea; a large urn with a central tube for live charcoal, and a spigot for drawing off the boiling water.

samp (American) Coarsely - ground maize, boiled, and eaten with milk.

samphire Piquant-flavoured coastal herb found along cliffs, whose leaves can be pickled or served fresh in salads.

samztah (Arabic) Arabian sweet *purée* of cream, dates, and cornflour.

San Pietro, sampietro (Italian) John Dory fish.

sancocho (Spanish) (i) Half-cooked meal. (ii) Latin-American stew of meat, vegetables, spices, yucca, banana, etc.

sand cake Madeira-type cake made with cornflour, ground rice or potato flour.

sand dab (American) One of several species of small flatfish, usually dipped in cornmeal before frying, or pickled in salt brine, with onion rings, and vinegar.

sand eel Small fish which burrows into the sand at low tide. Cooked as for smelt.

sander Miniature "Shepherd's Pie". Minced beef or mutton with a little onion, gravy and seasoning, put into a saucer or scallop shell, covered with mashed potato, and browned in the oven.

sandia (Spanish) Watermelon.

sandpiper Small edible water-sparrow cooked on the Continent as for snipe.

sandre (French) Pike-perch, wall-eyed perch.

Sandtorte (German) (i) Sponge-cake. (ii) Madeira cake.

sandwich Two pieces of bread with

sweet or savoury filling, said to have been invented by the Earl of Sandwich. There are numerous variations on the basic idea – open sandwich, pinwheel sandwich, rolled sandwich, decker sandwich, hot sandwich, neapolitan sandwich, sandwich loaf. (See separate entries).

sándwich (Spanish) Sandwich.

sandwich cake Victoria sponge.

sandwich knife Knife with long, slim blade, for cutting sandwiches.

sandwich loaf Loaf cut horizontally into 4 slices with crusts removed and with varying fillings placed between each slice. The outside is coated with cream cheese and garnished with cut olives, sliced cucumber or tomato, etc.

sandwich spreader Flexible wide-bladed spatula with a serrated cutting edge.

sandwich tray Tray for serving sandwiches, *canapés*, biscuits, etc.

Sandwichtorte (German) Sandwich cake.

sangaree (Indian) Punch drink made with sherry, water, lemon juice, and sugar.

sangler (French) To freeze water-ice or ice-cream by packing ice or ice and salt around its container.

sanglier (French) Wild boar.

sangnat (French) Syngnathe.

sangre (Spanish) (i) Mexican version of "Bloody Mary" made with tequila. (ii) Blood.

sangri (French) Drink made from Madeira, sugar, water and nutmeg.

sangría (Spanish) Iced summer drink of red wine, lemon juice, and sweetening.

sangue, al (Italian) Rare, with the blood running, said of meat cuts such as steak.

sanguine (French) (i) Type of "pancake" made from cooked white onions mixed with chicken's blood. (ii) Blood orange.

sanguinaccio (Italian) Black pudding.

santé (French) Your health! A toast.

santoreggia (Italian) Savory.

sapaceau (French) Egg punch.

sapid Savoury, tasty.

sapidless Insipid.

sapodilla Evergreen West Indian tree yielding the sapodilla plum, with reddish-yellow flesh and apricot-like flavour.

sapotille (French) Sapodilla.

sapsago (American) Greenish cheese, similar to the German *Schabzeiger*.

saracen corn Buckwheat.

Saratoga water (American) Mineral water bottled in Saratoga Springs, New York.

Sarawak pepper White pepper from Sarawak, Borneo.

sarbotière (French) *Sorbetière*.

sarcelle (French) Teal.

sarda, sardella (Italian) Pilchard.

Sardelle (German) Anchovy.

Sardellensauce (German) Anchovy sauce.

sardenaira (Italian) Pizza, a special type found on the Riviera.

sardina (Italian and Spanish) Sardine. (See also *agone d'Istra*).

sardina all'olio (Italian) Sardine in oil.

sardina en escabeche (Spanish) Soused sardine.

sardina en lata (Spanish) Tinned sardine.

sardine Small migratory fish (young pilchard) of the genus *Clupeidae*. Originally fished off Sardinia, from whence it derives its name. In America and Russia small herrings are known as sardines; in Norway they are called silds. The Norwegians also pack young sprats (brisling) as for sardines. Newly-caught sardines are delicious and are eaten fresh but because of their rapid deterioration are more generally known in canned form, preserved in oil or brine, and served as *hors d'œuvre*, snacks, etc.

sardine butter Sardines pounded in oil and butter and rubbed through a cloth.

sardinha (Portuguese) Sardine.

sardinha grehalda (Portuguese) Grilled sardine.

sardo (Italian) Sardinian ewe's milk cheese.

sargasse (French) Sargasso.

sargasso Seaweed eaten as salad, especially in Spain.

sarma le umplute (Rumanian) Stuffed cabbage.

sarpents de vigne (French) Vine prunings used as fuel for cooking.

sarrasin (French) Buckwheat flour used in Breton pancakes.

sarriette (French) Savory.

sarsaparilla Flavouring derived from the dried roots of a tropical American plant, used to make a cold beverage and to flavour carbonated drinks.

sartén (Spanish) Frying-pan.

sartù (Italian) Neapolitan dish of rice and other ingredients such as vegetables, poultry, game, rissoles, etc.

sasarie South African dish of small pieces of skewered meat laid in a curry mixture for three days before being cooked.

sassafras (American) Tree of the laurel family which yields a volatile aromatic oil. Its dried root bark is used to flavour various foods and drinks.

sassenage (French) Semi-hard, blue-veined cheese similar to *Roquefort*.

sasser (French) To stir; to lift a spoonful of food from the bottom of a cooking pan and drop it back.

satay, sate (Indonesian) Meat or chicken skewered and marinaded before being barbecued, and served with satay sauce.

satay sauce (Indonesian) Hot thick chilli and peanut butter sauce served with skewered barbecued meat and chicken.

satsuma Variety of tangerine, grown in Spain and parts of the United States of America.

Saubohne (German) Broad bean.

sauce Dressing poured over or served with food to decorate or enhance its flavour. Sauces are infinite in variety, can be thick, thin, white, coloured. Famous sauces include *espagnole, béchamel, velouté, Hollandaise, Allemande* and *Béarnaise*. Many are based on (i) White sauce (*roux* or blended method) and (ii) Brown sauce. Sweet sauces are made by omitting salt and pepper from basic white sauce and adding sugar, together with required flavour such as grated fruit, chocolate, rum, etc., etc.

sauce (French) (i) Sauce. (ii) Gravy.

sauce Béarnaise (French) See *Béarnaise* sauce.

sauce béchamel (French) See *béchamel* sauce.

sauce bigarade (French) Sauce made of diluted juices from cooked duck, with added orange juice and orange peel cut in strips. In some versions, white wine is added, or port or Madeira.

sauce boat Vessel for holding sauce or gravy.

sauce bordelaise (French) Brown sauce with added Bordeaux wine.

sauce Bourguignonne (French) Burgundy sauce.

sauce Bretonne (French) Combined sauce made from *consommé, sauce Espagnole*, and onions.

sauce brune (French) Basic brown sauce.

sauce Espagnole (French) Sauce made by a slow cooking process of brown *roux*, carrot, onion, bacon, herbs, tomato *purée* and light brown stock.

sauce Espagnole maigre (French) Basic *Espagnole* sauce but with fish stock in place of meat stock.

sauce mère (French) Basic or great sauce, used in the preparation of many other sauces.

sauce poivrade (French) Pepper sauce.

sauce suprême (French) Rich white cream sauce served with poultry, eggs, vegetables, etc.

sauce tomate (French) Tomato sauce.

sauce tureen Small covered dish, usually with a matching ladle.

saucepan Cooking utensil, usually handled, and available in various sizes, used for many processes such as sauce-making, boiling vegetables, stewing meat, etc.

saucer (i) Dish for sauce or salt. (ii) Shallow concave dish placed beneath a matching cup.

saucer (French) To sauce a dish; to cover with a sauce.

saucier (French) Sauce cook.

saucière (French) Sauce-boat; a deep, narrow-shaped dish or bowl, in which sauce is served.

saucisse (French) Small sausage.

saucisson (French) (i) Large sausage. (ii) Smoked sausage.

saucisson de Bologne (French) Bologna sausage.

saúde e gozo (Portuguese) Health and happiness! A toast.

Sauerbraten (German) Beef marinated in vinegar, water, garlic and seasonings, then pot-roasted.

sauerkraut (German) Fermented pickled cabbage, a national dish of Germany, served with bacon or sausages, etc.

Sauerteig (German) Leaven.

sauge (French) Sage.

sauge sclarée (French) Clary.

saugrené (French) Process of stewing food in a little water with butter, salt, and herbs.

saumon (French) Salmon.

saumon bouilli (French) Boiled salmon.

saumon braisé (French) Whole braised salmon with or without stuffing, usually garnished with pike forcemeat.

saumon glacé (French) Glazed salmon.

saumon rôti (French) Salmon roasted whole or in large cuts.

saumoneau (French) Grilse, a young salmon.

saumure (French) Culinary pickling brine.

saumuré (French) Pickled, or marinaded.

saupiquet (French) (i) Wine sauce thickened with bread and served with roast hare. (ii) Spiced vinegar sauce.

saur (French) Herring which has been salted and smoked.

sauré (French) Cured in smoke.

saurel (French) Long, mackerel-like fish (sometimes known as Horse-mackerel). Cooked as for mackerel though less fine in flavour.

saurer (French) To cure.

saus (Norwegian) Sauce.

sausage (i) Uncooked mixture of meat, fat, cereal or bread, packed into a skin and twisted into "links". (ii) Ready-cooked preparation such as salami, liver sausage, breakfast sausage, smoked continental sausage, etc.

sausage-meat Uncooked sausage mixture sold in the mass and not in skins like sausages. Used as forcemeat, or made into patties, croquettes, pie fillings, etc., etc.

sausage roll Small pastry roll filled with sausage meat.

sausageburger (American) Hamburger made of sausage-meat.

sauté (French) Food lightly tossed in fat in a frying-pan; sometimes parboiled, as for potatoes.

*sauté-*pan Shallow, thin-bottomed cooking pan, originally copper.

sauter (French) To fry food lightly.

sauterelle de mer (French) Sea-grasshopper. See squill fish.

sauternes (French) Sweet white wine from the Gironde, including *Château Yquem*, *Barsac*, *Preignacs* and *Fargues*. They are served with fish, poultry and white meat, also with the sweet course.

sautoir (French) *Sauté-*pan.

savarin Rich light yeast cake baked in a ring mould, soaked with rum syrup and accompanied by cream or fruit salad. The sweet was named after Brillat-Savarin.

Savarin, Brillat See Brillat-Savarin.

saveloy Short, thick sausage of salted pork, seasoned and coloured red with saltpetre, dried, smoked and sold ready-cooked as an *hors d'œuvre* or savoury. Originally, saveloys were made of brains and were sold hot by butchers.

saveur (French) Taste, flavour.

savory Aromatic herb of two types: (i) Summer savory, an annual with pointed leaves, and a flavour resembling thyme but milder and more fragrant. (ii) Winter savory, a perennial which grows like thyme. Both are used (fresh or dried) for flavouring salads, soups, stews, stuffings, etc.

savoury (i) Tasty titbit eaten in the fingers. (ii) Highly seasoned dish, served after the sweet course and before the dessert at a formal dinner. (iii) Substantial dish forming the main course of a simple meal. (iv) Description of tasty, seasoned food.

Savoy (French) Mountainous territory in south east France with excellent vineyards on the south-facing hillsides, and fruit orchards, walnut and chestnut trees. Game flourishes on the aromatic herbs of the grasslands and the fish from the lakes and rivers is of excellent quality. Cheese, sausage and pâtés have a high reputation.

savoy Hardy variety of cabbage in season throughout the winter.

savoy biscuit Small sponge finger, used for making such sweets as Charlotte Russe and for serving with ice creams.

savoy finger Ladyfinger, boudoir biscuit, savoy biscuit.

savoyarde, à la (French) (i) Pancake omelette filled with sautéed potato and gruyère cheese. (ii) Chopped raw potatoes and grated gruyère cheese mixed with *consommé* and cooked in an earthenware dish.

sayadiah (Arabic) Lebanese fish and rice dish.

sazerac (i) Cocktail of bourbon or rye whisky, Pernod, ice, sugar syrup, and angostura bitters. (ii) (American) Proprietory brand of bottled cocktail produce in New Orleans.

scald (i) To pour boiling water over food to clean or skin it. (ii) To bring milk nearly to the boil.

scaillín (Gaelic) Heated drink made from butter, sugar, milk, and Irish whiskey.

scale (i) Balance for weighing food. (ii) To remove the scales of a fish before cooking.

scallion Onion which has developed no bulb. Shallots, leeks or spring onions can be used as substitutes.

scallop (i) Species of bivalve mollusc with ribbed rounded shells and delicate flavour. In season from October to March, when the flesh is white and the roe bright orange. Scallops should be removed from their shells, thoroughly washed and cleaned of the beard and black portion. They can be fried, sautéed, devilled, served in sauce after simmering, etc. (ii) To serve food baked in a scallop shell topped with breadcrumbs. (iii) To decorate the double edge of a pastry pie by making close horizontal cuts round the edge, then pulling the edge up vertically at intervals to give the appearance of scallops.

scalloped egg Hard-boiled egg sliced and served in scallop shells with anchovies and white sauce, sprinkled with breadcrumbs, and re-heated in the oven.

scalloped potato Potato sliced, seasoned and baked in milk.

scalogno (Italian) Shallot.

scaloppa (Italian) Escalope of veal.

scaloppa farcita (Italian) Veal "sandwich" filled with cheese, ham, etc.

scaloppina (Italian) Escalope.

scamorza (Italian) Cheese of a *mozzarella* type but made with cow's milk.

scampo (Italian) (i) Prawn, large shrimp. (ii) Dublin Bay prawn.

scapece (Italian) Pickled fried fish.

scare (French) Scarus, also called Parrot fish.

scarlet runner beans See French beans.

scarola (Italian) Endive lettuce.

scarole (French) Escarole, variety of salad greens, used as for endive and chicory.

scarus Mediterranean fish (known as "Parrot fish" because of its bright colours) which is cooked in *court bouillon*, or *à meunière*.

scatula (Italian) Tin; can.

sceau de Salomon (French) Solomon's seal.

Schabzeiger Käse (German) Hard whey cheese used in cooking.

Schale (German) (i) Eggshell (ii) Nut shell. (iii) Fruit peel or rind.

schaleth, cholet (Jewish) Jewish Sabbath dish of meat, rice, and peas (or barley and peas) set to cook on Friday and left until Saturday.

Schaumtorte (German) Confection consisting of fruit placed between layers of meringue.

schav borsht (Russian) Sorrel soup.

Scheibe (German) (i) Slice (of bread). (ii) Rasher of bacon.

Scheibenhonig (German) Honey in the comb.

Schellfisch (German) Haddock.

Schenke (German) Tavern, public house.

schiedam, schnapps (Dutch) Holland gin liqueur distilled from grain and flavoured with juniper berries.

Schildkrote (German) Turtle.

Schinken (German) Ham, gammon.

Schinkenbrot (German) Ham sandwich.

Schinkenspeck (German) Bacon.

Schinkenmousse (German) Ham pudding.

Schlachtplatte (German) Assortment of various types of fresh pork sausages and meat.

Schlagsahne (German) Whipped cream, double cream.

Schleie (German) Tench.

Schlesisches Himmereich (German) Silesian speciality of *sauerkraut* and *purée* of peas.

Schlosskäse (German) Strong-smelling cheese resembling Camembert.

schmackhaft (German) Savoury, tasty.

Schmalz (German) Fat, dripping, grease or lard.

schmalz Hering (German) Fat herring.

Schmaus (German) Feast.

Schmierkäse (German) Soft cheese.

Schmierwurst (German) Soft sausage.

Schmorbraten (German) Stewed meat, usually beef, garnished with mushrooms, gherkins and braised vegetables.

Schnapps (German) Brandy, gin, spirits.

Schneidebohne (German) French beans string bean.

schneiden (German) To carve.

Schnepfe (German) (i) Snipe. (ii) Woodcock.

Schnittbohne (German) French bean.

Schnitte (German) Slice (of bread).

Schnittlauch (German) Chives.

Schnittlauchsauce (German / Austrian) Chive sauce.

Schnitzel (German) (i) Thin slice of meat, usually veal, which is egged, crumbed and fried. (ii) Cutlet of meat.

Schokolade (German) Chocolate.

Schokoladebirnen (German) Pears in chocolate sauce.

Schokoladeeisschnitte (German) Iced chocolate pastry slice.

Schokoladefondant (German) Chocolate fondant.

Schokoladeglasur (German) Chocolate icing.

Schokolademokkaglasur (German) Chocolate mocha icing.

Schokolademousse (German) Chocolate mousse.

Schokoladeroulade (German) Chocolate roll.

Schokoladesauce (German) Chocolate sauce.

schooner Large drinking goblet or glass.

Schote (German) Pod.

Schrotbrot (German) Wholemeal bread.

Schüssel (German) Bowl, dish.

Schwamm (German) Mushroom.

Schwammerlpudding (German) Mushroom pudding.

Schwammerlstrudel (German) Mushroom *strudel*.

Schwammerlsuppe (German) Mushroom soup.

Schwarzbrot (German) Brown bread, rye bread.

Schwarzbrot mit Butter (German) Rye bread and butter.

schwarzer Kaffee (German) Black coffee.

Schwarzwalder Kirschtorte (German) Type of cherry cake served as a dessert in the Black Forest region.

Schwein (German) Pig.

Schweinebraten (German) Roast pork.

Schweinefleisch (German) Pork.

Schweineschmalz (German) Lard.

Schweinsgullasch (German / Austrian) Pork goulash.

Schweinshaxe (German) Pork shank.

Schweinskeule (German) Leg of pork.

Schweinssulz (German) Pork brawn.

schloer Non-alcoholic apple juice.

scollop gourd (American) Custard marrow.

scone Light, plain cake containing very little fat, baked in a hot oven or cooked on a griddle. Scones are usually split, buttered, and spread with sweet or savoury filling. Oven scones are made in a great variety of flours (wheatmeal, wholemeal, barley, etc.) and flavoured to taste. Girdle scones are made like oven scones but cooked on a hot girdle or electric hot plate, or in a thick iron pan. Drop scones are thin, light, spongy and made from a batter mix (Scotch pancakes).

scoop (i) Small concave shovel for scooping up flour, sugar, etc. (ii) Utensil used for gouging out portions of food such as ice cream, cheese, apple cores, etc.

scordalia (Greek) Pipe-fish in potato garlic sauce.

score To cut narrow crosswise incisions on the surface of food to facilitate cooking. Meat is scored to prevent curling; pastry is scored to release steam.

scorsonère (French) Scorzonera.

scorza amara (Italian) Dry red wine from Romagna.

scorzonera Plant virtually the same as salsify but with a root that is black instead of white on the outside. Cooked in the same way.

Scotch bap Round, slightly flattened bread roll with a soft crust and floury top.

Scotch broth Rich soup made of beef or mutton and vegetables, thickened with barley.

Scotch bun, black bun (Scottish) Spiced plum cake with a pastry crust, also known as Black Bun, eaten at Hogmanay, New Year's Eve. It is made well beforehand, so that it has time to mature.

Scotch egg Hard-boiled egg shelled, wrapped in sausage-meat, coated with breadcrumbs, and deep-fried, then halved.

Scotch kail (Scottish) Thick broth of which kale or kail is a component part.

Scotch lovage See lovage.

Scotch mist Cocktail of Scotch whisky served with a lemon twist.

Scotch oatmeal Unrefined ground oats used in making porridge, oatcakes, etc.

Scotch pancake Soft flat scone made from a batter mix, cooked on a girdle and eaten either hot or cold.

Scotch pudding Eggs and rum beaten and added to breadcrumbs, milk, dried fruit, beef marrow and crystallised fruit, then cooked in a *bain marie*.

Scotch whisky Whisky distilled in Scotland from malted barley.

Scotch woodcock Toast spread with anchovy paste and topped with scrambled egg.

scrambled egg Egg beaten with milk or water (or a mixture), seasoned and stirred gently in a saucepan in which butter has been melted. When thickened, the eggs can be flavoured to taste with herbs, chopped bacon, mushrooms, etc., and served on buttered toast.

scraper Pliable spatula for scraping bowls and plates.

screwdriver (American) Highball of vodka, ice and orange juice.

scrod (American) Young fish, generally cod.

scullery Room for rough kitchen work such as washing up and cleaning utensils.

scum (i) Froth which forms on top of a boiling liquid. (ii) Skin which forms on cooled boiled liquid through coagulation of proteins.

scurvy grass Cochlearia.

sea anemone Common name for starfish, edible mollusc found in quantity in the Mediterranean.

sea-bass Large edible perch-like marine fish in many varieties.

sea bread See hardtack.

sea-bream Delicately-flavoured Mediterranean fish sometimes found in the English channel, and distinguished by its brilliant golden crescent between the eyes. May be grilled, baked, boiled or fried.

sea cole Seakale.

sea-cow, manatee Herbivorous sea-mammal whose flesh (rather like pork in flavour) is highly esteemed in the West Indies.

sea crayfish Spiny lobster.

sea cucumber Trepang.

sea ear Abalone.

sea-grasshopper See squill-fish.

sea lettuce Green seaweed in several varieties used in soups and stews, and widely used in Japanese cookery.

sea mantis See squill fish.

sea pie Beef stew with a suet-crust lid.

sea purslane Orach or French spinach.

sea slug Trepang.

seafood Crustaceans and shellfish of various kinds served separately, or mixed, raw or cooked in many ways.

seafood bar (American) Counter or restaurant specialising in crabs, lobster, oysters, etc.

seafood cocktail (American) Cold crab,

lobster, or prawns, served with sauce as an appetizer.

seafood fork (American) Small three-tined fork for picking crab or lobster meat from its shell, or for eating seafood cocktails, clams or oysters.

seakale Celery-like vegetable with an earthed-up root to keep it away from the light. Seakale should be used whilst still fresh and crisp. Cooked in boiling water, drained and served in a sauce, or braised, or served *au gratin*.

seal Marine mammal whose flesh is eaten by Eskimos.

sear (i) To brown meat quickly in a little fat to seal in the juices during later cooking such as gilling or roasting. (ii) To brown vegetables in fat before using in soup or sauce.

seasoning Addition of salt and pepper, and any other herb or condiment to improve the flavour of a savoury dish.

seaweed Vegetable marine growth in sundry varieties and eaten in many countries, especially those where fresh vegetables are not easily available in winter. Dulse, laver or sloke are among the types eaten or used in cooking in Great Britain. Carrageen moss is used in place of gelatine.

sec, sèche (French) Dry.

sèche (French) Cuttlefish.

séché (French) Dried.

sécheur (French) Drying apparatus.

Sechsämtertropfen (German) Bitter-sweet fruit liqueur made in Bavaria.

seco (Spanish) Dry; dried up.

sedano (Italian) Celery.

sedano al forno (Italian) Baked celery.

sedano alla milanese Celery served in a green sauce with grated cheese.

sedano alla parmigianna (Italian) Celery cooked in broth, onion and ham, served with Parmesan cheese.

seed cake Madeira-type cake flavoured with caraway seeds and lemon rind or essence.

Seehund (German) Literally "sea-dog", a beverage of wine, rum and lemon.

Seesalz (German) Bay salt, sea salt.

Seezunge (German) Sole.

seigle (French) Rye.

Seim (German) Strained honey.

Sekt (German) Sparkling wine, German champagne.

sel (French) Salt.

Selbstbedienungsrestaurant (German) Self-service cafeteria.

self-raising flour Flour sold already mixed with a raising agent.

selin (French) Mountain parsley.

sella (Italian) Saddle (of veal, etc.)

selle (French) Saddle.

selle de mouton (French) Saddle of mutton.

Sellerie (German) Celery.

Selterwasser (German) Soda-water, mineral water.

Seltz, eau de (French) Selters or *Selterwasser*.

seltzer water Carbonated mineral water which originated in the German town of Nieder Selters, and is now widely imitated in manufacture table waters.

selvaggina (Italian) Game; venison.

seme di cumino (Italian) Cumin seed.

seme de finocchio (Italian) Fennel seed.

seme di papavero (Italian) Poppy-seed.

semi-sparkling wine Wine which, although not quite sparkling, is slightly effervescent.

Semillon (French) White wine grape from *Semilion* in the Bordeaux region of south-west France.

Semmelknödel (German) White bread dumpling.

semolina Particles of fine, hard wheat which do not pass into flour in milling, used in making pasta, puddings, soup-thickenings, etc.

semolina pudding Baked pudding of milk, semolina, sugar and egg. The pudding can be varied by addition of flavours such as chocolate, fruit *purée*, etc.

semoule (French) Semolina.

senape (Italian) Mustard.

senelle, cenelle (French) Haw; fruit of the whitethorn.

Senf (German) Mustard.

sentarse a la mesa (Spanish) To sit at a table.

separator Device used to separate cream from milk.

"serpent's tooth" Iced drink of Irish

whiskey, sweet vermouth, kummel, lemon juice and angostura bitters.

serpolet (French) Wild thyme.

service (i) Set of dishes for a particular meal, i.e., tea service, dinner service. (ii) Waiting at table.

service (French) (i) Personnel responsible for serving meals at a restaurant. (ii) Gratuity.

Service (German) Dinner-set, dinner-service.

servicio de mesa (Spanish) Table service.

servidor (Spanish) Waiter.

servidora (Spanish) Waitress.

servieren (German) To serve, to wait at table.

serviette (French) Table napkin.

Serviette (German) Table napkin.

servilleta (Spanish) Table napkin.

sesame East Indian plant whose seeds are used to decorate or flavour breads, buns, confectionery, biscuits, etc.

sesame oil Oil derived from sesame seeds, used in salads and also to flavour sweet and savoury dishes.

set (i) Culinary term for liquids co-agulated by cold, such as ices, jellies, etc., or by heat, such as custards. (ii) Term used for a collection of items forming a unit, such as tea-set, etc.

seta (Spanish) Mushroom.

sévigné (French) French soup named after the Marchioness *Sévigné* of *Rabutin-Chantal*, a French authoress (1626–1696).

Seville orange Spanish orange too bitter to be eaten as dessert, but used for making marmalade, wines, cordials, also for sauces and relishes, especially those served with duck.

Seyssel (French) White wine from the *Ain* department of France.

sfogliata (Italian) Thin flaky pastry.

sfogliatella (Italian) Flaky pastry filled with *ricotta* cheese and candied peel.

sgombro (Italian) Mackerel.

shad White fish of the herring family which migrates from the sea to the rivers for spawning. Shad may be pickled, boiled, grilled, or baked either plain or stuffed and served with a piquant sauce. Shad roe is especially delicious.

shadbush, juneberry (American) Several trees and shrubs of the genus *Amelanchier* with edible red or purple fruit.

shaddock Large coarse species of citrus fruit named after Captain Shaddock, who first introduced it into the West Indies from China in the 17th century. Called Pomeloe in the East.

shaggy ink cap Edible mushroom with black spores, prepared as for cultivated mushrooms but should only be eaten when very young and pink-gilled.

shaker Covered container for mixing and dispensing foods or liquids.

shallot Herb of the lily family, whose root forms small clusters of bulbs with a mild garlic flavour. Used in salads, soups, sauces, etc.

shallow-frying Frying food in a shallow pan in a small quantity of fat or oil, a method suitable for chops, sausages bacon, etc.

shamrock Drink consisting of Irish whiskey, dry vermouth, dashes of *crème de menthe* and green *Chartreuse*, stirred with ice.

shandy gaff Mixture of ale and ginger beer or lemonade.

shank (American) Shin of beef, leg of beef. Upper part of the foreleg of a meat carcase.

shark Carnivorous fish in several varieties and sizes, eaten in some parts of the world.

shark's fin Fin of a type of shark found in the Indian Ocean and used to make a soup regarded as a great delicacy in China.

sharpen To spice food, or acidulate it by the addition of vinegar, lemon juice or citric acid.

sharpening steel Butchers' or cooks' steel instrument for sharpening knives.

shashlik (Russian) Shish kebab of lamb roasted on skewers.

shchav (Russian) Sorrel soup.

shchavel (Russian) Sorrel.

shchi (Russian) Green vegetable soup of meat *bouillon* and cabbage.

shebeen Illegal Irish drinking den.

sheep Mammal of the goat family domesticated for its wool, meat, hide and milk (for cheese-making).

sheepshead (American) (i) Large striped marine fish caught off the Atlantic coasts. (ii) West Indian black drum fish. (iii) Dollarfish.

Sheffield Silver-plated tableware as made in Sheffield, Yorkshire.

shell (i) To remove outer casings from nuts, peas, etc. (ii) Casing of a crustacean such as crab, lobster, winkle, etc.

shellbean (American) Broad bean and any other bean (lima, mung, etc.) shelled before being cooked.

shellfish Edible crustacea (fish which have shells) such as clams, cockles, crabs, crawfish, crayfish, limpets, lobsters, mussels, oysters, prawns, Dublin Bay prawns, scallops, shrimps, whelks and winkles. They contain protein, vitamin B, iodine and mineral salts.

shellfish oil Trimmings and shells of shellfish pounded with olive oil, strained and used as a seasoning for fish salads, mayonnaise, etc.

shepherd's pie Leftover meat, usually lamb or mutton, (although beef is often used) and, according to the purists, sliced rather than minced, cooked under a mashed-potato crust.

shepherd's purse Corn salad or lamb's lettuce.

sherbet (i) Oriental fruit-juice drink with cooling properties. (ii) Effervescent powder used in confectionery and to make drinks. (iii) Type of ice cream made from sweetened fruit juice and beaten egg whites, sometimes with added gelatine and milk. (iv) (American) Sorbet, water ice-flavoured to taste with citrus or berry fruits.

sherbet cup (American) Glass cup used for serving sorbets and other desserts.

sherry English name for Xeres, the Spanish fortified wine originating from Jerez de la Frontera, Spain, and made there each year from the best of the vintage, blended with brandy. The light, dry sherries are: *Amontillado*, *Manzanilla*, *Fino*. The dark sherries to which a special sweet liqueur wine is added, are: Brown, *Amoroso*, *Oloroso*. Sherry is also made in Cyprus and South Africa. Sherry is served as an *apéritif*, also at table according to taste, (i.e.,) brown sherry with dessert. The less expensive brands add greatly to the flavour of soups and sauces as well as to certain sweets such as trifles, etc.

sherry cobbler (American) Mixed drink of sherry, brandy and curaçao, served with a slice of orange.

sherry glass Stemmed wine glass holding 2 to 2½ ounces of liquid.

shin of beef Fore portion of a leg of beef, used for stock, soups, etc.

ship's biscuit Hardtack.

ship's galley Ship's kitchen.

shirr To bake food such as eggs, in small, shallow dishes.

shirred eggs Eggs baked in a dish with cream and breadcrumbs and cooked in a hot oven until set.

shish kebab (Turkish) Skewered lamb cubes served with rice pilaff, chick-peas or between wheat *galettes*.

shivowitza (Hungarian) Slivovitz.

shoestring potato (American) Very thin French-fried potato.

shokudo (Japanese) Dining-room.

short broth *Court bouillon.*

short rib (American) Beef cut from between the ribs and the shoulder of a meat carcase.

shortbread Thick, crisp cake of biscuit-like texture, particularly associated with Scotland.

shortcake (American) Dessert made of sweet rich scone dough, baked, split, buttered, and filled with strawberries or similar soft fruit, topped with whipped cream and decorated with whole berries or fruit segments.

shortcrust pastry Crumbly-textured pastry made by rubbing the shortening into the flour until the mixture is of a bread-crumb consistency. Suitable for pies, tarts, etc.

shortening Butter, fat, lard, or any fat used in baking pies, tarts, etc.

shot glass (American) Small glass for serving a single whisky.

shot pepper Mignonette pepper made from white peppercorns broken into grains about the size of mignonette seed.

shoulder roast (American) Cut of carcase

meat, including the upper joint of the foreleg and surrounding portions.

shoveller Wild duck.

shred To slice food so finely with a sharp knife or coarse grater that the shreds curl.

shredded chipped beef (American) Breakfast dish of fine shreds of beef in white sauce.

shredder Metal utensil with sharp-edged perforations used to shred and grate foods.

Shrewsbury biscuit Biscuit made of butter, sugar, egg, plain flour and grated lemon rind.

Shrewsbury cake Old English baked cake made of flour, butter, sugar, caraway seeds, nutmeg, eggs, rose-water and sack or sherry.

shrimp (i) Small shellfish in several varieties of the crayfish and prawn family. Shrimps, usually sold ready cooked, may also be obtained frozen, potted and canned. Served as *hors d'œuvre* and used for garnishing, flavouring and adding to savouries and salads. Also made commercially into an inexpensive paste spread. (ii) (American) Prawn.

shrimp biscuit (American) Scone containing chopped prawns.

shrimp cocktail (American) Prawn cocktail.

shrimp creole (i) Shrimps cooked in spiced tomato sauce and served with rice. (ii) (American) Prawns served as above.

shrub Popular 18th century drink of spirits, sugar and spices. Later versions had fruit juices as an ingredient, and were bottled.

shuck (i) To remove the outer covering from food. (ii) Outer covering, such as husk, or pod.

sich stärken (German) To take refreshment.

side Half a carcase of a meat animal.

side meat (American) Bacon or salt pork cut from a side of pork.

sidecar Cocktail made of brandy, *Cointreau*, and lemon juice.

sidra (Spanish) Cider.

Sieb (German) Sieve, colander.

sieben (German) (i) To sift. (ii) To strain.

sieve (i) Kitchen utensil with meshed or perforated base through which food is pressed to make a *purée*. (ii) To rub or press food through a meshed utensil, as above.

sift To pass dry food such as flour through a sieve in order to remove lumps, masses, and foreign objects; also to blend with other dry ingredients.

sifter Kitchen utensil for sifting flour.

sikbaj (Arabic) Stew made of sheep's head.

sild Small herring, caught off the coast of Norway and exported in tinned form like sardines.

sild (Danish) Herring.

silent spirit See neutral spirit.

sill (Swedish) Herring.

sillbullar (Swedish) Herring ball or *croquette*.

Sillery (French) Famous champagne harvested in *Sillery*, department of the Marne.

sillsillat (Swedish) Herring salad.

silure (French) Wels, or catfish.

silver, silver-ware Utensils in silver or silver-plate used at table, such as cutlery, bowls, salt cellars, etc.

silver beet, seakale beet Swiss chard.

silver birch Northern hemisphere tree whose springtime sap makes a refreshing drink. In America it is fermented to make Birch beer.

silver fizz (American) Summer drink of soda water, gin and egg white.

silver hake (American) Species of whiting fished off the New England coast.

silver streak *Frappé* drink of gin and Kummel, or shaken as a cocktail with lemon juice.

silverside of beef Joint cut from the top of the round of beef which is boiled, either salted or fresh.

silverskin onion See pearl onion.

simmer To keep food in liquid cooking just below boiling point, having first brought it up to the boil, then lowered the heat accordingly. A method suitable for stews and other dishes needing long, slow cooking.

simnel cake Traditional Mothering Sunday, Lenten or Easter fruit cake, with a layer of almond paste on top and often another baked inside. Decorated with small balls of almond paste. Sometimes also made at Christmas time.

simple syrup Sugar and water boiled to a syrupy consistency.

Singapore gin sling Drink of dry gin, lemon or lime juice, powdered sugar *cointreau*, cherry brandy, ice and soda water.

singe To pass a plucked bird over a flame so as to burn off the remaining down.

singer (French) To dust or sprinkle with flour to thicken a sauce.

singin' hinnie North of England (especially Northumbrian) girdle-cooked cake of flour, lard, butter, salt, bicarbonate of soda, cream of tartar, currants and milk, split and served hot with butter.

singing kettle Whistling tea-kettle.

single cream See cream.

siphon Thick glass carafe holding effervescent soda water which is released by means of a metal lever on top.

siphon bottle (American) Soda siphon.

sippet Small shape of bread, fried or toasted, served as a garnish with meat, with *entrées*, soup or to border savoury dishes. *Croûton*.

Sir Robert Walpole's dumpling Eighteenth-century boiled pudding of currants, grated bread, suet, orange and citron peel, cinnamon, sugar and eggs boiled in a net made of pack-thread.

sirloin Joint of beef taken from the lumbar region between the end rib and the rump. Its name derives from *surlonge* (French – over long) although the legend persists that King Charles II, having enjoyed a meal of this joint, asked its name and, on being told said, "For its merit I will knight it. Henceforth it shall be called 'Sir Loin' ".

sirloin steak Beef steak cut from the sirloin.

sirnaya (Russian) Vanilla-flavoured pudding made from cottage cheese, dried fruit, sugar, flour and hard-boiled eggs.

sirnichky (Russian) (i) Ukranian cottage cheese patties. (ii) Sweet patties, with jam. Both served with sour cream.

sirop (French) Syrup.

sirop d'érable (French) Maple syrup.

sirop d'orgeat (French) Orgeat syrup, once a barley decoction, now made with almonds.

siroper (French) To mask with or steep in syrup.

Sirup (German) Syrup, treacle.

sis kebebi (Turkish) *Shish kebab*.

skål (Danish, Norwegian and Swedish) Good health! a toast.

skate (ray) Flat, scaleless fish with wing-like fins and a long, thickish tail. It is cut into chunks and fried, or baked in milk and served with a piquant sauce. Skate liver is highly regarded by some connoisseurs, and is jellied, poached, served in *croûtes*, made into fritters, etc., etc.

skewer (i) Thin metal or wooden rod to hold meat in shape whilst cooking. (ii) To insert skewers into meat, as above.

skillet (i) Frying pan. (ii) Spider, or iron frying pan on legs.

skilly Gruel or porridge once the staple diet of prisoners and able-bodied paupers in work-houses.

skim To remove cream from the top of milk, fat or grease from soup or cooled cooked dishes, and scum from broth or jam, etc., etc.

skimmed milk That part of milk left after the cream has been separated.

skink (Scottish) Strong beef soup.

skinkestek (Norwegian) Roast ham.

skip mackerel (American) Bluefish.

skoblianka (Russian) Stroganoff made with veal in place of beef.

skuet Eighteenth-century English recipe of bacon and sweetbreads or oysters cooked on a skewer.

sla (Dutch) Lettuce; salad.

sladky perezs (Russian) Sweet-pepper salad.

slainte (Gaelic) Your health! A toast.

slaw Coleslaw.

slicer Hand or power-driven apparatus for slicing foods.

sling Toddy or cocktail made with gin, brandy or whisky, with lemon or lime.

slipcote Soft cheese ripened between cabbage leaves which slip off when the process is completed, hence the name.

slivovitz Plum brandy from central Europe and the Balkans, particularly Yugoslavia.

sljivovica (Yugoslavian) Plum brandy.

sloe Small wild plum, fruit of the blackthorn, with a purple skin and sharp yellow flesh. Used with other fruit to make jellies, also made into liqueurs and cordials such as sloe gin.

sloe gin Cordial made from sloes, sugar and dry gin.

sloe gin fizz (American) Highball made from sloe gin, sugar, lemon juice, and soda water.

sloke Edible seaweed.

slotted server Slotted spoon.

slotted spoon Perforated cooking and serving spoon.

small beer Weak beer.

small salad (American) White mustard and cress served as salad or sandwich filling.

smallage Wild celery.

smaltost (Swedish) Soft cheese.

smash (American) (i) Crushed-fruit drink similar to lemonade. (ii) Alcoholic drink made with crushed mint, fine sugar, plain or soda water, and a spirit, either gin, rum, or whisky. When made with bourbon whiskey this is Mint Julep.

smelt Small, delicately flavoured fish which goes up the rivers to spawn, in the same way as salmon. Usually rolled in seasoned flour, egg-and-crumbed and fried in hot, deep fat. Served garnished with fried parsley and accompanied by *Hollandaise*, tomato or shrimp sauce, or with lemon slices and thin brown bread and butter.

smetana (Russian) Sour cream.

smitane (French) Sauce of sour cream and onions.

Smithfield ham (American) Aged and smoke-cured meat from acorn and peanut-fed pigs reared near Smithfield, Virginia.

smoke To preserve food by drying with wood smoke, thus killing the bacteria that cause food to spoil. Method suitable for many kinds of fish, meat, poultry, and cheese.

smoked fish Fish cured by smoking.

smoked haddock Haddock cured by wood-smoke process. (See smoke).

smoked ham Ham cured by smoking.

smoked herring (*bloater*, *kipper*) Fish salted then strung on rods and smoked by a wood fire.

smoked salmon Salmon cured by wood-smoke process. (See smoke).

smoked salmon paste Smoked salmon pounded into a spread for use on *canapés*, etc.

smoking (Spanish) Dinner jacket.

smör (Swedish) Butter.

smörgas (Swedish) Buttered bread.

smörgasbord (Swedish) Traditional Scandinavian buffet meal or cold table ranging from an *hors d'œuvre* course to a full meal, commencing with bread and butter and herrings, piquant dishes, salads, cold meats, aspics, etc., according to the scale of the meal.

smørkage (Danish) (i) Butter cake. (ii) Rich pastry.

smøorrebrød (Danish) Traditional open sandwich of buttered, rye bread topped with fish, meat, *pâté*, salami, cheese, egg, etc., and gaily garnished. Served for lunch, tea, supper or any informal occasion.

snack Light or quick meal.

snack bar Place where light meals and beverages are served.

snack table (American) Portable table, for holding snacks and drinks.

snail, edible Cultivated land gastropod, low in food value but highly regarded as a delicacy especially in France. After cleaning and boiling, the snail flesh is fried, baked, cooked in wine and herbs, etc., then returned to the shells before serving. Snails are obtainable in tins, together with ready-cleaned serving shells.

snake Edible gourd.

snap bean (American) Bean grown primarily for its pod, such as French bean or Scarlet runner.

snapdragon Traditional Christmas game in which raisins are placed in a shallow platter, soaked in brandy and ignited. Participants in the game snatch the fruit from the flaming dish.

snapper (American) Marine food-and-game fish rather like bass, found off the Florida coast.

snickerdoodle (American) Nutmeg-flavoured biscuit, a speciality of Connecticut.

snipe Small migratory marsh bird with a long bill and striped plumage, in season from August 15 to March 15. Snipe should be eaten very fresh and prepared as for woodcock.

snoek Large edible fish related to the mackerel, tuna and swordfish found in South African waters. (See also barracuda).

snow (i) Mixture of sweetened fruit pulp and egg whites; usually accompanied by biscuits or sponge fingers, or served on sponge cake previously soaked in a little fruit juice. A similar sweet may be made with gelatine. (ii) Froth of whipped cream or whisked white of egg and sugar, to which any flavour may be added which does not alter its colour; used as a covering of sweet dishes and for general decoration. (iii) Bed of grated ice upon which certain cold dishes are served.

snow partridge Variety of grouse, cooked similarly.

snow pea Pale green pea eaten complete with pod, used in salads and in Chinese cookery.

snowball (i) Spherical mould lined with chocolate ice cream, filled with vanilla *mousse* mixture and diced crystallised fruits. When set and turned out, the sweet is covered with *Chantilly* cream. (ii) Drink of Advocaat and lemonade. (iii) (American) Round cake or biscuit covered with white icing, especially coconut, or round ice-cream ball covered with coconut.

so ba (Japanese) Thin green buckwheat noodles.

soak To steep food in liquid to soften, de-salt, or impregnate with a special flavour.

Soave (Italian) Dry light wine from the Verona district of Italy.

sobronade (French) Country soup of the *Périgord* area, rather solid and containing diced salt pork and vegetables.

sockeye Highly esteemed salmon famed for its deep-red flesh and fine flavour.

socle (French) Base, pedestal, plinth or ornamental stand. Made of rice, fat, sugar, etc., formerly much used in the presentation of cookery and confectionery.

soda (i) Bicarbonate of soda. (ii) Soda water.

soda bread Irish bread in which the raising agent is bicarbonate of soda mixed with buttermilk.

soda fountain Bar where ice cream sodas and ices are served.

soda pop Flavoured effervescent drink such as ginger ale, colas, etc.

soda water Effervescent carbonated water.

sodium bicarbonate Baking soda, bicarbonate of soda.

sodium glutamate, monosodium glutamate Sodium salt of glutamic acid which accentuates the flavour of other foods, especially savoury types.

soep (Dutch) Soup.

sofrito (Greek) Veal in garlic sauce.

sofrito (Spanish) Lightly fried food.

soft-ball stage Stage in sweet-making when syrup dropped into cold water forms a soft ball. (240 degrees F.).

soft drink Non-alcoholic beverage in can or bottle, either carbonated (such as tonic water, etc.) or still (squashes, etc.)

soft roe The milt or sperm of the male fish, rich in fat and phosphorus. Cleaned and stripped of the side blood vessel, soft roes can be served in numerous ways – poached, fried, in pastry *barquettes*, in fritters, as a garnish, etc.

soft-shell clam (American) Thin-shelled edible clam, usually steamed.

soft-shelled crab (American) Moulting

stage of the common American blue crab.

softening (i) Over-ripening of fruit, such as the "sleepiness" of pears which indicates the on-set of decay. Some fruits, such as medlars and persimmons are not, however, ready for eating until this stage has been reached. (ii) Immersing food in liquid prior to cooking.

sogliola (Italian) Sole.

soirée (French) Evening party.

soisson, haricot blanc (French) French white bean.

soja (French) Soya bean.

sole Highly-regarded flat fish in season all the year round. Cooked by all usual methods, especially grilling and frying, or baked or poached and served with a well-flavoured sauce. The true (Dover) sole has the finest flavour and is recognised by its brown-grey back skin. Other varieties are lemon sole, (broader and with a red-brown back), Torbay sole, and witch sole.

sole (French) Sole.

Sole, Salzsole (German) Brine, salt water.

sole au vin rouge (French) Sole poached in red wine.

sole dorée (French) Floured sole cooked in clarified butter and served topped with skinned lemon slices and *noisette* butter.

sole frite (French) Fried sole.

sole marinière (French) Poached sole served with mussels and garnished with shrimps.

sole meunière (French) Butter-fried sole served with lemon juice, parsley and melted butter.

sole paysanne Sole cooked with vegetables.

sole Saint-Germain (French) Fillets of sole coated with butter and breadcrumbs, grilled, and served with potatoes cut to cook like olives, and *Béarnaise* sauce.

sole véronique (French) Filleted sole simmered with stock, wine, shallots and mushrooms and served in a sauce of cream with grapes.

Solei (German) Pickled egg.

solferino (i) Clear soup, with small batter *quenelles*. (ii) Tomato and other vegetables garnish.

solianka (Russian) Fish soup traditionally made with sturgeon, but other firm white fish sometimes substitutes.

solilem, solimeme (French) Alsatian cake of flour, sugar, yeast, eggs and cream, baked when raised; split and sandwiched with melted butter, served very hot.

sollaghan Traditional Christmas Day breakfast in the Isle of Man of crisped oatmeal.

sollo (Spanish) Pike, sturgeon.

solomillo (Spanish) Sirloin, chine or loin of meat carcase.

solomon's seal Woodland plant whose young shoots are edible and prepared like asparagus.

somen (Japanese) Thin wheat flour noodles.

sommelier (French) Wine steward or waiter.

son (French) Bran.

soor dook (Scottish) Buttermilk.

sopa (Portuguese and Spanish) Thick soup.

sopa a Portuguesa (Portuguese) Fish soup.

sopa borracha (Spanish / American) Puerto Rican trifle of sponge cake, sugar syrup, egg-white and muscatel, sometimes sprinkled with small sweets.

sopa clara (Spanish) Clear soup.

sopa de albóndigas (Spanish) Soup served with meatballs.

sopa de almendras (Spanish) Almond soup.

sopa de cebollas (Spanish) Onion soup.

sopa de fideos (Spanish) Noodle soup.

sopa de gato (Spanish) Thin soup.

sopa de habas (Spanish) Lima bean soup.

sopa de legumbres (Spanish) Vegetable soup.

sopa de mariscos (Spanish) Shellfish soup.

sopa de mondongo (Spanish) Tripe soup.

sopa de pescado (Spanish) Fish soup.

sopa de pollo (Spanish) Chicken soup.

sopa de verduras (Spanish) Green-vegetable soup.

sopa espesa (Spanish) Thick soup.

soppa (Swedish) Soup.

sorb-apple (i) Fruit of the Sorb or Service tree, used when over-ripe to make a kind of cider. (ii) Highly astringent fruit of the Rowan or Mountain ash tree, sometimes used in distilling.

sorbe (French) Sorb-apple.

sorbet (French) (i) Iced Turkish drink. (ii) Soft water-ice with fruit or liqueur flavour, usually served in goblets.

sorbetière (French) Pewter freezing-pot or freezing-pan.

Sorbett (German) Water-ice, sorbet.

sorbetto (Italian) Water-ice.

sorbitol Sugar substitute suitable for diabetics but not for slimming diets.

sorghum Tropical genus of grasses akin to sugar-cane, including durra and Kaffir corn. Cultivated for animal food and for sorgo.

sorgo Variety of durra or sorghum grass cultivated for making molasses.

sorrel Acid-tasting herb of the dock family in many varieties whose pointed leaves are used in soups, and in spinach and egg dishes.

sosaties (Afrikaans) Skewered lamb with cornflour and curry sauce.

sot-l'y-laisse (French) Rump or oyster of the chicken. Literally translated, "The fool leaves it".

soubise (French) Smooth mixture of onion pulp and cream served with meat *entrées*. The name is said to derive from Prince Charles Soubise (1715–1787) a celebrated epicure who served as Field-Marshal in the reign of Louis XIV. Dishes *à la soubise* generally indicate that onions enter largely into their composition or have a garnish of onion *purée*.

souchong Fine black tea grown mainly in China.

souci (French) Marigold.

soufflé (French) Sweet or savoury dish, baked or steamed or set with gelatine, lightened by the addition of stiffly beaten egg whites. Served hot or cold, according to type.

soufflé de saumon (French) Cooked salmon sieved, mixed with *béchamel*

sauce and egg yolks, with added whipped egg-whites.

soufflé glacé (French) Very light sweet cream mixture, iced, and served in a *soufflé* case.

soufflé omelette (French) Sweet or savoury omelette made by whisking the egg whites separately before adding to the beaten yolks.

soult South African dish of pigs' trotters boiled till tender, marinaded for some days and eaten cold.

soumaintrin (French) Burgundian round yellow cheese also called *Saint-Florentin*.

sound Fish's swimming bladder.

soup Liquid food of infinite variety, ranging from clear soups (*consommées*) to *purées* or cream soups made of meat, fish or vegetables; also thick broths with solid matter such as meat, vegetables or pasta suspended in the liquid. Soups are obtainable in canned or packet form, or can be home-made, using *bouillon* cubes or stock from soup-bones as the basic foundation. Soups are also made from fruit juices or puréed fruit, thickened, sweetened and with cream added.

soup cup Two-handled cup for serving soup.

soup dish Large shallow bowl or deep plate for serving soup.

soup ladle Serving implement with a deep round bowl at the end of a curved or straight handle.

soup spoon Round, deep spoon used for eating soups, chowders, etc.

soup tureen Large, deep, covered vessel for bringing soup to the table, often supplied with matching ladles.

soupa (Greek) Soup.

soupe (French) Thick *potage* or soup of various ingredients put into a broth, usually garnished with bread.

soupe à la bière (French) German beer soup.

soupe à la bonne femme (French) Soup of leeks, potatoes, *consommé*, butter and chervil.

soupe à la fausse tortue (French) Mock turtle soup.

soupe à l'oignon (French) Onion soup.

soupe aigre-douce (French) German

sweet-sour soup of leeks, onion, flour, stock, thick cream and butter.

soupe albigeoise (French) Substantial soup of beef, salt, pork, preserved goose, vegetables and garlic.

soupe arlégeoise (French) Substantial soup or *potée* of onions, carrots, leeks, potatoes, salt pork, garlic, etc.

soupe aux huîtres (French) Oyster soup.

soupe de veau aux herbes (French) Dutch soup of thickened veal stock garnished with veal dumplings or *quenelles*.

soupbone Marrow bone suitable for soup-making.

soupçon (French) Slight trace of some ingredient, usually a condiment, herb, or spice.

souper (French) Supper; evening meal.

souper de bal (French) Ball supper.

soupière (French) Soup-tureen.

soupies (Greek) Cuttlefish cooked in a sauce.

soupir de nonne (French) Light *soufflé* fritter ("nun's sigh") made of *chou* pastry. More commonly known as "Pet de nonne".

sour (i) Food possessing an acid or piquant taste or smell. (ii) Spirit-based mixed drink made sour by the addition of lemon or lime juice, but with mineral water and sugar added.

sour-cake (American) Cake-shaped oatmeal or rye bread.

sour cream Cream soured by lactic acid.

sour-cream biscuit (American) Scone made with sour cream instead of milk.

sour-cream dressing Salad dressing made with sour cream, vinegar, onion, sugar, salt and pepper.

sourdough (American) Leven; a piece of fermented dough reserved to act as a starter for the next batch.

sourdough bread Bread made with a starter of sourdough.

soursop (i) Tropical (American) tree of the custard apple genus. (ii) The ovoid succulent fruit which it bears.

sourire (French) To simmer gently.

souris (French) Mutton-knuckle.

sous cloche (French) Baked under a closed lid, as in a glass casserole.

souse (i) To pickle, to immerse food in vinegar and water or similarly preserve it.

Souse (German) Pork and veal jellied in a vinegar solution.

soused herring Herring filleted and baked or pressure-cooked in water and vinegar with added onion and tarragon or pickling spice.

southern comfort (American) Liqueur (100% U.S. proof) based on whisky, originating in New Orleans. May be used in place of whisky in composite drinks.

souvarov (French) (i) Type of *petit-four* consisting of ovals or rounds of pastry sandwiched with thick apricot jam and sprinkled with icing sugar. (ii) Method of cooking poultry in an earthenware casserole with *fois gras* and truffles.

souvlakia (Greek) Meat cooked on a spit over charcoal.

sow-belly (American) Belly of pork, salted.

sow-thistle Plant containing a milky substance, with a flavour of both chicory and lettuce, cooked like spinach or used in salads when young and tender. Its roots are prepared as for black and white salsify.

sowens (Scottish) Flummery.

soya Most nutritious of the bean family, grown in many varieties chiefly in the Far East, America and Germany. It has high protein and fat content plus calcium, iron and vitamin B1 but very little starch. Cooked like haricot beans or made into flour, soya sauce, etc. (See separate entries).

soya bean (soy bean) See soya.

soya bean curd Cooked and fermented soya beans, used in Eastern and American cookery.

soya bean oil Oil expressed from soya beans.

soya cheese Ancient Chinese cheese made from fermented soya beans.

soya flour Flour made from soya beans and, added to other flour, used in pastry, cakes, puddings, soups, sauces, etc.

soya sauce, soy sauce Dark brown, pungent sauce made from fermented soya beans, used as a flavouring agent and seasoning.

Soyer, Alex., 1809–1859 French chef and reformer who advocated English dishes prepared in French style. Went to Ireland 1848 to cook during the famine, and to the Crimea in 1854. Was chef at the Reform Club, invented a camp stove and was the author of many culinary books.

spaghetti (Italian) Pasta made in strands of many sizes, and served with a wide variety of sauces.

spaghettini (Italian) Fine spaghetti.

spalla (Italian) Shoulder (of meat, etc.).

spalla disossata (Italian) Boned shoulder of meat.

Spam (American) Brand name for a canned pork product, highly popular in Britain during the food shortage in and immediately after World War II. Still available.

spanakopeta (Greek) Spinach rolled up in pastry.

Spanischer Pfeffer (German) Red pepper, cayenne.

Spanish chestnut Large sweet chestnut grown in Mediterranean countries; the true chestnut.

Spanish licorice Extract of dried licorice root used as a flavouring.

Spanish lime West Indian genipap.

Spanish mackerel Mackerel with long dorsal fins found in both the Atlantic and Pacific oceans.

Spanish onion Large, mild-flavoured onion.

Spanish paprika Spanish-type pimento.

Spanish pear (American) Avocado.

Spanish potato (American) Sweet potato.

Spanish rice Savoury garlic-flavoured dish of rice cooked with tomatoes, onions and green peppers.

spare rib of pork (i) Back of a pig's neck, together with attached ribs. (ii) (North-country) The chine and ribs separated from the side or flitch and eaten fresh. (iii) (American) End of ribs, separated from the bacon strip.

Spargel (German) Asparagus.

Spargelsuppe (German) Asparagus soup.

sparklet Small ampoule of liquid carbon dioxide for making soda water in a syphon.

sparkling water Soda water.

sparkling wine Wine allowed to complete fermentation after bottling, thus producing an effervescent beverage.

spatchcock (i) Fowl, killed and immediately cooked, for some sudden occasion, said to be a corruption of "despatch" and "cock". (ii) Chicken split down the back, flattened out, and grilled. (See spread eagle).

Spatel (German) Spatula.

Spätlese (German) High-quality, rather sweet wine made from late-picked grapes.

spatula Broad-bladed kitchen utensil, usually flexible, for spreading icing, etc.

spatule (French) Spatula.

Spatzle (German) Flour ball cooked in a wide variety of ways and added to many dishes.

spearmint True aromatic mint used for sweets, chewing gum, mint sauce, etc.

speciality cut (American) Offal.

Speck (German) Bacon.

Speckgriesknodel (German) Semolina dumpling with bacon.

Specklinsen (German) Bacon with lentils.

Speckseite (German) Flitch of bacon.

Speech House pudding Gloucestershire recipe for a steamed pudding made of flour, eggs, sugar, butter, bicarbonate of soda, milk and raspberry jam.

Speigelei (German) Fried egg.

Speise (German) Food, nourishment, dish.

Speisekammer (German) Larder, pantry.

Speisekarte (German) Bill of fare, menu.

speisen (German) To eat.

Speisewagen (German) Railway dining-car.

Speisezimmer (German) Dining-room.

Sperrkäse (German) Dry hard German cheese.

spezzatino di manzo (Italian) Beef stew.

spezzatino di vitello (Italian) Veal stew.

spicchio d'aglio (Italian) Clove of garlic.

spice General term for the wide variety of aromatic seasonings used to flavour sweet and savoury dishes, including allspice, aniseed, cardamon, cayenne, chillies, cinnamon, cloves, cumin, curry powder, ginger, mace, mustard, nutmeg, pepper, etc. Sold individually or in combination, they should be used in moderation as a flavouring agent to stimulate the appetite.

spice shelf or cabinet Shelf or series of shelves intended for storing herbs and spices, usually in uniform-sized glass or porcelain containers designed to fit.

spiced vinegar See vinegar.

spider Iron frying pan on legs high enough to hold the pan above an open fire.

spider crab Species of crustacean allied to crabs, and prepared in the same way.

spiedini (Italian) Small pieces of meat and other foods grilled on a skewer.

spiedo (Italian) Spit, for roasting joints, etc.

Spiegelei (German) Fried egg.

spigot Wine-cask peg.

spinacio (Italian) Spinach.

Spinat (German) Spinach.

Spinatstrudel (German) Spinach *strudel*.

spiny lobster Crustacean with a spiny shell, no claws, two long antennae, a fan-shaped tail and a more barrel-shaped body than the true lobster. Found in the Atlantic and Mediterranean, and in other seas, though varying slightly in appearance. Cooked in innumerable ways as is the true lobster.

spinach Green plant of the goosefoot family whose green leaves, picked when fresh and tender, are an excellent vegetable or salad ingredient and high in vitamins C and A. Spinach can also be creamed, added to soups, etc.

spinach beet See Swiss chard.

Spinatsuppe (German) Spinach soup.

spirit lamp Small lamp burning methylated or other spirit, used to heat a chafing dish or other food receptacle.

spirits Distillate of wine, fruit, cereal, etc., containing alcohol, and including gin, whisky, brandy, rum, etc. In addition to their use as beverages, they can be used to flavour or preserve fruit, added to rich cakes, mincemeat, etc.

Spirituosen (German) Spirits.

Spiritusgehalt (German) Alcoholic strength; proof.

spisestue (Danish and Norwegian) Dining-room.

spisevogn (Danish and Norwegian) Dining car.

spit Rod on which fish, meat, or poultry can be barbecued or roasted, either vertically or horizontally according to type.

spit-roasting Meat cooked by rotating on a spit before an open fire, resulting in even cooking of meat, poultry, game, etc., as the meat is basted by its own juices. Many modern cookers have a rotary spit included in their design.

spitchcocked eel Filleted eel cut in pieces, stirred in melted, herbed butter, egg-and-breadcrumbed and grilled till crisp.

Spitzkäse (German) Well-flavoured rennet cheese produced in Switzerland.

split (i) West country yeast bun, split and served with cream or butter and jam (Devon split, Cornish split, etc.) (ii) Liquid measure containing 8 ounces. (iii) Half glass of spirits. (iv) Half bottle of aerated water.

split pea Green pea, dried, split, and used in soups, stews, etc.

spondias Indian tree bearing an edible fruit, hog apple, used for preserves and fermented into a drink.

spongada (Italian) Preparation of semi-frozen water-ice and stiffly-whipped white of eggs.

sponge cake Cake containing flour and a high proportion of eggs and sugar but no fat. (The true sponge). See also Genoese sponge and victoria sponge.

sponge pudding Light cake mixture, steamed or baked, and flavoured to taste or cooked with a fruit, preserve or syrup foundation.

spoom Sherbet-type ice-cream made from fruit juice or wine with added Italian meringue, served in glasses.

spoon Shallow bowl at the end of a handle, varying in size and design.

spoon dumpling Norfolk dumpling.

spoonbread (American) Cornmeal bread of an egg-custard like consistency, scooped out with a spoon and traditionally served with ham.

spotted dick, spotted dog Steamed or boiled suet pudding containing raisins or other dried fruit and shaped into a roll.

sprat Small fish of the herring family, sold fresh or smoked. Cooked fresh, they are usually grilled or fried, served with lemon or mustard sauce.

spread eagle chicken Young chicken split down the back, flattened, breast-bone removed, seasoned, oiled or buttered, and grilled or baked.

sprig Small herb such as mint, parsley, etc., used as an aromatic flavouring agent or garnish.

spring chicken Young pullet.

spring-form pan (American) Baking tin held together by a hinged clamp, so that it can be opened to release the contents when cooked or set.

spring greens Fresh young cabbage.

spring lamb Young lamb born in late winter or early spring.

spring of pork Thin flank or breast and belly.

spring onion Small type of onion with a green or white outer skin, used in salads and in flavouring savoury dishes.

spring water Water from a spring or natural well.

Springerle (German) Anise-flavoured biscuit with a design imprinted by a carved rolling pin.

sprit (Dutch) Crisp biscuit made of flour, custard powder, butter, sugar and egg yolks.

Spritz (German) Buttery biscuit made from dough pressed through a forcing bag on to a baking sheet.

spritzer White wine and soda water.

spritzig (German) German equivalent description of wines which the French call "Petillant".

Spritzkuchen (German) Fritter.

Sprout (i) Brussels sprout. (ii) Seed sown in a compact mass and cut for use when a few inches high, i.e., bean sprout, etc., etc.

sprout top Green-leaved top of Brussels sprout plant, cooked as for cabbage or spring greens.

spruce beer (i) Beer made from boiled molasses and spruce twigs, fermented with yeast. (ii) Spruce-flavoured soft drink.

spud Slang for potato.

spugnola (Italian) Edible fungus; morel.

spuma di fegato (Italian) Calf's liver *mousse*.

spuma di pesce (Italian) Fish *mousse*.

spumante (Italian) Sparkling (as of wine).

spumone (Italian) Ice cream dessert with nuts and strawberries or raspberries.

spuntino (Italian) (i) Snack. (ii) Snack bar.

squab Young pigeon.

squab chicken Young chicken.

squab pie West country dish of pigeon meat, apples and onions.

square-egg skillet (American) Square pan for frying an egg to be used as a sandwich filling.

squash (i) Fruit drink made with sweetened pulp, either home-made or commercially-produced. (ii) (American) Gourd-like vegetables such as vegetable marrow, zucchini, acorn squash, pumpkin, in many varieties and often well-flavoured, which are baked, boiled, sautéed or made into various dishes.

squeezer Utensil or press for extracting juice from fruit, etc.

squid Certain varieties of cephalopod called ink-fish (cuttlefish) common in Mediterranean countries, fried or cooked in sauces, etc.

squill-fish Crustacean, also known as sea-grasshopper and sea mantis, fished off Spain and Italy and in the English Channel. Cooked as for lobsters.

squille (French) Squill-fish.

squirrel Wild rodent, eaten as game in some countries, and cooked as for rabbit.

Stachelbeere (German) Gooseberry.

stachys Chinese artichoke.

"staff of life" Bread.

stag Male red deer.

Stahlwaren (German) (i) Hardware. (ii) Cutlery.

stainless steel Acid-resistant non-rusting

kitchenware, including cutlery, coffee and tea pots, cooking utensils, etc.

stainless-steel sponge Scouring pad of stainless-steel shavings for cleaning cooking utensils.

stalk (i) Main stem of a plant, like celery. (ii) To remove grapes, berries, etc., from their stalks.

stammpot (Dutch) Dutch national dish of smoked sausages served on a raised bed of cabbage, potato and veal fat hash.

star anise Badian anise or Chinese anise. Fruit of a tree of that name. See badian anise.

star-gazy pie West-country dish of pilchards with their heads showing above a shortcrust pastry or potato crust.

Star of Bethlehem Plant with edible roots prepared as for salsify.

starch Carbohydrate which is broken down into sugar before being absorbed by the body. The chief source of calories in human diet, it is found in small quantities in foods such as green vegetables and fruits, but in much larger quantities in cereals, grains, root vegetables and foods such as bread, cake, biscuits, etc. Starches such as potato starch, manioc (arrowroot) and cornflour are used to thicken soups, stews, sauces, etc.

Stärkemehl (German) Starch-flour.

starling Bird similar to, but smaller than, the blackbird. Cooked in France as for the thrush.

starna (Italian) Grey partridge.

steak (i) Cut from a beef animal (rump, fillet, porterhouse, *entrecôte*) etc., usually grilled or fried, (see separate entries) and served with pan juices, a sauce, and/or sundry garnishes and accompaniments. (ii) Cheaper cut of beef, such as chuck or skirt, cooked by a slower method. (iii) Thick cut from a fish, such as cod or salmon.

steak-and-kidney pie Beef steak and kidney placed in a piedish with flavourings and gravy, covered with a layer of pastry, and baked.

steak-and-kidney pudding Beefsteak and kidney steamed, with gravy, in a deep dish or basin lined and covered with suet pastry. The best puddings include oysters and mushrooms.

steak griller Electric grill for cooking chops, hamburgers, steaks, etc.

steak hammer Spiked tool used to tenderise meat by pounding and breaking down the muscle tissue.

steak knife Knife with a serrated edge for cutting steaks etc.

steakburger Hamburger made of minced steak.

steam To cook food in the steam from boiling water to preserve its flavour and vitamins, etc. Various utensils can be used, the best being a steamer with a perforated base. But a large basin standing in a pan of boiling water is a good substitute. It is essential in any case that the saucepan must not be allowed to boil dry, thus spoiling the food. Pressure-cookery is a further form of cooking by steam. Meat, poultry and puddings can all be cooked by steaming, the exact method and time depending upon the recipe concerned.

steam-bake To slow-cook food and keep it moist by a combination of steaming and baking in the oven.

steamer Double utensil for steaming food which rests on a perforated platform above boiling water.

stearin Chief constituent of solid fats, such as mutton suet, used for moulding *socles*, etc.

steeg (Danish) Steak.

steel Rod, sometimes fluted, used to sharpen knives, usually part of a carving set.

steel wool Scouring pad made of fine steel threads, sometimes impregnated with soap, for cleaning cooking pots, etc.

steep To cover food in hot or cold liquid and leave it to stand, either to extract flavour or colour, or to soften.

steer (i) Young ox. (ii) Castrated bull calf bred for meat production.

steer beef Meat of a castrated bull calf.

steerburger (American) Hamburger.

stegt al (Danish) Fried eel.

stein Earthenware mug or beer tankard.

Stein (German) Fruit stone or kernel.

Steinbutt (German) Turbot.

Steinobst (German) Stone-fruit.

Steinpilz (German) Stone mushroom.

sterilise To destroy harmful micro-organisms in foods and cooking utensils by raising the temperature to the necessary level. This varies according to the particular food, as does the time taken.

sterilised milk Milk subjected to further heat after pasteurisation, to impart almost indefinite keeping properties without refrigeration. It has a distinct flavour.

sterlet Small sturgeon whose flesh is highly regarded. Its roe yields top-quality caviare and its swimming bladder is used to make isinglass.

stew (i) To cook by a long, slow, moist process at simmering point, a method suitable for tougher cuts of meat. (ii) Dish of meat (see individual entries, brown stew, white stew, Irish stew). (iii) Dish of fruit or fruits cooked in water either in the oven or on top of the stove.

stifado (Greek) Beef stew.

still wine Non-sparkling wine.

Stilton Blue-moulded whole milk cheese originating in Stilton, Huntingdonshire, and left for six months to mature. A whole Stilton should be served wrapped in a napkin. The top is cut off to form a lid, and the cheese scooped out. If it becomes too dry, it can be moistened by pouring a little port wine into holes made in the top.

stinger (American) Mixed drink of brandy and *crème de menthe*.

stir To mix food in a circular motion by means of a whisk, fork, spoon or other utensil.

stir fry To cook rapidly over high heat, stirring and tossing ingredients constantly.

stirabout Oatmeal stirred constantly during cooking; the Irish equivalent of porridge.

stoccafisso (Italian) (i) Stockfish. (ii) Dried cod.

stock (i) Liquid or broth in which meat and bones have been boiled, of which soups and sauces are made. (ii) Liquid in which fish bones and skin have been boiled, as a basis for sauces, etc. (iii) *Bouillon* cube dissolved in water.

stock pot Large pot for making beef, chicken, fish or other stock. Some cooks keep a permanent stock pot at the ready.

Stockfisch (German) Dried cod.

stockfish Air-dried, unsalted cod, hake, etc.

stone cream Seventeenth-century Hampshire sweet made from lemon, sugar, cream, white wine, isinglass and water, cooled and poured over preserve spread in the bottom of a dish.

Stollen (German) Loaf fruit cake.

stolovaya (Russian) Dining-room.

stone Whetstone for sharpening cutlery, some using oil, or water, according to type.

stone fence Highball made with cider.

stoneware Coarse pottery.

stopper Shaped cork, glass, rubber, plastic or other substance used to insert in the tops of bottles, jars, etc.

Stör (German) Sturgeon.

stör (Swedish) Sturgeon.

store cheese (American) American cheddar cheese.

storione (Italian) Sturgeon.

stout Beer made with a dark malt and sweeter than ale.

stove (i) To heat or bake in a stove or oven. (ii) Cooker.

stracchino (Italian) Soft goat cheese.

stracciatella (Italian) Chicken or beef broth with added beaten egg, semolina and grated cheese.

stracotto (Italian) Beef, vegetables and sausage stewed in wine.

stracotto de vitello (Italian) Veal stew.

strainer Sieve-like kitchen utensil for straining sauces and other liquids.

straining bag Felt or cloth funnel used to clarify liquids.

strapazzate al pomodoro (Italian) (i) Scrambled egg with tomato. (ii) Tomato omelette.

straw (i) Stalk of grain remaining after threshing. (ii) Oven-baked strip of puff pastry. (iii) Deep-fried thin strip of potato. (iv) Hollow tube used for sipping liquid from a glass.

straw wine Pressings of grapes which have been dried on straw.

strawberry Low-growing plant with delicious red fruit now cultivated in most parts of the world. Strawberries are eaten as dessert, with sugar and cream to taste, or used to make a wide variety of sweets, desserts, creams, ices, etc., though generally uncooked, since cooking spoils their colour, flavour and shape. Strawberries can be made into jam, but need extra pectin or acid (e.g. lemon juice, tartaric acid) to aid setting. They do not bottle well, but will freeze with moderate success.

strawberry guava (American) Sub-tropical shrub related to the true guava whose dark-red fruit is used in making preserves.

strawberry omelette Beaten eggs with added strawberries previously steeped in Kirsch or rum, glazed under the grill.

strawberry tomato Cape gooseberry, a yellow seed fruit the size of a cherry (sometimes called Winter cherry) originating in Mexico but grown in Europe and South Africa, and used in jams, syrups, *compôtes*, confectionery, etc.

strega (Italian) Sweet citrus liqueur. Literally, "witch".

streusel topping (American) Crisp, crunchy topping made from flour, sugar, and cinnamon mixed with butter used on coffeecake, etc.

Streuzucker (German) Caster sugar.

string bean See bean.

strip To take leaves and petals off a plant.

striped bass (American) Rockfish, caught off both East and West coasts of the United States.

Stritzel (German/Austrian) Classic Austrian Christmas cake of yeast dough divided into nine pieces of varying sizes, plaited, set atop one another, brushed with egg and sprinkled with salt and caraway seeds.

stromateus, rudderfish Mediterranean fish with delicate flesh, prepared as for turbot.

strömming (Swedish) Small species of herring found in the Baltic Sea.

Strudel (German) Tissue-thin layers of pastry filled with chopped apples, nuts, currants, and spices. The national cake of Bavaria.

strudel leaves Ready-made raw *Strudel* pastry packed in polythene bags.

strutto (Italian) Lard.

Stückzucker (German) Lump sugar.

stud To force cloves, garlic or other seasoning into food surfaces, e.g., cloves in a glazed ham, onion in bread sauce.

stufa (Italian) Stove, oven.

stufa economica (Italian) Kitchen range.

stufaiola (Italian) Stewpan, casserole.

stufatino (Italian) Florentine dish of veal stewed in wine.

stufato (Italian) Stew.

stufato di maiale Stewed or braised pork.

stufato di manzo Beef stew.

stuffed cabbage roll Cabbage leaf stuffed with a savoury mixture and baked in a casserole.

stuffed egg Hard-boiled egg with yolk removed, beaten with cheese, anchovy, essence, tomato *purée* or other flavouring and replaced in the hollows of the egg-white halves.

stuffed potato Potato baked in its jacket, then split, the cooked flesh removed, blended with butter and cheese or other savoury flavouring, then re-packed into the shell and browned under the grill.

stuffed tomato Tomato with slice cut from the top, the pulp scooped out and blended with a savoury mixture, then re-packed into the hollow, topped with the "lid" and baked or eaten raw, according to recipe.

stuffing Savoury mixture of breadcrumbs, vegetables, herbs, spices, minced meat or fish, etc., bound with egg, stock, sauce, lemon juice, milk, etc., to enhance a dish. Stuffing is placed in meat or poultry cavities, rolled up in cabbage or vine leaves, spread on rolled fillets, used to fill eggs, aubergines, tomatoes, etc., etc. The variety of flavours and uses of stuffing is enormous, and serves not only to improve the flavour of the original dish, but also to add bulk, preserve shape and provide interest to the palate.

sturgeon Large shark-like migratory, river-spawning fish of fine flavour whose roe is made into caviare. It is found from the Caspian Sea to North America and occasionally in the River Thames. In season August to March. By tradition, the first sturgeon caught each season is offered to the sovereign. It is cooked filleted, in steaks, braised, etc.

sturgeonburger (American) Hamburger made with sturgeon meat.

suave (Spanish) See *taco*.

suc (French) Liquid squeezed from animal or vegetable substance.

suc de viande (French) (i) Juice pressed from raw meat. (ii) Juice which runs from roast meat. (iii) *Consommé* greatly reduced.

succo (Italian) Juice.

succo d'arancia (Italian) Orange juice.

succo di pomodoro (Italian) Tomato juice.

succo di pompelmo (Italian) Grapefruit juice.

succotash (American) American-Indian dish of green sweetcorn cooked with lima beans.

succory Variant of chicory.

succulent (French) Juicy.

sucker Any fish which has a cup-shaped sucker or a sharp spine on a fin.

sucre (French) Sugar.

sucre d'erable (French) Maple sugar.

sucre filé Spun sugar.

sucrerie (French) Confections; sweet-meats.

sucrose Sugar derived from sugar cane, maple, syrup, palm, sorghum, etc. When cooked with acid sucrose divides into glucose (less sweet) and fructose (more sweet).

Südfrüchte Tropical or Mediterranean fruit.

suédoise (French) Fruit cooked in syrup then arranged in a mould and covered with jelly flavoured with fruit or liqueur.

Suédoise, à la (French) Food cooked in Swedish style.

suet Fat found around the kidneys and loins of sheep and bullocks, bought either from the butcher in lumps, or from the grocer, packeted in shreds, ready for use. Suet is used in stuffings, mincemeat, steamed puddings and suet-crust pastry.

suet-crust pastry Pastry made with flour and suet and used for steamed or baked dishes.

suet pudding Sweet or savoury pudding made either with suet-crust pastry or with a slacker mixture, which is steamed or boiled. The pudding can take the form of layer or roly-poly pudding, or be made in a basin.

Suffolk ham Sweet-cured, darkish ham.

sugar Sweet crystalline substance high in energy-producing carbohydrates and obtainable from many sources (see also fructose, glucose, lactose, maltose and sucrose). Commercially-prepared sugars include cane and beet in consistencies ranging from icing sugar to "pieces", the dark brown moist and least refined-sugar. Sugar is a basic essential in cakes, puddings, etc., as well as of confectionery in general. It is used as a preservative in jam and marmalade-making, etc. Sugar can be flavoured in many ways – with anise, cinnamon, ginger, clove, lemon, orange, etc.

sugar beer Old Suffolk light effervescent drink made from hops, honey or sugar and yeast, taken as "elevenses" by harvesters in the field.

sugar beet White-rooted beet, the second most important source of sugar.

sugar bowl Dish for holding sugar; sometimes with accompanying spoon or tongs.

sugar candy Strings suspended in a strong solution of sugar, left standing in a cool place until the candy is deposited on the strings in angular crystals.

sugar cane Tall reed with a spongy marrow, the principal source of sugar.

The juice is pressed from the cane and subjected to sundry processes which produces molasses, and yellow or brown sugar. This is further refined to produce granulated, castor, icing, lump sugar, etc.

sugar cube Square of compressed sugar.

sugar pea Pea from a pod with no inner lining, so therefore eaten complete with pod. Cooked as for garden peas.

sugar tongs Silver or plate tongs for handling cube sugar.

sugee (Indian) Powdered white grain grown around Calcutta, used for bread and puddings and resembling semolina and tapioca in flavour.

sugo (Italian) Juice, gravy.

sugo, al (Italian) With sauce.

suif (French) Mutton suet; tallow.

suimono (Japanese) Clear soup.

Suisse, à la (French) Food cooked in Swiss style.

sukiyaki (Japanese) Thinly-sliced beef cooked at the table with bamboo shoots, onions, mushrooms, and other vegetables.

süllö (Hungarian) Fish.

sultana Seedless grape originating in Turkey but now in world-wide cultivation. Sultanas vary in colour from pale yellow (the best variety) to dark brownish-yellow, and are used in confectionery, cakes, puddings, mincemeat, pickles and curried dishes. They have a high iron and sugar content.

sultane (French) (i) Sultana. (ii) Elaborate confectionery dish of lattice-work sugar surmounted by sugar-plums.

sultane, à la (French) Dishes, especially sweets and pastries, characterised by the inclusion of pistachio, usually pistachio butter.

Sülze (German) Brawn.

summer flounder (American) Small edible Atlantic flatfish cooked as for similar fish.

summer pudding Cold sweet made by lining a basin or mould with bread or sponge cake and filling the centre with stewed fruit, such as red-currants, black-currants, raspberries or logan-

berries. The basin is covered with more bread or cake, and pressed so that the juice is absorbed. After several hours, the pudding is turned out onto a platter and served with cream.

summer savoury Savory.

summer squash (American) Pumpkin.

Sunday pudding Nineteenth-century West country boiled pudding of flour, breadcrumbs, suet, raisins, currants, sugar or treacle, and eggs.

sundae Ice cream topped with flavoured syrup or sauce and whipped cream, and decorated with nuts, fruits, etc.

sundew Aromatic insectivorous bog-plant whose leaves can be cooked or used in salads.

sunflower Tall plant (Helianthus) with large yellow flowers, the seeds of which are (a) processed for their oil which is used extensively in cooking, (b) dried and salted, particularly in America, for eating as a snack.

sunflower oil Oil extracted from sunflower seeds, used for frying and in salad dressing.

sunny side up Method of frying an egg on one side only, so that the yolk is clearly visible.

suolasilli (Finnish) Pickled herring.

suomaleinen pannukakku (Finnish) Finnish pancakes.

superburger (American) Large-size hamburger.

Suppe (German) Soup.

Suppenfleisch (German) Stock-meat.

Suppenkelle (German) Soup ladle.

Suppenterrine (German) Tureen.

supper Last meal of the day.

suprême (French) Best; most delicate.

suprême sauce (French) Rich, delicately-flavoured cream sauce, made from chicken stock, etc.

suprême de volaille (French) Breast of chicken.

surard (French) Elderberry vinegar.

sureau (French) Elderberry tree.

surf clam (American) Large clam from New England.

surlonge (French) Sirloin of beef.

surtout (French) Epergne; centre-piece.

sushi (Japanese) Boiled rice, wrapped in

brown kelp, purple seaweed, or fresh raw fish.

susina (Italian) Plum.

susina secca (Italian) Prune.

susina verde (Italian) Greengage.

Sussex dumpling Boiled ball of flour, salt and water (hard dumpling).

Sussex pond pudding Nineteenth-century recipe of a boiled-in-a-cloth pudding made of suet crust with currants wrapped round a ball of butter and demerara sugar.

sutliash (Bulgarian) Rice pudding.

suze (French) Proprietory brand of *gentiane* liqueur.

svíčková pecene (Czechoslovakian) Pickled beef with sour cream.

svinestek (Swedish) Roast pork.

swallow Bird protected in Britain and France, but the Far Eastern swallow makes a nest which is processed into Swallow's Nest Soup, chiefly for its gelatinous substance produced by the bird from feeding on seaweed. In Eastern cookery the birds are also eaten as garnishes to other dishes.

swallow's nest See swallow.

swallow's nest soup See swallow.

swan Graceful, long necked bird which in the Middle Ages was considered a delicacy and ranked with peacock as banquet fare. Today it is rarely eaten, and then only when very young (cygnet), when it is stuffed and cooked in a pastry case which is removed to brown the breast.

sweat To heat food (usually vegetables) gently in butter in a lidded pan, to extract flavour.

swede, swedish turnip Rather coarse but well-flavoured root vegetable of a golden yellow colour. Boiled till tender, then mashed or puréed. It can also be cut into pieces and roasted, or included in soups, stews and Cornish pasties.

Swedish meatball (American) Meatball seasoned with nutmeg and served with a cream sauce.

sweet (i) Chocolate or confectionery. (ii) Food served at the pudding course.

sweet and sour Mixture of sweet and sour ingredients, much used in Oriental cookery.

sweet basil Basil.

sweet butter (i) Unsalted butter. (ii) Rum butter, a Cumberland delicacy which used to be made before the birth of a baby and offered to visitors.

sweet cicely Aromatic umbelliferous herb formerly used in cookery.

sweet corn Maize, corn on the cob, Indian corn.

sweet flag Aromatic pond plant whose rootstock is sometimes candied.

sweet marjoram See marjoram.

sweet martini Gin and sweet Italian vermouth served with a twist of orange peel.

sweet orange wine Wine made from sweet oranges, sugar and yeast.

sweet potato Tropical vegetable cultivated for its sweet tuber, but not allied to the common potato. Sweet potatoes are served baked, boiled souffléed, stewed, sautéed, etc., and much used in Créole cookery.

sweet roll Danish pastry.

sweet sorghum Sorgo.

sweetbread Pancreas or thymus gland of fully developed calf or lamb. Soft and whiteish, this is considered one of the chief delicacies of butchery. It is in two parts, the kernel (*noix*) and throat (*gorge*) and is prepared in a wide variety of ways.

sweetmeat Chocolate or other confectionery.

sweetsop (American) Custard apple.

Swiss chard Vegetable also known as Spinach beet or Seakale beet. The green parts of the leaves are cooked as for spinach and the mid-ribs as for celery.

Swiss cheese (American) Cheese with large holes originally imported from Switzerland but now also manufactured in the U.S.A.

Swiss roll Sponge cake spread with jam, cream or other filling and rolled up. Served as a cake, hot pudding with sauce, made into a trifle, or sliced as a base for sweets using fruit, cream, etc.

Swiss steak (American) Cut of beef

topside floured, pounded, browned, and served with vegetables.

swizzle Mixed iced drink of bitters, lime juice, sugar, and spirit such as rum or whisky.

swizzle stick Glass, plastic or wooden rod used for stirring mixed drinks.

swordfish (American) Large oceanic fish with delicate white flesh and long, sword-like upper jaw. It can be baked, smoked or cooked as for fresh tuna.

syllabub Traditional old English sweet made (i) by pouring fresh milk from a height over cider, ale or wine and sweetening and spicing the resultant frothy mixture, (ii) by whisking together cream, wine, sugar and grated lemon rind.

sylt (Swedish) Jam.

Sylter Welle (German) Strong beverage of mixed red wine and brandy.

Sylvaner Rhineland grape which gives its name to wines made from it.

syngnathe Pipe-fish, sometimes called sea-serpent.

Syrian coffee Sweetened black coffee flavoured with black cardamom seeds.

syrup (i) Saturated solution of sugar, generally flavoured with fruit essence; used for various culinary purposes, such as preserving fruits, etc. (ii) Liquid sweetener such as corn syrup, molasses, golden syrup, etc.

szekely (Hungarian) Ewe's milk cheese sold in sausage skins.

t-bone steak (i) Steak cut from the sirloin containing a T-shaped bone, grilled, fried, etc. (ii) (American) Cut from beef short loin.

Tabasco (American) Proprietory brand of red condiment sauce of hot pepper and vinegar.

taberna (Spanish) Tavern; public house.

tabernero (Spanish) Tavern-keeper.

table à manger (French) Dining-table.

table d'hôte (French) (i) Table at which the principal meals at an hotel or restaurant are served to guests. (ii) Meal of several courses served at a fixed price.

table napkin Serviette.

table jelly Commercial gelatine, coloured and flavoured, in either solid or crystal form, needing only the addition of hot water.

table linen Napkins and tablecloths, place mats, etc.

table salt Finely ground, refined salt usually mixed with a little added calcium phosphate and magnesium carbonate to help keep it dry.

table water Bottled water, either still or carbonated.

tablecloth Covering for a dining or luncheon table.

tableware Cutlery, china, etc., used in setting a table.

Tablett (German) Tray.

tacaud (French) Variety of cod, cooked in the same ways.

tacchina (Italian) Turkey hen.

tacchino (Italian) Turkey.

tacchino arrosto (Italian) Roast turkey.

tacchino arrosto ripieno (Italian) Stuffed, roast turkey.

tacchino bollito (Italian) Boiled turkey.

tacchino in maionese (Italian) Cold, sliced turkey with mayonnaise.

tacchinotto (Italian) Young turkey.

taco (Spanish) Tortilla filled with mixture of beans, cheese, fish, poultry or meat and vegetables.

tafia Unrefined rum.

taffy (American and Old English) Pulled hard toffee.

Tagesplatte (German) Dish of the day.

tagliatelle (Italian) Ribbon macaroni.

tagliatelle verde (Italian) Green noodles, spinach macaroni.

taglierini (Italian) Ribbon macaroni.

tahn (Armenian) Yoghurt-and-water summer drink.

taille Thin slice or crust of bread put in a soup tureen.

tailler la soupe (French) To place thin slices or crusts of bread in a soup tureen.

Taillevent, Guillaume (1326–1395) Famous cook and author of one of the oldest cookery books, *Viandier*. He was head cook to many French notables.

tailloir, tranchoir (French) (i) Slices of bread which in earlier times acted as plates. (ii) Wooden platter on which meat is cut up.

talisker Famous malt whisky from the Isle of Skye.

Talleyrand, Marquis de Nineteenth-century French epicure, statesman and diplomat whose *chef* was once Carême.

tallow Renderings of mutton or beef fat.

talmouse (French) Cheese cake or tartlet, usually served as *hors d'œuvre*.

tamago-yaki (Japanese) Baked egg roll.

tamale Mexican dish of corn (maize) cake stuffed with chicken, fish, meat, or vegetables and steamed in a banana leaf or maize husk.

tamara Mixture of spices such as cinnamon, coriander, fennel seed, cloves, etc.

tamarin (French) Tamarind.

tamarind Tropical tree and its acid, pod-like fruit. The leaves and flowers are eaten as a vegetable; the juicy pulp is used to make preserves, sauces and chutneys and figures largely in Eastern cooking. The seeds are ground into a meal and baked as cakes. The fruit has laxative properties.

tamarind ball (American) Jamaican confection made of brown sugar and tamarind.

tambour (French) (i) Fine sugar sieve. (ii) Small dessert biscuit.

tamis (French) Tammy. Fine sieve. Woollen or canvas cloth used for straining soups and sauces.

tamisé (French) Rubbed through a tammy cloth or tammy sieve.

tammy Cloth or sieve through which a sauce is squeezed to strain it and make it glossy.

tanche (French) Tench.

tangelo Ugli, a hybrid fruit resulting from a cross between a tangerine orange and a pomelo.

tangerine Small loose-skinned variety of mandarin orange, originally imported from China. Delicious in flavour, it is eaten raw or used in desserts, confections, etc.

tango (American) Mixed drink of gin, vermouth and orange juice.

tangoa (American) Tangerine liqueur.

tankard Tall glass, silver, pewter, stainless steel or stone drinking vessel with a handle, often also a hinged lid.

tansy Herb with bitter, aromatic leaves, once widely used for flavouring puddings like egg custard.

tansy mustard (American) Herb of the mustard family similar to the true tansy.

tapioca Farinaceous food obtained from the roots of the cassava (manioc plant), a native of tropical Asia, America, and Africa. One of the most easily digested farinaceous foods, it is used to thicken broths and soups, and to make milk puddings.

tapioca (Italian) Tapioca.

tappit hen (Scottish) (i) Buck rarebit. (ii) Lidded drinking tankard with a knob on top.

taramosalata (Greek) Smoked cod roe *pâté*.

targhana (Russian) Dried yeast and yoghurt dough used for soup-making.

tari Liquor obtained from palm trees.

taro Tropical plant grown for its starchy root (also known as Coco Yam) which is boiled, baked, or made into bread. A staple article of diet in the Pacific islands, it is also used to make the fermented paste, Poi, much used by Hawaiians.

tarragon Spicy, tangy herb with small

olive-green leaves, used to flavour stews, sauces, omelettes and salads, especially in France.

tarragon vinegar White vinegar flavoured with tarragon.

tart (i) Open pastry case with a filling of fruit, jam, lemon curd, golden syrup, etc. usually made of shortcrust or flan pastry. Sometimes called a Flan. (ii) Sharp, sourish flavour.

tarta (Spanish) Cake.

tarta de manzana (Spanish) Apple tart.

tartare sauce Mayonnaise sauce flavoured with herbs, capers, gherkins, etc. served with fish, salads and certain vegetables.

tartaric acid Acid found in many fruits especially unripe grapes; it is extracted from the lees of wine and is used commercially as a raising agent, also in mineral drinks and sweet-making.

tartaruga (Italian) Turtle.

tarte (French) Open tart, flan.

tarte aux pommes (French) Apple tart.

tartelette (French) Small tart.

tartina (Italian) Slice of bread spread with butter, paste, jam, etc.

tartine (French) (i) Small tart. (ii) Slice of bread spread with butter, jam, jelly, etc. (iii) Sandwich.

tartlet Small tart.

tartrique (French) Tartaric acid.

tartufo (Italian) Truffle.

Tascherin (German/Austrian) Stuffed turnovers containing cheese, meat, nuts, jam, etc.

tassard (French) Kingfish.

tasse (French) Cup.

Tasse (German) Cup.

tassie (Scottish) Small cup.

tâte-vin, tastevin (French) Small silver saucer for wine-tasting, now antique rather than in common use since the advent of clear glass.

Taube (German) Pigeon, dove.

tava kebab (Russian) Lamb patty.

Tavel (French) Red wine from the *Languedoc* area of France.

tavern Bar or combined bar and restaurant.

tawny port Port fully aged in the cask for up to 15 years, thereby losing some of its natural red colour.

taza (Spanish) Cup.

taza de té (Spanish) Cup of tea.

taza para té (Spanish) Tea-cup.

tchadi (Russian) Georgian maize-bread baked with feta cheese.

te (Danish and Norwegian) Tea.

tè (Italian) Tea.

té (Spanish and Swedish) Tea.

tè di Ceilan (Italian) Ceylon tea.

tè di China (Italian) China tea.

tè dell' India (Italian) Indian tea.

te-komplet (Danish) Light meal usually including bread, cake, and tea.

tea Beverage derived from the leaves of *Thea sinenis*, a tree akin to the camellia. Although all tea comes from the same plant, the variations are produced by differences in climate, soil, etc., and by processing, i.e. fully, partially or non-fermented. Tea was first introduced into England in 1661 and for many years it was the beverage of the wealthy, who kept their supplies locked in caddies. It can be served with or without milk or sugar, with lemon, hot or iced, or mixed with alcoholic drinks to make punches. Chief types of tea are: Green, Brown, Black, but they are obtainable in many blends and varieties.

tea bag Cloth or filter-paper bag containing tea leaves which is immersed in boiling water to make leafless tea.

tea ball; tea spoon Perforated metal infuser, ball- or spoon-shaped, made in two hinged parts, opened and filled with tea and used like a tea bag.

tea bowl (i) Chinese or Japanese style teacup without handles. (ii) Original early English teacup, made without handles.

tea bread Sweet bread, bun, or cake served for tea.

tea caddy Small box or chest for holding tea.

tea cloth (i) Small decorative tablecloth for a light meal. (ii) Glass-cloth.

tea cozy Cloth or knitted cover used to keep a teapot warm.

tea kettle (i) Spouted utensil in light-weight metal, with top handle, lid and sometimes a whistle, for boiling water for tea-making. (ii) Electrically-heated vessel similar to the above, but heavier and without a whistle device.

tea maker (i) Tea-ball. (ii) Automatic electric apparatus time-set to release boiling water into a tea-pot.

tea punch (i) (Non-alcoholic) Beverage of strong tea, orange and lemon juice, pineapple cubes and crushed ice, sugared to taste. (ii) (Alcoholic) Beverage of very strong hot tea, lemon juice and zest on lump sugar, with added rum and brandy, flamed.

tea service Set of ceramic or metallic utensils, for serving tea; if of metal (stainless steel, silver, etc.) teapot, tray, milk jug, sugar bowl, hot-water jug; if of ceramic (usually fine china) teapot, sugar bowl, milk jug, teacups, saucers and plates.

tea set Tea service, usually ceramic, including cups, saucers, and plates. (See tea service.)

tea towel Wiping-up cloth.

tea tray Tray large enough to hold teapot, milk jug and sugar basin; often also large enough to hold teacups and saucers.

teacake Light, flat yeast bun served at tea, often toasted, split and buttered.

teacup Drinking cup, usually part of a tea service, with a matching saucer.

teapot Spouted vessel of metal or earthenware, provided with a handle and a lid, used for making and serving tea.

teal Small, highly prized wild duck, in season from October to February. Usually roasted and garnished with watercress and slices of lemon.

teaseed oil Oil extracted from the seeds of a plant of the tea family, used commercially to replace olive oil for salad dressings, frying, etc.

tee (Finnish) Tea.

Tee (German) Tea.

Teedose (German) Tea-caddy.

Teegebäck (German) Tea-cake.

Teekanne (German) Teapot.

Teelöffel (German) Teaspoon.

Teesieb (German) Tea-strainer.

teff Abyssinian small-grained cereal grass ground into meal and made into bread which forms the staple diet of that country.

teflon Compound of tetrafluoroethylene, a non-sticking plastic used to coat cooking utensils such as saucepans and frying pans. Utensils thus treated are easily cleaned, and reduce the amount of oil or fat needed in cooking.

Teig (German) Dough, paste.

Teigrolle (German) Rolling-pin.

Teller (German) Plate.

telur (Malay) Egg.

temp. Abbreviation for temperature.

temperature Degree of heat required for cooking a particular dish, its accuracy being essential to its ultimate success. Oven temperatures are thermostatically controlled. For other processes such as preserving, sugar-boiling, etc., thermometers are obtainable.

tempura (Japanese) Food dipped in batter and deep-fat fried.

tench Small freshwater fish of the carp family soaked in salted water before being fried or grilled.

tenderloin (American) Part of the sirloin of beef; the *contre-filet*.

tendon Fibre attaching the muscular mass of flesh to the bone.

tenedor (Spanish) Fork.

tener hambre (Spanish) To be hungry.

tener sed (Spanish) To be thirsty.

tendron (French) (i) Tendon; gristle. (ii) Cut from the breast of lamb or veal, in which the gristle is found.

tepary bean (American) Mexican drought-withstanding bean grown in the Southern States.

tequila Mexican alcoholic beverage or beer distilled from pulque, the fermented sap of the maguey cactus.

ternera (Spanish) Veal, calf.

terrapène (French) Terrapin.

terrapin Small turtle originating in North America, whose flesh is considered a great delicacy. It is soaked, boiled or steamed, then cooled.

terre-noix (French) Earth-nut.

terrine (i) Earthenware dish or pot, used for *pâtés*, and for potted meats, game, fish, etc. (ii) The *pâté* itself such as terrine of duck or chicken.

Terrine (German) Tureen.

terrine du chef (French) Chef or cook's own *pâté*.

terrón d'azúcar (Spanish) Lump of sugar.

testa (Italian) Animal head or face.

testugine de mare (Italian) Turtle.

tête (French) Head.

tête d'aloyau (French) End of the rump of beef.

tête de cuvée (French) Choice wine obtained by crushing the grape before it is subjected to the press.

tête de moine (French) Cheese made in the Jura. Literally "monk's head".

tête de veau (French) Calf's head.

tetera (Spanish) Tea-pot.

tétine (French) Udder.

tétine de veau (French) Calf's udder.

tétras (French) French grouse; prairie chicken.

texel (Dutch) Green sheep's-milk cheese.

thé (French) Tea.

thé-complet (French) Light meal of tea, bread and cake.

The Dean's Cream Eighteenth-century Cambridge pudding made from sponge cakes, raspberry jam, marmalade, sherry, brandy and cream, decorated with cherries and angelica.

thee (Dutch) Tea.

therid (Arabic) Soup whose principal ingredients are broth, olive oil, eggs, vinegar, and breadcrumbs.

thermometer Instrument to measure and register degrees of temperature, oven heat, etc.

thermos Vacuum container used (a) to keep hot such foods as tea, coffee, soup, etc., and (b) to keep iced drinks, etc. cold.

thiamine Part of the vitamin B group (once called B1) found in pork, liver, yeast (B1) wheat germ, milk, eggs and other foods.

thickening Culinary process of rendering gravies, soups, or other liquids thicker by the addition of egg yolk or certain farinaceous substances, such as flour, tapioca, etc.

thistle Wild plant in sundry varieties, some eaten for their flower-head (like the globe artichoke) some for

their stems and leaves, (like the cardoon).

thon (French) Tuna fish.

thon mariné (French) Pickled tuna fish.

thonine (French) Mediterranean variety of tuna fish.

thonné (French) Method of cooking veal preceded by long marination.

thorins (French) Fine Burgundy wine from the *Saône-et-Loire* department of France.

thourins, tourin (French) Onion-based soup thickened with egg-yolks.

thread stage Stage in sweet-making when syrup dribbled from a spoon into cold water forms into threads. (230 degrees – 234 degrees F.)

thrush Speckled song bird protected in Britain but eaten on the Continent, usually roasted and served on a piece of bread fried in the cooking fat.

Thunfisch (German) Tuna fish.

thyme Garden herb with a strong flavour, used sparingly in soups, sauces, stews, etc. Lemon thyme is excellent for veal stuffing.

Thymian (German) Thyme.

thymus Sweetbread, the ductless gland in the upper part of the thorax in young animals.

Tia maria Coffee-flavoured Jamaican liqueur.

tidy: Sink tidy Perforated receptacle used for straining waste materials.

tied house British public house owned by a brewery.

tiffin Anglo-Indian term for a light mid-day or late morning meal.

tiger melon Melon, segmented, and striped in green and yellow.

timbale (French) (i) Originally, a small metal receptacle for a beverage. (ii) Large bowl in which food is served. (iii) Moulded food, hot or cold, the mould lined with noodle paste, macaroni, sieved potato, noodles, or similar preparation, filled with a mixture of fish or meat or poultry, etc. *Timbales* can be large or in small individual moulds.

timbale iron Long-handled metal mould for shaping and baking moulds or shells for *timbales*.

timballo (Italian) *Timbale*, a savoury mixture of food placed into a dish lined with breadcrumbs or other commodity suitable as a mould. (See *timbale* (iii))

timer (i) Clockwork device for timing in cookery. (ii) Device incorporated in a gas or electric cooker to indicate when food is ready.

timo (Italian) Thyme.

tinca (Italian) Tench.

tinned food Canned food.

tinplate, tin ware Pressed iron covered with tin, used for kitchen cooking utensils such as cake tins, baking tins, graters, etc. Many such items are now being replaced by aluminium, fireproof glass, cast iron, etc.

Tintenfisch (German) Cuttle-fish.

Tio Pepe Dry Spanish sherry.

tip of sirloin (American) Thin hind-quarter flank of beef.

tipsy cake (i) Tall sponge cake soaked in fruit juice and sherry or wine, coated with custard and decorated with almonds. Its name is derived from the fact that its moist texture often causes it to tilt over. (ii) Colloquialism for sherry trifle.

tipsy pudding Tipsy cake.

tiré (French) Pulled, as *sucre tiré* – pulled sugar.

tire-bouchon (French) Corkscrew.

tinto (Spanish) Red (wine).

tisane (i) Originally, barley water. (ii) Nowadays, any infusion of herb tea such as jasmine, camomile, etc.

tisane de champagne (French) Lighter-than-ordinary champagne.

Tisch (German) Table.

Tischdeck (German) Table-cloth.

Tischtuch (German) Table-cloth.

Tischzeit (German) Meal-time.

tiste (Spanish) Central American drink made of toasted maize flour, cacao, anatto and sugar.

tizer Aereated soft drink.

tjener (Danish) Waiter.

toad-in-the-hole Sausages, cutlets or chopped cooked meat, baked in Yorkshire pudding batter.

toast (i) Toasted bread. (ii) To brown by direct heat, in a toaster or under a grill, or in front of a fire.

toast melba Thin slices of bread toasted slowly until they become crisp.

toast rack Slotted utensil for holding toasted bread so that it retains its crispness.

toaster Electric appliance for toasting bread, etc. many fitted with timing devices to make the toast pop up when ready.

toasting fork Long-handled tined implement used for toasting foods such as bread, buns, etc., in front of an open fire.

tobasco Tabasco.

toby jug Beer-mug shaped like a fat man in the three-cornered hat. Nowadays, more an ornament than put to actual use.

tocan (French) Parr, a very young salmon.

tocană (Rumanian) Creamed chicken.

tocane (French) (i) New juice of grapes. (ii) New champagne wine in its first stage.

tocino (Spanish) Bacon, salt pork.

toddy (i) Drink made with rum or whisky, hot water, sugar and lemon. (ii) Fermented drink made from the sap of various tropical palm trees.

toddy palm Tropical palm tree (also known as the Milk tree) which produces a sap fermented into a strong alcoholic beverage.

toffee Chewy sweet made from a sugar mixture usually containing butter, boiled at a high temperature, flavoured and coloured, sometimes with added nuts, fruits, etc.

toffee apple Apple coated with reddish toffee and served on a stick.

toffy Toffee.

toheroa Edible but scarce New Zealand clam. The soup made from it is a great delicacy.

toilette (French) Another name for caul or *crépine*.

Tokay Sweet Hungarian wine made from grapes allowed to shrivel in the sun before being gathered. Tokay, when fully matured by keeping, will remain unchanged for a hundred years.

Tokai (French) Tokay.

tom and jerry (American) Hot punch of rum, boiling water, eggs, cinnamon and clove.

Tom Collins (American) Cocktail made from sugar syrup, lemon juice, gin, ice and soda water.

tomar la cena (Spanish) To dine.

tomar un trago (Spanish) To have a drink.

tomate (French and Spanish) Tomato.

Tomate (German) Tomato.

tomate frite (French) Fried tomato.

tomate grillée (French) Grilled tomato.

Tomatensaft (German) Tomato juice.

tomato ("love apple") Pulpy fruit of a plant of South American origin, at first considered to be poisonous, introduced into Europe by the Spanish in the 16th century. In the last 80 years it has developed into a major horticultural industry. Tomatoes vary in shape and colour from red to yellow, and are a good source of vitamins A and C. Best of all eaten raw and freshly picked, they nevertheless contribute greatly to cooking, in soups, stews, or individually grilled, fried, stuffed, baked, etc. They are a colourful addition to salads and garnishes, and their juice makes a refreshing beverage.

tomato bouillon Beef *bouillon* with tomato juice.

tomato catsup (American) Tomato ketchup.

tomato fondue Peeled, pressed and butter-cooked tomatoes, seasoned and used as a garnish or as filling for *bouchées*, etc.

tomato juice Juice extracted from ripe tomatoes, used in cookery or as a drink. Combined with vodka, it forms the cocktail Bloody Mary.

tomato ketchup Piquant tomato sauce, bottled commercially.

tomato paste Concentrated tomato *purée*.

tomato sauce (i) Tomato ketchup. (ii) (American) *Purée* of tomato, flavoured with onions, parsley, fat and sugar.

tomato scone Scone made from dough containing tomato juice in place of milk.

tomber (French) To cook meat in no liquid other than that produced by the meat itself. The ultimate result will be juice of a syrupy consistency. (See *Tomber à glace*).

tomber à glace (French) To reduce a liquid until it has the appearance of a thick syrup or glaze.

tome au raisin (French) Soft cheese covered with a 'crust' of grape-pips.

tonalchile Guinea pepper.

tonic water Carbonate quinine water used as an additive to gin.

tongs Instrument for holding food, varying in size according to its particular use, i.e. sugar tongs, asparagus tongs, etc.

tongue Animal delicacy, braised, pickled or smoked, served hot or cold. Also available ready-packed in tins or jars. Hot tongue is usually accompanied by a suitable sauce; cold tongue is often glazed in aspic and served with salad.

tongue cress Garden cress in several varieties – golden, large leaf, common cress. Used in salads and as a garnish for roast or grilled meat or poultry.

tonnato (Italian) Food cooked with tuna fish sauce.

tonno (Italian) Tuna fish.

tonno sott'olio (Italian) Tuna fish in oil.

toothpick Short pointed stick of wood, plastic or quill used to remove food shreds from between the teeth, to spear olives, gherkins, etc., or to secure double-decker sandwiches.

Topfenknödel (German/Austrian) Cottage cheese dumpling.

Topfenschnitzel (German/Austrian) Cottage cheese rissole.

Topfenstrudel (German) Cottage cheese *strudel*.

Topfentorte (German/Austrian) Cottage cheese *gâteau*.

Töpferware (German) Pottery, earthenware.

topinambour (French) Jerusalem artichoke.

topinambur (Italian) Jerusalem artichoke.

tordo (Italian) Thrush.

toronja (Spanish) Grapefruit.

torpedo Large skate-like fish, common in the Mediterranean, prepared as for skate.

torpille Torpedo fish.

torrone (Italian) Nougat.

torrone gelato (Italian) Iced nougat pudding.

torsk (Danish and Norwegian) Cod.

torta (Italian) (i) Cake. (ii) Tart or pie.

torta (Spanish) Round cake or loaf.

torta de banana (Spanish) Banana cake.

torta di frutta (Italian) Fruit flan.

torta di frutta alla panna (Italian) Fruit flan with cream.

torta di mandorle (Italian) Venetian almond tart.

torta di noci (Italian) Nut tart.

torta pasqualina (Italian) Savoury pie of eggs, cheese, artichokes and onion eaten on Fast days.

tortada (Spanish) Large pie of meat or chicken.

torte Large cream cake, originating in Austria, usually decorated with or incorporating fruits and nuts and served on festive occasions.

Torte (German) (i) Cake. (ii) Pastry, flan or tart.

tortellino (Italian) Macaroni or pasta rings stuffed with meat, ham, cheese, etc.

tortello (Italian) (i) Fritter. (ii) Pasta cushions stuffed with cottage cheese.

tortera (Spanish) Deep baking dish.

tortilla (Spanish) Omelette.

tortilla (Mexican/Spanish) (i) Maize-flour pancake spread with spicy sauce, beans or meat, then rolled up. (ii) Thin bread-cake made from yucca or manioc flour.

tortilla de camarónes (Spanish) Prawn or shrimp omelette.

tortilla española (Spanish) Spanish omelette.

tortilla francesa (Italian) Omelette.

tortina (Italian) Tartlet.

tortino di carciofi (Italian) Artichoke-heart omelette.

tortue (French) Turtle.

tortue claire (French) Clear turtle soup.

tortue, en (French) Turtle garnish.

tortue-fausse (French) Mock turtle.

tortue liée (French) Thick turtle soup.

tostada (Spanish) Toast, toasted bread.

tostar (Spanish) To toast; to brown.

tostino (Italian) (i) Toaster. (ii) Coffee roaster.

tostón (Spanish) (i) Buttered or oil-covered toast. (ii) Roasted pea.

tostón (Venezuelan/Spanish) Green plaintain cut into long sticks and fried to resemble toast.

tot Small drink.

tôt-fait (French) (i) Cake made with cake-flour, sugar, lemon rind and eggs, baked in a buttered mould. (ii) Pancake.

totano (Italian) Cuttlefish, squid.

Töttchen (German) Highly seasoned stew made in Münster.

touffe (French) Bunch of stalks tied together.

touffe de persil (French) Bunch of parsley.

Toulousaine, à la (French) Food served in Toulouse style, usually applied to a *ragoût* bound with white sauce and served with roast or poached poultry, or as a filling for tarts, etc.

Touraine (French) Area of France around *Tours*, noted for its excellent cookery in general as well as fruit, *charcuterie* fish and vegetables, but with few local specialities. Also known for its dry, smooth, aromatic wines (*Vouvray, Candes, Bourgeuil*, etc.)

tourne-broche (French) Turnspit.

tournedos (French) Small fillet of beef first served in Paris in 1855. The name implies that it is cooked in a twinkling, or, while the cook's back is turned.

tourner (French) To "round" or shape certain vegetables, such as shaping potatoes like olives, etc.

touron (French) Sweetmeat like the Spanish *turron* but varying in flavour and decoration.

tourte (French) (i) Round meat-filled pie. (ii) Round sweet or fruit pie.

tourte aux abricots (French) Round tart of puff pastry filled with ripe, halved apricots before baking.

tourte corse (French) Corsican pie of chestnut flour, dried fruits and pine kernels, baked in a pie-dish.

tourteau (French) Large edible crab.

tourtelette (French) Tartlet.

tourterelle (French) Turtle dove.

tourtière (French) Tart mould, pie dish, baking dish.

toute-bonne (French) Kind of Bartlett pear.

towel Edible gourd.

tovuk palov (Russian) Uzbek chicken pilaff.

toyo (Filipino) Soy sauce.

tragacanth Gum derived from several species of plants, used by confectioners and pastry-cooks to bind their oils and firm their pastes. Also used in ice-creams, jellies, etc.

trago (Spanish) Draught of liquid; drink.

trago de vino (Spanish) Drink of wine.

traguito (Spanish) Small drink.

trammel Contrivance for adjusting a pothook in a fireplace so that a cooking pot can be raised or lowered.

tranche (French) Slice, rasher.

tranche grasse (French) Butchery term for leg of beef extending the length of the topside as far as the rump.

trancher (French) To cut or carve.

trancheur (French) Restaurant waiter in charge of carving the meat.

tranchieren (German) To carve (meat).

Tranchiermesser (German) Carving-knife.

trancia (Italian) Slice, rasher.

trancia di torta (Italian) Slice of cake or tart.

transparent icing Very thin icing applied to give a professional finish to royal-iced cakes.

Trappist cheese Cheese made in the Trappist monastery of *Port du Salut* in France.

Traube (German) Grape.

Traubensaft (German) Grapejuice.

Traubenstrudel (German) Grape *strudel*.

Trautmannsdorff Austrian Count (1749–1827) after whom several sweets are styled.

travailler (French) (i) To beat food such as batter, pasta, etc., to ensure a smooth blend. (ii) To change the nature of food, i.e. dough, by allowing it to rise.

treacle Molasses, golden syrup: viscous liquids which are the by-products of sugar-refining.

treacle mustard Old Suffolk recipe of shortcrust pastry filled with mixed syrup and egg, baked brown and eaten cold.

treacle tart Short-crust pastry flan filled with treacle or golden syrup and breadcrumbs, usually with pastry strips in lattice pattern on top.

treacle toffee Sweetmeat made of brown sugar, treacle, water and cream of tartar.

treble palma Highest grade of quality in sherry.

trefah (Hebrew) Foods forbidden to Jews, like pig, shellfish and scaleless fish, and certain parts of Kosher animals: also animals not killed in accordance with dietary laws, or other dietary violations.

trempage (French) Soaking food to soften, desalt or impart a particular flavour.

tremper la soupe (French) To pour soup over thin slices or crusts of bread placed in the soup-tureen.

tremper le vin (French) To mix wine with water.

trempette (French) Small slice of bread soaked in liquid such as soup.

trepang Sea slug or sea cucumber, a holothurian eaten by the Chinese.

trianon, à la (French) Trianon style, usually a dish or garnishing in three colours.

trifle Cold sweet made with a basis of sponge cake soaked in wine, sherry or fruit juice, then covered with custard sauce and whipped cream, and decorated with cherries, angelica, etc. Made either in a large glass dish or in individual portions.

triggerfish, pigfish Genus of fish in several species with an erect, spined dorsal fin. All have bright metallic colouring, with delicate flesh prepared as for tuna fish. Some make a pig-like grunting noise when caught.

triglia (Italian) Red mullet.

trigo (Spanish) Wheat.

trim To pare; to cut off portions of

meat or vegetables in order to improve their appearance.

trimmings Parts of meat removed before cooking, many of which can be used to make a stock-base for sauce.

trinken (German) To drink.

tripa (Spanish) Tripe.

tripe Inner lining of the stomach of the ox or cow, with a texture resembling a blanket or honeycomb, depending whether it comes from the first or second stomach. It is usually sold cleaned and blanched and parboiled. It is then simmered in milk, served with boiled onions or a white sauce. Blanket tripe can be cut into small pieces after cooking, dipped in batter, or egged-and-crumbed and fried. In France, tripe from pigs is used for certain dishes, such as *Tripe à la mode de Caen*. Tripe in general is cooked in a variety of ways, and much more highly regarded than in Britain.

triperie (French) Shop where tripe and other offal is sold.

tripes (French) Tripe.

trippa (Italian) Tripe.

trippa di bue (Italian) Ox-tripe.

trippa di maiale (Italian) Pig's tripe.

trivet (i) Three-legged metal stand for holding a hot dish on a table. (ii) Three-legged pot. (iii) Bracket with three projections for fixing on to the top bar of a fire grate.

trocken (German) Dry.

Trockenbeerenauslese (German) Expensive sweet German wine made from grapes left to shrivel on the vine.

Trockenkäse (German) Hard dry cheese.

trognon (French) Edible heart of a vegetable or fruit.

tronçon (French) Small slice of fish or meat cut longer than it is wide.

tronçon de saumon (French) Middle-cut of salmon.

tropical lemon Additive for gin or vodka with a flavour lying between tonic water and bitter lemon.

trota (Italian) Trout.

trota affumicata (Italian) Smoked trout.

trota salmonata (Italian) Salmon-trout.

trotter (i) Pig's foot, usually braised or stewed. (ii) Calf's foot, cooked as above or used to make calf's foot jelly.

trousse (French) Sheath to hold butcher's knife or implements.

trout Freshwater fish of the salmon group, its delicate flesh varying in colour according to the waters in which it lives. Varieties include salmon trout, lake trout, rainbow trout, river trout, brown trout (also known as brook trout and speckled trout). Lake and salmon trout are mostly prepared as for salmon, but all trout can be cooked and served in a wide variety of ways.

trucha (Spanish) Trout.

truelle (French) Curved-handled spatula used to serve fish and pastries.

truffe (French) Truffle.

truffe blanche (French) White truffle.

Trüffel (German) Truffle.

truffer (French) (i) To garnish or stuff a dish with truffles. (ii) To stud a dish with small pieces of truffle.

truffle Globular edible fungus which grows below ground, a much prized and expensive delicacy, rare in this country but widely available on the Continent. The prime varieties come from Italy and France, particularly those from the Périgord district of S.W. France, where trained pigs and dogs are used to find them. Fresh truffles are usually served cooked in a wine sauce, but bottled truffles are used to flavour savoury dishes and to garnish all manner of food, also to stuff poultry and game. The value of truffles lies not so much in their own flavour but in their ability to impart flavour to other food.

truie (French) Sow; female pig.

truite (French) Trout.

truite au bleu (French) Variety of trout which is caught, killed and cooked instantly.

truite de rivière (French) River trout.

truite saumonée (French) Salmon trout.

trunkfish, cofferfish Small edible fish enclosed in a box of bony scales, and often baked in this shell-like covering.

truss To tie a bird with string, which is passed through and fastened in such a manner as to keep its shape and retain its juices during the process of cooking.

Truthahn (German) Turkey cock.

Truthenne (German) Turkey hen.

tuba (Filipino) Wine of the Philippines made from fermented palm sap.

tube pan (American) Deep ring-shaped cake tin with a central cavity used for baking angel cakes, and other deep, light-textured cakes. It ensures that they cook in the middle as well as round the edges.

Tuborg (Danish) Lager brewed in Copenhagen.

tuica (Rumanian) Rum-flavoured plum liqueur.

tuile (French) Type of *petit four* which, when baked, is bent over to resemble a curved tile.

tukum dolma (Russian) Uzbek stuffed meat-balls.

tulip Tulip-shaped wine glass.

tulip, wild Plant growing in the South of France whose edible root is prepared as for Jerusalem artichoke.

tumbler Straight-sided stemless drinking glass, usually intended for water or milk.

tumeric Turmeric.

tun Large cask.

tuna, tunny Fish found in warm and temperate seas, with firm and well-flavoured flesh, ranging in size up to 10 feet long. When cooked fresh, it can be fried, grilled or boiled, and served with a sauce. Canned tuna, preserved in oil, can be used in salads and savoury *hors d'œuvre* items, cooked in a fish pie, etc., etc.

tunge (Danish) Tongue.

Tunke (German) Sauce, gravy.

turban (i) (American) Edible gourd cooked as for pumpkin. (ii) Ornamental chicken *entrée* dressed in the form of a turban. (iii) Cold fowl and cold veal, sliced, garnished with tongue and truffles arranged in the shape of a turban. (iv) Other foodstuffs similarly arranged. (v) Forcemeat cooked in a border mould.

turbit Variety of domestic pigeon, with a very short beak.

turbot Highly-esteemed flat sea-fish, firm, white and delicate and capable of weighing up to 50 lbs. In season all year round. Usually sold in slices or cutlets, which can be grilled, baked, braised, fried, depending on size, and served with various garnishes and sauces.

turbotière (French) Turbot-kettle or pan in which turbot is cooked.

turbotin (French) Small turbot.

tureen Large deep dish in which soup is served.

turkey Large fowl native to North America, domesticated by the early settlers as a good source of food and now the traditional dish on American Thanksgiving Day. Turkey was introduced into Europe in the 16th century, and for many years has been traditional Christmas fare in Britain, although it is now available all the year round in frozen form, ready for cooking. The hen bird is more tender than the cock and carries less bone. Turkey can be roasted in a variety of ways and with differing accompaniments and stuffings. The cold leftover meat lends itself to excellent *rechauffée* dishes, moulds, minced preparations, etc., etc.

turkeyburger (American) Hamburger made of turkey meat.

turkish blood Beverage of red burgundy and strong ale.

Turkish coffee Powdered coffee boiled three times in a sugar-syrup. A few drops of rose-water are added.

Turkish delight Sweetmeat made of sugar, gelatine or other thickening agent such as cornflour, and icing sugar. Boiled till transparent then flavoured and coloured. When set, it is cut into squares and tossed in icing sugar.

Turkish pepper (i) Bonnet pepper. (ii) Paprika, which is made from the bonnet pepper.

turk's cap Edible gourd cooked as for pumpkin.

turk's head pan (American) Fluted ring-shaped deep cake tin alleged to resemble a turban.

turmeric Plant of the ginger family,

whose aromatic root is ground into an orange-yellow powder used to colour curry powder, mustard pickles, etc., and to flavour meats and eggs.

turn To trim or pare vegetables into neat round or oval shapes.

turner Broad-bladed perforated tool for turning food over during frying or grilling.

turnip White bulbous root vegetable said to have been introduced into Britain from Germany in the reign of George I. Is served as a vegetable, tossed in butter or with white sauce, or used in moderation to flavour soups, and stews. The swede, or rutabaga is a yellow variety of turnip, used similarly.

turnip cabbage (American) Kohlrabi or rutabaga.

turnip radish Variety of radish with a bulbous root.

turnip-top Pungent young leaves of the turnip or swede, cooked as for cabbage or other greens.

turnover Semi-circular large or small pie made by folding a round of pastry in half, filling it with a sweet or savoury mixture and sealing the edges before baking.

turnspit Young person or trained dog formerly used to turn a joint roasting on a spit before a fire. This is now performed mechanically.

turrón (Spanish) Sweetmeat of nougat or almond paste, incorporating candied fruits and nuts, either hazel, pistachio or almonds.

Turteltaube (German) Turtle-dove.

turtle (i) Terrapin (land turtle) (ii) Edible marine or sea tortoise brought to England in the middle of the 17th century. The green turtle is considered the most highly prized as a food delicacy. In addition to the famous turtle soup, numerous other dishes are made from it, especially from the flippers. Ready-made turtle soup is available in cans or bottles.

turtle-dove Member of the pigeon family prepared as for pigeon.

turtle herbs Ready-prepared mixture of thyme, bay, basil and marjoram, for seasoning stews, sauces, etc.

tushi (Armenian) Vegetable pickles.

tutter (Dutch) To your health! A toast.

tutti-frutti (Italian) (i) Various kinds of fruits. (ii) Mixture of cooked vegetables. (iii) Ice-cream mixed with different sorts of candied fruits.

twelfth cake Large, old-English ceremonial cake, into which a bean, ring, or other article was introduced, made for Twelfth Night festivals. The person finding the article in his or her piece of the cake was recognised as king for the occasion.

twin-spout teapot Teapot with two sections and two spouts, with tea poured from one and hot water from the other.

twist (i) Piece of lemon, lime, or orange peel served with a drink. (ii) Bread, pastry or roll formed into a twisted shape.

twister (American) See cruller.

two-bean succotash (American) Mixture of green beans, lima beans, and yellow corn, a speciality dish of Iowa, U.S.A.

tzimmes, tzyimes (Jewish) Blended food, slowly cooked in a casserole; combinations include meat with dried fruit, vegetables with fruit, etc., varied to taste.

udder Cow's and calf's udder, prepared like escalopes of veal, or salted or smoked.

Ude, Louis Eustache (French) Famous chef, once cook to Louis XVI and the Earl of Sefton. Author of *The French Cook* published in 1827.

udon (Japanese) Thick corn or wheat noodles.

ugli Hybrid cirtrus fruit of a pleasantly sweet flavour developed in Jamaica by crossing a grapefruit with a tangerine. In the West Indies it is baked in cinders.

uisgebeatha (Gaelic) Whisky.

uitsmijer (Dutch) Open sandwich, sometimes topped with a fried egg.

ukha sucha (Russian) Fish soup.

ullage Quantity by which a bottle, flagon, or other vessel is short of being full.

ultra heat·treated milk Milk treated to a minimum of 270 degrees F (132 degrees C) for two seconds, then packed into cartons. Its keeping properties are extended to several months, without need for refrigeration.

ulva Sea lettuce eaten in oriental countries, notably Japan. Used in salads, soups, and stews, but lacking in food value.

ulve (French) Ulva.

umbles Edible entrails of a deer, once made into a pie for servants, hence the expression "to eat (h)umble pie".

umbrine Perch-like Mediterranean fish with delicate flesh and prepared as for bass.

umbra Grayling, a freshwater fish.

umido (Italian) Stew.

umrühen (German) To stir.

uncork To remove the cork from a bottle; an operation requiring skill so as not stir up the sediment.

unfermented tea Green tea.

unfermented wine Grape juice or other fruit, cereal or vegetable juices not yet fermented into wine.

univalve Edible mollusc whose shell is

composed of a single piece, such as snail, whelk, etc.

unleavened bread Flat, crisp bread made from flour from various grains, plus salt and water. Examples are matzos and chapattis.

Untertasse (German) Saucer.

Untersatz (German) Table-mat.

untruss To remove the trussing string from birds, after cooking.

uovo (Italian) Egg.

uovo abattato (Italian) Beaten egg.

uovo affogato (Italian) Poached egg.

uovo affogato in pomodoro (Italian) Egg poached in tomato sauce.

uovo al burro (Italian) (i) Oven-cooked egg in butter. (ii) Fried egg.

uovo al latte (Italian) Soft-boiled egg.

uovo all'ostrica (Italian) Prairie oyster.

uovo alla fiorentina (Italian) Poached egg on spinach with a cheese sauce.

uovo bollito (Italian) Boiled egg.

uovo crudo (Italian) Raw egg.

uovo di alosa (Italian) Shad roe.

uovo di tonno (Italian) Tuna-fish roe.

uovo farcito (Italian) Stuffed egg, devilled egg.

uovo freddo con salsa maionese (Italian) Egg mayonnaise.

uovo fresco (Italian) New-laid egg.

uovo fritto (Italian) Egg fried in olive oil.

uovo fritto al bacon (Italian) Bacon and egg, fried.

uovo guasto (Italian) Stale egg.

uovo molletto (Italian) Soft-boiled egg.

uovo ripieno (Italian) Stuffed egg.

uovo sodo (Italian) Hard-boiled egg.

uovo sodo con salsa maionese (Italian) Hard-boiled egg in mayonnaise.

uovo strapazzo (Italian) Scrambled egg.

upper crust Top crust of pastry.

upside-down cake or pudding Sponge mixture baked over fruit such as pineapple, apricots, peaches, etc., and turned out after baking so that the fruit is uppermost.

unranoscopus Species of fish found in temperate or warm seas, such as the white hogfish used in *bouillabaissé*.

urda (Rumanian) Sheep's-milk cheese.

ushky (Russian) Tiny dumplings served in soup.

usquebaugh (Corrupt Gaelic) (i) Whisky. (ii) Irish liqueur.

uszka (Polish) Stuffed dough envelopes.

utrennii (Russian) Breakfast.

uunijuusto (Finnish) Milk dish made from beestings baked in a slow oven.

uva (Italian, Portuguese, and Spanish) Grape.

uva passa (Italian) Dried grape. Raisin.

uva seca (Spanish) Dried grape. Raisin.

uva spina (Italian) Gooseberry.

uvaggio (Italian) Wine made from mixed grapes.

úzhin (Russian) Supper.

vaca (Spanish) (i) Beef. (ii) Cow.

vaca en conserva (Spanish) Corned beef.

vache (French) Cow.

vache à lait (French) Milch-cow.

vacherin (French) Sweet made of meringue or macaroon mixture built up in rings on a pastry base, filled with cream or ice cream and fruit.

vacherin (Swedish) Creamy, aromatic cheese spread.

vacuum carafe Vacuum-insulated jug for keeping ice water cold.

vacuum container Container with an inner and outer wall divided by a vacuum, maintaining liquids at their original temperature.

vacuum flask Flask used to keep liquids hot or chilled, as required. See vacuum container, also thermos.

vaffel (Norwegian) Waffle.

vagão restaurante (Portuguese) Dining-car.

vagón-restaurante (Spanish) Dining-car.

vagon-restoran (Russian and Turkish) Dining-car.

vagone ristorante (Italian) Dining-car.

vainilla (Spanish) Vanilla.

vairon (French) Minnow.

vaisselle (French) Collective term for table plates, dishes, etc.

vaisselle plate (French) Collective term for table silver-ware.

vajilla (Spanish) Crockery.

valdepinas (Spanish) Dry, full-flavoured wines, both red and white.

valdespino (Spanish) Fine brand of sherries.

valence (French) Oranges, particularly Spanish oranges.

Valencia (i) District of Spain famous for its oranges and its vineyards. (ii) (American) Sweet orange cultivated in the United States.

valenciennes (French) Food, particularly chicken, served with a garnish of rice.

valesniki (Russian) Cream-cheese *croquette*.

valosniski polonais (Polish) Thin, unsweetened pancake filled with cream cheese and then deep-fried.

Valpolicella (Italian) Dry red wine.

van der hum (Africaans) South African tangerine-flavoured liqueur.

vand (Danish) Water.

vaniglia (Italian) Vanilla.

vanilla Mexican climbing orchid yielding seed pods which are dried and fermented and used as a flavouring agent. (See also vanilla pod and vanilla sugar).

vanilla essence See vanilla pod.

vanilla pod Dried pod of the vanilla plant, used whole for flavouring dishes; also used commercially to produce bottled vanilla essence by soaking in alcohol or spirit of wine.

vanilla sugar Sugar flavoured by placing a vanilla pod in an airtight jar of sugar and allowing it to absorb the flavour.

vanille (French) Vanilla.

vanilline Synthetic product used as a substitute for real vanilla.

vann (Norwegian) Water.

vanneau (French) Lapwing; peewit.

vanner (French) Culinary term, to stir a sauce quickly in order to make it smooth and prevent a skin from forming.

varéniki (Polish) Square or round noodle paste filled with savoury food such as meat or cheese, and poached.

vareniky (Russian) Ukranian stuffed dumplings.

variety meats (American) Offal.

vaso (Spanish) Glass.

vasque (French) Shallow bowl for serving cold foods, both sweet and savoury.

Vatel (French) Celebrated *maître d'hôtel* (1635–1671) said to have been chef to Louis XIV and to have committed suicide because fish for a special banquet did not arrive on time. There is, however, some doubt about the truth of the legend and of his standing as an actual chef.

vatrushka (Russian) Cheese-cake.

vatrushky (Russian) Cottage cheese tarts.

vatten (Swedish) Water.

veal Flesh of calf, at its best when just under 3 months old, and milk-fed. Once it is grass-fed, the flesh darkens. Veal fillets, shoulder, loin and best end of neck are roasted; sliced fillets are fried or made into a *fricassée*, or beaten thin for escalopes. Loin chops and neck cutlets can be fried or grilled. Veal flesh lacks fat, is not highly flavoured and benefits from being served with a good sauce and accompanied with more strongly-flavoured food in stews, pies, etc.

veal and ham pie Diced or minced veal cooked with ham or bacon in a pastry case.

veal bird Stuffed rolled veal cutlet, sautéed in butter and then braised.

veal *blanquette* See *blanquette* (i).

veal tendon See tendron.

veau (French) Veal. The flesh of the calf.

veau, tête de (French) Calf's head.

vegan Strict vegetarian who eats no food of animal origin.

vegeburger (American) Vegetarian meatless hamburger.

vegetable General term covering non-animal foods – roots, tubers, bulbs, leaves, fruits, flower-heads, pods, seeds, pulses, seaweeds. All contribute valuable vitamins of varying types and in varying degrees (see separate entries) as well as protein in some cases and carbohydrates in others. Vegetables are obtainable fresh, canned, frozen, and dehydrated, and should be stored and cooked with care to preserve their nutrient values. They can, according to type, be boiled, pressure-cooked, steamed, sautéed, fried, braised and stewed. or eaten raw in salads.

vegetable brush Hard-bristled brush used for scrubbing vegetables which are to be cooked whole.

vegetable caviar Cold Russian vegetarian dish of chopped aubergines, onions, parsley and tomatoes cooked in olive oil.

vegetable cheese Bean curd.

vegetable chowder Thick soup of assorted vegetables, diced, sautéed and cooked in water or stock.

vegetable colouring Colouring matter of vegetable origin.

vegetable dish Large dish for taking cooked vegetables such as baked potatoes, cauliflower, sprouts, etc. to the table.

vegetable gelatine Agar-agar.

vegetable gold Saffron.
vegetable jelly Pectin.
vegetable marrow Oval variety of pumpkin, cooked as a vegetable (see marrow).
vegetable milk (American) Synthetic milk derived mainly from soya beans.
vegetable oil Essential oil extracted from a plant.
vegetable oyster Salsify.
vegetable pear Chayote.
vegetable peeler Utensil for removing the outer skins of vegetables such as potatoes, carrots, etc.
vegetable pickles Mixture of different fruit and vegetables covered with a spiced marinade, and sealed.
vegetable stock Liquor obtained by boiling vegetables for making soups and stews.
vegetable strainer Perforated sieve to hold boiled vegetables so that the water can be poured away.
vegetarian One who eats only fruits, nuts, and other vegetables; some less strict vegetarians include dairy products and eggs (See vegan).
vegetal (Spanish) Vegetable.
vegetarianismo (Spanish) Vegeterianism.
velouté (French) (i) Rich white sauce made with a foundation of chicken or veal stock, used as the basis of more elaborate sauces such as *Allemande*, *Mousseline*, etc. (ii) Thick soup of a creamy consistency.
venado (Spanish) Deer, venison, stag.
venaison (French) Venison or any deer flesh.
venison Deer-flesh, hung until slightly "high" before being eaten. The haunch, fillet and loin will roast or fry, but neck and breast require slow cooking. Sliced fillet can be cooked as for beef steak but requires more fat.
ventresca (Italian) Paunch of pork (Cooked).
ventresca di tonno (Italian) The prime portion of tuna-fish, its stomach.
venus Cockle mollusc.
verbena Herb native to Chile and Peru but cultivated in Europe. It has a faint lemon fragrance and is used to make a tea which is credited with being an aid to digestion.

verderol (Spanish) Type of green shellfish.
verduleria (Spanish) Greengrocer's shop.
verdura (Ialian and Spanish) Green vegetables.
verduresse (French) (i) Green vegetables. (ii) Salad herbs. (iii) Pot herbs.
verenika (Jewish) Noodle dumpling.
verjuice Juice of unripe grapes, apples or crab-apples once used in place of lemon juice or vinegar.
verjus (French) Verjuice. Juice of unripe grapes or other fruit.
verlorenes Ei (German) Poached egg.
vermicelle (French) *Vermicelli* (Italian).
vermicelli (Italian) Very thin pasta used in soups and milk puddings.
vermouth Fortified white wine flavoured with herbs and spices, including wormwood, which gives it its distinctive flavour. French vermouth is drier and lighter than Italian vermouth. It is used in cocktails, served with gin, etc.
vermouth cassis (American) Highball of French vermouth, *crème de cassis*, and soda water.
verpflegen (German) To cater, to provide food.
Verpflegung (German) (i) Food. (ii) Catering.
verre (French) Glass.
vert, au (French) Served with or in green sauce.
vert-pré (French) (i) Grilled meats garnished with potato straws and watercress. (ii) Food such as poultry or fish coated with green mayonnaise.
verveine (French) Verbena.
verza (Italian) Cabbage.
vesi (Finnish) Water.
vesop Concentrated vegetable extract used in oriental cooking.
vesou (French) Cane juice.
Vesperbrot (German) Light afternoon luncheon.
vessie de porc (French) Pig's bladder.
vetch Name of sundry pulses, some edible. The cultivated vetch yields seed eaten like peas. The starchy root of the tuber-vetch tastes rather like chestnuts and is baked in hot ashes.
viande (French) Meat, viands.

viande de carême (French) Lenten food.

viande de soja (French) Vegetarian "meat" prepared commercially from soya beans.

viande faisandée, hasardée (French) Meat kept till it is "high".

vichy carrots Carrots cooked in water and butter until the liquid evaporates and the carrots appear glazed. Originally this recipe used Vichy water because both it and carrots are considered to be beneficial to afflictions of the liver.

Vichy water Effervescent mineral water imported from a spring in *Vichy*, France.

vichyssoise (French) Cold leek and potato cream soup.

vicia (Spanish) Carob bean.

victoria sponge sandwich Cake made with a creamed mixture of equal amounts of flour, sugar, fat and eggs which keeps moist longer than the true, fatless sponge.

videlle (French) (i) Gadget to remove stones from fruit. (ii) Wheel pastry-cutter.

vidriado (Spanish) Crockery; glazed earthenware.

vielle curé (French) French liqueur originating in an abbey near Bordeaux, sweet, brown, aromatic and highly intoxicating.

Vienna loaf Milk-enriched bread, steam-baked, with crisp glazed crust and tapered ends.

Vienna steak Cake of minced beef, onions, herbs and ketchup, cooked in a covered frying pan.

vierge (French) Frothy concoction of well-beaten butter, pepper, salt and lemon-juice, served with boiled vegetables.

vigne (French) Vine.

Villeroi (French) Famous 19th-century French family after whom several dishes are named.

Villeroux (French) Chef and friend of Carême, said to have invented the *omelette au jambon*.

vin (Danish, French, Norwegian and Swedish) Wine.

vin blanc (French) White wine.

vin blanc, au (French) Cooked in white wine.

vin coupé (French) Diluted wine.

vin d'honneur (French) Wine served in honour of a distinguished guest.

vin de paille (French) Straw wine.

vin de sureau (French) Elderberry wine.

vin de table (French) Table wine.

vin des noces (French) Marriage wine offered to the officiating priest.

vin du pays (French) Local wine.

vin du Rhin (French) Rhine wine.

vin fou (French) Very effervescent wine from the Jura region; literally "crazy wine".

vin mousseux (French) Sparkling wine.

vin ordinaire (French) Common table wine, usually cheap claret or inferior Sauterne.

vin pur (French) Undiluted wine.

vin rosé (French) Pink wine. Light and slightly sweet rose-coloured wine served with cold cuts and salads.

vin rouge (French) Red wine.

vinagre (Spanish) Vinegar.

vinagrada (Spanish) Cooling drink made with vinegar and sugar.

vinagreta (Spanish) Sauce made with oil, vinegar and onion.

vinaigre (French) Vinegar. Literally sour wine, *vin-aigre*, used for pickling, in sauces, and for salads.

vinaigre de framboises (French) Raspberry vinegar.

vinaigrer (French) (i) To season with vinegar.

vinaigrette (French) Sauce mixture of oil, vinegar and seasonings, (sometimes with added herbs) served with vegetables, fish, salads, etc.

vinaigrier (French) Small barrel in which vinegar is made.

vinazo (Spanish) Very strong wine.

vincent sauce *Purée* of herbs and chopped, hard-boiled eggs added to mayonnaise, served cold.

vine leaf Leaf from the vine used to wrap around game birds before cooking; or stuffed with a rice and meat mixture (Turkish dolmas).

viñedo (Spanish) Vineyard.

vinegar Dilute impure acetic acid made from beer, poor quality wine, apples, sugar, etc. Malt is the chief source of ordinary British table vinegar. Vinegar is used for pickling, sousing, preserving, marinading, and as a table condiment. It can be flavoured with herbs and spices, such as tarragon, cayenne, chilli, etc. White wine vinegar is used in sauces.

vinepress Winepress for expressing grape juice.

viner Vine-grower.

vinho (Portuguese) Wine.

vinho de Madeira (Portuguese) Madeira wine.

vinho do Porto (Portuguese) Port wine.

vinho verde (Portuguese) "Young" wine, literally "green" wine.

viniculture Cultivation of the vine.

vinillo (Spanish) Very weak wine.

vinjak (Yugoslavian) Cognac.

vino (Italian and Spanish) Wine.

vino añejo (Spanish) Old wine.

vino asciutto (Italian) Dry wine.

vino bianco (Italian) White wine.

vino blanco (Spanish) White wine.

vino corriente (Spanish) Spanish equivalent of *vin ordinaire*.

vino de Jerez (Spanish) Sherry.

vino de mesa (Spanish) Table wine.

vino de Oporto (Spanish) Port.

vino de pasto (Spanish) Table wine.

vino dolce (Italian) Sweet wine.

vino espumante (Spanish) Sparkling wine.

vino rosso (Italian) Red wine.

vino secco (Spanish) Dry wine.

vino spumante (Italian) Sparkling wine.

vino tinto (Spanish) Red wine.

vintage (i) Wine yield of a certain year. (ii) Gathering of the grape harvest.

vintage port Unblended port allowed to age in the bottle.

vintage wine Wine grown and processed naturally, its quality varying from one year to another because of climatic conditions.

vintner Dealer in wines.

violet Dark blue-mauve flower of a low, herbaceous plant with a delicate perfume. Crystallised and used for decorating chocolates, sweets, desserts, etc.

violeto (Spanish) Clingstone peach.

violette (French) Violet.

Virginian ham (American) Hickory-smoked, specially spiced ham from pigs fed with peaches.

virgouleuse (French) Winter pear grown near *Limoges*.

virtiniai (Russian) Lithuanian stuffed dumplings.

vis (Dutch) Fish.

viscera Internal organs of an animal; heart, kidneys, liver, lungs, etc. Most are edible (see offal and separate entries).

visniski (Russian) Rissole of *coulibiac* dough stuffed with fish forcemeat, and fried.

vitamins Chemical substances needed to maintain health and obtained by way of food. Deficiency in a particular vitamin can set up a particular illness, but most people who adopt a normal varied diet take in sufficient vitamins for their needs. Absence of vitamin A causes eye troubles; of the B group, nervous, skin and digestive complaints; of C, scurvy; of D, rickets and tooth decay; of E, stunted growth and probable sterility. Vitamin sources include: A: Egg-yolks, butter, fish oil, cheese and vegetable foodstuffs; B: Bread, meat, liver, fruits, nuts, vegetables, milk; C: Oranges, blackcurrants, grapefruit, green vegetables, etc.; D: Fish liver oils, herrings, sardines, salmon, eggs, cheese, butter, milk, etc.; E: Seed oils and leafy vegetables.

vitello (Italian) Veal.

vitello al forno (Italian) Roast veal.

vitello alla genovese (Italian) Veal cooked in butter and white wine, with artichoke hearts.

vitello tonnato (Italian) Veal with tuna fish sauce.

vitelotte Peachblow potato. Red kidney potato.

viticulture Cultivation of the vine.

vittles Colloquialism for food.

vivares (Spanish) Victuals, provisions.

vive (French) Weever fish.

viveur (French) Culinary term for a dish highly seasoned with cayenne or paprika.

vlattero (Greek) Currant-flavoured liqueur.

vodka Russian national drink now imitated in other countries. Fiery and colourless, true Russian or Polish vodka is distilled from wheat, rye or potatoes and is used as an *apéritif*, a liqueur, a base for other drinks both hot and cold. Vodka is used in cocktails like Bloody Mary, Moscow mule and Black Russian.

voileipäpöytä (Finnish) Finnish equivalent of *smørgasbord*.

vol-au-vent (French) Round, square or oval case of puff pastry, filled with a ring *ragoût* of cooked meat, game, chicken, fish, shellfish, mushrooms or sweetbreads, etc., or with fruit mixed with whipped cream.

volaille (French) Poultry, collective name for all domesticated birds, chicken, turkey, duck, pigeon, guinea-fowl, goose, etc.

volière, en (French) Ostentatious presentation of game birds, now discontinued, by bringing them to table adorned with their plumage.

Volnay (French) Excellent Burgundy from the *Côte d'Or*.

vongola (Italian) (i) Mussel. (ii) Clam.

vongole, alla (Italian) Dish with shellfish sauce.

vopallière (French) Small chicken fillet, larded and braised, served with truffle sauce.

Vorratskammer (German) Store-room, larder.

Vorspeise (German) Appetizer.

Vosne (French) Red wine from the *Côte d'Or*.

Vougeot (French) Highly-esteemed Burgundy from the *Côte d'Or*.

Vouvray (French) Light wines from the *Vouvray* district of the Loire.

vraie tortue (French) Real turtle. See turtle.

V.S.O. Very special old brandy.

V.S.O.P. Very special old pale brandy.

V.V.S.O.P. Very, very special old pale brandy.

Wabe (German) Honeycomb.
Wachsbohne (German) Wax bean.
Wachtel (German) Quail.
wafer Thin, crisp, sweetened biscuit, served with ice cream, or desserts, made in oblong or fancy shapes, sometimes sandwiched together with a sweet or savoury cream filling.
wafer-paper (American) Rice paper.
Waffel (German) Waffle.
waffle Large, crisp cake made by cooking waffle-batter mixture in a waffle-iron which makes deep indentations and cooks on both sides simultaneously. Served as a savoury with grills, or as a sweet with a sauce poured over it, particularly maple syrup, or to accompany fruit, fools, etc.
waffle-batter Mixture of flour, salt, sugar, baking powder, egg, milk and melted butter, beaten into a batter and cooked in a waffle-iron.
waffle-iron Hinged utensil, usually electric, for cooking waffles.
wagon-restaurant (French) Dining car.

wagtail Small bird cooked in France as for lark.
waiter (i) One who waits at table to serve drinks and meals. (ii) Serving tray for carrying food or holding crockery.
Waldmeister (German) Woodruff.
waldorf salad (American) Salad made of diced apples, celery, walnuts, and mayonnaise.
Waldschnepfe (German) Woodcock.
walewska (French) Fish, especially sole fillets, poached and garnished with spiny lobster and truffles, mornay sauce and spiny lobster butter.
wall-eyed perch (American) Edible freshwater fish with prominent eyes.
wall-eyed pike (American) Another name for wall-eyed perch.
Walnuss (German) Walnut.
walnut Fruit of the walnut tree, grown throughout the world, and used as dessert, as a source of oil, in cakes, puddings etc., whole or chopped, and as a decoration. Unripe (green) walnuts

are pickled in brine (which turns them black) or made into a ketchup.

walnut ketchup Crushed green walnuts, steeped in rock salt, strained to remove the juice. The juice is boiled with spices, then mixed with the crushed walnuts, bottled and sealed and kept for some time before use.

walnut oil Pure oil extracted cold from dried walnuts and used in cookery.

Warmeeinheit (German) Thermal unit, calorie.

Wärmegrad (German) Temperature, degree of heat.

warmer (i) Chafing-dish. (ii) Hot-plate.

WarmerKrautsalat (German) Hot white cabbage salad.

warming tray Tray incorporating an electric heating element, to keep food warm.

wasabi (Japanese) Green root used similarly to horseradish, and served with fish.

wassail Spiced ale, generally containing roasted apples, traditionally served on Christmas Eve.

wassail bowl Bowl in which wassail was served.

Wasser (German) Water.

Wasserkanne (German) Ewer, pitcher.

Wasserkessel (German) Kettle.

Wassersuppe (German) Water-gruel.

waste disposal Garbage disposal.

wastelbread (American) Bread made from the finest flour.

water Colourless, tasteless, odourless liquid essential to life, and the largest constituent of animal and plant life, which boils at 100 degrees C (212 degrees F) and freezes at 0 degrees C (32 degrees F). Some water contains soluble calcium and is described as "hard" water. Water is used extensively in cooking, making drinks, etc., etc.

water apple Custard apple.

water biscuit Thin, crisp biscuit made with water instead of milk, usually served with cheese.

water bottle Carafe, or other container for holding liquids.

water-brose (Scottish) Gruel made of meal and water.

water-chestnut Nut-like seed of an acquatic plant, widely used in Chinese cooking.

water ice Frozen sweet made from sugar syrup flavoured with fruit juice. Sorbet.

water kale (American) Meatless vegetable broth.

water parsnip Acquatic plant whose leaves are similar to celery and are eaten in salads. The root, however, is poisonous.

water pitcher (i) Earthenware jar for holding water. (ii) (American) Large jug containing a supply of ice water at table.

water rice Wild rice.

water softener Appliance used to soften hard water by neutralising calcium carbonate deposits with salt.

water-souchet See *waterzoetje*.

watercress Perennial green-leaved plant found growing in running water and used for salads, garnishing, soup-making, etc.

waterfisch (French) Dutch word meaning fresh-water fish and used in connection with a sauce served with perch and other freshwater fish.

waterless cookery Cooking food with a minimal amount of liquid in a special heavy aluminium pan which has a steam vent in the lid to prevent build-up of pressure; suitable for pot-roasting, braising, etc.

waterzoï (French) See *waterzoetje* (Dutch)

waterzoetje (Dutch) (i) Fish stew served in a soup tureen and eaten with a spoon, also called water-souchet. (ii) Chicken cooked in a similar manner.

watermelon Fruit of a plant of the cucumber family, growing in many varieties, with flesh ranging from white to red. Eaten as dessert or used for jam-making. In some countries the seeds are roasted, salted and eaten as a snack.

waxbean (American) Kind of French bean with a yellow pod that can be cooked whole.

waxed paper Paper coated with white wax to protect it from water and grease, used for storing food, etc.

waxwing Small bird caught and cooked in France as for lark.

weakfish (American) See croaker fish.

wedding cake Traditional rich fruit cake, with one or more tiers, covered with almond paste and decorated with royal icing, served at the wedding reception.

Wedgwood Superior pottery, lightly glazed and cameo-decorated, designed by Josiah Wedgwood (1730–1795).

weever European fish found along sandy coasts, in two species, the Greater weever being the most esteemed for flavour. Cooked as for whiting. The stiff spines along its dorsal fin are capable of inflicting poisonous pricks.

Wein (German) Wine.

Weinbau (German) Viticulture, wine-growing.

Weinbeere (German) Grape.

Weinberg (German) Vineyard.

Weinbrand (German) Brandy.

Weinekellerei (German) Winestore.

Weinekneipe (German) Wine tavern.

Weinernte (German) Vintage.

Weinessig (German) Wine vinegar.

Weingeist (German) Spirits of wine; alcohol.

Weinhandler (German) Wine merchant.

Weinkaltschale (German) Cold wine soup.

Weinkarte (German) Wine list.

Weinkeller (German) (i) Wine-cellar. (ii) Wine-tavern.

Weinkelter (German) Wine-press.

Weinkraut (German) White cabbage cooked with wine.

Weinlaub (German) Vine-leaves.

Weinlese (German) (i) Vintage. (ii) Grape harvest.

Weinschenke (German) Wine-house, tavern.

Weinstock (German) Vine.

Weintraube (German) Bunch of grapes.

weisse Glasur (German) White icing.

weisse Rube (German) White turnip.

Weisswein (German) White wine.

Weisswurst (German) Small white un-smoked spicy veal sausage, a speciality of Munich.

Weizen (German) Wheat.

Weizengriess (German) Semolina.

well (i) Space made in the middle of flour in which other ingredients are put for gradual working in, such as eggs or milk in batter-making. (ii) Space left in food for insertion of garnishes, fillings, etc. (iii) Metal sleeve placed in certain types of cooking tins.

wels (i) Catfish, freshwater fish prepared like burbot. (ii) Large European fresh-water fish.

Welschkohl (German) Savoy cabbage.

Welschkorn (German) Indian corn, maize.

Welsh bean (American) Kidney bean.

Welsh onion Hardy plant with a leek-like bulb and tubular leaves. Pieces of leaf may be broken off without dis-turbing the main plant, and used for flavouring.

Welsh rarebit Commonly called "Welsh rabbit". Toasted bread covered with melted cheese and butter, seasoned with pepper and mustard.

Welsh venison Cambridge college dish of braised glazed loin of mutton, with port added to the reduced braising liquid.

Wensleydale cheese Two distinct types of Yorkshire cheese made in Wensley-dale: (i) Cylindrical double cream cheese, like Stilton, and "blue" when ripe; made from June to September. (ii) Flat, well-flavoured white cheese made at the beginning and end of the year, and eaten fresh.

Werderkäse (German) Rennet cheese originating in Werder, Germany.

Wermut (German) (i) Vermouth. (ii) Absinthe.

West Indian gherkin Small prickly cucumber used mainly for pickling.

Westphalian ham Ham cured by the Westphalian (Germany) method of smoking over beechwood and juniper fire, thus imparting a distinctive flavour.

wether Castrated ram.

whale Cetaceous mammal in many orders, some of which have been over-fished and are in danger of extinction. Whale oil was once used in making margarine but has been replaced by vegetable oils. Whale-flesh is edible if soaked first and well cooked.

whale oil See whale.

wheat Cereal grass grown in most parts of the world for its edible seed which is threshed and ground into flour. Wheat products contain carbohydrate protein, B vitamins, iron and calcium, and include cereals, flours, bread, pastas, etc. There are several varieties of wheat which fall into two categories: (a) hard grain, which is richer in gluten. (b) soft grain, which is richer in flour.

wheat germ Seed of the grain, a rich source of the vitamin B group largely removed during the milling of white flour, but available as a commercial preparation to be sprinkled on cereals and other foods, and added to proprietary breads.

wheatcake (American) Pancake.

wheatear Small bird esteemed for the table in France, cooked as for lark.

wheatmeal See flour.

whelk Small marine gasteropod with a conical twisted shell, cooked and eaten like winkles.

whey Uncoagulated portion of milk; the watery liquid which separates from the curd when milk is clotted, little used in human diet, but often included in pig-food.

whey wig Nineteenth-century Westmorland beverage made of mint or sage leaves infused in buttermilk, and served during hay-harvest.

whinberry Bilberry.

whip (i) To beat into a froth or thickened consistency by means of a fork or special tool. (ii) Dessert of fruit *purée* blended with beaten egg-whites, cream or jelly.

whipped butter Creamed butter.

whipped cream Double-cream beaten or whipped to a consistency thick enough to be piped onto dishes as decoration.

whipping cream (American) Double cream.

whisk Wire utensil for beating, stirring, and whipping.

whiskey (i) (American) Whisky made from rye or maize. (ii) (Irish) Whisky made from rye.

whisky spirit distilled from cereal grains or other starch-yielding foods such as potatoes.

whisky (American) Scotch whisky.

whisky collins (American) Tom Collins cocktail made with whisky.

whisky sour Cocktail made of bitters, lemon juice, orange juice and whisky.

whistling kettle Tea kettle with a whistle in the spout activated by steam when boiling point is near.

white fish General name for fish such as whiting, cod, haddock, etc. which are rich in protein and low in fat.

white meat Pork, lamb or veal, or the white meat of poultry.

white pepper Powdered berries of the pepper-plant with the outer husks removed.

white pudding Variety of farmhouse sausage made at pig-killing time from the cooked brain, tongue, and other offal mixed with cooked pearl barley, oatmeal, or breadcrumbs, seasoned and flavoured, then fried and eaten hot.

white sauce Sauce made either by the *roux* method (flour stirred into melted butter and liquid then added) or the blended method (mixing flour with milk or milk and stock) used as a basis for sweet or savoury sauces.

white stew Mutton, rabbit or veal cooked slowly in a closely-lidded vessel. Neither the meat nor any accompanying vegetables are fried before the stewing process is started.

white wine Wine made from the juice only of white or black grapes, light coloured or uncoloured, such as *Chablis, Sauterne*, hock, etc.

white wine cup Cup made of white wine, brandy, ice, fruit slices and a garnish such as mint or cucumber.

whitebait Tiny fish, the young of the herring genus, fried as fresh as possible and served with slices of lemon and thinly-cut brown bread and butter.

whitepot Ancient preparation of cream, eggs, pulp of apples, etc., baked in a dish or in a crust. A kind of custard fruit *purée* pie.

whiting Easily-digested white fish, fried and served with lemon when very fresh, but otherwise requiring a good sauce as it lacks flavour. It can be baked, or egged-and-crumbed, and fried. Salted and dried, it is sometimes sold as Buckhorn.

wholemeal flour See flour.

wholemeal loaf Bread made from wholemeal flour, sometimes sprinkled on top with cracked wheat.

whortleberry Small, acid, reddish berry used in *compôtes* and as an accompaniment to game and red meats. It resembles the bilberry and cranberry.

wicker bottle Bottle covered with woven wicker-work.

wicker flask Wine flask covered with woven wicker-work.

wickerwork Articles such as bread basket, fruit or vegetable container etc. made of wicker.

widgeon Small wild duck in season from September to January. Prepared as for duck but requiring only short cooking at a high temperature, it is served with a rich gravy flavoured with redcurrant jelly or port wine.

Wiener (German/Austrian) (i) Sausage. (ii) (American) Frankfurter, hot dog.

Wiener schnitzel (German/Austrian) Viennese dish of egg-and-crumbed veal fillet, fried, and served either with lemon, or garnished with eggs, olives and anchovies.

wienerbrod (Danish) Viennese-type bread or pastry.

Wienerwurst (German) Viennese sausage.

wijn (Dutch) Wine.

Wild (German) Game, venison.

wild basil Aromatic herb of the mint family.

wild boar Wild mammal whose flesh, when young, is marinated and then cooked as for pork. Up to a year old, the entire carcase makes good eating – leg, saddle, loin, shoulder, etc. Thereafter, is only edible if left to marinate for a long time. The wild boar is a night-time feeder on roots and truffles. The flesh of those with access to truffles has a distinctive and delicate flavour.

wild chicory Salad vegetable, slightly bitter; blanched by being grown in a dark place. It can be cut up and pickled in vinegar.

wild duck Mallard.

wild goose Bird whose flesh has a more gamey flavour than that of the domesticated bird.

wild honey Honey made by wild bees.

wild rice Tall acquatic grass growing in North American bogs and swamps, also in parts of France and Italy. It was cultivated by the American Indians but has proved difficult to grow elsewhere, therefore is extremely expensive. It is not related to true rice, requires longer cooking and is regarded as a great delicacy.

wild sweet potato (American) Morning glory plant with a large starchy root.

wild thyme Scented aromatic herb used for making infusions, also as a condiment.

wildfowl Game bird such as wild duck, geese, snipe, etc.

Wildgullasch (German / Austrian) Venison goulash.

Wildpret (German) Venison, game.

wilfra tart Small jam tart or cheesecake traditionally made in Ripon, Yorkshire, to mark the celebration of Wilfra (or St. Wilfrid) week at the beginning of August.

william pear Sweet, juicy variety of eating pear.

willow pattern White china-ware patterned in blue, originating in China and purporting to tell the story of two lovers pursued by angry parents. Made into dinner services, tea services, etc.

Windbeutel (German) Cream puff.

windsor bean Broad bean.

wine (i) Alcoholic beverage produced from fermented grape juice or fresh or dried grapes, black or white. The flavour of the wine is conditioned by the species of vine, the soil, the climate and the method of production, which varies from district to district. The countries best known for wine production are France, Germany, Italy,

Spain and Portugal. Other wine-producing countries include Yugoslavia, Hungary, Australia, South Africa, Cyprus. Wines fall into three principle categories: Standard, vintage and fortified, but the sub-divisions are very numerous. Wine is drunk as a beverage in its own right; as an accompaniment to and embellishment of food; also used as an ingredient in all manner of cookery, such as sauces, desserts, casseroled dishes, etc., etc. (ii) Beverage produced by fermenting commodities other than grapes – fruits, vegetables, etc., mostly home-made, some very potent. (See separate entries).

wine bag Wine skin.

wine-berry (i) Grape. (ii) Redcurrant, gooseberry or bilberry. (iii) Raspberry of China and Japan.

wine-bibber Habitual drinker of wine.

wine biscuit Arrowroot biscuit originally intended to be served with wine.

wine bottle Glass container of varying shape and size designed to hold wine.

wine card Wine list.

wine-cask Cask for holding and storing wine.

wine cellar (i) Basement room or cellar, for storing wine. (ii) Stock of wines kept in a convenient place.

wine coaster Rimmed container for a wine bottle, designed to catch drips.

wine cooler Ice bucket for chilling a bottle of wine before serving.

wine cradle Serving basket which holds a bottle of wine at a slant so the sediment will not be disturbed.

wine ferment Wine yeast.

wine glass Small glass, usually stemmed, in which wine is served. Its shape varies according to its intended contents.

wine grape Any grape used in wine production.

wine herring Herring pickled in wine-flavoured and spiced vinegar.

wine jelly Jelly dessert flavoured with wine.

wine lees Wine dregs.

wine list List of wines served in a restaurant, hotel or elsewhere.

wine press Machine for expressing grape juice for wine manufacture.

wine rack Metal or wooden rack used for storing bottles of wine at the correct angle.

wine sap Variety of deep red winter apple.

wine skin Bag made out of animal skin for holding wine.

wine-taster One whose business is to sample wines.

wine-vat Vat in which grapes are pressed in wine-making.

wine vault Underground cellar where wine is stored.

wine vinegar Vinegar made from fermented red or white wine, used in salad dressings, sauces, marinades, etc.

wine yeast Yeast used in making wine.

winery Place where wine is made.

winkle, periwinkle Small black shell-fish, washed and boiled, the "meat" then being extracted from the shell with a pin.

winter apple Apple ripening late in the autumn and on sale during the winter.

winter cherry See strawberry tomato.

winter cress See barbarea.

winter pear Any variety of late-ripening pear.

winter savory Aromatic labiate herb used fresh or dried to flavour food.

wintergreen Evergreen herb whose aromatic leaves yield oil of wintergreen, used for flavouring confectionery, and also in medicine.

Winterkohl (German) Winter cabbage. Kale.

wintersweet Wild marjoram.

wirken (German) To knead; (dough).

Wirtshaus (German) Inn; tavern.

wisniowka (Polish) Cordial liqueur made from black cherries.

witch Type of flounder caught in the Atlantic.

witloof (Belgian) Endive blanched in cellars.

Wittwenkuss (German) Almond-filled pastry.

wood grouse, capercailzie Largest European game bird, with delicate flesh, found in Northern European countries. See capercailzie.

wood pigeon Bird which should be hung for a few days, then cooked as for ordinary pigeon.

woodcock Small wild migratory game bird with mottled plumage and a long bill, in season from October (September in Scotland) to January, and considered by many to be the best winged game because of its excellent flavour. Woodcock are not drawn before cooking and their heads are left on. They are roasted and served on toast. Also made into *pâté*, casseroled, etc.

woodruff Sweet-scented plant with small white flowers, sometimes used to flavour wine.

woof Yorkshire name for catfish or dory.

Worcestershire sauce Proprietary brand of piquant sauce, thin, dark and spicy, used to add to soups, stews, etc.

work To knead or mix with a tool or by hand until smooth.

wormseed Mexican tea.

wormwood Various wild plants whose bitter leaves are used to flavour absinthe, vermouth, wine, tisanes and liqueurs.

wrap To enclose meat in a wrapping such as foil, cooking film, parchment, pig's caul, then in a cloth, suitably prepared, before cooking.

Wurst (German) Sausage, fresh or smoked.

Wurst im Saft (German) Sausage in gravy.

Wurstbrot (German) Sausage sandwich.

Würstchen (German) Sausage links or strings.

Würzburger (German) Dark beer brewed at Würzburg in Bavaria.

Würze (German) Seasoning, condiment, spice.

würzen (German) To season, to spice.

wyandotte (American) Bread of domestic poultry, originating in America and named after a North American Indian tribe.

xanthia (American) Cocktail of brandy, gin, and yellow chartreuse.

xanthin Yellow food colouring extracted from madder.

xapoipa (Spanish) Type of pancake.

xavier (French) Clear soup said to have been introduced by King Louis XVIII in honour of Count Xavier of Saxony, who died in 1806.

Xérès, vin de (French) Sherry. Spanish fortified wine of deep amber colour and aromatic flavour; so-called from Xeres, (Jerez) near Cadiz.

xeres (Italian) Sherry.

Xereswein (German) Sherry.

xerophagy Limiting diet to dry foods or bread, vegetables and water, as a form of fasting.

ximenia Several species of small plant yielding edible fruit known as mountain plums or wild limes.

xiphias (Greek) Swordfish.

Xmas fruitcake (American) Christmas cake.

X.O. Extra old cognac.

xynogala (Greek) Clabber; sour milk that has thickened.

yablouchni (Russian) Chilled apple soup.

yack (French) Yak.

yahni (Greek) Food braised in olive oil then boiled with tomatoes.

yak Long haired domesticated Tibetan ox, yielding edible flesh as well as abundant milk rather resembling goat's milk.

yakimono (Japanese) Grilled food.

yam Tropical climbing plant with a tuberous potato-like root which can be baked, boiled, fried, and eaten in the same way as potatoes.

yam bean Tropical vine yielding edible pods, and edible tubers resembling turnips. Its seeds are a source of oil.

yam potato Sweet potato.

yamadon Oil from the yellow nutmeg.

yaourt (French) Yoghurt.

yapok, yapock South American water oppossum.

yapon, yaupon, yupon Bushy evergreen shrub whose leaves yield the "black drink" of the American Indians.

yeast Microscopic, single-celled plant which multiplies very rapidly and produces ferments capable of converting starch and sugars into carbon dioxide and alcohol. Used in making bread, certain cakes, wines, beers, etc. A good source of vitamin B and available in several forms – compressed, granulated (baker's yeast) or semi-liquid (brewer's yeast).

yeast cake Yeast compressed into a small cake.

yeast-extract Product made by treating yeast with acid, a good source of vitamin B. Used to flavour soups, casseroles, etc. or as a spread.

yeast granules Yeast sold commercially in granular form.

yeen wor (Chinese) Bird's nest.

yellow chartreuse Sweeter and less potent of the two liqueurs invented in the 17th century by the Carthusian monks in the Grenoble area, who used well over 100 herbs in its making. The other is the more costly green chartreuse.

yellow perch (American) Common perch found in lakes and streams.

yellow pike (American) Wall-eyed pike or perch.

yellow plum (American) Wild plum.

yellow yam (American) Sweet potato.

yema (Spanish) Egg yolk.

yerba (Spanish) Herb, grass.

yerba doncella (Spanish) Periwinkle, a creeping woodland plant.

yerba marina de mar (Spanish) Seaweed.

yerba mate South American shrub, the leaves of which are dried and used to make Paraguay tea by putting the leaves in a hollowed-out gourd and pouring on boiling water. The tea is sucked up through a small tube, like a metal straw.

yerbabuena (Spanish) Mint (herb).

yering Delicate red dry Australian wine.

yiaourti (Greek) Yogurt.

yoghurt, yoghourt, yogurt Semi-solid fermented milk product available in plain form or flavoured with fruit, chocolate, coffee, etc. and eaten as a dessert or used in place of cream or custard. In its plain form it is also widely used in savoury dishes, salad dressings, etc. It can be made at home by procuring a supply of culture.

yoghurt dressing Salad dressing made of yoghurt, onion, vinegar and herbs.

yolk Yellow centre of the egg of a bird or reptile.

York ham Ham cured by a process originating in York, resulting in meat with a mild, delicate flavour, pale pink lean flesh and pink-tinged fat.

Yorkshire Breed of white pigs originating in Yorkshire.

Yorkshire apple cake Apple "cheese" made by boiling sugar, adding apples and lemon and boiling till stiff.

Yorkshire pudding Light baked batter made of flour, eggs, and milk, served with roast beef, or separately with gravy as a first course.

Yorkshire rarebit Welsh rarebit topped with a slice of boiled bacon and a poached egg.

yu chi tong (Chinese) Shark-fin soup.

yucca Genus of plants of the lily family native to South Western America. The fruit is roasted, the young stalks eaten like asparagus.

yule log Traditional Christmas cake; a butter-cream-filled Swiss roll coated with chocolate butter icing and forked to simulate the bark of a wood log.

yvette cream Violet-flavoured liqueur.

zabaglione Egg yolks, Marsala wine and sugar beaten to a thick froth and served warm in a glass.

zabaione (Italian) Zabaglione.

zachtegekookt ei (Dutch) Soft-boiled egg.

zafferano (Italian) Saffron.

zahari (Spanish) Variety of pomegranate.

Zahlen, bitte (German) The bill, please.

Zahlkellner (German) Head waiter.

zahora (Spanish) Luncheon party.

zakuska (Russian) Hot or cold appetizer served ahead of a main meal and consisting of mixed delicacies such as marinaded herrings, caviar, sausages, cooked vegetables with fish or meats, hot cheese pastries, etc.

zalbarsčiái (Lithuanian) Cold *borsch* (beet soup) served with hard-boiled eggs and diced cucumber.

zalm (Dutch) Salmon.

zamia Genus of palm-like trees, some species of which yield an edible pith.

zampino (Italian) Stuffed pig's leg.

zampone (Italian) Boiled, stuffed pig's trotter.

zanahoria (Spanish) Carrot.

zander, zant, sander European pike perch.

Zander (German) Pike.

zandía (Spanish) Water-melon.

Zante currant Small seedless raisin grape from *Zakinthos*, Greece.

zapote (Spanish) Sapodilla tree, and fruit.

zapotilla Sapodilla and its fruit.

Zara (Yugoslavian) Maraschino liqueur made in the Dalmatian village of *Zara*, used in pastry-making and in flavouring confectionery, ices and sweets.

zara (Spanish) Maize; Indian corn.

zaragoci (Spanish) Variety of plum.

zarf Ornamental coffee-cup holder.

zarzamora (Spanish) Blackberry.

zarzuela (Spanish) Dish including many varieties of fish which is first lightly fried then boiled in garlic and onion sauce. Literally, a "musical comedy".

zato (Spanish) Piece of bread.

zatta (Italian) Variety of melon.

zavtrak (Russian) Breakfast.

zdrowie twóje (Polish) Your health! A toast.

zebu Humped domestic ox from India, China and West Africa, whose flesh is prepared and eaten as for beef. It has been imported into the southern United States because of its ability to withstand drought and disease and has been crossed with other breeds.

zedoary Powerful sudorific; a bitter pungent root grown in India and China.

Zeeland oyster Famous oyster from the mouths of the rivers *Scheldt* and *Maas*.

zeevis (Dutch) Fish; seafood.

Zellersuppe (German/Austrian) Celery soup.

Zeltingen (German) White *Moselle* wine mostly used for cups.

zenzero (Italian) Ginger.

zéphire (French) (i) Small oval forcemeat dumpling poached and served with a rich sauce. (ii) Anything shaped in a *zéphire* mould. (iii) Any light and frothy preparation.

Zeppelinwurst (German) Liver sausage speciality of Frankfurt.

zest (i) Thin, oily outer skin of citrus fruits. (ii) Thin shaving of orange or lemon peel. (iii) Coloured part of the peel, sometimes rubbed off on to lumps of sugar. (iv) Skin covering the walnut kernel.

zeste (French) Zest.

zesté (French) Flavoured with the outer skin of the orange or lemon.

zesteuse (French) Citrus fruit peeler.

Zichorie (German) Chicory.

Ziege (German) Goat.

zimino (Italian) Fish stew, speciality of Genoa.

Zimtstern (German) Cinnamon biscuit baked in a star shape.

Zimt (German) Cinnamon.

zingara (French and Italian) Tomato and tarragon-flavoured garnish for small cuts of meat and poultry, made from ham, tongue, mushrooms and truffles bound with sauce.

Zingel (German) Fish of the perch family, found in the Danube.

zingiber Genus of tropical herbs which includes ginger.

zirrak (Russian) Mixture of braised meat and vegetables used in pilafs.

ziste (French) Pith beneath peel of citrus fruits.

ziti (Italian) Large macaroni.

zitoni (Italian) Long unfluted macaroni.

Zitronat (German) Candied lemon peel.

Zitrone (German) Lemon.

Zitronenglasur (German) Lemon icing.

Zitronenlimonade (German) Lemonade, lemon drink.

Zitronensaft (German) Lemon-juice.

Zitronensäure (German) Citric acid.

Zitronenschale (German) Lemon-peel.

zizanie (French) Wild rice.

zolletta, zollettina (Italian) Lump of sugar.

zoma (Spanish) Coarse flour.

zombie Drink of dark rum, lime juice, unsweetened pineapple juice and papaya juice, apricot brandy and powdered sugar, shaken over cracked ice and decorated with mint, pineapple cube and cherry on a stick.

zrazy (Russian) Roulade of beef (stuffed).

zubrovka (Russian) (i) Buffalo grass. (ii) Vodka in which buffalo grass has been steeped.

zubrowka (Polish) Vodka made from *zubrowka* grass, also made in Russia. (See *zubrovka*).

zucca (Italian) Gourd; pumpkin.

zucchero (Italian) Sugar.

zucchero a velo (Italian) Icing sugar.

zucchero fino in polvere (Italian) Caster sugar.

zucchero granulato (Italian) Granulated sugar.

zucchero in pezzi (Italian) Lump sugar.

zucchetta (Italian) (i) Small pumpkin. (ii) Vegetable marrow.

zucchino (Italian) Baby marrow, *courgette*.

zucchino in agrodolce (Italian) *Courgette* or baby marrow in sweet-sour sauce.

zucchino fritto (Italian) Fried *courgette*.

zucchino ripieno (Italian) Stuffed baby marrow, or *courgette*.

Zucker (German) Sugar.

Zuckerbäcker (German) Confectioner.

Zuckerguss (German) Sugar-icing.

Zuckerkandis (German) Sugar candy.

Zuckerkrank (German) Diabetic.

Zuckerrohr (German) Sugar-cane.

Zucherrübe (German) Sugar-beet.

Zuckerwerk (German) Confectionery.

Zuckerzange (German) Sugar-tongs.

zugo (Italian) Sweet fritter.

zumo (Spanish) Juice.

zumo de naranja (Spanish) Orange juice.

zumo de uvas (Spanish) Grape juice.

zumoso (Spanish) Juicy, succulent.

Zunge (German) Tongue.

Zungenscheiben (German) Sliced tongue.

Zungenwurst (German) Tongue sausage.

zupa (Russian) Soup.

zupa grzybowa (Polish) Soup made with sour cream and dried mushrooms.

zuppa (Italian) Soup.

zuppa al brodo (Italian) Fish broth with toasted bread and cheese.

zuppa alla marinara (Italian) Fish stew.

zuppa di cozze (Italian) Mussel stew.

zuppa di pesce (Italian) Fish chowder or stew.

zuppa di tartaruga (Italian) Turtle soup.

zuppa di verdura (Italian) Vegetable soup.

zuppa di vongole (Italian) Clam stew.

zuppa inglese (Italian) Literally "English soup", the Italian name for trifle.

zuppiera (Italian) Soup tureen.

zurano (Spanish) Wood-pigeon.

zurrapa (Portuguese) Cheap wine.

Zutat (German) Ingredient.

zuurkool (Dutch) *Sauerkraut*.

Zweitfrühstück (German) Second breakfast, a late-morning meal of sausage, sandwiches, etc. as opposed to the First breakfast of coffee and a roll.

Zwetsche (German) Damson.

Zwetschgenknödel (German) Plum dumpling.

Zwetschgenwasser (German) Plum brandy.

Zwetschkenröster (German / Austrian) Austrian plum jam.

Zwieback (German) Rusk; dry sweet bread sliced and browned crisp.

Zwiebel (German) Onion.

Zwiebelrindfleisch (German) Beef with onions.

Zwiebelsauce (German) Onion sauce.

Zwiebelsuppe (German) Onion soup.

Zwiebelrostbraten (German) Meat pot-roasted with onions.

Zwischengericht (German) *Entrée*.

zyme (Greek) Leaven.

zymology Science of fermentation.

zymometer Instrument for measuring the degree of fermentation of liquids.

zymurgy Branch of technological chemistry concerned with brewing, wine making and other fermentation processes.

zythos (Greek) Ancient beer.

zythum Kind of beer made from barley by the ancient Egyptians.